CURRENT PERSPECTIVES

FOR

MANAGING ORGANIZATIONS

CURRENT

FOR

MANAGING

Prentice-Hall, Inc., Englewood Cliffs, New Jersey

PERSPECTIVES

ORGANIZATIONS

EDITED BY

BERNARD M. BASS   SAMUEL D. DEEP

MANAGEMENT RESEARCH CENTER / UNIVERSITY OF ROCHESTER

CURRENT PERSPECTIVES FOR MANAGING ORGANIZATIONS
edited by Bernard M. Bass and Samuel D. Deep

13-195594-2

Printed in the United States of America

Library of Congress Catalog Card Number:
76-111524

Current Printing (last digit):
10 9 8 7 6 5 4 3 2 1

Prentice-Hall, International, Inc., London
Prentice-Hall of Australia, Pty. Ltd., Sydney
Prentice-Hall of Canada, Ltd., Toronto
Prentice-Hall of India Private Ltd., New Delhi
Prentice-Hall of Japan, Inc., Tokyo

Preface

This collection of readings will be generally useful to students of management as well as managers themselves. The idea for this particular effort was to provide an up-to-date review of what is currently available in behavioral science, psychological, management and trade-related publications of reviews, field studies, surveys, cases, essays and experiments.

We feel this collection can also answer a specific need of several hundred management educators with whom the editors have been working in the past few years. These educators from universities, institutes and industrial training departments are members of the International Research Groups on Management in North America, Latin America, Europe, India and Japan. They employ participative educational approaches to engage small groups of managers in various standardized organizational problems concerning objectives, attitudes, communications, supervision, interpersonal behavior, formal organization, conflict resolution, executive decision-making, management and organizational development and their own futures. The educators find it useful to assign relevant readings following critiques of the style and adequacy with which each problem has been handled. The collection of such readings in this volume can serve these groups of managers by providing them with recent research and theory on the subject of each of the organizational issues with which they must deal. Beyond this, we think such a collection will be useful for business students and managers, in general, particularly if the connections between articles and chapters are shown as we try to do with our relevant introductory statements and presentation of study questions concerning managerial implications.

The book is divided into three parts. The first part deals with what the manager must understand about the interface between man and his organization. The material is arranged around the concept of management by objectives and covers in turn, behavioral issues involved in setting objectives, organizing for goal attainment and compensating for goal attainment.

The second part deals with individual behavioral issues such as attitudes, motivation, interpersonal communication, supervision, teamwork, decision-making and conflict resolution.

The third part is an attempt to describe both organizational and individual trends likely to be of consequence to today's manager.

As we looked through the 40-odd journals and other sources in the past decade, we judged each article according to our estimate of its interest and importance to managers and students of management. Naturally, these subjective judgements were matters of opinion. However, subsequently we were able to try out about half the final collection on one group of senior executives who, despite their criticisms of other portions of the graduate course in which the readings were assigned, felt quite positive as a group about the interest, quality and utility of the readings. Similarly, we obtained corresponding evaluations from professional colleagues and students in the Management Research Center.

To provide additional familiarity of the reader with different ways of developing understanding of management, we pursued as a second criterion of selection, the formation of a diversified portfolio according to methodology. The extent to which we succeeded is indicated by the distribution of articles. Of the 43 readings in the book, approximately 40 percent are theoretical or critical reviews, 40 percent are field studies, surveys or cases, 10 percent are essays, and 10 percent are experiments.

A further important consideration was that each article was to be readable to the manager or student without requiring highly specialized training in the particular field with which the article dealt. But we did not rule out articles necessarily because they contained simple descriptive or analytical statistics for we believe that familiarity with such statistics is now common among educated managers and students.

Another related—but less significant—criterion was to achieve some variety in source publications. To this end our final collection contained 20 articles from management or trade-related journals, 16 articles from psychological or behavioral science journals, and 7 extracts from other varied sources.

A fifth criterion was recentness. We strove to locate the most up-to-date and complete statement on an issue. As a consequence, half of the articles chosen appeared between 1968 and 1970, and only five of the remaining selections appeared before 1966. We assumed that a more recent article on a given issue was often likely to incorporate or build on earlier works, whereas older articles might miss more recent progress on a subject. Wherever possible, we made a deliberate effort to choose readings which built on or included reviews of earlier ideas on the issues discussed.

Controversial positions were welcomed, but only those which presented data to buttress their positions were included.

Preparing such a volume would have been impossible without the help of many. In addition to the authors and publishers who were kind enough to consent to our use of their works, we are indebted to the entire staff of the Management Research Center for their suggestions and advice as the project progressed. Dean Joseph W. McGuire of the University of Illinois, Professor Herbert Simon of the Carnegie-Mellon University, and Professor Edgar H. Schein of the Massachusetts Institute of Technology were all very helpful in the preparation of this manuscript; we owe our thanks to them for their encouragement and suggestions. We also appreciate the help from Edel Deep in typing various drafts and assembling the chapters. Finally, we are grateful to Mrs. Joyce Colletti for typing the manuscript, compiling the references, preparing the indexes, and keeping our heads above water.

Editing this book was a rewarding educational experience for us. We recommend the experience to others.

BERNARD M. BASS
SAMUEL D. DEEP

ROCHESTER, NEW YORK

Contents

PERSONAL GROWTH AND INTERPERSONAL DYNAMICS

CURRENT PERSPECTIVES FOR FOR MANAGING ORGANIZATIONS

OBJECTIVES
AND
HUMAN PERFORMANCE

Since the landmark publication by Peter Drucker[1] on the subject, progressive managements have seriously attempted to shift from management-by-responsibilities to management-by-objectives. But it is easier said than done. That is, the ideas involved are simple, the mechanics are easy to understand, but the social and emotional components of management behavior that need to be accepted and internalized meet with much conscious and unconscious resistance. To accomplish true management-by-objectives, rather than the appearance of it, requires managers to develop a sense of mutual trust with their subordinates to permit real attitudes, expectations, hopes, and fears to be communicated between them. Moreover, managers must develop patience and a willingness to depend on their workers to follow through the attainment of objectives that have been set by means of joint consultation.

---

[1] *The Practice of Management.* New York: Harper & Brothers, Publishers, 1954.

Management-by-objectives assumes that subordinates are better motivated to do their best if they have clear accepted goals to achieve than if they are aware only of the work they are responsible for doing. These goals are more clear and acceptable to the subordinates if they participate in identifying and clarifying these objectives and if in the process they become committed to achieving them.

The approach calls for periodic meetings between manager and subordinate to set mutually acceptable goals and development of plans to reach them. The period between meetings depends on the nature of the subordinate's job. Meetings may be once a week for blue-collar employees or once a year for higher level bench scientists. The following meeting on the subject is a review of the extent to which the goals agreed to at the first meeting have been attained and how objectives have to be reset as a consequence for the next period of effort.

At least seven behavioral requirements are needed by managers to make management-by-objectives a success: (1) skill in consulting, (2) skill in coaching, (3) skill in group leadership, (4) analytic skills to diagnose problems, (5) concern and consideration for subordinates, (6) interest in developing subordinates, and (7) understanding one's self and others involved in the implementation process. These requirements of the individual manager will be dealt with more fully in the second part of the book; the first part concentrates on examining the social, psychological, and managerial issues involved in setting objectives, organizing to meet those objectives, and evaluating and compensating performance in attaining the objectives.

Setting
Objectives

This chapter deals with the goals and motives of business managers. The readings included go into the issues of individual perception of the importance of goals, organizational correlates of management's goals, and the relation of organizational goals to survival and success.

Concentration on some objectives rather than others in making business decisions may depend on managerial values held about human, technical, and monetary issues. Thus, given the same objective information concerning company policy, two managers may adopt opposing positions. Why? Because their personal values differ. England finds that businessmen continually deal with a great number and variety of goals, and he distinguishes among four subsets of these goals in terms of their behavioral relevance and content. His finding that personal variables account for more of the goal differences reported by managers than do organizational characteristics sheds revealing light on the objective setting function within organizations.

Graham suggests that the influence an organization member has on setting goals, the information he has concerning them, and his extent of formal education are all positively correlated with his perceived importance of the goals. Like England, he places the source or organization objectives at the feet of the individual manager and his own characteristics.

It is easy to say that managers have one simple goal—to make money—or, in the case of nonprofit activities, to produce a maximum quality and quantity of goods or services; but we rarely see such single-minded direction. Perhaps it is more realistic to look upon the manager as a system balancer working in a complex environment with multiple objectives. Certainly England and Graham both imply this to be the case. In a more direct approach, Friedlander and Pickle look at the effect on survival and growth of an organization in terms of its ability to concurrently fulfill the complex needs of its owners, its employees, and its contacts with the outside world. This approach destroys the myth that organization decision makers can be guided by only one or a few objectives, and presents a clear connection between the complexity of organizational goals and systems analysis.

1

Organizational Goals
and
Expected Behavior of American Managers

George W. England
University of Minnesota

This study complements (16), also by the author. In the current analysis the author compares four levels of organizational goals with their assumed behavior importance and content. Organizational efficiency, high productivity, and profit maximization form a subset of goals that are behaviorally very important and are viewed as maximization criteria and as alternative generators.

This research was completed under a Ford Foundation Faculty Fellowship for Research on Business and while the author was a Senior Specialist, Institute of Advanced Projects, East-West Center, University of Hawaii. Appreciation is expressed to both institutions. Reprinted by permission from *Academy of Management Journal*, X, No. 2 (1967) 107–17.

There has been considerable discussion and interest in "organizational literature" about the importance and relevance of the concept of an organizational goal or a set of organizational goals in understanding organizational behavior. Simon's analysis in this area is particularly helpful in identifying important issues and suggesting logical solutions. He proposes that ". . . the concept of goal appears indispensable to organization theory." However, he points out that "the goal of an action is seldom unitary, but generally consists of a whole set of constraints the action must satisfy. It appears convenient to use the term 'organizational goal' to refer to constraints or sets of constraints, imposed by the organizational role, that have only an indirect relation with the personal motives of the individual who fills the role. More narrowly, 'organizational goal' may be used to refer particularly to the constraint sets that define roles at the upper levels of the administrative hierarchy."

Simon further suggests that goals may be utilized in two different ways in decision making. ". . . The goals may be used directly to synthesize proposed solutions (alternative generation). Second, the goals may be used to test the satisfactoriness of a proposed solution (alternative testing)" (37).

The present paper is concerned with these and related issues concerning the goals of business organizations. Specifically, it presents data concerning the way in which organizational goals are viewed by a sample of American managers. The empirical data for this report were obtained through the same study which provided the factual base for the article in the March *Journal,* "Personal Value Systems of American Managers" (16). In the present article the previously discussed personal values of American managers are complemented by the responses of the same managers to concepts about goals of business organizations.

ORGANIZATIONAL GOALS AND EXPECTED BEHAVIOR

A summary of the responses of 1072 managers to the organizational goal concepts is shown in Table 1. The columns of data in Table 1 represent: 1) the percentage of the total group of managers who rated each goal as "highly" important, 2) the percentage of the total group of managers who ranked "successful" as best indicating the meaning of each goal to them, and 3) the percentage of the total group of managers who both rated the goal as "highly important" and ranked "successful" as best indicating the meaning of the goal to them. The vertical lines beside the percentage figures indicate groupings of similar values.

For example, the percentages 81, 80, and 72 in the first column signify approximately equal rated importance for the three goals (Organizational Efficiency, High Productivity, and Profit Maximization). Likewise the percentages 60, 58, 58, and 65 in the first column signify approximately equal rated importance for the four goals (Organizational Growth, Industry Leadership, Organizational Stability, and Employee Welfare). The rated importance of the former three goals is higher, however, than the rated importance of the latter four goals.

TABLE 1
BEHAVIOR ANALYSIS OF ORGANIZATIONAL GOAL CONCEPTS

Goals of Business Organizations	% High Importance	% Successful 1st Ranked	% High Importance and Successful 1st Ranked
Organizational Efficiency	81	71	60
High Productivity	80	70	60
Profit Maximization	72	70	56
Organizational Growth	60	72	48
Industrial Leadership	58	64	43
Organizational Stability	58	54	38
Employee Welfare	65	20	17
Social Welfare	16	8	4

Total Group (N=1072).

A theoretical rationale and considerable data from the larger Personal Value System study suggest that a useful general measure of the behavioral relevance of each goal concept is represented by the percentage in the third column of Table 1 (e.g., the percentage of the total group that responds both "high importance" and "successful" as most descriptive)[1] If one accepts this joint probability statement—column 3 also can be expressed in probability terms as P (High Importance Ω Successful first ranked) or $P(I\Omega S)$ as a measure of the general behavioral relevance of a goal, the data in Table 1 clearly show that the eight goals constitute four subsets of goals as indicated by the horizontal lines.

The first subset includes the goals Organization Efficiency, High Productivity, and Profit Maximization. Both the high behavioral relevance and the content of the goals in this subset would argue that these are what Simon calls maximization criteria. They are the goals which managers attempt to influence by their actions, decisions, or behavior. It would also seem that this subset of goals could be described as alternative generators (e.g., goals which are used to directly synthesize proposed solutions in situations where possible courses of action must be discovered, designed, or synthesized). This subset of goals is perhaps best understood as indicating "general efficiency," a dimension of organization efficiency that is discussed by Mahoney (27).

The second subset consists of the goals Organizational Growth, Industry

---

[1] (16) A highly abbreviated version of the rationale would be as follows. Managers are basically pragmatically oriented individuals; that is, when they say something is important they also say it is successful (data from the larger study support this statement). Therefore, in such a group the behavioral relevance of an idea or concept to an individual may be best indicated as a joint function of its importance to him and the extent to which it fits his primary orientation. $P(I\Omega S)$ was chosen as the function of these two variables to represent the behavioral relevance.

Leadership, and Organizational Stability. The secondary position of these goals in terms of behavioral relevance and their content would suggest that they should be viewed as associative constraints. They generally are not sought in and of themselves (actions are not usually taken to directly influence them); rather they are utilized in alternative testing. A manager may decide on a given action to influence the "general efficiency" goals and then check to see what the impact is on the goals in this second subset. Perhaps the term "associative status goals" reflects both that these goals are often associated with the "general efficiency" goals and their status nature.

The third subset of goals includes only Employee Welfare. The data suggest that Employee Welfare is a professed goal but one which will not influence managerial behavior to any great extent. Employee Welfare is considered "highly important" by 65 per cent of the total sample, while only 20 per cent view it as successful. In other words, it does not fit the pragmatic orientation of managers and thus will not be high in behavioral relevance (this is shown in the percentage figure of 17 in column 3 of Table 1). Other data not included in this article suggest that Employee Welfare as an organizational goal probably represents an Intended Value which is socioculturally indiced but which has relatively low behavioral relevance.[2]

The final subset of goals includes Social Welfare which is seen as neither important nor successful by managers. In other words, it is not important and it does not fit the pragmatic mode of valuation which is characteristic of managers; thus it would be expected to have low behavioral relevance, as is indicated by its low percentage in column 3 of Table 1.

The general validity of separating the organizational goal concepts into four subsets is further supported by analyses which show the same behavioral relevance patterns emerge, as shown in Table 1 for 61 of 65 subgroups formed from categories of the organizational and personal variables (taken one at a time). The four exceptions to this pattern are all cases where the goal Organizational Growth has the third highest joint probability $P(I\Omega S)$ and becomes a part of the first subset of goals.

RELATED RESEARCH

Dent reports the interview responses of 145 chief executives (or their deputies) in businesses in five cities to the question, "What are the aims of top management in your company?" (14). A rearrangement of Dent's results as shown in Table 2 is generally consistent with the present results, although the samples, questions, and methods of data collection are different. The stated aims "to make money, profits, or a living" are viewed as general indicators of

---

[2] Other concepts from the larger study which are grouped with employee welfare are trust, loyalty, honor, dignity, individuality, government, property, rationale, and religion. They form what is commonly called a "motherhood" set of values, highly professed but perhaps less operative in terms of behavior.

the "general efficiency" subset of goals, while "to be efficient, economical" and "to pay dividends to stockholders" are more specific indicators of the "general efficiency" goals and are therefore not mentioned as frequently. "To provide a good product; public service" is a general indicator of the "associative status goals," while "to grow," "to operate or develop the organization," and "to meet or stay ahead of competitors" are specific instances or examples of the associative status goals. "To provide for the welfare of employees" clearly is similar to Employee Welfare. Dent was not able, however, to distinguish the professed nature of this goal with his data as is done in the present study. "To contribute to the community; community relation" is an expression of the goal Social Welfare which is of low behavioral relevance in both studies.

Table 2 summarizes the distinctions that have been made concerning the eight organizational goals studied. The reader should be aware that this classification of organizational goals by type, major function, and behavioral relevance is made at a high level of generality and does not imply rigid and nonoverlapping subsets of goals. Rather, it attempts to suggest the essence of each type of goal in terms of function and behavioral relevance.

TABLE 2
SUMMARY CLASSIFICATION OF ORGANIZATIONAL GOALS

Type of Goal	Major Functions of Goals	Behavioral Relevance of Goals
Maximization Criteria Organizational Efficiency High Productivity Profit Maximization	Alternative Generation	High
Associative Status Goals Organizational Growth Industry Leadership Organizational Stability	Alternative Testing	Moderately High
Intended Goals Employee Welfare	Alternative Testing	Relatively Low
Low-Relevance Goals Social Welfare		Very Low

ORGANIZATIONAL GOAL VARIABILITY

As previously indicated, the general pattern of four subsets of goals shown in Table 2 remains constant when analyzed with respect to organizational and personal variables. Within this general pattern, however, there are a number of differences relating to a specific goal and a specific organizational or personal variable. Table 3 summarizes the extent of such differences.

TABLE 3
AIMS OF MANAGEMENTS IN FIVE CITIES ($N = 145$)
(AFTER DENT, 1959)

Aims of Management	Percentage of managers giving various aims among first 3 aims
To make money, profits, or a living	52
To be efficient, economical	12
To pay dividends to stockholders	9
To provide a good product; public service	39
To grow	17
To operate or develop the organization	14
To meet or stay ahead of competitors	13
To provide for the welfare of employees: a good living, security, happiness, good working conditions	39
To contribute to the community, community relations	3
Miscellaneous other aims	18

Table 4 shows that there is a statistically significant relationship between a specific goal and an organizational or personal variable in 14 out of a possible 88 instances. The nature of these relationships is considered in the following sections.

TABLE 4
ORGANIZATIONAL AND PERSONAL VARIABLE DIFFERENCES
IN RESPONSE TO GOALS
ORGANIZATIONAL GOALS

	High Productivity	Profit Maximization	Organizational Efficiency	Industry Leadership	Organizational Stability	Organizational Growth	Employee Welfare	Social Welfare
Company size		X			X	X		
Type of Company				X				
Line–Staff position								
Department								
Organizational level								X
Income								
Years as manager				X				
Job satisfaction				X				
College major	X		X			X		
Amount of education					X			
Age					X	X		X

X denotes instances where there is a chi-square which is significant at the 0.05 level or above between classification on an organizational or personal variable and a goal's behavioral relevance score.

SIZE OF FIRM (NUMBER OF EMPLOYEES)

The relationship between size of firm and the behavioral relevance of organizational goals, $P(I\Omega S)$, is similar for the general efficiency goals (Organizational Efficiency, High Productivity, and Profit Maximization). Managers from small firms (under 500 employees) have the *lowest* behavioral relevance scores (54, 54, and 48, respectively, for the three goals). Managers of medium-size companies (500–999 employees) have the *highest* behavioral relevance scores (64, 64, and 61, respectively, for the three goals). Large firm managers (10,000 or more employees) have behavioral relevance scores that are *between* those of the other two size groups (61, 58, and 56, respectively, for the three goals). While these results are rather clear cut, undoubtedly their explanation is not. The nonlinear nature of the relationship between size of firm and the behavioral relevance of the general efficiency goals suggests that several explanatory variables may be involved. Most frequently mentioned in the literature are differences in ownership equity, in competitive pressures, in public attention focused on various size firms, and in the relative affluence of different size firms (9).

The Associative Status Goals (Organizational Growth, Industry Leadership, and Organizational Stability) are not consistently related to size of firm. There are, however, two significant relationships. Managers of medium size firms have *higher* behavioral relevance scores on the goal Organizational Growth than do managers of either small or large firms (53 as compared to 42 and 43). These findings appear reasonable if one assumes that managers from medium size companies can most logically expect growth and perhaps most desire it. Small firms may well accept their size status, and large firms have already achieved the goal of Organizational Growth so it is less meaningful to them. Managers of large firms have *lower* behavioral relevance scores on the goal Organizational Stability than do managers of either small or medium size firms (29 as compared to 40 and 41). Perhaps this finding indicates that large firms already have sufficient stability to absorb minor shocks; thus their stability is seldom seriously threatened. There are no significant relationships between size of firm and behavior relevance for the goal Employee Welfare or for the goal Social Welfare.

TYPE OF COMPANY

Wholesale and Retail Trade managers have *high* behavioral relevance scores on the goal Industry Leadership (48 as compared with 43 for all managers). This finding suggests that brand leadership and industry marketing figures are stressed in the highly competitive trade areas. There are no major types of firm differences on the other seven organizational goals.

ORGANIZATIONAL LEVEL

Presidents of companies indicate *greater* behavioral relevance for the goal Social Welfare than managers at other levels in the organization (16 as compared to 4 for the total group). Approaching statistical significance were organizational level differences on the goal Employee Welfare. Here also, presidents had *higher* behavioral relevance scores than did other groups (29 as compared to 17 for the total group). These findings would seem to reflect the social class position of presidents as well as the fact that presidents represent their company to society and generally have more contact with society than do others in the organization. There are no significant organizational level differences on the general efficiency goals or on the associative status goals.

MANAGERIAL EXPERIENCE (YEARS AS A MANAGER)

Managers with over 30 years of managerial experience have *high* behavioral relevance scores on the goal Industry Leadership (53 as compared with 43 for the total group). As will be seen, Industry Leadership becomes a more relevant goal with increased age and job satisfaction as well as with increased managerial experience. There are no significant differences between experience levels on the other seven organizational goals.

GENERAL JOB SATISFACTION

Hoppock's Job Satisfaction Blank (a four-item general satisfaction measure) was included as a part of the personal information obtained from managers (21). For purposes of the present analysis, the scores on the four items were combined for each manager and the distribution of total scores was divided into three groups: low group (satisfaction scores—approximately 25 per cent of managers), middle group (middle satisfaction scores—approximately 50 per cent of managers), and high group (highest satisfaction scores—approximately 25 per cent of managers).

There is a significant linear relationship between job satisfaction scores and the behavioral relevance score on the goal Industry Leadership. The high satisfaction group has a behavioral relevance score of 50, the middle satisfaction group has a score of 44, and the low satisfaction group has a score of 36 on the goal Industry Leadership. There are no significant relationships between job satisfaction level and any of the other seven organizational goals.

COLLEGE MAJOR

Managers who majored in humanities, fine arts, or social sciences have significantly *higher* behavioral relevance scores on the general efficiency goals High Productivity and Organizational Efficiency (71 and 73, respectively, as compared to 60 for the total group of managers on the two goals). Managers who majored in the social sciences have *higher* scores of the goal Organizational Growth (56 as compared with 48 for the total group). Perhaps these findings indicate that those managers who have been able both to survive organizationally and who have formal training about human behavior recognize the difficulty and complexity involved in achieving organizational goals and assign more behavioral effort to the task. There are no significant college major differences on the goal Employee Welfare or on the goal Social Welfare.

AMOUNT OF FORMAL EDUCATION

Managers with less education (those without college degrees as contrasted with college degree holders) have *higher* scores on the goal Organizational Stability (46 as compared to 37). Managers with less education would seem to be less secure and less able to change; thus stability is highly valued. There are no significant differences in amount of education on the other seven organizational goals.

AGE

Middle-aged managers (45–54 years of age) have *low* behavioral relevance scores on the goals Industry Leadership and Organizational Growth (36 and 44 respectively as compared to 43 and 48 for the total group). Older managers (60 or over) have relatively *high* scores on the goal Industry Leadership (53), while younger managers (under 35) have *high* scores on the goal Organizational Growth (56).

There is a significant linear relationship between age and the behavioral relevance score on the goal Social Welfare. Older managers have *higher* scores while younger managers have *lower* scores (7 as compared to 1).

VARIABLES NOT SIGNIFICANTLY RELATED TO ORGANIZATIONAL GOALS

There are no significant relationships between behavioral relevance scores on any of the eight organizational goals and Line–Staff Position, Departmental Affiliation, and Income Levels of Managers.

SUMMARY AND CONCLUSIONS

The present study strongly supports the notion that it is generally more meaningful to talk about a set of organizational goals as opposed to a single organizational goal. We would agree with Simon that decisions are most often directed toward courses of action that satisfy a number of constraints and that it is this set (rather than any one of its members) that is most accurately viewed as the goal of an action.

The present analysis, however, does distinguish between four levels of organizational goals in terms of their behavioral importance and their content. The goals Organizational Efficiency, High Productivity, and Profit Maximization form a subset of goals that are behaviorally very important and could be viewed as maximization criteria and alternative generators. In this sense, one is justified in saying that this subset of goals is the most important subset. A second subset of goals includes Organizational Growth, Industry Leadership, and Organizational Stability. This subset of associative status goals is moderately important behaviorally and probably serves largely an alternative testing function in the decision-making process. The goal Employee Welfare is viewed as an intended goal which has low behavioral relevance and will most often serve in an alternative testing function. Finally, the goal Social Welfare was found to have low behavioral relevance as an organizational goal.

There is a very high degree of similarity of goal patterns in different types and sizes of organizations and as expressed by different groups of managers. The pattern of four subsets of goals seems to cut across organizational and personal variables and probably represents a highly stable hierarchical arrangement of the goals as viewed by American managers in general.

When the relationships between specific goals and organizational or personal variables are examined, two major implications are suggested. There are only three significant relationships between the general efficiency goals and the organizational or personal characteristics as compared to nine significant relationships for the associative status goals. This would imply that differences in decision making or in behavior among groups (as opposed to within groups) may be more a function of the associative status goals than of the general efficiency goals. The general efficiency goals are "more important behaviorally" within an organization, but since they are internalized more equally by different groups of managers, they are less responsible for differences across or between organizations. In this sense, alternative testing may contribute to decision differences between organizations to a greater extent than does alternative generation.

Second, the finding that personal variables account for more of the specific goal differences than do organizational variables (nine differences associated with personal variables as compared with five for organizational variables) suggests that the actual goals of business may be related more closely to personal characteristics of its managers than to broad characteristics of the business. This finding is in direct contradiction to Dent's conclusion and questions the extent to which organizational goals can be understood without reference to personal goals, personal values, or motives of individuals. To paraphrase Simon, organizational goals (rather than personal motives) may enter the decision process as fixed constraints (only courses of action that satisfy the constraints are considered, but the constraints have no influence on the choice of action within the set).

Finally, it should be quite clear that there is a great deal of variation in the behavioral importance of organizational goals at the level of the individual manager even within the generally stable pattern found. It is this individual variation in terms of organizational goals, coupled with the fact that goals are only one part of the decision process, that accounts for much of the richness of behavior within organizations.

2

Correlates of Perceived Importance of Organizational Objectives

Gerald H. Graham
Wichita State University

A survey of 315 organizational members suggests that influence, information, and formal education are positively and significantly correlated with one's perception of the importance of organizational objectives, whereas years of experience and organizational level are not significantly correlated to perceived importance of objectives.

Reprinted by permission from *Academy of Management Journal*, XI, No. 3 (1968), 291–300.

Organization theorists generally conceive that the establishment and identification of departmental objectives are important to the efficient functioning of the department and, thus, to the entire organization (17, 20, 33). Below are a few of the more common reasons why objectives are considered to be important:

1. they serve as a priority system over opposing interests,
2. they serve as standards by which accomplishments can be compared,
3. they make possible decentralization of authority by allowing commonly held objectives to serve as coordinators, and
4. individuals tend to participate in group activity to the extent that they perceive group goals as providing degrees of satisfaction for their individual needs (26, 29).

We can generalize and say that organizational objectives are important to efficient departmental functioning because of the coordinating influence that objectives have upon human behavior. Further, it has been demonstrated that specific individual behavior is partially a function of (1) a person's perception of tangible and intangible variables that exist external to his nervous system, and (2) other mental concepts that comprise a portion of his cognitive field. Put differently, an individual's reaction within a situation is a function of his perception of the situation rather than his interaction with a solitary combination of "real" stimuli and constraints (7, 19, 36).

Perception, as Young expresses it, refers to sensing, interpreting, and appreciating physical and social processes (41). However, as in the Dewey and Bentley connotation, it is probably more valid to regard perception as a transaction with one's environment rather than to think of it as a stimulus–response relationship. Meanings which are assigned to events are not intrinsic in the events, but they exist internally within the skin of the individual. Although physical and social worlds are dynamic, people build up constancies within their minds which tend to remain relatively stable over a period of time. These internal dimensions of a person's inner state are largely learned as a result of the individual's totality of previous experience; and in any given interaction, a portion of an individual's internal state may remain unevoked and a portion of his environment may go unnoticed (28).

The purpose of this study is to examine the extent to which certain organizational variables are related to a member's perception of the importance of departmental objectives to the efficient functioning of the department. The specific hypothesis may be stated as follows:

There is a positive and significant relationship between a member's perception of the importance of departmental objectives to the efficient functioning of the department and:

1. perceived amount of influence the member has upon setting or altering the objectives of his department,

2. perceived amount of information the member has concerning the objectives of his department,
3. formal organization level,
4. years of experience with the organization,
5. member's extent of formal education.

The hypothesis, by focusing on the perception of a relationship—importance of objectives to efficiency—reflects Berelson and Steiner's contention that persons respond to relationships rather than to discrete elements one at a time or the sum total of the whole picture (6).

We can reason that a person is inculcated by his culture to associate his perceived ability to influence with a mental construct labeled "importance." It adds to one's self-significance to perceive the objects of his influence as being relatively important. Conversely, if we postulate importance as the independent variable and perceived influence as the dependent variable, then it is plausible that an individual would function to amplify personal influence over that which he conceives as being important.

It is further suggested that the degree to which information is dispersed inherently connotes importance to whatever the information concerns. If persons in relatively high-power positions expend significant amounts of energy transmitting information, it is implied that the object of the information is important enough to justify such actions. Or, if information is the dependent element of the relationship, then we can accept the proposition that an individual would seek to gain information about that which he considers important. In a similar, but more general vein, Kelly found that information about something ahead of time influences the perception of the event (24).

Some studies have indicated that organizational position (level) influences the manner in which the individual perceives himself and other organizational components (13, 32). There are at least two reasons why managers in upper levels might be expected to attach more importance to the relationship between objectives and efficiency than would managers at lower levels. One, upper-level managers are more concerned with the establishment and evaluation of objectives at various organizational levels; and two, they probably have more exposure to information which stresses the importance of objectives.

Finally, some writers have indicated that the selection and accentuation of certain features of one's environment are colored by the perceiver's education, learning, and experiences (6, 39). Parts 4 and 5 of the hypothesis are assumed to relate to some degree to particular segments of a person's education and experience. Specifically, formal education, in a general sense, is associated with intelligence and a greater understanding of one's environment; thus, the more formal education that one acquires, the more likely he is to be cognizant of the importance of departmental objectives. Similarly, it would seem that additional years of experience would have tendencies to make it easier for members to understand and appreciate the environment in which they operate.

METHODOLOGY

To test the hypothesis, 250 names of managers of manufacturing companies were randomly selected from a directory which listed the top official of each manufacturing company located in a heavily industrialized state.[1] The list included companies which had branch offices as well as those with home offices in the state, but it included only one representative from each company. Companies with less than 200 employees were excluded from the study.

Two identical questionnaires were mailed to each person selected from the list. The recipients of the questionnaires were instructed to complete one of the questionnaires and pass the other along to the first member of his company, at the next lower managerial level, with whom he came into contact after receiving the letter. It is possible, of course, that this method of selection is not "purely" random because some individuals may have selected the second person according to personal preferences. However, this was discouraged by the instruction to present the "extra" questionnaire to the first person with whom he came into contact. After a follow-up letter, 315 (63 percent) usable returns were received.

The purpose of choosing a large number of firms with only two representatives from each firm was an attempt to reduce the possible biasing effect of a particular philosophy that may tend to permeate a given organization. When a study concentrates on a few firms, it becomes increasingly difficult to generalize the findings to other organizations because of the possibility of this biasing effect. It may appear to be more statistically sophisticated to select a large number of representatives from a few organizations, but the writer earnestly believes that a sample of a few members drawn from a large number of organizations is likely to be more representative of the universe. If there is a loss in statistical sophistication, this is more than offset by the reduction of the possible biasing effect of a particular philosophy.

Among other questions, the participants were asked to respond to the following three questions:

1. How important are the objectives of your department to the efficiency of operations within your department?
2. How much influence or say do you have in setting or changing the objectives of your department?
3. How much information do you have about the objectives of your department?

For Question 1, their alternatives were: "absolutely necessary," "very helpful," "some help," or "little or no help." The alternatives for Questions 2 and 3 were: "a great deal," "quite a bit," "some," or "little or none." The participants

---

[1] This study represents a portion of a more comprehensive study concerning organizational objectives.

were also classified according to organizational level, formal education, and years of experience with the company.

From these data, five contingency tables were constructed to relate responses to Question 1 to responses to Questions 2 and 3 as well as to organization level, education, and experience. Chi-square scores were computed for each contingency table.[2] For the complete hypothesis to be supported, the chi-square score for each table should be significant, and observation of the data should indicate that the relationship is positive.

To check the interrelatedness of the variables, additional contingency tables were developed to cross-classify each variable in the study with every other variable in the study.

FINDINGS

As shown in Table 1, the data suggest the existence of a significant relationship between perceived influence in setting or changing departmental objectives and perceived importance of departmental objectives to organizational efficiency. Observation of the data also indicates that the relationship is positive; *i.e.*, the more influence one perceives himself as having, the more important he perceives the objectives to be. Fifty-one and three tenths percent of those who indicated that they had "some or none" influence on evolving or altering organizational objectives classed objectives as being "absolutely necessary," but 76.0 percent of those who believed that they had a "great deal" of influence on objectives classed them as being "absolutely necessary." Contrarily, only 4.0 percent of the respondents who perceived their influence as being "great"

TABLE 1
RELATION OF PERCEIVED INFLUENCE
TO PERCEIVED IMPORTANCE OF OBJECTIVES

Importance of Objectives	Amount of Influence					
	Great		Quite		Some or None	
	Number	Percent	Number	Percent	Number	Percent
Absolutely necessary	95	76.0	49	60.5	56	51.4
Very helpful	25	20.0	26	32.0	33	30.3
Some or none	5	4.0	6	7.5	20	18.3
Totals	125	100.0	81	100.0	109	100.0

$Chi^2 = 22.186 < 0.05$.

[2] Because of limited responses in certain cells, the "little or no help" classification was combined with the "some help" category in Question 1, and "little or none" responses were combined with the "some" responses in Questions 2 and 3 for purposes of constructing the contingency tables.

checked the "some or none" classification under "importance of objectives." And the figure in the "some or none" classification under "importance of objectives" increased to 18.3 percent of those who felt that they had "some or none" influence on setting the objectives. According to the data, we can accept Part 1 of the hypothesis.

TABLE 2
RELATION OF PERCEIVED INFORMATION
TO PERCEIVED IMPORTANCE OF OBJECTIVES

Importance of Objectives	Amount of Information					
	Great		Quite		Some or None	
	Number	Percent	Number	Percent	Number	Percent
Absolutely necessary	134	75.7	51	53.7	15	34.8
Very helpful	37	20.9	35	36.9	12	27.9
Some or none	6	3.4	9	9.4	16	37.3
Totals	177	100.0	95	100.0	43	100.0

$Chi^2 = 57.607 < 0.05$.

We observe in Table 2 a significant relationship between perceived amount of information concerning department objectives and perceived importance of the objectives. Again, the relationship appears to be positive because 34.8 percent of those who checked "some or none" under "amount of information" indicated that objectives were "absolutely necessary," and 75.7 percent of those who indicated a "great amount" of information related that they felt objectives were "absolutely necessary." Likewise, the percentage of those who perceived "some or none" information and "some or none" importance was 37.3 percent as compared to only 3.4 percent for those who indicated the cell which includes "great" information and "some or little" importance. Therefore, on the basis of this survey, we are able to accept Part 2 of the hypothesis.

As indicated in Table 3, the data reveal no significant relationship between

TABLE 3
RELATION OF ORGANIZATION LEVEL
TO PERCEIVED IMPORTANCE OF OBJECTIVES

Importance of Objectives	Organization Level					
	Top Management		Middle Management		Supervisory Level	
	Number	Percent	Number	Percent	Number	Percent
Absolutely necessary	49	69.1	79	68.2	72	56.3
Very helpful	17	23.9	25	21.5	42	32.8
Some or none	5	7.0	12	10.3	14	10.9
Totals	71	100.0	116	100.0	128	100.0

$Chi^2 = 6.080 > 0.05$.

perceived importance of departmental goals and organization level. More middle management members (69.1 percent) tended to perceive objectives as being "absolutely necessary" than did supervisors (56.3 percent), but more supervisors checked "very helpful" than did middle managers (32.8 percent as compared to 21.5 percent, respectively). At the 0.05 level, the chi-square score indicates that the rows and levels are independent; thus, Part 3 of the hypothesis must be rejected.

Table 4 presents data which show no significant relationship between years of experience with the company and perceived importance of objectives. In fact, there is some evidence of a trend for members with 31 years or more with the company to attach slightly less importance to objectives than do members with less experience. Sixty-six and three tenths percent of the members with 10 years' experience or less felt that objectives were "absolutely necessary" while only 60.8 percent of the members with 31 years' experience or more revealed that objectives were "absolutely necessary." However, at the 0.05 level, the relationship is not significant and Part 4 of the hypothesis must be rejected.

TABLE 4
RELATION OF EXPERIENCE WITH COMPANY
TO PERCEIVED IMPORTANCE OF OBJECTIVES

Importance of Objectives	Years of Experience With Company							
	31 or more		21 to 30		11 to 20		10 or less	
	Number	Percent	Number	Percent	Number	Percent	Number	Percent
Absolutely necessary	28	60.8	51	61.4	56	63.6	65	66.3
Very helpful	10	21.8	23	27.8	27	30.7	24	24.5
Some or none	8	17.4	9	10.8	5	5.7	9	9.2
Totals	46	100.0	83	100.0	88	100.0	98	100.0

Chi^2 = 5.768 > 0.05.

Finally, as Table 5 depicts, the relationship between formal education and perceived importance of objectives approaches significance at the 0.05 level, and the chi-square score is significant at the 0.10 level. In the "absolutely necessary" slot there appears to be a definite trend for perceived importance to increase as the amount of formal education increases. Whereas only 54.0 percent of the respondents with a high school diploma or less indicated that objectives were "absolutely necessary," 68.5 percent of those with post-graduate college education felt that objectives were "absolutely necessary." Therefore, for the moment at least, we can accept Part 5 of the hypothesis.

The empirical data are consistent with two of the five parts of the hypothesis (Parts 1 and 2) and another part (Part 5) may be tentatively accepted.

To determine the interassociation of the variables with each other, each variable was cross-classified, in the form of a contingency table, with every other

TABLE 5

RELATION OF FORMAL EDUCATION
TO PERCEIVED IMPORTANCE OF OBJECTIVES

Importance of Objectives	Level of Formal Education							
	Post Graduate		College Degree		Some College		High School Diploma or Less	
	Number	Percent	Number	Percent	Number	Percent	Number	Percent
Absolutely necessary	24	68.5	80	67.3	56	63.6	40	54.0
Very helpful	7	20.0	32	27.1	25	28.5	20	27.1
Some or none	4	11.5	6	5.0	7	7.9	14	18.9
Totals	35	100.0	118	100.0	88	100.0	74	100.0

Chi^2 = 11.463 > 0.05.
Chi^2 = 11.463 < 0.10.

TABLE 6

RELATION OF EACH VARIABLE
TO EVERY OTHER VARIABLE*

	Influence	Information	Organization Level	Formal Education	Experience
Importance	+	+	0	+†	0
Influence		+	+	+	+
Information			+	+	0
Organization Level				+	+
Formal Education					+‡

*+ indicates significant and positive relationship at 0.05 level.
†Significant at 0.10 level.
‡Significant relationship but not clearly positive.

variable, and the associations that were found significant at the 0.05 level are indicated by a plus (+) sign in Table 6.

Although there is no relationship between organization level and importance of objectives, there is a significant and positive relationship between influence and organization level and between amount of information and organization level. Since managers at the top strata perceive themselves as containing more information and exerting more influence, concerning objectives, than do managers at lower levels, these forces would apparently suggest that higher level managers also perceive objectives to be more important than would managers at lower levels. This follows because information and influence are correlated with perceived importance. To explain this paradox, we can postulate two opposing sets of forces operating within the same relationship. The preceding discussion suggests forces with proclivities for a peremptory correlation between organization level and perceived importance. But since lower level managers have less information and influence concerning objectives, it is rational to assume that they attach a relatively greater value to the information and influence, which they perceive themselves as possessing, than managers at higher levels. Additionally, objectives at lower levels are more specific, more tangible, and more closely fettered to the individual's immediate success or failure than are the rather general, abstract, and often ambiguous objectives of higher organization levels.

If there are forces which tend to start up proclivities in individuals at top organization levels to attach more importance to objectives than individuals at lower levels attach to objectives, these forces could be offset by relatively greater values which are federated with limited resources and immediate environmental constraints.

If a person's totality of experiences is an influence upon his perception, the segment of these experiences identified as years of experience with the company has no significant differentiating effect with regard to perceived importance of objectives. This might be attributed to the fact that most individuals do not enter a business organization until they are 18 to 22 years of age. It is quite possible that certain constancies have been developed before individuals enter organizations, and these constancies may be stable enough to consistently perceive a specific mental construct labeled "importance of objectives." It might also be argued that a person's later years of experience are interpreted so that they are supportive to the constancies acquired during his initial years of experience. In other words, later years of experience may be less differentiating than earlier years.

Finally, a glance at Table 6 shows that almost all the variables are significantly related with each other. More specifically, (1) "influence" is significantly related to each of the other variables, (2) "formal education" is related to each of the other variables, (3) "information" is related to each of the other variables with the exception of "experience," (4) "organization level" is related to each of the other variables with the exception of "importance," (5) "importance" is related to each of the other variables with the exception of "organization level" and "experience," and (6) "experience" is related to each of the other variables with the exception of "importance" and "information."

SUMMARY AND CONCLUSIONS

To generalize, we can conclude that an organization member's perception of the importance of objectives to the efficient functioning of the department varies with influence and information that the member perceives himself as having concerning the objectives. And the relationship between formal education and perceived importance can be tentatively accepted. Observation of the data tends to indicate that these relationships are positive.

Of course, statistical analysis cannot tell us which of the variables are independent and which are dependent; we can only conclude that they are closely related. (In reality, the independency–dependency relationship probably flows in both directions for most of the variables in this study.) When an individual perceives the objectives of his department to be very important to the efficient functioning of his department, the probabilities are that he will also have more formal education and he will perceive himself as having more influence and information concerning the objectives than individuals who perceive objectives to be of lesser import. Or, in a situation in which organization members perceive themselves as having relatively little influence and information concerning departmental objectives, and in addition, if they have relatively little formal education, the probabilities favor the proposition that these members also attach relatively minor significance to the relationship between departmental objectives and efficient departmental functioning.

3

Components of Effectiveness
in Small Organizations

Frank Friedlander
Case Western Reserve University

Hal Pickle
Southwest Texas State College

If is to become effective in terms of survial and growth, an organization must fulfill (or satisfice) the needs and demands of its employees, its owners, and the relevant members of the society with which it transacts (its community, its governments, its customers, its suppliers, and its creditors). In this study, 97 small-business organizations and their relevant societal components were surveyed in order to explore the extent to which the organization fulfilled the needs of these components. Data indicate relatively few significant relationships among various types of employee fulfillment, owner fulfillment, and societal fulfillment, and these few relationships are of a rather low magnitude. The feasibility of an organization concurrently fulfilling the variety of demands made upon it is discussed. The organization is viewed as an open system of interdependent components, with energy transfer within the organization as well as between the organization and the societal components.

Reprinted by permission from *Administrative Science Quarterly*, XIII, No. 2 (1968) 289–304.

A primary focus for those interested in understanding or changing organizations has been upon the internal dynamics of the organization. This focus has led to emphasis on methods of enhancing the worth of the employee (to himself or to the organization) through selection, training, group participation, job restructuring, etc.; and consequently to criteria of effectiveness that are limited to the internal dynamics of the organization. The criteria have typically been of two kinds: those dealing with individual human resources such as motivation, mental health, cohesiveness, satisfaction, etc.; and those concerned with individual performance, such as amount produced, quality of output, error rate, etc. The generally low relationship between these two sets of criteria has been disturbing for the researcher and has resulted in numerous dilemmas for the practitioner (34). Since these two criteria have for the most part been uncorrelated, it appears useless to attempt to maximize them both. On the other hand, favoring one over the other produces either inefficiency for the organization or dissatisfaction for the individual. This dilemma has spurred some researchers to expand the scope of their analyses to encompass situational determinants of the satisfaction-performance relationship (23). Others have, in one way or another, explicitly recognized the inescapable tension between the individual and the organizational goals (1, 25, 35) and have concentrated upon the reduction of these tensions.

For the most part, theories and research concerned with individual performance, employee satisfaction, and reduction of tension between individual and organizational goals are dealing only with internal aspects of the events, relationships, and structures that make up the total organizational system. If the organization is viewed as an open-energy system, however, it is apparent that it is dependent for survival and growth upon a variety of energy transfers not only within the organization, but also between the organization and its external environment (22). It is obvious, then, that the internal and external dynamics of the organization are complementary and interdependent. Modifications in one of these structures have an impact upon the other. This perpective of the organization is similar to the model proposed by Parsons, Shils, Naegle, and Pitts (30) in which four fundamental processes are specified for every social system: adaptation, goal achievement, integration, and latency. These functions provide a structural framework within which internal and external relationships may be explored.

A perspective that includes the organization's societal relationships can account for the full cycle of energy, since it incorporates both the importation of energy from this societal environment and the output of energy into that environment. The relationship between organization and environment is recognized by several research workers. For example, Bennis (5) claims that bureaucracy is least likely to cope and survive if unable to adapt to a rapidly changing, turbulent environment. Emery and Trist (15) stress that the primary task of managing an enterprise as a whole is to relate the total organizational system to its environment, and not just internal regulation. If the organization is to survive and grow, it must control its boundary conditions—the forms of exchange between the enterprise and the environment. Strother (40) reverses the direction of this influence process by claiming that one must allow for control of the organization by an outside and changing environment. Pepinsky, Weick, and Riner (31) observe that the organization must adapt to regulatory control by the environment. Typical models of organization behavior, however, treat the organization as a closed system and concentrate upon principles of internal functioning as if these problems were independent of the external environments (22).

SYSTEM EFFECTIVENESS

Parallel to the need to understand the total organization system as inter-dependent with its environment is the establishment of criteria of organizational effectiveness that reflect these interdependencies. Such criteria include those with some element of the organization's contribution *to society*, and those that describe effectiveness in terms of maximization of return *from society* to the organization. Bass (3), for example, suggests that an organization be evaluated in terms of its worth to the individual worker and the value of the worker and the organization to society. Similar criteria suggested by Davis (12) include broad social values, economic values, and the personal values. The emphasis is in a reversed direction for Katz and Kahn (22), who describe organizational effectiveness as referring to the maximization of return to the organization by all means—technological, political, market control, personnel policies, federal subsidies, etc.

Most behavioral scientists have come to realize that organizational effectiveness is not a unitary concept. Guion, for example, points out that "the fallacy of the single criterion lies in its assumption that everything that is to be predicted is related to everything else to be predicted—that there is a general factor in all criteria accounting for virtually all the important variance in behavior at work and its various consequences of value" (18). The assumption of unitary criteria of organizational effectiveness has its counterpart in the concept of utility maximization, in which utility is defined as the value to an individual of all things he can possibly enjoy or possess. All the nonmonetary components are assumed to be translatable into a single utility scale, which allows trade-offs between the nonmonetary and monetary components. The behavioral theory of the firm, by contrast, is rooted in the "satisficing" concept of individuals searching until a satisfactory (not an optimal) solution is found (37). Individuals are not likely to combine their various sources of satisfaction into a single function, and certainly are not likely to maximize such a function. They are likely to seek satisfactory solutions in the several areas of their activities, with few trade-offs.

These differences in assumptions parallel those of organizational behavior, not only in terms of the internal dynamics of the organization, but also in terms of the criteria of organizational effectiveness. In the behavioral theory of organizations, it is assumed that goals are formulated for organizational activity in several areas. The rational-man assumptions of economics for the individual become profit maximization for the organization. If organizational goals are extended beyond profit maximization, the organizational utility function must incorporate effectiveness in these other areas (8). If satisficing in these several activities rather than profit maximization is an organization goal, relative independence in their attainment might be expected.

Although the degree-of-fulfillment terminology is used in this article, fulfillment is probably more accurately represented in terms of the degree to which the organizational or environmental component is satisficed. Furthermore, it is probable that the expectations which a component holds of the organization in general, and the specific organization with which it transacts, affect the degree to which that component is satisfied with the organization.

Clearly, effectiveness criteria must take into account the profitability of the organization, the degree to which it satisfices its members, and the degree to which it is of value to the larger society of which it is a part. These three perspectives include system maintenance and growth, subsystem fulfillment, and environmental fulfillment. Each is obviously composed of several related components, and each component is hypothetically related to the other. The degree to which these several components of organizational effectiveness are interrelated is a primary focus of this paper.

The purpose of this study, then, was to explore the concept of total organizational effectiveness by studying the relationships between internal and external system effectiveness. Internal system components were those within the formal boundaries of the organization. Societal components with which the organization transacts by exporting and importing energy were considered part of the larger environment in which the organization is located. Effectiveness was viewed as the degree to which the needs of components were fulfilled (or satisficed) in their transactions with the organization. The specific interest was in the degree of interdependence in the satisfaction of components.

The particular subsystem components chosen for study do not exhaust the variety of components, but were selected to include seven of primary importance for the maintenance and growth of the organization in its society: the owner, the employees, and five societal components—the customers, the suppliers, the creditors, the community, and the government.[1]

---

[1] While customers, suppliers, creditors, communities, and governments were grouped in the general category of the organization's societal environment, other models are obvious. In accord with Parsons' AGIL model (adaptation, goal attainment, integration, latency), for example, owners and customers are crucial to goal attainment of product exchange; creditors, communities, governments, and suppliers provide necessary resources and support for the organization and are thus instrumental in the organization's adaptation to its environment; and employees perform integrative functions within the organizational system (30).

DATA

SAMPLE

Small organizations were preferred as sample units in the study, because it was felt that whatever relationships exist among components might be explored more adequately, since the links among these components are presumably shorter and less numerous. The sample included 97 small businesses, each with only one level of management, and each employing from 4 to about 40 employees.

A random stratified technique was used. The distribution of types of small businesses in the United States was determined from various census data and this distribution was approximated in a random selection of small businesses within the state of Texas. Since responses from two of the initial 97 business organizations were suspect, two additional organizations were substituted for these. The final sample of 97 small businesses was composed of 54 retail establishments, 26 service establishments, 8 wholesale establishments, 6 manufacturers, and 3 mineral extraction firms.

SOCIETAL COMPONENTS

The data for measuring the degree of fulfillment for each of the five societal components for each of the 97 organizations were gathered by questionnaires and interviews. All data were collected in quantified form, either in a Likert-type, multiple-choice format, or in specific dollar amounts or frequency information.

Initially, satisfaction for each of the five societal components was measured by from 5 to 37 items. Correlation coefficients were then computed among all items within each of the five components. Items within each of the five components which correlated highly with each other were then selected to represent that component, so as to maximize its internal consistency or cohesion. The items so selected were then given equal weight and averaged to form mean scores for each of the components. As a final check on this process and on the internal consistency of each component scale, reliability coefficients for internal consistency[2] were computed for each scale with the following results: custom-

---

[2] The internal consistency of each total societal component scale was computed using Kuder–Richardson's formula 20:

$$r_{tt} = \left[\frac{n}{n-1}\right]\left[\frac{\sigma T^2 - \Sigma pq}{\sigma T^2}\right].$$

Essentially, this formula measures the proportion of the total scale variance $[\sigma_T^2]$, which is composed of the sum of the inter-item covariances $[r_{12}\sigma_1\sigma_2]$. This formula was not applied to the creditor scale, since data were gathered from different types of statistical and financial records and were, therefore, not comparable.

ers, 0.96; suppliers, 0.77; owners, 0.92; communities, 0.65; and governments, 0.60. This method of scale construction, based upon maximizing the internal consistency of items within each scale, yielded improved results over some of our earlier procedures which did not utilize this method.

The data gathered and the methods used follow:

1. *Community.* Community fulfillment was measured in the general areas of membership and leadership in local and nonlocal organizations, the number of committees and drives that managers participated in during the past two years, and their attendance at community affairs such as fund-raising dinners, bazaars, etc. These data were obtained through a questionnaire survey administered to the managers in directed interviews.

2. *Government.* Relations with the federal, state, and local government were measured through the administration of a questionnaire to managers. Items concerned questioning by officials of the Internal Revenue Service on income tax returns, penalties paid on local, state or federal taxes, or reprimands or censures by tax officials. In general, these items reflected the degree to which the organization carried out its explicit and implicit responsibilities with governmental agencies.

3. *Customers.* Customers were surveyed by the use of a questionnaire administered in an interview. The sample size for each organization was proportional to its total number of customers within a framework of a minimum of 15 and a maximum of 25 customers per organization. Customers rated the respective business on a five-point scale on each of the following features: quality of goods or services; quantity of goods or services available; neatness, cleanliness, and uniformity of appearance of product; management's knowledge of product or service; speed of service; dependability of business; rank of this business in relation to others in its field; helpfulness, friendliness, and appearance of employees.

4. *Suppliers.* Supplier fulfillment was measured in the following areas: promptness of payment of accounts, fairness in transactions, receptiveness to suggestions, and over-all evaluation as a customer. Of 403 survey questionnaires mailed, 208 were completed and returned, representing a return of approximately 52 percent.

5. *Creditors.* Levels of creditor fulfillment with each organization were obtained from statistical data gathered during interviews with banks, retail merchant associations, and Dun and Bradstreet.

OWNER COMPONENTS

The degree of satisfaction for the owner of each organization was primarily financial. The score was composed of equal weights of the average yearly profit for the owner for the last ten years and the average yearly profit as a function of the hours per week that the owner worked for the organization. Since the correlation between these two measures was 0.95, the component was essentially a measure of owner financial profit.

EMPLOYEE COMPONENT

The SRA Employee Inventory, a measure of employee satisfaction, was administered to all employees of each organization having ten or fewer employees. For organizations having more than ten employees, ten were randomly selected to represent the organization. A total of 513 inventories were completed, representing an average of 5.29 employees per organization.

Five types of employee fulfillment were measured within each organization. These types of fulfillment had been previously derived from a factor analysis of the SRA Employee Inventory (10). Types of fulfillment included the following:

1. *Satisfaction with working conditions:* 9 items related to adequacy of working conditions, effects of these conditions on work efficiency, adequacy of equipment, reasonable hours of work, and absence of physical and mental pressures.

2. *Satisfaction with financial reward:* 7 items related to adequacy of pay, effectiveness of personnel policies with respect to pay, and benefit programs and pay in comparison with other companies.

3. *Confidence in management:* 19 items related to management's organizing ability, its handling of employee benefit policies, its adequacy in two-way communication, and its interest in employees.

4. *Opinion about immediate supervisor:* 12 items related to how well the supervisor organized his work, knowledge of the job, ability to get things done on time, supplying adequate equipment, letting employees know what was expected, emphasizing proper training, making employees work together, treating employees fairly, keeping his promises, giving encouragement, and interest in employee welfare.

5. *Satisfaction with self-development:* 5 items related to employee's feeling of belongingness, of participation, of pride in the company, of doing something worthwhile, and of growth on the job.

RESULTS

Correlation coefficients were computed in order to explore the relationships among the components. The relationships between external and internal criteria of organizational effectiveness were considered first. External criteria were those related to fulfillment of the needs of the five components of the societal system; internal criteria were those related to the five needs of the employees.

In a moderate number of instances, organizations were able to satisfice both societal needs and employee needs simultaneously, as indicated in Table 1. In almost all cases where significant relationships do exist, however, these are of a relatively low magnitude. Thus, while some mutual satisficing of employees and societal components does occur, the degree of this concurrent satisficing

TABLE 1
RELATIONS AMONG SOCIETAL FULFILLMENT, OWNER FULFILLMENT,
ORGANIZATIONAL SIZE, AND EMPLOYEE FULFILLMENT.

Components fulfilled	Employee fulfillment				
	Working conditions	Financial rewards	Confidence in management	Immediate Supervisor	Self-development
Societal components					
Community	0.33*	0.06	0.28*	0.23†	0.24†
Government	−0.09	0.00	−0.06	−0.03	−0.12
Customer	0.11	0.20†	0.21†	0.23†	0.32*
Supplier	0.10	0.12	0.16	0.05	0.10
Creditor	0.09	−0.03	0.09	0.15	0.16
Owner					
Financial profit	0.12	0.07	0.20†	0.22†	0.23†
Organizational size					
(size of work force)	−0.03	−0.21	−0.10	−0.03	0.01

*$p < 0.01$.
†$p < 0.05$.
$N = 97$.

is rather low. Of the five societal components, only community and customer satisfaction seem to vary consistently (and positively) with the several types of employee satisfaction. In the case of community fulfillment, this finding is understandable. Organizations that recognize community needs and fulfill them are likely to be effective in providing similarly for their employees. Furthermore, in smaller communities, the membership of community and employee groups may overlap to a considerable degree. The reasons for the employee–customer satisfaction relationship are perhaps similar to those of the finding on the employee–community satisfaction relationship. Furthermore, in retail and service organizations, close contact between customers and employee may serve as a mechanism of contagion of satisfaction. Customer satisfaction may fulfill employee service needs, thereby causing employee satisfaction which, in turn, is sensed by customers. Finally, both the community and customer components represent more personal and less organized entities within the society. A management which takes action to increase employee fulfillment might thus tend also to focus upon increased customer and community satisfaction.

In the association between employee satisfaction and owner fulfillment, several significant relationships were found. Financially successful organizations were also those in which employees had confidence in management, held higher opinions of the supervisor, and sensed opportunities for self-development. Although these correlations were not of a high magnitude, they do point to the tempting conclusion that satisfied employees contribute toward (or are a product of) an organization profitable for the owner. The relationship is highest between owner fulfillment and employee self-development, a finding that seems understandable since the self-development measure reflects the employee's feelings of belongingness, participation, and pride in the company—a sense of "psychological ownership" in the organization. Previous findings in this area are ambiguous, however. Bass, McGhee, and Vaughan (4) found that satisfaction with one's particular job in the company did not seem particularly related to financial performance of the company. Katzell, Barrett, and Parker (23), however, reported about three fourths of their attitude items correlated positively with organizational performance and no items correlated negatively with performance. They also reported consistently negative relationships between job satisfaction and size of work force, a finding validated to some extent in this study. Table 1 reveals consistent (but generally not significant) negative relationships between organizational size (as measured by size of work force) and employee fulfillment. The single significant relationship indicates that employees are less satisfied with pay policies in organizations composed of larger work forces.

Since the relationships between internal and external criteria of organizational effectiveness were relatively weak, the relationships among the several external criteria were of interest, as well as those between external criteria and owner fulfillment and organizational size.

The relationships among the external components of the organizational system show no definite pattern, as indicated in Table 2. Only five of the 15 relationships are significant. Customer satisfaction is correlated positively with supplier and owner fulfillment, which is understandable, since both are societal units with which the organization exchanges services directly for financial remuneration. This is also the case for exchanges with the employee components of the organization.

There was a negative relation between government and customer fulfillment, which was unexpected. It appears that organizations that focus upon goal achievement through customer interactions are less concerned with the adaptive

TABLE 2
RELATIONS AMONG SOCIETAL FULFILLMENT, OWNER FULFILLMENT, AND ORGANIZATIONAL SIZE.

Components fulfilled	Fulfillment of needs of					
	Government	Customer	Supplier	Creditor	Owner	Org. size
Societal components						
Community	0.00	−0.04	0.03	0.03	0.32*	0.29*
Government		−0.25†	−0.11	0.20†	−0.11	−0.07
Customer			0.20†	0.10	0.21†	0.20†
Supplier				0.09	0.08	0.13
Creditor					−0.02	0.10
Owner						0.28*

*p < 0.01.
†p < 0.05.
N = 97.

functions of fulfilling governmental obligations. However, the adaptive function of fulfilling community needs does appear to be related to the goal of achieving organizational profitability; organizations whose managers are actively involved in community afiairs are also those that are most profitable for the owner.

Perhaps one of the most direct exchanges leading to goal attainment is that between the owner and the customer of the organization. Table 2 indicates that organizations in which owner needs are fulfilled are also those in which customer fulfillment is high. The tempting conclusion is that the successful organization (for the owner) is one which satisfices customer needs also.

As might be predicted, government and creditor fulfillment were moderately correlated. The needs of both of these components can be viewed more as financial obligations of the organization. These needs are fulfilled as they are continually reduced to a minimum.

Organization size is also related to the ability of the organization to fulfill the needs of the societal component. The larger the organization (in number of employees), the more likely it is to fulfill the needs of its community, its owner, and its customers. Organizations with larger human and financial resources can be expected to provide greater support for the community in which they exist; they are able to offer a wider variety of products and services to customers, and thus greater psychological and financial satisfaction for the owner. Two notes of caution should be mentioned in connection with these inferences. First, one cannot be sure about the causal direction of these relationships. It is possible that because an organization provides fulfillment for its community, owner, and customers, it has grown larger. It is more probable that causality changes its direction over time: at one time the organization grows because it fulfills societal needs; subsequently, society's needs are fulfilled to a greater extent because the organization is larger and offers greater resources. Second, organizational size in this study was limited to organizations of 40 employees. In organizations with many more than 40 employees, it is probable that the size-fulfillment relationship becomes asymptotic; similar increments in size may produce decreasing gains in societal fulfillment.

DISCUSSION

In this study we have attempted to avoid the dichotomy of satisfaction versus productivity, by which organizational effectiveness is traditionally gauged. This dichotomy has left both organizational researchers and practitioners with discomforting dilemmas, and resulted in a focus on internal criteria to the exclusion of the demands of the organization's environment. Instead, the organization has been conceived as interdependent components or subsystems through which energy is transferred; and energy exchange occurs both within the organization and also between it and its environment. In this light, organizational effectiveness is the extent to which all forms of energic return to the organization are maximized.

The five societal components upon which the organization is dependent for its survival and growth include the community, government, customers, suppliers, and creditors. The organization is also dependent upon maximizing energy transformation within the firm, a process in which its employees play a major role. A third component important in the survival and growth of the organization is its owner. The focus of the study was on the degree to which fulfillment of the needs of the organization's environmental components was related to fulfillment of the needs of the organization's internal subsystem components, and whether organizational size was related to these.

Findings of this study indicate that there are only a moderate number of relationships between the degree to which the organization concurrently fulfills the needs of its internal subsystem components (its employees), its owner, and the components of its larger society. Concurrent fulfillment of the needs of the five societal components is also of a rather low magnitude.

Evidently, organizations find it difficult to fulfill simultaneously the variety of demands made upon them. Whether the organization *can* concurrently fulfill all or even a major share of the divergent demands made upon it is a provocative and hypothetical question. It is probable that organizations do not strive to maximize fulfillment of any one system component, but operate in accordance with a policy of satisficing several system components. A no-layoff policy, for example, may partially fulfill employee needs, but might do so at the cost of diminishing fulfillment of other societal components. Fulfillment of needs of the various organizational components must, therefore, be treated as separate and, apparently independent. Components in the organization's system are linked together more by the flow of energic activities than by common goal attainment.

From a broader vantage, then, the manager's task is not only to coordinate functions within the organization, but to relate these internal functions to the organization's societal environment. Lack of concurrent maximization of the organization's components calls for greater focus upon the role of the manager as a systems balancer as well as a mediator of the boundaries of the organization (3, 11).

The inability of the organization to fulfill concurrently the needs of its societal components, its owners, and its employees presents dilemmas for theorists in organizational behavior as well as for practitioners in industrial organizations. If prophesies and predictions (5) are correct, the tasks and goals of organizations will become far more complex in the future and will require greater adaptive and innovative capabilities. These increasing organizational complexities will demand the articulation and development of meta-goals that shape and provide the foundation for the goal structure. For example, one meta-goal might be the creation of a system for detecting new and changing goals of the organization or methods for deciding priorities among goals.

Finally, as Bennis (5) predicts, there will be an increase in goal conflict, more and more divergency and contradictoriness between and among effectiveness criteria. While at this date, the different effectiveness criteria among the variety of organizational functions appear unrelated and divergent, lethargy by management may allow these relationships to become negatively related to each other. Management's awareness of these relationships and of how they may change with differing goal structures seems a first step toward maximizing future organizational effectiveness.

Questioning the Managerial Implications of Setting Objectives

1. What explanation can you offer for the difference between the findings reported by England and those he ascribes to Dent?

2. What are some effective ways an organization can provide an appropriate amount of influence over, and information about, organizational goals pursued by its members to insure proper emphasis on certain objectives within the organization? If such a conscious manipulation is always possible, is it also always desirable?

3. Do you agree with Friedlander and Pickle that the complexities of the future will force managers to become more aware of the interacting model they describe, or will a new age of specialists mean that very few managers will need to be concerned with such wide-ranging and complex matters?

4. How would you summarize the thoughts presented in the three preceding articles? Can you find any one clear thread of conclusion from the three authors? What are some other important issues concerning the setting of organizational objectives not yet mentioned?

References

1. Argyris, C., *Interpersonal Competence and Organizational Effectiveness.* Homewood, Ill.: Irwin-Dorsey, 1962.

2. Bass, B. M., "Ultimate Criteria of Organizational Worth," *Personnel Psychology,* V (1952), 157–73.

3. ——, *Organizational Psychology.* Boston: Allyn & Bacon, Inc., 1965.

4. ——, W. P. McGhee, and J. A. Vaughan, "Three Levels of Analysis of Cost-Effectiveness Associated with Personnel Attitudes and Attributes," prepared for the *Proceedings of the Logistics Research Conference,* Warrenton, Va.: Department of Defense, May 1965.

5. Bennis, W. G., "Organizational Developments and the Fate of Bureaucracy," Address presented at the meetings of the American Psychological Association, Los Angeles, Calif., September 1964.

6. Berelson, B., and G. A. Steiner, *Human Behavior.* New York: Harcourt, Brace & World, Inc., 1964.

7. Cantril, H., *Psychology and Social Movements.* New York: John Wiley & Sons, Inc., 1942.

8. Charnes, A., and A. C. Stedry, "Quasi-Rational Models of Behavior in Organization Research" Management Sciences Research Report No. 31, Pittsburgh: Carnegie Institute of Technology, Graduate School of Industrial Administration, 1965.

9. Cyert, R. M., and J. G. March, *A Behavioral Theory of the Firm.* Englewood Cliffs, N. J.: Prentice-Hall, Inc., 1963. Particularly Chapters 1, 2, and 3.

10. Dabas, Z. S., "The Dimensions of Morale: An Item Factorization of the SRA Employee Inventory," *Personnel Psychology,* XI (1958), 217–34.

11. Davis, K., and R. L. Blomstrom, *Business and Its Environment.* New York: McGraw-Hill Book Company, 1966.

12. Davis, R. C., *Industrial Organization and Management.* New York: Harper & Row, Publishers, 1940.

13. Dearborn, D. C., and H. A. Simon, "Selective Perception: A Note on the Departmental Identifications of Executives, "*Sociometry,* XXI (1958), 140–44.

14. Dent, J. K., "Organizational Correlates of the Goals of Business Management," *Personnel Psychology,* VII (1959), 365–93.

15. Emery, F. E., and E. L. Trist, "Socio-Technical Systems," Paper presented at Sixth Annual International Meeting of the Institute of Management Sciences, Paris, France, September 1959.

16. England, G. W., "Personal Value Systems of American Managers," *Academy of Management Journal,* X, No. 1 (1967), 53–68.

17. Georgopoulous, B. S., "Normative Structure Variables and Organizational Behavior," *Human Relations,* XVIII, No. 2 (1965), 164.

18. Guion, R. M., "Criterion Measurement and Personnel Judgments," *Personnel Psychology,* XIV (1961), 141–49, esp. 145.

19. Haire, M., *Psychology in Management,* 2nd ed. New York: McGraw-Hill Book Company, 1964, p. 52.

20. Hicks, H. G., *The Management of Organizations.* New York: McGraw-Hill Book Company, 1967, p. 51.

21. Hoppock, R., *Job Satisfaction.* New York: Harper & Row, Publishers, 1935.

22. Katz, D., and R. L. Kahn, *The Social Psychology of Organizations.* New York: John Wiley & Sons, Inc., 1966.

23. Katzell, R., R. S. Barrett, and T. C. Parker, "Job Satisfaction, Job Performance, and Situational Characteristics," *Journal of Applied Psychology,* VL (1961), 65–72.

24. Kelly, H. H., "The Warm–Cold Variable in First Impressions of Persons," *Journal of Personality,* XVIII (1950), 431–39.

25. Levinson, H., "Role, Personality, and Social Structure in the Organizational Setting," *Journal of Abnormal and Social Psychology,* LVIII (1959), 170–80.

26. Litterer, J. A., *The Analysis of Organizations.* New York: John Wiley & Sons, Inc., 1965, p. 148.

27. Mahoney, T. A., Preliminary Report—"Studies of Criteria of Organization Effectiveness," University of Minnesota: Industrial Relations Center, April 1966.

28. March, J. G., and H. A. Simon, *Organizations.* New York: John Wiley & Sons, Inc., 1958, pp. 10–12.

29. Newman, W. H., and C. E. Summer, Jr., *The Process of Management.* Englewood Cliffs, N. J.: Prentice-Hall, Inc., 1962, pp. 136, 378, 347–48.

30. Parsons, T., E. Shils, K. Naegle, and J. Pitts, *Theories of Society.* New York: The Free Press, Inc., 1961, pp. 38–41.

31. Pepinsky, H. B., K. E. Weick, and J. W. Riner, *Primer for Productivity.* Columbus, Ohio: Ohio State University Research Foundation, 1965.

32. Porter, L. W., "Differential Self-Perceptions of Management Personnel and Line Workers," *Journal of Applied Psychology,* XLII, No. 2 (1958), 105–8.

33. Raven, B. H., and J. Rietsema, "The Effects of Varied Clarity of Group Goal and Group Path upon the Individual and his Relation to the Group," *Human Relations,* X, No. 1 (1957), 29–45.

34. Seashore, S., *Assessing Organization Performance with Behavioral Measurements.* Ann Arbor, Mich.: The Foundation for Research on Human Behavior, 1964.

35. Shepard, H. A., "Changing Interpersonal and Intergroup Relations in, Organizations," in *Handbook of organizations,* ed. J. G. March. New York: Rand McNally & Co., 1964, pp. 1115–43.

36. Sherif, M., *The Psychology of Social Norms.* New York: Harper & Row, Publishers, 1936, pp. 95–100.

37. Simon, H. A., *Models of Man.* New York: John Wiley & Sons, Inc., 1957.

38. —— "On the Concept of Organizational Goal," *Administrative Science Quarterly,* IX (1964), 1–22.

39. Stagner, R., "Psychological Aspects of Industrial Conflict; Part 1, Perception," *Personnel Psychology,* I, No. 2 (1948), 131–35.

40. Strother, G. B., "Problems in the Development of a Social Science of Organization," in *The Social Science of Organizations,* ed. H. J. Leavitt. Englewood Cliffs, N. J.: Prentice-Hall, Inc., 1963, pp. 3–37.

41. Young, K., *Social Psychology,* 3rd ed. New York: Appleton-Century-Crofts, 1956, pp. 59–60.

Organizing

for Goal Attainment

The consistent patterns of relations among large groups of men may be formal or informal. Classical organizational theorists provided what appeared to be a logical set of rules for formally promoting and maintaining task patterns. However, because the relations to be regulated are among people as well as among people and positions, the rules need to be qualified in the light of modern behavioral science.

A basic consideration to any organization is the form it will assume. Organizational planners have long wrestled with the structural issues of centralization vs. decentralization, committee management vs. individual authority, the staff–line dichotomy, and functional vs. product organization. Walker and Lorsch touch on these issues, concentrating on the latter. They analyze the characteristic nature of differentiation, integration, conflict management, effectiveness, and employee attitudes for the two approaches. Since managers are frequently faced with complex problem-solving tasks that can use the properties of each of these structures to advantage, they describe three compromises between product and functional bases that enable companies to deal with multiple tasks simultaneously.

Bass offers insight into one specific organizational process affected by the choice between product and function. The cross-cultural experiment he reports on indicates that real productivity gains and job satisfaction may accrue in the project-type organization where planners and doers are one in the same.

Certain forces in the organizational climate cause collections of people not otherwise grouped by the formal structure to band together. Delbecq asserts that a manager must understand the factors that determine interpersonal choice if he is to make use of the tendency for groups to attract people in planning for decision making and in selecting the most efficient organizational design. Specifically, he proposes "project-group" management as a strategy facilitating the kinds of social relationships that lead to organizational success.

4

Organizational Choice: Product vs. Function

Arthur H. Walker
Northeastern University

Jay W. Lorsch
Harvard Business School

Corporations, especially manufacturers, long have wrestled with the problem of how to structure their organizations to enable employees, particularly the specialists, to do their jobs with maximum efficiency and productivity. One perplexing issue has been whether to organize around functions or products. Here, two behavioral scientists look at the question in light of recent studies. They focus on two plants (of two of the largest consumer products companies), one organized by product, the other by function.

Reprinted by permission from *Harvard Business Review*, November–December 1968, 129–38. © 1968 by the President and Fellows of Harvard College; all rights reserved.

Of all the issues facing a manager as he thinks about the form of his organization, one of the thorniest is the question of whether to group activities primarily by product or by function. Should all specialists in a given function be grouped under a common boss, regardless of differences in products they are involved in, or should the various functional specialists working on a single product be grouped together under the same superior?

In talks with managers we have repeatedly heard them anguishing over this choice. For example, recently a divisional vice president of a major U.S. corporation was contemplating a major organizational change. After long study, he made this revealing observation to his subordinate managers:

We still don't know which choice will be the best one. Should the research, engineering, marketing, and production people be grouped separately in departments for each function? Or would it be better to have them grouped together in product departments, each department dealing with a particular product group?

We were organized by product up until a few years ago. Then we consolidated our organization into specialized functional departments, each dealing with all of our products. Now I'm wondering if we wouldn't be better off to divide our operations again into product units. Either way I can see advantages and disadvantages, trade-offs. What criteria should I use? How can we predict what the outcomes will be if we change?

Companies that have made a choice often feel confident that they have resolved this dilemma. Consider the case of a large advertising agency that consolidated its copy, art, and television personnel into a "total creative department." Previously they had reported to group heads in their areas of specialization. In a memo to employees the company explained the move:

> Formation of the "total creative" department completely tears down the walls between art, copy, and television people. Behind this move is the realization that for best results all creative people, regardless of their particular specialty, must work together under the most intimate relationship as total advertising people, trying to solve creative problems together from start to finish.
>
> The new department will be broken into five groups reporting to the senior vice president and creative director, each under the direction of an associate creative director. Each group will be responsible for art, television, and copy in their accounts.

But our experience is that such reorganizations often are only temporary. The issues involved are so complex that many managements oscillate between these two choices or try to effect some compromise between them.

In this article we shall explore—from the viewpoint of the behavioral scientist—some of the criteria that have been used in the past to make these choices, and present ideas from recent studies that suggest more relevant criteria for making the decision. We hope to provide a way of thinking about these problems that will lead to the most sensible decisions for the accomplishment of organizational goals.

The dilemma of product versus function is by no means new; managers have been facing the same basic question for decades. As large corporations like Du Pont and General Motors grew, they found it necessary to divide their activities among product divisions (7). Following World War II, as companies expanded their sales of existing products and added new products and businesses, many of them implemented a transition from functional organizations handling a number of different products to independently managed product divisions. These changes raised problems concerning divisionalization, decentralization, corporate staff activities, and the like.

As the product divisions grew and prospered, many companies extended the idea of product organization further down in their organizations under such labels as "the unit management concept." Today most of the attention is still being directed to these changes and innovations *within* product or market areas below the divisional level.

We are focusing therefore on these organizational issues at the middle and lower echelons of management, particularly on the crucial questions being faced by managers today within product divisions. The reader should note, however, that a discussion of these issues is immensely complicated by the fact that a choice at one level of the corporate structure affects the choices and criteria for choice at other levels. Nonetheless, the ideas we suggest in this article are directly relevant to organizational choice at any level.

ELEMENTS TO CONSIDER

To understand more fully the factors that make these issues so difficult, it is useful to review the criteria often relied on in making this decision. Typically, managers have used technical and economic criteria. They ask themselves, for instance, "Which choice will minimize payroll costs?" Or, "Which will best utilize equipment and specialists?" This approach not only makes real sense in the traditional logic of management, but it has strong support from the classical school of organization theorists. Luther Gulick, for example, used it in arguing for organization by function:

> It guarantees the maximum utilization of up-to-date technical skill and . . . makes it possible in each case to make use of the most effective divisions of work and specialization. . . . [It] makes possible also the economies of the maximum use of labor-saving machinery and mass production. . . . [It] encourages coordination in all of the technical and skilled work of the enterprise. . . . [It] furnishes an excellent approach to the development of central coordination and control (17).

In pointing to the advantages of the product basis of organization, two other classical theorists used the same approach:

> Product or product line is an important basis for departmentalizing, because it permits the maximum use of personal skills and specialized knowledge, facilitates the employment of specialized capital and makes easier a certain type of coordination (24).

In sum, these writers on organization suggested that the manager should make the choice based on three criteria:

1. Which approach permits the maximum use of special technical knowledge?
2. Which provides the most efficient utilization of machinery and equipment?
3. Which provides the best hope of obtaining the required control and coordination?

There is nothing fundamentally wrong with these criteria as far as they go, and, of course, managers have been using them. But they fail to recognize the complex set of trade-offs involved in these decisions. As a consequence, managers make changes that produce unanticipated results and many even reduce the effectiveness of their organization. For example:

A major manufacturer of corrugated containers a few years ago shifted from a product basis to a functional basis. The rationale for the decision was that it would lead to improved control of production costs and efficiencies in production and marketing. While the organization did accomplish these aims, it found itself less able to obtain coordination among its local sales and production units. The functional specialists now reported to the top officers in charge of production and sales, and there was no mechanism for one person to coordinate their work below the level of division management. As a result, the company encountered numerous problems and unresolved conflicts among functions and later returned to the product form.

This example pinpoints the major trade-off that the traditional criteria omit. Developing highly specialized functional units makes it difficult to achieve coordination or integration among these units. On the other hand, having product units as the basis for organization promotes collaboration between specialists, but the functional specialists feel less identification with functional goals.

BEHAVIORISTS' FINDINGS

We now turn to some new behavioral science approaches to designing organization structure. Recent studies (26), (32) have highlighted three other important factors about specialization and coordination:

As we have suggested, the classical theorists saw specialization in terms of grouping similar activities, skills, or even equipment. They did not look at its psychological and social consequences. Recently, behavioral scientists (including the authors have found that there is an important relationship between a unit's or individual's assigned activities and the unit members' patterns of thought and behavior. Functional specialists tend to develop patterns of behavior and thought that are in tune with the demands of their jobs and their prior training, and as a result these specialists (e.g., industrial engineers and production supervisors) have different ideas and orientation about what is important in getting the job done. This is called *differentiation*, which simply means the differences in behavior and thought patterns that develop among different specialists in relation to their respective tasks. Differentiation is necessary for functional specialists to perform their jobs effectively.

Differentiation is closely related to achievement of coordination, or what behavioral scientists call *integration.* This means collaboration between specialized units or individuals. Recent studies have demonstrated that there is an inverse relationship between differentiation and integration: the more two functional specialists (or their units) differ in their patterns of behavior and thought, the more difficult it is to bring about integration between them. Nevertheless, this research has indicated, achievement of both differentiation and integration is essential if organizations are to perform effectively.

While achievement of both differentiation and integration is possible, it can occur only when well-developed means of communication among specialists exist in the organization and when the specialists are effective in resolving the inevitable cross-functional conflicts.

These recent studies, then, point to certain related questions that managers must consider when they choose between a product or functional basis of organization:

1. How will the choice affect differentiation among specialists? Will it allow the necessary differences in viewpoint to develop so that specialized tasks can be performed effectively?

2. How does the decision affect the prospects of accomplishing integration? Will it lead, for instance, to greater differentiation, which will increase the problems of achieving integration?

3. How will the decision affect the ability of organization members to communicate with each other, resolve conflicts, and reach the necessary joint decisions?

There appears to be a connection between the appropriate extent of differentiation and integration and the organization's effectiveness in accomplishing its economic goals. What the appropriate pattern is depends on the nature of external factors—markets, technology, and so on—facing the organization, as well as the goals themselves. The question of how the organizational pattern will affect individual members is equally complex. Management must consider how much stress will be associated with a certain pattern and whether such stress should be a serious concern.

To explore in more detail the significance of modern approaches to organizational structuring, we shall describe one recent study conducted in two manufacturing plants—one organized by *product*, the other on a *functional basis* (43).

PLANT F AND PLANT P

The two plants where this study was conducted were selected because they were closely matched in several ways. They were making the same product; their markets, technology, and even raw materials were identical. The parent companies were also similar: both were large national corporations that developed, manufactured, and marketed many consumer products. In each case divisional and corporate headquarters were located more than 100 miles from the facilities studied. The plants were separated from other structures at the same site, where other company products were made.

Both plants had very similar management styles. They stressed their desire to foster employees' initiative and autonomy and placed great reliance on selection of well-qualified department heads. They also identified explicitly the same two objectives. The first was to formulate, package, and ship the products in minimum time at specified levels of quality and at minimum cost—that is, within existing capabilities. The second was to improve the capabilities of the plant.

In each plant there were identical functional specialists involved with the manufacturing units and packing unit, as well as quality control, planning and scheduling, warehousing, industrial engineering, and plant engineering. In Plant F (with the functional basis of organization), only the manufacturing departments and the planning and scheduling function reported to the plant manager responsible for the product (see Figure 1). All other functional specialists reported to the staff of the divisional manufacturing manager, who was also responsible for plants manufacturing other products. At Plant P (with the product basis of organization), all functional specialists with the exception of plant engineering reported to the plant manager (see Figure 2).

STATE OF DIFFERENTIATION

In studying differentiation, it is useful to focus on the functional specialists' differences in outlook in terms of:

Orientation toward goals.

Orientation toward time.

Perception of the formality of organization.

GOAL ORIENTATION   The bases of organization in the two plants had a marked effect on the specialists' differentiated goal orientations. In Plant F they focused sharply on their specialized goals and objectives. For example, quality control specialists were concerned almost exclusively with meeting quality standards, industrial engineers with methods improvements and cost reduction, and scheduling specialists with how to meet schedule requirements. An industrial engineer in Plant F indicated this intensive interest in his own activity:

> We have 150 projects worth close to a million dollars in annual savings. I guess I've completed some that save as much as $90,000 a year. Right now I'm working on cutting departmental costs. You need a hard shell in this work. No one likes to have his costs cut, but that is my job.

That these intense concerns with specialized objectives were expected is illustrated by the apologetic tone of a comment on production goals by an engineering supervisor at Plant F: "At times we become too much involved in production. It causes a change in heart. We are interested in production, but not at the expense of our own standards of performance. If we get too much involved, then we may become compromised."

FIGURE 1
ORGANIZATIONAL CHART AT PLANT F

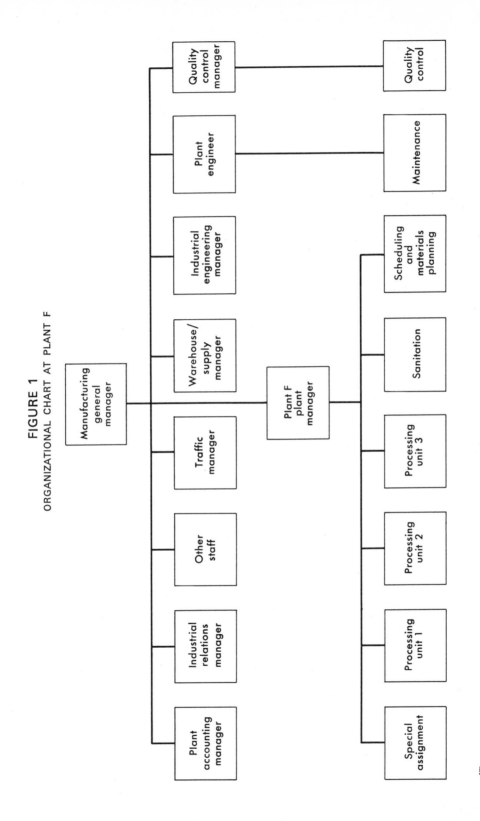

FIGURE 2
ORGANIZATIONAL CHART AT PLANT P

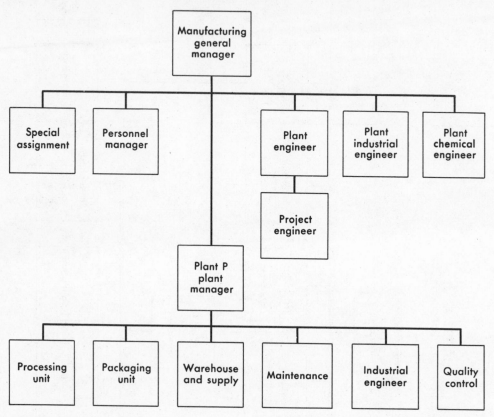

A final illustration is when production employees stood watching while members of the maintenance department worked to start a new production line, and a production supervisor remarked: "I hope that they get that line going soon. Right now, however, my hands are tied. Maintenance has the job. I can only wait. My people have to wait, too."

This intense concern with one set of goals is analogous to a rifle shot; in a manner of speaking, each specialist took aim at one set of goals and fired at it. Moreover, the specialists identified closely with their counterparts in other plants and at divisional headquarters. As one engineer put it: "We carry the ball for them (the central office). We carry a project through and get it working right."

At Plant P the functional specialists' goals were more diffuse—like buckshot. Each specialist was concerned not only with his own goals, but also with the operation of the entire plant. For example, in contrast to the Plant F production supervisor's attitude about maintenance, a Plant P maintenance manager said, under similar circumstances: "We're all interested in the same thing. If I can help, I'm willing. If I have a mechanical problem, there is no member of the operating department who wouldn't go out of his way to solve it."

Additional evidence of this more diffuse orientation toward goals is provided by comments such as these, which came from Plant P engineers and managers: "We are here for a reason—to run this place the best way we know how. There is no reluctance to be open and frank despite various backgrounds and ages.

"The changeovers tell the story. Everyone shows willingness to dig in. The whole plant turns out to do cleaning up."

Because the functional specialists at Plant F focused on their individual goals, they had relatively wide differences in goals and objectives. Plant P's structure, on the other hand, seemed to make functional specialists more aware of common product goals and reduced differences in goal orientation. Yet, as we shall see, this lesser differentiation did not hamper their performance.

TIME ORIENTATION The two organizational bases had the opposite effect, however, on the time orientation of functional managers. At Plant F, the specialists shared a concern with short-term issues (mostly daily problems). The time orientation of specialists at Plant P was more differentiated. For example, its production managers concentrated on routine matters, while planning and industrial engineering focused on issues that needed solution within a week, and quality control specialists worried about even longer-term problems.

The reason is not difficult to find. Since Plant P's organization led its managers to identify with product goals, those who could contribute to the solution of longer-term problems became involved in these activities. In Plant F, where each unit focused on its own goals, there was more of a tendency to worry about getting daily progress. On the average, employees of Plant P reported devoting 30 percent of their time to daily problems, while at Plant F this figure was 49 percent. We shall have more to say shortly about how these factors influenced the results achieved in the two plants.

ORGANIZATIONAL FORMALITY In the study, the formality of organizational structure in each functional activity was measured by three criteria:

1. Clarity of definition of job responsibilities.
2. Clarity of dividing lines between jobs.
3. Importance of rules and procedures.

It was found that at Plant F there were fewer differences among functional activities in the formality of organization structure than at Plant P. Plant F employees reported that a uniform degree of structure existed across functional specialties; job responsibilities were well defined, and the distinctions between jobs were clear. Similarly, rules and procedures were extensively relied on. At Plant P, on the other hand, substantial differences in the formality of organization existed. Plant engineers and industrial engineers, for example, were rather vague about their responsibilities and about the dividing line between their jobs and other jobs. Similarly, they reported relatively low reliance on rules and procedures. Production managers, on the other hand, noted that their jobs were well defined and that rules and procedures were more important to them.

The effects of these two bases of organization on differentiation along these three dimensions are summarized in Table 1. Overall, differentiation was greater between function specialists at Plant P than at Plant F.

TABLE 1
DIFFERENTIATION IN PLANTS F AND P

Dimensions of differentiation	Plant F	Plant P
Goal orientation	More differentiated and focused	Less differentiated and more diffuse
Time orientation	Less differentiated and shorter term	More differentiated and longer term
Formality of structure	Less differentiated, with more formality	More differentiated, with less formality

INTEGRATION ACHIEVED

While the study found that both plants experienced some problems in accomplishing integration, these difficulties were more noticeable at Plant F. Collaboration between maintenance and production personnel and between production and scheduling was a problem there. In Plant P the only relationship where integration was unsatisfactory was that between production and quality control specialists. Thus Plant P seemed to be getting slightly better integration in spite of the greater differentiation among specialists in that organization. Since differentiation and integration are basically antagonistic, the only way managers at Plant P could get both was by being effective at communication and conflict resolution. They were better at this than were managers at Plant F.

COMMUNICATION PATTERNS In Plant P, communication among employees was more frequent, less formal, and more often of a face-to-face nature than was the case with Plant F personnel. One Plant P employee volunteered: "Communications are no problem around here. You can say it. You can get an answer."

Members of Plant F did not reflect such positive feelings. They were heard to say: Why didn't they tell me this was going to happen? Now they've shut down the line.

"When we get the information, it is usually too late to do any real planning. We just do our best."

The formal boundaries outlining positions that were more prevalent at Plant F appeared to act as a damper on communication. The encounters observed were often a succession of two-man conversations, even though more than two may have been involved in a problem. The telephone and written memoranda were more often employed than at Plant P, where spontaneous meetings involving several persons were frequent, usually in the cafeteria.

DEALING WITH CONFLICT In both plants, *confrontation* of conflict was reported to be more typical than either the use of power to *force* one's own position or an attempt to *smooth* conflict by "agreeing to disagree." There was strong evidence, nevertheless, that in Plant P managers were coming to grips with conflicts more directly than in Plant F. Managers at Plant F reported that more conflicts were being smoothed over. They worried that issues were often not getting settled. As they put it:

"We have too many nice guys here."

"If you can't resolve an issue, you go to the plant manager. But we don't like to bother him often with small matters. We should be able to settle them ourselves. The trouble is we don't. So it dies."

Thus, by ignoring conflict in the hope it would go away, or by passing it to a higher level, managers at Plant F often tried to smooth over their differences. While use of the management hierarchy is one acceptable way to resolve conflict, so many disagreements at Plant F were pushed upstairs that the hierarchy became overloaded and could not handle all the problems facing it. So it responded by dealing with only the more immediate and pressing ones.

At Plant P the managers uniformly reported that they resolved conflicts themselves. There was no evidence that conflicts were being avoided or smoothed over. As one manager said: "We don't let problems wait very long. There's no sense to it. And besides, we get together frequently and have plenty of chances to discuss differences over a cup of coffee."

As this remark suggests, the quicker resolution of conflict was closely related to the open and informal communication pattern prevailing at Plant P. In spite of greater differentiation in time orientation and structure, then, Plant P managers were able to achieve more satisfactory integration because they could communicate and resolve conflict effectively.

PERFORMANCE AND ATTITUDES

Before drawing some conclusions from the study of these two plants, it is important to make two more relevant comparisons between them—their effectiveness in terms of the goals set for them and the attitudes of employees.

PLANT PERFORMANCE As we noted before, the managements of the two plants were aiming at the same two objectives:

1. Maximizing current output within existing capabilities.
2. Improving the capabilities of the plant.

Of the two facilities, Plant F met the first objective more effectively; it was achieving a higher production rate with greater efficiency and at less cost than was Plant P. In terms of the second objective, however, Plant P was clearly superior to Plant F; the former's productivity had increased by 23 percent from 1963 to 1966 compared with the latter's increment of only 3 percent. One key manager at Plant F commented: "There has been a three- or four-year effort to improve our capability. Our expectations have simply not been achieved.

The improvement in performance is just not there. We are still where we were three years ago. But our targets for improvements are realistic."

By contrast, a key manager at Plant P observed: "Our crews have held steady, yet our volume is up. Our quality is consistently better, too."

Another said: "We are continuing to look for and find ways to improve and consolidate jobs."

EMPLOYEE ATTITUDES   Here, too, the two organizations offer a contrast, but the contrast presents a paradoxical situation. Key personnel at Plant P appeared to be more deeply involved in their work than did managers at Plant F, and they admitted more often to feeling stress and pressure than did their opposite numbers at Plant F. But Plant F managers expressed more satisfaction with their work than did those at Plant P; they liked the company and their jobs more than did managers at Plant P.

Why Plant P managers felt more involved and had a higher level of stress, but were less satisfied than Plant F managers, can best be explained by linking these findings with the others we have reported.

STUDY SUMMARY

The characteristics of these two organizations are summarized in Table 2. The nature of the organization at Plant F seemed to suit its stable but high rate of efficiency. Its specialists concentrated on their own goals and performed well, on the whole. The jobs were well defined and managers worked within procedures and rules. The managers were concerned primarily with short-term matters. They were not particularly effective in communicating with each other and in resolving conflict. But this was not very important to achieve steady, good performance, since the coordination necessary to meet this objective could be achieved through plans and procedures and through the manufacturing technology itself.

TABLE 2
OBSERVED CHARACTERISTICS OF THE TWO ORGANIZATIONS

Characteristics	Plant F	Plant P
Differentiation	Less differentiation except in goal orientation	Greater differentiation in structure and time orientation
Integration	Somewhat less effective	More effective
Conflict management	Confrontation, but also "smoothing over" and avoidance; rather restricted communication pattern	Confrontation of conflict; open, face-to-face communication
Effectiveness	Efficient, stable production; but less successful in improving plant capabilities	Successful in improving plant capabilities, but less effective in stable production
Employee attitudes	Prevalent feeling of satisfaction, but less feeling of stress and involvement	Prevalent feeling of stress and involvement, but less satisfaction

As long as top management did not exert much pressure to improve performance dramatically, the plant's managerial hierarchy was able to resolve the few conflicts arising from daily operations. And as long as the organization avoided extensive problem solving, a great deal of personal contact was not very important. It is not surprising therefore that the managers were satisfied and felt relatively little pressure. They attended strictly to their own duties, remained uninvolved, and got the job done. For them, this combination was satisfying. And higher management was pleased with the facility's production efficiency.

The atmosphere at Plant P, in contrast, was well suited to the goal of improving plant capabilities, which it did very well. There was less differentiation between goals, since the functional specialists to a degree shared the product goals. Obviously, one danger in this form of organization is the potential attraction of specialist managers to total goals to the extent that they lose sight of their particular goals and become less effective in their jobs. But this was not a serious problem at Plant P.

Moreover, there was considerable differentiation in time orientation and structure; some specialists worked at the routine and programmed tasks in operating the plant, while others concentrated on longer-term problems to improve manufacturing capability. The latter group was less constrained by formal procedures and job definitions, and this atmosphere was conducive to problem solving. The longer time orientation of some specialists, however, appeared to divert their attention from maintaining schedules and productivity. This was a contributing factor to Plant P's less effective current performance.

In spite of the higher degree of differentiation in these dimensions, Plant P managers were able to achieve the integration necessary to solve problems that hindered plant capability. Their shared goals and a common boss encouraged them to deal directly with each other and confront their conflicts. Given this pattern, it is not surprising that they felt very involved in their jobs. Also they were under stress because of their great involvement in their jobs. This stress could lead to dissatisfaction with their situation. Satisfaction for its own sake, however, may not be very important; there was no evidence of higher turnover of managers at Plant P.

Obviously, in comparing the performance of these two plants operating with similar technologies and in the same market, we might predict that, because of its greater ability to improve plant capabilities, Plant P eventually will reach a performance level at least as high as Plant F's. While this might occur in time, it should not obscure one important point: the functional organization seems to lead to better results in a situation where stable performance of a routine task is desired, while the product organization leads to better results in situations where the task is less predictable and requires innovative problem solving.

CLUES FOR MANAGERS

How can the manager concerned with the function versus product decision use these ideas to guide him in making the appropriate choice? The essential step is identifying the demands of the task confronting the organization.

Is it a routine, repetitive task? Is it one where integration can be achieved by plan and conflict managed through the hierarchy? This was the way the task was implicitly defined at Plant F. If this is the nature of the task, or, to put it another way, if management is satisfied with this definition of the task, then the functional organization is quite appropriate. While it allows less differentiation in time orientation and structure, it does encourage differentiation in goal orientation. This combination is important for specialists to work effectively in their jobs.

Perhaps even more important, the functional structure also seems to permit a degree of integration sufficient to get the organization's work done. Much of this can be accomplished through paper systems and through the hardware of the production line itself. Conflict that comes up can more safely be dealt with through the management hierarchy, since the difficulties of resolving conflict are less acute. This is so because the tasks provide less opportunity for conflict and because the specialists have less differentiated viewpoints to overcome. This form of organization is less psychologically demanding for the individuals involved.

On the other hand, if the task is of a problem-solving nature, or if management defines it this way, the product organization seems to be more appropriate. This is especially true where there is a need for tight integration among specialists. As illustrated at Plant P, the product organization form allows the greater differentiation in time orientation and structure that specialists need to attack problems. While encouraging identification with superordinate goals, this organizational form does allow enough differentiation in goals for specialists to make their contributions.

Even more important, to identify with product ends and have a common boss encourages employees to deal constructively with conflict, communicate directly and openly with each other, and confront their differences, so they can collaborate effectively. Greater stress and less satisfaction for the individual may be unavoidable, but it is a small price to pay for the involvement that accompanies it.

The manager's problem in choosing between product and functional forms is complicated by the fact that in each organization there are routine tasks and tasks requiring problem solving, jobs requiring little interdependence among specialists and jobs requiring a great deal. Faced with these mixtures, many companies have adopted various compromises between product and functional bases. They include (in ascending order of structural complexity):

1. *The use of cross-functional teams to facilitate integration.* These teams provide some opportunity for communication and conflict resolution and also a degree of the common identification with product goals that characterizes the product organization. At the same time, they retain the differentiation provided by the functional organization.

2. *The appointment of full-time integrators or coordinators around a product.* These product managers or project managers encourage the functional specialists to become committed to product goals and help resolve conflicts between them. The specialists still retain their primary identification with their functions (25).

3. *The "matrix" or grid organization, which combines the product and functional forms by overlaying them.* Some managers wear functional hats and are involved in the day-to-day, more routine activities. Naturally, they identify with functional goals. Others, wearing product or project hats, identify with total product goals and are more involved in the problem-solving activity required to cope with long-range issues and to achieve cross-functional coordination.

These compromises are becoming popular because they enable companies to deal with multiple tasks simultaneously. But we do not propose them as a panacea, because they make sense only for those situations where the differentiation and integration required by the sum of all the tasks make a middle approach necessary. Further, the complexity of interpersonal plus organizational relationships in these forms and the ambiguity associated with them make them difficult to administer effectively, and psychologically demanding on the persons involved.

In our view, the only solution to the product versus function dilemma lies in analysis of the multiple tasks that must be performed, the differences between specialists, the integration that must be achieved, and the mechanisms and behavior required to resolve conflict and arrive at these states of differentiation and integration. This analysis provides the best hope of making a correct product or function choice or of arriving at some appropriate compromise solution.

5

When Planning for Others

Bernard M. Bass
University of Rochester

Reprinted in abridged form by permission from *Journal of Applied Behavioral Science*, VI, No. 2 (1970).

Much as each would have it otherwise, the completely rational organizational designer quickly runs into socio-emotional problems with which he must cope, while the behaviorally oriented designer finds that he will sacrifice effectiveness if he ignores simple rational demands of organization. A rational organizing principle, unity of command, may lead to many social and psychological failures of understanding and commitment. As a behavioral principle, shared leadership may produce low-level compromise, divided counsel, and system unreliability. Rationalists may design jobs which are too specialized and simple to hold the interest of the job holder; behavioralists may design jobs which are too complex for organizational efficiency. The rationalist's chain of command may speed the vertical flow of decisions while it obstructs horizontal interchanges among peers seen to be so important by the behavioralists.

Nowhere is the dilemma more apparent than dealing with the question of who shall plan and who shall execute. The rational approach is represented by Figure 1. One level of decision makers sets the desired performance levels and objectives based on the messages they receive from inside and outside the firm. Action takes place at a level below. A hierarchy of such levels complicates

FIGURE 1
GENERAL FRAMEWORK FOR ORGANIZATIONAL DESIGN.

Legend:
——————— Flow of matter
— — — — Flow of information
—•— •— •— Flow of energy

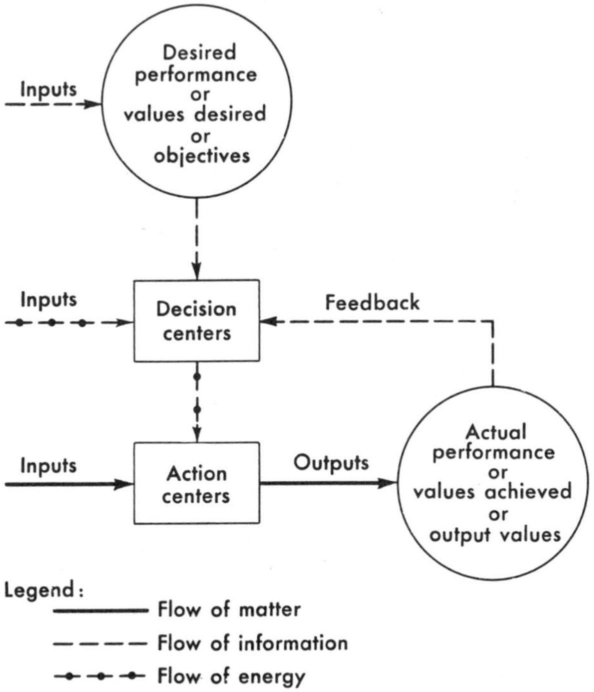

(From R. Carzo and J.N. Yanouzas, *Formal organization. A Systems Approach.* Homewood, Ill.: Irwin-Dorsey, 1967, p. 336. Reprinted by permission.)

matters in the larger firm. One level sets broad objectives, the next level narrows them, still a lower level proposes more specific goals to be achieved by the operators at this lower level. Already several layers of decision makers may separate some of the planners from some of the doers. And at the level above the doers, as shown in Figure 1, planners receive objectives from higher authority, and feedback from on-going actual performance of the doers, to plan the next steps for the doers.

This separation of planners from doers generates behavioral problems which lead the organizational theorist whose main concern is behavioral rather than rational to promote organizational designs which merge the planners and doers in temporary task forces and project teams (14). Or overlapping group designs are formed which move the decision making process down to the level at which the decisions will be executed (28). More generally, participative management is encouraged where the doers become informally involved in the planning although the rational, traditional structure of Figure 1 is maintained. But often, such mergers of doing with planning are physically, technically, economically, or rationally unsound or impossible and planners must remain apart from doers. We wish here to consider the consequences, as well as what countermeasures can be taken to mitigate the negative effects of such separation.

SOME EXPERIMENTAL EVIDENCE

In three controlled experiments, Bass and Leavitt (4) demonstrated the importance both to productivity and satisfaction of involving the doers in the planning. We devised several simple exercises for managers in programs of training. In each, trios of managers developed a plan for themselves, then exchanged plans with another trio. Each trio then had two plans, one self-developed and the other created by another trio. Following this, they executed both plans. Care was taken so that half the trios operated their own plan first and half operated their own plan second. Managers were both more productive and more satisfied when operating their own plan.

One of the exercises was translated into eleven other languages and recast into *Exercise Organization*, a self-instructional booklet (3) making it possible to broaden the national backgrounds of the managers subjected to the experience to test the universality of the results.

As it now stands, the exercise itself is simple. As part of a training activity, groups of six managers (usually from middle echelons of their companies) each are issued booklets in which are contained instructions to divide themselves into two trios. They are told about the *Numbers Task* which requires three operators, A, B, and C. Each operator is provided with his own list of numbers like A61324 or B41523. Their problem is to merge numbers they select from their own list with those selected by the other operators so that each selected number is bigger than the last, i.e. A02134, B24671, C29999, A31233, B42222, C42223, etc. Productivity is measured by how many such numbers can be successfully transferred by copying from each operator's list to a transfer file and thence to the final merged file of newly listed numbers in a correct order.

Each trio is given 30–60 minutes to complete a written plan on how to accomplish the task effectively. Then, plans are exchanged with the other trio in the group. Communications between trios are limited to information and questions about the plans.

Each trio operates the same plan first, so that half of the trios in all the groups engaged in the experience operate their own plan first, while half operate a plan assigned to them by the other trio in their group. Then, both trios operate the other available plan which is self-developed for half of the trios and assigned for the other half.

Table 1 shows the outcomes in productivity in Scandinavia, Holland, Belgium, Great Britain, the United States, and India for 600 managers working in 200 trios. As can be seen, regardless of nationality, trios assembled more numbers when they operated their own plan rather than the plan assigned to them by the other trio. For example, 78 Scandinavian managers (mostly Danes and Norwegians) produced an average of 71.7 numbers per trio in 20 minutes' operations when operating their own plan but only 62.2 numbers when operating the plan assigned from the other trio. As can be seen in Table 1, results were similar for the Dutch, Belgian, British, American, and Indian managers.

TABLE 1
PRODUCTIVITY OF MANAGERS OF DIFFERENT NATIONALITIES
THEIR OWN PLANS AND PLANS ASSIGNED TO THEM BY OTHERS

	Productivity When Operating:	
Number and Locatin of Managers	Own Plan (Self-Developed)	Other Plan (Assigned)
78 Scandinavian	71.7	62.2
108 Dutch	86.7	62.5
78 Belgian	68.9	49.1
132 British	94.9	79.2
162 American	80.9	69.9
42 Indian	63.0	41.1
600 All	77.0	64.8

In all, the 600 managers did almost 19 percent better operating their own plans than plans assigned to them by other trios. Productivity averaged 77.0 numbers when operating own plans and 64.8 when operating assigned plans. The probability by chance that results would be as predicted for managers from a single country was 0.5. For six independent replications, the probability is 1/64 or 0.016 that results would be as predicted for six independent replications.

Subjective results are the same. The 600 managers completed a questionnaire afterward as part of the exercise indicating how they felt about the two plans. As can be seen in Table 2, column 1, in each of the six national groups, a majority were more satisfied with their own jobs when operating their own plan rather than the plan assigned to them by the other trio. Effects were most striking for the Dutch and the Indian managers. Among the 108 Dutch managers, 83 percent were more satisfied with their own jobs when operating their own plan while only 4.3 percent were more satisfied with their jobs when operating the plan assigned to them by the other trio. Less than 13 percent felt the same about operating either plan. Among the 42 Indian managers, 76.5 percent were more satisfied when working on the other plan. A majority of Americans and British were like the Dutch and Indian managers, but as groups were less overwhelmingly as satisfied with their jobs when operating their own plans. For all 600 managers, 63.0 percent were more satisfied with their jobs when working on their own plans and only 20.2 percent preferred working on the other plan.

As can be seen in Table 2, column 2, similar results appeared when managers indicated how satisfied they were with their trio's efficiency when operating either of the plans. The Indian managers were most extreme in their differentiation of attitudes. Among them, 84.8 percent were more satisfied when operating

TABLE 2
SATISFACTION OF MANAGERS OF DIFFERENT NATIONALITIES WHEN OPERATING THEIR OWN PLANS AND PLANS ASSIGNED TO THEM BY OTHERS

Number and Location of Managers	(1) Satisfaction With Own Job As Operator (percent)	(2) Satisfaction With Own Trio's Efficiency (percent)
78 Scandinavian		
Own Plan	59.6	71.7
Other Plan	20.1*	20.9
108 Dutch		
Own Plan	83.0	68.4
Other Plan	4.3	11.2
78 Belgian		
Own Plan	64.6	62.2
Other Plan	24.3	26.5
132 British		
Own Plan	56.1	63.1
Other Plan	28.1	22.8
162 American		
Own Plan	52.8	62.2
Other Plan	24.9	34.7
42 Indian		
Own Plan	76.5	84.8
Other Plan	11.8	6.1
600 All		
Own Plan	63.0	66.3
Other Plan	20.2	22.9

*Does not add to 100 percent. Remaining respondents indicated there was no difference between plans.

their own plan. Only 6.1 percent felt operating efficiency was better with the other plan. For all 600 managers, 66.3 percent were more satisfied with trio efficiency when operating their own plans, 22.9 percent felt efficiency was higher with the other plan, and 10.8 percent found no difference when operating the two plans.

If structural arrangements could, in fact, succeed in merging all planning and executing in a firm, then there would be no purpose to this article on when planning for others except to add the evidence of the greater productivity and satisfaction associated with executing plans developed by oneself. But unfortunately, there are organizational imperatives which make the *separation* of planners and doers the common condition and the merger of planning and doing the exception. These imperatives make it worthwhile to consider what planners ought to take into account when planning for others if they would try to match productivity and satisfaction with what might have happened if plans had been self-developed. What keeps performing apart from planning?

First, in some instances, a division of labor is often more efficient and necessary. The doer is freed to operate because someone else is planning for him. Without a staff planning for him, an executive may literally have no time to execute the plans developed for him by others. The blueprints provided the carpenter increases greatly his speed and accuracy in building the housing framework. Even if he could develop his own blueprints, the allocation of his time to that effort might be much less profitable than using an already available set of standard blueprints at modest cost.

Second, in some cases, planning may require special skills. The simulation experiment to design a new marketing plan may be completely beyond the technical competence of the marketing executive. The architectural design of a new home is beyond the technical competence of the carpenter.

Third, the doer may dislike planning and may see himself spending his time more advantageously at other endeavors. The entrepreneur may prefer to rely on his accountant to estimate and plan his quarterly tax payment. The carpenter may be happier cutting wood to specifications than having to figure out in advance what size cuts will be required.

This article, then, is addressed to all those who must plan for others; managers, in general, as well as staff specialists, consultants, and professionals.

REASONS FOR PITFALLS IN PLANNING FOR OTHERS

The results with the 600 managers may be due to at least eight possible reasons on why planning for others tends to produce operations which are less productive and less satisfying. Looking at each of these reasons will provide ideas on what may be done when planning for others to yield the higher level of productivity and satisfaction that occurs when planning and doing are merged and self-planning is possible.

LESS SENSE OF ACCOMPLISHMENT

I infer that there is less sense of achievement when plans are assigned by others from the previously described results for the 600 managers for whom satisfaction with job and work group was less when operating the plan assigned by others. I assume that this reduced satisfaction was due not only to less actual success with the assigned plan, but also to less concern for its success as evidenced by reported less felt responsibility for it (results shown in column 2 of Table 3) to be discussed later.

TABLE 3
EVALUATION BY MANAGERS OF DIFFERENT NATIONALITIES OF OPERATING THEIR OWN PLANS AND PLANS ASSIGNED TO THEM BY OTHERS

Number and Location of Managers	(1) Which Was Better? (percent)	(2) Felt More Responsibility For Which? (percent)	(3) Which Was More Flexible? (percent)	(4) Which is Harder to Understand? (percent)	(5) Which Made Better Man-power Use? (percent)
78 Scandinavian					
Own Plan	61.4	53.0	30.1	18.2	66.0
Other Plan	31.0*	10.6	29.1	30.4	18.2
108 Dutch					
Own Plan	60.7	42.7	41.3	22.0	43.4
Other Plan	29.5	9.9	21.6	42.1	10.2
78 Belgian					
Own Plan	59.0	57.2	48.2	27.0	38.3
Other Plan	29.7	22.0	31.2	49.6	24.7
132 British					
Own Plan	61.4	43.9	33.3	10.5	40.4
Other Plan	21.0	17.5	21.0	28.1	17.5
162 American					
Own Plan	52.2	54.5	39.6	28.1	47.1
Other Plan	30.8	10.3	22.4	29.8	20.9
42 Indian					
Own Plan	79.4	64.7	51.5	23.5	66.7
Other Plan	14.7	17.6	15.2	50.0	12.1
600 All					
Own Plan	59.7	50.9	39.2	21.3	47.6
Other Plan	27.1	13.8	23.4	35.7	17.7

*Does not add to 100 percent. Remaining respondents indicated there was no difference between plans.

LESS CONFIRMATORY EFFORTS

A majority in all national groups were convinced that their own plan was better. The effect was greatest for the Indian managers, 79.4 percent of whom felt their own plan was better (Table 3, column 1). Americans were most charitable to the other plan. While 52.2 percent of 162 Americans favored their own plan, 30.8 percent acknowledged the superiority of the other plan. I infer that these convictions to some extent were "acted out"; that is, greater effort was expended to ensure that the judgments would be validated by outcomes. "I think this will happen; therefore, I will make it happen."

LESS COMMITMENT

As seen in column 2 of Table 3, the responsibility felt for the other plan was only 13.8 percent for the 600 managers while it was 50.9 percent for their own plans. In all six national groups, managers were less involved in the other plan and less committed to seeing that it worked. They were more curious about whether their own plan would work. They were more concerned that it would work. They tried harder to see that it did work.

LESS FLEXIBILITY

Based on the question: "Which plan was more flexible, allowing for individual initiative and unforeseen problems?" more managers from each of the six national groups agreed (Table 3, column 3), that their own plan was more flexible than the other assigned plan. The latter was seen by more of the managers to be less open to modification and to permit less initiative on the part of the operators to introduce changes in the plans. Of the 600 managers, 39.2 percent saw their own plan and 23.4 percent saw the other plan as more flexible.

However, 36.2 percent saw no difference in the flexibility permitted in the two plans.

LESS UNDERSTANDING

All but the American managers reported greater difficulty in understanding the plan assigned to them by the other trio than their own plan (Table 3, column 4). A plurality (35.7 percent) felt this way; 21.3 percent believed their own plan was more difficult to understand. Even allowing for ample time for explanations and clarifications of the other plan, it seems reasonable to expect that, as a whole, managers would find their own plan easier to understand since they had discussed all the details in developing their own plan and were more familiar with it.

LESS ADEQUATE USE OF AVAILABLE MANPOWER

In all six national groups, managers felt their own plan did a better job in this respect while few felt this way about the other plan. Of the 600 managers, 47.6 percent favored their own plan; 17.7 percent favored the other in regard to adequate use of manpower. Again, this seems reasonable. The other planners do not know how to make as good use of the human resources of a work group as do the members themselves who, if planning for themselves, can focus on the special talents and interests within the group. Outside planners cannot do this since they do not know the group as well as the members themselves.

COMMUNICATIONS PROBLEMS

There is obviously more room for error, distortion and misdirection where plans first formulated by one group need to be transmitted in their entirety to another group to be executed. Such errors, filtering of instructions, conscious and unconscious, took place according to post-session informal critiques of the transfer process. In some instances, receivers heard only what they wanted to hear. In other cases, senders failed to send key aspects of the plan because they made unreasonable assumptions about what the receivers would understand without being told.

COMPETITIVE FEELINGS

The intergroup conflict in this experimental situation is apparent. Two groups make plans. Each thinks its own plan is better (Table 3, column 1). Here, if the other trio's plans are executed as well as possible by our trio, we will lose and they will gain. Such competitive conditions can occur in any "we–they" situation in which "we" execute and "they" plan.

If "we," the doers, do as well as possible, "they" will look better than "us." If "they" look better, "we" will look worse. Often such competitive feelings may not be consciously perceived; nevertheless, they may produce reactions among those who carry out the plans given to them by planners which may be outright sabotage of the planners' efforts.

POSSIBLE REMEDIAL ACTIONS

Ideally, planners should be those who execute the plans. However, whenever planning must be for others (because of the need for division of labor, because planning requires special skills, or because the others prefer it that way) the eight interrelated factors just cited need to be considered by the planners. These eight factors adversely affect productivity and satisfaction in the implementation process when planning and doing are separated. . . .

FOSTERING
A SENSE OF ACCOMPLISHMENT

In self-planning, objectives often are implicit. In planning for others, it becomes most important to clarify objectives. A comparison of two large plants found workers much more satisfied in the one plant in which a great deal of attention was paid to explaining things that had to be done by workers when they were assigned tasks (18). In the same way, subjects in a simulation were much more productive and satisfied when they were told why they were doing a particular task of paper cutting (38).

In addition to clarifying objectives, plans need to be designed which provide satisfactory signals when those objectives are being reached. Means for providing more frequent feedback of success or failure must be built into plans for others. Thus, salary increases for meritorious performance could be scheduled at the time a project is completed rather than periodically.

PROMOTING CONFIRMATORY BEHAVIOR

After a plan has been presented, but before its execution is begun, the hopes and fears of the planners and doers can be explored. The planners can try to make the doers aware of provisions for various contingencies. The confidence of the planners in the adequacy of their plans can be communicated. Reservations of the doers need to be brought into the open and discussed with the planners. If the doers believe the plans are unrealistic, even if the plans are actually sound, the doers may behave in a way to confirm their beliefs (12). Planners need to share with the doers the reasons for their optimistic expectations.

PROMOTING COMMITMENT

Many ways are open to planners to increase the commitment of the doers. Thus, labor–management consultation at TVA which resulted in vigorous employee participation, particularly in their immediate work groups, has been seen to promote feelings of solidarity with the work organization and with management, and to increase employee acceptance of work changes (36).

Doers can be consulted at various stages in the planning process. Wherever possible, the ideas of the doers can be incorporated in the plans or when such ideas are unusable, the reasons can be discussed with doers. The doers can be involved in preliminary trials of the plans with emphasis given to evaluations of the trials by the doers. The plans can provide for some discretion on the part of the doers to modify noncritical elements of the plans increasing the feeling that the doers have some control over the fate of the plans and hence responsibility for the successful execution of the plans. The plans can provide for periodic feedback of evaluations from the doers in the planning process.

PROVIDING FLEXIBILITY

"It is a bad plan that admits of no modification." This 2000-year-old maxim of Publius Syrus is still as valid as ever. Groups of 40 men each were assigned to operate a simulated air defense system. Plans had been carefully engineered to maximize the load which could be handled safely by the men and their equipment. However, built into the plan was permission for the operators to modify their relations with each other in dealing with the load as they saw the need to do so. Following a period of trial and error, organizational innovations occurred, not foreseen by the planners, which resulted in the ability of the groups to handle much heavier loads than had been thought possible by the planners (8).

While those who plan for themselves will display more initiative in making needed changes in a plan, specific provisions to encourage such initiative are required when planning for others. In our exercise, it can take the form of an instruction: "Stop work after five minutes. Evaluate how well the plan has worked so far. If it is not working as well as it might, consider making suitable corrections to improve it before proceeding to continue work." In a real organization, it can take the form of an instruction asking doers to report back regularly to the planners the extent the plan is working satisfactorily and where it may need modification. As in the novel *The Bridge on the River Kwai*, planners may also need to allow for the completely unforeseen contingency, the critical event whose occurrence could not have been anticipated except by the general instruction to the doers to modify the plan in a suitable way if such an unsuspected event occurs.

PROMOTING UNDERSTANDING

No one package of approaches can be suggested since each situation will call for different means for promoting understanding of the plans by the doers. In one production situation, understanding may be promoted by pretests and modifications of presentations, demonstrations, and instructions. In another, it may best be aided by testing for individual differences in understanding of the plans, then working further with those who fail to understand the plan. What we are proposing here is that what is necessary is concern by the planners for understanding and suitable attention to this in the implementation process.

MAXIMIZING
THE EFFECTIVE USE OF AVAILABLE MANPOWER

This is a matter of making the most of what is available by whatever means the situation allows. One case may call for self-assessments by the doers which are incorporated in the plans. Another case may permit objective assessments of the differential capacities of the doers, so that men and jobs are similarly matched. Still another scheme may permit rotation of assignments until the optimum arrangements are found, or rotation may be continued to reduce boredom. Or, discretion may be allowed so that individual doers use what they regard as their own best ways to implement the plans. The organizational level (and capacity) of the doer may be paramount in deciding how much discretion can be built into the plan for him. The higher the level, the greater the discretion possible.

IMPROVING COMMUNICATIONS

If the planners and doers use the same codes, shorthand, or language, if the plans are simple for the doers to understand, one-way communication from the planners to the doers is likely to be fast, effective, and satisfying to both planners and doers. But, if the planners are using different concepts, "speak a different language," are presenting what is a complex set of instructions to the doers, then it becomes important for the communications to be two ways, from planners to doers and from doers to planners. The doers must have (and feel that they have) plenty of opportunity to question the planners for clarification of the presentation of the plans (27).

The planners need to attend to whether or not they are overestimating or underestimating the ability to comprehend of those who are receiving the plans. The planners need to judge whether they are transmitting too much or too little, too fast or too slowly, with too great or too little enthusiasm, with too much or too little confidence. The planner-senders have to be alert to the extent messages are being filtered by the receiver-doers, who may only "hear" what they want to "hear" or what fits with their past understandings.

MINIMIZING COMPETITION

When planning for others, the planners need to avoid creating a situation in which the doers see themselves in a zero-sum game with planners. If the plans succeed, relative to the planners, the doers must not lose status, prestige, power, or material benefits. Conditions must be established in which the doers share with the planners the same superordinate goals. The division of labor should be seen to benefit the doers as well as the planners. What is required is maintaining a non-zero sum game where both win, if the plans succeed.

6

How "Informal" Organization Evolves: Interpersonal Choice and Subgroup Formation

André L. Delbecq
University of Wisconsin

Reprinted by permission from *Business Perspectives*, IV, No. 3 (1968), 17–21.

Every student of management knows that the "official" organization (the hierarchy of positions and tasks) is constantly being modified by individual and group behavior, thus affecting the decision-making process. What is often less clear is the nature of the inexorable forces contained within the formal organizational design which contribute to the development of subgroups. The purpose of this brief article is to examine the relationship between structural properties of formal organizations and the formation of informal groups. It is hoped that this study concerning the manner is which the subgroup "overlay" comes into being can be understood in social psychological terms rather than merely intuitively (37, pp. 16–32).

FACTORS UNDERLYING
INTERPERSONAL CHOICES

Attractions and repulsions occur among individual members of an organization, often under conditions of short-lived acquaintanceship. Moreover, individual sociometrically isolated choice patterns are shown in a number of studies to persist over time, and even to become more apparent (19, p. 139). Therefore, we can talk of the configuration of such choice patterns as an element of informal group structure, and of such group structures as part of the informal-organization overlay which permeates formal organizational decision making (37, p. 19).

However, to understand that such interpersonal choices are a ubiquitous aspect of organizational life and that the choice pattern remains relatively stable is not sufficient. In order to relate interpersonal choice to formal organizational designs, the manager must understand the factors which underlie interpersonal choices.

A number of research studies have been devoted to this question (19, p. 127; 34), in which light the following factors appear particularly salient:

1. Proximity
2. Similarities or attractiveness in terms of
   a) work activities
   b) interests or values shared
   c) complementary personality profiles
   d) individual social characteristics (social class, status, rank, etc.).

While it is perilous to rank-order these variables in terms of importance, certain propositions appear defensible. To begin with, proximity is clearly a necessary precondition for group formation, and, thus, is the primary variable (13; 19, p. 139). Unless physical distance is overcome in some manner, interaction is impossible; since man mediates his behavior conceptually, it is not conceivable that a truly "human" relationship between individual group members could evolve without symbolic interaction (29). The feasibility of interaction must be assured by some form of proximity (either actual physical proximity or simulated proximity by means of modern communication methods) in order for other structural group characteristics to evolve.

Variables dealing with similarities or attractiveness manifest the following relevant considerations:

1. Individuals can and do distinguish between two dimensions, alternatively conceptualized as "affectional" choices as opposed to "instrumental" choices, (32, 43) and "private" or person-to-person friendships (41) as opposed to "public" choices (feelings toward a person arising from the group as a whole due to the role of the individual in the group).[1]

2. The degree to which task–instrumental or social–emotional considerations pertain to individual choices differs depending on the degree of achievement desires vs. affiliation desires of individuals (15).

3. Individuals (particularly in task-oriented groups) tend to make fewer choices on the basis of personality or social characteristics than on the basis of work criteria (16, 19, p. 139; 22).

4. Groups formed initially on the basis of personality or social characteristics (friendship) tend to be less stable (19).

5. Regardless of the basis of group formation, the stability of the groups and the continuance of the groups are secure only if shared values of interests are present or evolve (35, 39).

It should be noted that sociologically oriented theory has not integrated clinical psychological orientations to group formation. In clinical psychological theory, it is proposed that group formation can be studied from the standpoint of drive relationships and emotional procedures within each member of a group out of which the basis of group formative processes evolves. In one school of clinical thought, it is proposed that groups often polarize around a central person. Ten different roles which the central person might play are then discussed, including such roles as the patriarchal sovereign, the central person as love object, and the central hero.

Our objective is not to elaborate on the theory underlying the propositions themselves, but rather to relate these propositions to group formation in formal organizations. We will, therefore, move directly to the issue of formalization.

FORMAL "POSITIONS" AND INTERPERSONAL CHOICE

One does not talk about forming groups in classical management models. Rather, one forms a hierarchy of positions. Indeed, the prescriptive classical

---

[1] Obviously these alternative classifications are not conceptually equal. The first dimension (affectional–instrumental) refers to role played, and the second (public–private) to group situation or task content. Further, the correlation of all four choices often occurs, since there are some "great men" who have skills both "affectional" and "instrumental," and are seen as desirable members in both private and public groups. One of the methodological weaknesses in sociometric tests is the failure to make such distinctions. See (10).

maxim is to avoid building organizations around people, and to build around positions.

At the same time "position," as a concept, has largely been taken at face value in management literature. By definition, it has been thought of as an individual occupational role encompassing certain tasks. However, the concept "position" includes technical, socio-technical and social dimensions, and therefore, is a relatively complex notion. A more detailed discussion of the "position" concept and its dimensions is warranted.

TECHNICAL DIMENSION OF "POSITION"

All the physical artifacts which are part of the work activity (dictating machines, adding machines, etc.) are included in the technical dimension. Also, a cognitive content (conceptual program) is necessary so that ways of thinking are built into the "expertise" required of the positional incumbent. This work requires certain subcultural norms and values arising out of the socialization which takes place in the training and developing of "expertise." And finally, a degree of ecological separation according to process or function (departmentation) must exist.

Notice that these technical aspects of the work situation implicit in "position" already encompass several factors out of which subgroup formation is fostered: physical proximity of people engaged in similar work activities; common attitudes and values arising out of technical training; and, perhaps, certain social-class similarities which arise from the entrance and training requirements for acceptance into the position.

SOCIO-TECHNICAL DIMENSION OF "POSITION"

The socio-technical dimension refers to the fact that the total decision-making process (encompassing both problem solving and implementation) requires interaction between individuals occupying specific positions. This work-related interaction reinforces subgrouping and interpersonal choices.

SOCIAL DIMENSION OF "POSITION"

Finally, barring incompatible personalities, social relations grow out of contacts fostered by technical and socio-technical dimensions of work activity. These social activities again reinforce interpersonal choice and subgroupings within the complex organization.

Perhaps a brief example will make the matter clearer. John Doe joins XYZ Corporation as a personnel management trainee. He is assigned to an office on the sixth floor within the personnel management department (proximity). He finds that most of the staff in personnel have been similarly trained in several nearby graduate schools (common training leading to shared concepts, values, and attitudes). In carrying out his early work assignments, he must converse which colleagues primarily within the department (shared work activities and socio-technical interaction). After several months, he is asked to play golf with other members of the department, and soon the biweekly golf game is a standard recreational item (social dimension of position).

The interrelated technical, socio-technical, and social dimensions of John Doe's formal position as a personnel trainee create all the necessary conditions for a viable group structure. This subgroup structure, in turn, results in behavior patterns and normative concepts which may or may not be congruent with organizational objectives and the official decision system. John Doe may, for instance, become overattached to the personnel "gang," thereby tending to be overdefensive of their policy positions rather than adequately analytical. He may tend to interact too exclusively with the personnel group, thus limiting his exposure to other managers. This limited exposure mitigates the possibility of a promotion to a management position in an area related to, but outside of, the personnel department. He may tend to oversell programs initiated inside the department, and undervalue proposals originating outside the personnel department.

The relevant point here is that the type of subgroup suboptimization which has just been described should be the normal state of affairs rather than an aberration in the typical formal organization, since all the conditions for subgroup formation are present (shared activities, facilitated interactions, and common sentiments). By inserting the "positional" dimensions parenthetically into classical propositions about group formation, we can see this more clearly. For example,

> The more people associate with one another under conditions of equality (positional congruency and equal organizational influence bases), the more they come to share values and norms, and the more they come to like one another (6).
>
> Interaction between persons (due to technical work requirements) leads to sentiments of liking (reinforced by shared professional norms arising out of training in a functional specialization) and this leads to new activities (social), and these, in turn, mean further interaction. . . . The more frequently persons interact with one another (ecological proximity and socio-technical requirements), the stronger their sentiments of friendship for one another are apt to be. . . . The more frequently persons interact with one another, the more alike in some respects both their activities and sentiments become (20).

IMPLICATIONS FOR DECISION MAKING

Organizational subgroups (cliques and informal decision networks) well documented in research studies (9, 31) are not, then, to be seen as solely the result of political struggles for power and influence—a Machiavellian tone that permeates much discussion on informal organization. Rather, such cleavage also grows out of seemingly innocuous processes or organizational life such as assignments to work positions and departmentation. This implies that the integration of subgroups into an organizational structure which is cohesive and possessive of congruent norms throughout all subgroups requires conscious restructuring of interactions (away from the pattern of the bureaucratic model), in order to overcome fundamental propensities toward organizational cleavage.[2]

At the same time, political and affective dimensions are an inextricable aspect of subgroup interaction. Thus, political and affective overtones ultimately color the decision-making processes of complex organizations. Organizations are not, therefore, monocratic structures acting as a "corporate personality" with a simple preference function based solely on econological dimensions of a rationalistic choice situation. Attempts to reify organizations as "individual-choice mechanisms" and to ignore socialization within subgroups create an organizational model reinforcing the game of organizational charades (managers pretend to be totally rational while actually pursuing subgroup goals).

IMPLICATIONS FOR ORGANIZATIONAL DESIGN

This article's treatment of interpersonal choice points out several propositions which develop logically from, and are congruent with, revised organizational theories.

First, membership in organizational work groups should provide for "overlap" so that interaction between members of work groups from several functional areas and several hierarchical levels is facilitated. One theorist talks about this "overlap" as being developed primarily by the supervisor interacting in several groups (28). Others argue that overlapping membership should encompass more than one member of a relatively autonomous subgroup in order to provide better representation, both from the group to the organization, and from the organization to the group (23). The latter proposition seems sound, since representation by the supervisor alone is often dyadic, leading to all the dysfunctions of two-person interaction (11). In either case, the issue is quite similar. Unless the boundary between the relatively autonomous subgroup is overcome through interactions with personnel from outside the group, the increasing propensity for suboptimization is inevitable. Further, this need for overlapping membership is true of subgroups formed by means other than formal departmentation. For example, if the decision making of a college dean or a corporate vice-president is largely mediated by interaction with the same set of advisers (even though the advisers are taken from several functional groups), soon the advisers will form the much criticized self-contained managerial oligarchy relatively closed to other organizational personnel.

---

[2] Studies dealing with group size provide further evidence supporting the propensity toward organizational cleavage. In brief, such studies indicate that people cannot relate psychologically to more than seven individuals, and in general, prefer to interact with only two or three individuals (21). Thus, the proposition that cleavage rather than cohesiveness is the typical state of organizational affairs does not rest solely on the "interpersonal choice" dimension of group structure for theoretical justification.

Second, given the increasing complexity of much organizational decision making, no single expert of specialization can adequately claim total competence. Thus, mediation of decision making by specialists from several functional areas becomes necessary. However, if the mediation takes the form of power plays between specialist empires, then decision making is hardly satisfactory. Nonetheless, if specialists are generally self-contained within isolated subgroups and seldom interact outside these subgroups, this pattern of power plays is to be expected. Thus, the overlapping participation, while intermittent, cannot be so infrequent that parochialism remains intact.

Third, recent studies show quite clearly that personnel promotions are largely based on managerial acquaintance arising out of frequent socio-technical interactions, rather than based on a broad search process (1). However, if acquaintances are largely confined to subgroup "cronies," the possibility of adequate consideration of talented personnel from outside the very proximate subgroup is unlikely.

CONCLUSION

The organizational design which best provides for overlapping membership and which best facilitates work-relevant interaction between varied organizational positions is the task-force or project-group organizational design. Such an organizational strategy provides for overlapping group memberships of short to intermediate duration, bringing together decision-relevant groupings of specialists and administrators. Further, such groupings can be juxtaposed with departmentation for routine decision implementation. Finally, project management satisfies the need for overlapping group membership without artificially imposing the burden of "linking" groups solely on the departmental supervisors.

There are, of course, other arguments favoring the task-force organizational design (5, 30, 40). The social psychology of interpersonal choices is, however, one more stream of logic supportive of the reconceptualization of organizational structure in the direction of the more organic model of the task-force or project-management design.

Questioning the Managerial Implications of Organizing for Goal Attainment

1. What specific kinds of problems can you see arising within organizations from adoption of any of the three organizational structure compromises offered by Walker and Lorsch? Can you provide examples of kinds of organizations where each of these three proposals might be most useful?

2. In his case for the matrix organization, Delbecq has proposed one way to control and tap the potential value of the informal organization. Is the informal organization the employees' "sacred cow," or can an organization justify using employee groups to its own advantage?

3. Under what circumstances might it be most profitable to separate planning from doing in the organization? Which of the five organizational structures described by Walker and Lorsch would Bass prefer?

4. How is the "separation of line and staff" related to the issues previously discussed? How many other controversial organizational structure considerations can you identify in addition to the ones described in this chapter?

References

1. Alfred, T. M., "Checkers of Choice in Manpower Management," *Harvard Business Review,* XLV, No. 1 (1967), 157–69.

2. Bass, B. M., *Organizational Psychology.* Boston: Allyn & Bacon, Inc., 1965.

3. ——, *Exercise Organization.* Pittsburgh: INSTAD, 1967.

4. ——, and H. J. Leavitt, "Experiments in Planning and Operating," *Management Science,* IX, No. 4 (1963), 574–85.

5. Bennis, W., "Beyond Bureaucracy," *Trans-action,* Vol. III (1965).

6. Berelson, B., and G. A. Steiner, *Human Behavior.* New York: Harcourt, Brace & World, Inc., 1964.

7. Chandler, A. D., Jr., *Strategy and Structure.* Cambridge: The M.I.T. Press, 1962.

8. Chapman, R. L., J. L. Kennedy, A. Newall, and W. C. Biel, "The Systems Research Laboratory's Air-Defense Experiments, in *Simulation in Social Science: Readings,* ed. H. Guetzkow. Englewood Cliffs, N. J.: Prentice-Hall, Inc., 1962.

9. Dalton, M., *Men who Manage.* New York: John Wiley & Sons, Inc., 1959, p. 20.

10. Delbecq, A. L., "The Social-Psychology of Executive Roles Re-Examined," *Business Perspectives,* II, No. 3 (1966).

11. ——, "The World Within the Span of Control: Managerial Behavior in Groups of Varied Size," in press.

12. Festinger, L., *A Theory of Cognitive Dissonance.* Evanston, Ill.: Row, Peterson, 1957.

13. ——, S. Schlacter, and K. Back, *Social Pressures in Informal Groups.* New York: Harper & Row, Publishers, 1960. pp. 431–44.

14. Fisch, G. G., "Line Staff is Obsolete," *Harvard Business Review,* XXXIX, No. 5 (1961), 67–79.

15. French, J. R. P., "A Formal Theory of Social Power," *Psychological Review,* LXIII (1956), 181–94.

16. Gibb, C. A., "The Sociometry of Leadership in Temporary Groups," *Sociometry,* XIII (1950), 226–43.

17. Gulick, L., "Notes on the Theory of Organization," in *Papers on the Science of Administration,* eds. L. Gulick and L. F. Urwick. New York: New York Institute of Public Administration, 1937, pp. 23–24.

18. Habbe, S., "Does Communication Make a Difference?," *Management Record,* XIV (1952), 414–16, 442–44.

19. Hare, A. P., *Handbook of Small Group Research.* New York: The Free Press, Inc., 1962, p. 139.

20. Homans, G. C., *The Human Group.* New York: Harcourt, Brace & World, Inc., 1950.

21. James, J., "A Preliminary Study of the Size Determinant in Small-Group Interaction," *American Sociological Review,* XVI (1959), 474–77.

22. Jennings, H. H., "Sociometric Differentiation of the Psycho-Group and the Socio-Group," *Sociometry,* X (1947), 71–79.

23. Kahn, R. L., D. N. Wolfe, R. P. Quinn, J. D. Snork, and R. A. Rosenthal, *Organizational Stress: Studies in Role Conflict and Ambiguity.* New York: John Wiley, & Sons, Inc., 1964, pp. 388–92.

24. Koontz, H. D., and C. J. O'Donnell, *Principles of Management,* 2nd ed. New York: McGraw-Hill Book Company, 1959, p. 111.

25. Lawrence, P. R., and J. W. Lorsch, "New Management Job: The Integrator," *Harvard Business Review,* VLV, No. 6 (1967), 142.

26. ——, and ——, *Organization and Environment.* Boston: Harvard Business School, Division of Research, 1967.

27. Leavitt, H. J., "Some Effects of Certain Communication Patterns on Group Performance," *Journal of Abnormal and Social Psychology,* (1951), IVL 16–30.

28. Likert, R., *New Patterns of Management.* New York: McGraw-Hill Book Company, 1961.

29. Lindesmith, A. R., and A. L. Strauss, *Social Psychology.* New York: Holt, Rinehart & Winston, Inc., 1956, pp. 159–97.

30. Mee, J. F., "Ideational Items: Matrix Organization," *Business Horizons,* 1964, 70–72.

31. Merton, R. K., "Bureaucratic Structure and Personality," in *Complex Organizations,* ed. A. Etzioni. New York: Holt, Rinehart & Winston, Inc., 1961, pp. 48–61.

32. Miller, E. J., and A. K. Rice, *Systems of Organization.* London: Tavistock, 1967.

33. Moment, D., and A. Zaleznik, *Role Development and Interpersonal Competence.* Cambridge: Harvard University Press, 1963, pp. 42–45.

34. Newcomb, T. M., "The Prediction of Interpersonal Attraction," *American Psychologist,* XI (1956), 575–86.

35. ——, "Varieties of Interpersonal Attraction," in *Group Dynamics;*

Research and Theory, eds. D. Cartwright and A. Zander. Evanston, Ill.: Row, Peterson, 1960.

36. Patchen, M., "Labor-Management Consultation at TVA: Its Impact on Employees," *Administrative Science Quarterly,* X (1965), 149–74.

37. Pfiffner, J. M., and F. P. Sherwood, *Administrative Organization.* Englewood Cliffs, N. J.: Prentice-Hall, Inc., 1960, pp. 16–32.

38. Raven, B. H., and J. Rietsema, "The Effects of Varied Clarity of Group Goal and Group Path upon the Individual and his Relation to the Group," *Human Relations,* X, No. 1 (1957), 29–45.

39. Redl, F., "Group Emotion and Leadership," *Psychiatry,* V (1942), 575–84.

40. Shull, F. A., *Matrix Structure and Project Authority for Optimizing Organizational Capacity.* Carbondale, Ill.: Southern Illinois University, Business Research Bureau, Business Science Monograph 1.

41. Taylor, F. K., "The Therapeutic Factors of Group-Analytical Treatments," *Journal of Mental Science,* IVC (1950), 967–97.

42. ——, "Quantitative Evaluation of Psychosocial Phenomena in Small Groups," *Journal of Mental Science,* IIIC (1951), 698.

43. Walker, A. H., "Behavioral Consequences of Contrasting Patterns of Organization" (Doctoral dissertation, Harvard Business School, 1967).

Compensating
Management and Employees

Management and economists have overestimated the importance of pay, but psychologists have underestimated it. Dissatisfaction with pay may be symptomatic of more deep-seated disgruntlement, and low pay in itself may spread in its disturbing effects to other issues.

The actual amount of pay is not as significant as how much a person believes he should be paid. This belief depends on whom he compares himself with.

The readings that follow examine the importance of financial reward to both managers and employees, and attempt to provide an understanding of the compensation patterns for subordinates preferred by managers.

Dunnette offers advice to company compensation administrators. He proposes six questions, the answers to which he claims will enable an organization to gain the maximum benefit from its pay policies.

The study presented by Lawler and Porter represents an attempt to answer some of the questions asked by Dunnette. The specific value of this effort is that it examines the relationships between managers' perceptions regarding their pay and their position in the managerial hierarchy.

Vroom turns our attention to the compensation issues relevant to the motivation of employees. He analyzes the effect of pay under three separate approaches to reward systems: (1) paternalistic, (2) scientific, and (3) participative. Vroom envisions an integration of the scientific and participative techniques that will both reward employees objectively and create a motivating environment.

How do managers determine what salary increases will be awarded subordinates? Is the current practice as arbitrary as Dunnette indicates it might be, or do managers follow consistent patterns in salary administration? Bass provides some answers to these and other questions with the data he collected from the administration of a management training simulation exercise to 133 graduate business students. His results indicate that, although merit based on performance is a prime factor in establishing pay rates, the abilities and values of salary recommenders play a role in the increases they are willing to award.

7

Compensation: Some Obvious Answers to Unasked Questions

Marvin D. Dunnette
University of Minnesota

Reprinted by permission of the publisher from *Compensation Review*, first quarter, 1969. © 1969 by the American Management Association, Inc.

A somewhat caricatured history of my own compensation experiences will point up the many untested assumptions—obvious answers to unasked questions—implied by compensation practices in most firms today. These "answers" will then form the backdrop for raising and commenting on research questions that most compensation administrators and behavioral scientists have failed to ask and to research. These questions are what might be called the six P's of industrial compensation—*Purposes, Preferences, Perceptions, Persons, Performance,* and *Practices.*

I received my Ph.D. degree in the summer of 1954 and became an assistant professor of psychology and industrial relations. My salary was $5400 for the 12-month year. During that first year, I received no feedback about how I was doing. I wondered about the possibility of a pay raise, but received no word of any change until I noted a large July pay check, apparently reflecting an increase in annual salary to $6,000. Having more money was nice, but it was disturbing not to know what the raise was based on or what it meant.

Was this a standard raise that everyone received? Or had I been singled out for special treatment because of unbelievably great competence as a researcher? Was it a clerical error or a computer slipup?

None of these explanations could legitimately be ruled out; each seemed a distinct possibility. But I decided to keep quiet lest the raise turn out to be an error.

About that time, the employment magager of a large midwestern manufacturing firm inquired about my setting up a personnel research department. After being interviewed by nearly everyone, I was offered a job with a proposed starting salary of $7500. I wondered how they arrived at that salary figure. When I asked, my future boss mumbled something about "qualifications," "going rate," "survey," and "comparability with others of your age." In turn, I mumbled about "consulting contacts," "extra income," and "needed inducement to leave academia." Eventually, I went to work there at a salary of $8400.

I behaved like any good industrial psychologist—validating tests, interpreting them for applicants, bringing common sense to bear on personnel decisions, and seeking to talk the language of businessmen while maintaining enough of the vocabulary to retain the label of "expert." I liked the job, and people seemed to like me.

Periodically, my boss would summon me and say something like, "Well, Mary, we've just had a salary review, and your pay level has been increased to—(shuffling of papers, looking up data, hemming and hawing, some embarrassment)—$X." Occasionally, I cranked up enough courage to ask, "How'm I doing?" and he would respond, "Great, just great! If there are ever any problems, I'll let you be the first to know."

I remember one significant salary action that was shrouded in even deeper mystery. I was made a member of the management profit-sharing club; and at quarterly intervals after that, I received bonus checks equivalent to about a week's pay. I remember feeling very honored and happy about being placed in the profit-sharing group, even though the actual compensation advantage was not gigantic.

In the four years I was there, my salary increased to $12,000. In 1960, when I followed my intended objective of returning to academia, I found that the clerical errors at my previous institution had apparently continued and I was now worth $10,400 for the nine-month academic year—equivalent to $13,800 on a 12-month basis.

Since then, I have had occasionally startling salary experiences—some involving gallant financial action in response to job offers from elsewhere. But, by and large, the basis for salary increments has seemed well-grounded in merit. Each year—around New Year's Day—our department head asks us to prepare a memorandum describing all our experiences and accomplishments during the year—books and articles, research grants, honors and awards, competing job offers—anything that showed our "worth" as scholars, researchers, teachers, or even as human beings. None of us knows (I assume that my colleagues share my ignorance) by what mystical means these diverse elements of merit are combined to produce dollar values. But I feel content that somehow they are; and I am convinced that what I do as a professor *does* very directly affect the level of my compensation and the amount of my annual raise.

SO WHAT?

From this slightly caricatured story certain stark generalizations can be gleaned about the current state of the art in industrial compensation.

To begin with, it is assumed that compensation practices must be shrouded in secrecy. People not only do not know how much their compatriots make, they rarely know very accurately the basis underlying their own pay or what it may mean in terms of what they have done or may be expected to do.

Apparently, it is assumed that something damaging will occur if information about pay levels and their determination becomes widespread. It seems that pay and salary are viewed with embarrassment, a matter not to be discussed openly in polite company, merely an accounting detail to be handled as efficiently and with as little fanfare as possible. Open comparisons with others are viewed as indiscreet. Actual determinations of pay levels for different people should be done according to certain regulations that must not be publicized widely in the organization.

Second, it is assumed, apparently, that pay policies and pay practices can be formulated simply by asking what other companies are doing. Surveys of other firms, of "going rates" for similar jobs, of the latest gimmicks (profit sharing, stock-purchase agreements, turkeys at Christmas) and of current "thinking" about "salary growth," "career pay," and "pay for merit" are apparently seen as the best bases for fixing pay rates and for determining pay actions for a person as he "progresses" with a company.

Third, it is assumed, apparently, that money spent for pay should simply be regarded as a capital investment—spent merely to purchase a certain amount of human machinery in much the same way as other funds are spent to purchase plants and equipment.

In other words, the compensation dollar is spent merely to purchase a manpower commodity—work or labor; and, very important, it is assumed that the nature of the commodity received in return is not affected in any fundamental way by the manner in which the expenditure (or the purchase) is made.

Many additional assumptions stem from this last assumption:

1. Level of pay should be based mostly on longevity, "staying power," seniority, or whatever you may wish to call it. The notion seems to be that the long-running, older human machine is always worth more than the brand new one.
2. It doesn't matter how people are paid; whatever fits the accounting system most efficiently is the best. Hence, a monthly pay check or merely implanting a blip on a computer tape is just as "good" as handing out silver dollars or bags of gold.
3. The worst sin of salary administration is to overpay a person because overpayment implies a "bad deal" for the company in the purchase agreement.
4. As long as no one is complaining about pay, everything is OK.
5. People will take as much as they can get and will always be looking for more.
6. Pay policies and practices should be engineered to be the same for everyone; individual differences among different human elements may be taken into account in determining the cost of each element, but the strategies of salary determination and the techniques of payment needn't differ from person to person.

These assumptions are enough to illustrate the present pattern of stereotyped, accounting-based thinking and cataloging prevalent in most company compensation practices.

HOW DID IT HAPPEN?

It is difficult to understand how these assumptions came about or how they could have gained such credence as they have, for they seem not to recognize the behavioral side of the work equation. Probably they arose from an over-attention to the cost side of the equation. Because dollars were involved in labor purchasing and payment, a commodity purchasing and cost accounting philosophy took hold of salary administrators' thinking, and the assumptions were transported essentially intact from the cost accounting domain into the area of industrial compensation. Lip service was, of course, paid to the so-called "human element"—but nothing was said out loud about any possibility that the transported assumptions might not really apply. They came to be honored, with no new questions being asked, and the practices that evolved perpetuated them further—to a point where the unwary observer might even now be willing to argue that they have been tested (time-tested, perhaps?) and shown to be valid.

THE UNASKED QUESTIONS

Let us then consider the behavioral side of the work equation and state explicitly some of the questions that have gone unasked, what we may or may not know in our efforts to answer them, and what implications they have for the practice of industrial compensation.

PURPOSE

Here we ask whether money used for pay should rightfully be considered to be just another capital investment—a way of purchasing the manpower commodity. Should we attach motivational and broader behavioral significance to its use? No matter how reluctant some compensation administrators may be to admit it, their purpose in paying people is multifaceted—to attract competent persons, to retain effective performers, to dislodge ineffective performers, and to elicit job behavior leading to excellence. These purposes all involve volitional behavior—coming, staying, leaving, persisting, and striving—which need, in part at least, to be discussed within a motivational framework.

This does not mean that commodity concepts of labor should be disregarded or that there may not be many industrial situations in which market value may not actually be the sole basis for developing wage payment principles. Nor does it mean that there are not situations in which volitional components are unimportant. It does mean, however, that broader recognition should be accorded to the motivational purposes that most compensation plans have, that these purposes should be made explicit, and that their behavioral implications should be given research attention.

IMPLICATIONS FOR PRACTICE Ask the question: What purpose do we hope to accomplish with our salary administration dollars?

PREFERENCE

The issue of preference refers to what people want. Why do they work? What are their aspirations? What outcomes do they want from the job situation? How do people differ from one another in their preferences or motivations? Most important, how are different preferences ordered for different persons? Which preferences are complementary and which are antagonistic? How do they develop, grow, and mature? How do they wax and wane under the influence of different situations?

We know—in spite of many efforts to develop and espouse oversimplified "theories" of man's nature—that people differ substantially in what they want from a job. Many, of course, want recognition, accomplishment, and responsibility. But what for one man may be a rich and rewarding pat on the back may for another be merely empty praise. Tangible rewards (such as money) are far more important for some than for others. Some employees have strong security needs; others seek material advantage. Some are fully content to be in jobs with intrinsically interesting activities; others seek external factors as primary means of gratification. More effective managers have been shown to be those who strive not only for recognition and higher status, but who also give greater value to power and material advantage than do less effective managers.

We know little or nothing of the behavioral effects of these differential preference systems under different plans or strategies of compensation.

IMPLICATIONS FOR PRACTICE Recognize individual differences in people. Recognize that these differences extend into motivational areas as well as ability areas. Forget simple "theories" of job motivation. Do research necessary to determine the differential behavioral effects of different pay plans designed in accord with individual differences.

PERCEPTIONS

Questions about perceptions are so numerous that we can sample them only sparsely. First, what is the "meaning" of money? Certainly, it has meaning in terms of what it can buy. But, for many, it is also a sign of accomplishment—a sort of merit badge showing that somebody (one's boss, the company, somebody "up there") thinks they are worthy and valuable people.

Edward E. Lawler has developed data from which he argues—with a good degree of justification—that company policies of compensation secrecy have the net effect of stripping much of the symbolic reward value away from people's perceptions of money by not allowing them to display their merit badges and sometimes by not even giving them sufficient comparison information to allow them to attach "meaning" to their pay treatment.

IMPLICATIONS FOR PRACTICE Find out how money is perceived by employees. Experiment with different approaches designed to reveal more about compensation strategies and compensation levels.

PERSONS

Questions about persons must be asked in the context of others in an employee's job or social environment who may be chosen by him when he makes pay comparisons. Salary administrators have painfully learned that it is necessary to maintain equitable pay levels among jobs judged to be similar in what they require, and many practices and many textbooks revolve around the techniques of fixing pay rates. Unfortunately, such techniques always assume essentially that jobs are static entities, and they take little account of changes in people—with the possible exception of aging.

We know now, however, that attitudes toward pay and even job behavior are strongly affected by much more complicated comparisons than the ones that have traditionally been obvious to salary administrators. For example, with whom does any given person compare himself when he ponders what he gets from his job against what he puts into it? More highly educated persons—particularly those in the professions—lawyers, doctors, psychologists—usually choose persons outside the firm (other professionals) for their comparison mates. But whom do general managers look toward? Under what circumstances? How should facts about the persons who are chosen as social comparison objects be taken into account in a firm's salary administration practices?

IMPLICATIONS FOR PRACTICE Forget the old time slogan "Equal pay for equal work" because it implies that some basis exists (in the abstract) for measuring a job and how much it is worth. Recognize that people make their own "factor comparisons" based again on their perceptions—whom they see as their legitimate comparison mates—and what they see them as putting into and getting from the job. Adopt a perceptual framework based on inputs and outcomes instead of the overly simplistic concept of equal pay for equal work.

PERFORMANCE

Performance refers, of course, to behavior—specifically, job behavior. The major practical issue here is to decide what we can say about money's effects on behavior. Unfortunately, up to now research in industry has been almost exclusively restricted to behavior inferences derived from anecdotes and stories in response to interviews or on answers to items in job attitude and satisfaction measures. The crucial need is to learn whether or not other aspects of job performance—particularly coming, staying, leaving, persisting, and striving—are related to money rewards and pay practices.

It should be clear to any observer that in spite of such confused comment to the contrary, people do behave as if they value money highly. Executives strive mightily to advance to high-paying jobs; gamblers gamble; professors do research and publish books; and so on, and so on.

The question becomes not whether money is an appropriate incentive for goal-directed behavior, but what strategies are best for assuring that desired job behaviors are elicited by financial incentives.

A seemingly obvious, but little used answer in industry is to make more explicit exactly what a given job behavior can mean in terms of financial returns. Currently, about the only time this is made very explicit in industry is when a given salary offer is used as an inducement for the volitional act of coming to a firm. Other salary–job behavior linkages—often even the financial effects of promotion—are likely to be shrouded in mystery in most companies.

IMPLICATIONS FOR PRACTICE Define the part of an employee's job over which he has direct control. Moreover, define exactly how changes in that part of the job may affect his pay. Many jobs will be shown not to be subject to any substantial variation in job behavior. Others will allow great variation. Communicate exactly how and under what circumstances pay is related to what one does on the job.

PRACTICE

The implications of these questions for compensation practices may be summarized under four primary principles:

1. First, the compensation system for each employee should be individualized. As we have seen, people differ in what they want from a job. Moreover, they differ in what they perceive money to be and in what they believe money can do. In other words, pay systems should be tailored individually to fit the motive system, the individual perceptual and belief systems of each employee.

2. Second, the relationship between what a person does on the job and his salary must be specified very explicitly. This principle means that each employee should know exactly the nature of the linkage between his own job behavior and his pay. It demands that criteria be specified and developed for describing what employees do on the job. It demands career-long compensation planning, as opposed to the haphazard practices so prevalent now. Most of all, the principle demands that companies ask a simple but absolutely crucial first question as they plan compensation activities: What is our purpose; what do we hope to accomplish with our compensation dollars?

3. Third, every compensation plan must diagnose individual employee competence, the nature of organizational constraints, and the relative probability that an employee can, through his own efforts, accomplish the job outcomes desired by the organization. This principle requires that an employee be neither rewarded nor penalized for organizational outcomes that are not clearly within his control. It leads directly to the idea that it makes eminently good sense to divide the pay dollar into portions—some amount related to market value, some amount to type and length of job experience, but the most important portion to what the employee actually does on the job and how successful he is in doing it.

4. The fourth—and final—principle is that compensation plans should be attached directly to the preference, motive, or need systems of employees. Since the motives of achievement, recognition, and responsibility are quite prevalent in our industrial society, it will usually become necessary to attach the financial rewards of a job to these important motives. The most direct strategy for realizing this aim is to make pay procedures and actual salary actions much more public than they now are. Only when the aura of mystery is removed from present pay practices will it be possible to use pay action *directly* as merit badges, signifying work well done, recognition, and solid accomplishment—with the accompanying increased social and material status.

These guidelines for setting the compensation world in motion again should not be viewed as radical or extreme. They suggest only that:

1. You should ask what your purpose is.

2. You should increase your concern for using money to motivate men rather than just to placate them.
3. You should recognize that people differ and gear your programs around that fact.
4. You should tell the people in your company—everybody—what you are doing.

8

Perceptions Regarding Management Compensation

Edward E. Lawler, III
Yale University

Lyman W. Porter
University of California at Irvine

The assistance of the American Management Association, and particularly Robert
F. Steadman, in obtaining the sample respondents to our questionnaire is gratefully
acknowledged. Reprinted by permission from *Industrial Relations*, October 1963, 41–49.

Despite widespread interest in the problems of compensation, experimental investigation in the field has only recently begun (7, 8). The present study differs from most of the work in this area for two reasons: first, it is concerned with members of management and, second, it deals with the psychological aspects of compensation. Previous studies have dealt with such topics as the effectiveness of different methods of payment (13) and the incomes of different demographic groups. Research has been neglected on such aspects of pay as: (1) the importance attached to pay, (2) perceptions regarding the amount of pay received, (3) satisfaction with regard to pay, and (4) the needs which pay satisfies. The purpose of the following study is to investigate, at all levels of management and at all income levels, each of these four aspects of managers' perceptions regarding their pay.

QUESTIONNAIRE

The data for this study were obtained by means of a questionnaire. The relevant part of the questionnaire contained 13 items classifiable into a Maslow-type need hierarchy system (9), plus one item concerned with pay. The instructions for this part of the questionnaire stated:

On the following pages will be listed several characteristics or qualities connected with your management position. For each such characteristic, you will be asked to give three ratings:
a. How much of the characteristic is there now connected with your management position?
b. How much of the characteristic do you think should be connected with your management position?
c. How important is this position characteristic to you?

For each of the 14 items, the respondents were instructed to answer the above three questions by circling a number on a rating scale extending from 1–7, where "low numbers represent low or minimum amounts, and high numbers represent high or maximum amounts." Each item, such as the one on pay, appeared as follows on the questionnaire:

The pay for my management position:
(a) How much is there now?   (min) 1 2 3 4 5 6 7 (max)
(b) How much should there be?   (min) 1 2 3 4 5 6 7 (max)
(c) How important is this to me?   (min) 1 2 3 4 5 6 7 (max)

The items were randomly presented in the questionnaire. However, each of the 13 items pertaining to the Maslow-type need hierarchy theory had been preclassified into one of the following five types of needs: security needs, social needs, esteem needs, needs for autonomy, and needs for selfactualization (10).

PROCEDURE AND SAMPLE

The questionnaire was mailed to a random sample of 3000 members (approximately 10 percent) of the American Management Association and to another random sample of some 3000 managers whose names were on mailing lists available to the Association. Responses were received from 1958 managers, with the number of usable questionnaires for this study being 1913. (It should be noted that for a psychological research study dealing with managers this is an exceptionally large sample.) The method of distribution of the questionnaire resulted in a nation-wide sample, one in which any particular company would not be represented by more than a few individual respondents.

From personal data questions asked on the last page of the questionnaire, it was possible to classify respondents on a number of independent variables. The three relevant variables for this study were salary, level within management, and staff or line management (11). Table 1 shows the distribution of the sample by management level and pay group.

TABLE 1
DISTRIBUTION OF N FOR TOTAL SAMPLE
BY FIVE MANAGEMENT LEVELS AND TEN PAY GROUPS

	Pay groups										
Management level	1 Below $5,900	2 $6– 8,900	3 $9– 11,900	4 $12– 14,900	5 $15– 19,900	6 $20– 24,900	7 $25– 34,900	8 $35– 49,900	9 $50– 74,000	10 Over $75,000	Total N for level
President	1	1	2	4	13	15	28	16	23	11	114
Vice-president	2	9	27	80	111	108	154	78	30	11	610
Upper middle	2	34	127	159	177	92	51	14	3		659
Lower middle	3	63	129	130	77	21	4	1	1		429
Lower	4	30	34	17	14	2					101
Total N of pay group	12	137	319	390	392	238	237	109	57	22	1913

For this study the amount of annual pay was the major independent variable. However, since pay is correlated with management level, it was felt necessary to classify individuals both by management level and by pay. In this way, the effects of the two variables could be assessed independently. This was particularly important since previous studies have found that satisfaction of psychological needs varies with level of management (11). In this study we held pay level constant in order to see the effects of management level on perception of pay.

RESULTS AND DISCUSSION

IMPORTANCE ATTACHED TO PAY

The data concerned with the importance attached to pay were obtained from respondents' answers to part (c) ("How important is this to me?") of the item, "The pay for my management position." A study by Kahn showed that superiors consistently perceived their subordinates as attaching more importance to pay than they themselves did (8). Kahn's finding suggests that lower level managers attach greater importance to pay than do higher level managers. Since the size of a man's salary is highly correlated with management level, and is also a major determinant of the importance he attaches to pay, we held amount of pay constant in our analysis of differences among management levels. When we did this, we found no difference among managers at various levels in the importance attached to pay.

Then, to assess the effect of the amount of pay on the importance attached to pay, management level was held constant. When this was done, we found that higher paid managers attached *less* importance to pay than did lower-paid managers at the same level. If we assume that higher paid managers are better satisfied than lower paid managers, then these results support current motivational theories which state that as a need becomes better satisfied it tends to decrease in importance (9).

Line and staff managers who received the same pay and were at the same level in the organization showed no significant difference in the importance they attached to pay. The frequently stated opinion that the staff manager is less concerned with pay than the line manager is not supported by the data and, in fact, the trend, though not statistically significant, was in the direction of staff managers attaching more significance to pay. A study by Haire, Ghiselli, and Porter pointed out that the importance attached to different psychological needs seems to be largely a function of the individual and does not vary significantly with organizational variables (5). The importance attached to pay appears to operate in a similar manner, since no differences were found on the organization variables investigated (management level and line–staff type of position).

HOW CURRENT PAY LEVEL IS PERCEIVED

The answers to part (a) ("How much is there now?") and part (b) ("How much should there be?") of the question concerned with pay provide data on managers' attitudes toward how much pay they receive and how much pay they feel they should receive. The answers to the first question are particularly interesting because the ratings of "How much pay is there now for your management position?" on a seven-point attitude scale can be compared with an objective measure in dollars of the respondent's actual pay as revealed by him in the personal data items at the end of the questionnaire. It is valuable to make such a comparison, because in any attitude study the question always arises as to whether or not expressed attitudes have any relationship to reality.

Figures 1 through 5 represent the answers to "How much should there be?" and "How much is there now?" for each of the five management levels classified by actual pay groups. As each of the charts shows, the managers who in fact got the most pay, also *felt* that they got the most pay. This is shown by the fact that the'dotted line for "How much is there now?" rises from lower to higher paid groups within each graph. In contrast to this finding, when actual pay was held constant, managers at different levels showed no difference in their answers to this question. Therefore, actual pay rather than management level is the most important determinant of a manager's perception of how much pay he receives.

When management level was held constant, higher paid managers did not respond differently from those who were lower paid when asked, "How much pay should there be for your management position." The agreement between managers at the same level on what pay they should receive is shown in Figures 1 through 5 by the solid line ("How much should there be?"), which runs parallel to the X axis in each figure and indicates similar expectations regardless of present pay. When actual pay was held constant, higher level managers indicated there should be more pay for their management position than did lower level managers. The influence of management level on what managers feel they should be paid is indicated in Figures 1 through 5 by the tendency for the position of the solid line (for "expectations") to drop as management level decreases between Figure 1 and Figure 5. Apparently the key determinant of managers' expectations as to what they should be paid is not present pay, but management level.

SATISFACTION WITH PAY

The data relevant to the topic of *satisfaction* with pay were obtained from the difference in answers to part (a) ("How much is there now?") and part (b) ("How much should there be?") of the item, "The pay for my management position." The advantages and rationale for using these questions together as a measure of satisfaction were discussed in detail in a previous article (11). An a priori assumption was made that the smaller the difference—part (a) subtracted from part (b)—the larger the degree of satisfaction or the smaller the degree of dissatisfaction. In other words, it is the relationship between expectations and perceived outcomes that determines satisfaction. Since it is established that actual pay is an important determinant of an individual's perception of how much he receives, and that level is an important determinant of how much an individual feels he should be paid, these two variables must be considered in any analysis of satisfaction with pay.

Figures 1 through 5 illustrate the effect of actual pay on managers' satisfaction with their pay. Notice that at each management level, as pay increases, the difference between the solid line ("How much should there be?") and the broken line ("How much is there now?") decreases. Thus when management level was held constant, higher paid managers were found to be better satisfied with their pay than were lower paid managers. Holding management level

FIGURE 1

RESPONSES OF PRESIDENTS TO PARTS (A) AND (B) OF THE PAY ITEM, AS A FUNCTION OF ACTUAL PAY*

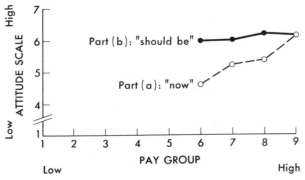

*Pay Groups 1-9 in Figure 1 through 5 are the same dollar groups as indicated ia Table 1.

FIGURE 2

RESPONSES OF VICE-PRESIDENTS TO PARTS (A) AND (B) OF THE PAY ITEM, AS A FUNCTION OF ACTUAL PAY

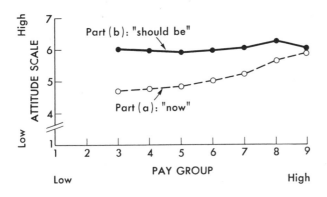

FIGURE 3

RESPONSES OF UPPER-MIDDLE MANAGERS TO PARTS (A) AND (B) OF THE PAY ITEM, AS A FUNCTION OF ACTUAL PAY

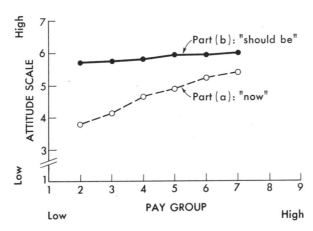

FIGURE 4

RESPONSES OF LOWER-MIDDLE MANAGERS TO PARTS (A) AND (B)
OF THE PAY ITEM, AS A FUNCTION OF ACTUAL PAY

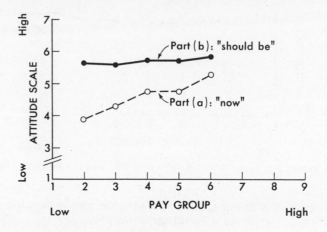

FIGURE 5

RESPONSES OF LOWER MANAGERS TO PARTS (A) AND (B) OF THE PAY
ITEM, AS A FUNCTION OF ACTUAL PAY

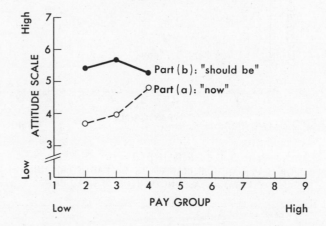

constant has the effect of holding expectations constant, and the effect of increasing pay is to increase the individual's perception of how much he receives, resulting in a decrease in the difference between the individual's expectations and perceptions with regard to his pay.

When actual pay was held constant, higher level managers were found to be *less* satisfied than lower level managers. (Note in Figures 1 through 5 the differences between the lines for perceived pay and expected pay for a given amount of objective pay at different management levels.) Since lower level managers have lower expectations with regard to pay than do higher level managers and since both groups receive the same pay, it follows that there is a smaller difference between expectations and perception of reality for lower level managers.

The question of which managers are the best satisfied with their pay can now be answered by looking again at Figures 1 through 5. At each management level, the smallest differences between expectations and perceptions of amount of pay received occur for the highest paid managers at *that* level. For example, first-line supervisors making between $12,000 and $14,900 (Pay Group 4) are better satisfied with their pay than are company presidents who make less than $49,000 (Pay Group 8 or below). It appears that a manager is very satisfied with his pay if he is paid well in relationship to others at his *same* level of management. As would be expected, since the lowest paid managers at *each* level are the worst paid relative to others doing a similar job, they are the most dissatisfied. However, even the highest paid groups at each management level are not completely satisfied.

There was no tendency for line and staff managers at the same level and receiving the same pay to report different satisfaction with pay. Apparently, not only do staff managers attach the same importance to pay as do line managers, but when pay and management level are held constant, they report the same degree of satisfaction as do line managers.

RELATIONSHIP BETWEEN PAY RECEIVED AND SATISFACTION IN FIVE NEED AREAS

Most discussions of pay emphasize that it does not satisfy a single need in the individual, but rather a variety of psychological needs (e.g., security and esteem needs) (4). In those need areas which are thought to be satisfied by pay, higher paid managers should report greater satisfaction than lower paid managers. Since management level has been shown in a previous study (11) to be correlated with satisfaction in the five need areas (social, esteem, security, autonomy, and self-actualization) considered in the present study, this variable was held constant in the analysis of the relationship of amount of pay to satisfaction in these need areas. When this was done, higher paid managers reported no greater satisfaction in the social and self actualization need areas than did lower paid managers. However, higher paid managers did show definitely greater satisfaction in the esteem and autonomy need areas and somewhat greater satisfaction in the security need area than did lower paid managers. It is interesting to note that the needs most frequently discussed as being satisfied by pay, namely, esteem and security needs, are according to the present study better satisfied for higher paid individuals.

CONCLUSIONS

1. The importance attached to pay varied with objective pay received, but not with level of management. Higher paid managers on each level attached *less* importance to pay.

2. There were no line vs. staff differences in either importance attached to pay or satisfaction with pay.

3. Managers' expectations about what pay they should receive were related to management level, but not to present actual pay.

4. Managers' perceptions about how much pay they received were realistic with tegard to actual pay.

5. At a given management level, as pay increased, satisfaction with pay also increased.

6. For any given amount of pay, the amount of satisfaction with pay *decreased* the higher the level of management.

7. Higher paid managers reported that they were better satisfied in the security, autonomy, and esteem need areas than did lower paid managers at .equivalent levels of management.

9

The Role of Compensation in Motivating Employees

Victor H. Vroom
Carnegie-Mellon University

From a talk delivered at the annual conference of the Life Office Management Association. Reprinted by permission from *Best's Insurance News* (Life ed.), April 1967, 67–74.

For a long time, compensation and the issues which surround it received little attention from behavioral scientists. The important research problems of the 1940s and 1950s involved the effects of supervisory behavior and work group characteristics on individual behavior and productivity. Company executives could read in the writings of behavioral scientists about how appraisal interviews should be conducted, about when groups should be used in making decisions, about the best relationship between staff and line, etc., but could receive little guidance in making compensation decisions or in formulating compensation policy. In the absence of sound data on the consequences of different compensation systems, they were forced to rely for decision making on surveys about what other companies were doing. This undoubtedly had the effect of decreasing the variance in corporate practices but it is doubtful that it contributed significantly either to collective understanding concerning the processes underlying the effects of compensation systems on people or to the rational design of compensation systems.

Fortunately, there are indications that the deficiencies in research which characterized the 1940s and 50s are being remedied in the 1960s. More and more behavioral scientists, particularly the younger representatives of their disciplines, are directing their research efforts toward issues and problems in the area of compensation. There appear to me to be three organizational strategies for motivating their members. Certainly, most companies utilize all three, sometimes at different levels in the hierarchy; however, I think that keeping the three separate will help to bring into focus the issues involved in compensation.

The first of these answers or organizational strategies for motivation can be called a parternalistic theory. It assumes that people dislike work but can be made to work effectively out of a feeling of gratitude to the organization. It is based on the assumption that if workers are rewarded they will work harder. The more their needs are satisfied the greater the extent to which they will respond with gratitude and loyalty by producing effectively on their jobs.

The essence of this approach is to make the company a source of important rewards—rewards for which the only qualification is employment within the company. In other words, the rewards which are utilized in this theory may be termed unconditional rewards. The amount of reward that any individual receives is not dependent in any way on how he behaves within the organization but rather on the fact that he is a member of that organization.

Some of the practices and programs within organizations which are consistent with this paternalistic view are the various forms of indirect compensation— things like pension plans, group insurance, free medical care, subsidized education programs, and the like. Also qualifying are employee clubs, recreation programs, the company golf course, attractive and comfortable working conditions, subsidized meals, and pleasant cafeterias. One might also add to this list high wage levels, across the board wage increases, implicit or explicit assurance of job security, paying the job and not the man, and promotion on the basis of seniority rather than merit.

How would a manager behave so as to be consistent with the paternalistic approach? He would seek to arrange conditions of work so that his people would feel comfortable, happy, and secure. His primary goal is to see to it that his subordinates are able to get the things they want and he assumes, as a consequence of this support, that his subordinates will display enthusiasm and loyalty. He would try to make his unit one big happy family and to avoid disagreement and conflict.

The one common property of all these rewards is that they are attractive and valued by individual employees—in that sense they are rewards—but none of them are allocated on the basis of differential effort and performance within the organization. As long as one retains his membership in the organization he receives these rewards. The moment he relinquishes his membership, he ceases to receive them.

REWARDS ARE EFFECTIVE

These unconditional rewards have proven to be quite effective in attracting people into organizations. There is no doubt that a company with high wage levels, good fringe benefits, and pleasant working conditions is in a better competitive position to recruit personnel than one with lower wage levels, less liberal fringes, and less pleasant working conditions. It is quite possible, however, that paternalistic practices have some less desirable effects on the type of persons that are recruited. I know of one large corporation that has been making concentrated effort to change its paternalisic image in an effort to attract more college graduates with management potential.

The existing evidence also suggests that, other things being equal, increasing the amount of rewards that people derive from their jobs increases their job satisfaction and decreases the probability that they will voluntarily resign. Thus, other things being equal, an increase in a person's pay will make him more satisfied with his pay, an increase in his chances for promotion will make him more satisfied with his promotional opportunities. While this relationship seems to hold within any given person for any given dimension of reward, it should not be concluded that one can predict the level of a person's satisfaction from knowing the amount of reward he receives. For example, in one study it was observed that first-level supervisors making more than $12,000 a year were substantially more satisfied with their pay than were company presidents making less than $49,000. The explanation of this apparent anomaly brings to light an important psychological principle. A person compares his level of reward with that received by others who in his judgment are of comparable rank, merit, or worth. Information about what others receive provides the basis for the establishment of what is, to him, a fair or equitable level and he becomes satisfied when his level of reward reaches or exceeds the fair or equitable level. Thus, dissatisfaction is a matter of relative rather than absolute deprivation. Two people might be receiving exactly the same level of compensation but one might be highly satisfied and the other dissatisfied because they are comparing their salary level to different sets of persons or groups. Furthermore, an increase in compensation for one person may actually increase, rather than decrease, his dissatisfaction with his pay if it was accompanied by a larger increase to someone who he believed to be of comparable worth.

There is a related question which has received some attention, pertaining to the effects of secrecy concerning salary schedules. Some organizations, including state and local governments, have publicized salary schedules which permit the free flow of information about salaries within the organization. Others, and these are probably in the majority, encourage secrecy with respect to level of compensation. The assumption is that such a practice will prevent comparisons and mask what might be perceived and interpreted as inequities. While by no means definitive, a recent investigation by a psychologist at Yale University shows that secrecy does not prevent people from making wage comparisons but merely means that the comparisons will be based on imperfect and incomplete information. Managers, in the absence of reliable information about the compensation level of others, tend to overestimate the compensation of peers and of subordinates and to underestimate the compensation of superiors. Believing that one's peers and subordinates are receiving more compensation than, in fact, they were, was contributing to considerable dissatisfaction with their pay; and believing that one's superior was receiving less compensation than he was seriously reduced the promotional incentive.

PATERNALISTIC SYSTEM

The paternalistic system—which emphasizes providing people with large amounts of rewards primarily of an unconditional nature, undoubtedly has helped to attract and hold on to employees and, with the exception of the problems associated with perceived unfairness and inequity, has contributed to increased satisfaction on the part of employees. It is exceedingly doubtful, however, whether this system did anything significant by way of motivating employees while they were in the organization.

The distinction suggested is a distinction between a person's satisfaction with his job and with his company and his motivation to perform effectively in his job within that company. Once it was assumed that these two things went hand in hand, that a person who is satisfied with his job would necessarily be an effective performer within that job and, conversely, that a person who is dissatisfied with his job would necessarily be an ineffective performer. During the last 10 to 15 years, there have been approximately 50 research investigations conducted in order to test the correctness of this assumption. In each of these investigations, measurements were taken of the job satisfaction of individual, typically through interviews or questionnaires, and these were correlated with measurements of the effectiveness of their performance. The obtained results indicate quite conclusively the inaccuracy of this assumption. There was no consistent or meaningful relationship between job satisfaction and job performance. Effective performers were as likely to be dissatisfied with their jobs as they were to be satisfied with their jobs, and ineffective performers were as likely to be satisfied with their jobs as they were to be dissatisfied.

A fairly consistent relationship has been observed between job satisfaction and turnover. The relationship is, as one might expect, a negative one. In other words, people who are satisfied with their jobs are much less likely to leave the organization than people who are dissatisfied with their jobs.

It is now fairly clear that the paternalistic approach was not a very effective strategy for dealing with the motivation problem. It operated primarily on job satisfaction and indirectly on people's decisions concerning whether to leave or stay in the organization and had relatively little, if any, effect on people's decisions about how much they would produce while in the organization. It was also in no sense a complete and integrated approach to management. While it is possible, and indeed necessary, for an organization to devote some of its resources to attracting future members to the organization and binding its members into the system, the paternalistic model was hardly a suitable guide for the decision-making process in organization. Clearly, there are other criteria for evaluating decisions than whether they will make the existing members of the organization happy.

SCIENTIFIC MANAGEMENT APPROACH

The second approach or strategy concerning how to motivate people within organizations is the scientific management approach. Like the paternalistic theory, this approach is also predicated on an assumption that people dislike work and that special conditions have to be created in organizations in order to induce them to work effectively. The scientific management approach also makes extensive use of rewards. However, these rewards are conditional rather than unconditional. The rewards are attached to and made conditional upon effective performance. Each person is rewarded in accordance with his contribution to the system.

The scientific management approach represents an attempt to create, on the part of members or employees of organizations, something which is akin to the motivation of the independent entrepreneur. Such persons are in the position of receiving rewards in direct relationship to their accomplishment. If their business goes bankrupt, they lose their investment; if it prospers, they reap the benefits.

There are two related methods of simulating these conditions for members of organizations who do not share directly in the financial profits. One involves the establishment of standard rules, policies, or procedures and punishing those who deviate from them. Examples of this are warnings, reprimands, or even dismissals for violating rules or procedures. The other is to establish standards of good performance on each job and to reward people in accordance with the degree to which they meet these standards. The clearest example of the latter method may be found in individual wage incentives. Here the size of an individual's paycheck is presumably directly related to the amount of his performance. It is also manifest in such practices as promoting individuals on the basis of their merit and in recognizing and rewarding people for special accomplishments.

While there are some differences between the behavioral consequences of conditional punishments and of conditional rewards (for example, people are more likely to feel coerced, threatened, and antagonistic under a conditional punishment system), they tend to be used together in organizations and because the steps which must be taken to create these conditions are, in fact, quite similar.

If one is actually to set up a system based on these principles, at least three different steps have to be taken. First, one has to define the standards used in allocation of the rewards and punishments, i.e., to decide what behaviors are going to be rewarded and what behaviors are going to be punished. This involves a set of rather precisely defined rules and practices and an attempt on the part of the manager to specify in as exact terms as possible what he expects of each of his subordinates. Secondly, a system must be set up whereby the behavior of the subordinate is monitored or observed so that errors, misbehavior, or violation of rules, as well as superior performance can be observed and detected. Finally, in order to be effective, the system must actually allocate rewards or punishments on the basis of these observations of performance. Thus, in order to implement the principle of rewarding good performance and punishing poor performance, one must incorporate into the system centralized planning and control and close supervision.

In an organization founded on scientific management motivational principles, one would expect to find well-defined job descriptions. Each person would understand what is expected of him, i.e., the criteria on the basis of which he is to be evaluated. While there might be a job evaluation system, the range allocated to individual jobs or positions would be large, permitting considerable latitude for merit increases. Rates of promotion would be highly variable even for persons starting in the same positions. Some persons with objectively demonstrated merit would advance rapidly while others would advance more slowly if at all. The rate of dismissals or involuntary turnover would be high, particularly in comparison with the paternalistic system.

How would a manager behave in strict accordance with the scientific management approach? Quite clearly the burden would be on him to make, within his area of freedom and responsibility, decisions with respect to the behavior of his subordinates. He must communicate these policies and decisions as accurately and precisely as possible and check up on his subordinates to make sure that their actions are in accordance with them. Whenever an error is made or a violation of rules occurs, his reaction is to find out who is responsible and to mete out the appropriate disciplinary action as quickly as possible. Whenever a person exhibits behavior above and beyond the call of duty, he receives special commendation.

SCIENTIFIC MANAGEMENT

Unlike the paternalistic approach, which has little foundation in psychological research or theory, the scientific management approach is predicated on a strong psychological foundation. The foundation in this case is what psychologists have termed the law of effect or principle of reinforcement. Succinctly, it states that if a person undertakes an action, and this action is rewarded, that behavior or action will tend to be repeated. On the other hand, if the person undertakes an action which is followed by punishment, that behavior will tend not to be repeated. Research has provided support for this proposition in a large number of different situations and many of the techniques for controlling behavior outside of industry rest on the same foundation. It is also consistent with dramatic increases in performance obtained from the installation of wage incentives in some situations and with evidence from studies of managers and hourly workers showing that effective performers are more likely than ineffective performers to view performance on their present job as a means to the attainment of wage increases and a promotion to a higher level job.

The motivational basis of scientific management consists of external or organizational control over the worker while he is performing his job. When this system is functioning optimally, the individual does his job well not because he gets any particular satisfaction from so doing, but because he is compelled to do so by his environment. Effective performance is necessary in order to get the things he desires or avoid the things he fears.

It is clear that the techniques associated with the scientific management approach have been useful in many instances in industrial organization. I assume that life insurance companies, for example, have benefited greatly from the fact that their salesmen work on an incentive basis. Wage incentives have also demonstrated their usefulness in many production jobs and it is clear to me that our large universities have increased the research output of their faculty by the introduction of a publish-or-perish philosophy.

On the other hand, the scientific management approach does not appear to be universally applicable. Wage incentives, for example, require some basis for measuring performance and for communicating the standards to be used in measurement to those who are affected. This is quite clearly difficult for many jobs, particularly those of a staff or managerial nature.

If one considers only those situations in which performance can be measured, I believe it true that the conditional reward–punishment strategy is of greatest value when individuals have control over the outcomes on the basis of which the rewards and punishments are allocated. By control, I mean that the individuals can produce or not produce the outcomes at will. It would make little sense to reward individuals on sunny days and punish them on rainy days even if good weather were indispensable to the success of the operation. Similarly, it makes little sense from a motivational standpoint, to pay a person who works on a mechanized conveyer belt in accordance with the speed with which he works, or to reward a company director who has no control over the company profits, with a stock option plan.

Somewhat less obvious are instances of partial control. These are situations in which the individual can not completely determine the outcomes which are linked to rewards or punishments. There are two primary sources of partial control in organizations. One source lies in the nature of the task or job performed by the individual. In some task or jobs there is less than a one-to-one relationship between the behavior of the incumbent and the effectiveness of the incumbent and the effectiveness of his performance. Other events not under his control also affect how well he does. The physician may perform a perfect operation but the patient may die; the salesman may make an effective presentation but fail to get the sale, and the manager may do an unusually effective job of administering his division but fail to make a profit due to adverse market conditions. Other "chance" factors influence the level of performance and, to the degree to which this occurs, the conditional reward–punishment strategy fails to achieve its intended purpose. Success or failure is a matter of luck rather than skill or conscientious application of effort.

A similar result occurs as a consequence of the fact that a set of jobs are interdependent rather than independent. The performance of worker *A* is dependent on the performance of worker *B*, which in turn is dependent on the performance of worker *C*, and so on. In such instances, and they are quite common, it is difficult or impossible to trace errors or superior performance to the efforts of one individual. It is only the group or team effort which can be adequately evaluated and each person has but partial control over the team outcome.

There is clearly much more evidence for the scientific management approach to motivation than was the case for the paternalistic approach. However, it would seem to be more useful in some situations than in others. Specifically, the conditional reward–punishement system is most applicable to the degree to which (1) the assessment of the outcomes of individual performance is feasible, (2) the basis for the reward system is comprehensive and is made clear to the person, and (3) the attainment of the outcomes on the basis on which the rewards and punishments are allocated is under the individual's control. Under these three conditions, the scientific management system can and has played an important part in motivating individuals to high productivity.

PARTICIPATIVE MANAGEMENT THEORY

A third strategy for motivation is the participative management approach. This strategy is more recent than the other two but appears to have had, during its relatively short existence, an important influence on managerial practice.

Whereas paternalistic management assumed that man can be induced to work out of a feeling of gratitude to the system and scientific management assumed that man can be induced to work by the expectation of gain for so doing or the expectation of loss for not doing, participative management assumes that conditions can be created such that people derive satisfaction from doing an effective job per se. They can become ego involved in their jobs—emotionally committed to doing them well and taking pride from evidence that they are effective in furthering the goals of the company.

Little mention is made in these ideas of either compensation or promotion. The incentives for effective performance in the participative management approach are in the task or job itself, not in the consequences of task performance. In other words, it seeks to create conditions under which effective performance can be the goal, not the means to the attainment of the goal. It is based on self-control rather than organizational control.

There is in this proposal a great deal of contact and interaction between supervisor and subordinate, but it takes a form different from more traditional conceptions of management. Instead of telling a subordinate exactly what is to be done and how he is to do it, checking up on him to make sure that instructions have been carried out, and rewarding or punishing him depending on an assessment of his performance, this system entails working with the subordinate in defining and structuring his job responsibilities, and problem solving with him in a joint manner about difficulties or problems which he is experiencing in doing his job.

There is much more reliance in the participative management approach on the group as a problem-solving and decision-making unit. On matters affecting the entire unit, the supervisor does not make decisions autocratically and issue orders for subordinates but rather meets with the subordinates as a group, sharing problems with them and encouraging them to participate with him in finding solutions to these problems. Thus, the president of an organization can meet with his vice presidents as a group and they can work on problems ordinarily handled by the president alone or by the president meeting individually with his vice presidents. In turn, each vice president meets with his department heads, department heads meet with their division heads, and so on down to the rank-and-file work group.

In effect, this entails participation by subordinates in the decision-making process which is assumed, with considerable justification, to create ego involvement on the part of subordinates in the decisions and identification with corporate goals.

This participative management approach to motivation is quite consistent with existing research results. A tremendous amount of research has been conducted within the last 10 to 15 years into the sources of differences between managers of high-productivity and low-productivity units. While there are some exceptions, the results generally support the notion that the managers of highly productive units are acting in accordance with the third strategy. This does not mean that this approach is equally effective under all conditions. In fact, it has been much more influential at higher than at lower organizational levels. One is more likely to find managers acting in accordance with the participative management strategy at upper and middle levels of management than on the shop floor.

Even at higher organizational levels I do not believe that we can afford to overlook the effects of compensation and promotion. Is a person who is highly ego involved in his job and identified strongly with corporate goals going to continue to produce at the same high level even though circumstances convince him that he is being greatly undercompensated relative to his peers? Even though he learns that his chances of promotion to a higher level position are nonexistent?

This raises the interesting possibility of an amalgam of the scientific management and participative management approaches.

There is no inconsistency between the notion of setting up conditions in organizations such that people are rewarded through wage increases and promotions for effective performance at the same time as they derive pleasure or satisfaction from observing that they have executed their responsibilities well. We can envision a system in which individuals are challenged by their jobs and are rewarded by the organization for doing them well.

An effective integration of the two sets of proposals would entail giving people as much freedom in planning their jobs as is consistent with the existing technology and tailoring the amount of rewards they receive with how effective they are. Evaluations of performance and hence compensation levels and promotional possibilities are based on results, not on adherence to arbitrary rules or supervisory whims and fancies.

10

Ability, Values, and Concepts of Equitable Salary Increases in Exercise Compensation

Bernard M. Bass
University of Rochester

One hundred and thirteen American graduate business students recommended annual salary increases for 10 fictitious engineers, each with a different reason for being given a raise. The mean recommendation was 9.3 per cent. Recommenders were more generous if the students were of lower intelligence and achievement, and if they held strong social and service rather than theoretical and economic values. They also were more willing to spend company money for other social and personnel purposes.

Reprinted by permission from *Journal of Applied Psychology*, LII, No. 4 (1968), 299–303. Copyright 1968 by the American Psychological Association.

Several recent reviews point to increasing interest in psychological aspects of pay (1, 6, 12). A modest amount of available research has probed the effects of pay differentials on attitudes and performance of those receiving the money, but little has been done to ascertain what motivates those who decide on what salaries will be paid when they respond to requests for salary increases and how their own ability and values affect their monetary decisions. These latter issues are the concern of this report.

METHOD

SUBJECTS

Forty-four per cent of the 113 male graduate business students who participated in this study held undergraduate engineering degrees, the other 56 per cent had earned undergraduate degrees in the liberal arts or in business administration. They averaged close to "B" in undergraduate grades and earned a mean of 566 on the Admissions Test for Graduate Schools of Business (ATGSB).

PROCEDURE

During the fourth week of a course in behavioral science, each participant was involved in a series of small group exercises (2, 3). One of these, *Exercise Compensation* (1st ed.), required that each participant, by himself, make a set of 10 salary recommendations prior to a group discussion about the matter. He was given the instructions which in essence were as follows:

You will have to recommend increases for 10 engineers in your company, all of whom are unmarried, 22-year-old college graduates who have just completed their first year with the company and are now to be considered for an annual raise. Keep in mind that you may be setting precedents, that you need to keep down salary costs, that you need to consider equity, that you want to retain all the engineers if possible. Your company has no job evaluation schedule but tries to match community and industry norms and to be competitive.

The 10 engineers are as follows:

Al, an average performer (50th percentile);

Bill (90th percentile in merit);

Charlie (10th percentile in merit).

All the remainder are like Al in merit, but in addition:

Dan is working on an insecure government contract. Because of his specialty, transfer is difficult.

Ed is on a "dead-end" job lacking advancement potential.

Frank has a dirty, unpleasant, hazardous, uncomfortable job.

Garry has a low-prestige job in a low-prestige subsidiary.

Henry has to work closely with a crew of uncongenial, unfriendly, competitive co-workers.

Irwin has a boring, dull, and monotonous job.

Jim has a definite job offer from a competitor substantially better than his current salary.

OTHER MEASURES

Of the 113 participants, during other weeks of the course, 112 completed the Allport–Vernon Study of Values and ranked their own life goals on the first edition of Exercise Life Goals (2). The goals were defined as follows:

(*a*) Leadership: To become a community leader, to become influential in public affairs, to become influential among co-workers.

(*b*) Comfort: To have the time and means to enjoy life, to become happy and content, to have financial security, to be well liked.

(c) Creativity: To produce original and unique plans and ideas, to devise new approaches, to be expressive.

(d) Expertness: To become an authority on a special subject in any field, to persevere to reach a hoped-for expert level of skill and accomplishment.

(e) Technology: To make contributions to technical or scientific knowledge, to invent apparatus or equipment.

(f) Prestige: To become well known, to obtain awards and recognition.

(g) Service: To contribute to the satisfaction of others, to be helpful to others who are in difficulty.

(h) Wealth: To earn a great deal of money, to build a large financial estate.

(i) Independence: To be free to do what one likes, to be one's own boss, to control others rather than be controlled by them.

Exercise Objectives (2) also was completed by the 113 participants. In this activity, after reading a company's last annual profit and loss statement, each participant made five budgeting decisions. In one of these he had the option to spend or not to spend $225,000 to correct a safety hazard likely to produce a serious injury. In another, he could spend or avoid spending $15,000 to modify a plant that was polluting a stream. In still others, he had to spend money on managers, products, and to settle a strike, but in these cases his problem was on which way to spend the money to handle each case. These latter decisions were not expected to relate to salary recommendations and in fact they did not do so.

RESULTS

MEAN RECOMMENDATIONS

The mean increase awarded the 10 engineers by the 113 graduate business students (Table 1, column 5) was 9.3 per cent. As is common with most other groups of managers and students tested here and abroad, the largest source of variance in recommendations was merit. Bill, of high merit, was assigned 1.5 times the increase awarded Al, the average man, while Charlie, the man of low merit, was given approximately 0.7 as much as average Al. The hypothesis has been advanced (3) that half of the increase given Al, the average man, will be denied to Charlie. This half will be added to Bill's increase so that Bill gets 1.5 times as much as Al, and Charlie is left with only 0.5 of the increase given Al. But the hypothesis did not hold completely in Charlie's case. Here, the ratio of mean recommendations that occurred for Bill:Al:Charlie was 3:2:1.5, rather than 3:2:1.

As seen in Table 1, column 5, next to meritorious performance the participants were most willing to pay for poor working conditions (Frank) and were relatively least responsive to Ed who lacked opportunities, although in comparison to what they awarded average Al, they were willing to give a premium for everyone from Dan to Jim who had special problems.

TABLE 1
RELATION BETWEEN TESTED INTELLIGENCE ACHIEVEMENT
AND COMPENSATION DECISIONS

Recommendations for	ATGB			Under-graduate grades[b]	Mean % increase in recommen-dations[c]	SD of recommen-dations[c]
	L[a]	Q[a]	T[a]			
Al (average)	−0.08	−0.18*	−0.17*	−0.19*	8.02	2.62
Bill (best)	−0.08	−0.14	−0.15	−0.25†	11.96	3.78
Charlie (poor)	−0.17*	−0.17*	−0.23*	0.00	5.55	2.38
Dan (no security)	−0.09	−0.11	−0.15	−0.03	9.83	3.24
Ed (no opportunity)	−0.12	−0.21*	−0.22*	−0.09	9.05	3.00
Frank (poor conditions)	−0.01	−0.24†	−0.16*	−0.04	10.18	3.08
Garry (no prestige)	−0.10	−0.21*	−0.20*	−0.14	9.49	3.16
Henry (unfriendly co-workers)	−0.05	−0.21*	−0.18*	−0.13	9.72	3.10
Irwin (uninteresting work)	0.00	−0.19*	−0.12	−0.14	9.83	3.26
Jim (competitive offer)	−0.02	−0.16*	−0.11	−0.08	9.34	3.32

Note.—ATGSB = Admissions Test for Graduate Schools of Business. L = Linguistic; Q = Quantitative; T = Total.
[a]N = 101.
[b]N = 99.
[c]N = 113.
*$p < 0.05$.
†$p < 0.01$.

CORRELATIONAL ANALYSES

The main purpose of this report is to see what personal factors influenced the recommendations. For this, correlational analyses will be presented in four sections. First, the extent that salary recommendations are associated with the intelligence and achievement of the recommender will be examined. Next, will be seen how the self-reported values of the recommender may enter the picture. Third, a look will be taken at how the recommender's own stated life goals correlated with his recommendations for raises in salary. Finally, the author will note how generosity in recommending raises also may relate to willingness to spend company money on other personnel and organizational needs.

ABILITY AND COMPENSATION DECISIONS

Table 1 shows the product–moment correlations between the salary increases each participant was willing to award each of the 10 engineers and each participant's tested intelligence and undergraduate record (columns 1–4). It can be seen that differences among the participants' decisions were unrelated to verbal aptitude as measured by the ATGSB, except possibly the salary decisions about Charlie, who was lacking in merit. However, a modest association was found between quantitative aptitude and the tendency to recommend smaller raises in salary. Participants with greater tested quantitative aptitude awarded smaller salary increases, particularly ($p < 0.01$) when the increases were being justified by poor working conditions ($r = -0.24$). When verbal and quantitative scores were combined and total intelligence test scores were correlated with compensation decisions, the effect was most pronounced in dealing with the salary increase for Charlie, the engineer low in merit. Those with greater tested intelligence were significantly likely to recommend a smaller raise for Charlie ($r = -0.23$).

Perplexing was the significant correlation ($p < 0.01$) of -0.25 between undergraduate quality-point averages and the raise awarded Bill, suggesting that achieving students recommended smaller salary increases for the most meritorious engineer. They awarded Al, the average engineer, a smaller raise also. There was little other evidence of the influence of undergraduate achievement on the other compensation decisions.

To sum up, some tendency was seen for brighter and more academically successful participants to recommend smaller raises (or for the duller and less successful to recommend bigger salary increases). Quantitative aptitude was more of a factor than verbal aptitude.

VALUES, LIFE GOALS, AND COMPENSATION DECISION

The correlations among the Allport–Vernon Study of Values scale scores and the salary recommendations are shown in Table 2. It can be seen that holding certain values predisposed recommenders to be generous, while strong values in other directions did the reverse. Those with strong social values tended to recommend bigger raises in general to all engineers, but the effects were less marked when dealing with Bill (most meritorious), Frank (poor working conditions), and Jim (competitive offer). Evidently, lack of security, opportunity, prestige, congenial co-workers, and interesting work weighed heavier as an excuse to grant bigger raises for recommenders scoring high in social values.

The correlations also were uniformly positive between religious value scores and the size of salary recommendations, but they were generally lower. Strong social values played a greater role than strong religious values. At the other extreme, recommenders holding strong economic and theoretical values according to their self-reports were likely to offer smaller raises to the engineers. Those holding strong economic values were particularly unlikely to be generous to Al (average merit) and Charlie (low merit). Those holding strong theoretical values were particularly unlikely to be generous to George (no prestige) and Irwin (unfriendly co-workers).

TABLE 2

RELATION BETWEEN ALLPORT–VERNON STUDY OF VALUES
AND COMPENSATION DECISIONS

Recommendations for	Allport–Vernon scores					
	Theoretical	Economic	Aesthetic	Social	Political	Religious
Al (average)	−0.23†	−0.38†	0.10	0.34†	−0.03	0.16*
Bill (best)	−0.13	−0.18*	−0.09	0.20*	0.07	0.11
Charlie (poor)	−0.20*	−0.38*	0.08	0.33†	−0.06	0.17*
Dan (no security)	−0.14	−0.20*	−0.10	0.24†	0.11	0.10
Ed (no opportunity)	−0.23†	−0.27†	−0.01	0.33†	0.04	0.14
Frank (poor conditions)	−0.16*	−0.26†	−0.05	0.19*	0.09	0.19*
Garry (no prestige)	−0.29†	−0.27†	0.03	0.32†	0.04	0.16*
Henry (unfriendly co-workers)	−0.24†	−0.29†	0.04	0.29†	0.08	0.12
Irwin (uninteresting work)	−0.30†	−0.30†	0.05	0.29†	0.09	0.17*
Jim (competitive offer)	−0.20*	−0.24†	0.02	0.17*	0.07	0.17*

Note.—N = 112.
*p < 0.05.
†p < 0.01.

Table 3 shows how self-ranked life goals were related to compensation recommendations. Here one goal stands out. Recommenders with relatively

TABLE 3

RELATION BETWEEN SELF-RANKED LIFE GOALS
AND COMPENSATION DECISIONS

Recommendations for	Self-ranked life goals								
	Leader-ship	Com-fort	Crea-tivity	Expert-ness	Tech-nology	Pres-tige	Service	Wealth	Inde-pend-ence
Al (average)	0.10	−0.07	−0.11	−0.10	−0.09	0.02	0.26†	−0.03	0.01
Bill (best)	0.15*	−0.14	−0.00	−0.13	−0.03	0.09	0.22†	−0.06	−0.10
Charlie (poor)	0.09	−0.11	−0.09	−0.00	−0.12	−0.00	0.18*	−0.03	0.02
Dan (no security)	0.10	−0.08	−0.14	−0.11	−0.19*	0.06	0.27†	−0.00	0.04
Ed (no opportunity)	0.12	−0.09	−0.15*	−0.07	−0.19*	−0.01	0.29†	0.02	0.02
Frank (poor conditions)	0.12	−0.07	−0.11	−0.07	−0.13	−0.00	0.31†	−0.04	−0.04
Garry (no prestige)	0.11	−0.12	−0.10	−0.13	−0.16*	0.03	0.27†	0.04	−0.01
Henry (unfriendly co-workers)	0.09	−0.06	−0.06	−0.12	−0.18*	0.03	0.27†	0.02	0.06
Irwin (uninteresting work)	0.07	−0.05	−0.06	−0.14	−0.20*	0.02	0.27†	−0.00	0.04
Jim (competitive offer)	0.15*	−0.03	−0.15*	−0.16*	−0.21*	0.03	0.27†	0.02	0.02

Note.—Signs reversed. N = 113.
*p < 0.05.
†p < 0.01

greater concern for service as an important life goal tended to be more generous—almost uniformly so.

To a lesser extent, those concerned about technical success were likely to be less generous than the average recommender.

Different reasons for being generous may or may not be involved. For those high in economic value, it may be that the same amount of money is worth more and is considered to be a larger raise than would be seen by those low in economic value. For those high in concern for theory, understanding, and technical success, less need may be seen to grant large increases in compensation for effort. For those with strong concerns for social service and religion, pure generosity may be operative in their salary recommendations.

WILLINGNESS TO SPEND MONEY

How general is generosity? Two of the five budgeting decisions on Exercise Objectives invovved whether or not to spend money (not how to spend it) primarily for human or social rather than immediate economic returns. As can be seen in Table 4, there was a slight positive association between the size of salary increases recommended and a willingness to spend money on fixing a plant to end pollution of a stream. There seemed to be an even greater tendency to provide extra money for raises for all kinds of special reasons other than merit (rs ranged from 0.18 to 0.23) and a willingness to spend money on safety equipment to avoid the possibilities of a serious accident.

TABLE 4
RELATION BETWEEN WILLINGNESS TO SPEND MONEY
ON SAFETY AND STREAM CLEANING AND
COMPENSATION DECISIONS

Engineer	Spend on safety	Spend on stream clean-up
Al (average)	0.07	0.09
Bill (best)	0.10	0.14
Charlie (poor)	0.09	0.11
Dan (no security)	0.23*	0.11
Ed (no opportunity)	0.20*	0.13
Frank (poor conditions)	0.18*	0.11
Garry (no prestige)	0.21*	0.11
Henry (unfriendly co-workers)	0.21*	0.13
Irwin (uninteresting work)	0.19*	0.16*
Jim (competitive offer)	0.22†	0.13

Note.—N = 113.
*p < 0.05.
†p < 0.01.

CONCLUSIONS

Despite the observation that "Pay, in one form or another, is certainly one of the mainsprings of motivation in our society" (6), little data are available on what bases decisions about pay are made. Many people would like to believe that highly objective analyses produce highly objective job evaluations and merit rating and manpower plans which yield highly objective standards for establishing pay and pay raises. In fact, the author suggests that much subjectivity of judgmenet is involved at every phase in these schemes and that it would be useful to develop some understanding of what may affect these judgments. In the present study, one sees that while merit overshadowed other factors in consideration by the recommenders of salary increases, at the same time, as might have been anticipated, the abilities and values of the recommenders played some role in what values they were willing to recommend.

Higher salary increases were recommended by those lower in intelligence and achievement, by those who held strong social and religious rather than theoretical or economic values, who were more interested in service rather than technical achievement and who also were more willing to spend their company's money for other personnel and social purposes.

Questioning
the Managerial Implications of
Compensating Management and Employees

1. Dunnette chides salary administrators for ignoring individual differences and needs of managers in establishing pay policies. Evaluate each of his four "implications for practice" in terms of their applicability to submanagerial-level employees.

2. Which of the seven conclusions reached by Lawler and Porter are surprising to you? Do you attribute any conflicts between these findings and your own perceptions to the particular methodology used, to a lack of sensitivity on your part, or to some other factor?

3. Why does Vroom feel the need to recommend a combination of the participative *and* the scientific approach in compensating employees? Would not strict adherence to participative methods alone avoid the evils he ascribes to paternalistic management?

4. If business student responses described by Bass are generalizable to business managers, do his results infer that company pay policies will suffer from lack of objectivity even if the recommendations of Dunnette, Vroom, and others are adopted?

5. What are your recommendations for establishment of an effective reward system? Can an organization expect its compensation practices to be a principal source of managerial motivation? Of employee motivation?

References

1. Adams, J. S., and P. R. Jacobsen, Effects of Wage Inequities on Work Quality," *Journal of Abnormal and Social Psychology,* LXIX (1964), 19–25.

2. Bass, B. M., *"A Program of Exercises in Management and Organizational Psychology,"* Pittsburgh: INSTAD, 1967.

3. ——, "Combining Management Training and Research," *Training Directors Journal,* XXI, No. 4 (1967), 1–7.

4. Haire, M., *Psychology in Management.* New York: McGraw-Hill Book Company, 1956.

5. ——, E. E., Ghiselli, and L. W. Porter, "Cultural Patterns in the Role of the Manager," *Industrial Relations,* III (1963), 95–117.

6. ——, ——, and ——, "Psychological Research on Pay: An Overview," *Industrial Relations,* III (1963), 1–8.

7. Jaques, E., *Equitable Compensation.* New York: John Wiley & Sons, Inc., 1961.

8. Kahn, R. L., "Human Relations on the Shop Floor," in *Human Relations and Modern Management,* ed. E. M. Hugh-Jones. Amsterdam: North-Holland, 1958.

9. Maslow, A. H., *Motivation and Personality.* New York: Harper & Row, Publishers, 1954.

10. Porter, L. W., "A Study of Perceived Need Satisfactions in Bottom and Middle Management Jobs," *Journal of Applied Psychology,* VL (1961), 1–10.

11. ——, "Job Attitudes in Management: I. Perceived Deficiencies in Need Fulfillment as a Function of Job Level," *Journal of Applied Psychology,* IVL, (1962), 375–84.

12. Weick, K. E., "The Concept of Equity in the Perception of Pay," *Administrative Science Quarterly,* XI (1966), 414–39.

13. Whyte, W. F., *Money and Motivation.* New York: Harper & Row, Publishers, 1955.

PERSONAL GROWTH
AND
INTERPERSONAL DYNAMICS

Three assumptions underly the material of this section. First interpersonal competence is assumed to be important to managers if teamwork is required in their organization. Second, it is assumed that managers need to remain open to changes that are occurring around them in order to avoid obsolescence in attitudes and knowledge. Third, both interpersonal competence and the avoidance of obsolescence are assumed to be dependent on interest in self-development leading to adequate self-understanding. However, such self-understanding may be at the expense of satisfactory adjustment to current environmental conditions. A recent lead article in *The Wall Street Journal* began as follows:

Last year a big New York consumer products company sent Mrs. D, a product manager, to a week-long sensitivity training program. She got so sensitive she quit the company.

That isn't what is supposed to happen, of course. Ideally, sensitivity training produces better bosses and better employees. Meeting in group discussions with no planned agenda, participants are encouraged to respond to each other with brutal candor and on intensely personal levels. Through analysis of their behavior by the rest of the group, participants are supposed to gain a deeper understanding of themselves and others.

Mrs. D loved that part. "It was a whole week of truth serum, all openness," she recalls. "But then I came back to work and found it shrouded in the usual unnecessary tactfulness and diplomacy. I discovered that the training had so opened me up that I was tired of the Mickey Mouse." When her superiors wanted to delay a decision on a new product development program she had been working on for more than a year, she told them she was tired of their procrastination and quit to take a comparable job elsewhere, where she has more latitude. Her old employer dropped the sensitivity training program in which she participated.[1]

Part II begins with a systematic examination of how organizations cope with their own development and the development of their management. It is clear that sensitivity training is not enough. However, much of the newer approaches build upon what has been learned through experience in sensitivity-training efforts.

Next, the importance of expectations is considered, and how such hopes affect subsequent performance. This is followed by further examination of what motivates employees and managers, problems in improving communications between employees and managers as well as general supervision and development of team effort. Finally, consideration is given to the fact that the manager must live in a world of limited rationality, which puts him in need of understanding about how decisions are made and how conflicts may be more expeditiously resolved.

---

[1] B.E. Calame, "The truth hurts," The Wall Street Journal, IL (1969) p. 1.

Developing
Management and
the Organization

The industrial culture is characterized by its dynamic nature, its continuing development and change. Both managers and organizations need to remain open to changes in their environment and even to initiate change if they are to keep pace with the evolution process at work in society.

The readings that follow treat the issues of management development and organizational development both as separate concepts and as one entity. They deal with some of the important aspects particular to each area, but they are perhaps more valuable in that they emphasize the interface between these two really inseparable notions.

Pym dwells on the relation between the development of managers and their organizations. He identifies individual characteristics of managers that separate more successful from less successful change agents. His ideas are neatly extended into implications for management skills training.

127

Patten offers a different variation on this theme in his interview study of upper managers in a large organization. He proposes some theories on more effective use of organizational resources to develop managers based on responses to questions concerning identification of high performers, sources of contributions to personal development, and methods of getting outstanding men for vital jobs. He concludes that the "critical" job assignment is the best management developer.

The remaining two articles of this chapter examine the outcomes of the laboratory approach on the education of managers in organizations. This methodology, involving some form of sensitivity training, has generated a vast literature[1], rather sharply divided on the advantages and disadvantages of this alternative for developing managers and solving organizational problems.

Golembiewski and Blumberg describe an application of sensitivity training to change the attitudes of members in a complex business organization. Their technique, termed "confrontation design" is presented as an analog to the T-group. Its intent is to provide a means for raising and dealing with specific organizational problems by involving in the design those organization members most concerned with the issues.

The perspective assumed by Bass is quite different. In drawing comparisons between the pure T-group and anarchy, and in describing the inadequacies of sensitivity training when it does not provide for transfer of learning into real organizations, he substantiates an argument that T-groups are necessary but not sufficient for organizational learning.

---

[1] For a comprehensive review and critique see M. D. Dunnette and J. P. Campbell, "Laboratory Education: Impact on People and Organizations," *Industrial Relations*, VIII, no. 1 (1968), 1–27.

11

Effective Managerial Performance in Organizational Change

Denis Pym
London Graduate School
of Business Studies

This paper is concerned with identifying the characteristics of managers who are able to perform their tasks effectively in conditions of change. In sharp contrast to much of the work of British social scientists in industry, therefore, it is concerned with differences between individual managers rather than with the influence on performance of differences in the conditions in which men work. It emphasizes change not only because change is widespread and pervasive but because it is now generally recognized that in many of our institutions change is not taking place fast enough.

After referring briefly to a series of six earlier studies of performance in conditions of change, the paper describes a study of managers concerned with the installation and servicing of computers. Particular attention is paid to differences in what their superiors and subordinates expected of these managers, and in how they rated them. It is shown that inability to cope with change is closely related to a belief that there is only "one best way" of doing most things, and to a system of values of which this is a key feature. Finally, the implications of these findings for management training are discussed.

This article is based on a paper read to a symposium on "Training Industrial Managers" at the 127th Annual Meeting of the British Association for the Advancement of Science, Cambridge, England, September 1965. Acknowledgements are due to I.B.M. (U.K.) Ltd. who gave permission for these results to be published. This study took place in the Company's Customer Engineering function. Reprinted by permission from *Journal of Management Studies*, III, No. 1, February 1966.

AN INQUIRY INTO
PERFORMANCE IN CONDITIONS OF CHANGE

The inquiry of which a part is reported here is not yet complete. It is composed of a series of investigations into work behavior in a variety of changing circumstances. Seven of the studies are reported in one place (79) where the reader may find the methods and instruments of measurement explained in some detail. We will begin with an explanation for this approach.

Two factors call for diversity in the design and the populations to be investigated. One of these lies in the difficulty of conducting industrial research and the other in the complexity of studying organizational change. Sofer (98) has already referred to the difficulties of assessing the effects of innovation. In an environment continually in transformation, there can be no clearly definable independent variable and therefore no research design of the before-and-after type. Indeed in only one of the studies outlined here is it possible to claim that the design approached the laboratory kind of experiment.

The textbook procedure for conducting social research suggests that the investigator begins with a statement of the problem and the hypotheses, then develops his research design and methods of data collection, and only subsequently chooses a population on which to test his ideas. This procedure is frequently unsuited to industrial research and is one cause of the failure of some projects. On the one hand, the organization to which we look for facilities may turn out to be unhappy about the design or method. On the other hand, after beginning an inquiry we sometimes find that changes in the conditions of the organization (e.g., transfer of manpower, new regulations, industrial conflict) upset the research design and render some of the original hypotheses untestable. It is generally more practicable, having defined the general aims of the enquiry, to find organization(s) that are prepared to offer facilities and then tailor the method to suit the firm.

As it is difficult to study industrial populations and organizational change on a scientific basis, extra efforts are needed to preserve the empirical status of this kind of research. One course of action is to study a number of different populations by differing methods, hoping to arrive at similar or complementary conclusions. Ideally, the researcher should be able to develop hypotheses as a result of his first investigation and then in subsequent studies advance their status towards a theory or have them rejected within a single enquiry. This is the pattern followed here.

The purposes of the first study were to investigate the correlates of attitudes to work-related change and to try to identify a factor resembling the flexibility/rigidity construct using the principal-components, factor-analytic technique described by Hotelling (48). To this end 408 young people drawn from three populations, two of them at work, completed a battery of tests and questionnaire scales measuring abilities, achievements, job interests, and aspirations and attitudes to work and to change.

In the second study (80) a number of instruments, linked with attitudes to change and loaded on the flexibility/rigidity factor identified in the first investigation, were administered to 99 female operatives before and after a change in the manufacturing processes of sports wear. The output of the operatives was also measured, at several periods before and after the innovation, over the course of two and one-half years. Five of the instruments identifying attitudes, interests, and aspirations were found to point to shifts in performance following the innovation. As a result of this second study it became possible to specify certain attributes which appeared to be associated with versatility.[1]

Most changes cannot be studied in the manner outlined above for the reasons already given. However, one method of checking upon the earlier findings is to observe the characteristics of men doing a job which specifies a high degree of adaptive behavior. In the third study, 85 electronic maintenance engineers engaged in work demanding considerable versatility were assessed by means of job studies, group discussions, and questionnaires. These data were then related to selection-test scores, training-school reports, and on-the-job evaluations by managers. The results supported and expanded upon the earlier findings.

Fourth, fifth, and sixth studies dealt with organizational features which facilitate or hinder individual performance in change. One was a survey of the organizational constraints on professional employees. Another was a case study of the outcomes of a decision to increase organizational control over the conduct of a marketing force. Yet another involved case and comparative studies of the differing effects of organization structure upon the attitudes and performances of personnel in data-processing units.

In a seventh study, described in some detail below, attention was focused on the manager. Using job studies, questionnaires, group discussions, and assessments of performance, we were able to develop a framework of expectations of the first-line manager by both subordinates and superiors. Having identified the most and least effective managers from two viewpoints, it was then possible to relate the information we had obtained about these men to the characteristics of versatility identified on previous occasions.

EXPECTATIONS AND RATINGS
FOR FIELD MANAGERS

The department in which the seventh study took place is part of a firm that manufactures and markets data-processing equipment in Britain and looks after the installation, maintenance and repair of the equipment. The men who perform these functions are engineers. The machines and the systems for which

---

[1] Versatility is operationally defined as the concept embracing those aspects of personality associated with continuing effective performance in a changing work environment; e.g., work tasks, the work group, production methods.

they are responsible range from simple card and tape punches and verifiers to sophisticated computer systems. In little more than a decade several radical changes have taken place in the technology of the equipment. Indeed, at the time of the inquiry the engineers were spending an average of one-fifth of their working time in the training school. Change is an essential part of the engineer's occupational existence. Each man is normally assigned responsibility for a specified number of machines and customers. He has his objectives clearly defined, although the methods and routes by which he carries out his duties are largely left to the engineer's own discretion. He has fairly limited contact with his manager, referred to here as the field manager, and normally works on his own. Between eight and fourteen engineers report to a field manager and above him there are three additional organizational levels including the manager for the whole country.

We began by finding out through interviews and group discussions what the field manager's boss and subordinates expect of him. Many studies of the first-line manager picture him as a sort of marginal man torn between two conflicting sets of expectations. In this particular case, according to personnel above and below the field manager, he should, if he is doing his job well, perform the functions shown in Table 1.

TABLE 1
SUBORDINATE AND SUPERIOR EXPECTATIONS
OF THE FIRST-LINE MANAGER

Subordinates' expectations	Superiors' expectations
Leave the engineer to get on with the job	Keep all installations in the territory running smoothly
Keep the engineer informed about company operations	Deploy men effectively and inform, appraise, reward, and encourage them
Ensure that the engineer gets technical backing	Ensure that all company policies and decisions are implemented
Help the engineer when in difficulties with customers	Supply the company with reports on the operations of the territory
Champion his own men in difficulties with the company	Maintain liaison with customers

We note that the engineers' expectations are mostly of a communications kind. They do not look to the manager for technical advice though they do want him to know where to get it and to assist them to this end when necessary. The two sets of expectations are reasonably complementary, though there are one or two points on which differences occur. On the top of the engineers' list come autonomy. They want the manager to leave them to handle the work and the customer. Now senior managers, our investigations showed, are divided on whether the field manager's responsibilities are to the engineer or directly to the customer. Those field managers who believe that they are answerable to the customer may seem, to the engineers, to be encroaching upon their domain.

Table 2 shows this particular conflict in interests at closer quarters. We have here questionnaire assessments of the 32 field managers by both superiors

TABLE 2

DIFFERENCES IN EVALUATIONS
BETWEEN THOSE ABOVE AND BELOW THE FIELD MANAGERS

Assessments of Field Managers by superiors	Number of Field Managers	Percentage of favorable assessments made by subordinates on four aspects of the manager's conduct			
		Decisiveness	Planning	Giving reponsibility	Familiarity with engineers' work
High	7	86	71	89	78
Above average	10	89*	89*	91	94*
Below average	9	80	63	95*	83
Low	6	74	53*	81*	79

= Represents the group of managers most highly regarded by the engineers.
*Percentages significantly different from the mean.
There were 10 senior managers, 32 first-line managers, and 360 engineers in this exercise.

and subordinates. The senior managers' ratings have been categorized in four classes of effectiveness, whereas the engineers evaluated their bosses according to a number of activities, four of which are shown in the table.

Field managers who are least effective according to their bosses also obtain the poorest ratings from the engineers. There is some diversity of opinion at the other end of the scale. We find, generally speaking, that those field managers rated by their bosses as "above average" get the highest assessment from their subordinates. There is marked disagreement between the more senior managers and the engineers with respect to the engineers' autonomy. We have then some differences in standards of excellence between managers and men and even, as we have already observed, between managers.

In an additional analysis of the wide range of the engineers' attitudes to the boss, thirteen items including the four in Table 2 were used. A factor-analysis of this data did not reveal Fleishman's two dimensions of leadership behavior, "consideration," and "initiating structure" (36); this provided evidence to support Moos's (71) suggestion that in these kinds of circumstance it is not possible for employees to perceive the differences between the two dimensions.

Now if we are to draw up a picture of effective managerial performance encompassing the points listed here, we must, in some cases, choose between the evaluations of superiors and subordinates. Normally we might argue that the middle managers' assessments should hold the greater weight. However, in the present circumstances, the engineer is in some respects more aware of the technical and changing realities of the job. We might therefore decide to seek the attributes of the "better manager" among those about whom there is greatest agreement between management and engineers.

If we take these "better managers" as well as the least competent, we find that the former display characteristics which closely overlap with the features listed on the right of Table 3. On the other hand, the less competent managers have attitudes, aspirations and interests which are in many ways in line with those shown on the left of Table 3. Throughout this entire engineering function, the majority of personnel are inclined to possess characteristics congruent with those already shown to be associated with versatility, one important factor contributing to the success of this concern.

CHARACTERISTICS ASSOCIATED WITH SUCCESSFUL PERFORMANCE IN ORGANIZATIONAL CHANGE

In Table 3, the results of the seven studies are summarized under individual and managerial characteristics associated with effective and less effective performance in conditions of change. For the most part the evidence suggests that the lists of features go together, i.e., managers who prefer a structured and formalized work existence and who can generally be described as rigid in their

TABLE 3

INDIVIDUAL AND MANAGERIAL CHARACTERISTICS
ASSOCIATED WITH MORE AND LESS SUCCESSFUL PERFORMANCE
IN ORGANIZATIONAL CHANGE

Less successful	Individual characteristics	More successful
Toward equilibrium Deficiency motivated, concern for safety and security Preoccupation with means	Orientation	Toward growth Enthusiasm for change, desire for new experiences, risk taking Greater attention to ends
Belief in a "one best way"	Sentiments	Openness to more than one course of action
Regularity/order, financial security, prestige/status	Work aspirations	Freedom to be responsible, concern for achievement interesting work
Limited and conventional	Leisure interests	More diverse and less conventional
	Managerial characteristics	
Boss is the "expert" on subordinate's job	View of technical skills	Boss no longer expects to be, nor is regarded as, the "expert"
Efficiency and human relations are separate features of behavior	View of dimensions of leadership	Efficiency and human relations are merged
Submissive	Relations with superiors	Equality in relations with others, authority according to contribution
Directive and authoritative	Relations with subordinates	
Decisions are of a serial kind, i.e., based upon assumptions that previously successful solutions can be applied to new problems	Decision making	Less dependence on experience and more on the evaluation of the evidence

behavior possess one set of characteristics and those whose behavior can be described as more versatile, the other.

The attitudes and conduct, which distinguish men who can cope with innovation from those less able to do so, are linked in several respects with findings on the differences between growth and deficiency motivation (65), the authoritarian personality (1), and on the open and closed mind (84). They also parallel aspects of "divergent" and "convergent" behavior which form the nucleus of some of the current work on creativity.

There is not space to comment on all of the points in Table 3 here, though perhaps we should look more closely at two of the characteristics most relevant to the behavior of the manager.

It has often been said that the manager of the future will need to be a technical specialist. If the future, say the next twenty years, holds a greater degree of industrial stability than we know now, then that prediction may be fulfilled. It seems more likely that the conditions of accelerated change we now face will go on for some time. In this case it may be impossible for any manager to maintain a high level of expertise in any technical aspects of his job. The results here suggest that the more successful manager in conditions of change does not regard himself as a technical expert, nor do his subordinates, who are, in many cases, much more knowledgeable on such matters than he could expect to be. However, the same manager does know where to get technical advice and how to use it.

We observe that there are important differences in decision making. In conditions of rapid change, one finds that some important verdicts can be evaluated fairly quickly; their time span is short. I have been particularly interested in less successful decisions. One striking feature about most of them is their logic. They are not based on guess-work as we so often think but on assumptions that past conditions still prevail. Managers who are less successful in variable conditions are those who rely too heavily on their experience. Rapid change renders obsolete much of our experience.

These findings are not new; for the most part they complement the work of a number of management theorists (4,62). They can be integrated also into the organizational frameworks conducive to change advanced by Shepard (94) and Burns and Stalker (19), and examined by Spencer and Sofer (100) in this journal.

THE "ONE BEST WAY" AND INNOVATION

We have, up to this point, been concentrating attention on the individual; however we have noted that a firm which is successfully coping with change has among its employees a large number who possess characteristics associated with versatility. This suggests that the "organizational climate" is important and that the information in Table 3 reflects two opposing systems of values.

A number of researchers have found evidence which points to the existence of a new system of values in industrial management directly opposed to traditional values. Features of these two cultures are to be found in both organizations and people. Their differences are historically and technologically determined. One, let us call it the traditional or mechanical culture, provides the basis for resistance to change since its roots are in the past; the finest period in its long history stretches from the middle of the eighteenth century to about the time cars begin rolling off Henry Ford's assembly-line. The other, let us call it the scientific or progressive culture, derives from the development of electronics, atomic energy, and automation, and calls for the inculcation of attitudes generally associated with scientific endeavor.

Let us elaborate a little further on these two systems of values. The society which developed around the machine suffered from some of the limitations which are inherent in the simple one-way mechanical sequence of the early machine. Its growth was largely controlled by fragmentation and the strict application of law, two pillars of the mechanical era and incidentally of early theories of management. The essential features of the traditional culture are underlined by assumptions that there would be no change but only enlargement and extension. The automatic system with its feed-back loop upsets all this, for by definition it is adaptable and multipurpose. The progressive culture is founded more closely upon the realities of our time and brings with it the evolution of systems based upon assumptions of growth. Integrated functioning, self-regulation, and decentralized controls are some of its attributes.

It is really a coincidence that social standards and educational practices came into line with the demands the era of the machine made upon man? The severity of eighteenth and nineteenth century socializing processes must have helped to mould the closed minds best able to cope with an increasingly regulated environment. In many ways the prevailing sentiment of Victorian society was a belief in the "one best way of doing things" and they thought they had found the answer. My own generation heard much about this from our elders but changing circumstances have made it possible for us not to have to accept it.

Is it also a coincidence that the shift to more permissive child-rearing practices and our concern about our mechanical systems of education since the last war should come at a time when industry demands an increasing amount of adaptability on man's part? Of course, Marx and Weber told us a long time ago about the link between technical and social systems and the Tavistock Institute of Human Relations have demonstrated this fact empirically. I must confess that I had not really begun to be aware of the implications until my own researches showed that a belief that there is "only one best way of doing most things" is closely linked with the *inability* to maintain effective performance in changing conditions. May I repeat the point because it seems to me to be very important: the belief that there is "only one best way of doing most things" is a useful predictor of the individual's *inability* to cope with change. Yet it is also another important assumption underlying much of early management theory.

What I have been arguing is that the individual characteristics associated with effective performance in conditions of change are part of the scientific or progressive culture, just as the individual features linked with less effective performance are aspects of another system of values, the mechanical culture.

There are a number of additional points we can make about these two systems of values.

(a) Most occupational concerns have their roots in the mechanical era.

(b) Both systems of values are present in all people and organizations to some degree.

(c) Individuals are attracted to concerns with a similar climate of beliefs, e.g., mechanistic organizations and rigid people are mutually attracted. An organization with the traditional climate facing the need for rapid change is likely to be hampered by the kinds of people attracted to it. This state of affairs will not necessarily be helped if the Personnel Department has the power to recruit employees since this department is frequently among the most conformist sections, with respect to values, in industrial concerns.

(d) In most internal clashes between the two value systems, the mechanical is the more powerful. This follows the prevailing practice whereby responsibility is largely dependent on age and experience, a practice which can be justified in the mechanical culture since all previous experience is believed to be relevant in any new situation.

(e) If the people in power have predispositions toward the traditional culture and the circumstances demand the progressive system of values, then we have the basis for differences in concepts of what constitutes effective managerial performance and all that that implies.

(f) The growth in technical and social pressures for a change in attitude will produce camouflaging activities on the part of those who hold traditional values but not necessarily any real shift in sentiment.

THE RESPONSE TO INNOVATION OF MANAGERS WHO HOLD TRADITIONAL VALUES

Managers who hold sentiments congruent with the mechanical culture will respond to innovation in one of two ways: either they will cling more resolutely to the old and once successful customs and habits or they will grasp it as the answer to all their problems, as the drowning man clings to a passing piece of driftwood.

Most of us have at some time found ourselves alone in the crowded street of a strange city. If you can remember such an experience, you may also recall that you kept seeing people in the mass of faces around you, whom you thought you knew. In times of uncertainty and stress, managers, like any other people, hold closely to the familiar. They may seek to bolster their own security by promoting those who most closely resemble themselves in attitudes and beliefs. In other cases they may conveniently close ranks to ensure the failure of a new project. Burns and Stalker (19) give us a number of examples of this kind of response to change.

The second form of resistance, grasping an innovation as the answer to all one's problems, is in some ways a more serious form of resistance since, on the surface, the participants appear to be in favor of innovation. Managers who possess a low threshold for tolerance of ambiguity, when they find one set of rules or systems of operation failing to work, may search round for some alternative structure. Rapid developments demand the extensive assimilation of new industrial techniques. If the highest returns are to be obtained from these aids, not only must we make use of them but when they no longer serve their original purposes we must modify or disband them. Many innovations fail to pay off because the new method is considered to be beyond question, a kind of restorer of some lost equilibrium, as for example a wage incentive plan or a new piece of equipment or machinery frequently are.

IMPLICATIONS FOR MANAGEMENT TRAINING

This point of "belief in techniques and systems of operation" is relevant to the consideration of management training. Unfortunately many vocational courses are run with just this objective in mind and this includes management training. The efforts of many management educators are directed toward obtaining their students' dependence on and belief in traditional values. It is another manifestation of our old friend "the one best way." Indeed so many students in management courses are themselves preoccupied with finding *the answer* to problems and questions that one begins to wonder about the kinds of people who are attracted, or sent, to formally run courses in the first place. Let us conclude this discussion with reference to an example given by Joan Woodward in her recent book (109). She describes the unusual organizational structure of a successful concern in which 30 departmental supervisors all reported to five senior executives. Miss Woodward notes that the system appeared to work well and 28 of the supervisors endorsed this observation. Two of the supervisors disagreed.

They were very disgruntled and said that a functional type of organization was a constant source of frustration and irritation. Both felt that they would be a lot happier if they were responsible to one person only. They talked a lot about "the principle of unity of command" and about management organizational in general. Both had taken the British Institute of Management and Ministry of Education Joint Diploma in Management Studies, and were more organization conscious than their colleagues, none of whom had been given any formal management training. They had definite views about what was right and wrong in organization and much of their discontent arose from comparing their own situation with what they thought was the ideal one.

This example would appear to justify some skepticism about the worthwhileness of management training as it is widely conducted in industry and the technical colleges. It can no longer be treated as so many of us seem to, as merely an extension of conventional education. Training, like any other business venture, needs some recognized and accepted goals. It can only be evaluated in the light of knowledge about the kinds of characteristics which differentiate the competent from the less satisfactory manager.

This article has, therefore, concentrated on the characteristics of people who work effectively in conditions of change, so that the findings may be incorporated into the aims and methods of management training. This course has been pursued because it is fairly clear that those responsible for training industrial managers need to come to grips more closely with effective performance and its correlates. This must be done within the context of conditions which prevail in industry today.

In circumstances of rapid change, we have observed that attitudes and sentiments assume considerable significance in their effects upon the behavior of managers and other employees. Indeed, technical change is associated with the evolution of new organizational values which are similar to those found in scientific endeavor and which are at variance with traditional, mechanical values.

In organizations where these two value systems exist side by side, we have the basis for disagreement over standards of performance. In this conflict, the mechanical culture is likely to hold the upper hand since its support is most widely found among those people with the greatest authority in industry. The personnel and training departments, where change in the organization is concerned, are frequently lined up with the more conventional elements of the firm. We should not be surprised, therefore, to find that traditional values frequently hold sway in the methods of management training, in management ideology, and among people vocationally attracted to the subject.

This paper has outlined a number of attributes by which those people who are likely to be effective managers in conditions of change may be identified. These are also features of a "managerial climate." The results demonstrate that the basic framework of management training, both in method and in subject matter, should be built upon the development of sentiments and beliefs suitable to the individual's conditions of work. To achieve this end, the training establishment will need to be run more like the research laboratory and less like the conventional secondary school. It will also need, in the first instant, to shift the focus of attention from teaching skills to investigating the systems of values which operate within the organization.

12

Organizational Processes
and the Development of Managers:
Some Hypotheses

Thomas H. Patten, Jr.
Michigan State University

Reprinted by permission from *Human Organization*, XXVI, No. 4 (1967), 242–55.

In recent years complex organizations of all kinds, but particularly industrial bureaucracies, have given widespread attention to an elusive phantom called "management development." The importance of the subject cannot be gainsaid, for as one leading manpower expert has put it: "Whether a company is well run or not depends on the policies it follows in developing executives" (39). Yet as far as running the firm is concerned one of our most distinguished contemporary industrial sociologists has stated: "In the area of managing managers we have minimal knowledge and a great deal of speculation" (32, 33). This paper attempts to fill some of the lacunae in sociological knowledge of managers, managing, and management, fields certainly not unplowed by sociologists but, equally, areas in which we require more empirical work to assess existing sociological theory (42). The paper attempts an inductive contribution to the development of theory in industrial sociology by relating one empirical study to some of the best known and most pertinent literature.

Gleanings from the trade literature of management and what managers say to each other at professional meetings suggest that companies believe their needs for managers will not immediately be met by letting uncontrolled organizational processes operate on the recruitment, selection, placement, development, movement, and retention of managerial personnel (40). As a result, firms continue to spend a great deal of time and money on "management development," a term which embraces for some firms all the previously mentioned personnel actions but which for other firms is limited to one or two of these activities.

This article reports the findings of a study of management development based on depth interviews with 79 managers in a large firm employing more than 100,000 persons. At the time of the study, total annual compensation for these managers (salary plus executive bonuses) ranged from $15,000 to more than $100,000; the average was probably around $30,000 to $35,000. Depending on one's terminology, the men may be regarded as high middle management or top management. Rarely have individuals at this organizational level been intensively studied by industrial sociologists using the methods of interviewing and observation, although at least one well-known recent study approximates this type (27).

METHODOLOGY

The principal research method was a semistructured or focused interview (68). Four basic questions were asked; each question was probed deeply by the researchers, who were employed in a research capacity by the firm studied. Some of the interviews lasted as long as four hours; the shortest was about one hour. The research situation involved tandem interviewing whereby one researcher asked questions while the other took notes (6, 27, 51, 83). The note-taker asked questions in some interviews as the interview moved from one of the four main question areas to the next. For many of the interviews the interviewer in one situation became the recorder in the next interview session. Several days after the interview, the notes were submitted to the interviewee for review as to accuracy and interpretation, although changes in the latter were avoided as far as possible. The notes were then returned to the research team for final analysis. Occasionally specific names of individuals and certain ideas were deleted by the interviewee, but the returned interviews were in substance unchanged from the original notes.[1]

The managers interviewed represented a wide variety of functional fields: general management (i.e., management of multiple functions in a large division), production, industrial relations, engineering, financial control, purchasing, plant management, administrative services, research and development, and most of the manufacturing-related activities associated with production such as quality control, production control, industrial engineering, etc. There was an underrepresentation of sales and marketing personnel because in the firm studied the marketing and sales functions are organizationally separate entities. The managers to be interviewed were chosen for ease of geographical access and because of a stated willingness to participate by top management of the selected division. Undoubtedly these considerations influenced the results; had other segments of the organization been studied, the findings might be different.

The interviewing commenced at the highest levels of management and cascaded downward to the lower levels. In this way, cooperation was easily obtained, and the researchers were able to move rapidly through the organization. Two large divisions of the firm were intensively studied in an attempt to differentiate a "good" from a "bad" organizational "climate" for managment development (47). These components were classified good or bad on the basis of such designations by higher management, which were very consistent.

As employees of the organization, the researchers had access to personnel records, appraisals, and job evaluation data for most of the men included in the study. This information proved of limited value except to provide descriptive factual details. The personnel records, for example, revealed that on the average respondents were in their forties, had two to four years of college, and had about twenty to twenty-five years of work experience in the same or related fields of management. They were clearly "professional managers." Most had been with the organization ten to fifteen years; some longer. Because this particular company had undergone an extensive reorganization about twelve years prior to the study, many of the managers had been attracted from other firms. To some extent, therefore, it can be asserted that these men were "developed" elsewhere, for they had obtained their first supervisory work experience

---

[1] There nevertheless remained significant problems in analyzing the interview data even though reasonably concrete agreement was reached by this method as to the substance of what was communicated in the interview. The kinds of problems that can be expected and advantages of this approach despite these problems are discussed in Whyte (108).

outside the present firm. This finding had interesting implications for the study because many respondents were able to compare their current experience with that in other leading firms of the same general type.

The interviews began with an explanation that the researchers were conducting a study to determine what action, if any, the company should take to provide outstanding people for future management positions. The interviewee was asked: "To begin, we would like to have you select from among your current subordinates the man who, in your opinion, is performing the best all-around management job. We are not interested in this man's name or position. We merely want you to have him firmly in mind as a basis for your answers." Then the interviewer asked, "Why did you select this man?" We were interested in isolating the standards, criteria, or guideposts used by managers in evaluating managerial personnel. If the respondent answered with broad general categories such as personality traits, management responsibilities, functions, or similar ad hoc terminology, he was asked to explain and give examples, if possible, of what he meant. Since much research on executive behavior reports findings in terms of broad traits and abstract job functions, we wished if possible to secure more concrete data (37, 81, 99). The respondent was then asked to indicate in what ways the man he was discussing could improve. If the man discussed was a line man, the interviewer was asked if there would be any difference in standards if he were talking about a staff man (and vice versa). The obvious objective of the first main question and the line of probes was to obtain criteria by which the respondent evaluated the managerial performance of subordinates.

The second major question was: "In your opinion, which of your organizational components is contributing most toward producing managerial personnel for the company?" The respondent was then asked why he chose this organizational component, and whether he had noticed if there was anything significant about where this component obtained its people. He was also asked if he had noticed anything significant about the kinds of people it got; and if he knew of anything in the component which he considered significant that helped managers develop. Then he was asked the opposite side of the coin: "In your opinion, which one of your organizational components is contributing least toward producing managerial personnel for the company?" He was subsequently asked why he chose this component and then the three probes regarding whether or not he noticed anything about where this component got its people, the kind of people it got, and anything significant that helped managers develop there. The objective of this second line of questions was to obtain the respondent's concept of what contributes to managerial growth and to have the respondent identify organizational components reporting to him which were, from his viewpoint, contributing the most and the least toward producing managerial personnel for the company.

The third major question was: "What do you think have made the most important contributions to your career success and personal development?" Like the previous questions this one was deliberately left vague to secure the respondent's thoughts in his own framework. He was then asked why he considered these important and to state if there was anything that in retrospect he thought he missed which he would now consider helpful in his development. To assist the respondent in answering, it was sometimes necessary to ask him to consider contributions made before his first fulltime job, after this first job but prior to his present employment, after coming to the present position and, lastly, any experiences not job related that might have contributed to his development. To balance his ideas about positive contributions, the respondent was asked what, if anything, he considered might have delayed or interfered with his development. He was also asked if he had ever had formal on- or off-the-job management development training, and if so, what such training was, where it took place, and what he thought of it. In seeking the respondent's concept of these positive and negative contributions to his career success and personal development, no definition of development was given. If the respondent asked what the researchers meant by that term, he was invited to define it in his own way.

The final question was designed to elicit the respondent's opinion of "what action, if any, the company should take to provide outstanding people for management positions." The last probe encouraged an elaboration of his answer: "Is there anything you would change, discontinue, or add to what the company is now doing?"

INTERVIEW FINDINGS

The analysis of these four main lines of questioning was necessarily qualitative, since it was based on data of uneven quality with all the gaps, diverse emphases, and incompatabilities to be expected in this type of open-ended exploratory study (23, 53, 96).

INDIVIDUAL PERFORMANCE

In answering the first question concerning the individual performing the best all-round management job, the interviewees talked, in part, about the nature of management work. Specifically, they discussed management performance as having both individual and supervisory aspects. In his *individual* role, the manager performs as a functional expert. He assesses reports (originated by subordinates, peers, or others) either as a member of a committee contributing specialized knowledge or as a separate individual reacting to problems in his sphere of competency (25).

In addition to assessing reports, the manager frequently provides advice on problems both in his own area and in other areas in which he is reputedly proficient. Thus, a comptroller explained that he did not have time for the close supervision of his subordinates because he was constantly away from his office giving advice to others.

Committee duties occupy much of a manager's time. One of the interviewees, an industrial relations manager, had extended duties as a member of a production planning committee. And the operating committee, both at the division and plant levels, typically included managers from a number of functional areas.

In discussing the *supervisory* role, most interviewees talked in some detail about their relationships with a specific group of subordinates doing analytical work and/or work closely related to sustaining adequate production. Yet they only briefly mentioned relations with other employees who reported to them. For example, comptrollers consistently stated that financial analysts were performing best as all-round managers and dismissed subordinates in general accounting as of little importance. One interviewee said, "If a man is willing to go into general accounting in the first place, he either doesn't know what being a manager is, or isn't interested." A purchasing agent designated production purchasing as crucial because as he put it, "Errors made there can shut down the line" (103). In this vein, an industrial relations manager stated: "I am afraid to replace the man in labor relations (as opposed to salaried personnel) because there is danger there and we can get into a mess." The mess would, of course, be failure to meet the production schedule. Three product engineering managers designated design areas and design personnel as of key importance. The choice reflected the kind of work for which the managers were held accountable. As one of them put it: "Whenever I meet [with my organizational superiors] it is on engineering problems. They ask me, 'How is the [next year's] model progressing?' or, 'Will this aspect give us problems?' or, 'How about die castings; will they give us trouble?' These are the questions we discuss, never anything else."

In commenting on the supervisory role, interviewees stressed the results of supervision, namely, assessing reports and communicating findings to other members of management. They had little to say about techniques for getting the work done. A few did remark that selecting and developing people was part of the manager's supervisory role, but this was of less importance then skill in evaluating information and making recommendations.

Respondents touched only briefly on relationships with subordinates other than those in the previously mentioned specific groups. Interviewees simply indicated that they used all their subordinates to meet commitments established by higher management or by themselves and other managers working as a committee. Among the commitments mentioned were profit objectives, cost standards, production quotas, and meeting report deadlines.

What do these managers consider the qualifications of a good manager? First, a manager should have analytical ability. This was generally described as the ability to diagnose problems rapidly and propose solutions quickly. Comments such as "mentally alert," "sound judgment," "curiosity," and "quick perception and fine reasoning," apparently are to be included under this concept of analytical ability. Obviously it is difficult to prove that the point of reference for these rather vague terms is something called "analytical ability," but this seemed to be the common denominator (17, 26, 35, 57, 91). At least we could not find an alternative term which gave due consideration to other data as well.

Next, there was considerable emphasis on the need for skill in obtaining information and communicating facts and ideas to other managers. As one respondent noted, " . . . Nobody in supervision can do an effective job without the ability to communicate." To paraphrase another, his subordinate's strength is that "he sees the problem, can analyze it, and show us what to do about it."

Third, there was almost unanimous agreement that managers should be college graduates. It is noteworthy that many did not necessarily consider the knowledge acquired in college as essential for acceptable managerial performance. Instead, emphasis was placed on "having the degree," which is apparently a credential for finding and holding a management position. Several interviewees agreed that the highest position to which "grease boys" (people without college degrees) might aspire was that of plant manager, but actual achievement of such a position was considered very unlikely for anyone with less than a college degree.

In addition to the above generally applicable criteria, a smaller number of managers regarded technical proficiency as important. Others who failed to mention this may have taken it for granted. Interviewees usually discussed technical proficiency in terms of functional specialty: the comptroller should have knowledge of the technicalities of finance and accounting; an engineer should know his engineering specialty; and a production control manager should know materials handling, scheduling, and routing.

Finally, there was frequent comment on the need for the manager to get along with other and be receptive to their ideas, "to listen with wonderment in his own mind," as one interviewee put it. However, there was general agreement that getting the work done was more important than getting along with people. In fact, there were several favorable comments about overly aggressive individuals who single-mindedly achieved work results. Such men were highly valued even though the interviewees were aware of the human relations problems they created.[2] One interviewee criticized his outstanding subordinate for "showing impatience too much," "being too fast in his judgment of personalities," suggesting "he could be just as effectivd by being a less apparent task-master." Several interviewees talked about effective performers "stepping on the toes" of others

---

[2] Students of the sentimental school of human relations may have a hard time reconciling this finding with what is nowadays derisively called "soft" organization theory. We indicate subsequently in the paper that some of our interviewees favored effective human relators. However, it is of interest to note that in recent years many writers have reassessed the post-World War II "nice guy" syndrome, and have touted instead the values of "aggressiveness," "drive," "impatience," etc. See "Broadside at U.S. Management" (14), where Cameron Hawley, author of best-selling novels of business, is quoted as saying that what U.S. management needs is the "blunt, straight-forward man who would drive ahead in spite of Hell and high water." Fisch (35) p. 6 has stated that the best people in a company "are usually blessed with impatience and a personal sense of urgency." Reed M. Powell (77), as a consequence of study of 263 top managers in forty companies, writes that "the personality trait best described by ambitiousness, aggressiveness, and drive is the top consideration in job advancement."

or being "unsympathetic" to the problems of people in other functional areas. A certain amount of rigidity and tenacity, even if possession of these qualities meant alienating others, was considered a virtue, provided it got results: in the words of one engineering executive, "If you are right engineering-wise, don't give up." This conception is clearly opposed to the bland other-directed social ethic of the "organization man."

Several other criteria discussed in the literature of management were mentioned only occasionally; the ability of a manager to select and develop people, "physical and mental fitness," "the need for good health," "an abundance of energy," and "having the over-all view"—being able to approach the solution of problems from a multifunctional or multicomponent perspective. The few interviewees above the general manager level, however, did stress having the over-all view. At this highest level, there also appeared to be greater emphasis on the importance of what one interviewee called "collateral as opposed to vertical" organizational relationships: managers must be aware of the impact of their actions and decisions on the total organization. Few of the middle management interviewees spoke in these terms; instead, they stressed qualifications needed for positions specifically concerned with day-to-day production operations. It should be noted that this generalization included engineers involved in research and development work, and executives earning between $35,000 and $100,000 per year. Thus, individuals at very high organizational levels (immediately beneath the top) stress a conception of managerial work at variance with the managerial textbook dogma of the supposed necessity of the over-all view. In an age of bureaucracy, it is perhaps not particularly surprising to find a parochial emphasis even among relatively high-level and certainly highly paid managers on narrow areas and day-to-day problems, since their jobs are ultraspecialized despite their high level. This may simply be a variant on Thorstein Veblen's "trained incapacity."

DEVELOPMENTAL EXPERIENCES

Turning now to the second main objective of the study, we were successful in obtaining information on how managers considered they "developed." To accomplish this objective, each of the interviewees was asked to describe what he thought had most contributed to or interfered with his own career success and personal development, and whether he had ever participated in any formal off-the-job management education or training activities. Five factors were mentioned recurrently in this broad area.

1. Almost every manager discussed "Luck." Some interviewees regarded luck as "being in the right place at the right time." Others may have mentioned luck either because they were modest, unwilling to discuss their careers, or simply because they did not know how they reached their present occupational status; but most interviewees clearly perceived that at least once in their careers they were exposed to what they considered an opportunity, presumably through "luck" rather than any effort of their own (15, 64, 97, 101, 102). This opportunity

made their work "visible" to organizational superiors having control over their destiny (60). Thus, middle managers seemed to think of "development" as the period between starting a career and arriving later at a managerial position, a period governed in large part by luck.

2. Interviewees generally agreed that a second factor affecting their development was the chance to observe organizational superiors at work. Some of these former superiors were considered inept managers: "He did so many things that went haywire that he was eventually fired," as one interviewee put it. Other interviewees considered their former superiors as outstanding: "They listened to your recommendations and seriously considered them." (This would indicate that at least a few of the interviewees placed some premium on that old chestnut of human relations, "good communications.") However, the important point appears to be that the interviewees reporting these instances were themsevles alert to the possibilities of either learning by observation or learning vicariously and had been placed in positions where they could observe and reflect on the experience. One manager commented, "I tried to see the strong points of each [former organizational superior] and avoid the weaknesses of each."

3. Work assignments, as a third factor, were often described as "challenging" in the sense that the individual was, as one put it, "constantly . . . thrown into situations which were over my head." Sometimes interviewees described being assigned, while young men, to resolve problems of increasing difficulty as a result of having dealt successfully with a series of less complex problems. Others talked about having been delegated broad responsibilities or having been given general assignments in which they were expected to develop the specifics and accomplish the principal objectives.

4. Interviewees mentioned the value of having worked in firms other than the present organization, and having been exposed to other managerial techniques. As reported previously, most top managers of this firm were employed during a period of reorganization; as many as one-third had formerly worked for another leading firm in the same industry earlier in thier careers. Since many considered early work experience influential to their development, the stress on experience with another firm could be expected. However, it is difficult to draw any general conclusions about the specific developmental value of experience in the other company, especially since the interviewees came from a spectrum of divisions in that company where developmental techniques differed. It is nevertheless significant that few of the informants had anything but praise for the work experience in that firm. This may have been a manifestation of myth-making, the embellishment that may accompany retrospection or, indeed, reality.

5. The final factor connected with development was that of related developmental training or experiences. Not more than half a dozen of those interviewed had direct experience with formal university management education programs; but these expressed satisfaction with such programs. About two dozen of the interviewees reported that they had participated in brief seminars (of two days'

to one week's duration) concerned with management problems or related topics. These individuals endorsed such participation, noting that seminars provided them with significant information about what other companies were doing. As one said, "Just to go out and sit with these people is very good training." Another noted that at some seminars, "the company is more of a contributor than a recipient," but indicated that only attendance at such seminars could provide this reassuring knowledge. Several suggested that formal provision be made for the exchange of information among people in different components of the company, and the exchanges of various kinds be made between company managers and those in other firms. Managers who had visited other companies were enthusiastic about what they learned and recommended such visits for others. As one interviewee stated, the type of firm visited is irrelevant: "You can get ideas in a slaughterhouse!" All this would seem to suggest that bureaucratic experience is parochial and that managers, at least in this large-scale organization, hungered for knowledge of what other firms were doing. This may very well explain the endemic curiosity among American managers, reflected in their constant surveys of one another either directly through mail and phone inquiries or by means of the National Industrial Conference Board or similar agencies—all apparently designed to exchange experiences and information, to find out how IBM, GM, or Triple M does it!

GETTING OUTSTANDING MEN

The third objective of the study was to solicit opinions about what action the firm should take to provide outstanding people for management positions. Interviewees were asked specifically to suggest changes in existing programs; to suggest what, if anything, now being done should be continued or discontinued; and to indicate what should be added.

The firm had a management appraisal and replacement planning program as well as training programs covering all levels of hourly and salaried employees. These training programs included on-the-job training, supervisory training sessions for line and staff supervisors, programs for college graduate trainees and cooperative trainees, apprentice and trade training, a tuition refund plan, and a policy for permitting employees to take an educational leave of absence.

In general, the management appraisal and replacement planning programs were favorably regarded by higher echelon interviewees, but reactions were more varying at lower levels. It is possible that the programs as administered are most meaningful to higher level managers. They valued the replacement planning program perhaps because it encouraged planning by getting a deadline for submitting reports. As one top manager described it, "When you take your whole organization and sit down and lay out every guy's age, every guy's position, and every guy's potential, and then you have to plan developmental experiences for every single individual, you do it. You are facing a deadline with a program and it forces you to report." Others thought the program was worthwhile but needed strengthening, particularly by making it more than a paper program. As one interviewee said: "Greater accountability must be determined with regard to management development." A third believed that payoff would come in time: "The concept is embedded and after a few years, it may pay big dividends." Finally, all higher echelon managers interviewed agreed that the job of management development must be done by the general manager.

Interviewees occupying positions below the general management level reacted differently to replacement planning. They are of course the planned-for rather than the planners and, reflecting this role, tended to regard themselves as separate from "the company." Although they generally accepted as an idea the management appraisal and replacement planning program, they had some reservations about its practical application. They reacted in some instances with feelings of anxiety and uneasiness since they did not know how the program might affect their future progress. Some talked about "lip service" and another said, "It has been too much a matter of putting together a pretty book for our top people." Similarly, the appraisal program was generally endorsed but with such qualifying remarks as, "The forms should be thrown away after we use them," and "Only one out of a hundred of us would dare put down on paper what we really think of a guy." It was also pointed out that the ratings were only as good as the individuals doing the evaluating; one manager said, "You cannot do Rembrandts without being Rembrandt."

Many interviewees wanted more managerial job rotation. They felt the need for knowledge of other business functions in order to qualify for higher positions but believed it highly unlikely that such rotation would be instituted. As one stated, "It would be far easier for me to move to [another company] than to another division within [the company in which the research was conducted]."

There were also varying reactions to company-sponsored training programs. Programs designed to select and develop young people with potential were given widespread endorsement, but comments on training for already employed management personnel were more qualified. Several interviewees questioned the value of training sessions using the conference leadership technique, except perhaps where policy or other leadership information was communicated. Many stressed that development depended upon individual initiative, indicating that they had learned through correspondence courses, college courses taken after working hours and through reading. (The latter may surprise those who suspect most executives read with their ears, whether because of a lack of time or a positive proclivity.)

THE ORGANIZATIONAL CLIMATE

The fourth and last objective of the research study was to differentiate between organizational components which were contributing most and those contributing least toward developing managerial personnel. This was an attempt to identify the phenomenon known in management literature as "organizational climate" and to see what this concept might refer to in reality. Each interviewee was asked to identify the best and worst components along this dimension from among those reporting directly to him. On the basis of a composite of the judgments of the first 34 interviewees, two divisions were selected for study. Twenty-six interviews were held with managerial personnel in these two divisions, using the questions utilized in interviewing other managers. (The remaining 19 interviews—of the total 79—were held with research and development personnel.)

The author is unable to identify from these 26 interviews any themes or items of substance which would meaningfully differentiate the two components. This may not prove that there were no differences; it may simply indicate that other questions should have been formulated to probe for differentiating factors. The two divisions were functionally quite different: One was involved in basic manufacturing of raw materials, the other concerned with numerous fabrication processes. The division that was successful in developing managers was highly profitable in the year of the study; the one that was reportedly having difficulty in developing managers was not making money. In the recent past the relative profitablity of the two divisions had been the reverse, and still more recently both were very profitable. Both divisions had been reorganized. The unsuccessful division had also had a fairly recent reorganization of such a fundamental nature that it could be termed an "earthquake." Interviewees considered the changes demoralizing for all levels of personnel.

The concept of organizational climate, a bothersome one, may not be very fruitful for social research until it is redefined in more specific terms. Perhaps other research, using a different approach and different tools, might have been more successful, in the present case, in identifying organizational climate. It is possible that designations of "good" and "bad" components were consistent among the interviewees because at the time of the study the production process was well under control in the profitable division but constituted a serious problem in the less profitable component.

INTERPRETATION

The separate answers to the interview questions provide valuable insight into how managers perceive their own development. The perception per se might interest the social psychologist. The individual answers become much more meaningful, as Roethlisberger and Dickson have shown, when they are integrated to form a pattern (82). In this study the integration takes the form of sociological interpretation that can be confidently set forth because the author had intimate knowledge of the broad culture and organization of the firm studied. The interpretation consists of a description of the pattern and restatement of the answers. In the process of spelling out the hypothetical pattern, the author has drawn upon a number of publications in the sociological literature (55, 89, 96). These include materials on communication theory (20, 29, 30, 31), organization theory (24, 63, 85), and the literature of industrial sociology.

Many of these materials have a common meeting ground in the fields of problem solving and decision making about which we heard so much in our interviews.

We take as a starting point the defensible assumption that the way an organization functions determines the kinds of managers it will produce. The interpretation highlights first the relationships which enable managers in key positions to carry out their organizational responsibilities; and second, how these relationships affect management development. We have deliberately avoided the use of specific organizational terminology, such as job titles or written descriptions of job responsibility and authority, in order to emphasize the underlying social pheonomena rather than the formal organizational structure of the particular firm.

The pattern begins to appear when we consider that the managers interviewed, with the possible exception of a few at higher echelons, regard themselves as primarily concerned with controlling the production process. This is undoubtedly associated with the fact that the mission of the divisions studied is production, with only a minor emphasis on sales. Most of the products manufactured and fabricated are sold internally to end-product divisions within the firm and only incidental nonusable byproducts are marketed externally. (These by products, of course, are usable by firms in other industries.) This view of the managerial assignment is important because it determines the ultimate standard used by the interviewees in assessing themselves and others. This standard is hypothesized as: *How much does the manager's performance contribute to the control of the production process?*

The size of the company and the attendant physical distance between processes is another factor determining the form of the pattern. Most of the interviewees were physically and organizationally removed from the actual point of production. They controlled through reports. The information obtained in the interviews may thus be comprehanded in terms of communication theory, looking upon the organization as a complex network of decision centers, information channels, and learning systems (20,31).

In essence, there appear to be two kinds of reporting activities which bridge the distance between the point of production and the managers' locations. Using the terminology of Selznick (89) which also seems implicit in the work of other scholars (18, 25, 50, 76, 104, 105), the first may be viewed as a series of recurrent "routine" and/or administrative reports which are based upon an assumed standard of performance. The manager is alerted to a problem when one or more of these reports reflects a deviation from previously determined standards; for example, an off-budget condition, an inability to produce according to engineering specifications, or an increase in the accident frequency rate. The second kind of reporting involves individuals doing "critical" work. These separate reports are analyses of the causes underlying deviations from the standard, with recommendations for remedical action. With these recommendations in hand, the manager who is physically and organizationally removed can take the necessary action to bring the production process back under control.

Two factors account in part for the manner in which interviewees described their work. These factors are (1) their "orientation" (or role-set, as Simon terms it) toward control of the production process[3], and (2) the fact that they are physically and organizationally separated from this process. These considerations make it necessary for managers to work through reports and provide technical assistance and advice which enable other managers of varying backgrounds to react to the reports. In addition, the managers themselves must function as analysts since they synthesize reports for presentation to committees. This functioning by the manager at least a part of the time as an individual analyst has been noted by other students of management; nevertheless, the evidence from this study provides an additional dimension for understanding how and why the manager must act as what we would call a "superanalyst." We do not see the manager performing the abstract functions of classical–traditional organization theory, such as planning, organizing, staffing, directing, and the like, as described by Urwick (106), Koontz and O'Donnell (52), Allen (2), and others identified essentially with the deductive school of management theory.

Turning to another aspect of the pattern, we can now understand hypothetically why the interviewees' conception of the requirements of their work governs their utilization of subordinates reporting to them. Specifically, relationships with subordinates are determined by the manager's self-assessment of his strengths and weaknesses. He makes this assessment, in part, in terms of what he thinks he needs for control of the production process and in terms of his conceptions of the particular assignments most vital to control. As Simon (96) and Cyert and March (24) in their "attention-focus" concept suggest and as Churchman (22) notes[4], managers control two very scarce commodities, their own time and attention; their most conscious problem is one of determining to what they should pay attention, on what they should focus. As a consequence, the managers develop their closest relationships with those subordinates who complement them with technical skills they believe they lack, or with those whose work is, in their opinion, most vital to the control of production. These are the subordinates who are performing "critical" assignments. Under similar circumstances different managers may depend upon different individual subordinates in different positions to carry out these "critical" assignments; therefore, we do not see manifest consistencies in these functional specialty background

---

[3] The concept of orientation is, of course, a basic one in sociology and social psychology. Simon (96) regards orientation as a role set. This concept has great pertinence here. See also Selznick (89), Schumpeter (88), Mauser (66), Lewis (61), Fisch (35), C. Shepard (90), H. Shepard (91–93), Kornhauser (54), Burns (18), and Patten (75).

[4] Norman Berg (9) states the matter somewhat differently, getting perhaps to the nub of the matter:

> At each level considerations of stability, profits or growth *at that particular level* are better understood and of more immediate concern than are similar considerations for other levels. Executives at each level tend to view the process and the problems from the standpoint of their own interests and environment. (Italics in original.)

relationships in pairs of managerial superiors and subordinates across the firm studied, although we would hypothesize that latent complementarity is there.

Interviewees stress their relationships with those carrying out "critical" assignments almost to the complete exclusion of "those doing routine work." These critical assignments are in such areas as financial analysis, production purchasing, labor relations, and design. The common denominator which seemingly accounts for these designations is that, at the manager's request, these individuals obtain information about production problems and make recommendations which enable higher managers to bring the production process under control when there are deviations from standards.

Another dimension of the interview data contributes to the emerging pattern of managerial development. The individuals designated as outstanding managers were considered qualified because they had analytical ability, could identity problems, could propose solutions, and displayed skill in communication. College education was deemed necessary. Even the overly aggressive individual who created human relations problems was considered acceptable if he had these qualifications. The qualifications interviewees required of managerial candidates are significant because they are identical with the qualifications of the individuals who perform "critical" work. These men are professionals who, after securing employment in the firm through an academic degree, the initial passport, master the aforementioned anaytical and communication skills. Inasmuch as the interviewees designated these individuals as their potential replacements (and in a few instances actually were replaced by them), the characteristics of the managers of the future in the organization studied have, in large part, already been defined.

Thus managers develop largely from among those who are given the special assignments inherent in "critical" work. It will be recalled that interviewees repeatedly stated that they had developed through challenging assignments and through observing organizational superiors at work. We strongly suspect that special analyses and reports inherent in "critical" work involving control of the production process are precisely these challenging assignments. The fact that these reports are essential to higher management in carrying out their duties enables the individuals involved in "critical" assignments to observe and be observed by their own, as well as other, organizational superiors. This gives these fledgling managers visibility; they become known and are asked for when vacanices occur (12, 34, 49). Because they are "hot shots" they can easily obtain "sponsors" and become the "coat-tail riders" of older mobile managers.

The requirement that managers have reporting, communication, and analytical skills tends to disqualify others for management positions: men who work close to the physical processes of production, who take direct action and make minute-to-minute or day-to-day decisions, as well as those who provide recurrent reports, are not as likely to master the skills considered most necessary for higher management positions. They are disbarred because they do "routine" work of minor significance. In other words, those who work in "critical" areas are the potential managers and those who work in the "routine" areas are likely to remain in their present status level.

As a consequence of the hypothesized organizational relationships, the higher level manager will exercise more care in the selection of those who will be given "critical" work than in making assignments to others. From the manager's point of view, individuals doing "critical" work solve his most important problems, those for which he may be gigged if they become visible to higher management. In fact, in selecting subordinates for "critical" work, a manager may deliberately seek a person whose skills specifically complement his own, which would be a particularly rational decision in a results-oriented production organization. Furthermore, the performance of persons doing "critical" work will be constantly under surveillance. The manager must trust them because their performance affects his tenure: he is clearly dependent upon their skill in getting accurate information and correctly analyzing it. Also, those performing "critical" assignments can establish relationships with many organizational superiors. Since their work requires them to deal with many ramifications of the particular problem, it brings them in contact with managers from varying fields. This, as previously suggested, gives them visibility and the opportunity to be observed and assessed. Finally, since there are relatively few individuals involved, the very variety of their assignments enables them to move around the organization sufficiently to attract relatively widespread attention, which further enhances their opportunity for upward managerial mobility.

CONCLUSION

What are the implications of this interpretation for developing managers? Or, what are the implications of the management orientation identified and of the patterns resulting from the ways in which managers carry out their organizational responsibilities? Here we may be turning from industrial to educational sociology and even into the field of business administration.

Effective use of organizational resources in the development of managers necessitates an awareness that there are the two kinds of assignment, "routine" and "critical." The first provides an opportunity to learn routine operations and existing organizational relationships. The second requires individuals to analyze problems and propose solutions. Positions of the first kind provide training and job-induction for less-experienced people and familiarize potential managers with the procedures of a variety of departments. However, positions of the second kind hypothetically contribute most to the development of managers because individuals working on special assignments in "critical" areas will learn what is considered "important" in the industrial and occupational culture in which they find themselves. Also, they are directly observed and assessed by organizational superiors and promoted if they perform acceptably. Individuals doing routine reporting work ordinarily do not have this visibility or attention and, because they are involved in organizational minutiae, will be less apt to be considered for promotion. They are the organizational hewers of wood and drawers of water. Here it is of interest to recall a perceptive quotation cited earlier: "If a man is willing to go into general accounting in the first place, he either doesn't know what being a manager is, or isn't interested."

Effective placement planning requires the calculated development of managers, but the positions in a firm are not all equally suited for this purpose. There are relatively few developmental positions in which individuals can receive the special analytical and reporting assignments inherent in "critical" work. Such individuals are already visible to their organizational superiors and are being developed as long as they remain in their jobs. However, individuals occupying other positions will not be visible even if they have the potential managerial capacity. A deliberate technique is needed to identify such individuals and to rotate them selectively into positions culturally defined as having developmental value where they can be observed and assessed.

Furthermore, it is possible to use the organization more effectively for developing managers (21). When, for example, there is an anticipated vacancy in a key managerial position, a sufficient period of planning for the transfer and placement of selected individuals should be allowed, to give the manager who is responsible for the selection time to test the performance of candidates against qualifications required for that position. For obvious reasons, managers are reluctant to place in vital managerial positions individuals they have not personally assessed (74). "Zig-zag mobility" (41) probably reflects position trials for managers whose qualifications are questionable and who need to be tested before they are awarded relatively permanent managerial berths. Advance transfer provides the manager with an opportunity to assess the risk involved in accepting a candidate for a key position. Effective placement planning thus requires an awarencess of future vacancies in key positions and also the advance placement of designated candidates in positions where they can be observed by the manager ultimately responsible for recommending promotion. The manager may select someone other than the candidate, in which case the passed-over candidate can be placed in another department under a different manager, if he is considered to deserve further consideration as a managerial possibility. If it is considered he should be "cooled out," he can be left there to "die" or drift according to the vagaries of the organization.

Underlying all this is the social psychological fact that the management development situation brings two personalities together and that development is as much dependent upon this relationship as upon the position itself (58, 86). Clashes in personality can frustrate the use of organizational resources in social learning. Correspondingly, changes in personnel among organizational superiors will probably change the developmental opportunities inherent in any particular situation (70). In this context a social psychological perspective on management development can be exceptionally meaningful.

Replacement planning must also provide for attracting people of management potential into the company. This includes, on the one hand, bringing in experienced individuals needed to provide skills not available among present employees, and further emphasis on recruitment for training of college graduates who may ultimately develop the skills necessary for occupying key management positions. As needed, work experience may be supplemented by management education and by providing formalized opportunities to exchange information and ideas with other personnel in the organization, as well as with people from other selected firms.

These suggestions for management development, having some theoretical integrity and consistency based upon the hypothetical interpretation of the data in the study, may be worth a trial by industrial firms. Such an application of industrial sociological knowledge need not imply that research in this field should have as its chief objective the improvement of techniques of business administration (73). Yet feed-back of this knowledge to management may provide clues to how organizational processes and the culture of the factory affect the development of managers. It may thereby carry a sociological lesson of its own on managing managers.

13

The Laboratory Approach to Organization Change: "Confrontation Design"

Robert T. Golembiewski
University of Georgia

Arthur Blumberg
Syracuse University

This study reports one "spin-off" from the basic technology of sensitivity training, which is now widely used for inducing attitudinal and behavioral change in organizations. Changes in attitudes of members of a complex business organization are reported in this paper, and they support the value of the "confrontation design." Similar results have been obtained in other business and government settings.

Reprinted by permission from *Academy of Management Journal*, XI, No. 2 (1968), 199–210.

This article provides specific research counterpoint to the summary description in an earlier paper (44) of the laboratory approach to organization change. That piece sketched the major properties of the laboratory approach, and particularly stressed the uses made of sensitivity training groups, or T-Groups. That article made two major points. Without question, considering personal learning, T-Groups are valuable vehicles for increasing interpersonal sensitivity, for demonstrating to individuals a sharper sense of what they need to function more fully and effectively, and for beginning the development of skills that permit individuals to attain more of what they desire in their interpersonal relations. Organizational applications of the laboratory approach were shown to raise more complicated issues.

The thrust of this article is directed toward the complex issues of organization applications of the laboratory approach. The argument is basically dual. For some purposes, T-Groups are not the only or the unqualifiedly best vehicle in the laboratory approach to organization change. Moreover, designs can be developed which at once exploit the learning potential associated with T-Groups while they aovid many of their major drawbacks in large organizations.

Basically, this paper views the T-Groups as an ideal learning environment that need not or cannot be duplicated in many ways in the "real world" of organizations. Thus the intense interaction characteristic of T-Groups cannot (and, perhaps, should not) be generated in some organizations. At the same time, knowledge of T-Group dynamics can generate spin-offs of applied techniques useful in complex organizations.

The usefulness of seeking analogical spin-offs of T-Group dynamics suitable for complex organizations will be illustrated. The focus is on a program of change in a large business organization, the over-all purpose of which program is to improve relations between several middle-managerial levels and functions. This paper deals with one spin-off of the laboratory approach used as part of this program of change, namely, the confrontation design. More specifically, this paper summarizes some of the attitudinal changes experienced by a diversified group of middle managers from the marketing area of a large firm who participated in a confrontation design. Similar results have been obtained in public agencies as well as in other business organizations.

INTERPERSONAL AND ORGANIZATIONAL PARALYSIS: A SIMPLIFIED CASE

A wide range of problems exist to which the T-Group and its analogs may be applied usefully. Consider only one way in which communication between individuals and their suborganizations can degenerate. A hypothetical but typical sequence of worsening relations between individuals A and B in an organization takes such a general form:

1. A does not *own up* to his attitudes or feelings toward B;

2. B, in turn, is less likely to *be open* with A;
3. A and B, consequently, experience a diminishing *mutual trust* as the number of unresolved issues between them increases;
4. A degenerative, self-heightening process can be set in motion as:
   a. A and B feel a diminished *interpersonal competence*, that is, as they experience an increased *risk* of recognizing and acknowledging their attitudes and feelings, as their *processes* for decision making become increasingly burdened by unfinished business, and as A and B consequently become less effective in *isolating and resolving substantive problems*, if indeed any such exist when decision-making processes function well;
   b. A and B consequently feel diminished *psychological success* in solving problems that remain solved without creating other problems; and
   c. A and B become *more dependent* on their superiors, with lessened openness and owning being associated with (for example) informing on peers or with "don't rock the boat" attitudes.

Now if A has a typical initial experience in a T-Group—usually two weeks at an isolated location spent working with individuals who are strangers—he very probably will gain valuable insights and skills in sensing and reversing such degenerative sequences in his relations with some C within the laboratory context. Thus A's self-esteem may be enhanced when he proves to himself he really can establish meaningful and authentic relations with others in a T-Group. Or A may sharpen his sensitivity to the early stages of degenerating communication sequences as well as augment his skill in dealing with them effectively. The other possibilities are numerous.

However, A faces many problems in attempting to transfer such new or augmented skills into his organization. He might reason: "If I could only get organization member B in a T-Group, he would see the light just as C and I did." The if is often a big one. Thus there are some things a T-Group can do poorly or not at all, when such degenerative experiences occur in organizations. For example, A's efforts to recreate in his organization the supportive environment typical of T-Groups may be frustrated for a variety of reasons. Typically, that is, degenerative communication sequences in organizations involve large numbers of people, diversely organized into units often having long histories of rivalry that might inhibit the intimacy and sharing characteristic of a T-Group, and each performing myriad day-to-day jobs that must be done. In contrast, "stranger" T-Groups typically involve only a dozen people or so with no past history, who will predictably go their largely separate ways after training, and who have no task in the interim but learning about each other from one another. Or finally, some powerful organization figures might argue that the desirable consequences of a common laboratory experience for members of the same organization are outweighed by the risks involved. T-Groups can range broadly, after all, and a man in that context thus might say things harmful to his career that had no relevance to his work. A similar revelation in a stranger T-Group would involve far less career risk, in contrast.

AN ORGANIZATIONAL ANALOG OF THE T-GROUP: SEVEN FEATURES OF THE CONFRONTATION DESIGN

The "confrontation design" attempts to capitalize on basic laboratory dynamics while doing what the T-Group in large organizations can only do weakly or not at all. Confrontation designs share an intent with organizational applications of sensitivity training, that is, but the two differ in critical ways. Although confrontation designs can vary widely in specifics, seven core features particularly distinguish them from learning designs using T-Groups.

First, confrontation designs involve as participants individuals who are hierarchically and/or functionally involved in some common flow of work. The attitudinal changes reported here concern four levels of the same marketing organization and some nine of its component activities. Immediately, then, the confrontation design seeks learning that has direct, on-the-job applications. In contrast, applications of sensitivity training in organizations often provide for an initial experience in "stranger" groups composed of individuals who do not know one another, or in "cousin" groups of individuals from the same organization who do not work together. Only after such a first experience, if then, is relational learning typically attempted in "family" groups of individuals who commonly do work together.

Second, confrontations involve two or more organizational entities whose members have real and unresolved issues with one another, e.g., "labor" and "management." In this case, the focus was on the relations between various headquarters activities and supervisors of a field salesforce.

Third, confrontation designs involve the mutual development of images as a basis for attempting to highlight unresolved issues. In this case, five Basic Learning Aggregates were instructed to individually choose "Relevant Others," that is, any organization positions or units with which more effective relations were considered necessary to do an effective job. For each of these Relevant Others, participants were instructed to develop "3-Dimensional Images" based on these questions:

1. How do we see ourselves in relation to the Relevant Other?
2. How does the Relevant Other see us?
3. How do we see the Relevant Other?

The 3-D Images were to be written on large sheets of newsprint. Each Learning Aggregate prepared its images in isolation.

The learning design in this case was complicated by a variety of factors. For example, only four of the five Basic Learning Aggregates were units of organization; the fifth was a categorical group composed of the specialites of various headquarter units. Moreover, the former units only recently were established. Such factors probably reduced the potency of the design. In general, we expect the confrontation experience to be more potent as each Basic Learning Aggregate is not merely a categorical group, that is, as its members share social norms and mutually identify (43). To the degree that a Basic Learning Aggregate possesses such qualities of real "groupiness," so should they be able to consensually validate and reinforce the learning of each group member.

Fourth, confrontation designs provide for sharing 3-D Images. This confronting-via-images is the first step toward mutually working through any relational problems. In this case, consultants scheduled blocks of time during which willing Relevant Others could confront one another. A consultant was present at each confrontation.

Fifth, confrontation designs assume that significant organizational problems often are caused by blockages in communication. Confrontations "free up" people "to level" in communicating, and thus set the stage for authentic interaction and for effective problem solving.

Sixth, confrontations are short-cycle affairs. The confrontation design about which data will be reported here, for example, took some 12 scheduled hours. In contrast, a typical stranger experience in sensitivity training lasts two weeks.

Seventh, confrontation designs typically are seen as springboards for organizational action. Since such a design is typically brief, however, real limits exist as to what can be accomplished. We instructed participants to try to do only two things: to try to understand the 3-D Images communicated to them, and to seek some areas of agreement where mutually beneficial accommodations might be made. In addition, Core Groups were set up following the confrontations to work on specific organizational issues. These Core Groups were formed as a terminal training activity, some work was begun in the groups, and plans were made for future meetings.

The learning in confrontation designs does not have to be transferred or made relational, in sum. *It is relational.*

ONE APPLICATION OF A CONFRONTATION DESIGN: SELECTED RESULTS

The effects of one application of the confrontation design will be illustrated in two ways. First, the representative 3-Dimensional Image in Table 1 reveals that participants did not trifle with the design. That table reflects many unresolved issues. Some of the issues were surprises, and none had been admitted to public dialog between the parties.

Second, providing more rigorous support of the efficacy of the confrontation is an involved matter. Our primary data concern before/after attitudinal changes and derive from a questionnaire administered before and immediately after the experience (45, 46). Only impressionistic data about behavioral changes are available, but they are consistent with the pattern of attitudinal changes that seem due to the confrontation.

Expectations about intended changes in attitudes were not simple. For

TABLE 1

A SAMPLE 3-D IMAGE BY REGIONAL SALES GROUP I
WITH THE PROMOTION DEPARTMENT AS THE RELEVANT OTHER

A. *How Members of Regional Sales Group I See Themselves in Relation to Promotion Department*

1. Circumvented
2. Manipulated
3. Receiving benefits of their efforts
4. Nonparticipating (relatively)
5. Defensive
6. Used
7. Productive
8. Instrument of their success
9. Have never taken us into their confidence in admitting that a promotion "bombed"
10. The field would like to help but must be a two-way street

B. *How Members of Regional Sales Group I Feel Promotion Department Sees Them*

1. Insensitive to corporate needs
2. Noncommunicative upward, as holding back ideas and suggestions
3. Productive in field saleswork
4. Naïve about the promotion side of business
5. Unappreciative of promotion efforts
6. As lacking understanding about their sales objectives
7. Belligerent
8. Overly independent operators
9. Not qualified to evaluate the promotions sent to us
10. Honest in opinions

C. *How Members of Regional Sales Group I Characterize Promotion Department*

1. Autocratic
2. Productive
3. Unappreciative of field efforts
4. Competent with "things" but not "people"
5. Industrious
6. Inflexible
7. Unrealistic
8. Naïve
9. Progressive in promotion philosophy and programs
10. Overly competitive within own department
11. Plagiarists who take field ideas but do not always give credit

From Robert T. Golembiewski and Arthur Blumberg, "Confrontation As A Training Design in Complex Organizations," *Journal of Applied Behavioral Science*, III (December, 1967), 534.

example, four of the organization units about which data were gathered were either represented at the confrontation by one participant or by none at all. No definite pattern of changes in attitudes toward these four targets was expected, consequently. For crude purposes, they are "control groups." And two of the remaining five units or positions—representing some 15 percent of the sample—were perceived by the consultants as creating substantial "new business" during the design (45). Before the data were processed, then, consultants distinguished three types of units or positions about which data were gathered and made three different predictions concerning them. Consultants distinguished:

1. Units which were deeply involved in the design, toward which the most favorable[1]

---

[1] The terms "favorable" and "unfavorable" are convenient shorthand only. On the Volitional Criteria-Questions, attitudinal changes reporting a greater desire to work together are considered "favorable," for example. Lessened desire to work together is considered to be "unfavorable." On the Objective items, for example, changes reporting a lower degree of perceived productivity are "unfavorable." On both kinds of items, the directions of scales were varied on the questionnaire to inhibit the development of response sets. However, the data were uniformly processed so that favorable changes are scored + and unfavorable changes are scored −.

shifts in attitudes were expected, as measured by pre- and post-confrontation administrations of the questionnaire.

2. Units which had little or token representation in the design, toward which was anticipated only a slight drift toward more favorable attitudes due to a "halo effect."

3. Units which had created substantial "new business" during the design, toward which the least favorable shifts in attitudes were expected. Basically, these two units did not participate fully in the confrontation. For example, one produced only a 2-Dimensional Image, neglecting to describe how they saw themselves.

In addition, three types of criteria-questions were distinguished a priori, for each of which different predictions seemed appropriate. The three types of questions are:

1. *Volitional Criteria-Questions* which tapped attitudes considered relatively easy to change (e.g., How much do you want to collaborate with Unit Z?) or attitudes deemed particularly sensitive to the confrontation design (e.g., How much information have you received from Unit X?).

2. *Objective Criteria-Questions* which tapped attitudes that could hardly be changed positively on the basis of the confrontation design, but which might very well drift negatively as people felt more free to be open about their attitudes toward self and others (e.g., What is the level of productivity of Unit Z?).

3. *Combined Criteria-Questions*, composed of 11 Volitional and 10 Objective Criteria-Questions, on which a general drift toward favorable changes in attitudes was expected.

These expectations may be conflated and summarized in a 3 × 3 matrix, as in Table 2. Interpretively, pre- and post-confrontation administrations of the questionnaire were expected to reveal that the most favorable shifts in attitudes would be reported towards the Deeply Involved organization units on the Voli-

TABLE 2

		Types of Units		
		Deeply Involved	Underrepresented	Unfinished Business
Types	Volitional	Most favorable shifts in attitudes	Moderately favorable shifts in attitudes	Least favorable shifts in attitudes
of	Objective	Least unfavorable shifts in attitudes	Moderately unfavorable shifts in attitudes	Most unfavorable shifts in attitudes
Criteria-				
Questions	Combined	Strong favorable shifts in attitudes	Slight favorable shifts in attitudes	Least favorable shifts in attitudes

tional items. On the Objective items, the expectation was that attitudes toward all organization units would tend to change negatively, and most sharply for the Unfinished Business units.

The pattern of attitudinal changes above was not only expected, it was intended. Designing for "negative" or "unfavorable" shifts in attitudes on the Objective Criteria-Questions may seem perverse, that is, but it is not. Basically, the learning design was a dilemma/invention model that captures much of the essence of the dynamics of T-Groups. Let us simplify grievously. Consultants concluded that members of the host organization had entered into a mutual-defense pact expressed, for example, in terms of unrealistically high but mutual public estimates of performance[2]. Lack of openness, in short, obscured basic orgnization dilemmas. The confrontation design attempts to induce the public recognition of such dilemmas via greater openness and risk taking, by explicitly dealing with the "real reality" perceived by organization members. Hence negative changes in attitudes on the Objective Criteria-Questions do not signal a dangerous deterioration of morale. Rather, such changes establish that dilemmas requiring attention have been acknowledged. During a confrontation, that is, organization members are encouraged to activate the "dilemma" part of the dilemma/invention learning model, as by seeing themselves and others as less productive than they were willing to admit previously. At the same time, however, the confrontation design encourages organization members to work harder on the "invention" aspects of the learning model. That is, the confrontation design is intended to favorably change the attitudes of organization members on the Volitional Criteria-Questions, e.g., toward a greater desire to cooperate in coping with organizational dilemmas.

The matter may be summarized briefly. In its basic intent, then, the confrontation design proposes to raise to public attention unacknowledged but real dilemmas in an organization that must be dealt with. The confrontation design also intends to induce greater commitment and effort toward developing inventions capable of minimizing or eliminating the dilemmas, as in the Core Groups built into the confrontation design or in the back-home situation. These two intents are realized, in turn, as participants accept norms for giving and receiving feedback consistent with the laboratory approach (44).

Table 3 establishes that these complex expectations were generally supported by attitudinal changes in the host population. The ratios in Table 3 are derived from changes in before/after attitudes of all participants toward each of nine target positions or units of organization, including their own. A ratio greater than 1.0 indicates that favorable changes in attitudes outnumbered unfavorable changes; a ratio less than 1.0 indicates that negative or unfavorable changes in attitudes were more numerous.

---

[2] Illustratively, organization norms prescribed vigorous applause following a presentation, no matter how bad the performance.

TABLE 3

SUMMARY DATA CONCERNING ATTITUDINAL CHANGES
TOWARD NINE UNITS OF ORGANIZATION,
BASED ON PRE- AND POST-CONFRONTATION ADMINISTRATIONS
OF A QUESTIONNAIRE

			Types of Organization Units or Positions		
			Deeply Involved	Underrep-resented	New Business
	Volitional	Ratio +/− changes	14.00 (28/2)	2.33 (28/12)	1.86 (13/7)
Types		Ratio +/− Stat. sig. changes	Infinity (14/0)	4.45 (9/2)	1.67 (5/3)
of	Objective	Ratio +/− changes	0.65 (13/20)	0.42 (13/31)	0.38 (6/16)
Criteria-		Ratio +/− Stat. sig. changes	0.25 (1/4)	0 (0/10)	0.18 (2/11)
	Combined	Ratio +/− changes	1.86 (41/22)	0.95 (41/43)	0.83 (19/23)
Questions		Ratio +/− Stat. sig. changes	3.75 (15/4)	0.82 (9/11)	0.58 (11/19)

N.B. The numbers in the parentheses indicate the raw number of positive/negative changes.

The data in Table 3 may be sampled.[3] For example, Deeply involved units attracted the most favorable shifts in attitudes, as expected. Favorable changes in attitudes toward those units at a minimum were 14 times more likely than unfavorable changes. The other two types of units, in contrast, experienced approximately a 2 : 1 ratio of positive/negative changes. All three types of units, within a narrow range, experienced unfavorable attitudinal shifts on Objective items. Roughly, unfavorable attitudinal changes outnumbered favorable changes by 2.5 to 1. The negative trend was anticipated. As anticipated, also, the data do not even suggest wholesale rejection. Thus the Deeply Involved units were the targets of roughly the same proportion of favorable/unfavorable changes on the Objective Criteria-Questions as the New Business units[4].

---

[3] Malcolm Parsons of Florida State University raised issue with the original classification of Criteria-Questions 14 and 16 in the Volitional category. We are now persuaded that his instincts are sharper than ours were, as Table 3 reflects. Early published reports of our findings were based on the original classification and, if Parsons is as accurate as we now feel he is, they underestimated the impact of the design on attitudes. The ratios for All Criteria-Questions and for the Objective Criteria-Questions changed not at all and relatively little, respectively. But the three ratios for Volitional Criteria-Questions in Table 3 rose sharply to 14.0, 2.33, and 1.86, for example. In contrast, the original ratios were 5.0, 1.7, and 1.4.

[4] The data are not reported here, but individuals describing their own unit saw themselves just as "unfavorably" on the Objective Criteria-Questions after the confrontation as did others describing them. So the pre/post drift toward negative changes was not an "us good guys" and "those bad guys" phenomenon.

As the summary in Table 3 suggests, then, a confrontation design imbedded in the context of a complex organization induced some of the same kinds of dynamics that are characteristic of T-Groups. The sharp favorable drift in attitudes on the Volitional Criteria-Questions implies that the confrontation attitudinally prepared people to improve relations that were not critically bad but which were of growing concern. At the same time, as the data on the Objective Criteria-Questions suggest, participants tended to describe their reality in somewhat sharper negative terms.

A capsule characterization seems appropriate. After the confrontation, individuals seemed more willing to undertake a task that they saw as more demanding than they had thought. This describes an orientation that is conducive to effective learning and change.

Without making too much of such data, more broadly, the summary data in Table 3 suggest the antithesis of a degenerative communication process. In the following particulars, that is, the data suggest an alleviation of the processes leading to interpersonal and organizational paralysis:

1. A as a member of an organization unit was encouraged by the confrontation design to *own up* to his feelings and attitudes concerning B and/or his unit in developing a 3-D Image;
2. B as a member of an organization unit, in turn, was encouraged to *be open* in developing a 3-D Image about A and his unit;
3. Both A and B experienced a growing *mutual trust* as the amount of unfinished business between them was reduced by the confrontation design, especially as it provided that A and B share their 3-D Images of each other and/or of each other's organization units;
4. A healthy, self-correcting process can be set in motion as:
   a. A and B as members of organization units feel an increased *interpersonal competence*, that is, as they experience a lessened *perceived risk* of recognizing and acknowledging their attitudes and feelings, their *processes* for decision making are less burdened, and as A and B can be more effective in their *problem solving*;
   b. A and B consequently feel greater *psychological success* by mutually solving problems that stay solved without creating other problems;
   c. A and B become less *dependent* on formal superiors, and hence need concern themselves less with "tattling" or "not making waves."

CONCLUSION

Although data support the efficacy of one spin-off of sensitivity training, in sum, several points must be stressed by way of qualification. First, the data trends in Table 3 probably understate the power of the confrontation design. Briefly, the learning situation was very complex in the present case, desirable "closure" often was not possible when confrontations were held, and some mutually desired confrontations were not held because of lack of time. More favorable attitudinal changes should show up in cases where there are fewer loose ends.

Second, however, a variety of research is necessary to establish the specific conditions under which various consequences might be exected from applications of confrontation designs. For example, the results above strongly suggest one application was useful in modifying the attitudes of organization members. In turn, these *attitudinal changes* reasonably could be expected to facilitate *behavioral changes* that would (for example) improve degenerating communication sequences. No direct evidence about behavioral change is presented here, however, although various "soft" data strongly imply behavioral changes. For example, the history of the Core Groups was characterized by an excess of zeal, if anything. Specifically, some Core Groups attempted to engage in problem solving in areas beyond their jurisdiction, against which consultants had strongly cautioned and advised. Predictably, superiors in the broader control system restrained some of the Core Groups. That superiors did so, of course, suggests that the attitudinal changes summarized above did induce behavioral changes in at least some participants.

Third, the confrontation design seems widely applicable, but some potential host organizations are not culturally prepared for it. No doubt, most culturally unprepared organizations would be aware enough to avoid soliciting such an experience. But consultants still face a real responsibility of judging the preparedness of the host organizations and its personnel to profit from what is for most organizations a novel vehicle for exerting influence.

Should the consultant misjudge an organization's preparedness, however, the most probable damage is the loss of a useful opportunity for development. That is, the confrontation design includes a wide array of safety features. For example, the present design provided that only mutually willing Relevant Others would confront one another. Avoiding a confronatation perceived as dangerous or unprofitable would not be difficult, then. And members of an organization are very likely to avoid explosive situations. In addition, confrontation designs include a massive safety factor, the large number of points at which participants must make collaborative judgments about the degree of openness they are willing to risk. For example, the groups used in confrontation designs give each individual a range of resources which can advise against or support various statements in a 3-D Image. Elements of a 3-D Image are neither offered without conscious risk taking, in short, nor without testing for commitment. And that is intended by the design. For we only can really learn as we risk and make real commitments.

Safeguards also inhibit taking the easy ways out, of avoiding a confrontation or of weaseling in the preparation of images. That is, any group developing a 3-D Image will be alert to the design property that watering down their image so as to guarantee safety may invite ridicule as their image is compared unfavorably to image(s) developed by others. The derivative tension is very real and seems to result in a kind of escalation of truthfulness in which the relative merits of openness and closedness are very consciously weighed. As it should be, then, a major share of the responsibility for the success or failure of a confrontation design rests with members of the host organization. They are, after all, the ones who basically must live with the results.

Fourth, no particular skills are required of participants in a confrontation design, but skilled consultants should be provided each time images are actually shared. Such a resource person can intervene if things go badly. Far more likely, however, his particular usefulness lies in encouraging participants to confront each other at "deeper levels." Our original expectation was that consultants could intervene if (for example) a Basic Learning Aggregate began roughly confronting a "weak" individual. The only individuals confronted, however, were the top organizational officials. They required no aid, although consultants did intervene to point up what seemed to them defensive reactions by these officials during the sharing of the images.

14

The Anarchist Movement and the T-Group: Some Possible Lessons for Organizational Development

Bernard M. Bass
University of Rochester

Spanish anarchism was an extremely cohesive but ineffective movement espousing many of the ideals similar to those advanced in laboratory training. This paper argues that there may be some parallels between the history of Spanish anarchism and the contributions of T-Group training to organization development, if insufficient attention is paid to the organizational learning that must take place along with the personal and interpersonal learning of the T-Group experience. Eight approaches are described for increasing organizational learning in the context of laboratory training and follow-up.

Reprinted by permission from *Journal of Applied Behavioral Science*, III, No. 2 (1967), 211–27.

T-Group theorists often imply that what is good for an individual's mental health and maturity is good for the organization's well being. Therefore, they maintain that if we can train people to be better diagnosticians with greater tolerance and social awareness, organizations composed of such people will be the better for it. But this position may be as wrong as assuming that what is good for the organization is good for its members. Sensitivity training may be necessary for organizational development, but it is not sufficient. By itself, T-Grouping is not enough.

Consider the following experimental results: Nine quasi-T-Groups (T-Groups without trainers) met for 15 weeks as part of a graduate business management program. After another 15 weeks had passed, three of the nine groups were each splintered into three parts and the parts reassembled into three new teams. Three other groups were divided in half and reassembled as three new teams. Three groups were left intact. Then the teams competed for 15 weeks with one another in the Carnegie Tech Management Game. Interpersonal comfort, openness, familiarity, communication ease, and cohesiveness were greatest in the three intact groups, according to member ratings made five weeks after company operations began. Nevertheless, it was these three intact groups that lost an average of $5.37 million in the competition with the remaining splintered groups. The splintered groups broke even or made a good profit, on the average. Yet these splintered groups were less successful interpersonally, according to member descriptions. These firms were felt to be less cohesive and were seen as less open. Members were less familiar with one another and had more difficulty in communicating. But they were much more successful in operating as business firms. Why? We think the answer may lie in the tendency we observed for these financially successful groups to make better use of management controls that avoided too heavy reliance on interpersonal confidence.

In the intact groups, with better interpersonal feelings, members expected more from one another as persons than they could actually receive; and for 15 weeks, at least, they were unable to correct this error of overdependence on one another. For instance, one team member might ask another to complete a budget analysis in time for the company to use it to make an important buying decision. In the intact group, the team member who made the request was likely to expect that it had been done. In the fractured groups, the members were more likely to depend on formal controls to see that such action had been taken. And thus it was that the intact groups made many more forecasting errors, failed often to take advantage of discount opportunities, had more shortages or overstocked inventories, and so on (28). In many respects, the intact groups were reliving, in 15 weeks, a half century of the history of the Spanish anarchists.

The Spanish anarchists[1] were a primitive social movement, yet seem to have nurtured many of the values often stressed in a T-Group. Although the following

---

[1] I have relied heavily on Brenan (13) for the description and evaluation of Spanish anarchism presented here.

sounds like Bethel, 1967, it was written by the anarchist, Francisco Pi y Margall, a Catalan writer and politician of the mid-nineteenth century:

> True order supposes cohesion, yet not a cohesion obtained by the presence of exterior forces, but an intimate and spontaneous cohesion which external constraints inevitably inhibit. Every man who has power over another is a tyrant. . . . In place of power relationships which should be eliminated, there can develop a natural system of relationships in their stead.

As soon as the old social order was destroyed (or as T-Groupers might say, as soon as unfreezing had been accomplished), "then nature would cause new and better social organisms to arise to fill their place."

The anarchist emphasis on freedom of individuals and freedom of groups of individuals produced effects that may be seen in many an assembly of T-Groups. At a congress of anarchists, the delegates assembled with the wishes and capacities of the groups they represented carefully in mind. Each would get up and say what his group was prepared and able to do. No group was urged to take any action which it did not feel itself prepared to take. No group was ever overruled by another group or had pressure put on it to act against its private convictions. Similarly, no objections were raised to local groups' or individual members' cooperating with a particular proposal, if they desired to do so.

The Spanish anarchist movement was an attempt to recover the equality and dignity of the individual faced with the everincreasing complexities of modern industrialization. It was an expression of nostalgia for the past: a fight against the strain of factory life. To some degree, the T-Group experience is seen in a similar way by Schein and Bennis: "Laboratory training is singularly appropriate for dealing with some of the core crises facing contemporary society" (87, p.6). They add that for the individual, life has become more problematical. He is alienated, lonely, anxious, and desperately seeking purpose and identity. Presumably laboratory training can help, just as anarchism could help the individual to cope better with his industrial environment.

Nevertheless, 60 years of anarchist leadership brought to its members practically nothing. The movement was much more effective than the competing movement of socialism in creating a feeling of need for change, yet anarchism lacked the necessary programs for bringing it about (13).

Here, what may be a poor analogy ends. For the anarchists were intolerant of those who did not share their views. They were uncompromising, unsophisticated, and uninterested in social reform. They were a puritanical movement. They aimed to destroy modern society and had little to recommend in its place. Nevertheless, there may be some lessons to be learned from analyzing why they failed, lessons which may have implications for efforts to develop organizational effectiveness through T-Grouping. The anarchists always put individual freedom ahead of organizational necessities. This resulted in the organization's suffering one defeat after another, despite which it usually was stronger in cohesiveness after defeat than before. The anarchists insisted that their adherents remain free and unfettered, organized in local groups, and without bureaucratic ties. They emphasized the importance of the primary group and its individual members, and de-emphasized the formal organization, even to the point of providing no salaries or centralized financial resources for the movement's central leadership.

The anarchists represented a movement in which enthusiasm, interpersonal acceptance, mutual support, individual freedom, and cohesiveness of membership were maximized, yet where their effects on society were the reverse of what they had intended.[2]

The anarchists failed because they refused to accept supergroup goals, goals to which all or most of the local units could subscribe. They refused to accept building a formal organization to coordinate and direct the primary groups toward any such supergoals. This emphasis on freedom of the individual and the small group made it impossible to predict what others would do, which, in turn, made coordinated effort impossible. There was a refusal to submerge individual and small-group needs to advance organizational interests.

A second reason they failed, or more often had a reverse influence on the course of events, was the destructiveness of their unfreezing efforts. These aroused counterforces in reaction which were even stronger in support of reaction or the status quo.

It seems to me that both of these causes of failure in the anarchist movement may be present in laboratory training programs purporting to foster both individual as well as organizational development, for what may be good for individual growth may not always be good for the organization's health. If we wish to increase our understanding of how to optimize the development of the individual *and* the organization, it may be profitable to review the parallels between the ineffectiveness of the anarchist movement and what goes on in the training laboratory.

For example, the T-Group laboratory does in miniature what the anarchists attempted to do in macroscopic proportions. Unfreezing is accomplished in the laboratory by removing the familiar props and customary social mechanisms, by violating the expectations of trainees, and by creating an ambiguous, unstructured situation for them of unclear goals and minimum cues.

The staff is aware of the need to avoid patterns of dependence and counterdependence of staff with trainees. Yet this unfreezing process may foster feelings within some trainees that echo Bakunin, the founder of the anarchist movement, who declared: "All exercise of authority perverts and all submissiveness to authority humiliates." That is, given a severe, structureless experience, it may be that some laboratory participants lose their confidence to use authority which may

---

[2] This is not an unusual circumstance. There are many situations where a group's success at its tasks may be negatively related to its success in its interpersonal relations. For instance, the highly cohesive group may lack resources to cope with its tasks. Conversely, the group that is low in cohesion may be highly productive if the tasks are simple and the members are constrained from withdrawing by threat of punishment or promise of reward (7). Again, satisfactory interpersonal relations may be necessary in many circumstances for organizational productivity, but they are no guarantee of it.

be needed in the future for organizational reasons. This may be neither the intent of the program nor a ligical outcome, but it may occur just the same[3]. At the same time, there may be a correspondingly reduced acceptance of submissive behavior that may be necessary at times for the interests of good organization. In short, the "destruction" of the customary authority structure in the T-Group in order to promote exploration and change in the individual participants, coupled with an emphasis on the values of democracy and consensus, may produce, in some participants at least, sufficient antiauthoritarian leadership attitudes to reduce their contributions to the organization at times when such directive leadership is required.

Yet one can catalog many organizational circumstances in which shared, permissive leadership would be less effective and acceptable than more authoritarian approaches, such as when interaction in the organization between superior and subordinate is restricted by infrequent meetings or poor communications; in large groups, where the superior is in the center of a communication network; when higher authority or the marketplace imposes arbitrary deadlines; or where subordinates expect authoritative direction. The culture may require more directive leadership. Recently, in a classroom role-play I conducted in Spain, the participants rejected the democratic supervisor and showed preference for one who tried to persuade them. They felt the persuasive leader was according them the dignity to which they were accustomed. The democratic supervisor, since he did not try to change their minds, appeared to them to show less interest in them as persons.

T-Group theory emphasizes learning through discovery. It tends to ignore other powerful learning processes that may be going on simultaneously in the highly ambiguous setting where motivation is strong and coping behavior is vigorous and where reinforcement and fixation are unclear and uncertain to both staff and trainees. What is being reinforced and how and when it occurs may be unclear to both. Imitation, vicarious learning, incidental learning, and persuasion all may be operating in subtle directions counter to what is being learned through discovery. Despite these offsetting possibilities, T-Groups are effective training grounds. A reasonable amount of controlled research evidence by Bunker (16), by Miles (69), and by Boyd (11), among others, attests to the increased interpersonal competence, back on the job, of trainees that results from a laboratory experience. Just as important are the observable changes which are seen in the trainee's increased awareness of interpersonal dynamics. (Ask any trainer!)

Thus we have considerable evidence that the T-Group experience is likely to

---

[3] In one industrial laboratory, I recall overhearing some executives who were wandering around and muttering to themselves, "I must not be a leader. I must not be a leader!" Similarly, at the conclusion of another laboratory, many executives commented that they had removed their protective outer shells and were more open to experience than before but wondered whether, as a consequence, their confidence in themselves to play the authority figure "back home," as demanded, had been undermined.

increase a trainee's willingness, back in the organization, to try to foster mutual trust, shared decisions, and openness of communication. At the same time, the experience may decrease his willingness to withhold the release of information, to maintain social distance, or to make political alliances. Indeed, he may fail completely to recognize how differently he may need to behave when he is negotiating in the interests of his department or organization from when he is problem solving with others. Minimally, greater internal conflict and guilt feelings may be aroused in him when he is forced by organizational demands to adopt Machiavellian approaches.

There seems to be a generally accepted assumption that a considerable amount of frustration must be built up during the unfreezing process in the T-Group and that the greater this frustration, the greater will be the search for solutions to the dilemmas imposed on the trainees by the ambiguous situation. This is predicated on a homeostatic model. One must need or want to change before he will change; and the greater the felt need, the greater will be the change. But one wonders whether the learning process may be hindered rather than helped by this emphasis on a model of frustration-search-fixation, a model that may be more applicable to rats than to man. Counterdependent feelings may be raised that increase rather than decrease resistance to change. All too often the trainer may become a leadership model that may be inappropriate for the organization. While I do not suggest that trainers, in general, engender more hostile counterreactions by their role repertoire, it is possible that some, perhaps out of their own aggressive needs, do make a considerable effort to knock the past out of trainees and to arouse a great deal of frustration in them.

One wonders whether all or any of this preliminary frustrating experience is necessary. More learning might occur about process and interpersonal awareness by beginning the group with a task, say, an in-basket test or a review of an organization survey—this to be followed by a shared process analysis of the experience. What would be learned might have more direct relevance for organizational affairs. We would be dealing with "How am I doing?" in the context of a simulation of an organizational issue or in the context of real organizational problems rather than "How am I doing?" in my interpersonal relations as simulated by the T-Group of which I am a member. Less feeling might be aroused, but more significant learning might take place.

The question of goals which transcend the primary group goals in the laboratory often is given little emphasis. The paramount authority of the T-Group is stressed. Most of the reinforcement is given for agreements, compacts, and "ground rules" established within the T-Group. Participant responsibilities to the collectivity of T-Groups are secondary. As a consequence, the staff faces difficulties when one T-Group is ready for a lecture and another is not, or when one T-Group feels it wants more T-Group time and another does not.

Competitive intergroup exercises have focused attention, in some degree, on this issue of superordinate problems. With good reason, intergroup exercises focus on the dynamics of competition; for much is learned here about in-group behavior and attitudes toward out-groups. Occasionally in laboratories, organizational simulations are run that require the establishment of organizational goals to which the subordinate T-Groups must subscribe; but I do not think we have achieved equal success in creating for learning purposes such cooperating experiences as we have achieved in designing competing ones. Somehow, we are going to have to provide training experiences in which we develop the same socio-emotional intensity of commitment to laboratory as to the T-Group, then place these laboratory commitments in conflict with commitments to the T Group. This will require participants to deal with the common organizational experience of superordinate goals that conflict with department goals.

As it was among the anarchists, individual freedom is fostered in the T-Group laboratory, where "the delegate is free—and is encouraged—to question (and reject) all inputs from the staff or other delegates. Self-control. . . is vigorously sanctioned; delegates are viewed. . . as free agents, autonomous volunteers in the learning process" (87, p.33). This emphasis on freedom is not usually matched by an equally important emphasis on the need for individual responsibility which may constrain the individual. This need to restrict one's freedom to maintain a more responsible stance for the good of the organization is seldom seen in the laboratory situation. Most emphasis is likely to be placed on tolerance of others' needs and on individual liberty rather than on the need for individual responsibility. For instance, the laboratory will stress that an individual is free to accept or to reject ideas, that he is free to change or not to change, that he is free to take roles or not to take them. It will be less likely to stress that he also has the responsibility to communicate to others what he has accepted or rejected, his intentions to change, and his assumption of particular group tasks. That is, if we wish to promote *both* individual and organizational effectiveness, then we need to point out that if an individual member of an organization is given considerable discretion and freedom he, in turn, must make it possible for others to take account of his actions and changes of plans. He is not free to act without ensuring that others are aware of his changes of plans. Mutual predictability seems of paramount importance to the organization if coordinated effort is to be achieved, although it may be of less consequence to a given individual.

Other important organizational needs may be underplayed when they conflict with individual values. For instance, in the intergroup competition held in many laboratories, we see increased loyalty to one's own group and increased cohesiveness within one's group. The bias of members toward their own group's product is exposed. Members who might defect are prospective traitors. The need for greater objectivity under such circumstances is seen, but I doubt whether most trainers call attention to the other aspect of the situation; e.g., on occasion, such blind loyalty may have positive organizational value. Thus, if I shared a foxhole with a fellow soldier, I would prefer that he remain blindly loyal to our side in the midst of a fire fight rather than suddenly deciding that the other side had more merit and that he was going to switch sides.

Or, consider the question of tolerance for deviant opinion. Here again, from the organization's point of view, there is a need for a two-way give and take. The deviant has to have some sense for tolerating the majority opinion, just as the majority needs to be able to tolerate deviants if the organization is to prosper.

Where, in the laboratory experience, is much learned about when and where individual interests may need to be subordinated for reasons of organization? Where is much learned about how to cope with the need to protect individual interests without jeopardizing the interests of the organization?

Schein and Bennis (87) see the earlier emphasis on personal development (the yogi approach) as now being supplemented, in some degree, by concern for organizational development (the commissar approach). However, they do not seem to share with Pugh (78) the thought that the yogi approach may reduce the contribution and effectiveness of the individual to the organization. They seem to be more in agreement with Argyris (3), for whom interpersonal competence[4] is prerequisite to effective decision making, organizational flexibility, and freedom from defensiveness. Individual maturity is seen as essential for increasing organizational effectiveness. Pugh (78) is not so sure.

Pugh (78) assumes, rightly, that T-Group training, as such, is oriented toward increasing personal maturity and understanding. What happens, he asks, when the ex-T-Grouper returns to a mechanistic organization? Pugh is uncertain. It may be that such an organization calls for little initiative from the ex-T-Grouper and only a routine, shallow use of his skills, which results in his increased frustration and job dissatisfaction. Or it may be that the rigid, mechanistic system requires sophisticated personnel to operate it so that the increased perceptual sophistication of the ex-T-Grouper increases his effectiveness.

Similarly, returning to an organic structure may be easier or more difficult for the ex-T-Grouper. He may be called upon to display initiative in setting goals and in diagnosing social problems which he now can do more effectively. Or, to quote Pugh, he may be ruined; for in a fluid, organic situation "only an immature, job-centered bastard can insensitively hack his way to achievement."

Bamforth (5) abandoned a pure T-Group effort in a firm where the T-Groups were composed of "diagonal slices" of the organization so that no man was in the same T-Group with his boss or immediate subordinates. Among the inadequacies of this program, Bamforth cited:

1. T-Group discussion became a ventilation area. Yet the real boss-subordinate problems were not explored or dealt with effectively.
2. Role conflicts at work were perceived in the T-Group discussions but were left unresolved.
3. T-Group meetings did not result in corresponding work group meetings; i.e., there was no transfer.

---

[4] Giving and receiving nonevaluative feedback, owning up to one's feelings and attitudes, openness, experimenting, and helping others to experience their own attitudes.

In sum, as with the anarchist movement, the pure T-Group experience may generate a great deal of individual development. The T-Group may bring about increased commitment to social understanding, greater self-awareness, and greater acceptance of individuality. Yet collectives of such more "mature" individuals may make less effective organizations. Moreover, the process of such individual growth, paralleling the anarchistic ideology of unfreezing, may carry with it some byproducts of negative import to the individuals as effective members of an organization.

It is assumed that increased diagnostic skill and increased self-awareness are transferred from the T-Group experience back to the organization. Yet learning research clearly suggests that for such transfer to occur one must teach for transfer. In the past eight years or so, we have seen a considerable increase in attention to this need to teach for transfer, either by introducing learning experiences simulating important organizational issues or by increasing the similarlity to the real organization of the setting in which the training experience takes place. Direct evidence of the utility of increasing the similarity of the training group to the work group comes from an analysis by Morton (72). Six T-Groups of men from the same aerospace company, from different departments and levels (diagonal slices of the organization), were contrasted with six T-Groups where men in a given T-Group came from the same department, so that bosses and their subordinates were together in the same T-Groups. Six months after training, the latter groups reported significantly more critical incidents of effectiveness back on the job that were attributable to the T-Group experience.

At least eight different approaches are now being employed to increase the transfer of training.

A common laboratory practice is to gradually reduce time in T-Groups, as well as in lectures and exercises concerning individual and small-group behavior, during the course of a laboratory. In their place, the program substitutes exercises generating organizational phenomena and discussions about these phenomena. The exercises are an effort to provide quasi-real organizational experiences for participants for which they can profitably criticize both the content and the process. These exercises may be business games of various degrees of sophistication and complexity. They may be miniature representations of the participants' back-home, real organization. They may be replications of organizational experiments such as the Bavelas-Leavitt communication network experiment (8) or the Leavitt one-way versus two-way communications experiment (56). I have prepared a program of such exercises which can be sandwiched in between T-Group sessions. The exercises involve organizational issues such as the multiplicity of management budgeting goals, expectations and satisfaction, compensation, leadership style, planning versus operating, and collective bargaining (7). The important staff input in dealing with these organizational exercises is to motivate participants to examine the processes by which they were confronted rather than to remain fixed on the more seductive structural and economic contents of the problems. At any rate, these exercises give participants an opportunity to transfer the analytic approaches they have developed in T-Groups to simplified replicas of organizational situations, which process analyses they all can share in the here-and-now.

A second way of promoting organizational learning, using here-and-now experiences, is to confront the whole laboratory with real problems they have, as a laboratory. They might have to deal with a T-Group that never comes into theory sessions on time, which holds up all the others. Or the staff may ask each T-Group to subdivide or merge for specific purposes. Or the staff may ask members to rearrange themselves. A particularly strong socio-emotional experience can be engendered by a sort of "sociometry in motion," in which these rearrangements are made physically in one large room. Members literally have to get up and leave their own groups or call for the formation of new groups. Again, the learning comes not from the doing so much as from the analysis of what was done and how it was done.

A third approach picks up real organizational issues on which to work, using T-Group and laboratory structures which have developed earlier in the program. This requires that the T-Groups contain men who work together in the real organization and face together real problems back on the job. For example, in the Aerojet program (72), in each laboratory each of four T-Groups was composed of men from the same department. The last three days of the 10-day program provided opportunities for the T-Groups to form consulting teams (one man from each T-Group) similar to ones used earlier in the laboratory to consult on T-Group problems, but now made available to consult with the T-Groups on real work problems since, as all men within a T-Group were from the same department, they also could consult on real interdepartmental problems between T-Groups.

A fourth approach, which could begin during a laboratory or after it, organizes a continuing series of T-Groups to be held back home in the organization among men who must work together. An executive and his immediate subordinates might form such a continuing T-Group.

A fifth approach was pioneered by Bamforth (5) as a consequence of the failure of the within-plant T-Group members with whom he worked to transfer their learning to on-the-job problems. He dispensed with the T-Group experience altogether. He changed from the role of a T-Group trainer to that of a consultant to functioning, formal work-group meetings, where he helped the groups to recognize their boss-subordinate difficulties, anxieties about using or not using authority, colleague relations, role classifications, communications difficulties, resistance to the disclosure of initially unrecognized dynamics, and other sociopsychological problems.

In this approach, as a group works on its own real problems, the consultant slowly and gradually introduces process analysis of what is taking place, beginning possibly with some questions on how the group feels about its progress to date. The discussions about the group's performance may eventually move the group into a general program of education about group and organizational dynamics, using the group's own current experiences as the continuing basis for discussion and analysis (87).

Along lines similar to those developed by Bamforth, Friedlander (38) ran laboratory sessions for four work groups lasting four or five days. The work groups identified problems they faced and examined ways of solving them and implementing solutions. Interpersonal and intergroup processes affecting each work group were explored in this context.

In comparison with eight untrained groups, four work groups who received such training were found six months after training to describe themselves as more effective in problem solving, more mutually influential, and more involved in group meetings.

A sixth way combines several of the previously mentioned methods, again dispensing with the T-Group, per se. At International Mining, for instance, participants from the same real organizational group engage in a complex business game over an extended period of time. After each set of decisions has been completed, a formal session of process analysis is completed. Participants have an opportunity to examine their sociopsychological interplay when engaged in behavior simulating real behavior in an organization (107). The content of interaction among the trainees, who are an intact work group, is a simulation of real organizational problems. The process discussion gradually takes on T-Group qualities.

A seventh variant, employed by Matthew Miles (69), among others, is more directly focused on organizational improvement as the basis for work-group deliberations. The meetings of the group primarily concern the construction, development, and evaluation of an attitude survey of the organization for which the group is responsible. Such a group might consist of a department head, his four immediate assistants, and their subordinates. Again, staff personnel gradually focus attention on the processes for the organization as a whole.

Finally, Blake's managerial grid (10) represents still another approach that focuses a supervisor's attention on his own style of leadership and its likely effects on his contribution to his organization. The quasi-T-Group training aims to move the trainee to an optimum style of leadership and to help him see the effects of different styles of leadership on organizational performance.

These eight approaches all represent efforts to promote transfer of training. The more we can move in this direction, the more we are likely to increase the utility of laboratory methods for both personal and organizational improvement.

Thus it is that most of the recent organizational improvement programs, such as those of Esso, Pacific Finance, Space Technology Laboratory, Aluminum Company of Canada, U.S. Rubber, Hotel Corporation of America, General Electric, I.B.M., Eli Lilly, Hydro-Electric Commission of Canada, Beltone, and Aerojet-General. have involved much more than just T-Group training (87). And when one considers the newness of all these programs one cannot but feel that we are at the beginning of an era of exciting innovation in organizational psychology, an excitement not based on anarchistic destructiveness but resulting from creative developments and successes in the integration of individual and ororganizational well being.

From an organizational point of view, mere T-Grouping is not enough. Various supplementary activities which build upon the T-Group experience or take place in conjunction with T-Grouping or as substitutes for T-Grouping, in one way or another, need to be employed to promote organizational as well as individual learning and development. It should be clear that I still see the T-Group experience, or related approaches, as basic to organizational development. But as I stated in the introduction, T-Grouping is necessary but not sufficient.

Questioning
the Managerial Implications of Developing
Management and the Organization

1. Pym has outlined some pretty clear directions for an organization to take in overcoming the "traditional" change-resistant elements within itself. What are the implications for the individual manager who suddenly realizes that his attitudes and beliefs are in sharp conflict with those around him? Can management development bring about permanent change in the individual characteristics described by Pym, or is the deviant manager faced with either perpetual conflict or flight?

2. Do you agree with Patten's conclusion that aspiring managers must find their way into "critical" assignments before their potential managerial abilities can be meaningfully assessed?

3. What do Golembiewski and Blumberg mean when they say that some organizations are not "culturally prepared" for the confrontation design? How would you distinguish such an organization from one that would benefit from this technique?

4. How does the confrontation design fare in light of the criticisms of T-Grouping made by Bass?

5. Write the first paragraph to an article you have just decided to write entitled, "The Development of Managers and Organizations—An Interrelationship."

References

1. Adorno, W. T., *et al., The Authoritarian Personality.* New York: Harper & Row, Publishers, 1950.

2. Allen, L. A., *The Management Profession.* New York: McGraw-Hill Book Company, 1964.

3. Argyris, C., *Interpersonal Competence and Organization Effectiveness.* Homewood, Ill.: Irwin-Dorsey, 1962.

4. ——, *Understanding Organizational Behavior.* London: Tavistock, 1964.

5. Bamforth, K., "T-Group Methods Within a Company," in *ATM Occasional Papers,* vol. II, ed. G. Whitaker. Oxford, England: Basil Blackwell, 1965.

6. Barber, B., and R. C. Fox, "The Case of the Floppy-Eared Rabbits: An Instance of Serendipity Gained and Serendipity Lost," *American Journal of Sociology,* LXIV (1958), 129–36.

7. Bass, B. M., *"A Program of Exercises in Management and Organizational Psychology."* Pittsburgh: INSTAD, 1967.

8. Bavelas, A., "Communication Patterns in Task-Oriented Groups," *Journal of Acoustical Society of America,* XXII (1950), 725–30.

9. Berg, N., "Strategic Planning in Conglomerate Companies," *Harvard Business Review,* IIIL (1965), 91.

10. Blake, R. R., and J. S. Mouton, *The Managerial Grid.* Houston: Gulf Publishing Co., 1964.

11. Boyd, J. B., and J. Elliss, *Findings of Research into Senior Management Seminars.* Toronto: The Hydro-Electric Power Commission of Ontario, Personnel Research Department, 1962.

12. Braybrooke, D., "The Mystery of Executive Success Re-Examined," *Administrative Science Quarterly,* VIII (1964), 533–60.

13. Brenan, G., *The Spanish Labyrinth.* Cambridge: Cambridge University Press, 1943.

14. "Broadside at U. S. Management," *Business Week,* No. 1590 (1960), 129.

15. Brown, J. A. C., *The Social Psychology of Industry.* London: Penguin Books, 1954, p. 59.

16. Bunker, D. R., "The Effect of Laboratory Education upon Individual Behavior," in *Personal and organizational change through group methods,* eds. E. H. Schein and W. G. Bennis. New York: John Wiley & Sons, Inc., 1965.

17. Burck, G., "Management Will Never be the Same Again," *Fortune,* LXX (1964), 124–26, 199–204.

18. Burns, T., "The forms of conduct," *American Journal of Sociology,* LXIL (1958), 137–51.

19. ——, and G. M. Stalker, *The Management of Innovation.* London: Tavistock, 1961.

20. Cadwallader, M. L., "The Cybernetic Analysis of Change in Complex Social Organizations," *American Journal of Sociology,* LXV (1959), 154–57.

21. Chapman, J. F., "Thinking Ahead: Trends in Management Development," *Harvard Business Review,* XXXII (1954), 27–34, 159–66.

22. Churchman, C. W., "Managerial Acceptance of Scientific Recommendations," *California Management Review,* VII (1964), 36.

23. Collins, O. F., and D. G. Moore, *The Enterprising Man.* East Lansing: Michigan State University Press, 1964, pp. 25–27.

24. Cyert, R. M., and J. G. March, "Behavioral Theory of Organizational Objectives," in *Modern Organizational Theory,* ed. M. Haire. New York: John Wiley & Sons, Inc., 1959.

25. Dale, E., *Management: Theory and Practice.* New York: McGraw-Hill Book Company, 1965, pp. 300–12, 655–71.

26. ——, and L. F. Urwick, *Staff in Organization.* New York: McGraw-Hill Book Company, 1960.

27. Dalton, M., *Men who Manage.* New York: John Wiley & Sons, Inc., 1959, p. 20.

28. Deep, S. D., B. M. Bass, and J. A. Vaughan, "Some Effects of Business Gaming of Previous Quasi-T-Group Affiliations," *Journal of Applied Psychology,* LI, No. 5 (1967), 426–31.

29. Deutsch, K. W., "On Communication Models in the Social Sciences," *Public Opinion Quarterly,* XVI (1952), 356–80.

30. Dill, W. R., "The Manager as a Learner," in *Proceedings of the Eighteenth Annual Industrial Relations Research Association,* ed. G. G. Somers. Madison, Wis.: IRRA, 1965, pp. 68–75.

31. Dorsey, J. T., Jr., "A Communication Model for Administration," *Administrative Science Quarterly,* II (1957), 307–24.

32. Dubin, R., "Supervision and Productivity: Empirical Findings and Theoretical Considerations," in *Leadership and Productivity,* eds. R. Dubin, *et al.* San Francisco: Chandler Publishing Co., 1965, p. 17.

33. Dubin, R., and S. L. Spray, "Executive Behavior and Interaction," *Industrial Relations,* III (1964), 106.

34. Evans, W. M., "Organization Man and Due Process of Law," *American Sociological Review,* XXVI (1961), 540–47.

35. Fisch, G. G., *Organization for Profit.* New York: McGraw-Hill Book Company, 1964. pp. 240–48.

36. Fleishman, E. A., "The Description of Supervisory Behavior," *Journal of Applied Psychology,* XXXVI (1953), 1–6.

37. French, W., *The Personnel Management Process: Human Resources Administration.* Boston: Houghton Mifflin Company, 1964, pp. 498–516.

38. Friedlander, F., "The Impact of Organizational Training Laboratories upon the Effectiveness and Interaction of Ongoing Work Groups," China Lake, Calif.: Naval Ordnance Training Station.

39. Ginzberg, E., *Human Resources: The Wealth of a Nation.* New York: Simon and Schuster, Inc., 1958, p. 34.

40. ——, *What Makes an Executive?* New York: Columbia University Press, 1963.

41. Goldner, F. H., "Demotion in Industrial Management," *American Sociological Review,* XXX (1965), 714–24.

42. ——, "Managers—An Improper Subject for the Study of Management," in *Proceedings of the Eighteenth Annual Meeting, Industrial Relations Research Association,* ed. G. G. Somers. Madison, Wisc: IRRA, 1965, pp. 76–82.

43. Golembiewski, R. T., *The Small Group.* Chicago: University of Chicago Press, 1962.

44. ——, "The Laboratory Approach to Organization Change: The Schema of a Method," *Public Administration Review,* XXVI (1967), 211–21.

45. ——, and A. Blumberg, "Confrontation as a Training Design in Complex Organizations: Attitudinal Changes in a Diversified Population of Managers," *Journal of Applied Behavioral Science,* III (1967), 525–47.

46. ——, and ——, "Training and Rational Learning," *Training and Development Journal,* XXI (1967), 35–42.

47. Goode, W. J., and P. K. Hatt, *Methods in Social Research.* New York: McGraw-Hill Book Company, 1952, pp. 330–40.

48. Hotelling, H., "Simplified Calculation of Principal Components," *Psychometrica,* I (1935), 27–35.

49. Howton, F. W., "Work Participation Observations," *Administrative Science Quarterly,* VII (1963), 502–20.

50. Jaques, E., *Measurement of Responsibility.* London: Tavistock, 1956.

51. Kincaid, H. V., and M. Bright, "Interviewing the Business Elite," *American Journal of Sociology,* LXIII (1957), 304–11.

52. Koontz, H. D., and C. J. O'Donnell, *Principles of Management,* 3rd ed. New York: McGraw-Hill Book Company, 1964.

53. Kornhauser, A., *Mental Health of the Industrial Worker.* New York: John Wiley & Sons, Inc., 1965, p. 12.

54. Kornhauser, W., *Scientists in Industry.* Berkeley, Calif.: University of California Press, 1962.

55. Lazarsfeld, P., "Reflections on Business," *American Journal of Sociology*, LXV (1959), 1–31.

56. Leavitt, H. J., "Unhuman Organizations," *Harvard Business Review*, XL, No. 4 (1962), 90–98.

57. ——, "The Managers of Tomorrow," *Training Directors Journal*, XVII (1963), 45.

58. ——, and B. M. Bass, "Organizational Psychology," in *Annual Review of Psychology*, XV, ed. P. R. Farnsworth, 1964, 379–80.

59. ——, and T. L. Whisler, "Management in the 1980s," *Harvard Business Review*, XXXVI (1958), 41–48.

60. Leeds, R., and T. Smith, *Using Social Science Knowledge in Business and Industry.* Homewood, Ill.: Richard D. Irwin, Inc., 1963, pp. 24–26.

61. Lewis, R. F., *Management Uses of Accounting.* New York: Harper & Row, Publishers, 1961, p. 31.

62. Likert, R., *New Patterns of Management.* New York: McGraw-Hill Book Company, 1961.

63. March, J. G., and H. A. Simon, *Organizations.* New York: John Wiley & Sons, Inc., 1958.

64. Martin, N. H., "Differential Decisions in the Management of an Industrial Plant," *Journal of Business,* XXIX (1956), 249–60.

65. Maslow, A. H., "Deficiency Motivation and Growth Motivation," in *Nebraska Symposium on Motivation,* ed. M. Jones. Lincoln: University of Nebraska, 1955.

66. Mauser, F. F., *Modern Marketing Management.* New York: McGraw-Hill Book Company, 1961, pp. 10–11.

67. McGregor, D. M., *The Human Side of Enterprise.* New York: McGraw-Hill Book Company, 1960.

68. Merton, R. K., *et al., The Focused Interview.* Glencoe, Ill.: The Free Press, 1956.

69. Miles, M. B., "Learning Processes and Actions in Human Relations Training," in *Personal and Organizational Change through Laboratory Methods,* eds. E. H. Schein and W. G. Bennis. New York: John Wiley & Sons, Inc., 1965.

70. Miles, R. E., "Attitudes Toward Management Theory as a Factor in Managers' Relationships with their Superiors," *Academy of Management Journal,* VII (1964), 308–14.

71. Moos, S., "Automation: A Worker's Balance Sheet," *New Society,* August 6, 1964.

72. Morton, R. B., and B. M. Bass, "The Organizational Training Laboratory," *Training Directors Journal,* XVIII, No. 10 (1964), 2–18.

73. Patten, T. H., Jr., "Directions of Research in Industrial Sociology," *American Catholic Sociological Review,* XXIV (1963), 316–32.

74. ——, "Merit Rating: An Outmoded Personnel Concept?" *Hospital Administration,* VIII (1963), 26–38.

75. ——, "An Evaluation of the Marginal Man Concept in Industrial Sociology," *Social Science,* XL (1965), 11–21.

76. Porter, E. H., *Manpower Development.* New York: Harper & Row, Publishers, 1964, p. 74.

77. Powell, R. M., "How Men Get Ahead," *Nation's Business,* LII (1964), 56.

78. Pugh, D., "T-Group Training from the Point of View of Organizational Theory," in *ATM Occasional Papers,* vol. II, ed. G. Whitaker. Oxford, England: Basil Blackwell, 1965.

79. Pym, D., "Occupational Changes and Their Relations to Employee Satisfactoriness and Satisfaction" (Doctoral dissertation, University of London, 1965).

80. ——, "Identifying Some Characteristics of the Versatile Worker," *Occupational Psychology,* in press.

81. Randle, C. W., "How to Identify Promotable Executives," *Harvard Business Review,* XXXIV (1956), 122–34.

82. Roethlisberger, F. J., and W. J. Dickson, *Management and the Worker.* Cambridge: Harvard University Press, 1939, pp. 189–269.

83. Rogers, K., *Managers—Personality and Performance.* London: Tavistock, 1963.

84. Rokeach, M., *The Open and Closed Mind.* New York: Basic Books, Inc., Publishers, 1960.

85. Rubenstein, A. H., and C. Haberstroh, *Some Theories of Organization,* rev. ed. Homewood, Ill.: Irwin-Dorsey, 1966.

86. Schein, E. H., "Management Development as a Process of Influence," *Industrial Management Review,* II (1961), 59–77.

87. ——, and W. Bennis, *Personal and Organizational Change Through Laboratory Methods.* New York: John Wiley & Sons, Inc., 1965.

88. Schumpeter, J. A., *The Theory of Economic Development.* Cambridge: Harvard University Press, 1949, pp. 74–94.

89. Selznick, P., *Leadership in Administration.* Evanston, Ill.: Row, Peterson, 1958, pp. 31–38, 134–54.

90. Shepard, C. R., "Orientations of Scientists and Engineers," *Pacific Sociological Review,* XLII (1961), 79–83.

91. Shepard, H. A., "Patterns of Organization for Applied Research and Development," *Journal of Business,* XXXIX (1956), 52–58.

92. ——, "Superiors and Subordinates in Research," *Journal of Business,* XXXIX (1956), 261–67.

93. ——, "Engineers as Marginal Men," *Journal of Engineering Education,* IIIL (1957), 534 ff.

94. ——, "Organic and Mechanistic Models of Organization," paper presented at Esso Laboratories, Bayway, N. J., 1959.

95. Shils, E. B., *Automation and Industrial Relations.* New York: Holt, Rinehart & Winston, Inc., 1963, p. 271.

96. Simon, H. A., *Administrative Behavior,* 2nd ed. New York: The Macmillan Company, 1961, pp. 80–81.

97. Sims, J. H., "Thinking Ahead: Power Tactics," *Harvard Business Review,* XXXIV (1956), 25–36.

98. Sofer, C., "The Assessment of Organizational Change," *Journal of Management Studies,* I (1964), 128–42.

99. Sonthoff, H., "What is the Manager?" *Harvard Business Review,* XIIL (1964), 24–36, 188.

100. Spencer, P., and C. Sofer, "Organizational Change and its Management," *Journal of Management Studies,* I (1964), 26–47.

101. Stark, S., "Research Criteria of Executive Success," *Journal of Business,* XXXII (1959), 1–14.

102. Strauss, A. L., "Patterns of Mobility Within Industrial Organizations," *Journal of Business,* XXIX (1956), 101–10.

103. Strauss, G., "Work-Flow Friction, Interfunctional Rivalry, and Professionalism: A Case Study of Purchasing Agents," *Human Organization,* XXXIII (1964), 144.

104. Suojanen, W. W., "Management Theory: Functional and Evolutionary," *Academy of Management Journal,* VI (1963), 7–17.

105. Taylor, H., *The Statesman.* New York: New American Library, Inc., 1958, pp. 109 ff.

106. Urwick, L. F., *The Elements of Administration.* New York: Harper & Row, Publishers, 1943.

107. Wagner, A. B., "The Use of Process Analysis in Business Decision Games, *Journal of Applied Behavioral Science,* I, No. 4 (1965), 387–408.

108. Whyte, W. F., "Toward an Integrated Approach for Research in Organizational Behavior," in *Proceedings of the Sixteenth Annual Meeting, Industrial Relations Research Association,* ed. G. K. Somers. Madison, Wisc.: IRRA, 1963, pp. 2–20.

109. Woodward, J., *Industrial Organization Theory and Practice.* New York: Oxford University Press, 1965.

Managing
Attitudes

Employee attitudes can be assessed in many ways: by interviews, polls, attitude scales, and disguised projective and objective measures. Regardless of technique used, many reported analyses suggest that a small set of factors accounts for the differences among employees in how satisfied they report themselves to be. These include satisfaction with supervision, working conditions, opportunities for personal development, material benefits, and the organization as a whole. In the readings that follow we look at a few of these factors, and consider the effect of attitudes on motivation and job performance.

In the first article, Klein and Maher examine the expectations and satisfactions of college educated and non-college educated managers. They discover that the college educated manager begins his first job with a higher expectation of success and salary level than his less educated colleague. Dissatisfaction results when this manager learns that, although he is to receive a higher salary than the non-college graduate, the actual level is not commensurate with what he feels he is worth.

Gruenfeld examines a quite different shaper of expectations—personality needs. He emerges with a clear relationship between personality variables, expected benefits from training, and reported benefits from training. The results offer striking implications for the planning and conduct of management development programs.

The Sykes study differs in methodology from each of the first two articles. He describes an effort to change the hostile attitudes of workers which are rooted in stereotypes of their foreman based on traditionally, but false, perceptions. The rather impressive results achieved point to the value of self-analysis in overcoming prejudicial stereotypes.

The most pragmatic, yet perhaps most controversial, analyses of attitudes have dwelt upon the nature of the link between attitudes, motivation, and job performance. Porter and Lawler examine this relationship in depth. They integrate their findings into recommendations to top management for the proper assessment and understanding of the impact of attitudes in the work place.

15

Educational Level, Attitudes, and Future Expectations Among First-Level Management

Stuart M. Klein
University of Kentucky

John R. Maher
International Business Machines Corporation

Reprinted by permission from *Personnel Psychology*, XXI, No. 1 (1968), 43–53.

BACKGROUND OF THE STUDY

Because of the increasing number of individuals attending college prior to entering the nation's labor force, the need to understand the nature and dynamics of the relationship between education and job-related attitudes is rapidly becoming more urgent. In a recent study dealing with this problem (12), the following results were reported:

1. Managers who have attended college tend to be less satisfied with their pay than managers who have not attended college.

2. Compared to managers who have not attended college, college-educated managers tend to be more optimistic about their chances of getting their present salary at another company, but they tend to be less optimistic about making more money on their present job.

3. When internal and external optimism are controlled for, the differences between college-educated and non-college educated managers are considerably attenuated, especially in terms of satisfaction with pay "considering duties and responsibilities."

These findings were interpreted to be primarily a result of discrepancy between a person's previous expectations about his salary and his actual salary at present. Expectations, moreover, were assumed to be a function of what the individual considers to be relevant characteristics brought to the job, e.g., a college education. This interpretation draws heavily on equity theory (1) and, if correct, leads to predictions about other job-related attitudes among college-educated managers.

Presumably, higher education is perceived to be an important job input by the individual possessing it; thus it follows that, if college-educated managers see themselves as receiving the same treatment as managers who have not attended college, they will perceive some degree of inequity and be relatively dissatisfied with certain aspects of their job, i.e., those which are considered most relevant by the individual. While our last study focused exclusively on satisfactions with salary, here we will be extending this focus to include other common job outcomes, namely, (1) benefits, (2) immediate manager, (3) job, and (4) higher management. In addition, we have attempted to discover what differences, if any, exist regarding expectations about future inputs and outcomes between those individuals who have attended college and those who have not.

THEORY AND HYPOTHESES

Equity theory predicts that if the individual perceives some aspect of himself as being a relevant input to his job, this perception will influence his expectations of how much he will contribute and what he will receive in return for this contribution. Moreover, the more valuable he perceives a given input to be, the greater he will see his contribution as being and the greater will be the resulting outcomes he expects. If the expectations of the person regarding his outcomes are fulfilled, he then should perceive a situation of equity. If, on the other hand, these expectations are not fulfilled, feelings of inequity and dissatisfaction should result. Education, then, may function in two related ways. First, it may be perceived as a relevant input when the individual assesses what he brings to the job, and, secondly, because of this, it may affect the individual's expectation of his contribution to the job.

If we assume (1) that college education is perceived as a relevant input, and (2) that expectations about the future are primarily a function of this input, two interesting derivations follow. First of all, college-educated managers should expect to contribute more to their company than will non-college educated managers. Secondly, holding job level constant, college educated managers should be less satisfied with their job outcomes than will non-college educated managers.

PRESENT STUDY

One of these job outcomes—salary—has already been shown to be less favorably received by the college-educated than by the non-college educated (12). In this study we will focus on other job characteristics that may be considered job outcomes. As mentioned before, these are benefits, job itself, and satisfaction with immediate manager and higher management. Other areas of job satisfaction that have been identified, such as working conditions or co-workers (21), are not included in this study because we have no measurement of them. The present study was conducted by doing further analysis of the survey data used in our previous research on education level and satisfaction with pay. The respondents are all first-level managers in the electronics manufacturing division of a large manufacturing concern. While some manage direct labor departments and others supervise support labor, all are directly involved with the manufacturing operation. The population contains both college educated and non-college educated individuals, all of whom hold jobs at approximately the same level in the organization. Altogether we were able to obtain data from 727 such managers.

The instrument used to collect data was a 426-item questionnaire, which was administered on company time. The questionnaire was anonymous, and the subjects were assured that their responses would be reported only in terms of group results. Most respondents spent approximately two hours completing the questionnaire.

VARIABLES

The variables, together with the questionnaire items used to measure them, are listed on the next page.

1. Expectations of inputs and outcomes
   a. Expected contribution to the company (input)
      Question: Over the long haul, what do you think the chances are of your having the opportunity to help the company build its reputation as a first-class organization?
   b. Expected salary increases (outcome)
      Question: Over the long haul, what do you think the chances are of your receiving better than average salary increases?
   c. Expected advancement (outcome)
      Question: Over the long haul, what do you think the chances are of your advancing to a policy-making position in management?

These three items all utilized an 11-point scale, with possible responses ranging from 0 ("I definitely will not") to 10 ("I definitely will"). Thus the higher the score on these items, the higher (or more optimistic) the expectation in question.

2. Satisfaction with present outcomes
   a. Satisfaction with benefits
      Question: How would you rate your employee benefits?
   b. Satisfaction with immediate manager
      Question: How good a job is being done by your immediate manager?
   c. Satisfaction with top local management
      Question: How good a job is being done by top local management?

These three questions had five response categories varying from 1—"Very good" to 5—"Very poor." Thus, the lower the score the more favorable the response.

   d. Satisfaction with job
      Question: How would you say your job measures up to what you want in a job?

This question had response categories ranging from 0—"Very poorly" to 10—"Extremely well." Thus the higher the score the more favorable the response.

3. Education
   Question: How much education have you had?

There were six categories ranging from grade school to graduate degree (master's or doctorate). Subjects were grouped according to whether they had attended (not necessarily graduated from) college or not.

4. Age
   Question: How old are you?

There were eight categories ranging from "Under 25" to "60 or older." Those 40 and above were considered "older" and those under 40 were considered "younger."

5. Skill level
   Question: What is the average job code level of the people you supervise?

There were six ranges of code levels scaled in ascending order. Subjects were assigned to "higher" or "lower" skill levels according to whether they indicated the upper three or the lower three in response to this item.

Age and skill level are included in the analysis because of their strong tendency to correlate with education and also with salary in the sample population. Thus it was necessary to use the latter two items as controls in order to make certain that any significant results could be unequivocally attributed to the effects of education rather than some other demographic factor.

The method of analysis used here differs from that in our previous paper, where we were forced to employ a series of *t*-tests or chi-square analyses. A recently developed [IBM] 7090 series program now permits us to do analysis of variance on the data, taking into account the disproportionate number of observations in each cell and the possible violation of the assumption of orthogonality of the data. *F* ratios were computed using the general linear hypothesis model, of which the typical equal *n* analysis of variance is a special case. This method of analysis allows us more control over the possible confounding effects of the age and skill level parameters.

RESULTS

The results shown in Table 1 clearly confirm the first hypothesis that college-educated managers expect to contribute significantly more to their company than do non-college managers. The education main effect is significant at the 0.01 level of confidence, while none of the interactions involving education approaches statistical significance. This finding lends support to the assumption that higher education is in fact perceived as a relevant job input since its possessors believe themselves to be of more value to their organization than do those without it.

TABLE 1
EXPECTED CONTRIBUTION TO THE COMPANY

	Cell Means			
	College		Non-College	
	Under 40	40 or older	Under 40	40 or older
High Skill	7.49 ($N = 153$)	6.98 ($N = 83$)	6.83 ($N = 69$)	6.01 ($N = 70$)
Low Skill	7.36 ($N = 39$)	7.50 ($N = 16$)	6.98 ($N = 56$)	7.03 ($N = 124$)

Analysis of Variance		
Source	*F*	*p*
Education	7.88	<0.01
Age	1.66	N.S.
Skill	3.17	N.S.
Education × Age	0.19	N.S.
Education × Skill	0.79	N.S.
Skill × Age	2.97	N.S.
Education × Age Skill	0.06	N.S.

The data concerning optimism about future outcomes (Tables 2 and 3) are less clear-cut. Table 2 shows that education is siginificantly related to perceptions of future salary increases and the college-educated managers are actually more optimistic in this regard than are their non-college counterparts. However,

TABLE 2
EXPECTED SALARY INCREASES

	Cell Means			
	College		Non-College	
	Under 40	40 or older	Under 40	40 or older
High Skill	6.55 ($N = 154$)	6.33 ($N = 82$)	5.83 ($N = 70$)	5.83 ($N = 69$)
Low Skill	6.74 ($N = 38$)	6.63 ($N = 16$)	6.04 ($N = 57$)	6.19 ($N = 124$)

Analysis of Variance		
Source	F	p
Education	7.96	<0.01
Age	0.05	N.S.
Skill	1.59	N.S.
Education × Age	0.34	N.S.
Education × Skill	0.01	N.S.
Skill × Age	0.11	N.S.
Skill × Age × Skill	0.00	N.S.

TABLE 3
EXPECTED ADVANCEMENT

	Cell Means			
	College		Non-College	
	Under 40	40 or older	Under 40	40 or older
High Skill	3.81 ($N = 125$)	4.16 ($N = 70$)	4.07 ($N = 60$)	4.19 ($N = 63$)
Low Skill	4.36 ($N = 33$)	5.00 ($N = 16$)	4.63 ($N = 57$)	5.00 ($N = 120$)

Analysis of Variance		
Source	F	p
Education	0.32	N.S.
Age	2.26	N.S.
Skill	7.88	<0.01
Education × Age	0.25	N.S.
Education × Skill	0.00	N.S.
Skill × Age	0.30	N.S.
Education × Age × Skill	0.00	N.S.

education appears to have little effect on the perceived possibility of advancing to a high-level position in management, as is evident in Table 3.[1]

TABLE 4
SATISFACTION WITH BENEFITS

	Cell Means			
	College		Non-College	
	Under 40	40 or older	Under 40	40 or older
High Skill	1.39 ($N = 154$)	1.51 ($N = 83$)	1.69 ($N = 70$)	1.65 ($N = 69$)
Low Skill	1.39 ($N = 38$)	1.75 ($N = 16$)	1.54 ($N = 57$)	1.80 ($N = 126$)

Analysis of Variance		
Source	F	p
Education	6.05	<0.05
Age	7.61	<0.01
Skill	0.91	N.S.
Education × Age	1.02	N.S.
Education × Skill	0.80	N.S.
Skill × Age	4.08	<0.05
Education × Age × Skill	0.06	N.S.

TABLE 5
SATISFACTION WITH JOB

	Cell Means			
	College		Non-College	
	Under 40	40 or older	Under 40	40 or older
High Skill	7.12 ($N = 154$)	6.10 ($N = 83$)	6.59 ($N = 70$)	5.78 ($N = 69$)
Low Skill	7.66 ($N = 38$)	6.19 ($N = 16$)	6.61 ($N = 57$)	6.30 ($N = 125$)

Analysis of Variance		
Source	F	p
Education	4.86	<0.05
Age	20.09	<0.01
Skill	2.16	N.S.
Education × Age	2.94	N.S.
Education × Skill	0.01	N.S.
Skill × Age	0.00	N.S.
Education × Age × Skill	1.38	N.S.

---

[1] While the statistical significance of variables other than education in Tables 3, 4, 5, and 7 is most interesting, such results are not directly relevant to our major line of investigation, and hence they will not be included in the discussion section.

TABLE 6
SATISFACTION WITH IMMEDIATE MANAGER

	College		Non-College	
	Under 40	40 or older	Under 40	40 or older
High Skill	1.87 (N = 156)	1.99 (N = 83)	2.18 (N = 71)	2.17 (N = 70)
Low Skill	1.97 (N = 39)	2.31 (N = 16)	2.20 (N = 56)	2.18 (N = 126)

Cell Means

Analysis of Variance

Source	F	p
Education	2.56	N.S.
Age	1.38	N.S.
Skill	1.52	N.S.
Education × Age	1.71	N.S.
Education × Skill	1.21	N.S.
Skill × Age	0.36	N.S.
Education × Age × Skill	0.37	N.S.

TABLE 7
SATISFACTION WITH HIGHER LOCAL MANAGEMENT

	College		Non-College	
	Under 40	40 or older	Under 40	40 or older
High Skill	1.87 (N = 156)	1.98 (N = 82)	2.03 (N = 70)	2.20 (N = 70)
Low Skill	2.00 (N = 39)	2.19 (N = 16)	2.11 (N = 59)	2.30 (N = 126)

Cell Means

Analysis of Variance

Source	F	p
Education	3.45	N.S.
Age	4.15	<0.05
Skill	2.58	N.S.
Education × Age	0.05	N.S.
Education × Skill	0.27	N.S.
Skill × Age	0.10	N.S.
Education × Age × Skill	0.03	N.S.

The data clearly do not support the second hypothesis (Tables 4, 5, 6, and 7). The college-educated are more satisfied with benefits and with the job itself and there is no statistically significant difference between the college and non-college populations on satisfaction with immediate or top-level management.

DISCUSSION AND CONCLUSIONS

Several things are apparent from these results. First of all, college-educated managers expect to contribute more to the business over the long haul, but this contribution may be independent of their advancement to a "policy-making" position. Apparently these managers do perceive education as a relevant input to their job performance and, because of this, see themselves as contributing more to the company than their non-college educated counterparts even though the objective skill level and experience are approximately equal across the comparison groups.

Secondly, college-educated managers do not manifest dissatisfaction toward the job outcomes we have dealt with, with the exception of salary. In fact, they appear to be more satisfied with their job and with their benefits. Thus, it would appear that, for our population, the most relevant job-rated outcome in terms of predicting perceived inequity is that of salary. Outcomes such as the job itself or benefits apparently are not part of the equation that the college-educated man uses when comparing the ratio of his inputs and outcomes to that of his non-college educated counterpart.

There is one finding of the present study that is not entirely consistent with our previous results. While managers who have attended college are more pessimistic about getting more money on their present jobs, they are more optimistic about their long-terms salary prospects. It is unlikely that this finding is simply a result of college managers expecting to "go farther" in the company than non-college managers since Table 3 indicates that, with respect to high-level positions, this is not the case.

It appears that the respondent is using different reference points in answering the two questions pertaining to future salary prospects. Specifically, when asked about his chances of making more money on his present job, he is asked to make an evaluation ranging from "Very good" to "Very poor." This evaluation is based only partly on the absolute level of money he expects. More importantly, it is based on this level compared to an ideal level of where he feels he should be. If education is a relevant input, then it follows that the college-educated manager will rate salary increments that are roughly equal to his non-college educated counterpart as less good since he brings more to the job than his counterpart. However, when asked to rate the probability of his receiving "better than average" salary increases, he is reporting something that is more objectively based. Since college-educated managers do get somewhat larger salary increases than the non-college manager, it appears that he is responding factually to this item.

To summarize, the college-educated manager appears to come into his job expecting to contribute heavily to the success of his company, and at the same time expecting to receive rewards commensurate with his contribution. Even though his salary outcomes are in reality greater than those of managers without college educations, and are perceived by him as such, they apparently do not measure up to what he expects his education and talents are worth, and hence he is relatively dissatisfied with his salary. While his dissatisfaction does not generalize to other areas of satisfaction, these results strongly suggest that company representatives and recruiters should make every effort to provide potential manager trainees with information which will be useful in generating realistic expectations about a prospective job, in order to avoid morale problems that may occur when expectations and reality fail to coincide.

16

Personality Needs and Expected Benefits from a Management Development Program

Leopold W. Gruenfeld
Cornell University

A questionnaire prepared by Viteles for a study of the Institute of Humanistic Studies at the University of Pennsylvania (20) supplied a number of these objectives. The author expresses his gratitude to Dr. Viteles for allowing the use of his questionnaire in preparing his own. Other objectives were culled from the literature. Reprinted by permission of the editor from *Occupational Psychology* [XL (1966), 75–81], quarterly journal of the National Institute of Industrial Psychology, 14 Welbeck Street, London, W1M 8DR.

INTRODUCTION

The effectiveness of formalized educational programs is only in part due to the content of the program or the pedagogical techniques employed. Personality, motivation, and ability of participants also affect the program's impact. These latter factors are particularly pertinent when the participants do not actively and voluntarily seek out the program. Many executives arrive at university-sponsored management development programs because they were encouraged or even ordered by their employer to attend. They arrive with a variety of needs, expectations, and motivations which undoubtedly influence the effectiveness of the programs.

Several plausible relationships are apparent. The first is that participants who do not expect to derive benefit are not likely to do so, perhaps because they do not experience a need for change.

The second is that those individuals who are generally resistant to change will resist change in a particular program. Mahler (16) suggested that theory and research in management development should be related to what is known about this "resistance to change." The importance of such a relation receives considerable support from an exhaustive review of research by House (9) which showed that personality variables usually associated with individual resistance to change do account for some of the "effectiveness" of a variety of management development programs. The results of House's review overlapped with the findings of small group experiments on attitude change by Hovland, Janis, and Kelley (10).

It was the major purpose of this study (1) to examine the relationships among expectations, personality, and benefit from a management development program, and (2) to account systematically for these findings and to suggest their practical implications. The specific content of this study is best described by the following hypotheses.

HYPOTHESES

If an individual experiences a need for change, he feels inadequate. Hovland (10) has found that individuals who feel inadequate are more likely to change their attitudes and opinions than those individuals who feel secure. If the observation by Hovland is generalizable, it would follow that:

HYPOTHESIS 1   Participants who feel relatively inadequate will report more benefit from a management development program than those individuals who feel relatively adequate.

Measure of adequacy: The abasement scale of the Edwards Personal Profile (EPPS) (8) is an appropriate measure of the lack of adequacy.

It follows from the above that:

HYPOTHESIS 2 Participants in a program who experience need for change because they feel inadequate will expect to derive relatively more benefit from the program than those who experience little need for change because they feel relatively adequate.

Measure of expectation: A questionnaire was administered prior to exposure to the program to elicit expectations of benefit.

Furthermore,

HYPOTHESIS 3 Participants in a program who expect to derive more benefit from the program will report more benefit than those who do not expect much.

The above hypotheses were designed to test the proposition that perceived benefit from a formalized educational experience is in part a result of feelings of inadequacy and associated need for change and expectations of improvement.

Hovland identified another pertinent pattern: interpersonal hostility and its complement, social withdrawal, are usually associated with resistance to change. He suggests that "... It is difficult to discriminate sharply between overt aggressiveness and social withdrawal tendencies, both of which may be manifest by generalized attitudes of indifference toward others." These observations suggest the following hypotheses:

HYPOTHESIS 4 Participants who have strong needs for the overt expression of hostility toward others will report less benefit from the program than those who are low in need for overt expression of hostility toward others.

Measure of hostility toward others: The "aggression" scale of the EPPS is an appropriate measure of hostility toward others.

HYPOTHESIS 5 Participants who have strong needs for social withdrawal are less likely to report benefit than those who have strong needs for affiliation with others.

Measure of social withdrawal: The "affiliation" scale of the EPPS is an appropriate measure of the *inverse* of the need for social withdrawal.

Still another pattern was identified by House: an inverse relationship exists between benefit from management development programs and authoritarianism as measured by the F-scale. However, questions have recently been raised about the validity of the F-scale (18), whose critics suggest that it merely records the willingness of individuals to agree or disagree with attitude items and is therefore essentially a measure of response set. If this criticism is correct, there should be a positive relationship between the F-scale and reports of benefit from the program because the item format on both measures is identical. Such a finding would reflect adversely upon our measure of benefit. However, in view of House's report and our original intent it was predicted that:

HYPOTHESIS 6 Individuals high in authoritarianism will report less benefit from the program than those who score relatively low in authoritarianism.

In addition to the above-mentioned variables we also included for analysis the remaining scales of the EPPS (see Table 1), age and education.

DESCRIPTION OF THE PROGRAM

The Wabash Institute for Personal Development (WIPD) is a five-year program in the liberal arts for executives in business and industry. The content of the seminars, lectures, and readings relies equally upon the subject matter of the humanities, social and physical sciences. Faculty consists of regular staff members of the college. Formal instruction occurs during a period of ten weeks spread over five summers. By means of a developmental counseling program, participants also plan a program of reading and other activities to fit their own personal needs for the interim periods between summer sessions.

Although this particular program of management development differs from the more traditional "human relations," "sensitivity," and "problem-solving" programs in approach, it is similar to all these programs in terms of processes. First, most of the problems dealt with concern human behavior, interpersonal relations and the impact of society on the individual. Second, each participant has a number of opportunities to present his ideas, beliefs, and attitudes to the group. His ideas are evaluated by the group, he is asked to defend them, he is made aware of other alternatives, and he sees his influence fail or succeed. In other words, he receives immediate feedback on his attempts to influence without the protection of formally legitimated power. These programs provide both leadership and followership experiences, with opportunities for the participant to gain insight into his ability to influence others. Third, the educational part of the WIPD program is accompanied by personal counseling. Here the participants have an opportunity to reflect upon their values, to receive feedback from tests and questionnaires, to identify strengths and weaknesses, and to plan ameliorative actions. They bring up problems of family and work relationships. They have opportunities to discuss problems of transferring learned material and insights to their work environments.

The WIPD program approaches similar problems through different material content than do the traditional management development programs. It shares with similar programs the assumption that it can improve the effectiveness of an individual's behavior as a citizen and hopefully also as an executive.

METHODS AND PROCEDURES

MEASURE OF BENEFIT

A summated rating scale was designed to elicit reports of perceived improvement. Each of 71 items in the scale consisted of the description of an objective claimed for programs of this kind. Participants were asked to rate for each item the degree of improvement (or deterioration) they could attribute to the influence of WIPD.

A factor analysis of the total questionnaire revealed five major item clusters (factors), each one accounting for approximately 20 percent of the total variance. However, factor scores correlated substantially with each other (ranging from 0.06 to 0.90) as well as with total score on the questionnaire (0.75 to 0.88), warranting the conclusion that participants completed the instruments under a general evaluative set. Consequently, it was decided to use the total score of the 71-item questionnaire as the dependent variable.

The item content of the questionnaire is best summarized by the results of the factor analysis which showed clusterings of items about the following areas: (1) interest in subject matter content and improvement in (2) interpersonal sensitivity, (3) oral and written communication, (4) problem solving, and (5) insight into self.

The split half reliability for the total questionnaire consisting of 71 items was 0.98 ($N = 100$). It should be noted that 100 percent of the participants completed the questionnaire.

PERSONALITY MEASURES

The present study began after two groups ($N = 27$) had completed five years in the program. It was considered unfeasible to administer the personality instruments by mail; so of the remaining four groups ($N = 73$) 44 participants completed the EPPS and the *F*-scale and 32 completed the intelligence test. These instruments were administered on an individual basis in connection with the developmental counseling program on a voluntary basis. There is good reason to believe that under these auspices participants were motivated to give honest responses.

MEASURE OF EXPECTATION

The 71-item evaluation questionnaire was also administered to two incoming groups of 40 participants prior to exposure to the program with instructions to complete each item on the questionnaire in terms of improvement *expected*. After one year of participation in the program one of these groups ($N = 15$) completed the questionnaire again, this time in terms of perceived benefit. These two groups were not a part of the original sample of 100. They expected to be in the program for three instead of five years.

STATISTICAL PROCEDURE

The perceived benefit scores were positively affected by time spent in the program: in general, the longer an individual participated in the program, the higher his perceived benefit score. Therefore, average partial correlations were obtained (holding time constant) by correlating each personality measure with the questionnaire scores for each group, and obtaining an average coefficient of correlation across all groups after appropriate conversion to *Z*-scores.

THE SAMPLE

The participants in this program represented primarily the middle management strata from a variety of manufacturing, financial, insurance, and public utility corporations. Their ages ranged from 22 to 48. All subjects had finished high school, and approximately 60 percent had completed college. The number of individuals who completed the respective personality instruments is shown in Table 1.

RESULTS

MAIN FINDINGS

Table 1 shows the correlations of perceived benefit and expected benefit with several personality variables. The average correlation between perceived benefit from WIPD and abasement, the measure of inadequacy, is 0.41 ($p < 0.01$) in the predicted direction. Participants who are relatively high in abasement, and therefore are presumed to feel inadequate, report more benefit from the program than participants relatively low in abasement. Furthermore, the correlation between abasement and expected benefit, a measure that was obtained prior to participation in the program, is 0.33 ($p < 0.05$) in the predicted direction. In addition, the correlation between expected and perceived benefit based on a group of 15 participants is 0.65 ($p < 0.01$) in the predicted direction.

These findings converge to warrant the conclusion that those individuals who do not expect to benefit do not perceive benefit upon exposure. Moreover, those individuals who feel inadequate both expect and perceive more benefit than their relatively self-confident peers, because they are more likely to experience need for change and improvement. These findings clearly support the first three hypotheses, which were based on the notion that participants who expect to derive benefit are likely to do so because they experience a need for change.

Focusing now on the remaining hypotheses, which were designed to test the more general presumption that those participants whose personality and needs predispose them to resist change will report less benefit, we find the data in Table 1 consistent with predictions albeit not unequivocally as predicted. First, those participants who are indifferent toward others are less likely to report benefit from this program. Table 1 shows the average correlation between perceived benefit from the program and aggression, which is -0.29 ($p < 0.05$) in the direction predicted by hypothesis 4, although the magnitude of this relationship is relatively low. Participants who need to express hostility toward others (those who have previously been found to resist influence attempts and change) report less benefit from this program than those relatively low in this need.

Second, the correlation between perveived benefit and need for affiliation, a measure of the inverse of social withdrawal, is 0.25 ($p < 0.05$) in the direction predicted by hypothesis 5, but not statistically significant by conventional standards.

The correlation between perceived benefit from WIPD and authoritarianism (*F*-scale) is essentially zero. Participants who measure relatively high in authoritarianism report neither more nor less benefit from the program than those who score low in authoritarianism. This finding fails to support the hypothesis which predicted a relationship between authoritarianism and resistance to change or an alternative hypothesis based on the notion that the *F*-scale is a measure of response set.

TABLE 1

CORRELATIONS BETWEEN PERCEIVED AND EXPECTED BENEFIT
FROM WIPD AND PERSONALITY VARIABLES

Personality Variable	Perceived Benefit r_{obs}	N	Expected Benefit r_{obs}	N
Age	0.06	76	−0.09	40
Education	−0.22†	76	−0.01	40
Achievement	−0.20	44	−0.28	40
Deference	0.18	44	−0.10	40
Orderliness	0.01	44	−0.05	40
Exhibitionism	−0.30*	44	0.00	40
Autonomy	−0.40†	44	−0.10	40
Affiliation	0.25	44	−0.14	40
Introception	0.47†	44	0.40†	40
Succorance	−0.30*	44	0.05	40
Dominance	0.17	44	−0.22	40
Abasement	0.41†	44	0.33*	40
Nurturance	−0.30*	44	0.12	40
Change	0.08	44	−0.07	40
Endurance	−0.21	44	−0.12	40
Heterosexuality	−0.14	44	−0.02	40
Aggression	−0.29*	44	−0.05	40
Authoritarianism (*F* Scale)	0.03	44	not available	not available

*Significant at 0.05 level.
†Significant at 0.01 level.

OTHER SIGNIFICANT RELATIONSHIPS

Table 1 also shows several other significant relationships between perceived benefit and the remaining variables: years of education completed, and these scales from EPPS: exhibitionism (the need to be the center of attention in a group), autonomy (the need for independence), succorance (the need to obtain aid), and nurturance (the need to provide aid). All were negatively related to perceived benefit from the program.

It is also interesting to note that introception (the need to think about one's own motives and the motives of others) is positively related to both perceived (0.47) and expected (0.40) benefit from the program. Furthermore these correlations are of the highest magnitude as predictors for both perceived and expected benefit measures; the introception scale of the EPPS is the best single personality predictor of perceived and of expected benefit. It is important to remember that developing the ability to observe and define motives is one of the major objectives of this and similar programs. It is shown here that those participants who are already concerned with understanding behavior motives are most likely to report benefit from this program.

DISCUSSION AND CONCLUSIONS

This study has confirmed the predicted relationship between benefit from a management development program and participants' expectation and need for change. In addition its findings are strikingly similar to what is usually found in conformity studies (6), (7). The need for aggression and social withdrawal reflects not only "anti-people" oriented needs, but is typical of those individuals who are inclined to resist change. The observed negative relationship of need for autonomy and benefit is similar to Cartwright's observation that the need for independence is usually associated with resistance to change. Bernardin and Jessor (4) have also found the same autonomy scale to be negatively related to change. Although the lack of relationship between authoritarianism and reported benefit raises some doubt about the conformity syndrome, the other observed relationships support it rather strongly.

"Conformity" has a negative connotation which rests on a value judgment against individuals who exhibit a willingness to accept change. However, if one considers that organizations are not likely to accomplish their goals without a broad base of individuals who are prepared to accommodate themselves to social imperatives and that without this broad base of "consensually oriented" individuals coordination and change would be difficult indeed, these so-called conformists are not necessarily the least valuable members of organizations.

In sum, the findings of this study show clearly that perceived benefit in a management development program can be predicted in part by participants' expectations prior to exposure to the program. Both the expectations of benefit and subsequent perceived benefit can be predicted by measures of abasement (inadequacy) and introception (the concern with speculation over one's own motives and the motivations of others) as well as personality characteristics that are associated with conformity needs. These major findings warrant the following conclusion: Management development programs are more likely to achieve their immediate value objectives if greater care is taken to select individuals (1) who are unsure of their adequacy and therefore more likely to be willing to change; (2) who are already concerned with intra- and interpersonal motives and whose inclinations are therefore reinforced rather than changed; and (3) who prefer social involvement to aloofness and are generally less likely to resist change.

17

A Study in Changing
the Attitudes and Stereotypes
of Industrial Workers

A. J. M. Sykes
Scottish College of Commerce
Glasgow

Reprinted by permission from *Human Relations*, XVII, No. 2 (1964), 143–54.
© Tavistock Institute of Human Relations, 1964.

This study describes an attempt made to change the attitudes of hostility that certain workers held toward their foremen by changing the stereotype on which these attitudes were based. The study covered a period of fourteen months in the works. The occasion arose when the author was employed by a large company in the heavy engineering industry to investigate industrial relations in one of its Scottish works. The works had a staff of 680 workers, who, with the exception of the maintenance workers, were all members of the Transport and General Workers Union. The works constituted a complete T & GWU branch in its own right. The secretary, chairman, and committee of the branch were all employed in the works and acted as shop stewards within it, the branch secretary acting as convenor of shop stewards. It may be necessary to point out here that in British trade union practice—as distinct from theory—the post of branch secretary takes precedence over that of branch chairman, and this works was no exception, the branch secretary being the dominant figure to whom the branch chairman and the committee deferred.

METHOD

The aim of the investigation was to study industrial relations within the works and suggest ways in which relations could be improved. The company which owned the works was worried about the bad relations that existed within it: This particular works had frequent disputes, many of which ended in unofficial strikes, whereas other similar works belonging to the same company and situated in the same area were relatively free from disputes. It was known that pay and conditions were not as good in this works as in the other works belonging to the company, and it was thought that this was the reason for the bad relations.

The first step was to see the works manager and explain to him the object of the study and the method to be used. The method consisted of interviewing the shop stewards, the foremen, and a cross section of the workers. These were to be interviewed initially in an office made available by the manager. The interviews were nondirective and the office was in the works, distant from the administration block and out of sight of the workers on the shop floor. After the initial contact had been made through the formal interviews, informal interviews were held in the canteens, lavatories, and other places where workers congregated to smoke and gossip. The investigator was not a participant observer in the full sense in that he did not do a normal job within the plant and was not a member of the trade union, but he did move about freely within the works, observing activities and speaking to men at their work. As the company had trainee-managers who also wandered freely about the works, this was not regarded as unusual. In any event the workers in the plant soon grew accustomed to the investigator and stopped touching their heads when he appeared in the works—touching the head was the standard signal that a "hat," one of the management, was prowling about the works. The investigator also attended the T & GWU branch meetings by permission of the branch committee.

Good relations with the trade union were established at the beginning of the study. It was believed that if the investigator was first accepted by the shop stewards and the other active members of the branch, this would guarantee acceptance by the workers generally. To this end the branch officials were requested to allow him to attend a branch meeting in order to explain the nature of the study and to answer any questions that the members wished to raise. The officials agreed to this and, since in most trade union branches the normal attendance was very poor, they put pressure on the shop stewards and active members to attend. In all, thirty-three men attended the meeting, asked questions about the proposed study, and finally expressed themselves satisfied with the answers given by the investigator.

ATTITUDE TO THE FOREMEN

The most striking feature of this meeting was the attitude of the trade union members to the foremen in the works. During the course of the meeting, several aspects of conditions in the works were criticized. The men complained about wages and conditions, and these complaints were later found to be justified, but the most bitter complaints were made about the foremen. Over half the time spent discussing conditions was occupied in denunciations of the foremen expressed in the most bitter terms, saying:

"You'd scour Hell to get their match!"
"They are a crowd of ignorant bloody men who don't know how to speak to human beings!"
"They are the worst foremen in Britain, you couldn't get their equal anywhere!"
"The foremen in here are just slave-drivers, they treat you like dirt!"

Such remarks were in contrast with the men's expression of their other grievances which was moderate and reasonable.

Several of the men pointed out that they had complained about the foremen on a number of occasions to the full-time officials of the union, the district and regional organizers, but that nothing had been done. To this, the chairman and the secretary replied that, though they agreed with the members entirely on this question and had brought in the organizer, they had been unable to force the issue because of a lack of concrete evidence, and they asked the members to supply them with details of specific acts committed by the foremen so that they could take the matter up again. Further discussion indicated that this attitude was not assumed to impress the investigator but was held in all sincerity. The men were convinced that the foremen were bad, and believed that the company deliberately chose the most brutal men available to be foremen. It is by no means uncommon for foremen to get a bad name, whether they deserve it or not, but in this case the men showed such bitter hatred of the foremen that it seemed they must have some reason for it. As the trade union officials were moderate, reliable, and accurate in their statements and judgments in other matters it seemed reasonable to suppose they would be equally reliable about the foremen.

It did not appear that the men were using the foremen as a scapegoat and were projecting their real grievances upon them, since they did not confine their complaints to the foremen but complained also of pay and conditions in the works. In their relations with management the men complained much more of their other grievances, and it was not realized by management before the research that they regarded the foremen as a major source of grievance.

After the meeting, the research within the works was begun. A check with both management and the union had shown that the thirty-three men who attended the meeting included all the active memebers of the T & GWU in the works; it was therefore decided to interview them first. For convenience, these thirty-three are henceforth referred to as the active members. This implies not that they were the only members but that they were the members who took an active part in union affairs. These interviews were interspersed with observation within the works and informal discussions with workers and foremen. The interviews covered industrial relations in general within the works and the men were allowed to range freely over this field. The information obtained through them confirmed the impression gained at the trade union meeting—that the foremen were extremely unpopular and were regarded as the most objectionable feature of the works.

THE STEREOTYPE OF THE FOREMEN

During the interviews it became clear that the hostility to the foremen was directed not toward the foremen as individuals but to the stereotype of the foremen accepted by the men. Thus, when the men discussed the foremen they would abuse them in general, and then go on to attack particular individuals among them. Complaints were made about ten foremen: of these, six had retired, the last of the six having retired five years before the investigation. All the thirty-three active members interviewed complained of two or more of the retired foremen, five complained of two or more of the present foremen, seven of one of the present foremen; the other twenty-one had no complaints against any of the present foremen. In all, there were complaints about four out of a total of forty foremen in the works at the time of the investigation.

An extract from an interview with the branch chairman is given below. The pattern it displays—condemnation of the foremen in general, combined with approval of individual foremen—was typical of the interviews as a whole. The branch chairman, a man with thirty-eight years' service in the works, was one of the most bitter critics of the foremen and had pressed the trade union district organizer on several occasions to complain to the senior management of the company about the foremen. The interview began with the branch chairman denouncing the foremen as "a lot of ignorant men, just ignorant, they treat you like jailers!" He then went on to speak of the three he had contact with, the superintendent, senior, and junior foremen in his department, who had been his foremen for fifteen, seven, and five years respectively. The conversation went as follows:

"What's A [the junior foreman] like?"

"He's a very nice bloke, knows his job, got a very nice approach to the men, and is always ready to help you; A's a good lad."

"What about B?" [the senior foreman].

"He's all right too, never bothers you. C [the superintendent] is the same, never bothers you if you do your work. He chases some of the men, but it's their own fault, they need chasing, they don't want to work, they only come in here out of the way of the buses. No one who does his job needs to worry about C."

Yet at the end of the conversation he repeated his complaints about "the foremen."

This attitude of hostility to "the foremen," combined with very different attitudes to the individual foremen, was found to be typical of the men interviewed, as well as of the active members. During the period spent in the works a total of eighty-five men were interviewed in addition to the thirty-three active members mentioned above (see Table 1). Of these, seventy-nine complained of the foremen in general, the six who did not had all been in the works less than four months; fifty-two of the men complained about foremen who had left the works, including seventeen men who had no direct experience of the foremen they complained of. There were seventeen men in departments under one or more of the four foremen about whom the active members had complained—henceforth referred to as the four unpopular foremen. Each of the seventeen complained of those of the four unpopular foremen he had contact with. Nine of the men made complaints about foremen other than these four, but no two complained of the same foreman. In each case, the shop steward of the department knew of the man's dislike of the foreman and gave reason for it in terms of a specific incident in the past. In three of the cases, the shop steward blamed the foreman; in four, the worker concerned; in two, both foreman and worker.

TABLE 1
COMPLAINTS BY WORKERS ABOUT THE FOREMEN

	Of one or more of the four unpopular foremen	Of other individual foremen	Of one or more of the retired foremen	Of "the foremen"	Total inter- viewed
By active members	12		33	33	33
By other workers	17	9	52	79	85
Total	29	9	85	112	118

Thus there was consensus among the men interviewed that "the foremen" were "brutal," and they displayed an attitude of hostility to "the foremen." When dealing with individual foremen there was no general consensus, because *all* the men interviewed did not have experience of *all* the foremen. However, there was consensus among all the men interviewed who had experience of the four unpopular foremen that these were "brutal," and the men displayed an attitude of hostility toward them. There was no consensus about the other foremen: There were complaints about nine of them, but only one complaint was made about each of the nine. With the exception of these nine complaints the attitudes the men expressed toward their foremen ranged from acceptance to strong liking.

ORIGINS OF THE STEREOTYPE

The conclusion that only four foremen were generally unpopular was borne out by the past and present members of the branch committee who had experience of dealing with all the foremen in the course of handling complaints in all departments of the works. When interviewed, each of the committee members named the four unpopular foremen—and only these four—as being generally, and justifiably, disliked. Thus there was a distinct difference between the attitudes of the men to "the foremen" as a collective entity, and the attitudes expressed toward individual foremen. This was due to the fact that the attitudes to "the foremen" were a reaction to a stereotype of them; the attitudes to the individual foremen were based on direct experience of them as individuals.

The stereotype of the foremen was apparently based upon the fact that the foremen in the past had been very brutal: on this point the workers, the present foremen, and the management were all agreed. With the outbreak of war in 1939 and the end of unemployment in the area, a distinct improvement had begun, and by the early 1950s all the more brutal foremen had retired and had been replaced by more reasonable men. However, the stereotype of the foremen remained unaltered because the conditions which had led to its creation, the brutality of past foremen, were kept alive by oral tradition in the works. The older workers told the younger ones stories of the behavior of the foremen in the past, how men had to give them money or buy them drink on pay-nights in order to keep their jobs, and of their endless bullying and brutal treatment of the men. Some of these stories went back to before the First World War, and did not lie within the experience of even the oldest workers, but had been learned by them from a previous generation. Yet the men would become indignant when recounting or listening to these stories and they accepted them as being applicable to the present. In this way, belief in the stereotype was kept alive.

The shop stewards and the men got on well with the foremen as individuals; nevertheless, the existence of the stereotype of the foremen as "brutal" poisoned industrial relations in the works. As they had little contact with management proper, the men looked on the foremen as the true representatives of the management and the company. Consequently, the attitude of hostility the men had for "the foremen" was projected onto the company and its management, and embittered industrial relations.

ATTEMPT TO CHANGE THE STEREOTYPE

In the circumstances, it was felt that an attempt should be made to change the stereotype. This was difficult, because it was not considered practicable to make a direct approach to the men and attempt to show them that the stereotype was false. The stereotype was a belief, it was not rational, and it was unlikely to be disproved by logical arguments coming from an outsider. The men were certain to be very suspicious of any direct attack upon the stereotype that seemed to come from the management side. If they became suspicious, then no arguments would prevail, for they would probably refuse to listen and would fall back on the line of argument: "We know, we have experience of them and you haven't"—an argument to which there is no answer.

Thus the situation was that the stereotype had to be submitted to critical examination and analysis if it was to be disproved, and this had to be done by the men themselves. The method chosen was based upon observations made by the investigator during previous research. It had been noted that questions asked in the course of research had the effect of stimulating those interviewed into thinking about, and often questioning, their previous assumptions. Those who had only vague ideas about their work and their attitude to it found that they had to think about these ideas and clarify them before they could answer questions. Even those who already had clearcut ideas were stimulated to reconsider them while trying to justify them to the questioner, and they were often surprised at the conclusions they reached while doing so. As a result it was noticeable that after research had been conducted in a works or an office, the people in it had much clearer and more definite views on works or office matters than they had previous to the research. Sometimes the ideas of those interviewed changed, sometimes they remained the same, but usually they were clarified. For example, some individuals who had previously held a strong but vaguely defined sense of grievance against the employer now found that they had no real grounds for grievance; whereas others were confirmed in their sense of grievance and were now able to define their reasons for it.

As previous research had produced these results, it was decided to continue with the present study and see whether the research method alone would stimulate the men into analyzing and adjusting their stereotype of the foremen. The research was continued, no attempt was made to argue with the men on the subject of the foremen, and no disapproval was shown of even their wildest denunciations of them. But the men were reminded that, while any justifiable grievance would be taken up and an attempt made to remedy it, they had to *prove* that grievances were justified: Statements of opinion were not enough, evidence was required to support them. It was pointed out that this was in the interests of the men, for they had everything to gain by presenting a sound case in support of their claims. The branch committee members in particular saw the point of this and did all they could to collect concrete evidence about their grievances—including that concerning the foremen.

Once the need for evidence had been accepted it was possible to cross-question those interviewed without giving offense. It must be emphasized that this was done in a friendly manner. If a man said the foremen were bad, he was asked how many of those he knew personally were bad; how many good. If he said a particular one was bad, he was asked to give reasons. If he quoted actual cases, he was asked when these occurred, and, if they were pre-war as many were, he was asked if the foreman concerned was still in the works, and if he knew of any recent cases of this kind. It was necessary not to harass the men unduly, but at the same time no statement could be allowed to pass unchallenged. It must also be noted that the question of the foremen took up only a part of each interview. Interviews were nondirective and the men were allowed to discuss their work in general. Hence the subject of the foremen did not occupy the whole interview, as may appear from the accounts given above. It occupied an important part, but many other questions of pay, conditions, etc., were also covered. In the circumstances the men had no occasion to feel, and in fact it is known that they did not feel, that any special significance was being placed on the problem of the foremen.

This technique was adopted at a time when the thirty-three active trade unionists and twenty-six of the other men had already been interviewed. The investigator had reached the conclusion that the active members created opinion among the men generally, hence they were given informal follow-up interviews using the new technique. This created no problem since the investigator was in constant contact with the active members. The twenty-six others were not re-interviewed but the technique was applied in all new interviews.

RESULTS

These interviews led to frequent informal discussions among the active members about their grievances, and, at first, to increased discussion with the investigator. However, it became noticeable that the subject of the formen was soon dropped from these discussions and was deliberately avoided in conversation with the investigator. The first indication of a change of attitude came three months after the active members had been re-interviewed. The branch secretary, hitherto a very bitter critic of the foremen, when discussing with the investigator some recent negotiations with a foreman on pay, praised the foreman for his cooperation and ended his account by saying: "You know we are lucky in here, we have quite a decent sensible crowd of foremen."

However, the other active members remained evasive on the subject of the foremen. It was thought that they might well have ceased or be ready to cease believing in the stereotype but were afraid to declare themselves until they knew the opinion of their group. In short, the members were in a state of pluralistic ignorance about the group's present stereotype of and attitude to "the foremen." In order to force a public declaration of opinion, the investigator raised the question of the foremen with the branch secretary during an informal lunch-time meeting of the branch committee and other active members: a small group of these habitually lunched together in the Blacksmith's Shop belonging to the works. The branch secretary replied that the men "talked a lot of blethers about the foremen." At this the branch chairman, who had previously been evasive, broke in and told the investigator: "Don't take too much notice of what the men say about the foremen, they aren't really such a bad lot in spite of what they say; they could have a damn sight worse, in fact, they have had a damn sight worse in this works in the past." The other men present agreed with him and cited examples of how helpful and cooperative many of the foremen were.

After this incident, there was a marked change of attitude toward the foremen among all the active members who had been present. They were no longer evasive, but discussed the foremen freely and warned the investigator against paying too much attention to the men's complaints about them. The public declaration by the branch secretary of his new attitude to the foremen appeared to have provided the necessary sanction which the other active members had awaited before publicly committing themselves to this new attitude. The active members who had not been present at the meeting remained evasive until the branch meeting a week later, when the branch secretary, without referring to their previous grievances, stated that there had been "a lot of stupid complaints about the foremen by some of the men," and went on to give his opinion that the foremen were "a pretty decent bunch." In this, he was supported by the branch committee. After this event, none of the active members was found to be evasive or to be hostile to the foremen.

In subsequent interviews, none of the thirty-three active members complained of the foremen generally, although they still complained of the four unpopular foremen. It was noticeable that none of the active members ever admitted that there had been any change of attitude on their part. They said that the men had long had a foolish hostility to the foremen but they, the active members, had never shared it, and had tried to show the men how wrong their view of the foremen was—and from this point on, they did discourage criticism of the foremen by the men. At the same time, the active members, and the branch committee members in particular, expressed a view which contradicted their claim that they had always known the foremen were "a good crowd." This view was that the foremen had been *ordered* to be more cooperative. In spite of denials by the investigator, the active members claimed that he must have complained to the management and that they had put pressure on the foremen. As evidence of this, they cited instances of the new cooperativeness of the foremen in handling disputes and grievances; these instances did not include the four unpopular foremen who were still attacked as "men who will never learn." The investigator had found no discernible change in the behavior of the foremen and had not suggested to the management or the foremen that there ought to be any change. In fact the men themselves had cited similar examples of cooperation by individual foremen even when the stereotype of the foremen as brutal was still accepted.

Thus the active members had changed their stereotype of the foremen and had adopted a new attitude toward them. So far as the investigator could discover they realized that a change had taken place but were reluctant to accept that the change had taken place in their own perception of the foremen. They rationalized the situation by claiming: (a) that they had always known that the foremen were "all right;" and (b) that the foremen had changed their behavior toward the workers.

The rest of the men in the works did not abandon the stereotype and change their attitude to the foremen as rapidly as did the active members. The hostility to the foremen was discernible several months after the active members had changed. That the attitude did eventually change was owing to, or at least was speeded up by, the work of the active members. They became openly critical of any unsubstantiated complaints made about the foremen and, after negotiating on behalf of the men, would return and praise the fairness and moderation of the foremen to them. The long-term effect of this was to create a new stereotype of the foremen and a new attitude toward them.

It is difficult to assess the success or otherwise of such an exercise since it is not possible to measure and compare the various factors involved with any exactitude. From the strictly practical point of view the exercise was a success since it did result in the men adopting a new stereotype of and a new attitude to the foremen. In consequence, relations between the union officials and the foremen improved; as indicated above, these had not been bad before, but they could, and did, improve. The foremen reported that they found the shop stewards more cooperative and less aggressive, and the number of disputes declined considerably; incidents which had formerly led to strikes or at least to disputes which had to be settled at general-manager level were now settled amicably within the department. The subject of the foremen as a major grievance was dropped completely and the men concentrated on their other grievances, the most important being pay and conditions. As these were *real* grievances which the company could amend, and was willing to amend, this was no disadvantage. In short, an imaginary grievance which could not be settled was replaced by real ones which could—to the satisfaction of the men and the company. It must be emphasized that the grievances about pay and conditions were not tackled until after the active members had changed their attitudes to the foremen, hence there was no question of this change being due to a settlement of their other grievances.

SUMMARY

1. The investigator was asked to study industrial relations in a works and recommend any necessary changes. Relations were found to be bad, mainly owing to the attitude of hostility the men held toward the foremen generally.

2. It was found that this attitude of hostility was based upon a stereotype that the foremen were brutal. The stereotype proved to be false and the men in general complained of only four out of forty foremen.

3. An attempt was made to change the stereotype by causing the men to in-

vestigate the evidence for their complaints against the foremen. It was hoped that if the stereotype was changed the attitude of the men would change also.

4. As a result, the active members of the union did decide that the stereotype was false but were reluctant to admit this until the trade union leader, the branch secretary, openly stated that it was so. As a result of the change of stereotype, the active members dropped their attitude of hostility to the foremen.

5. The active members never admitted that they had changed their opinion of the foremen but claimed two contradictory things: (a) that they had always known that the foremen were "all right"; (b) that the foremen had changed for the better.

6. The workers in general were much slower in changing their stereotype of the foremen and their attitude of hostility to them, but eventually did so under pressure from the active members.

CONCLUSIONS

It is difficult to draw precise conclusions from a study of this kind because of the vague nature of much of the evidence. However, it is possible to indicate certain general points that were brought out by the research.

1. It has been suggested that where actual cultural differences between groups are small a false stereotype is often due to lack of contact and can be reduced by increasing contact between the groups concerned: "Contact by itself is a major weapon in the reduction of tension where groups are alike or similar, and where stereotypes are unrealistic" (19, p. 237). In the case described above this was not so; contact alone had no effect. The foremen had the same social background as the workers, they had worked their way up to their present rank within the same works, and they lived in the same small town. There were few or no cultural differences between workers and foremen and there was frequent contact between them. In spite of this, the stereotype of the foremen as brutal persisted among the workers.

2. Allport has claimed that stereotypes do not create prejudice, but rationalize or justify an existing prejudice: "Whether favorable or unfavorable, *a stereotype is an exaggerated belief associated with a category. Its function is to justify (rationalize) our conduct in relation to that category*" (2, p. 187).

Saenger and Flowerman have stressed the same point: "Stereotypes are only symptomatic. At most, they reinforce hostile attitudes, are supporting rationalizations" (19, p. 237).

This may be so in many, even in most, cases, but it is difficult to see how it fits the study described here. In this case the stereotype had fitted the facts: It was agreed by the foremen, management, and office staff, as well as by the workers, that the foremen had been brutal. The retirement of the brutal foremen and their replacement by others who were not brutal created a situation in which the stereotype was false. The workers displayed an attitude of hostility toward "the foremen" who, according to the stereotype, were brutal, but, as Table 1 shows, relatively few men regarded the individual foremen as brutal or displayed an attitude of hostility toward them. In these circumstances it is difficult to see what created and maintained the prejudice against the foremen as a group if it was not the stereotype, particularly as few of the younger men in the works had any direct experience of a brutal foreman. The stereotype did not justify the prejudice against the foremen but *was* the prejudice, and it was justified by an oral tradition in the works which embodied stories of brutal behavior by foremen in the past. In other words, it was justified by myths which formed part of the culture of the works. It may be argued that all workers are prejudiced against foremen because of their role, but even if this is admitted it remains that the prejudice in the works was intensified by the stereotype. In any case there was little prejudice displayed against individual foremen.

Allport further claims that, since the stereotype does not create the prejudice but is only a rationalization of it, removing the stereotype will not remove the prejudice:

> Stereotypes are not identical with prejudice. They are primarily rationalizers. They adapt to the prevailing temper of prejudice or the needs of the situation. While it does no harm (and may do some good) to combat them in schools and colleges, and to reduce them in mass media of communication, it must not be thought that this attack alone will eradicate the roots of prejudice (2, pp. 198–99).

In the case described here removal of the stereotype did end the prejudice against the foremen as a group, and it changed the attitude of hostility the men had toward them. This is not to argue that Allport is entirely wrong, but only that, in cases where the stereotype was once correct but is so no longer, owing to a change in circumstances, then the survival of the false stereotype does in itself lead to prejudicial attitudes, and a change in the stereotype can lead to a removal of prejudice.

3. Marrow and French have shown that stereotypes in industry can be changed by inducing those who hold a false stereotype to participate in an inquiry into its validity:

> Our experiment at the Harwood Manufacturing Corporation demonstrated that whereas arguments and persuasion had failed to uproot a strong institutional stereotype crystallized into company policy, other methods succeeded. Chief among them were participation of management in research and participation of supervisors in group discussion and decision. Thus, through a process of guided experiences which are equally his own, a person may be re-oriented so that he gradually takes on within himself the attitudes which he would not accept from others (17, p. 37).

The investigator did not know of this study at the time of his own research; nevertheless, the method he evolved was very similar to theirs. Thus, the workers, the active members in particular, were led to inquire into the validity of their stereotype of the foremen with the results shown above. It appears, therefore, that it is possible to remove or reduce prejudice by such methods; however, neither study was precise enough to allow one to draw conclusions as to *exactly* how the change occurred.

4. One interesting fact that emerged during the study was the group nature of the change. The active members did not display any open change of attitude to the foremen generally until this was sanctioned by the branch secretary and, later, by other committee members who first displayed in public a new attitude and denounced the old stereotype. The workers generally accepted the change only after it was pressed on them by the active members. This appears to support two points raised by Lewin: (a) that it is easier to change group standards than to change individual members of the group:

> Perhaps one might expect single individuals to be more pliable than groups of like-minded individuals. However, experience in leadership training, in changing of food habits, work production, criminality, alcoholism, prejudices, all seem to indicate that it is usually easier to change individuals formed into a group than to change any one of them separately (14, p. 34);

and (b) that in changing "group ideology" and "group action" one should try to change people in "key positions" rather than attempt to change the entire population (14, p. 143). This second point, that the approval of prestigeful members of a group may influence group members into changing their attitudes, is supported by Kelly and Woodruff (11) in their study of "apparent group approval of a counternorm communication."

5. A final point that may be of significance is the fact that the men concerned in this study did not admit that they had changed their stereotype of, and attitude to, the foremen. Instead they claimed that they had never held the stereotype of the foremen as brutal and had never been hostile to them; the active members said that the other men had held it; the men generally blamed each other; no one admitted that *he* had ever held the attitude and stereotype; at the same time, the active members claimed that the foremen had changed for the better. In discussing the situation with the active members it was clear that they were ready to resist strongly any attempt to make them admit that *they* had changed. In short, it was easier to bring about a change in their stereotype and attitude than it was to obtain admission of such change. This may seem an obvious point, but it is one that is important in industrial relations: that it may be much easier to make changes in stereotypes and attitudes if one does not insist on an admission that change has occurred, or if the change can be attributed to a fictitious cause—in this case, to the supposed change in the behavior of the foremen.

18

Attitude Surveys and Job Performance

Edward E. Lawler, III
Yale University

Reprinted by permission from the September-October 1967 issue of *Personnel Administration*, copyright 1967, Society for Personnel Administration, 485–87, National Press Building, 14th and F Streets, N. W., Washington, D. C. 20004.

Organizational attitude surveys have become a well-accepted tool in many organizations—a tool that can and often does shed considerable light upon the internal state of the organization. Likert has eloquently pointed out that attitude surveys allow for the assessment of the human resources of the organization (15). He also points out that only by assessing such factors as the satisfaction level of employees can organizations determine the impact of actions upon all relevant organizational resources. For example, looking just at the effects on productivity of an authoritarian leadership pattern while ignoring its impact on the job satisfaction of employees can be a costly type of myopia. It is all too clear that many practices can lead to short-term improvements in performance at the cost of using up the significant human resources of an organization—human resources that may be important determinants of the long-term success of the organization.

ATTITUDES AND PERFORMANCE

My own views are very much in agreement with those expressed by Likert. However, I do want to question the kinds of measures that are typically included in most attitude surveys.

Most attitude surveys, I feel, do not measure those attitudes that are most important in determining how motivated an individual will be to perform his job effectively. For example, most attitude surveys traditionally have focused on attitudes toward job satisfaction and on attitudes toward the importance of job factors like supervision and of job rewards like pay. One glance at the literature of industrial psychology is enough to establish that there are literally hundreds of research studies that have focused upon these two kinds of attitudes. Yet, there is a considerable amount of literature that suggests neither of these kinds of attitudes predicts the degree to which an individual will be motivated to perform his job effectively. Job satisfaction measures, however, have proved to be rather effective in predicting absenteeism and turnover rates (5). Attitudes toward the importance of job factors, on the other hand, have not been particularly effective in predicting any aspects of employees' job behavior.

Over-all, then, attitude surveys often find themselves in the rather unfortunate position of not measuring any attitudes that appear to be direct determinants of performance effectiveness.

If the purpose of attitude surveys is to predict employee behavior in a way that will lead to suggestions designed to increase the employees' motivation to perform effectively, this is a critical problem. How may attitude surveys be made more effective? Motivation theory provides a possible answer to this question. It suggests that attitudes toward job satisfaction and attitudes toward the potency of different job factors are not enough to understand human behavior in organizations.

THE MISSING LINK

What is needed are data on how employees feel important rewards can be obtained in their organizations. In the language of the theory, we need data on employees' path–goal or reward expectancy attitudes—on the employees' attitudes toward what factors influence the rewards they receive. It is these attitudes that provide the link between attitudes toward the importance of job factors and job performance, the link that is typically missing in attitude surveys. These attitude data, when combined with job satisfaction data, should allow for the understanding not only of issues involving turnover and absenteeism rates, but also of the motivational state of the organization with respect to performance effectiveness.

The psychological literature on motivation theory provides the basis for the statement that path–goal attitudes are the key to understanding employees' motivation to perform effectively. A number of motivation theorists have stated what Atkinson calls expectancy theories of motivation (3). According to expectancy theory, the amount of effort an individual will put into performing effectively is a function of two factors—the perceptions the individual holds about what rewards are associated with performing effectively and the importance or attractiveness of the rewards to the individual.

It is important to note that in expectancy theory, reward importance and path–goal attitudes combine multiplicatively. This means that there will be no motivation to perform effectively if the rewards that are seen to be tied to performance are unimportant or if the rewards available in the situation are not seen to be tied to performance. Thus, in order to understand behavior, data are needed on both the importance of job factors and on the perceptions of employees about how positively valued rewards are obtained.

JOB PERFORMANCE AND REWARDS

In terms of expectancy theory, then, the type of data on the importance of various rewards that are collected in many attitude studies is important in understanding employee behavior. It is important because it indicates what will be sought after by the employees. But it is not sufficient to predict how motivated they will be to perform effectively because it does not tell what paths employees will follow in order to obtain these rewards. Motivation theory clearly indicates that data are also needed on how the employees see the relationship between their own job performance and the rewards that are important to them.

Over the past several years, I have collected data from almost a thousand managers on the relationship between their perceptions of their pay and their job performance. These data rather consistently show that *the importance of money to managers has virtually no relationship to how hard they work*. Their perceptions of whether their pay is influenced by their performance has a somewhat higher but still low relationship to how hard they work.

When, however, these two measures are combined so that managers who say pay is important to them and that their pay is tied to their performance can be compared with those who say pay is relatively unimportant to them and not tied to their performance, a strong attitude performance relationship appears. The more motivated managers clearly are characterized by appropriate path–goal and reward importance attitudes. It would seem, therefore, that if organizations are going to predict how motivated their employees will be to perform effectively in the future, they need to know the path–goal attitudes of their employees.

PATH–GOAL ATTITUDE DATA

In terms of the theoretical framework developed so far, job satisfaction attitudes represent a kind of path–goal attitude and, thus, it is not surprising that they predict job attendance behavior. The evidence relative to over-all job satisfaction indicates that it is a function of the degree to which an individual feels his important needs are fulfilled as a result of holding a given job. Thus, asking an individual whether he is satisfied with his job is equivalent to asking him if he feels his needs are fulfilled as a function of holding his present job. The feeling that holding the job leads to need satisfaction is a path–goal attitude with respect to holding the job just the same as is the attitude that good performance leads to high pay.

It is not surprising, therefore, that employees who say they are not satisfied with their jobs are more likely to be absent and quit since they are in effect saying that they do not see any relationship between having the job and the satisfaction of their needs. Similarly, the employee who says he is satisfied should be expected to come to work since he is saying that he sees a strong relationship between the satisfaction of his needs and having the job.

It makes sense in terms of motivation theory, then, to continue collecting data on job satisfaction to the extent that organizations want to predict turnover and absenteeism. The data show that job dissatisfaction is an antecedent of absenteeism and turnover and as such can be a good barometer of what the future state of the organization is likely to be. In other words, collection of satisfaction data should allow an organization to diagnose itself and to anticipate the problems that are likely to appear in the future. This is clearly what many organizations attempt to do when they systematically measure the job satisfaction level of their employees.

However, the point of this article is that all too often they fail to assess the path–goal attitudes of the employee with respect to good performance. Just as job satisfaction data can provide a useful diagnostic tool that can help understand absenteeism and turnover problems, path–goal data with respect to performance can help to understand and predict job performance problems that are related to a lack of motivation. They also can be quite helpful in understanding differences between organizations as well as in measuring the impact of incentive and motivation plans. Let us then consider a few examples of where the collection of path–goal attitude data has been or might be particularly helpful in understanding the operation of a given organization.

PAY AND PERFORMANCE

Several years ago I had the opportunity to collect some data on the perceived path–goal relationship between pay and performance in a number of organizations. One of these was a rapidly growing aerospace manufacturer. I was particularly interested in the path–goal attitudes data provided by the managers in this firm because the personnel manager had told me that the motivation level of the employees seemed to be low despite the fact that the job satisfaction level of the employees was generally high. One look at the path–goal data with respect to pay suggested the reason for this problem. The managers felt that their pay was determined largely by their education level and by their job level but not by their performance.

Given this situation, it is hardly surprising that the managers were not very motivated to perform effectively since the organization was not seen by the employees as being likely to reward effective performance. When confronted with the path–goal perceptions of their employees, the top management admitted that these perceptions did have some basis in fact. The company had brought in a number of highly educated managers recently at high salaries and they admitted that perhaps pay was not always closely tied to merit. The latter point was confirmed when a low correlation was found between managers' salaries and their superiors' evaluation of their performance.

An interesting example of organizational differences on path–goal attitudes appeared between a sample of three government organizations and a sample of four private industrial organizations (13). There were some differences between the two samples on the degree to which seniority, educational level, and other factors were seen to be determinants of pay. However, major differences appeared between the two samples on the degree to which job performance and pay were seen to be related. The private industry saw job performance factors as being much more important in determining their pay than did the government sample. Interestingly, both samples said their pay was important to them and that pay should be based upon performance. However, if we accept the point made by "expectancy" theory that not only must pay be important, but it must be seen as being tied to performance, then it is apparent that for the managers in the government sample pay was not operating as a motivator.

PERFORMANCE AND PROMOTIONS

In a later study, path–goal data relevant to another reward—promotion—were collected. The path–goal data from one organization provided an increased understanding of the meaning of some job satisfaction data that were also collected. A relatively high level of dissatisfaction with the promotion opportunities available in the firm was noted, yet the head of the organization pointed out that a number of people had been recently promoted in the organization. Analysis of the employees' path–goal data with respect to promotion showed that they did not feel that promotion in the organization was based upon job performance.

This meant that promotion was not serving as an incentive in the organization. It also seemed to lead to general dissatisfaction with the promotion possibilities in the organization. This seemed to come about because the employees not only felt that promotion was not based upon performance, but that it should be. Similar data on pay have been obtained in another study. These data showed that the employees most dissatisfied with their pay were those who felt their pay should be based upon their performance but that it actually was not. These data, then, suggest that path–goal attitude data can not only indicate how effectively rewards like pay are being used, but can also help point to the underlying cause of the dissatisfaction that appears in the typical job satisfaction survey.

Potentially, the most useful kind of path–goal data that an organization could collect would involve repeated annual or semi-annual measurements of the employees' perceptions of the paths to a number of goals. Employees might be asked to report how helpful they feel a number of things (e.g., good performance, seniority, hard work) are for obtaining a number of important rewards (e.g., pay, promotion, security, status, feelings of achievemen).

It is important to include multiple rewards because "expectancy" theory clearly says that in order to know how much effort will be put forth to perform an act, it is necessary to know all the rewards and penalties that are seen to be tied to the performance of the act. The more rewards and the fewer penalties that are seen to be tied to the performance the greater will be the effort put forth to perform it.

Repeated periodic measurements of path–goal attitudes can give the company a method of systematically vaiidating changes that are made in the incentive systems of the organization. Typically, when organizations have changed their pay program or their promotion system, they have either had to take it on faith that this led to an increased level of motivation in the organization or they have tried to measure changes in performance. Neither of these approaches has proved to be successful. Obviously, companies cannot afford to assess their progress on the basis of mere conjecture or faith. And as far as measuring performance changes is concerned, not only is performance hard to measure but it is influenced by many things other than motivational factors. Therefore, performance changes are not likely to be perfectly correlated with changes in the motivation system of the organization.

THE MOTIVATIONAL CLIMATE

My suggestion is that organizations consider the employees' path–goal attitudes as the major dependent variable that should be used in measuring the effects of changes in such things as pay and promotion programs. That is, the effectiveness of the change would be measured by the degree to which it leads to increased feelings on the part of the employees that receiving important rewards is tied to job performance in the organization. Implicit in the use of this measurement process is the apparently valid assumption that positive path–goal attitudes with respect to performance are desirable because they lead directly to increased effort for effective performance and through increased effort to improved performance.

The use of path–goal attitude measures for the assessment of the motivational climate of the organization could have an additional advantage if the organization were to emphasize to each manager that part of his job is to create a situation where these would be positive. This would emphasize to the manager the importance of each decision he makes concerning pay raises or promotions on the path–goal attitudes of his employees. It would become necessary for the manager to maintain a consistent policy of rewarding performance if he is going to produce positive path–goal attitudes and to be sure that the employees realize the basis upon which these decisions are made. Interestingly, to do this he would need to consider not only his views of his subordinates' performance but also other employees' views of who is performing well. This would be necessary because employees base their path–goal attitudes on their view of who is performing well. Peer ratings and subordinate ratings would therefore become important supplements to normal decision-making data since they would suggest the impact of specific salary and promotion actions on employee path–goal attitudes.

In summary, this article has argued that if properly used, the addition of path–goal attitude measures to the typical company attitude survey can provide an important and often missing link—the link between attitude data and the degree to which the employees are motivated to perform their job effectively.

Questioning
the Managerial Implications of
Managing Attitudes

1. The final suggestion by Klein and Maher implies that telling a college-educated manager that his salary outcomes are unrealistic will reduce his feelings of inequity in comparing his salary with that of his less-educated counterpart. The danger with this approach is that the college-educated manager may find that reducing his job contribution expectations is the only way to bring his input/outcome ratio into parity. What other ways can be proposed to deal with the salary dissatisfaction claimed by the college-educated sample in this study?

2. Outline a plan for an application of the method used by Gruenfeld to an organizational situation or program (other than management development) in which you hypothesize that initial expectations will be powerful determinants of eventual satisfaction or performance.

3. The word "stereotype" takes on a rather negative connotation in Sykes's article. Are there any circumstances under which stereotyping of others is likely to yield positive interactional outcomes in an organization?

4. In your own words, explain how the application of "path-goal" attitude data can provide an understanding of the effect of employee expectations and attitudes on their job performance.

5. Which is more important for managers of organizations to understand—the shaping of attitudes or the effect of attitudes on behavior? Which can be more easily manipulated to provide the most benefit to the human organization?

References

1. Adams, J. S., "Inequity in Social Exchange," in *Advances in Experimental Social Psychology*, ed. L. Berkowitz. New York: Academic Press, Inc., 1965.

2. Allport, G. W., *The Nature of Prejudice.* New York: Doubleday & Company, Inc., 1954.

3. Atkinson, J. W., *An Introduction to Motivation.* Princeton: D. Van Nostrand Co., Inc., 1964.

4. Bernardin, A., and R. Jessor, "A Construct Validation of the Edwards Personal Preference Schedule with Respect to Dependency," *Journal of Consulting Psychology*, XXI (1957), 63–67.

5. Brayfield, A. H., and W. H. Crockett, "Employee Attitudes and Employee Preference," *Psychological Bulletin,* LII (1955), 396–424.

6. Cartwright, L., "Influence, Leadership, Control," in *Handbook of Organizations*, ed. J. G. March. Chicago: Rand McNally & Co., 1965.

7. Crutchfield, R. S., "Conformity and Character," *American Psychologist*, X (1955), 191–98.

8. Edwards, A. L., *Personal Preference Schedule.* New York: The Psychological Corporation, 1959.

9. House, R. J., *A Predicative Theory of Management Development: An Empirically Derived Explanation.* Preliminary draft of monograph, *The Harvard Business Review*, Readers' Service, Soldier's Field, Boston, Mass. 02166, 1963.

10. Hovland, C. I., I. L. Janis, and H. H. Kelley, *Communication and Persuasion.* New Haven, Conn.: Yale University Press, 1953.

11. Kelley, H. H., and C. L. Woodruff, "Members' Reactions to Apparent Group Approval of a Counternorm Communication," *Journal of Abnormal and Social Psychology,* LII (1956), 67–74.

12. Klein, S. M., and J. R. Maher, "Education Level and Satisfaction with Pay," *Personnel Psychology,* XIX (1966), 195–208.

13. Lawler, E. E., III, "Managers' Attitudes Toward How Their Pay Is and Should Be Determined," *Journal of Applied Psychology,* L (1966), 273–79.

14. Lewin, K., "Frontiers in Group Dynamics," *Human Relations,* I (1947), 5–42, 143–53.

15. Likert, R., *New Patterns of Management.* New York: McGraw-Hill Book Company, 1961.

16. Mahler, W. R., "What Is Needed to Improve Management Development Programs?" Paper presented to the American Psychological Association Symposium, St. Louis, Mo., September 4, 1962.

17. Marrow, A. J., and J. R. P. French, "Changing a Stereotype in Industry," *Journal of Social Issues,* 1945, 1, 33–37.

18. Milholland, J. E., "Theory and Techniques of Assessment," *Annual Review of Psychology,* XV (1964).

19. Saenger, G., and S. Flowerman, "Stereotypes and Prejudical Attitudes," *Human Relations,* I (1954), 8, 217.

20. Viteles, M. S., "'Human Relations' and the 'Humanities' in the Education of Business Leaders: Evaluation of a Program of Humanistic Studies for Executives," *Personnel Psychology,* XII (1959), 12, 1–28.

21. Vroom, V. H., *Work and Motivation.* New York: John Wiley & Sons, Inc., 1964.

Motivating
Management and Employees

Of the many causes of human behavior in organizations, motivation has proven one of the most resistant to understanding and classification. Perhaps the lack of a comprehensive and replicated theory of worker motivation can be attributed to the inability of researchers to settle on a unified definition of the term.

Gardner Murphy considers motivation as the "General name for the fact that an organism's acts are partly determined by its own nature or internal structure."[1] P. T. Young, on the other hand, sees motivation as ". . . the process of arousing action, sustaining the activity in progress, and regulating the pattern of activity."[2]

Other notable students of human behavior have approached the study of motivation in still other ways. The two preceding defini-

---

[1] *Personality: A Biosocial Approach to Origins and Structure*. New York: Harper & Row Publishers, 1947, p. 991.

[2] *Motivation and Emotion. A Survey of the Determinants of Human and Animal Activity*. New York: John Wiley & Sons, Inc., 1961, p. 24.

tions were chosen for consideration because they serve as bases for two study techniques dominating the recent management and behavioral science literature.

The approach implied by Murphy is characterized by the first two readings of this chapter. For example, Ghiselli examines managerial motivation in terms of internal desires for job security, financial reward, power, and self-actualization. He concludes that successful middle managers have less desire for security and high financial reward and place more value on self-actualization than those who are less successful. Hall and Nougaim further pursue an understanding of organizational motivation in terms of need satisfaction. Their efforts are aimed at an attempt to determine the applicability of Maslow's need hierarchy among managers in an ongoing organization. Although they are unable to find confirmation of the sequential need satisfaction claimed by Maslow's theory, they do identify changing need patterns for the advancing manager.

The definition of motivation previously attributed to Young generally characterizes the approach of Myers. Yet, even though many others have taken this pragmatic approach, few seem to have applied it so convincingly to the motivation of employees. Myers' framework is based on elimination of what he calls the "management–labor dichotomy." His plan for job enrichment opts for "self-managed" jobs where the worker has a say in the planning, execution, and control of his duties.

19

Some Motivational Factors in the Success of Managers

Edwin E. Ghiselli
University of California
Berkeley

Reprinted by permission from *Personnel Psychology*, XXI, No. 4 (1968), 431–40.

While there have been a fair number of studies examining the kinds of traits and abilities which are important in determining the degree of success achieved by those in management positions, relatively little attention has been given to the part played by motivational factors. There has been, of course, a good deal of speculation about the function of various motivational factors in the performance of managers. In these speculations there has been considerable discussion about four sorts of motivational factors, viz., the desires for job security, for high financial reward, for power over others, and for self-actualization.

It is generally held that the desire for security plays no part whatsoever in determining performance at the managerial level. The argument is that those who reach the managerial levels are so confident in their own talents that they are completely unworried about the continuation of their employment. Essentially the position is that the strength of the desire for job security is unrelated to quality of job performance on the part of those in management positions. Those managers who have a high desire for job security are no more likely to be successful than those who have no desire at all for such security.

It seems apparent to those who have considered the matter that high financial reward ought somehow to be an important motivator for those in management positions. Some hold that managers wish substantial financial reward for itself, desiring money for what can be bought with it. But others take the position that those in management positions feel they make a sufficient amount to buy what they want, and the amount of money a manager makes is important to him principally because it provides him, and those in his social milieu, with an index which precisely measures the level of success he has achieved. If the first notion be true, then there should be a positive relationship between strength of financial drive and success. If the second notion describes the role of money in management positions, then it is not clear just what the relationship between strength of financial drive and success should be. Money would be taken to be a result of effort rather than a cause of it. Probably it would be held that there should be no correlation at all between desire for high financial reward and success.

It would appear that a desire for power over others should play some part in the motivation of managers. This should be the case at least for those who are in so-called line positions where there is active supervision of subordinates, and the job involves the manipulation of them in order to achieve the organizational goals. If the desire for power over others is indeed a strong motivation among managers, then its effects very likely are subject to some sort of moderating effect by the organizational climate in which they work. If the climate is authoritarian one would expect that a positive relationship should hold between strength of desire for power, and if it is participative one would expect the relationship to be negative.

Most contemporary writers about managers hold that the opportunity to utilize one's talents in creative ways is the prime occupational objective of managers. This position is in contradistinction to the image of the organization man so popular a few years ago. It is also held that creativity is valued by the organization. On these grounds, then, it would be anticipated that a positive relationship should exist between strength of desire for self-actualization and performance among managers.

METHODS AND PROCEDURES

A 64-item forced-choice adjective check list was used in the development of scales measuring the four desires (12). Each item in the inventory consists of a pair of personally descriptive adjectives which are roughly equated for social desirability. Half of the items consist of adjectives describing desirable traits, and the other half adjectives describing undesirable traits. In the first half of the items the respondent chooses that member of the pair which he considers to better describe him, and in the second half he chooses that one which he considers less well describes him.

In a previous investigation which was concerned with another sort of motivational factor—initiative, the desire to operate on one's own—it was found that a scale, based on items which discriminated between college students who said that initiative was important to them in their occupational lives and those who said it was unimportant, did in fact have substantial construct validity (13, 14). So this same method was used here in the development of scales designed to measure the four sorts of motivational factors of concern.

Undergraduate students, 313 in number and enrolled in several different colleges and universities, filled out a questionnaire in which they were asked to evaluate their motivations with respect to their occupational lives. Eight types of motivations were presented to them, the desire for job security, high financial reward, power over others, self-actualization, independence of action, status, a kind and understanding supervisor, and fame. The motivations were presented by means of the paired comparison method, and every individual indicated which member of each pair was the more important to him. The students also took the 64-item forced-choice inventory.

For each of the first four types of motivational factors, the students were divided into two groups: those who said that the motivation was important to them, and those who said it was unimportant. An item analysis was performed against these two criterion groups, and for each of the four motivational factors the differentiating items were noted. The items which significantly differentiated between the highs and lows for each of the four factors are listed in Tables 1 through 4. The number shown before each pair of adjectives is the weight assigned to the item, and is proportional to the degree to which the item differentiated between the two criterion groups.

Each of these four sets of items forms a scale measuring a motivational factor. Because the individual filling out the forced-choice inventory does not know what is being sought by it, these four scales provide disguised, or indirect measures of the four motivational factors. Scales of this sort have a certain advantage over direct and explicit reports of motivation because the objective

TABLE 1
ITEMS SIGNIFICANTLY DIFFERENTIATING
THOSE FOR WHOM JOB SECURITY IS IMPORTANT
FROM THOSE FOR WHOM IT IS NOT

Job Security Important	Job Security Not Important
Describe themselves as:	
2 cooperative	important
1 dependable	loyal
1 determined	courageous
2 unaffected	alert
1 deliberate	sharp-witted
1 efficient	clear-thinking
1 thrifty	progressive
1 thoughtful	fair-minded
1 poised	ingenious
3 self-controlled	imaginative
2 stable	foresighted
Describe themselves as not:	
1 headstrong	emotional
2 quarrelsome	immature
1 dreamy	dependent
1 careless	foolish
1 selfish	weak
1 opinionated	pessimistic

TABLE 2
ITEMS SIGNIFICANTLY DIFFERENTIATING
THOSE FOR WHOM HIGH FINANCIAL REWARD IS IMPORTANT
FROM THOSE FOR WHOM IT IS NOT

High Financial Reward Important	High Financial Reward Not Important
Describe themselves as:	
1 independent	persevering
1 kind	jolly
1 intelligent	enterprising
1 thoughtful	fair-minded
1 logical	adaptable
Describe themselves as not:	
1 opinionated	pessimistic
2 hard-hearted	self-pitying
3 aggressive	cynical

of the questionnaire is not apparent to the respondent. As a consequence it might be expected that his responses would be more valid. Nevertheless, very likely the value of "masked" over direct and explicit measures of such subtle matters as motivation is overrated. Certainly indirect measures, too, have flaws, and it is quite possible to falsify responses to forced-choice questions.

TABLE 3
ITEMS SIGNIFICANTLY DIFFERENTIATING
THOSE FOR WHOM POWER OVER OTHERS IS IMPORTANT
FROM THOSE FOR WHOM IT IS NOT

Power Over Others Important	Power Over Others Not Important
Describe themselves as :	
1 loyal	dependable
1 deliberate	sharp-witted
1 progressive	thrifty
1 fair-minded	thoughtful
1 pleasant	modest
1 patient	sympathetic
Describe themselves as not :	
1 shy	lazy
1 unambitious	reckless
2 noisy	arrogant
1 immature	quarrelsome
1 shallow	stingy
1 nervous	intolerant
1 despondent	evasive
1 shiftless	bitter
2 hard-hearted	self-pitying
2 excitable	sly
1 irresponsible	impatient

TABLE 4
ITEMS SIGNIFICANTLY DIFFERENTIATING
THOSE FOR WHOM SELF-ACTUALIZATION IS IMPORTANT
FROM THOSE FOR WHOM IT IS NOT

Self-Actualization Important	Self-Actualization Not Important
Describe themselves as :	
2 inventive	cooperative
2 industrious	practical
1 alert	unaffected
2 sharp-witted	deliberate
2 clear-thinking	efficient
2 ingenious	poised
1 dignified	civilized
Describe themselves as not :	
2 lazy	shy
1 emotional	headstrong
1 foolish	careless
1 submissive	fussy
1 dissatisfied	outspoken

To standardize the four motivational scales, the forced-choice inventory was administered to 300 persons who constituted a reasonably good cross section of the general adult employed population. For comparison purposes, the inventory was also administered to 400 middle-management men. Finally, the inventories of six groups of persons in middle-management positions for whom measures of job success were available were scored for the four motivational scales. These six groups are listed in Table 7. For the first four groups success was gauged by means of ratings developed within their organizations. For the fifth group, executives in a financial organization, those who lasted three years or more with the establishment were taken to be successful, and those terminated in less than three years were taken to be unsuccessful. The final group, various middle managers, consists of men in middle-management positions in a number of different organizations, no two men in fact being members of the same organization. This group, then, provides a coverage of a wide variety of different firms. The degree of success they achieved on their jobs was judged by the writer, who interviewed each man and made a rating on the basis of information so obtained and from other employment data. Ratings of this sort appear to have some merit as measures of the success of persons who hold managerial positions (15).

The following evidence is suggestive of the validity of the four scales. Interviews pertaining to their careers were conducted by the writer with 170 men employed in higher occupations, primarily managerial and sales. Of these men, 60 were judged to be less well adapted to positions in which responsibility and individual initiative were required, but rather had a substantial need for occupational stability and job security. On the security scale the average score of these "lows" was significantly lower than the 110 "highs" at the 6-percent level of confidence. The 170 men were also rated in terms of their desire for high financial rewards from their occupational pursuits, and for their desire for self-actualization and full utilization of their talents. The coefficient of correlation between the former ratings and scores on the high financial rewards scale was 0.42, and the coefficient between the latter ratings and scores on the self-actualization scale was 0.41. We might expect those managers who seek and are placed in line positions to be more highly motivated to exercise power over others than those who are in staff positions. This in fact appears to be the case since the scores earned on the power scale by 189 persons in line-management positions were found to be higher than those earned by 92 persons in staff-management positions at better than the 0.01 level of confidence.

RESULTS

From Tables 1 through 4, which list the adjectives forming each of the scales measuring the motivational factors, some notion of the sorts of persons for whom each factor is important or unimportant can be ascertained. Those for whom job security is important appear to be persons for whom reliability, perseveration, and carefulness are significant values. They seem to be tidy-minded sorts of people. Those for whom job security is not important tend to emphasize self-reliance, intellect, and imagination. They seem to be persons who are willing to take chances. People for whom high financial reward is a matter of concern regard themselves as bright, nice sorts of persons. On the other hand people who do not stress high financial reward look like optimistic, easy-going folk. It is people who regard themselves as solid, mature, and careful for whom power over others is a matter of moment. Tolerant and considerate persons are likely to be those with little desire for such power. A desire for self-actualization seems to characterize those who are energetic and clear thinking. Contrariwise, those for whom self-actualization has no great value are likely to be socially alert but rather detached individuals.

The interrelationships among the four motivational scales are given in Table 5. These are based upon the coefficients of correlation among the scores earned by the sample of the general employed population. It is apparent that, with one exception, the interrelationships among scores on all of the scales are essentially zero. The one exception is the correlation between the scales for job security and for self-actualization. Scores on these two scales have a fairly substantial negative relationship. It would appear that job security and self-actualization are somewhat polar motivational factors.

The average scores on the four motivational scales of 400 persons holding middle management positions are given in Table 6. To make these values more meaningful, they are expressed as percentile ranks of the scores of the sample of the employed population. It is apparent that, compared with the general run of employed people, those persons who hold positions at the middle-management levels earn substantially lower scores on the job security and high financial reward scales, whereas on the self-actualization scale their scores are some-

TABLE 5
INTERCORRELATIONS AMONG THE FOUR MOTIVATIONAL SCALES

	Job Security	High Financial Reward	Power Over Others	Self-Actualization
Job Security		0.085	0.004	−0.682
High Financial Reward			0.137	0.054
Power Over Others				−0.021

TABLE 6
MEAN SCORES ON THE MOTIVATIONAL SCALES OF 400 MIDDLE MANAGERS EXPRESSED AS GENERAL POPULATION PERCENTILE RANKS

Job Security	High Financial Reward	Power Over Others	Self-Actualization
25	26	51	63

what higher. On the scale concerned with power over others, the average of the scores of middle-management people is precisely the same as that of the general population.

The relationships between the four motivational factors and success in managerial positions are shown in Table 7. The weighted averages, through Fisher's z, of the coefficients of correlation are shown at the foot of the table. It would appear that the desires for job security and high financial reward are negatively related to success in middle-management positions, with the former relationship being stronger than the latter. In all six samples the correlations between job security scores and success are negative, ranging from a low of -0.105 to a high of -0.794. The six coefficients of correlation are also negative for high financial reward. Power over others apparently is almost completely unrelated to success in middle-management positions. The average coefficient is not greatly different from zero; in half of the samples the coefficients are positive and in the other half they are negative. Finally, there appears to be some positive relationship between the measure of desire for self-actualization and success. While the average of the coefficients is not high, being only 0.204, in all the six samples the coefficients are positive, ranging from 0.141 to 0.368.

TABLE 7

COEFFICIENTS OF CORRELATION BETWEEN SCORES ON
THE FOUR MOTIVATIONAL SCALES AND MEASURES
OF MANAGERS' JOB SUCCESS

Job Security	High Financial Reward	Power Over Others	Self Actual- ization	No. of Cases	Group
−0.285	−0.289	0.151	0.144	89	District Managers, Insurance
−0.794	−0.131	0.091	0.187	21	Personnel Officers, Insurance
−0.527	−0.444	0.522	0.368	20	Managers, Food Processing Plant
−0.166	−0.425	−0.145	0.141	22	Managers, Chemical Plant
−0.387	−0.135	−0.062	0.177	81	Executives, Financial Organization
−0.105	−0.332	−0.072	0.296	54	Middle Managers, Various
−0.343	−0.208	0.081	0.204	287	Weighted Average

DISCUSSION

The results of the present investigation give some support to the popular notion that job security is of no great importance for those in management positions. The findings indicate that the desire for job security is far less strong among those who hold management positions than it is among the general employed population. Not only do managers as a group feel little need for assurance of continued employment, but those for whom such a need is important perform less well. It would appear that, if a person at the management level devotes his attention and efforts to the stabilization of his position in the organization, those who evaluate him are likely to regard him poorly.

It may seem strange that managers apparently have less desire for high financial reward than the average employed person, and that those with the least desire tend to be most successful. Unquestionably pay operates in a complex manner, especially with those in management positions. Furthermore, the way in which pay is perceived certainly is a relative matter. It seems unlikely that high financial reward is a paramount matter in the thoughts of those who already have an assured substantial income. Thus managers, who are well paid compared with other workers, will not be consumed with an urge to achieve yet higher levels of financial gain. This is not to say that they do not have any motivation at all in this direction, but rather that it is not a strong one. It would also seem that organizations do not regard favorably those in management positions whose primary goals are financial. Those who are so inclined are considered by the organizational "establishment" to perform less well in their jobs.

The fact that the average manager has no more desire for power over others than does the ordinary employed person negates the charge sometimes made that those who direct the operations of business and industrial establishments seek to do so by controlling the actions of their subordinates in an authoritarian manner. Furthermore, the desire to sway and control others is neither an asset nor a liability for a manager. Whether or not he seeks power has no bearing upon how good his performance in his organization is perceived to be.

Another common belief, that the desire for self-actualization is of importance for those in management positions, is supported by the findings of the present investigation. Not only do managers want to utilize their talents in creative ways more than do workers in general, but those who have the strongest wish to do so tend to be regarded as the better managers in their organizations. Apparently, then, the organizational "establishment" does recognize, distinguish, and value managers who seek to express their individual personalities in their work.

The general picture of the nature of managers which emerges from this study while obviously but a small fragment of the total, is diametrically opposite to that portrayed by Whyte (39) in his now classic *The Organization Man*. Rather the findings are congruent with the results of more recent investigations (e.g., 34), which indicate that business and industrial managers are not conformists, but are characterized by a substantial measure of individualism and creativity. Furthermore, contrary to Whyte's thesis, it appears that organizations value those managers who seek the opportunity to utilize their talents in creative ways rather than those who seek security and self-gain.

SUMMARY

As compared with the employed population as a whole, persons in middle-management positions appear to have a substantially lower desire for security and for financial reward, and a higher desire for self-actualization. They do not differ from the employed population in the desire for power over others. Those middle managers who are successful are likely to have less desire for security and high financial reward than those who are unsuccessful, and the successful ones are more likely to value self-actualization. The desire for power over others appears to be unrelated to success in positions at the middle-management levels.

20

An Examination of
Maslow's Need Hierarchy
in an Organizational Setting

Douglas T. Hall
Yale University

Khalil E. Nougaim
International Bank for
Reconstruction and Development

Data from the first five years of the careers of a group of managers were employed to test Maslow's hierarchy of human needs in three ways. No strong evidence for either Maslow's hierarchy or a revised two-level hierarchy was observed. However, as other studies have found, as the managers advance, their need for safety decreases, and the needs for affiliation, achievement and esteem, and self-actualization increase. It was argued that these changes could be explained by a model of sequential career stages, which may be more the result of regularized status passages than of lower-order need gratification. Some methodological issues involved in testing the Maslow model were also explored.

The authors wish to express their appreciation to David E. Berlew, principal investigator of the project in which the coded data were obtained, and to David A. Kolb, who collaborated with the authors in an early phase of the present project. Helpful comments were provided by Clayton P. Alderfer, Chris Argyris, Richard Campbell, J. Richard Hackman, Lyman W. Porter, and Edward E. Lawler.

The materials which form the basis of this research were collected by the American Telephone & Telegraph Company as part of the Bell System's Management Progress Study. In this regard, we are indebted to Dr. Douglas Bray, Director of the Management Progress Study, and to W. D. Bachelis and W. S. Felton. The planning and execution of the research are the sole responsibility of the authors, and the conclusions reached do not necessarily reflect the views of the Management Progress Study. Reprinted in abridged form by permission from *Organizational Behavior and Human Performance*, III, No. 1 (1968), 12–35.

Psychologists concerned with issues of motivation and personal change in organizations have been making increasing use of Maslow's hierarchical model of motive change. Inherent in this hierarchy is the belief that an individual develops a healthy personality to the extent that he realizes fully his human potential. The basic appeal of this notion has made the theory extremely popular, and it has gained further acceptance through the writings of organization theorists such as McGregor (27), Haire (18), Schein (36), and Leavitt (23). Despite the popularity of Maslow's model, there has been comparatively little work done to test it empirically. Thus, the present research was conducted to determine the validity of the theory in an organizational setting.

MASLOW'S NEED HIERARCHY

Maslow's theory of human motivation (25) asserts that human motives emerge in a sequential pattern according to a hierarchy of five need levels. Listed in order from lowest to highest, these levels are as follows:

1. *Physiological*—(tissue needs such as hunger and thirst)
2. *Safety*—(needs for security, absence of threat)
3. *Affiliation*—(need for close affective relationships)
4. *Achievement and Esteem*—(need for achievement and self-respect)
5. *Self-actualization*—(need for the utilization and growth of one's potential skills and abilities).

The hierarchical nature of these need levels manifests itself in two ways. First, Maslow predicts a process of successive prepotency among the five levels. For a given individual at a given point in time, one class of needs will be more salient than any other. Then, as those needs become satisfied, needs at the next higher level will become stronger (i.e., more salient).

The second important characteristic of the hierarchy is its prediction of a decrease in the strength of a given need following its satisfaction. Thus, for example, when the safety needs are largely satisfied, not only do the affiliation needs increase, but also the safety needs decrease. Similar decreases are asserted to occur at all other levels upon gratification at those levels. In short, "a satisfied need is not a motivator" (25, p. 105).

This theory, then, asserts that the importance of higher needs increases in a consistent, sequential pattern as lower needs become satisfied and decrease. This relationship between lower need satisfaction and higher need strength is the object of inquiry in the present research.

RELEVANT RESEARCH

Most research on need hierarchies has been cross-sectional rather than longitudinal. A review of this research is reported by Vroom (38). Davis (11) found that underprivileged workers lacked ambition or concern with the nature of their work. Hierarchy theory would explain this result with the assertion that their lack of safety-gratification prevents them from progressing to a concern with achievement or self-actualization, which would make them interested in the manner in which the nature of their work enabled them to utilize their skills. Other researchers have compared high- and low-status occupational groups (which presumably differ on lower-level need satisfaction) and tested for higher-level need differences. Pellegrin and Coates (32) found that executives are likely to define success as career accomplishment, while first level supervisors (whose achievement needs are less well satisfied) tend to view it in terms of security and income. Porter (33) found that top executives are more concerned with esteem and self-actualization than managers lower in the organization structure. Centers (10), Morse and Weiss (28), and Lyman (24) found that ratings of the importance of accomplishment and self-expression in work are directly related to job level and presumably, then, to lower-level gratification. Veroff, Atkinson, Feld, and Gurin (37) report that *n* Ach [ievement] scores are directly related to occupational level.

One problem with inferring the existence of a need hierarchy from the study of deprived and satisfied groups is that selection, situational, or cultural factors, and not personality processes, may be affecting the result. It may be true, as the hierarchy theory would predict, that top executives have high needs for achievement, ambition, or concern with work because their lower-order needs have become relatively satisfied. On the other hand, though, these qualities may have been present before the executives were promoted (either as intrinsic personality factors or in response to predominant values in the organizational culture). Thus, these higher level concerns may have been a cause, not an effect, of their high organizational status.

The problems inherent in testing a need hierarchy through intergroup analysis have been avoided in a careful study by Alderfer (1). The hierarchy he tested was similar to Maslow's, consisting of three levels: existence (physiological and material concerns), relatedness (affiliation), and growth (developing and using skills and abilities). Here the unit of analysis was the individual, and he tested his three-stage hierarchy by looking for correlations at one point in time between a person's satisfaction at a given level and his need strength at the next higher level.

Measuring need strength and satisfaction through interviews and two types of questionnaires, Alderfer found evidence for the link between existence satisfaction and relatedness need strength. However, his data did not support the hypothesized relationship between the strength of growth needs and the satisfaction of relatedness or existence needs. He also found that the growth needs tend to increase as they are satisfied, whereas the lower needs decrease upon gratification.

Although a number of studies are related to Maslow's theory, none that we have seen has explicitly employed *his* need levels and studied *changes* in need strength and satisfaction in a panel of subjects *over time*. The theory is basically one of personality change; Maslow predicts that as lower-order needs *become* more satisfied, higher-order needs *become* more important. Thus the theory is best tested with change (i.e., longitudinal) data.

What is needed, then, is the longitudinal equivalent of the Alderfer study. To test the hypothesis that increases in lower-need satisfaction are related to increases in higher-need strength requires correlating *changes* in lower-need satisfaction with *changes* in higher-need strength. Very simply, we need a test of the hierarchy in action.

DESIGN OF THE STUDY

The present study attempted to meet this need by utilizing five years of data for a panel of new management trainees in an operating company of the American Telephone & Telegraph Company (often referred to as the Bell System). This company is a participant in AT&T's Management Progress Study (7). The hierarchy was tested in the following three ways:

STATIC ANALYSIS. The first test, which was similar to the studies reviewed above, was a static analysis. Here all the satisfaction scores were correlated with all the need strength scores within each year. It was hypothesized that the satisfaction of a given need level would correlate strongly with the strength of the next higher level. Thus, high correlations were expected between Safety satisfaction and Affiliation need strength, between Affiliation satisfaction and Achievement and Esteem need strength, etc.

CHANGE ANALYSIS. The second test, unlike the previously described studies and hitting much closer to the dynamic nature of the hierarchy's developmental approach, was a change analysis. Here all the changes in need satisfaction from one year to the next were correlated with changes in need strength at the next higher level during the same period of time. This was done for all the four periods between each of the first five-years' data (i.e., the periods between year 1 and year 2, between year 2 and year 3, etc.). Again high correlations were predicted between change in satisfaction of a given need level and the change in strength of the next higher level.

SUCCESS ANALYSIS. Unlike the previous analyses which used self-reports and subjective data of need satisfaction, the third analysis, also a longitudinal one, used an objective measure of need satisfaction over the five-year period: fifth-year income. Since the sample consists of management trainees of approximately the same age, educational background, and initial salary level, fifth-year income was expected to discriminate between "successful" and "less successful" managers by company standards. No differences were expected between the two groups in the first year. However, by the fifth year it was expected that needs and satisfactions would change differentially. Since the more successful managers were more secure and better paid, this group was expected to score higher on satisfaction and lower on need strength in the Safety category. In the Self-actualization and Achievement and Esteem levels, the successful managers were expected to have higher need scores, since their lower level satisfactions would have engaged these needs more.

HYPOTHESES.   The formal statement of the hypotheses to be tested by these analyses is as follows:

Hypothesis I: Within a given year, the satisfaction of a given level of needs will be positively correlated with the strength of the needs at the next higher level (static analysis).

Hypothesis II: From one year to the next, changes in the satisfaction of a given level of needs will be positively correlated with changes in the strength of the needs at the next higher level (change analysis).

Hypothesis III: After five years of employment, successful managers will show lower need strength and higher satisfaction in the safety needs than will their less successful colleagues. Thus, they will show higher achievement and self-actualization need strength than will the less successful group (success analysis).

METHOD

SUBJECTS.   The subjects are 49 young management-level employees of an operating company of the American Telephone & Telegraph Company, who were hired in 1957 and remained with the company during the five years of the study. All subjects are college graduates, originally hired as management trainees; most were hired directly from college, although a few came from other companies.

The subjects were at considerably higher levels in the organization by the fifth year. Whereas they began as trainees for positions at the first level of management, most had been promoted to either the second (supervisor) or third (district manager) level by year five.[1]

MEASURING NEEDS.   McClelland defines a motive as a learned construct, "a strong affective association, characterized by anticipatory goal reactions and based on past associations of certain cues with pleasure or pain" (26, p. 226). Research has shown that these motives may be inferred from the specific associations individuals use when perceiving themselves or their environment (2). If a person thinks of others in terms of how friendly or unfriendly they are, one would infer that affiliation is an important motive for him. If on the other hand, when he is given complete choice to describe other people, he consistently uses terms like "passive," "stubborn," "a pushover," "a powerful leader," "domineering," then one would infer that he is motivated by a need for power or control.

In the present study, motives were assessed through interview data. Subjects participated in five annual three-hour interviews with consulting psychologists

---

[1] The company has seven levels of management from foreman to president.

(who, during the course of the study established a high degree of rapport and trust with the subjects). Among the topics covered were the following: attitudes toward the job; relationships with superiors, peers and subordinates; major sources of satisfaction and dissatisfaction; career aspirations and strategies; and major occurrences in the past year. The questions were open ended so that the subjects had free choice to discuss the topics in terms of their own most important constructs. Thus, the "vocabulary" or set of personally salient dimensions that each subject used in the interview provided a profile of his motive structure.

Nine need categories were empirically derived from these protocols. These categories, their definitions and their coding reliabilities are contained in Table 1.

To obtain motive scores, the interview protocols were content-analyzed and

TABLE 1
NEED CATEGORIES, DEFINITIONS, AND CODING RELIABILITIES
($N = 30$)

1. *Meaning and Sense of Purpose*: the need to serve some higher cause. A desire to see one's own work as related to some more all-encompassing goals. These goals may range from the religious and altruistic to the more immediate and general goals of the individual's work group, district, or division. (Need strength reliability = 0.55; satisfaction reliability = 1.00.)

2. *Personal Development*: the need for development and integration of personal skills. The desire to become competent, skillful, and effective in areas which are important to the individual and which are job related, within broad limits. Included here is the individual's desire to acquire new knowledge and skills. (Need strength reliability = 0.65; satisfaction reliability = 0.60.)

3. *Stimulation*: the need for activity which stimulates curiosity and induces excitement. The need for interesting work, for unique and varied experiences. (Need strength reliability = 0.60; satisfaction reliability = 0.41.)

4. *Achievement and Challenge*: the need to compete with some challenging standard of excellence, either internal or external. (Need strength reliability = 0.69; satisfaction reliability = 0.72.)

5. *Power and Responsibility*: the need to hold a responsible position and/or to control the means of influence over policy and other people. Responsibility is used here in the sense of accountability for the effects of one's own decisions. The need to be in positions where one's judgment and decisions are important to the progress and welfare of projects and/or people. This concern may also be expressed as a need to control or manipulate in a socially less acceptable sense. (Need strength reliability = 0.63; satisfaction reliability = 0.55.)

6. *Support and Approval*: concern over acts of notice, praise, or blame as a means of self-definition. Relying on the opinions of others for achieving self-esteem and self-confirmation. (Need strength reliability = 0.27; satisfaction reliability = 0.55.)

7. *Affiliation*: concern over establishing, maintaining, or restoring a positive affective relationship with another person or group in the work situation. (Need strength reliability = 0.42; satisfaction reliability = 1.00.)

8. *Structure*: the need to have the world predictable and ordered, to avoid ambiguous situations, and to be dependent on others for the initiation of activities. (Need strength reliability = 0.49; satisfaction reliability = 0.42.)

9. *Security*: the need to feel safe and prepared for anything that might happen, however unexpected. The need to avoid threat. (Need strength reliability = 0.59; satisfaction reliability = 0.36.)

given need strength ratings ranging from 1 (low concern) to 3 (strong concern) in each of nine categories.

A second score was also given to indicate the extent to which the person was satisfied or dissatisfied in each need category. These satisfaction scores ranged from +2 (oversatisfied)[2] through 0 (satisfied—the desired state) to −2 (highly dissatisfied).

Also coded each year for each subject was a global rating of the extent to which the satisfaction of his most important needs was occurring on the job as opposed to off the job. This measure of relative on-the-job satisfaction, coded on a scale from 1 to 10, was labeled *work centrality*.

CODING.   Two doctoral candidates in psychology coded the cases. After a month of practice their intercoder scoring reliability coefficients ranged from 0.27 to 0.69 (median = 0.59) on the need strength categories, and from 0.36 to 1.0 (median = 0.55) on the satisfaction categories. Reliability on the work centrality index was 0.81.

Because the coding reliability was not as high as we would have preferred, each coder scored each case. Then they resolved whatever differences their scores contained, and arrived at final, jointly-determined scores.

Cases were scored on a completely random basis in terms of subject and year. This procedure assured us that the coding of each year for each subject would be an independent operation.

DETERMINING NEED LEVELS.   The nine need categories were collapsed into four a priori need levels approximating the four highest proposed by Maslow. Only the physiological concerns were not included. These levels and their component categories are as follows:

(1) Self-actualization: meaning and sense of purpose, personal development, and stimulation; (2) Achievement and Esteem: achievement and challenge, and responsibility; (3) Affiliation: affiliation; and (4) Safety: support and approval, security, and structure.

On the basis of the writers' understanding of Maslow's theory, the levels were placed in the preceding order, with Self-actualization being the highest level and Safety the lowest. There was some hesitation about the Support and Approval category, since on an a priori basis we would have been inclined include it in the Achievement and Esteem level. It was placed in Safety, however, because of its heavy dependence on the element of external approval, which Maslow feels does not belong to a healthy self-esteem level (11, pp. 90–91).

Level scores for both need strength and need satisfaction were obtained by summing the respective unweighted category scores for that need level. In addition to giving us a more manageable number of need groupings to analyze,

---

[2] This unusual condition means that the person is actually receiving more gratification in a given area than he wants. An example would be too much safety or structure in a job. Instances of such overgratification were rare, and when present, could usually be coded as dissatisfaction in another need area.

this summing process also gave us dimensions which were probably more reliable than individual categories.

RESULTS

STATIC ANALYSIS

The results of the static analysis are shown in Table 2. The correlations, as was mentioned earlier, measure the relationship between need satisfaction and need strength for all levels within each of the five years. The hypothesized relationships, the correlations between satisfaction of a given need and the strength of the next higher level, are indicated by the boxed numerals.

An obvious conclusion that can be drawn from the static analysis is that none of the predicted correlations is very large; many, in fact, are smaller than the nonhypothesized relationships.

With the exception of Affiliation, the strength of each need correlated more strongly with its own satisfaction than with the satisfaction of any other need. Safety satisfaction and Safety intensity show a pooled r of 0.26; Affiliation satisfaction and intensity, 0.16; Achievement and Esteem, 0.54; and Self-actualization, 0.29.

TABLE 2
STATIC ANALYSIS: CORRELATIONS BETWEEN
LOWER-LEVEL SATISFACTION AND HIGHER-LEVEL NEED STRENGTH

Need Satisfaction	Need Strength			
	Safety	Affiliation	Achievement and Esteem	Self-Actualization
Safety	0.26	0.18	0.28	0.17
Affiliation	0.07	0.16	0.23	−0.00
Achievement and Esteem	0.09	0.15	0.54	0.10
Self-actualization	0.11	0.12	0.36	0.29

Note.—Each r is a "z"-transformed pooled equivalent, computed from correlation coefficients for years 1–5. Since these rs are not composed of independent yearly estimates, we cannot legitimately indicate significance levels.

CHANGE ANALYSIS

The results of the change analysis are reported in Table 3. Again the coefficients are not high. Among the predicted relationships, two received moderate degrees of support. Safety satisfaction and Affiliation strength show a pooled r of 0.22. Achievement and Esteem satisfaction and Self-actualization strength have a pooled coefficient of 0.20. The other predicted link—Affiliation and Achievement and Esteem ($r_{pooled} = 0.05$)—received no support from the change data.

The correlations between the satisfaction of needs and their own intensities yielded results similar to the static analysis. Again the strength of each need in a given year was positively related to its own satisfaction in the previous year. This relationship was especially strong for Achievement and Esteem ($r_{pooled} =0.53$).

TABLE 3
CHANGE ANALYSIS: CORRELATIONS BETWEEN
CHANGES OF LOWER-NEED SATISFACTION AND HIGHER-NEED STRENGTH
FROM ONE YEAR TO THE NEXT

Change in Need Satisfaction	Need Strength			
	Safety	Affiliation	Achievement and Esteem	Self-Actualization
Safety	0.25	0.22	0.13	0.09
Affiliation	−0.02	0.21	0.05	0.12
Achievement	0.12	0.15	0.53	0.20
Self-Actualization	0.14	0.17	0.28	0.28

Note.—Each *r* is a "*z*"-transformed pooled equivalent, computed from coefficients for each of the four one-year periods. Since these *r*s are not composed of independent yearly estimates, we cannot legitimately indicate significance levels.

SUCCESS ANALYSIS

The purpose of this third analysis was to assess the relative impact on need strength and satisfaction of high and low fifth-year managerial success (i.e., salary). Data for conducting this analysis are graphed in Figures 1 and 2.

NEED INTENSITY. Figure 1 contains need intensity scores for both the high and low fifth-year salary groups in both the first and the fifth years. It was predicted that there would be no differences between the two groups in the first year. This was the case, with one exception. Interestingly, the successful group showed a significantly lower need for Safety in the first year than did their less successful colleagues ($p < 0.05$, two-tailed).[3]

In the fifth year we see that *both groups* significantly decreased in their concern for Safety ($p < 0.001$). Furthermore, *both groups* increased in their needs for Achievement and Esteem ($p < 0.001$), and Self-actualization ($p < 0.001$). For Affiliation, the successful group showed a significant increase in need strength

---

[3] Mean differences between groups were tested with *t*-tests for independent samples. Mean changes within groups were tested with *t*-tests for dependent samples (6).

($p < 0.025$), while the other group showed a nonsignificant increase.[4] Thus, over time, both the successful and the less successful groups decreased in their concern for Safety gratifications and increased in their concern for Achievement and Esteem and Self-actualization.

FIGURE 1
FIRST- AND FIFTH-YEAR NEED STRENGTH SCORES
FOR HIGH- AND LOW-SUCCESS GROUPS
($N = 25$ AND 24, RESPECTIVELY)

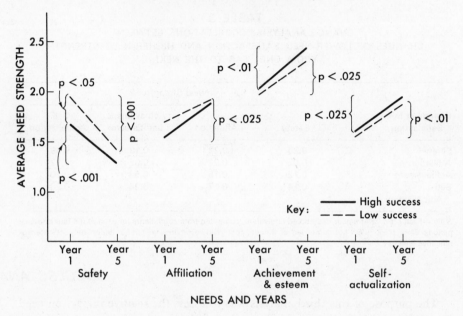

In the fifth year there were still no significant differences in need strength scores between the two groups. In fact, these intergroup differences were not markedly different from those of the first year. Therefore, both groups showed great interyear differences in need intensity, but no intergroup discrepancies. We conclude, then, that these need changes are not related to our objective measure of need gratification.

---

[4] Over the initial *eight* years of employment for this sample, Bray (personal communication, 1966) has found a significant decrease in affiliation concerns (as measured by the Edwards Personal Preference Schedule). In another Bell System operating company, Katkovsky (21) also found a significant decrease in TAT-measured need Affiliation over the first eight years of employment. These inconsistent results could have been due to the differences in time span, measuring instruments, or administration conditions. The latter is a distinct possibility, since over the years the interviewers for the present study developed increasing rapport and trust in their relationships with the subjects. This change may have manifested itself in the form of increased affiliation imagery during the later interviews.

NEED SATISFACTION.   Figure 2 shows the need satisfaction scores for both groups during the first and fifth years. In the first year there were no significant differences between the two groups.

By the fifth year, however, a large difference had developed in the Achievement and Esteem category; the less successful group decreased from their first year levels and reported significantly lower satisfaction than the more successful managers ($p < 0.05$). Thus a lack of objective success is related to decreasing satisfaction in one's need for Achievement and Esteem.

FIGURE 2

FIRST- AND FIFTH-YEAR NEED SATISFACTION SCORES
FOR HIGH- AND LOW-SUCCESS GROUPS
(N = 25 AND 24, RESPECTIVELY)

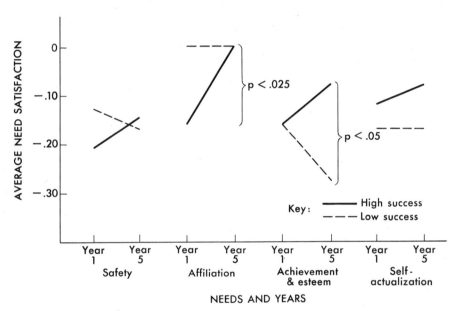

WORK CENTRALITY.   By the fifth year there exists a significant difference between the two groups on the Work Centrality dimension (cf. Figure 3). After five years of employment, the successful managers report that their needs are being satisfied on the job to a significantly greater extent than do the less successful managers ($p < 0.05$). Since no difference existed in the first year, this relative increase in Work Centrality must be related to the differences in success that have emerged during their first five years with the company. In other words, the more successful a man becomes, the more totally satisfying his job becomes.

FIGURE 3
WORK CENTRALITY AVERAGES SCORES, YEARS 1 AND 5,
FOR HIGH- AND LOW-SUCCESS GROUPS
(N = 25 AND 24, RESPECTIVELY)

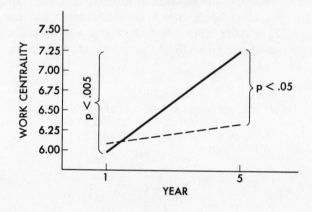

Key: ——— High success
      – – – Low success

DISCUSSION

In the static and change analyses no strong relationships were found to support the hierarchy of needs we hypothesized. Furthermore, none of the correlations between need and satisfaction levels was high enough to support the existence of a hierarchical order diffcrent from the one we tested.

The success analysis also yielded disconfirming results. For both the successful and the less successful groups, higher-level concerns increased and lower-level needs decreased in about the same ways; thus, changes in these needs were unrelated to an objective measure of gratification in the Safety and Achievement and Esteem areas.

An analysis of the changing need and satisfaction patterns of both groups, as shown in Figures 1 and 2, provides further group-level disconfirmation of the hierarchy. On the average, the groups decreased in their concern for the two lower needs and increased in the strength of he three higher needs. According to the theory, then, managers in the sample should have become more satisfied in at least the safety category, since the gratification of lower needs supposedly (1) reduces the strength of the lower needs, and (2) engages, or increases, the strength of the higher needs. The data, however, show that average satisfaction *decreased* in each of the lower needs, contrary to the theory's prediction.[5]

CAREER STAGES

As an alternative to the motive hierarchy, one could explain these changing needs in terms of developing career concerns rather than lower need gratification. In line with this reasoning, we could conceptualize a career as a series of salient personal issues, which emerge as the person passes through various status boundaries.[6]

The first phase is often characterized by a concern for security—gaining recognition and establishing oneself in a profession or organization. The beginning of the career is a new experience, and here the person is mainly concerned with defining the structure of his position and with feeling secure in it. At this point he is at the boundary of his organization, a very stressful location (20), and he is searching for means of integrating himself into the system. Being new, he does not have a strong identity relevant to his particular organization, and he is struggling to define more clearly his environment and his relationship to it.[7]

This is often a period during which the person feels highly disillusioned and sees little fit between his training and the organization's requirements. Even if the job is, in fact, highly challenging, he may not be aware of the choices he has in attacking a problem in his own way. Faced with little formal structure or with few clear organizational expectations, he may see this lack of structure as a lack of challenge. And if the job is, in fact, unchallenging for a man of his qualifications, he will not get really excited about his work and will probably be less successful than he would have been with a more demanding initial position (5).[8]

---

[5] The less successful group also either decreased or remained the same in satisfaction on the three higher-level needs, while strength of these needs increased. This phenomenon could fit with the theory since need strength levels could be increasing faster than gratifications, with the result that the gap between need and gratification would be increasing.

[6] For a more general discussion of the interaction between social structure and life stages, see L. D. Cain, Jr., "Life Course and Social Structure," in *Handbook of Modern Sociology*, ed. R. Faris (Chicago: Rand McNally & Co., 1964), pp. 272–309; A. Strauss, *Mirrors and Masks* (New York: Free Press of Glencoe, Inc., 1959); and E. Erikson, *Childhood and Society* (New York: W. W. Norton & Company, Inc., 1963).

[7] See Hall (19) for a discussion of the identity changes associated with a professional role transition.

[8] For a fuller discussion of early career issues from the points of view of the organization and the individual, see Edgar H. Schein, "How to Break in the College Graduate," *Harvard Business Review*, November and December, 1964, pp. 68–76.

In the present study, empirical support for the role of early safety concerns is found in the fact that in the first year the successful group had a significantly lower need for safety than the less successful group. Thus, while the first-year situation tends to arouse the safety needs for all employees, those who are relatively less concerned with safety are more successful in later years than their more security-conscious colleagues. This is corroborated by Berlew and Hall's (5) finding that Tolerance of Uncertainty correlated significantly with managerial success in their sample.

These data are further supported by Bray and Grant's (8) correlations found in other AT&T companies between managerial success and an index containing Tolerance of Uncertainty and Resistance to Stress.

Several other researchers have found empirical support for the key role of safety concerns in the early years of a career. In a study of scientists, Glaser (16) found that concerns with security and with "establishing themselves" distinguished junior investigators from senior investigators and supervisors. Caplow and McGee (9, p. 69) make similar observations about assistant professors. Becker and Straus (4, p. 260), Lazarsfeld and Thielens (22, p. 252), and Avery (3) provide additional data attesting to the early importance of the safety needs in other occupations.

Next might come a concern for promotion and achievement. At this intermediate stage a person is not so concerned with fitting into an organization (moving inside) as he is with moving upward and mastering it. This would, of course, be particularly true for our achievement-oriented line managers who would be "successful" to the extent that they moved up within the organization.

Our data support the importance of achievement in the intermediate career years in that both the high- and low-success groups showed a significant increase in the strength of Achievement and Esteem concerns between the first and the fifth years of employment. Furthermore, coupled with this increase in need strength is a significant difference in Achievement and Esteem satisfaction between the two groups in the fifth year. In no other need category was there a difference in need satisfaction between the two groups in either the first or the fifth year. Thus, in terms of both need strength and need satisfaction, Achievement and Esteem was a very active concern for the members of the sample between the first and fifth years of their careers.

In other Bell System operating companies Katkovsky (21) and Bray (personal communication) found significant increases in young managers' achievement and autonomy concerns (as measured by the Edwards Personal Preference Schedule) between the first and eighth years of employment. Glaser (16) similarly found promotion to be the dominant intermediate career concern in his sample.

Beyond the advancement stage we can only speculate, since our data cover only the first five years of the subject's careers. However, our subjective impression is that once the incumbent had cues that he was nearing the limit of this advancement, his career would start to level off, and the need—or opportunity—to compete would decrease. If he felt successful, he might become concerned with helping younger men—his successors—grow, in order to strengthen the organization and perpetuate his work. If he felt unsuccessful, he might still define his mission as helping these young men, or he might use his power to block their progress and thus punish them for his failure. Whatever the specific behavior at this later stage, the period does represent the onset of a terminal plateau. The man has achieved his own particular level of success, and he now must find some other means of gratification. The end, just as the beginning, can be a critical period, and the incumbent must adjust to a significantly altered self-definition.

We could also describe these phases in terms of Maslow's categories. The initial phase, of course, would be characterized by strong concerns for safety. The next stage, striving for advancement, would consist of high needs for achievement. The final stage would contain a different type of striving, one in which the person was attempting to relate his efforts to some higher-order cause, such as commitment to the organization or service to youth; and this concern for meaning and a sense of purpose in one's work would be a means of self-actualization.

In taking issue with this model, one could argue that a man moves on to the next stage in his career simply because he becomes satisfied in the needs experienced at the previous stage. We would not agree, and herein lies the difference between the stages model and the hierarchy. The career stages model asserts that a man moves on to a higher career stage as a result of fairly regular status passages which are facilitated by both the environment (i.e., role factors) and the individual (i.e., developmental life stages, à la Erikson). And these status passages can occur largely independent of the man's degree of perceived success in satisfying the concerns he experienced at the earlier stages (as witness the similar need changes for the high and low success groups in the present study, Figure 1).

If these career stages are, in fact, universal, it is not difficult to see how an observer might "read in" a hierarchical mechanism to aid in explaining the need changes which accompany them. If Maslow observed people at various stages in their careers—and he indicates clinical and observational data were important inputs in his model—he might see needs emerge in the order he describes. And he might also see people express more satisfactions in the lower-need areas (although the present data would not support this possibility). However, he could be incorrect in his inferences that lower-level gratification *causes* higher needs to emerge. If the model of successive stages is valid, these people may express less dissatisfaction with a lower need (such as safety, if we are considering a man at the midcareer stage) simply because that need is no longer so salient, and not vice versa.

More research—and quite sophisticated research at that—will be needed to answer the question of why these changing phases occur. If the changes are, in fact, due to the person's being in a certain social situation at a certain point in his life, it would be operationally difficult to untangle the effects of age, position, or role, and perceived lower-level need satisfactions, although a recent helpful article by Schaie (35) contains a promising methodology. Basically, we would test the hypotheses that the strength of the various needs is related more strongly to the interaction of age and role, than to the degree of lower-level need gratification.

21

Every Employee a Manager

M. Scott Myers
Texas Instruments

I am indebted to division training directors and line managers in Texas Instruments for their applications which have resulted in and are validating concepts presented in this paper. I am particularly indebted to Earl D. Weed, Corporate Manager of Training and Development, who helped formulate some of these concepts and plan the application of job enrichment at Texas Instruments. © 1968 by The Regents of the University of California. Reprinted from *California Management Review*, X (1968), No. 3, 9–20, by permission of The Regents.

This article is an extension of earlier studies in motivation made at Texas Instruments and published in the *Harvard Business Review* (29, 30, 31). These and similar studies done elsewhere provide corroborative evidence of the wastefulness of bureaucracy and the advantages of democracy. Terms made familiar through these publications include participative management, consultative supervision, theory Y leadership, self-direction and self-control, 9 to 9 supervision, goal setting, work simplification, team effort, personal commitment, and self-actualization. All have in common the fuller and more voluntary utilization of human talent and, as such, represent some form of job enlargement or enrichment of the job holder's life at work.

UNQUESTIONABLE BENEFITS

The informed manager no longer needs to be convinced of the merits of job enrichment. Experiments at Texas Instruments and elsewhere have shown tangible improvements in terms of such diverse criteria as reduced costs, higher yields, less scrap, accelerated learning time, fewer complaints and trips to the health center, reduced anxiety, improved attitudes and team efforts, and increased profits. Hence, the desirability of job enrichment is no longer in question, but, rather, the quest now is for definitions and implementation procedures. Most reports on job enrichment are situational descriptions which offer little guidance for supervisors in dissimilar circumstances, and slavish emulation of inappropriate models usually leads to failure.

The primary purpose of this article is to present a theoretical model for defining the characteristics of meaningful work and some techniques for analyzing work and enriching it. But, first, I will define and give some examples of job enrichment and analyze the traditional barriers to its implementation, then define the emerging role of the supervisor.

A BETTER USE OF TALENT

JOB ENRICHMENT

Though job enrichment is the new shibboleth of today's managers, few have had first-hand experience with it. But, McGregor's (27) message is getting through, and testimonials of the efficacy of theory Y are commonplace—people are responsible and creative when given the opportunity! Unfortunately, many managers still see job enlargement as a form of benevolent autocracy, and their unguided attempts to enlarge jobs fall more within the realm of manipulation than job enrichment. Job enrichment may result from horizontal or vertical job enlargement, or a combination of both, as illustrated in Exhibit 1. Horizontal job enlargement is characterized by adding a variety of similar functions, and, though it usually ameliorates the boredom of a simple job, it seldom offers the enrichment opportunity provided through vertical job enlargement. Vertically enlarged jobs enable employees to have a hand in doing some of the planning and control work previously restricted to persons in supervisory and staff functions.

EXHIBIT 1
EXAMPLES OF
HORIZONTAL AND VERTICAL JOB ENLARGEMENT

HORIZONTAL

• Assemblers on a transformer assembly line each performed a single operation as the assembly moved by on the conveyor belt. Jobs were enlarged horizontally by setting up work stations to permit each operator to assemble the entire unit. Operations now performed by each operator include cabling, upending, winding, soldering, laminating, and symbolizing.

• A similar transformer assembly line provides horizontal job enlargement when assemblers are taught how to perform all operations and are rotated to a different operation each day.

VERTICAL

• Assemblers on a radar assembly line are given information on customer contract commitments in terms of price, quality specifications, delivery schedules, and company data on material and personnel costs, breakeven performance, and potential profit margins. Assemblers and engineers work together in methods and design improvements. Assemblers inspect, adjust, and repair their own work, help test completed units, and receive copies of customer inspection reports.

• Female electronic assemblers involved in intricate assembling, bonding, soldering, and welding operations are given training in methods improvement and were encouraged to make suggestions for improving manufacturing processes. Natural work groups of five to 25 assemblers each elect a "team captain" for a term of six months. In addition to performing her regular operations, the team captain collects work improvement ideas from members of her team, describes them on a standard form, credits the suggestors, presents the recommendations to their supervisor and superintendent at the end of the week, and gives the team feedback on idea utilization. Though most job operations remain the same, vertical job enlargement is achieved by providing increased opportunity for planning, reorganizing and controlling their work, and earning recogition.

HORIZONTAL PLUS VERTICAL

• Jobs are enlarged horizontally in a clad metal rolling mill by qualifying operators to work interchangeably on breakdown rolling, finishing rolling, slitter, pickler, and abrader operations. After giving the operators training in methods improvement and basic metallurgy, jobs are enlarged vertically by involving them with engineering and supervisory personnel in problem-solving, goal-setting sessions for increasing production yields.

• Jobs in a large employee insurance section are enlarged horizontally by qualifying insurance clerks to work interchangeably in filing claims, mailing checks, enrolling and orienting new employees, checking premium and enrollment reports, adjusting payroll deductions, and interpreting policies to employees. Vertical enlargement involves clerks in insurance program planning meetings with personnel directors and carrier representatives, authorizes them to sign disbursement requests, permits them to attend a paperwork systems conference, and enables them to recommend equipment replacements and to rearrange their work layout.

Job enrichment sometimes results naturally from the intuitive practices of goal-oriented, emotionally mature managers who evoke commitment through a "language of action" which grants freedom and reflects respect, confidence, and high expectations. When job enrichment is attempted by reductive, authority-oriented managers by duplicating job designs evolved by goal-oriented managers, they may fail to inspire involvement and commitment, because their motives are suspect and their "language of action" comes through as manipulation and exploitation rather than as acts of trust, confidence, and respect.

Hence, job enrichment depends on style of supervision as well as job requirements and is not simply a matter of duplicating patterns of work and relationships found to be successful elsewhere.

MANAGEMENT FUNCTIONS

The role of the manager is explicitly defined in business administration textbooks in terms of functions generally labeled as planning, organizing, leading, and controlling, as illustrated in Exhibit 2. Despite the uniformity and universality of these management functions, their application mirrors a wide vari-

EXHIBIT 2
THE FUNCTIONS OF MANAGEMENT

Planning: objectives, goals, strategies, programs, policies, forecasts.
Organizing: manpower, money, machines, materials, methods.
Leading: directing, motivating, instructing, delegating, coaching, recognizing.
Controlling: auditing, measuring, evaluating, correcting.

ety of practices and management styles. In the eyes of the typical manager, management functions pertain to the job of a "manager," but not to the job of the "worker." For example, a manager in an automotive factory, if asked to describe his job, might say, "I am building automobiles, and my job includes planning, organizing, leading, and controlling. I have about 50 foremen who are leading and controlling." And, almost as an afterthought, he might add, "Oh

EXHIBIT 3
THE MANAGER'S TRADITIONAL PERCEPTION
OF HIS JOB

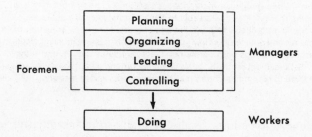

yes, I also have 2000 workers on the assembly line turning wrenches and screw drivers." This concept is reflected in Exhibit 3.

THE MANAGEMENT-LABOR DICHOTOMY

This typical point of view excludes employees from the realm of management and creates, subconsciously if not deliberately, a dichotomy of people at work—unintelligent, uninformed, uncreative, irresponsible, and immature workers who need the direction and control of intelligent, informed, creative, responsible, and mature managers. The consequences of this point of view are widely evident in industry and are reflected in Exhibit 4, which shows the cleavage between management and labor in terms of social distance and alienation.

EXHIBIT 4
THE MANAGEMENT–LABOR DICHOTOMY

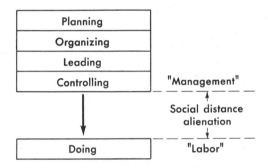

Though the gap between the employer and the employed has a long heritage and, in some respects, seems inescapably inherent to the relationship, it has become more formalized and widened through the efforts of labor unions whose charters depend on their success in convincing labor that management is their natural enemy. The union, while pressuring management to share its affluence and prerogatives, has at the same time clearly defined the laboring man's charter as being separate from, and indeed in conflict with, that of management. Managers typically and naturally align themselves with the goals of the company, but workers divide their allegiance between the union and the company, often with a feeling of closer identification with the union that with the company.

Two forces in America have the potential for rendering this labor–management dichotomy obsolete. One is the improving socioeconomic status and the consequent value changes of the previously less privileged, accelerated by legislated equality and increasing enlightenment in a democratic and increasingly affluent society. The second force is a growing awareness on the part of managers of the inevitability of democracy as the pattern for a healthful entrepreneurial society and the importance of their role in supporting it. This article is devoted more to this second force—defining a concept of meaningful work to guide tomorrow's managers in redefining their roles.

THE CHANGING NEEDS OF MAN

Maslow's (25) hierarchy of needs theory is useful in understanding the consequences of the increasing affluence of man. Primeval man's efforts were directed primarily toward survival needs—safety, food, and shelter—leaving little time or energy for preoccupation with his latent high-order needs. However, as his survival needs were satisfied, he became sensitized to social and status needs. Finally, in the affluence of recent decades, these lower-order or maintenance needs have been satisfied to the point that he is ready to realize his potential, to experience self-actualization in terms of intellectual, emotional, and esthetic growth, or to satisfy his motivation (29, p. 86) needs.

Management and the union have both contributed to the worker's readiness for self-actualization. Efficiency engineers of the Industrial Revolution, under the label of "scientific management," simplified tasks and created the mass production technology. Jobs were fractionated for efficiency in training (also to escape management's dependency on prima donna journeymen) and to satisfy the implicit assumption that workers would be happy and efficient doing easy work for high pay. And though mass-production technology made man an appendage of tools and destroyed his journeyman's pride and autonomy, it did price automobiles, washing machines, refrigerators, etc., within his reach. These and other effects of the mass production economy accelerated the satisfaction of man's lower-order needs and readied him to become aware of his dormant and unfulfilled self-actualization needs.

The union's role was just as vital in readying the worker for self-actualization, for it forced industrial managers to share company success with the worker, thereby narrowing the socioeconomic gap between the worker and the manager, further enabling him to buy the products of mass production. However, as noted earlier, the union sharpened the worker's identity as a member of labor rather than a member of management—preserving the cleavage that might otherwise have been reduced through economic trends.

WORK—PUNISHMENT OR OPPORTUNITY?

Work, in the eyes of many workers, is a form of punishment. It is uninteresting, demeaning, oppressive, and generally unrelated to, or in conflict with, their personal goals. But, it is an unpleasantness they are willing to endure to get the money needed to buy goods and services which *are* related to personal goals.[1]

---

[1] Furthermore, work (even uninteresting menial tasks) serves several other roles, such as removing role ambiguity, offering socializing opportunity, increasing solidarity through shared ritual, winning approval of authority figures, providing escape mechanisms for sublimating and channeling energy and thwarted intellectual capability, avoiding unpleasant home environments, and the prevention of guilt and anxiety feelings evoked by idleness in an achieving society. However, most of these roles tend to increase dependency and discourage self-actualization.

In contrast, the manager's job is often experienced as meaningful, satisfying, and at least partially aligned with his personal goals. This difference in job attitude between manager and worker is usually ascribed to immaturity of the worker rather than to the real causes: fundamental differences in the content of the worker's job and his opportunity to manage it. Workers are frequently only appendages of tools or links between them—doing what is necessary to satisfy the requirements of inflexible, inanimate monsters. Work itself, to be meaningful, must make tools the appendage of man and place man in a role not restricted to obedient doing. It must include planning and controlling, as well as doing, as illustrated in Exhibit 5.

EXHIBIT 5
MEANINGFUL WORK

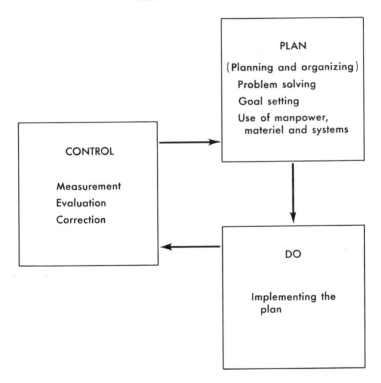

MEANINGFUL WORK

The *plan phase* includes the planning and organizing functions of work management and consists of problem solving, goal setting, and planning the use of manpower, materiel, and systems. The *do phase* is the implementation of the plan, ideally involving the coordinated expenditure of physical and mental effort, utilizing aptitudes and special skills. *Control is* the feedback and correction process for measuring achievements against planned goals. Feedback gives work its meaning, and its absence is a common cause of job dissatisfaction. The measurement, evaluation, and correction functions of the control phase are the basis for recycling planning, doing, and controlling. People who work for themselves generally have meaningful work in terms of a complete cycle of plan, do, and control.

The farmer, for example, plans and organizes in terms of crop selection, utilization of land, purchase of equipment, and the employment of manpower. He typically has a major role in implementing his plan, and, of course, he is the person most involved in measuring, evaluating, and correcting his program as the basis for future success. A similar analogy may be drawn for others in the entrepreneurial situation of working for themselves.

Managers in industry, though seldom having the autonomy of the entrepreneur, typically have jobs rich in plan, do, and control phases, particularly at the higher levels. Let's look at three levels of management jobs in Texas Instruments—operating vice-president, manufacturing manager, and foreman—in terms of planning, doing, and controlling. Organizational levels are as follows:

EXHIBIT 6

MEANINGFUL WORK—OPERATING VICE-PRESIDENT

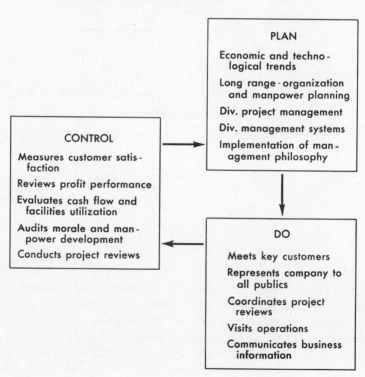

President
Operating Vice-President
Department Manager
Manufacturing Manager
Superintendent
Foreman
Operator

Note, first, the operating vice-president's job in Exhibit 6. As division manager he plans in the realm of economic and technological trends, facilities expansion, manpower and management systems, and has a hand in shaping policy. The doing aspect of his job involves him with key customers, in public relations roles, visits to various operating sites, and in the exchange of business information. His control functions include the measurement, evaluation, and correction of factors associated with customer satisfaction, profits, cash flow, facilities utilization, morale, and manpower development. Hence, the division director's job is rich in plan, do, and control, much like the self-employed individual.

EXHIBIT 7

MEANINGFUL WORK—MANUFACTURING MANAGER

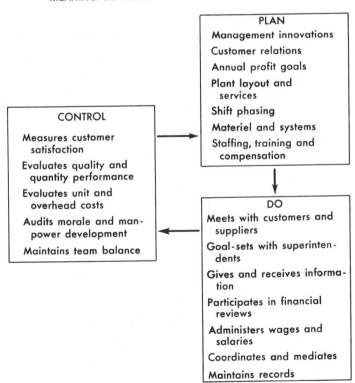

PLAN
Management innovations
Customer relations
Annual profit goals
Plant layout and services
Shift phasing
Materiel and systems
Staffing, training and compensation

CONTROL
Measures customer satisfaction
Evaluates quality and quantity performance
Evaluates unit and overhead costs
Audits morale and manpower development
Maintains team balance

DO
Meets with customers and suppliers
Goal-sets with superintendents
Gives and receives information
Participates in financial reviews
Administers wages and salaries
Coordinates and mediates
Maintains records

Similarly, Exhibit 7 shows the middle-management job of a manufacturing manager to be relatively rich in the meaningful aspects of work. Though two levels below the division manager's position and narrower in scope, it is nonetheless rich in plan, do, and control. A company is rarely plagued with a lack of commitment of a manufacturing manager.

Even the foreman's job, two levels below the manufacturing manager, may be rich in terms of meaningful work concepts. For example, we see in Exhibit 8 that the foreman's job, though narrower in scope than the superintendent's, offers him considerable latitude in managing his work. This example purposely portrays a traditional authority-oriented supervisor who will be contrasted later with a goal-oriented supervisor in Exhibit 12.

The foreman's job portrays a complete plan–do–control cycle, which, because it is authority-oriented, creates frustrations that do not plague the goal-oriented supervisor, who will be discussed later. Furthermore, the structuring of the *do phase* in accordance with this authority-orientation prevents the delegation of a complete plan–do–control cycle of responsibility to the operator. The operator lives in a world circumscribed by conformity pressures to follow instructions, work harder, obey rules, get along with people, and be loyal to the supervisor and the company, quashing any pleasure that work itself might otherwise offer. His role puts him in a category with material and other nonhuman resources to be manipulated by managers exercising their "management prerogatives" (as kings once exercised their "divine rights") in pursuit of "their" organizational goals. Conformity-oriented workers tend to behave like adolescent children responding to the punishments and rewards of authoritarian parents, and *their* prerogatives, which are generally expressed in terms of privileges wrested from management, are only incidentally aligned with company goals.

ANALYZING WORK

The foregoing examples show that meaningful work includes planning and controlling, as well as doing, and that the conformity pressures of the authority-oriented supervisor defined in Exhibit 8 prevent the expression of the full plan–do–control cycle of work for the operator. The meaningfulness of a job can be determined by answering questions related to each of the three phases of work as illustrated in Exhibit 9.

The supervisor's involvement in answering this type of question may give him his first insight into the scope of meaningful work. The planning and control items may at first appear unrealistic to him in terms of his perception of his people's competence, but they can be made more realistic by having him analyze a similar job managed by a person who works for himself.

For example, analysis of a company oil driller's job in the field may show it to be largely devoid of planning and control phases when compared to his entrepreneurial counterpart's job of managing his own drilling rig. The self-employed driller, who must manage the total plan–do–control cycle of his work to suc-

EXHIBIT 8
AUTHORITY-ORIENTED RELATIONSHIP BETWEEN FOREMAN AND OPERATOR

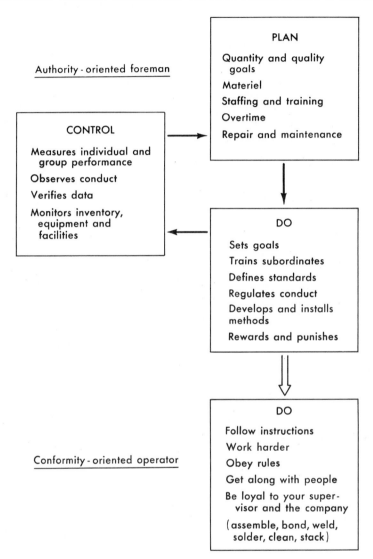

Authority - oriented foreman

PLAN

Quantity and quality
  goals

Materiel

Staffing and training

Overtime

Repair and maintenance

CONTROL

Measures individual and
  group performance

Observes conduct

Verifies data

Monitors inventory,
  equipment and
  facilities

DO

Sets goals

Trains subordinates

Defines standards

Regulates conduct

Develops and installs
methods

Rewards and punishes

Conformity - oriented operator

DO

Follow instructions

Work harder

Obey rules

Get along with people

Be loyal to your super-
  visor and the company

(assemble, bond, weld,
  solder, clean, stack)

ceed in business, thus serves as a model for planning the enrichment of the company driller's job.

Jobs may be analyzed with the help of job incumbents themselves by involving them in answering the questions in the Supervisor Worksheet, or they may assess their own work by completing checklist items illustrated in Exhibit 10. This checklist asks the incumbent whether his job permits him to perform

EXHIBIT 9
SAMPLE ITEMS FROM SUPERVISOR WORKSHEET
FOR ANALYZING MEANINGFULNESS OF WORK

PLANNING. Can the individual or group—
- Name customers and state delivery dates for products or services?
- State the product quality and quantity commitments?
- Organize their work layout and influence personnel assignments?
- Set goals and standards based on customer needs and fix priorities?
- State the sources of their materials and problems in obtaining them?
- List direct and overhead costs, selling price, and other profit and loss information?

DOING. Does the job—
- Utilize people's talents and require their attention?
- Enable people to see the relationship of their work to other operations?
- Provide access to all the information they need to do their work?
- Have a satisfactory work cycle—neither too long nor too short?
- Give people feedback on how well they are doing?
- Enable them to see how they contribute to the usefulness of the product for the customer?

CONTROLLING. Can the individual or group—
- State customer quality requirements and reasons for these standards?
- Keep their own records of quality and quantity?
- Check quality and quantity of work and revise procedures?
- Evaluate and modify work layout on their own initiative?
- Identify and correct unsafe working conditions?
- Obtain information from people outside the group as a means of evaluating performance?

EXHIBIT 10
SAMPLE ITEMS FROM JOB INCUMBENT CHECKLIST
FOR DESCRIBING MEANINGFULNESS OF WORK

	No	Some-times	Yes
PLANNING			
• Does my job allow me to set my own performance goals?	( )	( )	( )
• Is setting my own goals essential to good job performance?	( )	( )	( )
• Do I want more opportunity to set my own performance goals?	( )	( )	( )
DOING			
• Does my job provide variety?	( )	( )	( )
• Is variety in my job essential to good job performance?	( )	( )	( )
• Do I want more variety in my work?	( )	( )	( )
CONTROLLING			
• Does my job allow me to measure my work performance?	( )	( )	( )
• Is opportunity to evaluate my own work essential?	( )	( )	( )
• Do I want more opportunity to measure my own job performance?	( )	( )	( )

---

various plan, do, and control phases of his job, whether performance of each is essential to good job performance, and whether he wants more of this type of opportunity. This type of checklist provides a basis for assessing individual jobs, making intergroup comparisons, and for measuring time trends in the development of meaningful work opportunities. In Texas Instruments, items of this type have been added to the annual attitude survey to measure progress in the institutionalization of meaningful work.

THE SUPERVISOR'S SELF-EVALUATION

During the early applications of job enrichment, Texas Instruments supervisors found their traditional roles becoming incompatible with the increasing problem-solving, goal-setting responsibilities of the operators. For example, operators would often work directly with the engineers, taking the initiative in rearranging their workplace, and the problem-solving process did not always of necessity involve the supervisors. One supervisor, in joining his work group for a "problem-solving, goal-setting" session was told, "Look, Bill, we don't need to take up your valuable time in this meeting; we'll go ahead with it and keep you posted on what we come up with." Needless to say, this was a threatening experience, and a less secure person would have insisted on staying. Supervisors encouraged these new work roles of the operators, primarily because they resulted in improved performance, but they were understandably uncomfortable with the ambiguity of their own roles induced by this process. Consequently, a group of supervisors, with the assistance of the division training director, undertook the task of defining their new role.

The results of this group's efforts are reflected in Exhibit 11. Initial efforts of the group produced the traditional authority-oriented role outlined in the left column—not because they were committed to this role, but, rather, because their anxiety and haste regressed them temporarily to the typical textbook definition of the role of supervisor. After evaluating and rejecting this traditional role as an inaccurate description of their actual emerging role, they finally developed the items listed in the goal-oriented column.

Though most of the items in the left column are acceptable in the light of tradition, their collective effect tends to reinforce the authority-oriented relationship, depicted in the diagram at the foot of the column, in which people conform to the plan–lead–control directions received from their supervisors. Items in the goal-oriented column do not differ completely with the authority-oriented column, but their net effect provides opportunity for people to manage the full plan–do–control phases of their work, involving supervisors as resources.

During the discussion of the emerging role of the supervisor, the group concluded that an effective supervisor is one who *provides a climate in which people have a sense of working for themselves.* In terms of their day-to-day relationships, they further defined the supervisor's role as:

Giving visibility to company (customer) goals.
Providing budgets and facilities.

EXHIBIT 11
THE ROLE OF SUPERVISION

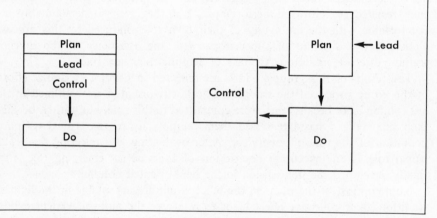

AUTHORITY-ORIENTED

Set goals for subordinates, define standards and results expected.

Train subordinates to do the job.

Check subordinates' performance to make sure they are doing things right.

Discipline to keep people in line and set examples.

Stimulate subordinates by forceful leadership and persuasion.

Develop and install new methods.

Develop and free subordinates for promotion.

Recognize achievements and point out failures.

GOAL-ORIENTED

Participate with people in problem solving and goal setting.

Create situation for learning to occur naturally.

Enable people to check own performance.

Mediate conflict and help people see the need for rules and consequences of violations.

Allow people to set challenging goals.

Provide opportunity for methods improvement by job incumbents.

Provide opportunity for people to pursue and move into growth opportunities.

Recognize achievements and help people learn from failures.

Mediating conflict.

But primarily, *staying out of the way to let people manage their work.*

This redefinition of the supervisor's role to provide opportunity for people to manage their own work is portrayed in Exhibit 12. In contrast to the authority–conformity–oriented roles of the supervisor and operator shown in Exhibit 8, each now has a goal-oriented role in which the revised *do phase* of the supervisor and *plan phase* of the operator comprise the realm of interface between them. Exhibits 11 and 12 both show the goal-oriented supervisor to be a resource person whose involvement is invoked primarily at the initiative of the operator.

Experience is showing that this relationship, illustrated in this article with

EXHIBIT 12
GOAL-ORIENTED RELATIONSHIP BETWEEN FOREMAN AND OPERATOR

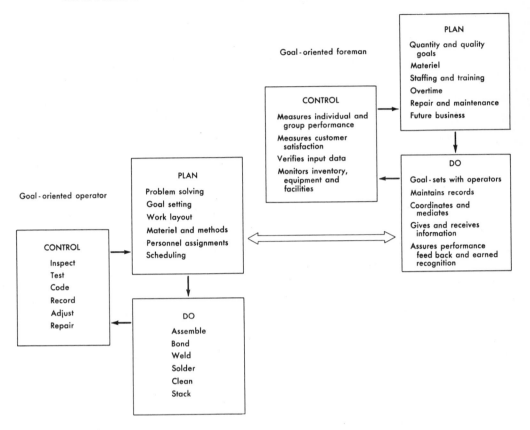

the foreman and operator, is a model representing ideal supervisory relationships at any level. Furthermore, enriching the operator's job has changed higher-level jobs. Two levels of jobs (assistant foreman and assistant superintendent) were eliminated, thereby reducing the division hierarchy level from eight to six. The foreman, now freed of many detailed maintenance and control functions, has more time to devote to higher-level planning functions and is also more available to meet his responsibility as a mediator and resource person when needed by the operators.

The new role of the supervisor is not always accepted easily. One manager in a multicompany seminar, in hearing a testimonial from another who solved a production problem by involving his operators, said, "You're a fool—you have just cut your own jugular vein! Now that your subordinates have solved your problem for you, they'll have no respect for you as their leader." Initial reactions of this type are not uncommon, as authority-oriented relationships fostered in many homes and schools find natural expression in most job situations. An authority-oriented supervisor does not switch roles by edict or as an immediate consequence of reading a book or hearing an inspiring speech. An intellectual message may sensitize him to his problem, but he must work through the process of self-evaluation, self-acceptance, adjusted values, and changed behavior at his own pace, in his own way, and in an atmosphere of approval. The pressure of an edict to "be democratic" will only regress him to familiar old authority-oriented patterns, from which stance he will obediently recite the intellectual message.

Gone are management prerogatives. The divine rights of "King Supervisor" are being relinquished by the self-imposed pressures of enlightenment. Their price in terms of quashed initiative and alienation is much too high for all but those with pathological needs for adulation. Prerogatives have given way to responsibility—to customers, shareholders, employees, and the community. Influence is still needed to satisfy this new role, but it is not the influence of supervisory authority, but, rather, the influence of all members of the group based on their competence and commitment to goals.

A WAY OF LIFE AT WORK

It is important that people, particularly supervisors, perceive meaningful work, not as another program (which has a beginning and an end) or current fad, but, rather, as a continuing way of life at work which finds expression not only through the pursuit of regular job goals, but also in administering systems which are outside the realm of normal responsibility. For example, methods improvement, job evaluation, wage surveys, insurance programs, attitude surveys, performance reviews, and employee recreation activities, traditionally administered by staff groups, are administered more effectively through the involvement of people being affected by these systems. This approach taps and develops unused talent, results in better systems, and provides a more sensitive feedback medium for keeping systems on track.

SELF-MANAGED JOBS

CONCLUSION

A framework has been presented to erase the management–labor dichotomy and give substance to a slogan "every employee a manager"—a manager being defined as one who manages a job. A self-managed job is one which provides a realistic opportunity for the incumbent to be responsible for the total plan–do–control phases of his job. Though many jobs in their present forms cannot be fully enriched, most can be improved and some can be eliminated. Whether the mission be to enrich, improve, or eliminate the job, it is achieved best by utilizing the talents of the incumbents themselves, provided, of course, this involvement will lead to equivalent or better opportunity. Job enrichment is

Though managers see it as a threat to their jobs

an iterative process. Though it finds most dramatic expression at the lower levels, it depends on supportive climate and action at the top. When achieved at the lower levels, its impact in terms of both organizational and human criteria reinforces its support from the top.

The application of meaningful work offers substantial short-range incentive for managers to support it. Judged as they are, year to year, in terms of profit, cost reduction, cash flow, and return-on-assets criteria, job enrichment is seen as a significant resource for achieving success. But it offers even greater rewards on a long-term basis, particularly if criteria of success are broadened to include aspects of human effectiveness, such as self-actualization of employees, responsible civic and home relationships, and the profitable and self-renewing growth of the organization. The role of business and industry in an entrepreneurial society such as the United States has a profound influence on the health of that society. Approximately 80 percent of people at work are in traditional conformity-oriented, nonexempt job categories. Hence, the implementation of job-enrichment principles in industry has great potential for developing a pattern of responsible behavior learned through a way of life at work which can influence people's behavior in their multiple roles in the community and family.

THERAPEUTIC VALUE

William Glasser's (17) new approach to psychotherapy points up the therapeutic value of enriched work. Rejecting a classical concept of mental illness and style of therapy, Dr. Glasser defines a process to help the individual face reality and accept responsibility for satisfying his needs in a way that does not deprive others of the ability to fulfill their needs. He shows that opportunity to love and be loved and to feel worthwhile to themselves and others is essential for responsible behavior—that is based largely on the here-and-now and need not probe the subconscious past. Enriched work offers such an opportunity for healthful interpersonal relationships by enabling people to act responsibly in the pursuit of meaningful goals.

Most people have the potential for maladjustment or mental health, and the quality of their vocational roles and relationships is a critical determinant. Hence, organizations applying these principles represent unequaled resources for character building and developing a nation's mental health.

Job enrichment can do much to conserve the competitive agility of the organization by avoiding the usual encumbering consequences of growth, such as excessive layers of supervision, proliferating control processes and conformity pressures, obscure charters, and inflexible systems. It provides a model of applied democracy to stem socialistic trends and represents a rich resource for influencing secondary schools and universities which are shaping candidates for tomorrow's work forces and managerial positions.

A COMMON MEETING GROUND

Management development results from job enrichment as a circular phenomenon. In the first instance, job enrichment requires action (or discontinuation of previous action) on the part of the supervisor to supply conditions of human effectiveness. The results of this action in turn reinforce it and encourage its application by others. Its application brings about subtle changes in the perceptions, values, and, finally, the habits of the supervisors, so that in a gradual branching and multiplying process a new way of life at work is put into motion which simultaneously changes and effects changes through the supervisor. Hence, the supervisor is the originator of, and medium for, change—providing conditions for the development of others and thereby bringing about his own self-development.

The business organization exists to serve society and survives only to the extent that it does so. Society's needs are served best in the long run by sustaining the health of the organization and its members. The health of a business organization is measured in terms of profitable growth, the health of its members in terms of realized potential. Hence, job enrichment is the common meeting ground of the hard-headed businessman and the altruist.

Questioning
the Managerial Implications of
Motivating Management and Employees

1. Ghiselli has identified differences in personal needs among managers and employees and among successful and unsuccessful managers. Of what possible value are findings like these? To whom might knowledge of such differences be important?

2. Are the findings of Ghiselli and Hall and Nougain comparable in any meaningful way? Would you have tested Maslow's hierarchy in the same way Hall and Nougaim did? What would you have done differently?

3. Myers has presented a pretty strong case for job enrichment. From your own experience, can you visualize any potential evils in this approach to motivation?

4. Which of the two definitions of motivation presented in the introduction to this chapter is most like your own? Can any one definition serve all purposes or situations? When might one be more useful than another?

References

1. Alderfer, C. P., "Differential Importance of Human Needs" (Doctoral dissertation, Yale University, 1966).

2. Atkinson, J. W., *Motives in Fantasy, Action, and Society.* Princeton: D. Van Nostrand Co., Inc., 1958.

3. Avery, R., "Enculturation in Industrial Research," *IRE Transactions in Engineering Management,* VII (1960), 20–24.

4. Becker, H. S., and A. L. Strauss, "Careers, Personality, and Adult Socialization," *American Journal of Sociology,* LXII (1956), 256–63.

5. Berlew, D. E., and D. T. Hall, "The Socialization of Managers: Effects of Expectations of Performance," *Administrative Science Quarterly,* XI (1966), 207–23.

6. Blalock, H. M., Jr., *Social Statistics.* New York: McGraw-Hill Book Company, 1960.

7. Bray, D. W., "The Management Progress Study," *American Psychologist,* XIX (1964), 419–20.

8. ——, and D. L. Grant, "The Assessment Center in the Measurement of Potential for Business Management," *Psychological Monographs,* LXXX, No. 625 (1966).

9. Caplow, T., and R. J. McGee, *The Academic Marketplace.* Garden City, N. Y.: Anchor Books, 1958.

10. Centers, R., "Motivational Aspects of Occupational Stratification," *Journal of Social Psychology,* XXVIII (1948), 187–217.

11. Davis, W. A., "The Motivation of the Underprivileged Worker," in *Industry and Society,* ed. W. F. Whyte. New York: McGraw-Hill Book Company, 1946, pp. 84–106.

12. Ghiselli, E. E., "The Forced-Choice Technique in Self-description," *Personnel Psychology,* VII (1954), 201–8.

13. ——, "A Scale for the Measurement of Initiative," *Personnel Psychology,* VIII (1955), 157–64.

14. ——, "Correlates of Initiative," *Personnel Psychology,* IX (1956), 311–20.

15. ——, "Managerial Talent," *American Psychologist*, XVIII (1963), 631–42.

16. Glaser, B. G., *Organizational Scientists: Their Professional Careers*. New York: The Bobbs-Merrill Company, Inc., 1964.

17. Glasser, W., *Reality Therapy*. New York: Harper & Row, Publishers, 1965.

18. Haire, M., *Psychology in Management*, 2nd ed. New York: McGraw-Hill Book Company, 1964.

19. Hall, D. T., "Peer and Authority Relationships During the Transition from Student to Professor" (Doctoral dissertation, Massachusetts Institute of Technology, Sloan School of Management, 1966).

20. Kahn, R., D. Wolfe, R. Quinn, J. Snoek, and R. Rosenthal, *Organizational Stress*. New York: John Wiley & Sons, Inc., 1964.

21. Katkovsky, W., "Personality and Ability Changes over Eight Years." Paper presented at Eastern Psychological Association Symposium, *The Young Business Managers*, April 22, 1965.

22. Lazarsfeld, P., and W. Thielens, *The Academic Mind*. New York: Free Press of Glencoe, Inc., 1958.

23. Leavitt, H. J., *Managerial Psychology*, 2nd ed. Chicago: The University of Chicago Press, 1964.

24. Lyman, E., "Occupational Differences in the Value Attached to Work," *American Journal of Sociology*, LXI (1955), 138–44.

25. Maslow, A. H., *Motivation and Personality*. New York: Harper & Row, Publishers, 1954.

26. McClelland, D., "Notes for a Revised Theory of Motivation," in *Studies in Motivation*, ed. D. McClelland. New York: Appleton-Century-Crofts, 1955, pp. 226–34.

27. McGregor, D. M., *The Human Side of Enterprise*. New York: McGraw-Hill Book Company, 1960.

28. Morse, N., and R. Weiss, "The Function and Meaning of Work and the Job," *American Sociological Review*, XX (1955), 191–98.

29. Myers, M. S., "Who Are Your Motivated Workers?" *Harvard Business Review*, XLII (1964).

30. ——, "Breakthrough in On-the-Job Training," *Harvard Business Review*, XLIV (1966).

31. ——, "Conditions for Manager Motivation," *ibid*.

32. Pellegrin, R., and C. Coates, "Executives and Supervisors: Contrasting Definitions of Career Success," *Administrative Science Quarterly*, I (1957), 506–17.

33. Porter, L. W., "Job Attitudes in Management: II. Perceived Importance of Needs as a Function of Job Level," *Journal of Applied Psychology*, XLVII (1963), 141–48.

34. ——, *Organizational Patterns of Managerial Job Attitudes*. New York: American Foundation for Management Research, Inc., 1964.

35. Schaie, K., "A General Model for the Study of Developmental Problems," *Psychological Bulletin,* LXIV (1965), 64, 92–107.

36. Schein, E., *Organizational Psychology.* Englewood Cliffs, N. J.: Prentice-Hall, Inc., 1965.

37. Veroff, J., J. Atkinson, S. Feld, and G. Gurin, "The Use of Thematic Apperception to Assess Motivation in a Nation in a Nationwide Interview Study," *Psychological Monographs,* LXXIV, No. 499, 1960.

38. Vroom, V. H., *Work and Motivation.* New York: John Wiley & Sons, Inc., 1964.

39. Whyte, W. H., Jr., *The Organization Man.* New York: Simon and Schuster, Inc., 1956.

Communicating
in the Organization

As the complexities of organizations increase, so do the difficulties of efficient and accurate communications. Centralized networks and one-way communications promote speed but not creativity or satisfaction, providing a dilemma for management. Other variables affecting the reception of communications are how the communicator is perceived, the medium employed, the order, style, and content of the message, as well as the ability and motivation of the receiver.

Leavitt opens this chapter with a discussion of the physical dimensions of the communication process. His presentation concentrates on the differences between one-way and two-way communication. In listing the relative advantages and costs of each method along with some common barriers to their effectiveness, Leavitt pinpoints potential communication bottlenecks for the practicing manager and student.

While limiting his analysis to upward communications, Anderson stresses interpersonal factors as determinants of accuracy in the exchange of information. He focuses on the human interaction between superior and subordinate in developing an extensive presentation of potential obstacles to upward information flow.

A study into the dimensions and characteristics of individual communications networks in an ongoing business firm leads Wickesberg to conclude that the range of contacts in an organization is far wider than traditional organizational analysis would indicate. His data demonstrate that the networks used for information flow are determined less by the organization chart than by immediate task requirements, goals, and individual initiative.

22

Communication :
Getting Information from A into B

Harold J. Leavitt
Stanford University

Reprinted by permission from *Managerial Psychology*, rev. ed., 1964, pp. 138–52.
© 1958, 1964 by the University of Chicago. All rights reserved.

People begin, modify, and end relationships by communicating with one another. Communication is their channel of influence, their mechanism of change. In industrial organizations it has become popular recently to communicate about communication—to talk and write about the importance of communication in problem solving. The talk about communication is appropriate because communication is indeed a critical dimension of organization.

Unfortunately, though, much of the talk has been either nonsensical or unusable. For one thing, the word "communication" has been used to mean everything from public speaking to mass merchandising. For another, most of the talk has been hortatory rather than explanatory. Managers are urged to use "two-way" communication, because it is "better" (what does "better" mean?) than one-way communication. The fad has extended to "three-way" communication, again without evidence or precise definition.

The purpose of this chapter is to describe some major dimensions of the communication process, to examine what can be meant by "better" or "worse" communication, and to relate the idea of communication to the ideas of interpersonal influence and behavior change.

SOME DIMENSIONS OF COMMUNICATION

Sometimes there are advantages to asking simple-minded questions. They can help to strip away some of the confusing gingerbread surrounding an idea so that we can see it more objectively.

Suppose we ask, simple-mindedly, what are the things that can happen when A talks to B? What is involved in two people's talking to one another?

First, A usually talks to B about something. The process has a content. They talk baseball or they talk business or they talk sex. The content is what usually hits us first when we tune in on a conversation. Content of communication, in fact, is what psychologists and businessmen alike are usually thinking about when they think about human relations.

We can see subclasses within content too. We can differentiate categories of content like, for example, fact and feeling.

Other things, quite independent of what is said, take place when A talks to B. Some conversations take place in the presence of a great deal of noise; others are relatively noiseless. In this context "noise" means things that interfere with transmission. We can encounter channel noise like the static on a telephone line that makes it hard for B to hear what A is saying. We can also usefully think of psychological noises, like B's thinking about something else, so that again it is hard for him to hear what A is saying; or like B's being so afraid of A that it is hard for him to hear what A is saying. Language or code noise may make it hard for B to hear: he doesn't understand the words A is using in the way A understands them.

All sorts of noise can occur independently of content. We can find noisy or noiseless communications about any content. We also can usually observe that A, in the presence of noise, is likely to communicate more redundantly—to repeat his message in the hope that B will be able to hear it better the second time, or to say the same thing in a different way. Redundancy is one of the most common weapons for combating noise. It is "inefficient" in the sense that repetition is wasteful of time and energy. It is "efficient" in the sense that, so long as noise exists, redundancy helps to push the content through.

Besides the content and noise dimensions of conversation between A and B, a third dimension is the communication net. Usually we think of A to B conversation as direct; but many such conversations, especially in organizations, are mediated through other people. One thing an organization chart is supposed to tell us is that A can speak to B only through C or D. The structure of the net a particular organization uses can have a lot to do with the speed and accuracy of members' talkings to one another.

One more dimension of the process is worth noting, especially since it has been ridden so hard in recent managerial literature. It is the direction of communication—its one-wayness or two-wayness. Again it is an independent dimension. No matter what A and B may be talking about, no matter how much static may be involved, no matter what the network, A may talk to B this way: A → B; or this way: A ⇌ B. A can talk and B can only listen, i.e., one-way communication; or A can talk and B can talk back, i.e., two-way communication.

This last aspect of the process, one-wayness versus two-wayness, gets special attention in the remainder of this chapter. Is two-way communication really better? What does "better" mean? Better for what and for whom? When?

ONE-WAY VERSUS TWO-WAY COMMUNICATION

Essentially our problem is to clarify the differences between these two situations: (1) One person, A, talking to another, B, *without* return talk from B to A; versus (2) conversation from A to B *with* return conversation from B to A. The differences can be clarified best by testing one method against the other. Here is such a test situation:

The pattern of rectangles in Figure 1 is an idea you would like to tell some B's about. Suppose you try to communicate it in words to a half-dozen of your friends who are sitting around your living room. Assume that the rectangles touch each other at "sensible" places—at corners or at midpoints along the line. There are no touch points at any unusual places. All the angles are either 90° or 45° angles; there are no odd ones. This pattern of rectangles is an idea comparable perhaps to a complicated set of instructions you may have to give to a subordinate or to the definition of a policy that you would like to pass along or to the task of explaining statistical quality control to a sales manager. This idea can be communicated to others under (1) one-way or (2) two-way conditions.

FIGURE 1

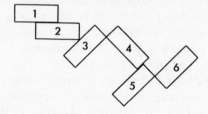

If you are the communicator, these are your one-way instructions:

1. Turn your back on your audience so that you cannot get visual communication back.
2. Give the audience blank sheets of paper, so that they can listen and draw exactly what you are communicating. Ask them to try to draw as accurate a picture of the pattern of rectangles as possible.
3. Describe the pattern of rectangles to them in words as fast as you can. The audience is not permitted to ask questions, or laugh, or sigh, or in any other way to communicate back to you any information about what it is receiving.

This game is a good parlor game, if you can find some people to try it on. Try it, time it, and then check the accuracy of your communication by determining whether or not your audience has drawn what you have described. If they received what you tried to send, so their pictures match the test picture, then you have communicated. To the extent that their pictures do not match the one in the drawing, you have not communicated.

Two-way communication can be tested for contrast in the same way. The same rules apply, and Figure 2 provides a similar test pattern. This time the basic job is the same, to describe the pattern verbally so that the people who are listening can draw it. But here are the differences:

1. This time you may face your audience.
2. They are allowed to interrupt and ask you any questions they want to at any time they want to.

Try it this way and time it. The differences between what happened the first

FIGURE 2

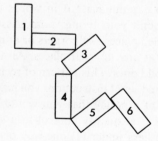

time and what happened the second time are the differences between one- and two-way communication. (The order in which the two methods are used does not matter.)

Under experimental conditions these findings have emerged from this game: (1) One-way communication is considerably faster than two-way communication. (2) Two-way communication is more accurate than one-way, i.e., more people in the audience correctly reproduce the drawing under two-way conditions. (3) The receivers are more sure of themselves and make more correct judgments of how right or wrong they are in the two-way system. (4) The sender finds himself feeling psychologically under attack in the two-way system, because his receivers pick up his mistakes and oversights and let him know about them. The receivers may make snide remarks about the sender's intelligence and skill, and, if the receivers are trying very hard and taking the task seriously, they may actually get angry at the sender, and he at them. (5) The two-way method is relatively noisy and disorderly—with people interrupting the sender and one another, with the slowest man holding up the rest, and so on. The one-way method, on the other hand, appears neat and efficient to an outside observer, but the communication is less accurate.

Such a demonstration points out both the advantages and the costs of one-way and of two-way communication. If speed alone is what is important, then one-way communication has the edge. If appearance is of prime importance, if one wishes to look orderly and business-like, then the one-way method again is preferable. If one doesn't want one's mistakes to be recognized, then again one-way communication is preferable. Then the sender will not have to hear people implying or saying that he is stupid or that there is an easier way to say what he is trying to say. Of course, such comments may be made about him whether he uses one-way or two-way communication, but under one-way conditions he will not have to listen to what is said, and it will be harder for anyone to prove that mistakes were made by A rather than B. If one wants to protect one's power, so that the sender can blame the receiver instead of taking blame himself, then one-way communication is again preferable. The sender can say: "I told you what to do; you just weren't bright enough to get the word." If he uses two-way communication, the sender will have to accept much of what blame there is, and it will be apparent to all that he deserves some of it; but he will also get his message across.

If one wants to simplify managerial life, so that even a rank amateur can handle it, one-way communication helps. It tightens and structures the situation so that A only has to make decisions about one kind of thing—content of the problem. When he opens up two-way communication, he has to be professional —for now he must make many kinds of decisions at once—content decisions and also decisions about people (Whom shall he recognize? How long should he work to make sure Joe understands while everybody else waits?), about personal strategies (When shall I cut off the discussion? Shall I accept sarcasm or fight it?), and about lots of other things. Like some formations in football, two-way communication is too powerful a device for safe use by people who are amateurs at management. But skilful use by a competent professional can be as beautiful and impressive as the work of a good T-formation quarterback.

Those are the major differences between one- and two-way communication. They are differences that most people are aware of implicitly. If a person gets a chance to ask questions, to double check what he might have missed, then he can make sure he has gotten exactly what he is expected to get. On the other hand, if he must only sit and listen, he may or may not get the word, and he is likely to feel frustrated and uncertain about what he does get. Moreover, that bit of frustration and uncertainty is likely to grow because he has no way of making sure of things he isn't sure of.

To put it another way, one-way communication is not likely to be communication at all. It is more likely to be talk. One can talk by passing words out into the air. Those words don't become communication until they enter meaningfully into somebody else's head.

Of course, it is simple for a communicator to claim that his responsibility is only to pass a message along, that the receiver's responsibility is to make sure that he understands it. But this is not a very adequate claim. If one really were to argue through the question of who is responsible for the success of communication, one would certainly conclude that communication is largely the communicator's responsibility. For if the communicator's job is to communicate—and if to communicate he must get his message through to the receiver—then his responsibility cannot end until the receiver has received. And he cannot be sure that the receiver has received until he gets confirming feedback from the receiver. On the other hand, the location of responsibility becomes a far less significant issue when one perceives communication as a two-party process to begin with.

A partial definition of communication is now possible. First, to communicate is to shoot information *and* to hit a target with it. Shooting alone is not communicating. Second, to have more than chance probability of hitting a target requires that the sender get feedback from the target about the accuracy of his shots.

If an artilleryman had to fire over a hill at an invisible target, he would have to fire blind and hope that by luck one of his shells would land on the target. He would spray the area with shells and go away, never being certain whether he had or had not destroyed his objective. But by the simple addition of a spotter standing on the hilltop, the likelihood of accurate shooting can be greatly increased. The spotter can feed back to the gunner information about the effects of the gunner's own shots. "Your last shot was a hundred yards short. The second was fifty yards over." And so on. The advantage is obvious, and it is precisely the advantage of two-way over one-way communication—the communicator can learn the effects of his attempts to communicate and can adjust his behavior accordingly. Like the learning machine, the decision maker needs inputs as well as outputs to correct his own behavior.

ONE-WAY AND TWO-WAY COMMUNICATION
ARE REALLY DIFFERENT METHODS

By this definition two-way communication is not just different from one-way in degree but also in kind. For when one switches from one-way to two-way, a great many changes take place, changes not only in the outcomes but in the inputs. For example, one-way communication usually calls for and gets much more planning than two-way. When you tell a sender in these experiments that he is to send one-way, and you show him the diagram and tell him he can take a few minutes to get ready to start, it is almost always true that he uses more minutes getting ready to start than he does in the two-way system. The reason is probably obvious. The sender needs to choose carefully the code he will use, even the precise words he will use. But in two-way communication he is apt to start out much more quickly, not worrying too much about a general plan or strategy, because he knows that the feedback will provide him with opportunities to correct himself. The first system is like a phonograph record. Once it starts, it must be played through. Hence it must be planned very carefully. Two-way communication is a different strategy, a kind of "local" strategy, in which the sender starts down one path, goes a little way and then discovers he is on the wrong track, makes a turn, discovers he is off a little again, makes another turn, and so on. He doesn't need to plan so much as he needs to listen, and to be sensitive to the feedback he is getting.

There are important differences associated with these two kinds of approaches. Planfulness, order, systemization, these are associated with one-way communication. The two-way method has much more a trial-and-error, "let's make a stab at it and see what happens" kind of flavor. It is understandable, therefore, that certain kinds of personalities tend to favor one of these or the other because one method or the other is apt to be much more consistent with one's personality.

With our definition of communication, the issue of one- and two-way communication in industry can be cast somewhat differently than is usual. For now one encounters apparent conflict between the short-run efficiency of two-way communication and the long-run need to maintain power and authority at various levels of the hierarchy. Two-way communication makes for more valid communication, and it appears now that more valid communication results not only in more accurate transmission of facts but also in reorganized perceptions of relationships. Authority, for example, may under ideal conditions of two-way communication cease to serve as a sufficient protection for inadequacy. The dictum that a well-informed citizenry is democracy's protection against autocracy may also be applicable to the well-informed staff or the well-informed employee. And though "democracy" may connote things desirable in government, its connotations for industrial organizations in our society are far from clear.

BARRIERS IN THE COMMUNICATION PROCESS

In our experiment we set up two-way communication simply by telling our subjects that we wanted them to talk back to the sender, to ask any questions they wanted to, any time they wanted to. Moreover, the experiment was just an experiment anyway, and nothing really rode on it. So there wasn't any reason why people shouldn't talk back—apparently. But, in fact, in almost every case, it turned out that some people in the two-way situation did not get complete and perfect answers. And it was also true that most of these people knew they were wrong—*yet they did not ask questions*. Why not?

When we asked people why not, we got a variety of answers. Some of them didn't ask questions because they were bored; they didn't much of the experiment anyway. Some of them didn't ask questions because they didn't want to occupy the group's time. Sometimes they were just plain mad at the sender because of the way he was encoding the material. They wouldn't give him the satisfaction of asking him a question. Sometimes they were scared. They had noticed that when Joe Blow asked a question earlier, the sender had given a curt and nasty answer. So they just quit asking questions. Some people said that they had wanted to ask questions, but so many other people were talking all at once that they couldn't get in.

So even in this gamey little experiment, where nothing much rode on what was going on, where the sender was not the boss—even in such a situation—there were lots of things that kept people from saying what they should have. Lots of barriers to two-way communication remained even after we had tried to set up a situation in which no such barriers would exist.

In the real world, of course, the barriers are likely to be greater and much more numerous. In the real world the boss's statement that his office door is always open has much, much less meaning, probably, than the experimenter's statement that people should feel free to ask any questions they want to, any time they want to.

There is, then, a moral to this tale. The moral is that if someone wants two-way communication in his organization, he had better plan to work for it. It does not come naturally or by issuing a proclamation. If a sender wants to make sure that two-way communication will in fact occur, he will need to be extremely sensitive to what the people in his group are thinking and feeling. He will have to have his eye open for the man who wants to talk but doesn't dare. He will have to be alert to the extent to which his own behavior is deterring people from asking the questions that need to be asked. He will have to worry about some degree of order or discipline in his group, so that people can get in questions they want to ask. He will even have to worry about the interpersonal relations among the members of the group, for sometimes people do not ask questions of the sender because they are fearful of one of their colleagues. He will have, in other words, to take many new kinds of responsibility.

COMMUNICATION ABOUT NOVEL AND ROUTINE PROBLEMS

In focusing on individual learning and problem solving, it is pointed out that people learn; they use their memories of past problems to solve similar present ones.

Correspondingly, it is obviously true that if the problem in the experiment on two-way communication had been a familiar instead of a novel one, the results might have been quite different. A, for instance, could probably have communicated the English alphabet accurately and rapidly through one-way communication alone. In fact, it has been shown that if we use two-way communication on these rectangle problems again and again with the same group, communication soon becomes one-way anyhow. People stop asking questions. They don't have to. They have learned the code; so A and B understand one another.

From the point of view of speed and accuracy, then, one could make this tentative generalization. Two-way communication improves the accurate communication of previously uncoded or insufficiently coded ideas. But two-way communication contributes considerably less to accuracy *after* the code has been clarified—after new problems have been programmed and routinized. Coupling this generalization with the notion that new unprogrammed problems tend to occur more frequently in upper organizational echelons, we can also tentatively conclude that two-way communication may be generally more useful for problem solving within the management group than further down the line—except when the problems are people problems, and those are unprogrammed everywhere.

WHAT GETS COMMUNICATED?

One aspect of the content problem deserves mention here, although it will be dealt with more fully later. The problem is that people usually communicate more than information to the target; they communicate feelings as well as facts. Suppose the artillery spotter, instead of simply announcing where the last shell had landed, decided to add a few typically human comments of his own. Suppose the spotter said to the gunner: "Look, you stupid s.o.b., your last shot was three hundred yeards over. Where the hell did you learn to shoot?" That kind of communication of unsolicited information will complicate the psychological picture, just as will the communication of inaccurate information, sometimes causing the now frustrated gunner to change his target from the farmhouse to the spotter.

IN SUMMARY

Communication is a primary tool for effecting behavior change. We can isolate at least four independent dimensions of the communication process: content, noise, network characteristics, and direction.

One-way communication has some advantages in speed over two-way. It also has the advantages of protecting the sender from having to recognize his own faults and protecting him from some more complex problems of managing. Two-way communication has the advantages of greater accuracy and greater feelings of certainty for the receiver. But two-way communication involves some psychological risks to the defenses of the sender. Two-way communication also means less planning work for the sender as far as the message itself is concerned but opens up a whole new series of managerial problems in maintaining and expanding the two-way system.

23

What's Blocking
Upward Communications?

John Anderson
Procter & Gamble Company

Reprinted by permission from the January-February 1968 issue of *Personnel Administration*, copyright 1968, Society for Personnel Administration, 485–87, National Press Building, 14th and F Streets, N. W., Washington, D. C. 20004.

When the subject of poor upward communications is discussed in management circles, analysis of the problem often turns to the concept of "effective vs. ineffective listening." The idea is that many managers don't listen very effectively to what people are saying to them, and this not only deprives them of valuable information, but is also bad for employee relations in general. So the solution sought is a way of helping managers develop their "listening skills."

In this article I want to present a framework for analyzing factors that may inhibit effective upward communication in an organization. There is little doubt that ineffective listening is often an important part of the communication problem. Many people do not listen very effectively, and even the most effective "receivers" are likely to have bad periods. But if an organization has problems with the quantity and quality of its upward communications, there may be several causes that have little to do with getting the beans out of management's ears.

First of all, to simplify the question with a model situation:

1. Suppose that B works for A.

2. B knows something that A needs to know, but doesn't.

3. This "something" might be knowledge of a current, developing, or potential problem in A's area of responsibility that A is unaware of. It might be factual information or a creative idea that could help solve a problem A *is* already aware of. It might be no more than a feeling of personal satisfaction or dissatisfaction with some situation that A is unaware of, but that may be affecting B's motivation on the job, or his ability to work effectively with A. Or it might be any combination of the three.

4. So the question is: "Under what circumstances will B probably communicate to A what he knows, and under what circumstances will he probably not?"

The task for any manager interested in improving the quality of communications coming up to him, then, would seem to be to look for these circumstances in his own organization, and in his own relationships with subordinates, and see which ones he might do something about.

FROM B TO A: POSSIBILITIES

In considering the likelihood of B's passing his information to A, one classification of requirements might be:

1. It must *occur* to B that he should tell A.

2. If he thinks of it, he must *choose* to do it.

3. If he chooses to tell, he must find an *opportunity* to do so.

4. If he finds an opportunity and takes it, A must *listen* to him.

5. Having listened to him, A must *act* on what he hears (at least sometimes) in ways recognizable and encouraging to B, or the next time around they will be right back at step 2 and B will choose *not* to bother.

Now, what obstacles might get in the way at each step, and what might A do about each if he were aware of it?

1. *It must occur to B that it matters whether he says anything.*

   a. B may not realize that the information he possesses has any value. For example, the cleanup man in a warehouse may see Product X stacked 8 high but not say anything because he doesn't know the stacking limit is 7. The more a man understands of the sense of his job, and the jobs of people around him (the whys of operating procedures, cost, quality, safety information, and salient department goals) the more likely he is to know when his observations are worth passing on. So, the solution for this obstacle to upward communication will usually be better downward or lateral communication through better initial job training, or continuing education on current departmental operating concerns.

   b. B may know the information he has is important, but he may think A already has the information, too, from his own observations or reports he receives from someone else. If erroneous assumptions of this sort ("Why, I thought you knew!") are often an obstacle to effective upward communication, a manager should check whatever systems he has for keeping informed for gaps and overlapping reporting responsibilities that could cause confusion.

2. *Once aware that he has significant information, B must choose to pass it on.*

   a. B may realize his information is important and that management doesn't have it, but he may still not pass it on because "it's not his job" to do so. If he has a narrow enough view of his job responsibilities (i.e., the organization's expectations of him), there may be several kinds of things he wouldn't think of talking about openly—for example, questioning his boss's judgment on anything to his face or making any kind of creative suggestion for solution of a problem himself. If he considers his management-expected role that of someone who does what he is told, suffers in silence, and questions or criticizes management judgment only privately with friends or through mechanisms provided in the union contract, he won't "communicate upward" in a way you might like him to because he doesn't think you would *want* him to. Corrective action for this obstacle probably lies initially in orientation and training practices, and then in the way individual managers respond when a B does volunteer information (see paragraphs under 4 and 5 below).

   b. Another consideration B will think about is who might be helped by his information, and who hurt, if he reveals it. If he thinks it might hurt his own pay, or the interests of someone he likes, or perhaps make life easier for a boss he doesn't like, this will encourage him to keep his mouth shut. Suggestions for management in avoiding this obstacle fall in areas of (1) consideration, fairness, and basic man–manager relationship development, (2) incentive system design that minimizes situations in which individual and organizational needs are at cross purposes, and (3) education again to broaden the perspective from which people view their responsibilities.

3. *B must have an opportunity to make his information available to A.*

a. If B doesn't have access to A, he can't communicate with him even if he wants to. One requirement is time. If B is so busy he can't find time, or if A is so busy, B can't find him, or if their available times don't coincide sufficiently for them to get together, B will often forget the whole thing.

b. A second requirement is a place to talk. Some kinds of things B might like to pass on to A he may not wish to unless it can be done privately (and "privately" may include out of sight, out of hearing, out of telephone access by others, or all three). The extreme example of a manager whose only desk is in a bullpen area may limit upward communications he receives regardless of his skills or his people's motivations.

4. *If B does speak, A must be able to receive his message.*

Once B has taken the step, placed himself in A's presence and started talking, the rest is up to A. In attempting to understand what B has on his mind, A must be able to compensate for any hesitancy or lack of clarity on B's part:

a. by his (A's) ability to set aside other pressing problems on his mind and concentrate his attention on B and what B is saying now;

b. by his own knowledge of B (his strengths, weaknesses, hopes, and concerns), and, therefore, his ability to see things from B's viewpoint and sense any pressures B may feel in the situation;

c. by his knowledge of technical aspects of B's job and how B's job relates to the department;

d. by his ability to question—to probe for information B doesn't clearly reveal —that is, to help B to get everything out that needs to be said. This implies both knowing what additional information to ask for to get at the heart of the problem, and how to ask (i.e., in a manner that is patient, interested, nonevaluative, appreciative—in general, supportive);

e. by his ability to keep his head in a situation where B's emotions might start to carry him away;

f. by his ability to summarize and keep straight in his mind the key points of B's message, even when it has been presented in a disorganized fashion.

What, then, can be done to build a management team with the ability to do these six things (*a–f*) well? First, ability in all six areas will be determined partly by well set and change-resistant qualities a manager brings to the company that hires him. So, selection and placement criteria will be important. Beyond this, however, factors that will affect managerial behavior in these areas, and that are within the control of management at some level, are:

MANAGEMENT WORK LOAD   If a manager is pressed by a work load beyond his capacity, his performance in factors *a* and *e* will be strained.

PRE-JOB TRAINING   Gaps in technical–operational aspects of pre-job training will affect his capacity in factor *c*.

SPECIAL TRAINING AND COACHING   Insight and ability in factors *b*, *d*, and *f* can be improved during pre-job training and/or after takeover by other special training programs now available to management.

JOB TENURE   Finally, since performance in factors *a*, *b*, *c*, and possibly *d* and *e*, will depend at least partly on the manager's experience in the area, too rapid job rotation can be detrimental.

Without even considering the time required to develop efficient administrative and technical competence in a department, the building of a man–manager relationship that is close, open, and trusting takes time, and some kinds of upward communication just won't take place unless and until such a relationship has had time to develop. Other things being equal, this means that larger numbers of people reporting to a manager, and such practices as shift rotation of managers and people on different schedules, as well as brief management job tenure, are going to have a negative effect on upward communications.

5. *Having listened to and understood B's message, A needs to act on it.*

If B doesn't see that anything happens once in awhile as a result of his communication to A (and results that please B, or at least don't displease him), he will probably not bother to give A the benefit of his thoughts as often, thereafter, and he may stop altogether (at least just short of what he needs to communicate to stay out of personal trouble).

The suggestion for A, then, is to make results plainly visible to B, or let B know quickly and plainly why he wasn't able to act. A's own manager should also recognize that if A is to continue to be a channel for good upward communications from B's, A must be seen as influential in the organization by B's. If A's manager can't support that image, A's effectiveness as an upward communications channel will be hampered or destroyed, no matter how effective a "listener" he may be.

SUMMARY OF OBSTACLES TO UPWARD COMMUNICATIONS (WHEN B DIDN'T COMMUNICATE TO A)

1. B didn't think of telling A what he knew because:
   B didn't know that what he knew was important.
   B thought A knew it already.
2. B chose not to tell it to A because:
   B didn't think it was his job to tell it.
   B thought if A learned of it, it might help (or harm) someone B wished not to help (or harm).
3. B couldn't get to A because:
   A was too busy.
   B was too busy.
   There was no good place for B to talk to A about it.

4. B tried, but A didn't get the message because:

A was thinking about something else while B talked.

A couldn't empathize with B's concerns, so he misunderstood and B gave it up (for a while).

A didn't know B's job (or his own) well enough to understand or appreciate what B was talking about.

A couldn't interview (question, probe) B well enough to get all the facts out clearly.

A didn't like what he thought he was hearing so he got mad.

By the time B finished, A had confused or forgotten important parts of the message.

5. B talked and A listened:

But A didn't do anything about it.

And he forgot to tell B why.

So B didn't talk to him any more.

He talked about A sometimes, but to somebody else.

24

Communications Networks in the Business Organization Structure

A. K. Wickesberg
University of Minnesota

The literature provides little information on actual dimensions and characteristics of individual communications networks within the firm. This study suggests such dimensions are extensive with surprisingly few differences between professional managerial and nonmanagerial organization members. Implications are discussed.

Reprinted by permission from *Academy of Management Journal*, XI, No. 3 (1968), 253–62.

In recent years there has been an increasing interest in the detailed workings of organization structure with particular reference to communications patterns. Harold J. Leavitt (4) and more recently Guetzkow and Dill (3) and others have constructed laboratory experiments in which communications patterns such as the "wheel," the "chain," and the "star" are artificially imposed to restrict communications ability and the effect on task performance noted. Another group of researchers, Burns (1), Sayles (6), Ponder (5), and Walker, Guest, and Turner (7), have sought to record communications as they occur in actual business conditions. A principal contribution stemming from these latter studies is the indication of the substantial amount of time individuals spend in communicating with others in the organization (2).

The bulk of the studies outside the laboratory setting, however, deal with factory (assembly) environments and record single firm experience. Data are lacking on what communications nets occur for what purposes, how many persons comprise any one individual's own communications network, and what differences there are between such networks for managers and for nonmanagers.

To secure some preliminary insights into the dimensions of individual network membership, a study was undertaken at the University of Minnesota to investigate the composition and nature of the several subnets, and the breadth of individual contacts throughout the firm as the individual builds his total communications net to carry out his task assignment. Ninety-one businessmen in Minnesota's Executive Master of Business Administration program recorded all communications, oral and written, issued or received, over a sample five-day period which consisted of Monday from Week I, Tuesday from Week II, Wednesday from Week III, Thursday from Week IV, and Friday from Week V. In all, 35 organizations in the Twin Cities were represented from a wide range of industrial, transportation, educational, retailing, and financial organizations. Participants were almost equally divided between managerial (those with subordinates formally assigned to them) and nonmanagerial positions. While occupational titles ranged widely, the principal functional areas of marketing, production, finance, engineering, and research and development were represented in about equal proportions.

No superior–subordinate pairs were present, nor were there any communications pairs among the participants. To include communications pairs (both issuer and receiver of a given communication) creates problems in analyzing the data to avoid double counting of a communication as received by one individual and reported as issued by another. Absence of communications pairs also serves to in effect double the size of the reporting group.

Each participant maintained a daily log of his communications including information on the nature or purpose of the communication, whether written or oral, the amount of time taken for each entry, and to whom or from whom the communication was issued or received. The log contained a brief description of the subject matter as well as a purpose code. In addition to the log, each participant provided the researcher with an organization chart and a brief statement pointing out any unusual features in his communications patterns for the period studied plus any other information he felt would contribute to better understanding of that individual's communications behavior.

DIMENSIONS OF
THE COMMUNICATIONS NETWORK

Examination of the data suggests the following as major categories for classifying the different purposes of the reported communications:

1. information received or disseminated,
2. instructions given or received,
3. approval given or received,
4. problem-solving activities, and
5. nonbusiness related communications or scuttlebutt.

GENERAL PURPOSES FOR WHICH
COMMUNICATIONS TAKE PLACE

The five categories into which data are grouped to study the purposes for which communications occur indicate several general conclusions (see Table 1). First, communications separate into four frequency levels with transmission of information by far the highest, followed by instruction and problem-solving in middle position, and with scuttlebutt and approval showing lowest frequency levels. In addition, there is little variation between manager and nonmanager in the frequency composition of his communications subject matter. While one might expect such frequencies to be identical where the participants consist of

TABLE 1
COMMUNICATIONS FREQUENCY
CLASSIFIED BY PURPOSE AND POSITION

Purpose	Position	Percentage of Total Communications	Frequency Level
Information	Manager	53.5	Level I
	Nonmanager	54.2	
Instruction	Manager	22.4	Level II
	Nonmanager	21.3	
Problem solving	Manager	11.1	Level III
	Nonmanager	12.5	
Scuttlebutt	Manager	6.6	
	Nonmanager	8.2	Level IV
Approval	Manager	6.2	
	Nonmanager	3.8	

communications pairs, where such pairs are lacking and where the respondents range widely over both position and industry categories, closeness of the data for each category is indeed of interest. It should also be noted that the findings showing the high frequency of information over other categories of communications are consistent with other research reports and with intuitive reflections on organization practice.

DIRECTION OF COMMUNICATIONS FLOW

In an organizational context, communications may be transmitted vertically up or down the scalar chain, horizontally to one's peers either within or outside one's own organizational unit, or diagonally to or from an organizational unit and hierarchical level outside the reporter's own formal organizational location. The data suggest very little difference between managers and nonmanagers in terms of the direction of communications flow analyzed by purpose with the exception of scuttlebutt or nonbusiness related communications. Nonmanagers restrict nonbusiness communications to horizontal organizational relationships to a far greater extent than do managers (see Table 2).

TABLE 2
DIRECTION OF COMMUNICATIONS FLOW
AS PERCENTAGE OF TOTAL ENTRIES
FOR EACH PURPOSE AND FOR ALL COMMUNICATIONS

Direction	Informa-tion	Instruc-tion	Approval	Problem solving	Scuttle-butt	All Com-munications
Horizontal:						
Manager	31.0	25.1	21.5	33.3	43.1	30.2
Nonmanager	41.3	43.7	33.4	45.6	67.9	44.7
Vertical:						
Manager	29.7	38.7	42.2	31.3	23.5	32.8
Nonmanager	22.8	23.2	34.5	22.8	19.1	23.1
Diagonal:						
Manager	39.4	36.1	35.8	35.4	33.3	36.9
Nonmanager	35.9	33.0	32.2	31.5	13.1	31.7

Of particular interest is the proportion of communications for all five purposes which utilizes *diagonal* relationships. Considerable contact between individuals regardless of position and unit takes place in the performance of the day-to-day activities related to their task assignment. Managers and nonmanagers alike seek out contributors to their task effectiveness and in so doing direct approximately one-third of their communications to persons in units and organizational levels other than their own. To the superior–subordinate and peer contacts reported in the literature, one must add and not overlook the presence and significance of the diagonal component.

Data on initiation of communications were submitted by 47 of the 48 managers and by 39 of the 43 nonmanagers. While perceptions undoubtedly differ on who is the initiator and who is the receiver, the data provided in the reporter logs clearly demonstrate that nonmanagers as well as managers initiate not only information and scuttlebutt but also play a sizeable role in the managerial communications activities of instruction, approval, and problem solving. These nonmanagers, as their communications networks indicate, are engaged in managing the accomplishments of those duties and tasks assigned to them regardless of where in the organization such activities may take them.

Of course, managers differ from nonmanagers in that nonmanagers have no opportunity for downward communications, for they are by definition the lowest members of the organizational hierarchy. In those organizational levels to which both managers and nonmanagers communicate, however, the bulk of these communications contacts occur at their own organizational level and at the level immediately above them. At these two levels, there are seldom any significant differences between managers and nonmanagers in the proportion of individuals in each category initiating communications for all five purposes. And the communications so initiated are directed by both managers and nonmanagers vertically, horizontally, and diagonally to every major segment of the organization at those two levels (see Table 3).

TABLE 3
ACCEPTANCE OR REJECTION OF THE HYPOTHESIS
THAT SIGNIFICANT DIFFERENCES EXIST BETWEEN
MANAGERS AND NONMANAGERS IN THE PROPORTION OF
INDIVIDUALS INITIATING COMMUNICATIONS FOR ALL PURPOSES
TO SELECTED ORGANIZATIONAL UNIT-LEVEL CELLS*

Organization Level Initiated to:	Organizational Unit Initiated to:			
	to own unit	outside unit, to own department	outside department, to own division	outside division, to own firm
to one level up	reject	reject	reject	accept
at own level	reject	reject	reject	reject

*Using chi-square test with acceptance at 0.05 level.

Questioning of respondents indicates that few horizontal or diagonal relationships are prescribed in the formal authority statements or procedures. This may be a function of the kinds of positions and the nature of the industries represented by the reporters. That such movement is so widespread, however, suggests that individuals move wherever in the organization information, advice, counsel, and expertise may be found to assist in gaining satisfactory accomplishment of the goals assigned. Managers and nonmanagers are alike in this behavior. Formal organization boundaries and levels yield to the demands of the task and situation.

NETWORK MEMBERSHIP

The composition of a communications network for a given individual may be considered in terms of (1) the total number of individuals with whom he communicates and their unit location in the organization, (2) the organizational level of these individuals in terms of communicating vertically, horizontally, or diagonally, and (3) the nature or purpose of the communication.

The data indicate that both managers and nonmanagers have communications network members who total far more than traditional spans of management or control would indicate and which are in excess of what one would conclude from examination of the organization charts and prescribed procedures alone (see Table 4). Furthermore, the scope of these networks varies only slightly between

TABLE 4
NUMBER OF MEMBERS IN AVERAGE INDIVIDUAL NETWORK
(BY ORGANIZATION UNIT)

	Within own unit	Outside unit, in own dept.	Outside dept., in own div.	Outside div., in own firm	Outside firm	Total net members
Manager	7	9	9	9	2	36
Nonmanager	4	6	10	6	2	28

manager and nonmanager. The very large proportion of members outside one's own immediate organizational unit should be noted. This amounts to 80 percent for managers and 85 percent for nonmanagers and confirms Leonard Sayles' experience (6, p. 39).

This sizeable component of net membership occurring outside one's own organizational unit and the substantial amount of communications movement regardless of formal organization and hierarchy boundaries are further supported in Table 5. Relatively few persons are present from the scalar chain, the vertical structure. The bulk of the network membership is to be found among one's peers in other units (the horizontal structure) and in persons at higher or lower levels in units other than the reporter's home base (diagonal structure).

TABLE 5
NUMBER OF MEMBERS IN AVERAGE INDIVIDUAL NETWORK
(BY DIRECTION OF COMMUNICATION)

	Vertical up	Vertical down	Diagonal up	Diagonal down	Horizontal	Total
Manager	2	5	5	10	14*	36
Nonmanager	2		10		16†	28

*in own unit—1 ; outside unit—13.
†in own unit—2 ; outside unit—14.

Taking into consideration the fact that nonmanagers have no subordinates and are at the lowest level in the hierarchy so they can have no "vertical down" or "diagonal down" communication, there is again close correspondence between managers and nonmanagers both in the total network size and in the network composition classified by direction of communication.

In addition to network membership examined in terms of organization location of the members and the direction of flow of communications issued or received, membership may be analyzed according to the function or purpose served by the individual network member (see Table 6). As in the case of

TABLE 6
NUMBER OF MEMBERS IN AVERAGE INDIVIDUAL NETWORK*
(BY TYPE OF COMMUNICATION)

Communication type	Position	Number of Members
Information	manager	25
	nonmanager	19
Instruction	manager	11
	nonmanager	9
Problem solving	manager	10
	nonmanager	7
Approval	manager	4
	nonmanager	2
Scuttlebutt	manager	4
	nonmanager	4

*Any one individual may be a member of more than one subnet.

communications frequency (see Table 1), network membership shows a predominance of individuals who serve the information function. The next highest number of members is less than one-half the number engaging in the information function. At this second level, the number of individuals in a network for instructional purposes is similar to those present for the problem-solving activity. The similar number of individuals for these latter two purposes departs from their volume characteristics as displayed in Table 1 where the number of instructional communications exceeds substantially the frequency of problem-solving items. As in Table 1, however, the approval and scuttlebutt purposes show the fewest number of subnet members. The magnitude for these two purposes is again less than one-half the number at the next higher level. Thus, with the exception of problem solving and instruction, there is close correspondence between the functional frequency of communications and the number of net members participating in the performance of that function.

While some network members are present for multiple communications purposes, it is of interest to note that a substantial proportion of a given network membership is present to service but a single function (see Table 7). In the average managerial network, 22 individuals (approximately 60 percent) participate in one function alone while for nonmanagers 16 persons (approximately 58 percent) are single-function participants. Once again, the information category has the highest proportion of persons present for a single activity.

TABLE 7

NUMBER OF MEMBERS SERVING SINGLE PURPOSE ONLY
IN AVERAGE NET

	Information		Instruction		Approval		Problem solving		Scuttlebutt		Total members
	This only	Total	This only	Total	This only	Total	This only	Total	This only	Total	
Manager	13	25	3	11	.7	4	4	10	1	4	36
Nonmanager	11	19	3	9	.3	2	1	7	1	4	28

QUALITATIVE OBSERVATIONS
FROM REPORTER LOGS

The large number of instances where communications take place outside the scalar chain indicates a substantial task orientation in the companies represented in the study. Such communications across organizational boundaries and in directions other than vertical suggest the existence of procedures regulating the flow of such communications. Little evidence, however, exists in the comments of participants to support the presence of formally prescribed procedures governing communications channels in the day-to-day activities. For the most part, reporting individuals were left to seek out and establish those network relationships which they believed to be useful or essential in the performance of their tasks.

The predominance of interunit and interlevel network membership and the substantial role of the nonmanager in initiating communications in all five purpose categories may well be a reflection of the high component among the reporters of professional or technical competence, of a sample bias toward aggressive, ambitious, younger individuals, and of a large component of so-called staff positions. At the same time, regardless of one's position title, his organization unit, his location in the hierarchy, and the presence or absence of formal structure, the qualitative as well as the quantitative data reflect the day-to-day emphasis on effective and economical task performance unrestricted by formal limits.

While one might feel that "staff" individuals would of course range widely through the organization, attempts at identification of "line" versus "staff" positions and relationships prove of little value. Position titles are of minor help in such classifications and give few clues to the actual relationships existing between individuals in a network. As one might suspect, examination of the communication itself provides the best indicator of the character of such relationships. And the data fail to provide any clear-cut distinction between "line" and "staff" or between "manager" and "nonmanager" based on the communications themselves. Any individual regardless of position title or organization location could be a member of either group depending on the time and the situation.

CONCLUSIONS

Several conclusions stem from the quantitative and qualitative data. First, the extent of the total communications network and therefore the range of individual contacts in an organization are far wider for both manager and nonmanager than one would gather from such traditional concepts as formal structure, span of management, and superior–subordinate relationships. This is illustrated in the large proportion of horizontal and diagonal contacts which exist outside the formal prescriptions of structure and procedure.

Second, on a day-to-day basis, the concept of manager should be expanded to include all individuals performing managerial functions whether or not these persons have subordinates assigned in the formal organizational hierarchy. Both managers and nonmanagers perform activities which are essentially managerial in planning for, implementing, and controlling those tasks assigned to them. Without recognition of the managerial characteristics of those traditionally classified as nonmanagerial individuals, these persons often are denied the official resources to perform satisfactorily and must rely primarily on their expertise and persuasive abilities to obtain from others those contributions necessary for effective goal attainment.

Performance of managerial functions by persons historically considered as nonmanagerial coupled with the substantial crossing of organizational boundaries and surmounting of hierarchical levels by both managers and nonmanagers suggest the growing contribution of informal relationships developed by individuals to further task accomplishment. This is a phenomenon which increases as complexity and sophistication of organizational requirements increase. Greater efforts must be made in the assignment of resources better to serve the activities and contributions of these informal relationships. More effective resource allocation is essential if informal relationships are to be relied upon to an ever-larger degree in solving complex tasks and in drawing to the maximum on the expertise present wherever it may be found in the organization.

That these are observations based on data from highly qualified professional reporters does not reduce their relevance for the nontechnical or less professionally dominated organization membership. These are observations drawn from individuals in organizations many of which are at the forefront of technological advance and therefore are indicators of structural changes and relationships likely to develop in any organization as its level of technology and the general expertise of its membership advance.

It is therefore suggested that management scholars and practitioners alike give greater attention to achieving organization balance by more carefully identifying the resource needs and structural relationships arising de facto from task requirements, project objectives, and individual expertise and initiative. Resource allocation based on formal power structures embedded in traditional concepts of superior–subordinate relationships, unit boundaries, and organizational hierarchy is no longer sufficient in meeting the demands produced by increasing levels of technology and higher levels of member competence.

Questioning
the Managerial Implications of
Communicating in the Organization

1. How would you describe the manager who is more likely to prefer one-way over two-way communications? What will be the advantages and costs of his practices in terms of subordinate performance and satisfaction?

2. What steps would you take as a manager if you were convinced that upward communication from your subordinates was being seriously hampered by the obstacles outlined by Anderson?

3. Put yourself in the role of the president of company XYZ, listening to the report of a management consultant who has just completed a three-month study of the communication processes within your firm. The content of the report is summarized by the conclusions reached by Wickesberg. Assuming that you have complete faith in the validity of his findings, what organizational changes would you consider instituting in response to the report?

4. What short-term and long-term benefits will accrue to an organization in which all relevant communications are passed to the right people? Are there any potential disadvantages to a fully effective system of information exchange?

References

1. Burns, T., "The Direction of Activity and Communications in a Departmental Executive Group," *Human Relations*, VII (1954), 73–97.

2. Dubin, R., "Business Behavior *Behaviorally* Viewed," in *Social Science Approaches to Business Behavior,* ed. G. Strother. Homewood, Ill.: Richard D. Irwin, Inc., 1962, pp. 11–55.

3. Guetzkow, H., and W. R. Dill, "Facets in Organizational Development of Task-Oriented Groups," *Sociometry*, XX (1957), 175–204.

4. Leavitt, H. J., "Some Effects of Certain Communication Patterns on Group Performance," *Journal of Abnormal and Social Psychology*, XLVI (1951), 38–50.

5. Ponder, Q., "Supervisory Practice of Effective and Ineffective Foremen" (Doctoral dissertation, Columbia University, 1958).

6. Sayles, L. R., *Managerial Behavior.* New York: McGraw-Hill Book Company, 1964.

7. Walker, C. R., R. H. Guest, and A. N. Turner, *The Foreman on the Assembly Line*. Cambridge, Mass.: Harvard University Press, 1956.

Supervising

Others

Considerable evidence supports the contention that the supervisor plays an important role in the success of his department. Particularly important is the extent to which he is considerate of the welfare of his subordinates and the degree to which he initiates the structure of relations between men and work in his department. He can use his power either to coerce his subordinates or to permit them to share in the setting of goals and in the structuring of the work situation. He can be either the supportive leader, willing to go to bat for his men, or he can remain aloof and relatively insensitive to their individual needs.

The now classic essay by Tannenbaum and Schmidt is a rather comprehensive description of the modes of leadership behavior open to managers. They stress an understanding of the forces at work in the manager, subordinate, and situation as being necessary before a manager attempts to make an informed choice of the most effective way to relate to his subordinates.

The study by Schein and Lippitt looks at the source of influence in the superior–subordinate relationship. In it they attempt to relate attitudes about the legitimacy of influencing subordinates to certain organizational variables with varying degrees of success. Their work points to the need for an understanding of the extent to which agreement or disagreement between superior and subordinate on what is legitimate influence and what is not leads to conflict in the relationship.

A critical review of the literature concerning the differences between authoritarian and democratic leadership is contributed by Sales. His explanation of the failure of many experimental studies to confirm the benefits of democratic leadership is a meaningful one.

25

How to Choose
a Leadership Pattern

Robert Tannenbaum
University of California at Los Angeles

Warren H. Schmidt
University of California at Los Angeles

Reprinted by permission from *Harvard Business Review*, March–April 1958, 95–101.
© 1958 by the President and Fellows of Harvard College; all rights reserved.

"I put most problems into my group's hands and leave it to them to carry the ball from there. I serve merely as a catalyst, mirroring back the people's thoughts and feelings so that they can better understand them."

"It's foolish to make decisions oneself on matters that affect people. I always talk things over with my subordinates, but I make it clear to them that I'm the one who has to have the final say."

"Once I have decided on a course of action, I do my best to sell my ideas to my employees."

"I'm being paid to lead. If I let a lot of other people make the decisions I should be making, then I'm not worth my salt."

"I believe in getting things done. I can't waste time calling meetings. Someone has to call the shots around here, and I think it should be me."

Each of these statements represents a point of view about "good leadership." Considerable experience, factual data, and theroretical principles could be cited to support each statement, even though they seem to be inconsistent when placed together. Such contradictions point up the dilemma in which the modern manager frequently finds himself.

NEW PROBLEM

The problem of how the modern manager can be "democratic" in his relations with subordinates and at the same time maintain the necessary authority and control in the organization for which he is responsible has come into focus increasingly in recent years.

Earlier in the century this problem was not so acutely felt. The successful executive was generally pictured as possessing intelligence, imagination, initiative, the capacity to make rapid (and generally wise) decisions, and the ability to inspire subordinates. People tended to think of the world as being divided into "leaders" and "followers."

NEW FOCUS

Gradually, however, from the social sciences emerged the concept of "group dynamics" with its focus on *members* of the group rather than solely on the leader. Research efforts of social scientists underscored the importance of employee involvement and participation in decision making. Evidence began to challenge the efficiency of highly directive leadership, and increasing attention was paid to problems of motivation and human relations.

Through training laboratories in group development that sprang up across the country, many of the newer notions of leadership began to exert an impact. These training laboratories were carefully designed to give people a first-hand experience in full participation and decision making. The designated "leaders" deliberately attempted to reduce their own power and to make group members as responsible as possible for setting their own goals and methods within the laboratory experience.

It was perhaps inevitable that some of the people who attended the training laboratories regarded this kind of leadership as being truly "democratic" and went home with the determination to build fully participative decision making into their own organizations. Whenever their bosses made a decision without convening a staff meeting, they tended to perceive this as authoritarian behavior. The true symbol of democratic leadership to some was the meeting—and the less directed from the top, the more democratic it was.

Some of the more enthusiastic alumni of these training laboratories began to get the habit of categorizing leader behavior as "democratic" *or* "authoritarian." The boss who made too many decisions himself was thought of as an authoritarian, and his directive behavior was often attributed solely to his personality.

NEW NEED

The net result of the research findings and of the human relations training based upon them has been to call into question the stereotype of an effective leader. Consequently, the modern manager often finds himself in an uncomfortable state of mind.

Often he is not quite sure how to behave; there are times when he is torn between exerting "strong" leadership and "permissive" leadership. Sometimes new knowledge pushes him in one direction ("I should really get the group to help make this decision"), but at the same time his experience pushes him in another direction ("I really understand the problem better than the group and therefore I should make the decision"). He is not sure when a group decision is really appropriate or when holding a staff meeting serves merely as a device for avoiding his own decision-making responsibility.

The purpose of our article is to suggest a framework which managers may find useful in grappling with this dilemma. First we shall look at the different patterns of leadership behavior that the manager can choose from in relating himself to his subordinates. Then we shall turn to some of the questions suggested by this range of patterns. For instance, how important is it for a manager's subordinates to know what type of leadership he is using in a situation? What factors should he consider in deciding on a leadership pattern? What difference do his long-run objectives make as compared to his immediate objectives?

RANGE OF BEHAVIOR

Figure 1 presents the continuum or range of possible leadership behavior available to a manager. Each type of action is related to the degree of authority used by the boss and to the amount of freedom available to his subordinates in reaching decisions. The actions seen on the extreme left characterize the manager who maintains a high degree of control while those seen on the extreme right characterize the manager who releases a high degree of control. Neither extreme is absolute; authority and freedom are never without their limitations.

FIGURE 1
CONTINUUM OF LEADERSHIP BEHAVIOR

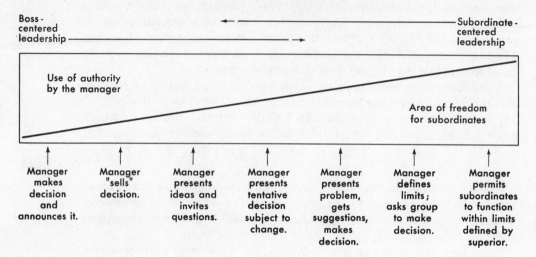

Now let us look more closely at each of the behavior points occurring along this continuum.

THE MANAGER MAKES THE DECISION AND ANNOUNCES IT. In this case the boss identifies a problem, considers alternative solutions, chooses one of them, and then reports this decision to his subordinates for implementation. He may or may not give consideration to what he believes his subordinates will think or feel about his decision; in any case, he provides no opportunity for them to participate directly in the decision-making process. Coercion may or may not be used or implied.

THE MANAGER "SELLS" HIS DECISION. Here the manager, as before, takes responsibility for identifying the problem and arriving at a decision. However, rather than simply announcing it, he takes the additional step of persuading his subordinates to accept it. In doing so, he recognizes the possibility of some resistance among those who will be faced with the decision, and seeks to reduce this resistance by indicating, for example, what the employees have to gain from his decision.

THE MANAGER PRESENTS HIS IDEAS, INVITES QUESTIONS. Here the boss who has arrived at a decision and who seeks acceptance of his ideas provides an opportunity for his subordinates to get a fuller explanation of his thinking and his intentions. After presenting the ideas, he invites questions so that his associates can better understand what he is trying to accomplish. This "give and take" also enables the manager and the subordinates to explore more fully the implications of the decision.

THE MANAGER PRESENTS A TENTATIVE DECISION SUBJECT TO CHANGE. This kind of behavior permits the subordinates to exert some influence on the decision. The initiative for identifying and diagnosing the problem remains with the boss. Before meeting with his staff, he has thought the problem through and arrived at a decision—but only a tentative one. Before finalizing it, he presents his proposed solution for the reaction of those who will be affected by it. He says in effect, "I'd like to hear what you have to say about this plan that I have developed. I'll appreciate your frank reactions, but will reserve for myself the final decision."

THE MANAGER PRESENTS THE PROBLEM, GETS SUGGESTIONS, AND THEN MAKES HIS DECISION. Up to this point the boss has come before the group with a solution of his own. Not so in this case. The subordinates now get the first chance to suggest solutions. The manager's initial role involves identifying the problem. He might, for example, say something of this sort: "We are faced with a number of complaints from newspapers and the general public on our service policy. What is wrong here? What ideas do you have for coming to grips with this problem?"

The function of the group becomes one of increasing the manager's repertory of possible solutions to the problem. The purpose is to capitalize on the knowledge and experience of those who are on the "firing line." From the expanded list of alternatives developed by the manager and his subordinates, the manager then selects the solution that he regards as most promising (19).

THE MANAGER DEFINES THE LIMITS AND REQUESTS THE GROUP TO MAKE A DECISION. At this point the manager passes to the group (possibly including himself as a member) the right to make decisions. Before doing so, however, he defines the problem to be solved and the boundaries within which the decision must be made.

An example might be the handling of a parking problem at a plant. The boss decides that this is something that should be worked on by the people involved, so he calls them together and points up the existence of the problem. Then he tells them:

> "There is the open field just north of the main plant which has been designated for additional employee parking. We can build underground or surface multilevel facilities as long as the cost does not exceed $100,000. Within these limits we are free to work out whatever solution makes sense to us. After we decide on a specific plan, the company will spend the available money in whatever way we indicate."

THE MANAGER PERMITS THE GROUP TO MAKE DECISIONS WITHIN PRESCRIBED LIMITS. This represents an extreme degree of group freedom only occasionally encountered in formal organizations, as, for instance, in many research groups. Here the team of managers or engineers undertakes the identification and diagnosis of the problem, develops alternative procedures for solving it, and decides on one or more of these alternative solutions. The

only limits directly imposed on the group by the organization are those specified by the superior of the team's boss. If the boss participates in the decision-
making process, he attempts to do so with no more authority than any other
member of the group. He commits himself in advance to assist in implementing
whatever decision the group makes.

KEY QUESTIONS

As the continuum in Figure 1 demonstrates, there are a number of alternative
ways in which a manager can relate himself to the group or individuals he is
supervising. At the extreme left of the range, the emphasis is on the manager—
on what *he* is interested in, how *he* sees things, how *he* feels about them. As we
move toward the subordinate-centered end of the continuum, however, the
focus is increasingly on the subordinates—on what *they* are interested in, how
they look at things, how *they* feel about them.

When business leadership is regarded in this way, a number of questions arise.
Let us take four of especial importance.

CAN A BOSS EVER RELINQUISH HIS RESPONSIBILITY BY DELE-
GATING IT TO SOMEONE ELSE? Our view is that the manager must
expect to be held responsible by his superior for the quality of the decisions
made, even though operationally these decisions may have been made on a
group basis. He should, therefore, be ready to accept whatever risk is involved
whenever he delegates decision-making power to his subordinates. Delegation
is not a way of "passing the buck." Also, it should be emphasized that the
amount of freedom the boss gives to his subordinates cannot be greater than the
freedom which he himself has been given by his own superior.

SHOULD THE MANAGER PARTICIPATE WITH HIS SUBORDI-
NATES ONCE HE HAS DELEGATED RESPONSIBILITY TO THEM?
The manager should carefully think over this question and decide on his role
prior to involving the subordinate group. He should ask if his presence will
inhibit or facilitate the problem-solving process. There may be some instances
when he should leave the group to let it solve the problem for itself. Typically,
however, the boss has useful ideas to contribute, and should function as an additional member of the group. In the latter instance, it is important that he indicate
clearly to the group that he sees himself in a *member* role rather than in an
authority role.

HOW IMPORTANT IS IT FOR THE GROUP TO RECOGNIZE WHAT
KIND OF LEADERSHIP BEHAVIOR THE BOSS IS USING? It makes
a great deal of difference. Many relationship problems between boss and subordinate occur because the boss fails to make clear how he plans to use his authority. If, for example, he actually intends to make a certain decision himself, but
the subordinate group gets the imporession that he has delegated this authority,

considerable confusion and resentment are likely to follow. Problems may also occur when the boss uses a "democratic" façade to conceal the fact that he has already made a decision which he hopes the group will accept as its own. The attempt to "make them think it was their idea in the first place" is a risky one. We believe that it is highly important for the manager to be honest and clear in describing what authority he is keeping and what role he is asking his subordinates to assume in solving a particular problem.

CAN YOU TELL HOW "DEMOCRATIC" A MANAGER IS BY THE NUMBER OF DECISIONS HIS SUBORDINATES MAKE? The sheer *number* of decisions is not an accurate index of the amount of freedom that a subordinate group enjoys. More important is the *significance* of the decisions which the boss entrusts to his subordinates. Obviously a decision on how to arrange desks is of an entirely different order from a decision involving the introduction of new electronic data-processing equipment. Even though the widest possible limits are given in dealing with the first issue, the group will sense no particular degree of responsibility. For a boss to permit the group to decide equipment policy, even within rather narrow limits, would reflect a greater degree of confidence in them on his part.

DECIDING HOW TO LEAD

Now let us turn from the types of leadership that are possible in a company situation to the question of what types are *practical* and *desirable*. What factors or forces should a manager consider in deciding how to manage? Three are of particular importance:

Forces in the manager.
Forces in the subordinates.
Forces in the situation.

We should like briefly to describe these elements and indicate how they might influence a manager's action in a decision-making situation (27). The strength of each of them will, of course, vary from instance to instance, but the manager who is sensitive to them can better assess the problems which face him and determine which mode of leadership behavior is most appropriate for him.

FORCES IN THE MANAGER

The manager's behavior in any given instance will be influenced greatly by the many forces operating within his own personality. He will, of course, perceive his leadership problems in a unique way on the basis of his background, knowledge, and experience. Among the important internal forces affecting him will be the following:

HIS VALUE SYSTEM. How strongly does he feel that individuals should have a share in making the decisions which affect them? Or, how convinced is he that the official who is paid to assume responsibility should personally carry the burden of decision making? The strength of his convictions on questions like these will tend to move the manager to one end or the other of the continuum shown in Figure 1. His behavior will also be influenced by the relative importance that he attaches to organizational efficiency, personal growth of subordinates, and company profits (3).

HIS CONFIDENCE IN HIS SUBORDINATES. Managers differ greatly in the amount of trust they have in other people generally, and this carries over to the particular employees they supervise at a given time. In viewing his particular group of subordinates, the manager is likely to consider their knowledge and competence with respect to the problem. A central question he might ask himself is: "Who is best qualified to deal with this problem?" Often he may, justifiably or not, have more confidence in his own capabilities than in those of his subordinates.

HIS OWN LEADERSHIP INCLINATIONS. There are some managers who seem to function more comfortably and naturally as highly directive leaders. Resolving problems and issuing orders come easily to them. Other managers seem to operate more comfortably in a team role, where they are continually sharing many of their functions with their subordinates.

HIS FEELINGS OF SECURITY IN AN UNCERTAIN SITUATION. The manager who releases control over the decision-making process thereby reduces the predictability of the outcome. Some managers have a greater need than others for predictability and stability in their environment. This "tolerance for ambiguity" is being viewed increasingly by psychologists as a key variable in a person's manner of dealing with problems.

The manager brings these and other highly personal variables to each situation he faces. If he can see them as forces which, consciously or unconsciously, influence his behavior, he can better understand what makes him prefer to act in a given way. And understanding this, he can often make himself more effective.

FORCES IN THE SUBORDINATE

Before deciding how to lead a certain group, the manager will also want to consider a number of forces affecting his subordinates' behavior. He will want to remember that each employee, like himself, is influenced by many personality variables. In addition, each subordinate has a set of expectations about how the boss should act in relation to him (the phrase "expected behavior" is one we hear more and more often these days at discussions of leadership and teaching). The better the manager understands these factors, the more accurately he can determine what kind of behavior on his part will enable his subordinates to act most effectively.

Generally speaking, the manager can permit his subordinates greater freedom if the following essential conditions exist:

If the subordinates have relatively high needs for independence. (As we all know, people differ greatly in the amount of direction that they desire.)

If the subordinates have a readiness to assume responsibility for decision making. (Some see additional responsibility as a tribute to their ability; others see it as "passing the buck.")

If they have a relatively high tolerance for ambiguity. (Some employees prefer to have clear-cut directives given to them; others prefer a wider area of freedom.)

If they are interested in the problem and feel that it is important.

If they understand and identify with the goals of the organization.

If they have the necessary knowledge and experience to deal with the problem.

If they have learned to expect to share in decision making. (Persons who have come to expect strong leadership and are then suddenly confronted with the request to share more fully in decision making are often upset by this new experience. On the other hand, persons who have enjoyed a considerable amount of freedom resent the boss who begins to make all the decisions himself.)

The manager will probably tend to make fuller use of his own authority if the above conditions do *not* exist; at times there may be no realistic alternative to running a "one-man show."

The restrictive effect of many of the forces will, of course, be greatly modified by the general feeling of confidence which subordinates have in the boss. Where they have learned to respect and trust him, he is free to vary his behavior. He will feel certain that he will not be perceived as an authoritarian boss on those occasions when he makes decisions by himself. Similarly, he will not be seen as using staff meetings to avoid his decision-making responsibility. In a climate of mutual confidence and respect, people tend to feel less threatened by deviations from normal practice, which in turn makes possible a higher degree of flexibility in the whole relationship.

FORCES IN THE SITUATION

In addition to the forces which exist in the manager himself and in his subordinates, certain characteristics of the general situation will also affect the manager's behavior. Among the more critical environmental pressures that surround him are those which stem from the organization, the work group, the nature of the problem, and the pressures of time. Let us look briefly at each of these.

TYPE OF ORGANIZATION.   Like individuals, organizations have values and traditions which inevitably influence the behavior of the people who work in them. The manager who is a newcomer to a company quickly discovers that certain kinds of behavior are approved while others are not. He also discovers that to deviate radically from what is generally accepted is likely to create problems for him.

These values and traditions are communicated in many ways—through job descriptions, policy pronouncements, and public statements by top executives. Some organizations, for example, hold to the notion that the desirable executive is one who is dynamic, imaginative, decisive, and persuasive. Other organizations put more emphasis upon the importance of the executive's ability to work effectively with people—his human relations skills. The fact that his superiors have a defined concept of what the good executive should be will very likely push the manager toward one end or the other of the behavioral range.

In addition to the above, the amount of employee participation is influenced by such variables as the size of the working units, their geographical distribution, and the degree of inter- and intra-organizational security required to attain company goals. For example, the wide geographical dispersion of an organization may preclude a practical system of participative decision making, even though this would otherwise be desirable. Similarly, the size of the working units or the need for keeping plans confidential may make it necessary for the boss to exercise more control than would otherwise be the case. Factors like these may limit considerably the manager's ability to function flexibly on the continuum.

GROUP EFFECTIVENESS.   Before turning decision-making responsibility over to a subordinate group, the boss should consider how effectively its members work together as a unit.

One of the relevant factors here is the experience the group has had in working together. It can generally be expected that a group which has functioned for some time will have developed habits of cooperation and thus be able to tackle a problem more effectively than a new group. It can also be expected that a group of people with similar backgrounds and interests will work more quickly and easily than people with dissimilar backgrounds, because the communication problems are likely to be less complex.

The degree of confidence that the members have in their ability to solve problems as a group is also a key consideration. Finally, such group variables as cohesiveness, permissiveness, mutual acceptance, and commonality of purpose will exert subtle but powerful influence on the group's functioning.

THE PROBLEM ITSELF.   The nature of the problem may determine what degree of authority should be delegated by the manager to his subordinates. Obviously he will ask himself whether they have the kind of knowledge which is needed. It is possible to do them a real disservice by assigning a problem that their experience does not equip them to handle.

Since the problems faced in large or growing industries increasingly require knowledge of specialists from many different fields, it might be inferred that the more complex a problem, the more anxious a manager will be to get some assistance in solving it. However, this is not always the case. There will be times when the very complexity of the problem calls for one person to work it out. For example, if the manager has most of the background and factual data relevant to a given issue, it may be easier for him to think it through himself than to take the time to fill in his staff on all the pertinent background information.

The key question to ask, of course, is: "Have I heard the ideas of everyone who has the necessary knowledge to make a significant contribution to the solution of this problem?"

THE PRESSURE OF TIME   This is perhaps the most clearly felt pressure on the manager (in spite of the fact that it may sometimes be imagined). The more that he feels the need for an immediate decision, the more difficult it is to involve other people. In organizations which are in a constant state of "crisis" and "crash programming" one is likely to find managers personally using a high degree of authority with relatively little delegation to subordinates. When the time pressure is less intense, however, it becomes much more possible to bring subordinates in on the decision-making process.

These, then, are the principal forces that impinge on the manager in any given instance and that tend to determine his tactical behavior in relation to his subordinates. In each case his behvior ideally will be that which makes possible the most effective attainment of his immediate goal within the limits facing him.

LONG-RUN STRATEGY

As the manager works with his organization on the problems that come up day by day, his choice of a leadership pattern is usually limited. He must take account of the forces just described and, within the restrictions they impose on him, do the best that he can. But as he looks ahead months or even years, he can shift his thinking from tactics to large-scale strategy. No longer need he be fettered by all the forces mentioned, for he can view many of them as variables over which he has some control. He can, for example, gain new insights or skills for himself, supply training for individual subordinates, and provide participative experiences for his employee group.

In trying to bring about a change in these variables, however, he is faced with a challenging question: At which point along the continuum *should* he act?

ATTAINING OBJECTIVES

The answer depends largely on what he wants to accomplish. Let us suppose that he is interested in the same objectives that most modern managers seek to attain when they can shift their attention from the pressure of immediate assignments:

1. To raise the level of employee motivation.
2. To increase the readiness of subordinates to accept change.
3. To improve the quality of all managerial decisions.
4. To develop teamwork and morale.
5. To further the individual development of employees.

In recent years the manager has been deluged with a flow of advice on how best to achieve these longer-run objectives. It is little wonder that he is often both bewildered and annoyed. However, there are some guidelines which he can usefully follow in making a decision.

Most research and much of the experience of recent years give a strong factual basis to the theory that a fairly high degree of subordinate-centered behavior is associated with the accomplishment of the five purposes mentioned (24, 29). This does not mean that a manager should always leave all decisions to his assistants. To provide the individual or the group with greater freedom than they are ready for at any given time may very well tend to generate anxieties and therefore inhibit rather than facilitate the atttainment of desired objectives. But this should not keep the manager from making a continuing effort to confront his subordinates with the challenge of freedom.

CONCLUSION

In summary, there are two implications in the basic thesis that we have been developing. The first is that the successful leader is one who is keenly aware of those forces which are most relevant to his behavior at any given time. He accurately understands himself, the individuals and group he is dealing with, and the company and broader social environment in which he operates. And certainly he is able to assess the present readiness for growth of his subordinates.

But this sensitivity or understanding is not enough, which brings us to the second implication. The successful leader is one who is able to behave appropriately in the light of these perceptions. If direction is in order, he is able to direct; if considerable participative freedom is called for, he is able to provide such freedom.

Thus, the successful manager of men can be primarily characterized neither as a strong leader nor as a permissive one. Rather, he is one who maintains a high batting average in accurately assessing the forces that determine what his most appropriate behavior at any given time should be and in actually being able to behave accordingly. Being both insightful and flexible, he is less likely to see the problems of leadership as a dilemma.

26

Supervisory Attitudes Toward the Legitimacy of Influencing Subordinates

Edgar H. Schein
Massachusetts Institute of Technology

Gordon L. Lippitt
Leadership Resources Inc.

This study attempts to relate attitudes about the legitimacy of influencing subordinates' behavior and attitudes to certain organizational variables. It is felt that the concept of legitimacy of influence is an important one to explore in the superior-subordinate relationship and in different organizational contexts.

The authors gratefully acknowledge the help of J. Steven Ott, Holly Crawford, and Robert Musser, whose work as assistants on this project has benefited it greatly. Thanks also go to the Air Force Advanced Management class, at The George Washington University, for gathering portions of the data.

A portion of this research was supported by the Office of Naval Research under Contract No. Nonr 1841 (83). Reprinted by permission from *The Journal of Applied Behavioral Science*, II, No. 2 (1966), 199–209.

One of the major issues in contemporary thinking about the relationship of employees to their company is the degree to which the company infringes on the private life of the employee. Some writers are concerned about the degree to which the managers and employees of today are so company-oriented that they willingly conform to any and all company norms which they may perceive (34); on the other hand, there is concern with the degree to which companies coercively demand conformity from their members and impose norms even in areas defined as private (7).

Whether voluntary and coerced conformity to company norms constitutes a problem for the organization depends to a large degree on the perceived legitimacy of attempts by superiors to influence the behavior of subordinates.

The purpose of this study is to explore whether differences of opinion among superiors concerning the number of areas in which they felt it was appropriate to influence subordinates are a function of the superior's (1) rank in the organization, (2) length of employment in the organization, or (3) the type of organization in which the superior is employed.

In a previous paper (23), data were presented on several areas of influence based on a large sample of students, labor leaders, and managers. It was found that there is considerable consensus on the rank ordering of items—almost all respondents consider immediate job-related attitudes and behavior as being more legitimate to influence than personal attitudes and behavior at home. However, the managerial sample in the earlier study tended to rate significantly more areas as legitimate than the other samples. The present study attempts to determine whether systematic differences would be present in different samples of managers.

UNDERLYING ASSUMPTIONS

The data collected in this study are primarily relevant to the effect of organizational culture and climate on a superior's opinion. One element of an organization's culture is its system of norms and the basic values and assumptions which underlie them. Such values and assumptions deal with the goals of the organization, the means to be employed in achieving the goals, the performance obligations of the members of the organization, and the "correct" way of handling the human resources of the organization. Thus, in reference to the two factors of length of service and type of organization to be examined in this study, one may find organizations varying in whether they assume people to be primarily self-motivated and trustworthy or primarily lazy, susceptible only to external motivation and in need of tight external control (18). These assumptions in turn define how superiors will deal with subordinates, how closely they will supervise them (12), and in what areas they will attempt to influence them.

PERCEIVED AREAS
OF LEGITIMATE INFLUENCE

The study of perceived areas of legitimate influence is an attempt to measure directly the perceptions and, by inference, the attitudes and values which govern this area of superior–subordinate relations. If there is consistency in these perceptions and attitudes within an occupational group, a company, a department, a rank level, or a group of equal length of service, we may assume that we are tapping a cultural element which relates either to the organization as such or to the reference group from which the sample was drawn. A group of "middle-level" managers may reflect primarily the values of "middle-level" management rather than the values of a particular company in which they are working. If there are systematic differences among groups within a single organization, and if these differences are not attributable to reference group norms, we may assume that we are tapping an element of the subcultures within the organization and can identify areas of potential conflict among subcultures. Differences among groups in their assumptions about what is legitimate and what is not are more likely to be sources of serious friction and conflict than disagreements about actual practices in attempted influence.

HYPOTHESES

No attempt is made in this study to explore personality dimension or "behavior styles" as a factor (32). The tendency to regard more or fewer areas as legitimate to influence can be related, however, to a number of organizational or occupational variables. In the previous study, it was found, for example, that labor leaders had the lowest influence index, students were next, and managers were highest. The variables which appear to be involved here are "proximity to the managerial role" and the intrinsic values which go with the occupational role. Supervisors regard a wider range of influence attempts as legitimate than do nonsupervisors, and a group such as labor leaders, who are ideologically committed to resisting infringement by management, are least likely to have a high influence score.

The concept of proximity to the managerial role suggested that there might be some other characteristics of this role itself which would influence the degree to which a person felt it legitimate to influence a subordinate. For example, the degree to which the person was integrated with and committed to the organization—as might be inferred from length of service and rank in the organization—should correlate positively with influence score. Second, influence score should be correlated with the degree to which the supervisory role is one which by its very nature demands close and extensive supervision because either the subordinates are not technically qualified to be given much independence or, as in the military service, the organization is highly centralized. Third, influence score should be correlated with the degree to which the subordinate's role is highly visible to others outside the organization. The more visible the subordinate, the greater the potential damage he can do to the organization's image by behavior out of line with norms. Therefore, the greater should be the superior's feeling that it is legitimate to influence the subordinate in many areas.

In the present study, we investigated the following hypotheses:

1. The higher the rank and greater the length of service of a manager, the higher will be his influence index.
2. The greater the degree to which the supervisory role demands extensive and close supervision because of a centralized and/or autocratic organization, the higher will be the influence index.
3. The greater the visibility of the subordinate's role, the higher will be the superior's influence index.

RESEARCH PROCEDURES

The data collected in this study are based on responses to an Influence Questionnaire (23), which consists of 55 items representing many possible behavior and attitude areas. These items range from highly job-related items (i.e., working hours, office neatness, supervisory habits) to highly personal items (i.e., fidelity to one's wife, attitude toward money, use of leisure time). The respondent is asked to write in Yes, No, or leave the item blank, depending on whether he considers it legitimate or not to influence a subordinate in that area. The instructions encourage nonresponse if for any reason the person is not sure or feels it depends on circumstances. In other words, the attempt is to identify those areas in which respondents have a clear attitude about whether influence attempts are or are not legitimate.

This instrument was administered to a variety of groups within government and industry in an attempt to obtain data on attitude variations which could be

TABLE 1
POPULATION SAMPLES*

30	Managers of supermarkets
30	County and city police chiefs
30	Civilian budget and fiscal officers
30	Military personnel directors of Air Force bases
324	Middle-level managers from three large companies
30	Sales managers of manufacturing concerns
30	Civilian personnel directors of government agencies
504	Total

*The samples of 30 were obtained by mailing the questionnaire to a large group and arbitrarily using the first 30 responses which came in. The sample of 324 managers was obtained during training and management development courses, both inside and outside the organization.

used to test our hypotheses. The conditions of administration varied only with respect to whether the questionnaire was mailed out or was administered to a group in a face-to-face setting. There is no evidence that method of administration made any difference in response patterns. The population samples obtained are shown in Table 1.

While the population sample differed in occupational role in accordance with the purposes of the study, it could be generalized that they all represented middle or upper managerial positions in the organization.

These responses were analyzed by obtaining for each group the average number of Yes answers, No answers, and items left blank. For each respondent, we computed an influence index based on all his responses by subtracting No's and 0.2 of the number of items left blank from the number of Yes's and adding 55 to make all scores positive. This index can vary from zero if a person gave 55 No's to $+110$ if he gave 55 Yes's.

RESULTS

INFLUENCE INDEX IN RELATION TO RANK AND LENGTH OF SERVICE

The relationship between rank and influence index is shown in Table 2. The data are shown for three different companies for which rank data were available: a large aircraft company (Co. 1) and two regional divisions of a public utility (Co. 2 and Co. 3). The results are inconsistent. In the manufacturing

TABLE 2
MEAN INFLUENCE INDEXES
AND FREQUENCY OF YES, NO, AND NA RESPONSES
IN RELATION TO ORGANIZATIONAL RANK

Organizational Rank N = 428	Index		Response Frequencies		
	Mean	S.D.	Yes	No	NA
Co. 1, Section heads (N 28)	49.1	11.8	22.2	26.6	7.2
Co. 1, Department heads (N 39)	52.0	13.3	24.8	24.9	6.3
Co. 2, Third-level supervisors (N 121)	52.8	13.0	24.3	25.2	5.4
Co. 2, Fourth and Fifth level (N 50)	47.8	11.5	20.8	26.8	7.4
Co. 3, Third-level supervisors (N 163)	46.5	11.1	20.4	27.5	7.0
Co. 3, Fourth-level supervisors (N 27)	44.5	12.6	18.6	27.2	9.2

concern, the higher the rank the higher the influence index, but in the utility divisions the reverse trend is evident. We also had available data on managers attending executive development courses at Massachusetts Institute of Technology. In comparing the M.I.T. Sloan Fellows with the senior executives at M.I.T. (who are roughly two to three ranks higher than the Sloan Fellows), we found again that the senior executives had lower indexes than the Sloan Fellows.

None of the differences reaches the 0.01 level of significance, but the fact that in three out of four groups of middle-level managers the trend was opposite to that hypothesized clearly fails to support our rank hypothesis. Either rank is a poor measure of commitment (defined as concern for the organization) to the organization, or commitment does not vary significantly among *middle*-level managers. We do not have data for a single organization which would permit comparing first-line supervisors with middle managers and senior executives.

Data on length of service are shown in Table 3 for the two divisions of the public utility. The results are shown for both rank levels and indicate a consistent but nonsignificant tendency for the mean influence index to rise with length of service. None of the interactions between ranks and length of service was significant, but it is of interest to note that in both companies the *lowest* influence score occurred in the higher ranking but shorter length-of-service group. If this trend reflects something other than chance, it would suggest that the rapidly rising young man in the organization is least likely to regard many areas as legitimate to influence.

The rank and length of service data are inconclusive. Whether this is due to the fact that rank and length of service are poor indicators of commitment to the organizations or whether commitment does not correlate with the influence index is not possible to determine from our data. It is suspected that a nonlinear relationship exists with low commitment at beginning and end of career. In a further study, we plan to measure commitment more directly to unscramble these relationships.

TABLE 3
MEAN INFLUENCE INDEX
AS A FUNCTION OF LENGTH OF SERVICE

	0–20 Years			21–40 Years		
Company 2 (N = 171)	Mean	S.D.	*N*	Mean	S.D.	*N*
Third Level	50.7	13.6	43	54.0	12.6	78
Fourth and Fifth Levels	43.4	11.8	14	49.5	11.4	36
Total	48.9	13.2	57	52.6	12.2	114
Company 3 (N = 190)						
Third Level	46.0	10.6	79	46.9	11.6	84
Fourth Level	42.6	10.0	11	45.8	13.9	16
Total	45.6	10.5	90	46.8	11.3	100

INFLUENCE INDEX
AS A FUNCTION OF TYPE OF
ORGANIZATION AND MANAGERIAL ROLE

Our samples permitted us to identify some organizations in which one could reasonably hypothesize that the managerial role would be different. In particular, two of the samples involved managers whose roles demand fairly close, centralized, autocratic supervision—supermarket managers and police chiefs. These groups were contrasted with civilian and military personnel directors, a group of budget and fiscal officers, and a group of sales managers of manufacturing concerns. The results are shown in Table 4.

TABLE 4
MEAN INFLUENCE INDEXES
AND FREQUENCY OF YES, NO, AND NA RESPONSES
FOR DIFFERENT SAMPLE GROUPS

Occupational Groups	Index				
	Mean	S.D.	Yes	No	NA
A. Managers of supermarkets (N 30)	59.6	11.4	29.1	24.2	1.6
B. County and city police chiefs (N 30)	57.3	7.6	26.4	22.9	5.7
C. Military personnel directors of Air Force bases (N 30)	52.5	11.1	23.5	23.9	7.6
D. Civilian personnel directors of government agencies (N 30)	44.5	8.4	18.0	25.7	11.3
E. Sales managers of manufacturing concerns (N 30)	49.4	13.0	22.6	27.1	5.2
F. Civilian budget and fiscal officers (N 30)	54.0	11.0	24.6	24.4	6.1
G. Middle-level managers from three large companies (N 324)	49.6	12.1	22.7	26.7	5.8

The results are clearly in the direction hypothesized. Supermarket managers and police chiefs are significantly higher than any of the other groups, and the military personnel directors are significantly higher than their civilian government agency counterparts. The supermarket managers are not only higher in the average number of Yes's, but they are more sure of themselves than any other group, as indicated by the low average number of No Answer responses. At the other extreme, the civilian personnel directors have the lowest average number of Yes's and highest average number of items left blank.

We examined the item data in order to determine whether the differences could result from certain items which would be especially relevant to a particular occupational role (e.g., the subordinate's sexual morals in the case of the police chiefs). We found that the tendency for a certain group to show higher indexes was not a function of particular items but rather expressed itself in higher rates of answering Yes across most of the items of the questionnaire. This finding confirms our earlier results (23): that the influence index measures a general attitude toward the legitimacy of influence which expresses itself across a wide variety of behavior and attitude areas. Police chiefs and supermarket managers, either by personal predisposition or by virtue of their managerial role, are generally more prone to regard influences as legitimate.

INFLUENCE INDEX IN RELATION TO THE VISIBILITY OF THE SUBORDINATE'S ROLE

The data relevant to this hypothesis can also be found in Table 4, if we compare the sales managers with budget and control officers and our other middle-management groups shown in Tables 2 and 3. The data clearly fail to support the hypothesis. The sales managers are lower than the budget and control officers and are virtually identical to the larger sample of middle management.

Informal data about sales organizations indicate that some of the severest pressures toward conformity which are generated in modern industry occur in sales departments, as contrasted, for example, with production departments. The fact that sales managers did not come out higher on the over-all index suggests either that these informal observations are false or that feelings about the legitimacy of influence are not correlated with actual influence attempts. Even an item like "whether the subordinate used the company product himself" did not receive a higher percentage of Yes's from the sales managers than from the other groups.

SUMMARY AND IMPLICATIONS

In this study we have attempted to relate attitudes about the legitimacy of influencing subordinates' behavior to certain organizational variables.

1. Contrary to our hypothesis, we did not find the number of areas regarded as legitimate to be related significantly to rank or length of service, although there was a consistent trend for middle managers with greater length of service to have higher indexes.
2. As hypothesized, managers whose organization and their role within it demand close line supervision and a high degree of centralization of responsibility regarded significantly more areas as legitimate to influence than other managerial groups. In particular, supermarket managers and police chiefs showed the highest influence indexes.
3. Contrary to the hypothesis, managers whose subordinates have more visible roles and who deal with members outside the organization, i.e., salesmen, did not show higher influence indexes than managers whose subordinates have less visible roles.
4. Differences between groups and between organizations tended to reflect an

over-all tendency to be higher or lower across all items. There were no clear-cut item categories in terms of which particular managerial groups or organizations could be identified.

These findings leave us with some puzzling implications. Originally, the Influence Questionnaire was intended to identify *content* areas in terms of which groups and organizations could be differentiated, as a way of getting concretely at organizational climate. Instead, we have consistently found that the over-all influence index, which measures simply the *number* of areas regarded as legitimate to influence, is a much more sensitive discriminator among groups. The influence index of managers is clearly different from nonmanagers, and some groups of managers are clearly different from others.

We attempted in this study to refine the characteristics of the managerial role which would correlate with the index, but we were only partly successful. Yet the consistent differences which show up in the index argue strongly that an important aspect of the managerial role is being tapped by it. The high scores of supermarket managers and police chiefs suggest something about a managerial role in which the manager is responsible for a great many people in a highly centralized kind of organizational structure. The higher scores of the military personnel chiefs relative to their civilian counterparts reflect this also. The key variable here may be the degree of risk associated with delegation to subordinates. If the superior feels that he is taking greater risks if a subordinate makes an error, he may well consider it more legitimate to influence the subordinate in many areas.

What we do not yet know is whether tendency to regard influence as legitimate is a personality characteristic which leads the high-influence person into roles in which his tendency can readily find expression or whether the realities of the role create certain attitudes toward legitimacy which the role occupant soon learns. Informal observations and clinical analyses of a few questionnaires done with Sloan Fellows at M.I.T. indicate that the latter explanation is more likely to be true. One respondent who has moved from a staff to a line position reports that he found himself saying Yes to more items because he suddenly had a much broader and deeper responsibility for the operation which made him less disposed to leave subordinates free in many areas. He was surprised at his own decrease in tolerance with the shift in role.

The ultimate importance of a variable such as the one we are attempting to delineate—attitudes about the legitimacy of influencing subordinates—lies in the fact that it may account for areas of superior–subordinate conflict and that it may provide a clue to the different kinds of superior–subordinate relationships which are established in different work settings. The findings that subordinates react favorably to superiors who show consideration and are employee centered (12) need to be refined in terms of some concept of *congruence* of attitudes. That is, it would be our hypothesis that more important than either consideration or employee centeredness is congruence or agreement as to what is a legitimate area of the superior's influence on the subordinate and what is not.

It is agreement at this level that might well determine whether the subordinate perceives the superior to be considerate or not. And, in different organizational settings, the area of agreement might well be different, as indeed Vroom (30) has shown in terms of subordinate preferences for authoritarian versus more democratic styles of supervision. On tasks requiring little contact which were low in interdependency, subordinates preferred more autocratic supervision.

In conclusion, we feel that the concept of legitimacy of influence is an important one to explore further in the superior–subordinate relationship and in different organizational contexts. In future studies, we hope to delineate more clearly the characteristics of the managerial role which lead to high or low indexes and the consequences for superior–subordinate relationships of disagreement about the amount and areas of legitimate influence.

27

Supervisory Style and Productivity: Review and Theory

Stephen M. Sales
University of Michigan

The author wishes to express his appreciation to Dr. Ned A. Rosen of the New York State School of Industrial and Labor Relations, Cornell University, for his constant assistance and encouragement. A grant from the Foundation for Research on Human Behavior, Ann Arbor, Mich., provided the time necessary for the preparation of this article. Reprinted by permission from *Personnel Psychology*, XIX, No. 3 (1966), 275–86.

It is widely assumed that employees will work harder for supervisors who employ given styles of supervision than they will for supervisors who use other styles. This supposition clearly underlies much of supervisory training; it is a basic tenet of the writings of Morse (20), Likert (12), and many others. However, the theoretical underpinnings of this assumption are often unclearly stated (when they are stated at all); furthermore, the wide variety of studies investigating the validity of this position are rarely fully described. The present article will sketch a theory which accounts for the predicted differential in productivity and will review and evaluate the literature relevant to this theory.

AUTHORITARIANISM AND DEMOCRACY

The styles to be discussed are the authoritarian and democratic dimensions. The distinction between these orientations has often been made in the literature; it will not be extensively elaborated here. Rather, we shall discuss only the major differences between these styles.

Authoritarian supervision, in general, is characterized by the relatively high degree of power wielded by the supervisor over the work group. As contrasted with democratic supervision, both power and all decision-making functions are absolutely concentrated in the person of the authoritarian. Democratic supervision, on the other hand, is characterized by a sharing of power and by participative decision making. Under democratic supervision, the work group becomes in some ways co-equal with the supervisor; responsibility is spread rather than concentrated.

DIFFERENTIAL EFFECTIVENESS

It is commonly assumed that, with other conditions held constant, employees will produce more under democratic supervision than they would have produced under autocratic supervision. (Such an assumption, of course, lies behind the entire human relations movement.) There is at least one good reason for this prediction. Specifically, the reinforcing value of work performed under democratic supervision should be higher than that of work performed under autocratic supervision.

It is a basic tenet of experimental psychology that high levels of performance will obtain in situations in which the reinforcement is large, whereas low performance levels will occur in those in which the reinforcement is small. In terms of industrial situations, the more reinforcement an employee receives for production, the higher his production should be. (This is, of course, the assumption which underlies incentive systems, although reinforcement is rather narrowly defined in such programs.) Vroom (31, pp. 26–43) in particular has explored the ramifications of this argument.

The importance of this point for the present consideration is that production is attended by two different levels of need-satisfaction under the two styles of supervision sketched above. Democratic supervision, by allowing subordinates freedom in determining the specific form and content of their work, implicates the personalities of the employees in the tasks they perform. This means that production, under democratic supervision, becomes a means for satisfying the employees' ego-esteem and self-actualization needs (see 4,15). That is, the "greater opportunity for regulating and controlling their own activities [provided by democratic supervision]. . . should increase the degree to which individuals could express their various and diverse needs and could move in the direction of fully exploiting their potential while on the job" (21). Authoritarian supervision, inasmuch as it makes work merely the carrying out of the supervisor's will, reduces the degree to which such need-satisfaction can be derived from production. Therefore, since productivity is less satisfying under autocratic than under democratic supervision, one would expect that workers would be less productive in the former condition than in the latter. (This effect, of course, should be accentuated for those individuals for whom the needs in question are most important.)

It should be noted that the above considerations do not involve between-style differences which rest upon uncontrolled factors (even when such factors might themselves follow from the style variation). For instance, if turnover were higher under one supervisory style than under the other, one would expect that the method resulting in higher turnover would be accompanied by the lower productivity rate (because of lowered effectiveness during learning periods). Factors of this sort would lead to productivity differences between the supervisory styles; however, such differences would not truly bear upon the question of effectiveness as usually posed. That is, statements about supervisory style center in general about the proposition that employees will work harder for some supervisors than for others. This statement cannot be supported by dependent variable differences which may be shown to result from between condition variations other than that of supervisory style. The present discussion is concerned solely with productivity differences which follow *directly* from the style of supervision.

RELEVANT INVESTIGATIONS

Any review of the literature on supervision must be in some way limited if both the reviewer and the readers are to escape total exhaustion. For this reason, investigations employing nonproduction criteria will be excluded from this review as will studies in which methodological looseness clouds interpretation of the findings reported. Thus, investigations which operationalize the effectiveness of the supervisory styles used in terms of "increased acceptance of decisions" (e.g., 5), morale, or similar criteria will not be reviewed, nor will unstandardized case studies of "participative management" or the Scanlon plan.

EXPERIMENTAL INVESTIGATIONS

The original and best known study in this area is the experiment of Lewin, Lippitt, and White (e.g., 13, pp. 496–510; 33). These investigators employed as subjects thirty ten-year-old boys who met in six groups which ostensibly were recreational clubs. These groups were supervised by adults who had been trained to act in either a democratic, autocratic, or laissez-faire manner. (The last condition is not considered in the present discussion.) Each club was exposed to each of the three styles for six weeks.

The results of this experiment, in terms of productivity, are extremely difficult to establish. When exposed to autocratic supervision[1] the boys spent more time at work than they did under democratic supervision (74 percent of the total time as opposed to 50 percent under democratic supervision). However, the "work-mindedness" of the democratically supervised boys appeared to be somewhat higher since under democratic supervision the groups engaged in a slightly larger amount of "work-minded conversation." (There were 63 work-minded remarks per child under the democratic condition, whereas in the autocratic condition this figure fell to 52.) However, no objective measure of productivity is reported by the authors, and therefore it is impossible to determine accurately which of the two styles evoked the higher production (a fact often overlooked by reviewers of this study).

McCurdy and Eber (16) examined supervisory style in an investigation on group problem solving. In this experiment, three-man groups participated in a task in which the group determined the proper setting of three switches. In the authoritarian condition one subject was given the power to order the others at will, making him an "absolute" supervisor. The other subjects were instructed merely to obey orders. In the democratic condition the instructions emphasized equalitarianism, specifying that each subject could offer suggestions and that no individual could order the others in any way. No differences whatever appeared between the two conditions on a productivity criterion.

Shaw (25), working with communication networks, also used problem solving as a dependent variable in an investigation of supervisory style effects. Employing three different "nets," he instructed the subjects assigned to the position with the highest independence score within each structure[2] to behave either in an autocratic manner (e.g., by giving orders) or in a democratic manner (e.g., by making suggestions). Shaw found that the autocratically supervised subjects (a) required less time to solve the problems, regardless of the communication net in which they were placed, and (b) made fewer errors.

Day and Hamblin (6) trained a female student to employ "close" and

---

[1] Only the "submissive reaction" to autocracy will be here considered; the "aggressive reaction" is felt to be a function of the subjects and the situation employed by the investigators.

[2] The research of Leavitt (11) clearly suggests that these positions are the ones from which leadership is exercised.

"general" supervisory styles in leading groups of female subjects in an assembly-line task. These researchers found that subjects exposed to close supervision produced less than did subjects exposed to general supervision.

Sales (22), like Day and Hamblin, replicated an industrial assembly-line setting in the laboratory. In Sales's experiment two male supervisors played democratic and autocratic roles over male and female groups. (Both role and sex of the subordinates were fully counterbalanced in this experiment.) Sales reports no differential effectiveness whatever between the two styles; the productivity means for the two conditions were virtually identical.

Spector and Suttell (26) report a relevant laboratory study with Naval trainees as subjects. These authors trained supervisors to use either "single leadership" or "leadership sharing" styles, patterns which seem to parallel the democratic–autocratic distinction. The task consisted of problems in which team members cooperated in receiving, processing, and recording information. No differences were detected in the productivity of the groups under the two styles.

In the most extensive of the investigations reported in this area, Morse and Reimer (21) created groups exposed either to democratic or to autocratic supervision by altering the style of supervision used in an on-going industrial setting. In two divisions ("participative treatment") an attempt was made to push down the level of decision making. Supervisors were trained to employ more democratic supervisory methods, and they were given greater freedom of action than previously had been allowed. In two other divisions an "hierarchically controlled treatment" was established by an increase in the closeness of supervision and a movement upward in the level at which decisions were made. The treatments were administered for a year's time to approximately five hundred employees.

Morse and Reimer found that both programs resulted in a significant increase in productivity. This increase was slightly higher for the hierarchically controlled divisions; however, the actual difference between the treatments was quite small.

On balance, then, the experimental studies reviewed above show no consistent superiority of one style over the other in terms of a productivity criterion. Of the six studies for which objective production data are available, one (6) reports democratic supervision to be more effective and one (25) reports authoritarian supervision to be more effective. The other four investigations note no differences of consequence between the two styles.

SURVEY INVESTIGATIONS

Survey researches applied to the problem discussed herein follow a standard methodology. The supervisory style which exists in each of the work groups in the situation is determined (usually by means of questionnaires administered to the employees), and this variable is then related to productivity. Researchers using this methodology generally have found a clear relationship between style of supervision and work group productivity.

The extensive investigations performed by the Survey Research Center at the University of Michigan during the early 1950s (8, pp. 146–71; 9, 10) are representative of this approach. In a wide variety of industrial situations (including railway maintenance crews, insurance office staffs, and heavy industry production lines), these authors found (1) that general supervision was associated with high productivity whereas close supervision was associated with low productivity, and (2) that "employee-oriented" attitudes in the supervisor were associated with high productivity whereas "job-oriented" attitudes were associated with low productivity. It is unclear exactly what relationship these independent variables have to the democratic–autocratic dimension; however, it can certainly be assumed that employee-oriented attitudes and general supervision will tend to be associated with democracy (as here used) whereas job-oriented attitudes and close supervision will tend to be associated with authoritarianism. The data of Morse (20) and Argyle, Gardner, and Cioffi (1) support these assumptions.

Argyle *et al.* (2) performed a successful replication of these earlier investigations in a British industrial situation. The authors report that foremen of high-producing work groups tended to use general rather than close supervision and were relatively more democratic in their behavior than were foremen of less productive work groups. Further, the attitudes of the more effective foremen tended to be more "employee-oriented" than those of the less effective foremen. In contrast to experimental findings, therefore, these survey data clearly seem to support the hypothesis that democratic supervision leads to higher production than does authoritarian supervision.

DISCUSSION

The usual explanations offered for the failure of the experimental method to replicate survey findings rest upon either (a) the brevity of the experimental sessions or (b) the peripheral nature of the experimental tasks. It seems to the present author, however, that these explanations are respectively (a) too facile and (b) inadequately elaborated for proper handling of the problem.

Of the two, the "brevity" argument is the more open to attack. Experimental sessions are, of course, of relatively short duration. However, the entire science of experimental social psychology rests upon the assumption that experimental periods are sufficiently lengthy for treatments to "take," an assumption which is supported in every significant finding obtained in an experimental laboratory. To argue that the experiments reviewed here failed to demonstrate predicted productivity differences because of inadequate time periods (especially when these same time periods are sufficient to evoke morale differences—favoring the democratic supervisor—between the groups exposed to the two styles) seems somehow an unscientific and unsatisfactory way of explaining the findings. Furthermore, such an explanation fails to account for the quite small productivity differential which existed between the conditions created by Morse and Reimer in an experiment which continued over the course of an entire year.

It appears to the author that, rather than looking to brevity, one may best explain the equal experimental effectiveness of the two supervisory styles by concentrating upon the nature of the tasks involved. (This is, of course, the approach incompletely hinted at in the "peripheral nature" argument.) Specifically, it seems that no differences in effectiveness have been found between the two styles because the tasks employed wholly fail to meet the conditions under which differential productivity was predicted.

Democratic supervision, it will be remembered, was expected to be the more effective style because of the greater extent to which it makes productivity a means to need-satisfaction. This prediction rests upon the assumption that democratic supervision allows productivity to be a path to the satisfaction of self-actualization and ego-esteem needs, whereas autocratic supervision does not serve such a purpose.

These conditions do not seem to have been generated by the experimental investigations reported above. Democratic supervision, in these experiments, can hardly be seen as allowing the subjects to see production on the task involved as a path to self-actualization. The thought is virtually absurd. Regardless of the intent of the investigators, the decisions allowed by the democratic supervisors (e.g., suggesting possible solutions to simple problems) do not seem to implicate the unique personalities of the subjects in their tasks. This seems to have been true even in the More and Reimer investigation, for the authors report that "both groups of clerks indicated that their jobs throughout the course of the experiment did not give them a very high degree of self-actualization." To the extent that experimental studies fail to make productivity under democratic supervision a path to significantly greater need-satisfaction than it would be under autocratic supervision, there is no reason to suspect that they should demonstrate democratic supervision to be more effective. Such investigations simply fail to provide the conditions necessary for a test of the hypothesis in question.

It should not be inferred, however, that survey investigations provide a more adequate test of the hypothesis that workers will work harder for democratic supervisors, in spite of the satisfying direction of the findings. There are at least two reasons for approaching the results of these studies with caution, both of which rest upon the fact that spurious variables which clearly affect work group productivity accompany both these styles. To the extent that the effects of such variables cannot be discounted, survey methodology is incapable of offering convincing evidence concerning the relative effort expended by workers exposed to the styles in question.

In the first place, the supervisory styles discussed herein are accompanied by differential turnover and absenteeism (e.g., 2, 14, 21). These effects do contribute to productivity differences between groups exposed to these styles, since the higher absenteeism and turnover evoked by autocratic supervision would lead to a productivity difference favoring democratic supervision. However, such a difference would be irrelevant to the hypothesis that democratic supervision leads directly to more concerted effort on the part of the employees involved. The effects of absenteeism and/or turnover could be removed from the analysis by means of simple statistical techniques, although no survey research known to the author has as yet attempted to do so.

A second consideration lies in the fact that supervisors who naturally affect a democratic style of supervision cannot be assumed to be otherwise similar to those who affect an authoritarian style. In particular, the author feels that democratically oriented supervisors can be expected to be more intelligent than are autocratically oriented supervisors. There are no direct data drawn from industry which bear on this statement. However, the fact that intelligence has clearly been shown to be negatively correlated with measured (F-scale) authoritarianism (e.g., 28), which in turn has been shown to be highly correlated with authoritarian behavior (17), seems sufficient to make the point.

It may be assumed that the intelligence of the supervisor should be of some importance in determining the productivity of the employees under him. The more intelligent supervisor might be expected to diagnose production difficulties more quickly than the less intelligent supervisor, and he might also be expected to take more effective remedial action. Therefore, inasmuch as authoritarian and democratic supervisors are differentiated on intelligence, one might expect them to be differentiated on their skill in dealing with day-to-day production problems. The advantage, of course, would go to the democratic supervisors.

The effect of this predicted difference between the two supervisory populations would be to make the work groups under democratic supervision more productive than those under autocratic supervision. However, as in the case of the different levels of turnover evoked by the two styles, such a finding would *not* necessarily imply that employees worked harder for supervisors affecting the democratic style. Like the effect of absenteeism, the effect of supervisory intelligence could be removed from the analysis by means of proper statistical techniques, but again there has been no survey research which has done so.

Therefore, in neither experimental studies nor survey investigations has an adequate test of the theory sketched above been made. Experimental studies have not created the conditions necessary for such a test; survey research has introduced at least two contaminating variables which render proper interpretation of the observed relationship extremely difficult. Such studies have not *disproved* the theory in question. They simply have not offered the unambiguous evidence administrative science must have in order to evaluate plans of action (e.g., supervisory training) tacitly based on this theory.

This should not be interpreted to mean that such a test cannot be made. Experimental investigations of the sort attempted by Morse and Reimer (21), using a technology in which self-actualization could occur under democratic supervision, would provide an adequate test, as would survey investigations in which the intelligence of the supervisors and the turnover (and/or absenteeism) levels existing in the various work groups were assessed and partialed out of the correlation between the style of the supervisor and the productivity of the subordinates. (Research now in progress is directed toward this latter objective.) Without such conditions, however, the hypothesis that democratic supervision will evoke greater effort from employees than will autocratic supervision cannot truly be either supported or rejected.

Questioning
the Managerial Implications of
Supervising Others

1. In describing "forces in the situation," Tannenbaum and Schmidt might have easily elaborated further on "the problem itself" and, more precisely, the nature of task involved in superior–subordinate interaction. What characteristics of tasks other than those already discussed would you expect to be telling forces in determining appropriate supervisory behavior?

2. Consider two situations: (1) a worker feels his boss should be more autocratic when it comes to making decisions, and (2) a worker feels his boss should be more democratic when a decision is to be made. Which situation is likely to be more disruptive in the work place?

3. Design in very brief form an experiment testing the relative effectiveness of the authoritarian and democratic leadership styles, in which participants have the opportunity to self-actualize. What are your hypotheses concerning worker satisfaction and performance?

4. Which role in your experiment above would be the most difficult for you to play? Why?

References

1. Argyle, M., G. Gardner, and F. Cioffi, "The Measurement of Supervisory Methods," *Human Relations*, X (1957), 295–313.

2. ——, ——, and ——, "Supervisory Methods Related to Productivity, Absenteeism, and Labor Turnover," *Human Relations*, XI (1958), 23–40.

3. Argyris, C., "Top Management Dilemma: Company Needs vs. Individual Development," *Personnel* (1955), pp. 123–34.

4. ——, *Personality and Organization*. New York: Harper & Row, Publishers, 1957.

5. Coch, L., and J. R. P. French, Jr., "Overcoming Resistance to Change," *Human Relations*, I (1948), 512–32.

6. Day, R. C., and R. L. Hamblin, "Some Effects of Close and Punitive Styles of Supervision," *American Journal of Sociology*, LXIX (1964), *69*, 499–510.

7. Goffman, E., *Asylums: Essays on the Social Situation of Mental Patients and Other Inmates*. Garden City, N. Y.: Anchor Books, 1961.

8. Katz, D., and R. L. Kahn, "Human Organization and Worker Motivation," in *Industrial Productivity*, ed. L. Reed Tripp. Madison, Wis.: Industrial Relations Research Association, 1951.

9. Katz, D., N. Maccoby, G. Gurin, and L. Floor, *Productivity, Supervision, and Morale Among Railroad Workers*. Ann Arbor, Mich.: Institute for Social Research, 1951.

10. ——, ——, and N. C. Morse, *Productivity, Supervision, and Morale in an Office Situation*, Part 1. Ann Arbor, Mich.: Institute for Social Research, 1950.

11. Leavitt, H. J., "Some Effects of Certain Communication Patterns on Group Performance," *Journal of Abnormal and Social Psychology*, XLIV (1951), 38–50.

12. Likert, R., *New Patterns of Management*. New York: McGraw-Hill Book Company, 1961.

13. Lippett, R., and R. K. White, "An Experimental Study of Leadership and Group Life," in *Readings in Social Psychology*, 3rd ed., eds. E. E. Maccoby, T. N. Newcomb, and E. L. Hartley. New York: Holt, Rinehart & Winston, Inc., 1958.

14. Mann, F. C., and H. D. Baumgartel, *Absences and Employee Attitudes in an Electric Power Company*. Ann Arbor, Mich.: Institute for Social Research, 1953.

15. Maslow, A. H., *Motivation and Personality*. New York: Harper & Row, Publishers, 1954.

16. McCurdy, H. G., and H. W. Eber, "Democratic Versus Authoritarian: A Further Investigation of Group Problem-Solving," *Journal of Personality*, XXII (1953), 258–69.

17. McGee, H. M., "Measurement of Authoritarianism and Its Relation to Teacher Classroom Behavior," *Genetic Psychological Monographs*, LII (1955), 89–146.

18. McGregor, D. M., *The Human Side of Enterprise*. New York: McGraw-Hill Book Company, 1960.

19. Moore, L., "Too Much Management, Too Little Change," *Harvard Business Review*, XXXIV, No. 1 (1956), 41.

20. Morse, N. C., *Satisfactions in the White-Collar Job*. Ann Arbor: University of Michigan, Institute for Social Research, 1953.

21. ——, and E. Reimer, "The Experimental Change of a Major Organizational Variable," *Journal of Abnormal and Social Psychology*, LI (1956), 120–29.

22. Sales, S. M., "A Laboratory Investigation of the Effectiveness of Two Industrial Supervisory Dimensions" (Master's thesis, Cornell University, 1964).

23. Schein, E. H., and J. S. Ott, "The Legitimacy of Organizational Influence," *American Journal of Sociology*, LXVII, No. 6 (1962), 682–89.

24. Schmidt, W. H., and P. C. Buchanan, *Techniques That Produce Teamwork*. New London, Conn.: Arthur C. Croft Publications, 1954.

25. Shaw, M. E., "A Comparison of Two Types of Leadership in Various Nets," *Journal of Abnormal and Social Psychology*, L (1955), 127–34.

26. Spector, P., and B. Suttell, *An Experimental Comparison of the Effectiveness of Three Patterns of Leadership Behavior*. Washington, D. C.: American Institute for Research, 1957.

27. Tannenbaum, R., and F. Massarik, "Participation by Subordinates in the Managerial Decision-Making Process," *Canadian Journal of Economics and Political Science*, 1950, pp. 413–18.

28. Titus, H. E., and E. P. Hollander, "The California F-Scale in Psychological Research: 1950–1955," *Psychological Bulletin*, LIV (1957), *54*, 47–65.

29. Viteles, M. S., *Motivation and Morale in Industry*. New York: W. W. Norton & Company, Inc., 1953.

30. Vroom, V. H., *Some Personality Determinants of the Effects of Participation*. Englewood Cliffs, N. J.: Prentice-Hall, Inc., 1960.

31. ——, "Human Relations Research in Industry: Some Things Learned," in *Research Frontiers in Industrial Relations Today*, ed. F. Baristow. Montreal: Industrial Relations Centre, 1962.

32. White, R. K., and R. O. Lippitt, *Autocracy and Democracy*. New York: Harper & Row, Publishers, 1960.

33. ——, and ——, "Leader Behavior and Member Reaction in Three Social Climates," in *Group Dynamics, Research and Theory*, 2nd ed., eds. D. Cartwright and A. Zander. Evanston, Ill.: Row, Peterson, 1962.

34. Whyte, W. H., Jr., *The Organization Man.* New York: Simon and Schuster, Inc., 1956.

Developing
Team Effort

Much of the behavior of the individual employee can only be understood in the context of the small group in which he works. Commitment to production goals, acceptance of leadership, satisfaction with work, and effectiveness of performance all tend to depend on the relations of a man with his immediate face-to-face workers.

A group reaches maturity when members have established mutual trust, open communications, shared decisions, and congruence of individual goals with the group's objectives. The article by Argyris analyzes the kinds of conditions that prevent such group self-actualization. He identifies the kind of executive behavior that inhibits openness, trust, and effective decision making in a committee or work group. In outlining productive group behavior, he stresses the importance of considered and accurate feedback.

The whole issue of feedback is one that deserves particular

attention. Anderson emphasizes the principal goal of feedback—
that it be helpful to the recipient. It should be offered in this spirit
so that the recipient can understand it, will accept it, and will be
able to do something about modifying his behavior toward others.

The group attains its maximum usefulness when it develops
into an effective consensual decision-making body. Before it can
realize this potential, however, its members must learn how to overcome the inherent inefficiencies and exploit the potential assets
of an interdependent collection of minds. Maier summarizes the
relevant research on group problem solving, and identifies the
forces of group assets and liabilities bearing on the decision-
making process. He concludes that an awareness and proper use of
these forces can measurably increase the process skills available to
a group.

28

Interpersonal Barriers
to Decision Making

Chris Argyris
Yale University

The actual behavior of top executives during decision-making meetings often does not jibe with their attitudes and prescriptions about effective executive action.

The gap that often exists between what executives say and how they behave helps create barriers to openness and trust, to the effective search for alternatives, to innovation, and to flexibility in the organization.

These barriers are more destructive in important decision-making meetings than in routine meetings, and they upset effective managers more than ineffective ones.

The barriers cannot be broken down simply by intellectual exercises. Rather, executives need feedback concerning their behavior and opportunities to develop self-awareness in action. To this end, certain kinds of questioning are valuable; playing back and analyzing tape recordings of meetings has proved to be a helpful step; and laboratory education programs are valuable.

These are a few of the major findings of a study of executive decision making in six representative companies. The findings have vital implications for management groups everywhere; for while some organizations are less subject to the weaknesses described than are others, *all* groups have them in some degree. In this article I shall discuss the findings in detail and examine the implications for executives up and down the line. (For information on the company sample and research methods used in the study, see the section on "Nature of the Study.")

WORDS VS. ACTIONS

According to top management, the effectiveness of decision-making activities depends on the degree of innovation, risk taking, flexibility, and trust in the executive system. (Risk taking is defined here as any act where the executive risks his self-esteem. This could be a moment, for example, when he goes against the group view; when he tells someone, especially the person with the highest power, something negative about his impact on the organization; or when he seeks to put millions of dollars in a new investment.)

Nearly 95 percent of the executives in our study emphasize that an organization is only as good as its top people. They constantly repeat the importance of their responsibility to help themselves and others to develop their abilities. Almost as often they report that the qualities just mentioned—motivation, risk taking, and so on—are key characteristics of any successful executive system. "People problems" head the list as the most difficult, perplexing, and crucial.

In short, the executives vote overwhelmingly for executive systems where the contributions of each executive can be maximized and where innovation, risk taking, flexibility, and trust reign supreme. Nevertheless, the *behavior* of these same executives tends to create decision-making processes that are *not* very effective. Their behavior can be fitted into two basic patterns:

Pattern A—thoughtful, rational, and mildly competitive. This is the behavior most frequently observed during the decision-making meetings. Executives following this pattern own up to their ideas in a style that emphasizes a serious concern for ideas. As they constantly battle for scarce resources and "sell" their views, their openness to others' ideas is relatively high, not because of a sincere interest in learning about the point of view of others, but so they can engage in a form of "one-upmanship"—that is, gain information about the others' points of view in order to politely discredit them.

Pattern B—competitive first, thoughtful and rational second. In this pattern, conformity to ideas replaces concern for ideas as the strongest norm. Also, antagonism to ideas is higher—in many cases higher than openness to ideas. The relatively high antagonism scores usually indicate, in addition to high competitiveness, a high degree of conflict and pent-up feelings.

Figure 1 summarizes data for four illustrative groups of managers—two groups with Pattern A characteristics and two with Pattern B characteristics.

FIGURE 1
MANAGEMENT GROUPS
WITH PATTERN A AND PATTERN B CHARACTERISTICS

	PATTERN A				PATTERN B			
Total number of units analyzed*	GROUP 1 198		GROUP 2 143		GROUP 3 201		GROUP 4 131	
Units characterized by:	Number	Percent	Number	Percent	Number	Percent	Number	Percent
Owning up to own ideas and feelings	146	74	105	74	156	78	102	78
Concern for others' ideas and feelings	122	62	89	62	52	26	56	43
Conformity to others' ideas and feelings	54	27	38	26	87	43	62	47
Openness to others' ideas and feelings	46	23	34	24	31	15	25	19
Individuality	4	2	12	8	30	15	8	6
Antagonism to others' ideas and feelings	18	9	4	3	32	16	5	4
Unwillingness to help others own up to their ideas	5	2	3	2	14	7	4	3

*A unit is an instance of a manager speaking on a topic. If during the course of speaking he changes to a new topic, another unit is created.

PRACTICAL CONSEQUENCES

In both patterns executives are rarely observed:

taking risks or experimenting with new ideas or feelings;
helping others to own up, be open, and take risks;

using a style of behavior that supports the norm of individuality and trust as well as mistrust;

expressing feelings, positive or negative.

These results should not be interpreted as implying that the executives do not have feelings. We know from the interviews that many of the executives have strong feelings indeed. However, the overwhelming majority (84 percent) feel that it is a sign of immaturity to express feelings openly during decision-making meetings. Nor should the results be interpreted to mean that the exectuives do not enjoy risk taking. The data permit us to conclude only that few risk-taking actions were observed during the meetings. (Also, we have to keep in mind that the executives were always observed in groups; it may be that their behavior in groups varies significantly from their behavior as individuals.)

Before I attempt to give my views about the reasons for the discrepancy between executives' words and actions, I should like to point out that these results are not unique to business organizations. I have obtained similar behavior patterns from leaders in education, research, the ministry, trade unions, and government. Indeed, one of the fascinating questions for me is why so many different people in so many different kinds of organizations tend to manifest similar problems.

NATURE OF THE STUDY

The six companies studied include: (1) an electronics firm with 40,000 employees, (2) a manufacturer and marketer of a new innovative product with 4000 employees, (3) a large research and development company with 3000 employees, (4) a small research and development organization with 150 employees, (5) a consulting-research firm with 400 employees, and (6) a producer of heavy equipment with 4000 employees.

The main focus of the investigation reported here was on the behavior of 165 top executives in these companies. The executives were board members, executive committee members, upper-level managers, and (in a few cases) middle-level managers.

Approximately 265 decision-making meetings were studied and nearly 10,000 units of behavior analyzed. The topics of the meetings ranged widely, covering investment decisions, new products, manufacturing problems, marketing strategies, new pricing policies, administrative changes, and personnel issues. An observer took notes during all but 10 of the meetings; for research purposes, these 10 were analyzed "blind" from tapes (i.e., without ever meeting the executives). All other meetings were taped also, but analyzed at a later time.

The major device for analyzing the tapes was a new system of categories for scoring decision-making meetings.[1] Briefly, the executives' behavior was scored

---

[1] For a detailed discussion of the system of categories and other aspects of methodology, see (3).

according to how often they

owned up to and accepted responsibility for their ideas or feelings;

opened up to receive others' ideas or feelings;

experimented and took risks with ideas or feelings;

helped others to own up, be open, and take risks;

did not own up; were not open; did not take risks; and did not help others in any of these activities.

A second scoring system was developed to produce a quantitative index of the norms of the executive culture. There were both positive and negative norms. The positive norms were:

1. *Individuality*, especially rewarding behavior that focused on and valued the uniqueness of each individual's ideas and feelings.
2. *Concern* for others' ideas and feelings.
3. *Trust* in others' ideas and feelings.

The negative norms were:

1. *Conformity* to others' ideas and feelings.
2. *Antagonism* toward these ideas and feelings.
3. *Mistrust* of these ideas and feelings.

In addition to our observations of the men at work, at least one semistructured interview was conducted with each executive. All these interviews were likewise taped, and the typewritten protocols served as the basis for further analysis.

WHY THE DISCREPANCY?

The more I observe such decision-making problems in different organizations possessing different technologies and varying greatly in size, the more I become impressed with the importance of the role played by the values or assumptions top people hold on the nature of effective human relationships and the best ways to run an organization.

BASIC VALUES

In the studies so far I have isolated three basic values that seem to be very important:

1. The significant human relationships are the ones which have to do with achieving the organization's objective. My studies of over 265 different types and sizes of meetings indicate that executives almost always tend to focus their behavior on "getting the job done." In literally thousands of units of behavior, almost none are observed where the men spend some time in analyzing and maintaining their group's effectiveness. This is true even though in many meetings the group's effectiveness "bogged down" and the objectives were not being reached because of interpersonal factors. When the executives are interviewed

and asked why they did not spend some time in examining the group operations or processes, they reply that they were there to get a job done. They add: "If the group isn't effective, it is up to the leader to get it back on the track by directing it."

2. Cognitive rationality is to be emphasized; feelings and emotions are to be played down. This value influences executives to see cognitive, intellectual discussions as "relevant," "good," "work," and so on. Emotional and interpersonal discussions tend to be viewed as "irrelevant," "immature," "not work," and so on.

As a result, when emotions and interpersonal variables become blocks to group effectiveness, all the executives report feeling that they should *not* deal with them. For example, in the event of an emotional disagreement, they would tell the members to "get back to facts" or "keep personalities out of this."

3. Human relationships are most effectively influenced through unilateral direction, coercion, and control, as well as by rewards and penalties that sanction all three values. This third value of direction and control is implicit in the chain of command and also in the elaborate managerial controls that have been developed within organizations.

INFLUENCE ON OPERATIONS

The impact of these values can be considerable. For example, to the extent that individuals dedicate themselves to the value of intellectual rationality and "getting the job done," they will tend to be aware of and emphasize the intellectual aspects of issues in an organization and (consciously or unconsciously) to suppress the interpersonal and emotional aspects, especially those which do not seem relevant to achieving the task.

As the interpersonal and emotional aspects of behavior become suppressed, organizational norms that coerce individuals to hide their feelings or to disguise them and bring them up as technical, intellectual problems will tend to arise.

Under these conditions the individual may tend to find it very difficult to develop competence in dealing with feelings and interpersonal relationships. Also, in a world where the expression of feelings is not valued, individuals may build personal and organizational defenses to help them suppress their own feelings or inhibit others in such expression. Or they may refuse to consider ideas which, if explored, could expose suppressed feelings.

Such a defensive reaction in an organization could eventually inhibit creativity and innovation during decision making. The participants might learn to limit themselves to those ideas and values that were not threatening. They might also decrease their openness to new ideas and values. And as the degree of openness decreased, the capacity to experiment would also decrease, and fear of taking risks would increase. This would reduce the *probability* of experimentation, thus decreasing openness to new ideas still further and constricting risk taking even more than formerly. We would thereby have a closed circuit which could become an important cause of loss of vitality in an organization.

SOME CONSEQUENCES

Aside from the impact of values on vitality, what are some other consequences of the executive behavior patterns earlier described on top management decision making and on the effective functioning of the organization? For the sake of brevity, I shall include only examples of those consequences that were found to exist in one form or another in all organizations studied.

RESTRICTED COMMITMENT

One of the most frequent findings is that in major decisions that are introduced by the president, there tends to be less than open discussion of the issues, and the commitment of the officers tends to be less than complete (although they may assure the president to the contrary). For instance, consider what happened in one organization where a major administrative decision made during the period of the research was the establishment of several top management committees to explore basic long-range problems:

As is customary with major decisions, the president discussed it in advance at a meeting of the executive committee. He began the meeting by circulating, as a basis for discussion, a draft of the announcement of the committees. Most of the members' discussion was concerned with raising questions about the wording of the proposal:

"Is the word *action* too strong?"
"I recommend that we change 'steps can be taken' to 'recommendations can be made.' "
"We'd better change the word 'lead' to 'maintain.' "

As the discussion seemed to come to an end, one executive said he was worried that the announcement of the committees might be interpreted by the people below as an implication "that the executive committee believes the organization is in trouble. Let's get the idea in that all is well."

There was spontaneous agreement by all executives: "Hear, hear!"

A brief silence was broken by another executive who apparently was not satisfied with the concept of the committees. He raised a series of questions. The manner in which it was done was interesting. As he raised each issue, he kept assuring the president and the group that he was not against the concept. He just wanted to be certain that the executive committee was clear on what it was doing. For example, he assured them:

"I'm not clear. Just asking."
"I'm trying to get a better picture."
"I'm just trying to get clarification."
"Just so that we understand what the words mean."

The president nodded in agreement, but he seemed to become slightly impatient. He remarked that many of these problems would not arise if the members of these new committees took an over-all company point of view. An executive commented (laughingly), "On, I'm for motherhood too!"

The proposal was tabled in order for the written statement to be revised and discussed further during the next meeting. It appeared that the proposal was the president's personal "baby," and the executive committee members would naturally go along with it. The most responsibility some felt was that they should raise questions so the president would be clear about *his* (not *their*) decision.

At the next meeting the decision-making process was the same as at the first. The president circulated copies of the revised proposal. During this session a smaller number of executives asked questions. Two pushed (with appropriate care) the notion that the duties of one of the committees were defined too broadly.

The president began to defend his proposal by citing an extremely long list of examples, indicating that in his mind "reasonable" people should find the duties clear. This comment and the long list of examples may have communicated to others a feeling that the president was becoming impatient. When he finished, there was a lengthy silence. The president then turned to one of the executives and asked directly, "Why are you worried about this?" The executive explained, then quickly added that as far as he could see the differences were not major ones and his point of view could be integrated with the president's by "changing some words."

The president agreed to the changes, looked up, and asked, "I take it now there is common agreement?" All executives replied "yes" or nodded their heads affirmatively.

As I listened, I had begun to wonder about the commitment of the executive committee members to the idea. In subsequent interviews I asked each about his view of the proposal. Half felt that it was a good proposal. The other half had reservations ranging from moderate to serious. However, being loyal members, they would certainly do their best to make it work, they said.

SUBORDINATE GAMESMANSHIP

I can best illustrate the second consequence by citing from a study of the effectiveness of product planning and program review activities in another of the organizations studied:

It was company policy that peers at any given level should make the decisions. Whenever they could not agree or whenever a decision went beyond their authority, the problem was supposed to be sent to the next higher level. The buck passing stopped at the highest level. A meeting with the president became a great event. Beforehand a group would "dry run" its presentation until all were satisfied that they could present their view effectively.

Few difficulties were observed when the meeting was held to present a recommendation agreed to by all at the lower levels. The difficulties arose when "negative" information had to be fed upward. For example, a major error in the program, a major delay, or a major disagreement among the members was likely to cause such trouble.

The dynamics of these meetings was very interesting. In one case the problem to present was a major delay in a development project. In the dry run the subordinates planned to begin the session with information that "updated" the president.

The information was usually presented in such a way that slowly and carefully the president was alerted to the fact that a major problem was about to be announced. One could hear such key phrases as:

"We are a bit later than expected."

"We're not on plan."

"We have had greater difficulties than expected."

"It is now clear that no one should have promised what we did."

These phrases were usually followed by some reassuring statement such as:

"However, we're on top of this."

"Things are really looking better now."

"Although we are late, we have advanced the state of the art."

"If you give us another three months, we are certain that we can solve this problem."

To the observer's eyes, it is difficult to see how the president could deny the request. Apparently he felt the same way because he granted it. However, he took nearly 20 minutes to say that this shocked him; he was wondering if everyone was *really* doing everything they could; this was a serious program; this was not the way he wanted to see things run; he was sure they would agree with him; and he wanted their assurances that this would be the final delay.

A careful listening to the tape after the meeting brought out the fact that no subordinate gave such assurances. They simply kept saying that they were doing their best; they had poured a lot into this; or they had the best technical know-how working on it.

Another interesting observation is that most subordinates in this company, especially in presentations to the president, tended to go along with certain unwritten rules:

1. Before you give any bad news, give good news. Especially emphasize the capacity of the department to work hard and to rebound from a failure.
2. Play down the impact of a failure by emphasizing how close you came to achieving the target or how soon the target can be reached. If neither seems reasonable, emphasize how difficult it is to define such targets, and point out that because the state of the art is so primitive, the original commitment was not a wise one.
3. In a meeting with the president it is unfair to take advantage of another department that is in trouble, even if it is a "natural enemy." The sporting thing to do is say something nice about the other department and offer to help it in any way possible. (The offer is usually not made in concrete form, nor does the department in difficulty respond with the famous phrase, "What do you have in mind?")

The subordinates also were in agreement that too much time was spent in long presentations in order to make the president happy. The president, however, confided to the researcher that he did not enjoy listening to long and, at times, dry presentations (especially when he had seen most of the key data anyway). However, he felt that it was important to go through this because it might give the subordinates a greater sense of commitment to the problem!

LACK OF AWARENESS

One of our most common observations in company studies is that executives lack awareness of their own behavioral patterns as well as of the negative impact of their behavior on others. This is not to imply that they are completely unaware; each individual usually senses some aspects of a problem. However, we rarely find an individual or group of individuals who are aware of enough of the scope and depth of a problem so that the need for effective action can be fully understood.

For example, during the study of the decision-making processes of the president and the 9 vice presidents of a firm with nearly 3000 employees, I concluded that the members unknowingly behaved in such a way as *not* to encourage risk taking, openness, expression of feelings, and cohesive, trusting relationships. But subsequent interviews with the 10 top executives showed that they held a completely different point of view from mine. They admitted that negative feelings were not expressed, but said the reason was that "we trust each other and respect each other." According to 6 of the men, individuality was high and conformity low; where conformity was agreed to be high, the reason given was the necessity of agreeing with the man who is boss. According to 8 of the men, "We help each other all the time." Issues loaded with conflict were not handled during meetings, it was reported, for these reasons:

"We should not discuss emotional disagreements before the executive committee because when people are emotional, they are not rational."

"We should not air our dirty linen in front of the people who may come in to make a presentation."

"Why take up people's time with subjective debates?"

"Most members are not acquainted with all the details. Under our system the person who presents the issues has really thought them through."

"Pre-discussion of issues helps to prevent anyone from sandbagging the executive committee."

"Rarely emotional; when it does happen, you can pardon it."

The executive committee climate or emotional tone was characterized by such words as:

"Friendly."

"Not critical of each other."

"Not tense."

"Frank and no tensions because we've known each other for years."

How was I to fit the executives' views with mine? I went back and listened to all the interviews again. As I analyzed the tapes, I began to realize that an interesting set of contradictions arose during many of the interviews. In the early stages of the interviews the executives tended to say things that they contradicted

FIGURE 2
CONTRADICTORY STATEMENTS

DURING ONE PART OF THE INTERVIEW AN EXECUTIVE SAID:	YET LATER IN THE SAME INTERVIEW HE SAID:
The relationship among the executive committee members is "close," "friendly," and based on years of working together.	I do not know how [my peers] feel about me. That's a tough question to answer.
The strength of this company lies in its top people. They are a dedicated, friendly group. We never have the kinds of disagreements and fights that I hear others do.	Yes, the more I think of it, the more I feel this is a major weakness of the company. Management is afraid to hold someone accountable, to say, "You said you would do it. What happened?"
I have an open relationship with my superior.	I have no direct idea how my superior evaluates my work and feels about me.
The group discussions are warm, friendly, not critical.	We trust each other not to upset one another.
We say pretty much what we think.	We are careful not to say anything that will antagonize anyone.
We respect and have faith in each other.	People do not knowingly upset each other, so they are careful in what they say.
The executive committee tackles all issues.	The executive committee tends to spend too much time talking about relatively unimportant issues.
The executive committee makes decisions quickly and effectively.	A big problem of the executive committee is that it takes forever and a day to make important decisions.
The members trust each other.	The members are careful not to say something that may make another member look bad. It may be misinterpreted.
The executive committee makes the major policy decisions.	On many major issues, decisions are really made outside the executive committee meetings. The executive committee convenes to approve a decision and have "holy water" placed on it.

later; Figure 2 contains examples of contradictions repeated by 6 or more of the 10 top executives.

What accounts for these contradictions? My explanation is that over time the executives had come to mirror, in their behavior, the values of their culture (e.g., be rational, nonemotional, diplomatically open, and so on). They had created a culture that reinforced their own leadership styles. If an executive wanted to behave differently, he probably ran the risk of being considered a deviant. In most of the cases the executives decided to forgo this risk, and they behaved like the majority. These men, in order to live with themselves, probably had to develop various defenses and blinders about their acquiescence to an executive culture that may not have been the one they personally preferred and valued.

Incidentally, in this group there were two men who had decided to take the other route. Both men were viewed by the others as "a bit rough at the edges" or "a little too aggressive."

To check the validity of some of the findings reported, we interviewed the top 25 executives below the executive committee. If our analysis was correct, we knew, then they should tend to report that the members of the executive committee were low in openness to uncomfortable information, risk taking, trust, and capacity to deal with conflicts openly, and high in conformity. The results were as predicted (see Figure 3).

FIGURE 3
HOW THE EXECUTIVE COMMITTEE WAS RATED BY 25 EXECUTIVES BELOW IT

Characteristic Rated	Number of Managers Rating the Committee As:		
	Low	Moderate	High
Openness to Uncomfortable Information*	12	6	4
Risk Taking	20	4	1
Trust	14	9	2
Conformity	0	2	23
Ability to Deal with Conflicts	19	6	0

*Three executives gave a "don't know" response.

BLIND SPOTS

Another result found in all organizations studied is the tendency for executives to be unaware of the negative feelings that their subordinates have about them. This finding is not startling in view of the fact that the executive problem-solving processes do not tend to reward the upward communication of information about interpersonal issues that is emotionally laden and risky to communicate. To illustrate:

> In one organization, all but one of the top executive committee members reported that their relationships with their subordinates were "relatively good to excellent."

When asked how they judged their relationships, most of the executives responded with such statements as: "They do everything that I ask for willingly," and "We talk together frequently and openly."

The picture from the middle management men who were the immediate subordinates was different. Apparently, top management was unaware that:

—71 percent of the middle managers did not know where they stood with their superiors; they considered their relationships as ambiguous, and they were not aware of such important facts as how they were being evaluated.

—65 percent of the middle managers did not know what qualities led to success in their organizations.

—87 percent felt that conflicts were very seldom coped with; and that when they were, the attempts tended to be inadequate.

—65 percent thought that the most important unsolved problem of the organization was that the top management was unable to help them over-come the intergroup rivalries, lack of cooperation, and poor communications; 53 percent said that if they could alter one aspect of their superior's behavior, it would be to help him see the "dog eat dog" communication problems that existed in middle management.

—59 percent evaluated top management effectiveness as not too good or about average; and 62 percent reported that the development of a cohesive management team was the second most important unsolved problem.

—82 percent of the middle managers wished that the status of their function and job could be increased but doubted if they could communicate this openly to the top management.

Interestingly, in all the cases that I have observed where the president asked for a discussion of any problems that the top and middle management men present thought important, the problems mentioned above were never raised.

Rather, the most frequently mentioned problem (74 percent of the cases) was the overload problem. The executives and managers reported that they were overloaded and that the situation was getting worse. The president's usual reply was that he appreciated their predicament, but "that is life." The few times he asked if the men had any suggestions, he received such replies as "more help," "fewer meetings," "fewer reports," "delay of schedules," and so on. As we will see, few of these suggestions made sense, since the men were asking either for increases in costs or for a decrease in the very controls that the top management used to administer the organization.

DISTRUST AND ANTAGONISM

Another result of the behavior patterns earlier described is that management tends to keep promotions semisecret and most of the actual reasons for executive changes completely secret. Here is an example from an organization whose board we studied in some detail over a period of two years:

The executives complained of three practices of the board about which the board members were apparently unaware: (1) the constant alteration of organizational positions and charts, and keeping the most up-to-date versions semiconfidential;

(2) shifting top executives without adequate discussion with all executives involved and without clearly communicating the real reasons for the move; and (3) developing new departments with product goals that overlapped and competed with the goals of already existing departments.

The board members admitted these practices but tended not to see them as being incompatible with the interests of the organization. For example, to take the first complaint, they defended their practice with such statements as: "If you tell them everything, all they do is worry, and we get a flood of rumors"; "The changes do not *really* affect them"; and, "It will only cut in on their busy schedule and interrupt their productivity."

The void of clear-cut information from the board was, however, filled in by the executives. Their explanations ranged from such statements as "They must be changing things because they are not happy with the way things are going" to "The unhappiness is so strong they do not tell us." Even the executives who profited from some of these moves reported some concern and bewilderment. For example, three reported instances where they had been promoted over some "old-timers." In all cases they were told to "soft-pedal the promotion aspect" until the old-timers were diplomatically informed. Unfortunately, it took months to inform the latter men, and in some cases it was never done.

There was another practice of the board that produced difficulties in the organization:

Department heads cited the board's increasing intervention into the detailed administration of a department when its profit picture looked shaky. This practice was, from these subordinates' view, in violation of the stated philosophy of decentralization.

When asked, board members tended to explain this practice by saying that it was done only when they had doubts about the department head's competence, and then it was always in the interests of efficiency. When they were alerted about a department that was not doing well, they believed that the best reaction was to tighten controls, "take a closer and more frequent look," and "make sure the department head is on top of things." They quickly added that they did not tell the man in question they were beginning to doubt his competence for fear of upsetting him. Thus, again we see how the values of de-emphasizing the expression of negative feelings and the emphasizing of controls influenced the board's behavior.

The department heads, on the other hand, reported different reactions. "Why are they bothered with details? Don't they trust me? If not, why don't they say so?" Such reactions tended to produce more conformity, antagonism, mistrust, and fear of experimenting.

Still another board practice was the "diplomatic" rejection of an executive's idea that was, in the eyes of the board, offbeat, a bit too wild, or not in keeping with the corporate mission. The reasons given by the board for not being open about the evaluation again reflected adherence to the pyramidal values. For example, a board member would say, "We do not want to embarrass them," or "If you really tell them, you might restrict creativity."

This practice tended to have precisely the impact that the superiors wished to *avoid*. The subordinates reacted by asking, "Why don't they give me an opportunity to really explain it?" or "What do they mean when they suggest that the 'timing is not right' or 'funds are not currently available'?"

PROCESSES DAMAGED

It is significant that defensive activities like those described are rarely observed during group meetings dealing with minor or relatively routine decisions. These activities become most noticeable when the decision is an important one in terms of dollars or in terms of the impact on the various departments in the organization. *The forces toward ineffectiveness operate most strongly during the important decision-making meetings.* The group and organizational defenses operate most frequently when they can do the most harm to decision-making effectiveness.

Another interesting finding is that the more effective and more committed executives tend to be upset about these facts, whereas the less effective, less committed people tend simply to lament them. They also tend to take on an "I told them so" attitude—one of resignation and noninvolvement in correcting the situation. In short, it is the better executives who are negatively affected.

WHAT CAN BE DONE?

What can the executive do to change this situation?

I wish that I could answer this question as fully as I should like to. Unfortunately, I cannot. Nevertheless, there are some suggestions I can make.

BLIND ALLEYS

First, let me state what I believe will *not* work.

Learning about these problems by listening to lectures, reading about them, or exploring them through cases is not adequate; an article or book can pose some issues and get thinking started, but—in this area, at least—it cannot change behavior. Thus, in one study with 60 top executives:

> Lectures were given and cases discussed on this subject for nearly a week. A test at the end of the week showed that the executives rated the lecturers very high, liked the cases, and accepted the diagnoses. Yet when they attempted to apply their new-found knowledge outside the learning situation, most were unable to do so. The major problem was that they had not learned how to make these new ideas come to life in their behavior.

> As one executive stated, pointing to his head: "I know up here what I should do, but when it comes to a real meeting, I behave in the same old way. It sure is frustrating" (2).

Learning about these problems through a detailed diagnosis of executives' behavior is also not enough. For example:

> I studied a top management group for nearly four months through interviews and tape recordings of their decision-making meetings. Eventually, I fed back the analysis. The executives agreed with the diagnosis as well as with the statement by one executive that he found it depressing. Another executive, however, said he now felt that he had a clearer and more coherent picture of some of the causes of their problems, and he was going to change his behavior. I predicted that he would

probably find that he would be unable to change his behavior—and even if he did change, his subordinates, peers, and superiors might resist dealing with him in the new way.

The executive asked, "How can you be so sure that we can't change?" I responded that I knew of no case where managers were able to alter successfully their behavior, their group dynamics, and so forth by simply realizing intellectually that such a change was necessary. The key to success was for them to be able to show these new strategies in their behavior. To my knowledge, behavior of this type, groups with these dynamics, and organizational cultures endowed with these characteristics were very difficult to change. What kind of thin-skinned individuals would they be, how brittle would their groups and their organizations be if they could be altered that easily?

Three of the executives decided that they were going to prove the prediction to be incorrect. They took my report and studied it carefully. In one case the executive asked his subordinates to do the same. Then they tried to alter their behavior. According to their own accounts, they were unable to do so. The only changes they reported were (1) a softening of the selling activities, (2) a reduction of their aggressive persuasion, and (3) a genuine increase in their asking for the subordinates' views.

My subsequent observations and interviews uncovered the fact that the first two changes were mistrusted by the subordinates, who had by now adapted to the old behavior of their superiors. They tended to play it carefully and to be guarded. This hesitation aggravated the executives, who felt that their subordinates were not responding to their new behavior with the enthusiasm that they (the superiors) had expected.

However, *the executives did not deal with this issue openly.* They kept working at trying to be rational, patient, and rewarding. The more irritated they became and the more they showed this irritation in their behavior, the more the subordinates felt that the superiors' "new" behavior was a gimmick.

Eventually, the process of influencing subordinates slowed down so much that the senior men returned to their more controlling styles. The irony was that in most cases the top executives interpreted the subordinates' behavior as proof that they needed to be needled and pushed, while the subordinates interpreted the top managers' behavior as proof that they did not trust their assistants and would never change.

The reason I doubt that these approaches will provide anything but temporary cures is that they do not go far enough. If changes are going to be made in the behavior of an executive, if trust is to be developed, if risk taking is to flourish, he must be placed in a different situation. He should be helped to (a) expose his leadership style so that he and others can take a look at its true impact; (b) deepen his awareness of himself and the dynamics of effective leadership; and (c) strive for these goals under conditions where he is in control of the amount, pace, and depth of learning.

These conditions for learning are difficult to achieve. Ideally, they require the help of a professional consultant. Also, it would be important to get away from the organization—its interruptions, pressures, and daily administrative tensions.

VALUE OF QUESTIONS

The executive can strive to be aware that he is probably programmed with a set of values which cause him to behave in ways that are not always helpful to others and which his subordinates will not discuss frankly even when they believe he is not being helpful. He can also strive to find time to uncover, through careful questioning, his impact on others. Once in a while a session that is focused on the "How am I doing?" question can enlighten the executive and make his colleagues more flexible in dealing with him.

One simple question I have heard several presidents ask their vice presidents with success is: "Tell me what, if anything, I do that tends to prevent (or help) your being the kind of vice president you wish to be?" These presidents are careful to ask these questions during a time when they seem natural (e.g., performance review sessions), or they work hard ahead of time to create a climate so that such a discussion will not take the subordinate by surprise.

Some presidents feel uncomfortable in raising these questions, and others point out that the vice presidents are also uncomfortable. I can see how both would have such feelings. A chief executive officer may feel that he is showing weakness by asking his subordinates about his impact. The subordinate may or may not feel this way, but he may sense that his chief does, and that is enough to make him uncomfortable.

Yet in two companies I have studied where such questions were asked, superiors and subordinates soon learned that authority which gained strength by a lack of openness was weak and brittle, whereas authority resting on open feedback from below was truly strong and viable.

WORKING WITH THE GROUP

Another step that an executive can take is to vow not to accept group ineffectiveness as part of life. Often I have heard people say, "Groups are no damned good; strong leadership is what is necessary." I agree that many groups are ineffective. I doubt, however, if either of the two leadership patterns described earlier will help the situation. As we have seen, both patterns tend to make the executive group increasingly less effective.

If my data are valid, the search process in executive decision making has become so complicated that group participation is essential. No one man seems to be able to have all the knowledge necessary to make an effective decision. If individual contributions are necessary in group meetings, it is important that a climate be created that does not discourage innovation, risk taking, and honest leveling between managers in their conversations with one another. The value of a group is to maximize individual contributions.

Interestingly, the chief executive officers in these studies are rarely observed making policy decisions in the classic sense, viz., critical selections from several alternatives and determination of future directions to be taken. This does not mean that they shy away from taking responsibility. Quite the contrary.

Many report that they enjoy making decisions by themselves. Their big frustration comes from realizing that most of the major decisions they face are extremely complex and require the coordinated, honest inputs of many different executives. They are impatient at the slowness of meetings, the increasingly quantitative nature of the inputs, and, in many cases, their ignorance of what the staff groups did to the decision inputs long before they received them.

The more management deals with complexity by the use of computers and quantitative approaches, the more it will be forced to work with inputs of many different people, and the more important will be the group dynamics of decision-making meetings. If anyone doubts this, let him observe the dry runs subordinates go through to get a presentation ready for the top. He will observe, I believe, that much data are included and excluded by subordinates on the basis of what they believe those at the top can hear.

In short, *one of the main tasks of the chief executive is to build and maintain an effective decision-making network*. I doubt that he has much choice *except* to spend time in exploring how well his group functions.

Such explorations could occur during the regular workday. For example:

In one organization the president began by periodically asking members of his top group, immediately after a decision was made, to think back during the meeting and describe when they felt that the group was not being as effective as they wished. How could these conditions be altered?

As trust and openness increased, the members began to level with each other as to when they were inhibited, irritated, suppressed, confused, and withholding information. The president tried to be as encouraging as he could, and he especially rewarded people who truly leveled. Soon the executives began to think of mechanisms they could build into their group functioning so they would be alerted to these group problems and correct them early. As one man said, "We have not eliminated all our problems, but we are building a competence in our group to deal with them effectively if and when they arise."

UTILIZING FEEDBACK

Another useful exercise is for the superior and his group members to tape-record a decision-making meeting, especially one which is expected to be difficult. At a later date, the group members can gather and listen to the tape. I believe it is safe to say that simply listening to the tape is an education in itself. If one can draw from skilled company or outside help, then useful analyses can be made of group or individual behavior.

Recently, I experimented with this procedure with an "inside" board of directors of a company. The directors met once a month and listened to tape recordings of their monthly board meetings. With my help they analyzed their behavior, trying to find how they could improve their individual and group effectiveness. Listening to tapes became a very involving experience for them. They spent nearly four hours in the first meeting discussing less than ten minutes of the tape.

"BINDS" CREATED.   One of the major gains of these sessions was that the board members became aware of the "binds" they were creating for each other and of the impact they each had on the group's functioning. Thus:

> Executive A was frequently heard antagonizing Executive B by saying something that B perceived as "needling." For example, A might seem to be questioning B's competence. "Look here," he would say, "anyone who can do simple arithmetic should realize that. . . ."
>
> Executive B responded by fighting. B's way of fighting back was to utilize his extremely high capacity to verbalize and intellectualize. B's favorite tactic was to show A where he missed five important points and where his logic was faulty.
>
> Executive A became increasingly upset as the "barrage of logic" found its mark. He tended to counteract by (a) remaining silent but manifesting a sense of being flustered and becoming red-faced; and/or (b) insisting that his logic *was* sound even though he did not express it in "highfalutin language" as did B.
>
> Executive B pushed harder (presumably to make A admit he was wrong) by continuing his "barrage of logic" or implying that A could not see his errors because he was upset.
>
> Executive A would respond to this by insisting that he was not upset. "The point you are making is so simple, why, anyone can see it. Why should I be upset?"
>
> Executive B responded by pushing harder and doing more intellectualizing. When Executive A eventually reached his breaking point, he too began to shout and fight.
>
> At this points, Executives C, D, and E could be observed withdrawing until A and B wore each other out.

PROGRESS ACHIEVED.   As a result of the meetings, the executives reported in interviews, board members experienced fewer binds, less hostility, less frustration, and more constructive work. One member wondered if the group had lost some of its "zip," but the others disagreed. Here is an excerpt from the transcript of one discussion on this point:

> *EXECUTIVE A:* My feeling is, as I have said, that we have just opened this thing up, and I for one feel that we have benefited a great deal from it. I think I have improved; maybe I am merely reflecting the fact that you [Executive B] have improved. But at least I think there has been improvement in our relationship. I also see signs of not as good a relationship in other places as there might be.
>
> I think on the whole we are much better off today than we were a year ago. I think there is a whole lot less friction today than there was a year ago, but there's still enough of it.
>
> Now we have a much clearer organization setup; if we were to sit down here and name the people, we would probably all name exactly the same people. I don't think there is much question about who should be included and who should not be included; we've got a pretty clean organization.
>
> *EXECUTIVE B:* You're talking now about asking the consultant about going on with this week's session?
>
> *EXECUTIVE A:* It would be very nice to have the consultant if he can do it; then we should see how we can do it without him, but it'd be better with him.

EXECUTIVE B: But that's the step, as I understand it, that should be taken at this stage. Is that right?

EXECUTIVE A: Well, I would certainly favor doing something; I don't know what. I'm not making a specific recommendation; I just don't like to let go of it.

EXECUTIVE C: What do you think?

EXECUTIVE D: I'm not as optimistic as A. I wonder if anybody here agrees with me that maybe we haven't made as much progress as we think. I've personally enjoyed these experiences, and I'd like to see them continued.

EXECUTIVE A: Would you like to venture to say why I think we have made progress and why I might be fooled?

EXECUTIVE D: Well, I think maybe you are in the worst position to evaluate progress because if the worst possible thing that can happen is for people to no longer fight and struggle, but to say, "yes, sir," you might call that progress. That might be the worst thing that could happen, and I sort of sense some degree of resignation —I don't think it's progress. I don't know. I might be all alone in this. What do you think?

EXECUTIVE C: On one level it is progress. Whether it is institutional progress and whether it produces commensurate institutional benefits is a debatable question. It may in fact do so. I think it's very clear that there is in our meetings and in individual contact less heat, less overt friction, petulance, tension, than certainly was consistently the case. Do you agree?

EXECUTIVE D: Yes, I think so.

EXECUTIVE C: It has made us a great deal more aware of the extent and nature of the friction and clearly has made all of us intent on fighting less. There's some benefit to it; but there are some drawbacks.

EXECUTIVE A: Well, if you and D are right, I would say for that reason we need more of the program.

LABORATORY TRAINING

Another possibility is for the executive to attend a program designed to help increase competence in this area, such as laboratory education and its various offshoots ("T-groups," the "managerial grid," "conflict management labs," and so on [1, 4, 38]). These learning experiences are available at various university and National Training Laboratory executive programs. They can also be tailor-made for the individual organization.

I believe outside programs offer the better way of becoming acquainted with this type of learning. Bear in mind, though, that since typically only one or two executives attend from the same organization, the biggest payoff is for the individual. The inside program provides greater possibilities for payoff to the organization.

At the same time, however, it should also be kept in mind that in-house programs *can* be dangerous to the organization. I would recommend that a thorough study be made ahead of time to ascertain whether or not a laboratory educational experience would be helpful to company executives individually and to the organization.

OPEN DISCUSSION

I have never observed a group whose members wanted it to decay. I have never studied a group or an organization that was decaying where there were not some members who were aware that decay was occurring. Accordingly, one key to group and organizational effectiveness is to get this knowledge out into the open and to discuss it thoroughly. The human "motors" of the group and the organization have to be checked periodically, just as does the motor of an automobile. Without proper maintenance, all will fail.

29

Giving and Receiving Feedback

John Anderson
Procter & Gamble Company

This article discusses several considerations involved in telling another person how you feel about him—"how to do it" considerations that are apt to be important, if your objective is to help him become a more effective person, and also to arrive at a more effective working relationship between him and yourself.

BACKGROUND

One of the central purposes of experience in a Managerial Grid Seminar or in a sensitivity training lab is to help the participant become more clearly aware of the impact he has on others. That is, during an experience of this kind, the participant has an opportunity to talk with others, solve problems with others, and in general interact with others in ways that are characteristic for him. The image he projects—the impression that others have of his behavior—is communicated back to him. And this sort of exchange is usually considerably more open than what is common in everyday life. The intent is that this feedback be useful to the recipient—that he may see, for example, some discrepancies between the effect he wished to create, in fact thought he was creating, and what actually took place, with the hope that he will be able to use this information in making a more intelligent choice of behavior with which to deal with similar situations in the future.

Such feedback, for reasons of content, timing, and the way it is given, may not always turn out to be useful to the recipient. While a large majority of managers who participate in public sensitivity training labs or grid seminars return saying that over-all the experience was a very useful one for them personally, many have felt that "That is a kind of thing you surely couldn't do with people you work with all the time!" The fear is that if the members of a work team did attempt to enter into an experience of this kind together, either:

1. They would not dare to be open and candid with one another, and the result, therefore, would be a superficial and useless experience, or
2. They would dare to be open with one another, and the result would be one of disruption in team working relationships, escalation of bad feelings carried over from old grievances, etc.

Several companies, however, *have* now experimented with some sort of work team development along these lines. In Procter & Gamble, the design we have used has varied considerably, depending on the needs of the particular group. But in no instance have these two fears—organized slumber or total destruction—materialized. Each has turned out to be, in the judgment of the large majority of participants, a very useful and very worthwhile experience from the standpoint of building more effective working relationships on the job. We have found that people seem to be both concerned enough for one another and trusting enough of one another that they are able to be *appropriately* open in exchanging feedback during a team discussion situation. Instances in which people have only hurt or confused one another in exchanges of this kind have been the result not so much of motivational problems as of problems of skill in giving feedback—that is, knowing *how* to do it well, and what kinds of pitfalls to watch out for.

SOME IMPORTANT CRITERIA

It is particularly important that the considerations which follow be given attention in teams that operate without the benefit of outside help—that is, where a trained, skilled, experienced, outside observer will not be available to get things back on track if they should begin to wander off in nonproductive directions. I'm thinking of Managerial Grid, or other instrumented, trainerless team-building designs. No doubt the following considerations also have some application to the conduct of "performance appraisal" discussions as well as other informal exchanges that often take place between people in or out of the workplace.

The most significant criterion that "useful feedback" must meet is simply that it be intended to be helpful to the recipient. That is, the sender of the message should ask himself beforehand, "Do I really feel that what I am about to say *is likely to be helpful to the other person?*" I need to examine my own motivation, to be sure that I am not simply about to unload a burden of hostility from my own breast and for my own personal benefit, quite regardless of the expected effect on the receiver. Otherwise, I may convince myself that my only obligation is to be open and honest—that the name of the game is "candor"—and that so long as I truly and completely "level," I have fulfilled the only necessary obligation. If my objective is to *help* the recipient of the feedback, then, three things are necessary:

1. The other person needs to *understand* what I am saying.
2. He needs to be willing and able to *accept* it.
3. He needs to be *able to do* something about it if he chooses to.

GETTING UNDERSTANDING

Two most important considerations in getting understanding of the message sent are:

1. Feedback should be specific rather than general. If I can give the man I am talking to specific examples of instances in which he has behaved in the way I am describing, it will be much easier for him to understand what I am talking about than it will if I speak only in terms of generalizations about "what he is like." For example, if I tell him that I think he talks too much, or doesn't express his thoughts very clearly, this is likely to be *less* helpful to him than if I am able to cite a particular situation, tied to time and place, where I thought he exhibited this behavior. If I can recall vividly to his mind a particular instance in which he rambled on long after I had gotten the idea of what he was trying to say, or when he had gone on and on without ever getting across clearly the idea of what he was trying to say to myself or to a group, he is more likely to be able to get a handle on what it is I am trying to tell him. Or at least I will have opened

up an area for him that we can then explore further to try to understand what was going on in the situation, so that he can come out of it with a clearer idea of some specific things he might consider doing differently in the future. The key here is, don't just generalize about what kind of a person he is. Give examples.

2. Another important factor in getting understanding is that recent examples of behavior are better than old ones. To understand what was happening in the situation, a person obviously has to be able to recall the situation somewhat vividly. What happened two minutes ago can be more vividly recalled than what happened an hour ago, which will in turn be more easily remembered than what happened yesterday, last week, last year, or five years ago.

GETTING ACCEPTANCE

There are circumstances in which anyone will find it most difficult to accept critical, negative, feedback—times at which it will be very difficult for anyone to face what is being said to him in an open, objective frame of mind. Some important considerations involved in gaining acceptance are:

1. There needs to be a foundation of trust among members of the group before this sort of experience is entered into. If B is to accept critical feedback from A, B must be somewhat convinced from his previous associations with A that A's motivations where B is concerned aren't entirely self-serving—that is, that A *does care* for B and can be trusted to be saying what he is saying because he really feels that it will benefit B to do so. Where B has a deep distrust of A going into this situation, there is probably very little that A can do to get B's voluntary acceptance of what he is telling him.

2. How A addresses himself to B in this specific situation, however, can also be an important factor. If A's tone of voice, the expression on his face, his choice of words, and everything about him communicates directly to B the impression that, "I value you, and I really would like to help you, and that is the only reason I am telling you this," then B is more likely to attend to the message with an open mind than if A simply rattles off a list of intellectual observations about B's behavior, perhaps without even looking directly at him while he does so.

3. A person will be more likely to listen to any negative feedback you wish to give him if you simply describe to him what you have seen, and the effect it has on you. If you want to be heard, avoid any suggestion of "judging" him as a person. Avoid the temptation to extrapolate far beyond the specific situational information you have to *generalize* to the other person about how foolish he is, how obstinate, how untrustworthy, or whatever. Suppose I tell you, for example, that "This may not be your problem; it may be mine. However, I want you to know that when you act toward me the way you do sometimes (describe a situation, in time and place), it is very difficult for me to (think straight, keep from getting mad, keep my mind on what we are talking about, keep from going to sleep—whatever fits the situation that I am trying to describe)." You

are much more likely to be able to accept such a message in an open frame of mind than if I tell you, "I think it is just terrible that you act toward people that way. I think you ought not to be that way, that's a completely senseless way to act. Why don't you grow up?..."

4. Before giving a person negative feedback of any kind, I ought to ask myself whether *now* is a good time to do it—whether he *appears* to be in a condition of readiness to receive information of this kind. If he appears, for example, to be angry, confused, upset, highly distraught, or defensive, the answer is probably no. I ought not to load any more on him right now.

This is one reason why feedback that is solicited by the recipient is somewhat more likely to be received in an open state of mind than feedback which is simply given whether he has asked for it or not. And the more specific the area in which feedback is solicited, the more likely it is to be *really* desired and received in an open frame of mind. For example, suppose the leader of a team says to his people, "How about the X decision I made last Friday. Do you feel that that was one I arrived at in an appropriate way, or do you feel that I should have involved you more before arriving at a conclusion?"

As a member of the team, I would feel that this solicitation of feedback was more genuine, and that I could respond to it more openly and with more confidence that I would be heard than I would feel when the leader of the team, perhaps a bit too intensely or with a laugh that is a little too loud, says something like, "O.K. men, this is my turn in the barrel! Really level with me now! I want to hear everything you don't like about me!" He may or he may not. If overt solicitation is indicative of probable acceptance, the former sort is apt to be more meaningful than the latter, all by itself.

5. Feedback given one man by another may be accepted as valid when in fact it ought *not* to be. For example, if I tell a man that there is a particular thing he does in our relationship that I find most upsetting, it may be that the problem isn't his at all, but rather that it's mine. One of the values of entering into this sort of exchange in a team, as opposed to doing so only in a one-to-one relationship, is that the feedback that each man gives another can be checked around the table to see whether anyone else has common experience of this kind which would support or clarify the meaning of what is being said. This should always be done, both as a check on the validity of the observation and to be sure that the recipient gets as many examples as are available to help him understand what is being said.

USING FEEDBACK

The third criterion of "useful" feedback (in addition to being able to understand and accept it) is that the recipient needs to be able to do something with it.

1. Suppose I feel that a man does not present his ideas as forcefully and

persuasively as he ought to, to get the attention they deserve from the team, and I decide I want to tell him about this. This is still a pretty general feeling, and before saying anything, therefore, I should consider what specifically there is about his delivery that makes me feel that way. Now if I think, for example, that he doesn't organize his thoughts as well under some circumstances as I know he is capable of (from other experience I've had with him), this is an example of something I might assume he could do something about, and so I probably should tell him I feel that way, especially if I can give him specific examples of instances in which he has done this. Or suppose I feel that he gets his ideas out all right, but that as soon as he receives any static from anyone about them, he withdraws, either from indifference, lack of confidence in his own ideas, or whatever. This too I might choose to tell him about, because I could expect that he might be able to do something about it.

On the other hand, suppose I feel that the only thing that interferes with his ability to persuade, to carry his ideas over forcefully, is that he is physically a very little fellow, and with a high squeaky voice, or that no matter how he sits or dresses he *looks* like he is only 14 years old. If I am really trying to be helpful to him, there isn't apt to be much value in calling these to his attention.

If I feel that he has a very limited vocabulary and this is getting in his way, there might be some point in his career when I would conclude that this was a helpful thing to tell him about—e.g., that he doesn't use words correctly, or that his grammar is poor. These are correctable problems. On the other hand, if he is nearing the end of his career and there is no likelihood that he is at this point in time going to try to do anything about his general skill with the English language, then there is no point in calling this to his attention.

So, by this criterion, you might or might not decide it would be helpful to tell the other person you felt he did not project his ideas in the group as forcefully or persuasively as he might. Whether you chose to do so or not would depend on your best estimate of his ability to do something about the particular barriers you saw to his effectiveness in this particular area.

2. During a discussion in which members are exchanging their views of and feelings about one another in this way, there may be a tendency to feel that you haven't really done a man justice unless you have told him "everything that bothers you" about him. It is not at all necessarily desirable, however, to be "complete" in the negative feedback you might give a person. It may be quite a large enough task, for example, for me to understand, accept, and consider doing something about my characteristic ways of behaving in two or three key areas. To give me more than this to think about may be simply spreading my attention beyond what I am capable of dealing with at this particular time. Also, other things being equal, the more you unload on me, the more threatening the experience is likely to be, and the more difficulty I am likely to have accepting any of it in an open frame of mind.

SUMMARY

To be maximally useful to the recipient, feedback should meet the following criteria. It should be:

1. Intended to help the recipient.
2. Given directly and with real feeling, and based on a foundation of trust between the giver and receiver.
3. Descriptive of what the receiver is doing and of effects he is having—not threatening and judgmental about what he *is* as a person.
4. Specific rather than general, with good, clear, and preferably recent examples.
5. Given at a time when the receiver appears to be in a condition of readiness to accept it.
6. Checked with other team members to be sure they support its validity.
7. It should also include only those things that the receiver might be expected to be able to do something about.
8. And he should not be told more than he can handle at any particular time.

IS IT POSSIBLE TO BE TOO CAUTIOUS?

Finally, the question might be asked, "Isn't there some risk that if all these cautions are followed, people might be induced to be overly cautious, and decline to take desirable risks in being open with one another?" Yes, being too cautious is a risk in itself. Many of us have a tendency to feel that we couldn't possibly share with other people the negative feelings we have about them. They would be crushed if we did so. Or they would never forgive us. All the criteria listed above are simply considerations that should be given some attention by the sender of feedback. But it will no doubt be impossible to meet all of them, all of the time, and still have something to say. In such cases it is appropriate to take prudent risks—to be open more than closed, experimentally, and see what happens. If you at least really *intend* to help—and there is no doubt that you intend to help by the manner in which you say what you say—then a good deal of clumsiness is almost certain to be overlooked by the receiver. Even if he doesn't understand or agree with what you are saying, he at least will probably not hold it against you. And if his defenses stay down, you may be able to clarify meanings, draw out essentials, and in general compensate for your initial clumsiness in trying to help.

RECEIVING FEEDBACK

There is less to say to the recipient of feedback about ways in which he might approach this opportunity:

1. First of all, he needs to make a sincere effort not to be defensive. This has

as much to say about what he allows to go on inside him as about what he allows himself to say overtly to those who are giving him feedback. He should try to look at what is being said with an open mind, trying to understand it, and not all the while explaining to himself and others, "They simply don't understand; it isn't what I meant at all."

2. If the recipient of feedback is having difficulty understanding what people are trying to tell him and they are unable to come up with examples that clarify things for him, he should begin to seek and speculate on possible examples himself with the group—to say, for example, "Remember the time we met last Friday, and I did such and so. Is that the kind of thing you are talking about?"

3. To be sure he understands, it is a good idea for the recipient of feedback to try to summarize briefly for the group what he understands them to be saying. This gives them a final opportunity to check misunderstandings that might have taken place.

4. I think it can be very helpful to an individual and to a group if the recipient of feedback from others is allowed, and encouraged, to share with the group some of his feelings about the kinds of thing they have been discussing—that is, his behavior in certain situations. The risk of defensiveness is one that all should be alert to. However, if a man can explore openly some of his feelings about why he tends sometimes to behave in "that" way, two things can happen. First, he may arrive at a better understanding himself of why he behaves in the way he does, simply in talking it through, and thereby be in a better position to consider what he might do about it. Secondly, if he does find it difficult or impossible to do anything about the behavior that has been negatively described to him by the group, even though he tries, if he has genuinely shared with them some of his concerns and some of the internal struggles he has in these situations, they may find it a little easier to understand and accept that behavior from him in the future.

5. As a final point, I believe some people react negatively to the very idea of doing this sort of thing—that is, meeting as a work team and exchanging in a quite open fashion their views of how they see one another, positively and negatively. The feeling may be that, "I am what I am, and I have a right to be that. And no group of people has a right to dictate to me what I should be like." My feeling is that this is exactly right. It does and should remain the right of each individual to evaluate what he hears, decide what he believes of it, and decide in what respects, if any, he feels it is personally worth his while to make the effort to change. The purpose of a team lab of the kind described here, and of the kind of information that is exchanged in it, is simply to give a man *better and clearer information* than he ordinarily receives on which to make his *own* judgment of his effectiveness in working with others, and his *own* judgment of how or whether he wishes to further develop that effectiveness.

30

Assets and Liabilities in Group Problem Solving: The Need for an Integrative Function

N. R. F. Maier
University of Michigan

Research on group problem solving reveals that the group has both advantages and disadvantage over individual problem solving. If the potentials for group problem solving can be exploited and if its deficiencies can be avoided, it follows that group problem solving can attain a level of proficiency not ordinarily achieved. The requirement for achieving this level of group performance seems to hinge on developing a style of discussion leadership which maximizes the group's assets and minimizes its liabilities. Since members possess the essential ingredients for the solutions, the deficiencies that appear in group solutions reside in the processes by which group solutions develop. These processes can determine whether the group functions effectively or ineffectively. The critical factor in a group's potential is organization and integration. With training, a leader can supply these functions and serve as the group's central nervous system, thus permitting the group to emerge as a highly efficient entity.

The research reported here was supported by Grant No. MH-02704 from the United States Public Health Service. Grateful acknowledgment is made for the constructive criticism of Melba Colgrove, Junie Janzen, Mara Julius, and James Thurber. Reprinted by permission from *Psychological Review*, LXXIV, No. 4 (1967), 239–49. Copyright 1967 by the American Psychological Association.

A number of investigations have raised the question of whether group problem solving is superior, inferior, or equal to individual problem solving. Evidence can be cited in support of each position so that the answer to this question remains ambiguous. Rather than pursue this generalized approach to the question, it seems more fruitful to explore the forces that influence problem solving under the two conditions (9, 15). It is hoped that a better recognition of these forces will permit clarification of the varied dimensions of the problem-solving process, especially in groups.

The forces operating in such groups include some that are assets, some that are liabilities, and some that can be either assets or liabilities, depending upon the skills of the members, especially those of the discussion leader. Let us examine these three sets of forces.

GROUP ASSETS

GREATER SUM TOTAL OF KNOWLEDGE AND INFORMATION

There is more information in a group than in any of its members. Thus problems that require the utilization of knowledge should give groups an advantage over individuals. Even if one member of the group (e.g., the leader) knows much more than anyone else, the limited unique knowledge of lesser-informed individuals could serve to fill in some gaps in knowledge. For example, a skilled machinist might contribute to an engineer's problem solving and an ordinary workman might supply information on how a new machine might be received by workers.

GREATER NUMBER OF APPROACHES TO A PROBLEM

It has been shown that individuals get into ruts in their thinking (6, 16, 44). Many obstacles stand in the way of achieving a goal, and a solution must circumvent these. The individual is handicapped in that he tends to persist in his approach and thus fails to find another approach that might solve the problem in a simpler manner. Individuals in a group have the same failing, but the approaches in which they are persisting may be different. For example, one researcher may try to prevent the spread of a disease by making man immune to the germ, another by finding and destroying the carrier of the germ, and still another by altering the environment so as to kill the germ before it reaches man. There is no way of determining which approach will best achieve the desired goal, but undue persistence in any one will stifle new discoveries. Since group members do not have identical approaches, each can contribute by knocking others out of ruts in thinking.

PARTICIPATION IN PROBLEM SOLVING INCREASES ACCEPTANCE

Many problems require solutions that depend upon the support of others to be effective. Insofar as group problem solving permits participation and influence, it follows that more individuals accept solutions when a group solves the problem than when one person solves it. When one individual solves a problem he still has the task of persuading others. It follows, therefore, that when groups solve such problems, a greater number of persons accept and feel responsible for making the solution work. A low-quality solution that has good acceptance can be more effective than a higher-quality solution that lacks acceptance.

BETTER COMPREHENSION OF THE DECISION

Decisions made by an individual, which are to be carried out by others, must be communicated from the decision maker to the decision executors. Thus individual problem solving often requires an additional stage—that of relaying the decision reached. Failures in this communication process detract from the merits of the decision and can even cause its failure or create a problem of greater magnitude than the initial problem that was solved. Many organizational problems can be traced to inadequate communication of decisions made by superiors and transmitted to subordinates, who have the task of implementing the decision.

The chances for communication failures are greatly reduced when the individuals who must work together in executing the decision have participated in making it. They not only understand the solution because they saw it develop, but they are also aware of the several other alternatives that were considered and the reasons why they were discarded. The common assumption that decisions supplied by superiors are arbitrarily reached therefore disappears. A full knowledge of goals, obstacles, alternatives, and factual information is essential to communication, and this communication is maximized when the total problem-solving process is shared.

GROUP LIABILITIES

SOCIAL PRESSURE

Social pressure is a major force making for conformity. The desire to be a good group member and to be accepted tends to silence disagreement and favors consensus. Majority opinions tend to be accepted regardless of whether or not their objective quality is logically and scientifically sound. Problems requiring solutions based upon facts, regardless of feelings and wishes, can suffer in group problem-solving situations.

It has been shown (32) that minority opinions in leaderless groups have little influence on the solution reached, even when these opinions are the correct ones. Reaching agreement in a group often is confused with finding the right answer, and it is for this reason that the dimensions of a decision's acceptance and its objective quality must be distinguished (22).

VALENCE OF SOLUTIONS

When leaderless groups (made up of three or four persons) engage in problem solving, they propose a variety of solutions. Each solution may receive both critical and supportive comments, as well as descriptive and explorative comments from other participants. If the number of negative and positive comments for each solution are algebraically summed, each may be given a *valence index* (13). The first solution that receives a positive valence value of 15 tends to be adopted to the satisfaction of all participants about 85 percent of the time, regardless of its quality. Higher quality solutions introduced after the critical value for one of the solutions has been reached have little chance of achieving real consideration. Once some degree of consensus is reached, the jelling process seems to proceed rather rapidly.

The critical valence value of 15 appears not to be greatly altered by the nature of the problem or the exact size of the group. Rather, it seems to designate a turning point between the idea-getting process and the decision-making process (idea evaluation). A solution's valence index is not a measure of the number of persons supporting the solution, since a vocal minority can build up a solution's valence by actively pushing it. In this sense, valence becomes an influence in addition to social pressure in determining an outcome.

Since a solution's valence is independent of its objective quality, this group factor becomes an important liability in group problem solving, even when the value of a decision depends upon objective criteria (facts and logic). It becomes a means whereby skilled manipulators can have more influence over the group process than their proportion of membership deserves.

INDIVIDUAL DOMINATION

In most leaderless groups a dominant individual emerges and captures more than his share of influence on the outcome. He can achieve this end through a greater degree of participation (valence), persuasive ability, or stubborn persistence (fatiguing the opposition). None of these factors is related to problem-solving ability, so that the best problem solver in the group may not have the influence to upgrade the quality of the group's solution (which he would have had if left to solve the problem by himself).

Hoffman and Maier (14) found that the mere fact of appointing a leader causes this person to dominate a discussion. Thus, regardless of his problem-solving ability a leader tends to exert a major influence on the outcome of a discussion.

CONFLICTING SECONDARY GOAL: WINNING THE ARGUMENT

When groups are confronted with a problem, the initial goal is to obtain a solution. However, the appearance of several alternatives causes individuals to have preferences and once these emerge the desire to support a position is created. Converting those with neutral viewpoints and refuting those with opposed viewpoints now enters into the problem-solving process. More and more the goal becomes that of winning the decision rather than finding the best solution. This new goal is unrelated to the quality of the problem's solution and therefore can result in lowering the quality of the decision (12).

FACTORS THAT SERVE AS ASSETS OR LIABILITIES, DEPENDING LARGELY UPON THE SKILL OF THE DISCUSSION LEADER

DISAGREEMENT

The fact that discussion may lead to disagreement can serve either to create hard feelings among members or lead to a resolution of conflict and hence to an innovative solution (8, 10, 12, 20, 22, 30). The first of these outcomes of disagreement is a liability, especially with regard to the acceptance of solutions; while the second is an asset, particularly where innovation is desired. A leader can treat disagreement as undesirable and thereby reduce the probability of both hard feelings and innovation, or he can maximize disagreement and risk hard feelings in his attempts to achieve innovation. The skill of a leader requires his ability to create a climate for disagreement which will permit innovation without risking hard feelings. The leader's perception of disagreement is one of the critical factors in this skill area (30). Others involve permissiveness (19), delaying the reaching of a solution (24, 33), techniques for processing information and opinions (22, 25, 31), and techniques for separating idea getting from idea evaluation (21, 22, 31).

CONFLICTING INTERESTS VERSUS MUTUAL INTERESTS

Disagreement in discussion may take many forms. Often participants disagree with one another with regard to solutions, but when issues are explored one finds that these conflicting solutions are designed to solve different problems. Before one can rightly expect agreement on a solution, there should be agreement on the nature of the problem. Even before this, there should be agreement on the goal, as well as on the various obstacles that prevent the goal from being reached. Once distinctions are made between goals, obstacles, and solutions (which represent ways of overcoming obstacles), one finds increased opportunities for cooperative problem solving and less conflict (11, 21, 22, 33, 40).

Often there is also disagreement regarding whether the objective of a solution is to achieve quality or acceptance (29), and frequently a stated problem reveals a complex of separate problems, each having separate solutions so that a search for a single solution is impossible (22). Communications often are inadequate because the discussion is not synchronized and each person is engaged in discussing a different aspect. Organizing discussion to synchronize the exploration of different aspects of the problm and to follow a systematic procedure increases solution quality (25, 31). The leadership function of influencing discussion procedure is quite distinct from the function of evaluating or contributing ideas (17,19).

When the discussion leader aids in the separation of the several aspects of the problem-solving process and delays the solution-mindedness of the group (20, 22, 33), both solution quality and acceptance improve; when he hinders or fails to facilitate the isolation of these varied processes, he risks a deterioration in the group process (40). His skill thus determines whether a discussion drifts toward conflicting interests or whether mutual interests are located. Cooperative problem solving can only occur after the mutual interests have been established and it is surprising how often they can be found when the discussion leader makes this his task (18, 22, 23).

RISK TAKING

Groups are more willing than individuals to reach decisions involving risks (42, 43). Taking risks is a factor in acceptance of change, but change may either represent a gain or a loss. The best guard against the latter outcome seems to be primarily a matter of a decision's quality. In a group situation this depends upon the leader's skill in utilizing the factors that represent group assets and avoiding those that make for liabilities.

TIME REQUIREMENTS

In general, more time is required for a group to reach a decision than for a single individual to reach one. Insofar as some problems require quick decisions, individual decisions are favored. In other situations acceptance and quality are requirements, but excessive time without sufficient returns also represents a loss. On the other hand, discussion can resolve conflicts, whereas reaching consensus has limited value (42). The practice of hastening a meeting can prevent full discussion, but failure to move a discussion forward can lead to boredom and fatigue-type solutions, in which members agree merely to get out of the meeting. The effective utilization of discussion time (a delicate balance between permissiveness and control on the part of the leader), therefore, is needed to make the time factor an asset rather than a liability. Unskilled leaders tend to be too concerned with reaching a solution and therefore terminate a discussion before the group potential is achieved (24).

WHO CHANGES

In reaching consensus or agreement, some members of a group must change. Persuasive forces do not operate in individual problem solving in the same way they operate in a group situation; hence, the changing of someone's mind is not an issue. In group situations, however, who changes can be an asset or a liability. If persons with the most constructive views are induced to change the end-product suffers; whereas if persons with the least constructive points of view change the end-product is upgraded. The leader can upgrade the quality of a decision because his position permits him to protect the person with a minority view and increase his opportunity to influence the majority position. This protection is a constructive factor because a minority viewpoint influences only when facts favor it (17, 18, 32).

The leader also plays a constructive role insofar as he can facilitate communications and thereby reduce misunderstandings (18, 40). The leader has an adverse effect on the end-product when he suppresses minority views by holding a contrary position and when he uses his office to promote his own views (24, 27, 32). In many problem-solving discussions the untrained leader plays a dominant role in influencing the outcome, and when he is more resistant to changing his views than are the other participants, the quality of the outcome tends to be lowered. This negative leader-influence was demonstrated by experiments in which untrained leaders were asked to obtain a second solution to a problem after they had obtained their first one (25). It was found that the second solution tended to be superior to the first. Since the dominant individual had influenced the first solution, he had won his point and therefore ceased to dominate the subsequent discussion which led to the second solution. Acceptance of a solution also increases as the leader sees disagreement as idea producing rather than as a source of difficulty or trouble (30). Leaders who see some of their participants as troublemakers obtain fewer innovative solutions and gain less acceptance of decisions made than leaders who see disagreeing members as persons with ideas.

THE LEADER'S ROLE
FOR INTEGRATED GROUPS

TWO DIFFERING TYPES OF GROUP PROCESS

In observing group problem solving under various conditions it is rather easy to distinguish between cooperative problem-solving activity and persuasion or selling approaches. Problem-solving activity includes searching, trying out ideas on one another, listening to understand rather than to refute, making relatively short speeches, and reacting to differences in opinion as stimulating. The general pattern is one of rather complete participation, involvement, and interest. Persuasion activity includes the selling of opinions already formed, defending a position held, either not listening at all or listening in order to be able to refute, talking dominated by a few members, unfavorable reactions to disagreement, and a lack of involvement of some members. During problem solving the behavior observed seems to be that of members interacting as segments of a group. The interaction pattern is not between certain individual members, but with the group as a whole. Sometimes it is difficult to determine who should be credited with an idea. "It just developed," is a response often used to describe the solution reached. In contrast, discussions involving selling or persuasive behavior seem to consist of a series of interpersonal interactions with each individual retaining his identity. Such groups do not function as integrated units but as separate individuals, each with an agenda. In one situation the solution is unknown and is sought; in the other, several solutions exist and conflict occurs because commitments have been made.

THE STARFISH ANALOGY

The analysis of these two group processes suggests an analogy with the behavior of the rays of a starfish under two conditions; one with the nerve ring intact, the other with the nerve ring sectioned (7, 35, 36, 39). In the intact condition, locomotion and righting behavior reveal that the behavior of each ray is not merely a function of local stimulation. Locomotion and righting behavior reveal a degree of coordination and interdependence that is centrally controlled. However, when the nerve ring is sectioned, the behavior of one ray still can influence others, but internal coordination is lacking. For example, if one ray is stimulated, it may step forward, thereby exerting pressure on the sides of the other four rays. In response to these external pressures (tactile stimulation), these rays show stepping responses on the stimulated side so that locomotion successfully occurs without the aid of neural coordination. Thus integrated behavior can occur on the basis of external control. If, however, stimulation is applied to opposite rays, the specimen may be "locked" for a time, and in some species the conflicting locomotions may divide the animal, thus destroying it (5, 36).

Each of the rays of the starfish can show stepping responses even when sectioned and removed from the animal. Thus each may be regarded as an individual. In a starfish with a sectioned nerve ring the five rays become members of a group. They can successfully work together for locomotion purposes by being controlled by the dominant ray. Thus if uniformity of action is desired, the group of five rays can sometimes be more effective than the individual ray in moving the group toward a source of stimulation. However, if "locking" or the division of the organism occurs, the group action become less effective than individual action. External control, through the influence of a dominant ray, therefore can lead to adaptive behavior for the starfish as a whole, but it can also result in a conflict that destroys the organism. Something more than external influence is needed.

In the animal with an intact nerve ring, the function of the rays is coordinated by the nerve ring. With this type of internal organization the group is always superior to that of the individual actions. When the rays function as a part of an organized unit, rather than as a group that is physically together, they become a higher type of organization—a single intact organism. This is accomplished by the nerve ring, which in itself does not do the behaving. Rather, it receives and processes the data which the rays relay to it. Through this central organization, the responses of the rays become part of a larger pattern so that together they constitute a single coordinated total response rather than a group of individual responses.

THE LEADER AS THE
GROUP S CENTRAL NERVOUS SYSTEM

If we now examine what goes on in a discussion group we find that members can problem-solve as individuals, they can influence others by external pushes and pulls, or they can function as a group with varying degrees of unity. In order for the latter function to be maximized, however, something must be introduced to serve the function of the nerve ring. In our conceptualization of group problem solving and group decision (22), we see this as the function of the leader. Thus the leader does not serve as a dominant ray and produce the solution. Rather, his function is to receive information, facilitate communications between the individuals, relay messages, and integrate the incoming responses so that a single unified response occurs.

Solutions that are the product of good group discussions often come as surprises to discussion leaders. One of these is unexpected generosity. If there is a weak member, this member is given less to do, in much the same way as an organism adapts to an injured limb and alters the function of other limbs to keep locomotion on course. Experimental evidence supports the point that group decisions award special consideration to needy members of groups (11). Group decisions in industrial groups often give smaller assignments to the less gifted (18). A leader could not effectually impose such differential treatment on group members without being charged with discriminatory practices.

Another unique aspect of group discussion is the way fairness is resolved. In a simulated problem situation involving the problem of how to introduce a new truck into a group of drivers, the typical group solution involves a trading of trucks so that several or all memebers stand to profit. If the leader makes the decision the number of persons who profit is often confined to one (27, 34). In industrial practice, supervisors assign a new truck to an individual member of a crew after careful evaluation of needs. This practice results in dissatisfaction, with the charge of *unfair* being leveled at him. Despite these repeated attempts to do justice, supervisors in the telephone industry never hit upon the notion of a general reallocation of trucks, a solution that crews invariably reach when the decision is theirs to make.

In experiments involving the introduction of change, the use of group discussion tends to lead to decisions that resolve differences (18, 19, 26, 28, 29). Such decisions tend to be different from decisions reached by individuals because of the very fact that disagreement is common in group problem solving and rare in individual problem solving. The process of resolving differences in a constructive setting causes the exploration of additional areas and leads to solutions that are integrative rather than compromises.

Finally, group solutions tend to be tailored to fit the interests and personalities of the participants; thus group solutions to problems involving fairness, fears, face-saving, etc., tend to vary from one group to another. An outsider cannot process these variables because they are not subject to logical treatment.

If we think of the leader as serving a function in the group different from that of its membership, we might be able to create a group that can function as an intact organism. For a leader, such functions as rejecting or promoting ideas according to his personal needs are out of bounds. He must be receptive to information contributed, accept contributions without evaluating them (posting contributions on a chalk board to keep them alive), summarize information to facilitate integration, stimulate exploratory behavior, create awareness of problems of one member by others, and detect when the group is ready to resolve differences and agree to a unified solution.

Since higher organisms have more than a nerve ring and can store information, a leader might appropriately supply information, but according to our model of a leader's role, he must clearly distinguish between supplying information and promoting a solution. If his knowledge indicates the desirability of a particular solution, sharing this knowledge might lead the group to find this solution, but the solution should be the group's discovery. A leader's contributions do not receive the same treatment as those of a member of the group. Whether he likes it or not, his position is different. According to our conception of the leader's contribution to discussion, his role not only differs in influence, but gives him an entirely different function. He is to serve much as the nerve ring in the starfish and to further refine this function so as to make it a higher type of nerve ring.

This model of a leader's role in group process has served as a guide for many of our studies in group problem solving. It is not our claim that this will lead to the best possible group function under all conditions. In sharing it we hope to indicate the nature of our guidelines in exploring group leadership as a function quite different and apart from group membership. Thus the model serves as a stimulant for research problems and as a guide for our analyses of leadership skills and principles.

CONCLUSIONS

On the basis of our analysis, it follows that the comparison of the merits of group versus individual problem solving depends on the nature of the problem, the goal to be achieved (high quality solution, highly accepted solution, effective communication and understanding of the solution, innovation, a quickly reached solution, or satisfaction), and the skill of the discussion leader. If liabilities inherent in groups are avoided, assets capitalized upon, and conditions that can serve either favorable or unfavorable outcomes are effectively used, it follows that groups have a potential which in many instances can exceed that of a superior individual functioning alone, even with respect to creativity.

This goal was nicely stated by Thibaut and Kelley (41) when they:

> wonder whether it may not be possible for a rather small, intimate group to establish a problem-solving process that capitalizes upon the total pool of information and provides for great interstimulation of ideas without any loss of innovative creativity due to social restraints (p. 268).

In order to accomplish this high level of achievement, however, a leader is needed who plays a role quite different from that of the members. His role is analogous to that of the nerve ring in the starfish which permits the rays to execute a unified response. If the leader can contribute the integrative requirement, group problem solving may emerge as a unique type of group function. This type of approach to group processes places the leader in a particular role in which he must cease to contribute, avoid evaluation, and refrain from thinking about solutions or group *products*. Instead he must concentrate on the group *process*, listen in order to understand rather than to appraise or refute, assume responsibility for accurate communication between members, be sensitive to unexpressed feelings, protect minority points of view, keep the discussion moving, and develop skills in summarizing.

Questioning
the Managerial Implications of
Developing Team Effort

1. Argyris has described six consequences of executive behavior that do not observe his principles of owning up, being open with others, or willingly assuming risk. How would you rank these consequences in terms of their dysfunctional effect on the organization? Can you perceive any organizational benefits arising from these consequences?

2. How would you go about telling your closest friend what you like least about him? How would you give your boss similar feedback?

3. To what extent do you agree with Maier's notions as to the appropriate role of the leader in a problem-solving group? How does your perception of the group leadership role differ from his?

4. What would be your reaction to a decision by higher-ups that you join a group of your contemporaries during the next year for the purpose of jointly accomplishing all anticipated studies, projects, programs, and routine work? Are your reactions any different now than they would have been before reading the preceding articles?

References

1. Argyris, C., "T-Groups for Organizational Effectiveness," *Harvard Business* Review, XLII (1964), 60.

2. ——, "Explorations in Interpersonal Competence II," *Applied Behavioral Science*, I, No. 3 (1965), 255.

3. ——, *Organization and Innovation*. Homewood, Ill.: Richard D. Irwin, Inc., 1965.

4. Blake, R. R., J. S. Mouton, L. B. Barnes, and L. E. Greiner, "Breakthrough in Organization Development," *Harvard Business Review*, XLII (1964), 135.

5. Crozier, W. J., "Notes on Some Problems of Adaptation," *Biological Bulletin*, XXXIX (1920), 116–29.

6. Duncker, K., "On problem solving," *Psychological Monographs*, LVIII, No. 270 (1945).

7. Hamilton, W. F., "Coordination in the Starfish, III: The Righting Reaction as a Phase of Locomotion (Righting and Locomotion)," *Journal of Comparative Psychology*, II (1922), 81–94.

8. Hoffman, L. R., "Conditions for Creative Problem Solving," *Journal of Psychology*, LII (1961), 429–44.

9. ——, "Group Problem Solving," in *Advances in Experimental Social Psychology*, Vol. II, ed. L. Berkowitz. New York: Academic Press, Inc., 1965, pp. 99–132.

10. ——, E. Harburg, and N. R. F. Maier, "Differences and Disagreement as Factors in Creative Group Problem Solving," *Journal of Abnormal and Social Psychology*, LXIV (1962), 206–14.

11. ——, and N. R. F. Maier, "The Use of Group Decision to Resolve a Problem of Fairness," *Personnel Psychology*, XII (1959), 545–59.

12. ——, and ——, "Quality and Acceptance of Problem Solutions by Members of Homogeneous and Heterogeneous Groups," *Journal of Abnormal and Social Psychology*, LXII (1961), 401–7.

13. ——, and ——, "Valence in the Adoption of Solutions by Problem-Solving Groups: Concept, Method, and Results," *Journal of Abnormal and Social Psychology*, LXIX (1964), 264–71.

14. ——, and ——, "Valence in the Adoption of Solutions by Problem-Solving Groups: II. Quality and Acceptance as Goals of Leaders and Members" (Unpublished manuscript, 1967 [mimeo]).

15. Kelley, H. H., and J. W. Thibaut, "Experimental Studies of Group Problem Solving and Process," in *Handbook of Social Psychology*, ed. G. Lindzey. Cambridge, Mass: Addison-Wesley Publishing Co., Inc., 1954, pp. 735–85.

16. Maier, N. R. F., "Reasoning in Humans. I: On Direction," *Journal of Comparative Psychology*, X (1930), 115–43.

17. ——, "The Quality of Group Decisions as Influenced by the Discussion Leader," *Human Relations*, III (1950), 155–74.

18. ——, *Principles of Human Relations*. New York: John Wiley & Sons, Inc., 1952.

19. ——, "An Experimental Test of the Effect of Training on Discussion Leadership," *Human Relations*, VI (1953), 161–73.

20. ——, *The Appraisal Interview*. New York: John Wiley & Sons, Inc., 1958.

21. ——, "Screening Solutions to Upgrade Quality: A New Approach to Problem Solving Under Conditions of Uncertainty," *Journal of Psychology*, IL (1960), 217–31.

22. ——, *Problem Solving Discussions and Conferences: Leadership Methods and Skills*. New York: McGraw-Hill Book Company, 1963.

23. ——, and J. J. Hayes, *Creative Management*. New York: John Wiley & Sons, Inc., 1962.

24. ——, and L. R. Hoffman, "Quality of First and Second Solutions in Group Problem Solving," *Journal of Applied Psychology*, XLIV (1960), 278–83.

25. ——, and ——, "Using Trained 'Developmental' Discussion Leaders to Improve Further the Quality of Group Decisions," *Journal of Applied Psychology*, XLIV (1960), 247–51.

26. ——, and ——, "Organization and Creative Problem Solving," *Journal of Applied Psychology*, XLV (1961), 277–80.

27. ——, and ——, "Group Decision in England and the United States," *Personnel Psychology*, XV (1962), 75–87.

28. ——, and ——, "Financial Incentives and Group Decision in Motivating Change," *Journal of Social Psychology*, LXIV (1964), 369–78.

29. ——, and ——, "Types of Problems Confronting Managers," *Personnel Psychology*, XVII (1964), 261–69.

30. ——, and ——, "Acceptance and Quality of Solutions as Related to Leaders' Attitudes Toward Disagreement in Group Problem Solving," *Journal of Applied Behavioral Science*, I (1965), 373–86.

31. ——, and R. A. Maier, "An Experimental Test of the Effects of 'Developmental' vs. 'Free' Discussions on the Quality of Group Decisions," *Journal of Applied Psychology*, XLI (1957), 320–23.

32. ——, and A. R. Solem, "The Contribution of a Discussion Leader

to the Quality of Group Thinking: The Effective Use of Minority Opinions," *Human Relations*, V (1952), 277–88.

33. ——, and ——, "Improving Solutions by Turning Choice Situations into Problems," *Personnel Psychology*, XV (1962), 151–57.

34. ——, and L. F. Zerfoss, "MRP: A Technique for Training Large Groups of Supervisors and Its Potential Use in Social Research," *Human Relations*, V (1952), 177–86.

35. Moore, A. R., "The Nervous Mechanism of Coordination in the Crinoid Antedon Rosaceus," *Journal of Genetic Psychology*, VI (1924), 281–88.

36. ——, and M. Doudoroff, "Injury, Recovery, and Function in an Aganglionic Central Nervous System," *Journal of Comparative Psychology*, XXVIII (1939), 313–28.

37. Osborn, A. F., *Applied Imagination*. New York: Charles Scribner's Sons, 1953.

38. Schein, E., and W. Bennis, *Personal and Organizational Change Through Laboratory Methods*. New York: John Wiley & Sons, Inc., 1965.

39. Schneirla, T. C., and N. R. F. Maier, "Concerning the Status of the Starfish," *Journal of Comparative Psychology*, XXX (1940), 103–10.

40. Solem, A. R., "1965: Almost Anything I Can Do, We Can Do Better," *Personnel Administration*, XXVIII (1965), 6–16.

41. Thibaut, J. W., and H. H. Kelley, *The Social Psychology of Groups*. New York: John Wiley & Sons, Inc., 1961.

42. Wallach, M. A., and N. Kogan, "The Roles of Information, Discussion, and Consensus in Group Risk Taking," *Journal of Experimental and Social Psychology*, I (1965), 1–19.

43. ——, ——, and D. J. Bem, "Group Influence on Individual Risk Taking," *Journal of Abnormal and Social Psychology*, LXV (1962), 75–86.

44. Wertheimer, M., *Productive Thinking*. New York: Harper & Row, Publishers, 1959.

Making

Decisions

In this section we look at the efforts of the organization's members, particularly its executives and managers, to reach decisions rationally. The elegant tools of applied mathematics aid the efforts of the decision maker when he can identify costs, risks, processes, and structures. But such complete rationality is seldom possible. Hence, the executive must develop a reliable method for solving ill-defined problems with an understanding of the motivational and perceptual distortions he is subject to when doing so.

The readings that follow imply that managerial decision-making behavior is a function of several factors both within the organization and within the manager. This is the principal finding by Stagner resulting from a questionnaire sent to executives representing widely varying business organizations. His complex analysis of the corporate decision process yields many other results concerning the effect of the profit motive, intracompany coalitions, participative management, communication patterns, and leadership styles.

Soelberg examines decision making as a heuristic process. His intent is to better equip the individual manager to make effective decisions by being aware of the influence of his own predispositions and prejudices on his problem-solving activities.

The impact of individual differences on decision making is also considered by Rim but for a more specific reason. In addition to discussing the phenomenon of the "risky shift" in problem-solving groups, he also seeks to identify the risk-taking manager in terms of a number of relevant personality factors.

31

Corporate Decision Making: An Empirical Study

Ross Stagner
Wayne State University

A questionnaire regarding corporate decision-making (dm) practices was mailed to 500 vice-presidents of 125 large firms. Response rate was 50 percent. Data indicate that many goals other than profit maximization are important in decisions, and that estimates of marginal costs and profits are not always carefully made. Profitability and executive satisfaction with decision-making practices are positively correlated. Factor analysis reveals at least three important dimensions of dm process: managerial cohesiveness, formal procedures in dm, and centralization–decentralization. Factor scores derived from these factors were significantly different for firms in top and bottom thirds on profitability. However, these scores did not predict increases or decreases in profitability over a 7-year time span. Interpretation favors the view of the corporation as a coalition, with social role and personal bias of the executive affecting his decisions. Participative practices are supported as both satisfying and profitable.

This research was financed by a grant from the Ford Foundation for the academic year 1963–1964. The Foundation is in no way responsible for the contents of this report. The author wishes to acknowledge the generous assistance provided by the staff of the Wayne State University Computing Center in adapting programs for this purpose, and the assistance of D. R. Jacobs, in cross checking many details in the data analysis. Reprinted in abridged form by permission from *Journal of Applied Psychology*, LIII (1969), 1–13. Copyright 1969 by the American Psychological Association.

Most of the literature on decision making in large corporations is of a highly abstract, theoretical, normative type. It sets forth, with impressive mathematical treatment, the decision processes in which corporation executives should engage if a number of quite unrealistic assumptions can be met. The articles have been characterized, perhaps unkindly, as our modern version of "how many angels can dance on the head of a pin?"

A second category, including most of the remaining publications on corporate decision making, includes memoirs of successful executives. Like case studies in the field of clinical psychology, these sometimes offer intriguing hypotheses about the process under investigation, but no acceptable data to support the proposed theory.

The field has been dominated by classical economic theory. The major assumptions about corporate decision making (dm) are as follows: (a) the firm is a unit; (b) the firm acts to maximize profit; (c) the firm is completely informed about alternative courses of action, consequences of each alternative, and the probabilities of these consequences (37). Some years of study of industrial conflict (44) were convincing that these were contrary to fact. In an industrial dispute, top executives usually produce recommendations for corporate action, many of which are mutually contradictory, and the settlement of the dispute inside management often is nearly as difficult as that with the union. Second, the firm often acts on power considerations, or even on the basis of maintaining a public image, rather than on profit considerations. Third, members of the firm are often woefully ignorant about alternative courses of action and their probable consequences.

In recent years there has been some increase in empirical research on corporate dm, most of which has had the effect of further shaking confidence in the relevance of the classical assumptions. Simon (37, 38) has cited numerous instances in which the unity of the firm was a fiction. White (48) documents many conflicts at the executive level, especially between functional departments. Dalton (11) provides intriguing instances of the conflict between outlying branches and a central corporate office. Stagner (45) offers various examples of disputes between vice-presidents in large- and medium-sized corporations. March (25) shows that a firm has some characteristics of a political coalition, composed of conflicting subunits.

With respect to profit maximization as a goal, the empirical data also lead to rejection of the assumption. Soelberg (43) has stressed the importance of individual goals which may have nothing to do with profit maximization. Simon (38) points out that most executives accept a "satisficing" policy rather than an optimizing alternative. Stagner (45) has shown that suboptimization may be quite common, as when a corporate policy is a compromise between what is optimal for a subunit and what is optimal for the entire firm. Feldman and Kantner (13) point out that the alleged rule of profit maximization, if defined precisely, often fails to predict the decision made by a firm; and Mueller, Wilken, and Wood (30) document this logical point with case studies in which an owner disregarded cost estimates in making plant location decisions.

Simon (38) has been particularly interested in the assumption of perfect knowledge and perfect rationality in dm. He notes that information costs money, and most managements stop searching for alternative courses of action when they locate a "satisficing" option. Relevant case studies are those of Cyert, Simon, and Trow (10), and Cyert, Dill, and March (9). Marschak and Radner (28) point out the difficulty of perfect communication from one member of the firm to another, and hence the unavailability of all the information in the dm process.

Psychologists have been concerned with the importance of perceptual bias in the handling of information. Cyert, Simon, and Trow (10) gave identical case histories of a firm to 23 executives in a training program. The selective perception of information is indicated by their answers to the question: "What is the most important problem facing the new president of this firm?" Of the sales executives, 83 percent named a sales problem, while only 29 percent of nonsales officials mentioned sales. Stagner (45) reports instances in which production and sales managers sponsored diametrically different solutions to what was ostensibly the same problem. Zalkind and Costello (49) have offered interpretations of the literature on perception as an aid in understanding differences in managers' choice of information to guide a decision. Appropriate to their remarks is the observation by Bowman (4) that the "operations analyst" may fail to perceive some important item which is obvious to a working manager. Bowman advocates use of varied information sources to minimize such oversights.

Much of the "information" used in dm is biased by executive wishes and expectations. Cyert, Dill, and March (9) suggest that staff personnel first decide whether the idea is good, then marshal data to support their view. Their paper gives a detailed account of the data-gathering process and cost estimates for installation of an electronic data processing unit in a medium-sized corporation. It sounds very impressive until they quote a staff member as saying, "In the final analysis, if anybody brings up an item of cost we haven't thought of, we can balance it by making another source of savings tangible (p. 340)." Similarly, Stagner (45) quotes a corporate vice-president on the question of cost figures: "The salesmen handling this line wanted to have unit cost data. I opposed giving it to them, partly because they might unintentionally reveal it to a competitor, but more because these cost figures are in some respects artificial (p. 17)." Thus the fancy mathematical solutions developed by the operations research staff apparently incorporate highly subjective estimates of various cost factors.

Not only is the information biased; in many instances it is ignored. Consider the instance in which careful market research led to "a proposal to set up three installations, each costing $5 million, two in the United States and one in Western Europe. The head of the English subsidiary and the head of the French subsidiary got into a feud over which would get the European unit. After considerable negotiating, the American controlling executives decided to put one each in France and England (45, p. 17). In this instance detailed staff work had indicated that one installation was adequate to the foreseeable European market. The key issue was the relative status and power of the two European executives, and $5 million was the "side payment" to keep peace in the organization. This is an instance of "suboptimization," a compromise between optimum for the subunit and optimum for the entire firm. It suggests that profit is only one of many goals which determine corporate decisions.

Economic theorists have not ignored absolutely the conflict of their assumptions with empirical reality. In an intriguing effort to incorporate some of these observations, Harsanyi (20) suggests that optimizing equations be rewritten to include such factors as the opportunity cost to A of getting and using power, the cost to B of refusing to yield to A, and the personal affection of B for A. Obviously such a formulation deviates rather far from the simple profit-maximization approach.

These observations suggest that there is an urgent need for research on corporate dm processes which is theoretically based but reasonably close to empirical reality. This study offers a beginning on that task.

METHOD

A THEORETICAL POSITION

It seems appropriate to approach the problem of corporate dm by making the following assumptions: (a) corporate policy is established by persons occupying certain role positions in the organization; (b) the behavior of these persons is determined in part by role prescriptions, and in part by personal motives; (c) perceptions of corporate resources, alternative actions, utilities, and probabilities of outcomes will be affected by role-induced experiences and by personal experiences; (d) policy proposals by different executives will reflect these divergent perceptions and motivations; and (e) corporate decisions will represent compromises among these, affected by the power of proponents as well as by logic and realistic data.

Research on this kind of complex phenomenon ideally should involve analysis of all relevant documents, video recordings of all relevant conversations and conferences, depth explorations of each executive to ascertain conscious and unconscious desires, symbols, etc., affecting his policy preferences, and an assessment of the power fields of the various executives. For many reasons such research is not presently feasible. As a substitute we may rely on reports of dm from participant executives, and try to ferret out the process from these subjective data. The task is difficult. Phenomenological reports are slippery even when made by trained observers having no aspirations likely to bias their observations.

Industrial executives are, for this purpose, untrained observers, and it is assumed that they will introduce biases into their reports. Nevertheless, this seems the only suitable source of data at this time for a study of high-level dm processes.

HYPOTHESES

While this was designed as an exploratory study, the following hypotheses were set up for testing:

1. Profit maximization will be the only goal reported by executives.
2. All corporations make decisions in the same manner, i.e., there are no significant differences in style of dm.
3. An executive's power status within the firm does not affect his part in the dm process.
4. Profitability is unrelated to variations of manner of making decisions.
5. Personality variables are nonsignificant in the corporate dm process.

PROCEDURE

This study develops from an earlier project (45) in which unstructured interviews explored executive perceptions of the corporate dm process. Analysis of the interview material led to the formulation of 28 questions which seemed to merit quantitative analysis. These were classified into six groups, although these categories are useful primarily for noting relations to theory, not for statistical analysis. The groups, and illustrative items, were: *goal variables:* cost and profit estimates, company tradition, corporate image; *means variables:* channels of communication, lines of authority, speed of decisions, formal routines, use of ad hoc committees, use of outside consultants; *leadership variables:* chief executive talks to one vice-president at a time, chief executive is concerned that all be satisfied; *role variables:* conflict between central office and divisions, vice-presidents exaggerate importance of their division; *interaction variables:* groups among top executives; tension among top executives; discussion among all persons affected, loser (on decision) feels defeated; *outcome variables:* satisfaction with decision-making procedure, morale of top executives. (In addition, profits as percentage of capital and profits as percentage of sales were used as outcome measures but these were not in the questionnaire.)

The questions were formulated so that they could be answered by making check marks on a seven-step scale, to avoid the objection to forced yes–no answers. The wording of the items and the definitions of the ends of each seven-step scale, with the answers from 217 vice-presidents, are given in Table 1.

SAMPLE OF FIRMS

The questionnaire as described was sent to 500 persons at the vice-presidential level (VPs). Sampling was as follows: from the *Fortune Magazine* list of 500 largest American corporations (18), 125 were selected by taking every

TABLE 1

QUESTIONNAIRE ITEMS AND RESPONSES

Item		Responses						"Very important"
1. Relative speed with which top-level decisions are made	2 :	4 :	22 :	48 :	39 :	73 :	29	87
	somewhat slower than similar companies						considerably faster than similar companies	
2. Concern over formal steps in decision making at top level (regular meetings, written records, etc.)	11 :	22 :	34 :	35 :	37 :	54 :	24	15
	much attention to formal routines						little attention to form	
3. Estimates of cost and anticipated profit to result from a decision	62 :	47 :	45 :	32 :	18 :	11 :	2	86
	always carefully computed						rough estimates only	
4. Discussion among all top executives	40 :	52 :	37 :	27 :	25 :	23 :	13	59
	discussions include all executives affected						most include only two men at a time	
5. Use of a top-level policy committee or operating committee	49 :	15 :	13 :	19 :	18 :	58 :	45	36
	we have none	it merely approves decisions already made					it is an active decision-making apparatus	
6. Use of ad hoc or special committees for single projects	29 :	27 :	41 :	37 :	25 :	38 :	20	7
	common practice						usually one person, not a committee	
7. Tendency of each vice-president to exaggerate importance of his own area	2 :	4 :	4 :	25 :	21 :	98 :	63	9
	serious problem here						not a serious problem	

TABLE 1—*(Continued)*

Item	Responses							"Very important"
8. Social interaction of top executives outside office hours (for nonbusiness purposes)	15 : frequent	16	27	44	25	70	20 : rare	1
9. Concern of chief executive for detailed information on which to base decision:	37 : wants substantial detail	41	30	22	23	47	17 : prefers broad outlines	40
10. Concern of chief executive that all executives are satisfied with the decision	23 : considerable concern	35	44	37	31	38	9 : minor concern	18
11. Concern with "going through channels"	7 : relatively little attention to this	22	32	39	47	52	18 : communications always observe channels	24
12. Importance attached to company tradition and past policies	19 : not much; easy to break tradition	36	43	36	35	33	15 : considerable weight attached to tradition	11
13. Concern of chief executive for "unanimous agreement"	1 : very reluctant to confirm policy if anyone opposes	7	8	19	31	101	50 : approves policy when he sees a clear majority	17
14. Reaction of executives to decisions which go against their preference	2 : often feel "defeated" in such a case	4	4	26	37	109	35 : usually accept decision without feeling "defeat"	14
15. Preferred style of chief executive	20 : talk with one man at a time	24	22	36	25	66	24 : talk with all interested men together	24

TABLE 1—(Continued)

Item	Responses							"Very important"
16. Normal operation of divisions within company	43 :	53 :	44 :	31 :	22 :	15 :	9	38
	most divisions highly independent						little divisional autonomy	
17. Tendency of chief executive to give the "losing" executive some other concession to make him feel better	3 :	10 :	18 :	34 :	44 :	84 :	24	1
	often happens						never happens	
18. Chief executive's preference for division heads to be partisan of division or look at company as a whole	5 :	10 :	19 :	30 :	28 :	82 :	43	37
	prefers strong division partisanship						wants all to think chiefly of company, not division	
19. Use of outside consultants	5 :	19 :	31 :	31 :	42 :	54 :	35	4
	used on most important issues						rarely used by this company	
20. Clear lines of authority	31 :	63 :	47 :	26 :	21 :	21 :	8	84
	everyone knows and respects lines of authority						lines of authority ambiguous, often ignored	
21. Importance attached to company "image" as seen by public	10 :	36 :	33 :	61 :	29 :	40 :	8	27
	often outweighs cost factors						would have little effect	
22. Importance of personalities in decisions at this level	6 :	18 :	39 :	35 :	38 :	76 :	17	21
	vigorous, persuasive individual often wins point						importance of function to company usually decisive	
23. Importance of divisional vs. central office disagreements	27 :	61 :	47 :	47 :	13 :	17 :	5	10
	few such disagreements						these are fairly common	

TABLE 1—(Continued)

Item	Responses							"Very important"
24. Ability of strong divisions to get their own way	: 7 : 40 : 52 : 31 : 30 : 42 : 15 : strong divisions win if deeply concerned / no differences among divisions							9
25. Groups within top executive echelon	: 2 : 13 : 14 : 14 : 35 : 89 : 50 : some men habitually vote together as a group / no tendency toward alignments							15
26. Amount of tension within top executive group over a difficult decision	: 22 : 59 : 47 : 36 : 34 : 14 : 5 : no tension or personal feelings / tension sometimes high, personal frictions							19
27. Your estimate of morale of top executive echelon	: 4 : 4 : 10 : 17 : 32 : 105 : 45 : low / high							81
28. Your feeling of satisfaction with the way these decisions are handled	: 48 : 70 : 42 : 18 : 23 : 11 : 5 : very well satisfied / some satisfaction							12

fourth name.[1] From Standard and Poor's Registry of Directors were obtained the names of four VP's (including when necessary treasurers, controllers, etc., if not enough VPs were listed). Thus, 500 questionnaires were mailed. These were coded to identify firms but not individual respondents.

Returns were received from about 260 individuals. All four officials replied from 6 firms; three from 29 firms; two from 46 firms; and only one from each of 28 firms; but a number of these were incomplete. The final analysis is based on 217 responses from 109 firms.

RESULTS

The distribution of 217 executives from 109 firms, in terms of their answers to specific items, is given in Table 1. Some interest will attach to these in the light of points made above. For example, it is obvious that in many firms, cost and marginal profit estimates are not carefully made (item 3). In fact, a substantial number (28 percent) indicated that "rough estimates" were made of such variables. Table 1 also indicates that company "image" may outweigh profit considerations (item 21) and adherence to tradition may also be an important value (item 12). These data merely confirm observations already made regarding the importance of goals other than profit maximization. They lead to rejection of hypothesis 1 (that profit will be the only goal reported).

The first seven columns in Table 1 show the number of VPs checking at each of the seven steps on the answer scale. Column 8 gives the number checking that item as very important. Various computations involving this datum led to absolutely no meaningful results, and the conclusion follows that these respondents were not good judges of the relative importance of various items in relation to dm procedure or outcome.

RELIABILITY OF DATA

To talk about the dm process in a firm, it must be shown that it can be described with sufficient precision as to be different from some other firm. To test this, the authors took 52 pairs of men from the multiple-responding firms and computed profile correlations (the pattern of responses on one questionnaire against that on another). Only one pair was taken from any given firm (Group A, Table 2). Then each of these 52 was paired against a man from a different firm. These are shown as Group B. As another control we took 190 random pairs from firms sending in only a single response (Group C). For pairs within the same firm the actual range of correlations was from +0.79 (rather high agreement) to +0.01 (no agreement at all). The mean (Table 2) is +0.43. For Group

---

[1] A few substitutions were made, e.g., when the above process turned up atypical organizations such as a large farmers' cooperative. In such instances the replacement was the next firm on the list.

TABLE 2
CORRELATIONS BETWEEN PAIRS OF EXECUTIVES
DESCRIBING THE DECISION-MAKING PROCESS

Group	Mean *z'*	Mean *r*
A (intra-firm)	0.463*	0.433*
B (random multiple-response)	0.330	0.319
C (random single-response)	0.310	0.300

Note.—*t* (A–B), 2.78, *p* < 0.05; *t* (A–C), 4.95, *p* < 0.05; *t* (B–C), 0.59, *ns*.

B (same men, paired across firms) the range is $+0.73$ to -0.27, with a mean of $+0.319$. In Group C (random pairs from firms with one respondent) the range is $+0.86$ to -0.53; mean, $+0.30$. The A–B and A–C differences meet the 0.05 level for a two-tailed test. Thus we can say conservatively that two VPs from the same firm will agree more in their responses than two from different firms, and the hypothesis of an observable event (the dm process) is sustained. (Conversely, it is a bit discouraging that the agreement within the firm is not higher; it suggests that the unity of the firm is even less than suggested earlier. We thus reject hypothesis 2 (that the dm process is the same in all firms.)

An examination of these profile correlations suggests that in some firms there is high communication and mutual understanding, while in others there is fractionation and dissociation. For one group of three VPs in the same firm, the correlations are 0.66, 0.79, and 0.64; for another set of three, the figures are 0.18, 0.13, and 0.38. This fact fits with other data to be mentioned later.

DIMENSIONS OF THE DM PROCESS

One major concern of the study was to identify styles of dm in corporations, and the tactic utilized for this purpose was factor analysis. Each of the 28 questionnaire items, plus size, profit on sales, and profit on capital, was correlated with all the others, and subjected to a principal axes analysis. Seven factors emerged, of which four had variances above 1.0. Only the first two seemed to make sense in terms of everyday knowledge of corporation functioning. Factor I is heavily loaded on executive morale (Table 3). This seems plausible in view of the number of questions asked which would bear, in one way or another, on the satisfaction of executives with the dm process. Teachers of industrial psychology and management courses will be pleased to note that "going through channels" and "clear lines of authority" favor high morale. Profitability is positively but not heavily loaded on this factor.

Factor II has its highest loadings on the two profitability indexes (Table 4). In addition, it includes several "means" items: "concern over formal steps," "use of ad hoc committees," "outside consultants," and relatively slow decisions. One possible interpretation, based partly on independent knowledge of the firms, is that this factor weights profitability based on strong decentralized divisions, as opposed to a cohesive central administration. Further support for this view

TABLE 3
ITEMS RECEIVING HIGHEST LOADINGS ON THE UNROTATED MATRIX, FACTOR I

Item	Loading
28. Your feeling of satisfaction with way decisions are handled (very well)	0.77
27. Your estimate of top executive morale (high)	0.73
20. Clear lines of authority (yes)	0.65
4. Discussion among all top executives (all incl.)	0.59
26. Tension within top executive group (rare)	0.57
25. Groups within top executive echelon (rare)	0.54
11. Concern with going through channels (yes)	0.54

Note.—The answer given in parentheses defines the positive end of the seven-step scale. See Table 1 for the complete items. For N = 217, a correlation of 0.30 is significant at the 0.01 level.

TABLE 4
ITEMS RECEIVING HIGHEST LOADINGS ON THE UNROTATED MATRIX, FACTOR II

Item	Loading
30. Profit as percentage of sales	0.47
31. Profit as percentage of capital	0.42
2. Formal routines (yes)	0.39
6. Ad hoc committees (common)	0.34
19. Outside consultants (often)	0.34
1. Speed of decisions (slow)	0.33
7. Losing executive feels defeated (yes)	0.31

derives from Table 5, showing items which reverse sign from factor I to II. It will be noted that the loadings in factor I point to an integrated structure, while II points to a number of autonomous units under a single corporate roof. Both factors point to rejection of hypothesis 4 (profitability not related to manner of dm).

Most factor analysts would argue that rotation of factors to simple structure provides the best approach to identifying meaningful dimensions in a mass of correlational data. The seven factors were rotated by Varimax, giving quite a different pattern from the unrotated structure.

Factor I' (Table 6) confirms the suggestion of a dimension of managerial cohesiveness. Firms high on this factor have managers skilled at working together; but the items give us no hint of how this coordination was achieved.

Factor II' (Table 7) might be called "formality in dm"; it has elements of participative management style and also essential bureaucratic procedures. The style of the chief executive seems to be important here in keeping a "tight ship" but at the same time listening to all concerned and maintaining high morale. It is a little surprising that, statistically, this is independent of factor I'.

TABLE 5

ITEMS WHICH REVERSE SIGN
FROM FACTOR I TO FACTOR II

Item	Answer positively loaded on	
	I	II
Each VP exaggerates importance of his division	No	Yes
Executives feel "defeated" if losing decision	No	Yes
Chief executive gives some other concession to loser	No	Yes
Lines of authority clear	Yes	Maybe
Corporate function more important than vigorous personality	Yes	Not always
Conflicts of divisions vs. central office	Few	Common
Strong divisions get own way	Not usual	If deeply concerned
Groups within top echelon of executives	No	Some
Tension among executives over tough decisions	No	Sometimes high

TABLE 6

ITEMS RECEIVING HIGHEST LOADINGS
ON THE ROTATED MATRIX, FACTOR I'

Item	Loading
27. Estimate of top executive morale (high)	0.67
26. Tension at top (low)	0.63
14. Losing executive feels defeated (no)	0.58
28. Your satisfaction with procedure (high)	0.57
23. Conflicts between central office and divisions (rare)	0.56
7. Vice-presidents exaggerate area importance (not serious)	0.53
25. Groups at top (no)	0.44

TABLE 7

ITEMS RECEIVING HIGHEST LOADINGS
ON THE ROTATED MATRIX, FACTOR II'

Item	Loading
4. Discussion among all executives affected (yes)	0.62
10. Chief shows concern that all are satisfied (yes)	0.52
15. Chief talks with one executive at a time (no)	0.52
11. Go through channels (yes)	0.52
20. Clear lines of authority (yes)	0.51
28. Your satisfaction with procedure (high)	0.51
2. Formal routines in decision making (yes)	0.47

Factor III' has precisely two items loading singificantly—profit on sales and profit on capital. This seems to confirm the factor analyst's belief that his procedure can extract a logically independent factor even if, in the raw data, it is thoroughly mixed in with other items.

Factor IV' seems to be a "fragmentation" or decentralization dimension (Table 8). It is plausible that such a dimension would exist in a population of corporations, but puzzling that it is independent of I'.

TABLE 8
ITEMS RECEIVING HIGHEST LOADINGS
ON ROTATED MATRIX, FACTOR IV'

Item	Loading
18. Chief executive prefers division heads to be partisan of division (yes)	0.48
16. Normal operation of divisions (highly independent)	0.46
24. Ability of strong divisions to get own way (win if deeply concerned)	0.45
12. Importance attached to company tradition and past policies (not much)	0.36
22. Importance of personalities in decisions (vigorous person often wins)	0.32

Factor V' seems to represent a group of firms with highly personalized management, by which is meant that personalities may weight more heavily than organization. However this factor accounts for only 10 percent of the common variance, which fits with other reports that corporate structure and power, not personality as such, determine dm outcomes. The two remaining factors were discarded because they had few significant loadings.

DM AND CORPORATE OUTCOMES

Major goals of corporation executives, as postulated, include profits and competitive stature. The variables of profit as percentage of sales, profit as percentage of capital, and size, represent indexes of such goal achievement. Does the type of dm activity within a firm have any relevance for such indexes of success?

We may first look at some specific items from the questionnaire, and then at factor scores based on the dimensional analysis. An item analysis was carried out by taking the top third and bottom third of all firms on each of the three outcome variables, and running *t*-tests on the difference in mean response to each item.

PROFIT ON SALES. The eight items which differentiated at the 0.01 level between firms most and least profitable are shown in Table 9. Some of these would be expected (costs and marginal profits are carefully estimated, as Adam Smith would have urged). Bureaucratic routines are also high. However, there

TABLE 9
PROFIT AS PERCENTAGE ON SALES

2. Concern over formal steps in decision making at top level (regular meetings, written records, etc.) (much attention to formal routines)
3. Estimates of cost and anticipated profit to result from a decision (always carefully computed)
4. Discussion among all top executives (yes)
8. Social interaction of top executives outside office hours (for nonbusiness purposes) (frequent)
11. Concern with "going through channels" (always observe)
20. Clear lines of authority (everyone knows and respects)
21. Importance attached to company "image" as seen by public (often outweighs cost factors)
28. Your feeling of satisfaction with the way these decisions are handled (very well satisfied)

Note.—Items differentiating at 0.01 level.

TABLE 10
PROFIT AS PERCENTAGE ON CAPITAL

5. Use of a top-level policy committee or operating committee (yes)
8. Social interaction of top executives outside office hours (for nonbusiness purposes) (frequent)
9. Concern of chief executive for detailed information on which to base decision (wants substantial detail)
15. Preferred style of chief executive (talk with all interested men together)
20. Clear lines of authority (yes)
28. Your feeling of satisfaction with the way these decisions are handled (very well satisfied)

Note.—Items differentiating at 0.01 level.

is evidence of the importance of interaction variables (discussion, outside socializing) which suggests that formal structure by itself is not enough. Some observers will be amused by the fact that "company image may outweigh cost factors" leads to more profitability, not to losses. And in this context one is not sure whether executive satisfaction helps earn profits, or whether firms that earn profits have satisfied VPs.

PROFIT ON CAPITAL. Six items meet the 0.01 criterion for profit on capital. Only minor differences are reflected if we compare these (Table 10) with those in Table 9. Profit on capital may be a bit more closely related to bureaucratic routines. However, much of this apparent difference would disappear if we published the items differentiating at the 0.05 level; in general, conditions favoring profit on sales are also those which favor profit as a percentage of capital. It should be noted that ranking for profit on sales correlates 0.71 (in this sample) with ranking for profit on capital.

SIZE. Only five items distinguish the top and bottom thirds of the size distribution (Table 11). Most of these are plausible in the sense that we would expect, in a larger firm, that cost estimates would be more carefully made, that the chief would not ask for much detail, and so on.

TABLE 11

ITEMS DIFFERENTIATING SMALLER FROM
LARGER FIRMS

3. Estimates of cost and anticipated profit (carefully made)
28. Your feeling of satisfaction (not very high)
5. Use of top-level policy committee (yes, active)
9. Concern of chief with detailed information (no)
20. Clear lines of authority (yes)
27. Estimated morale at top (high)

Note.—Answer for larger firms; items significant at 0.05 level.

The data were also analyzed to see if size functioned as a moderator variable to affect profitability/dm relationships. The exploration did not confirm the tentative hypothesis that profitable management of a smaller enterprise would follow a different pattern from that in a larger firm. In caution, it should be noted that this sample of firms was limited to rather large corporations—and highly profitable ones, too—so that such differences may not have been identifiable within the sample studied.

FACTOR SCORES AND PROFITS.   Table 12 shows the factor scores on rotated factors I', II', IV', and V' for the top and bottom thirds on profit on sales.[2] Similarly, Table 13 shows the mean scores for profit on capital.

TABLE 12

FACTOR SCORES RELATED TO PROFITABILITY
ON SALES 1963

Factor	High profit rank	Low profit rank	p
I' organizational cohesiveness	27.52	31.14	0.025
II' formality in decision making	37.32	46.14	0.001
IV' decentralization	26.15	25.70	ns
V' personalized management	25.49	24.74	ns

TABLE 13

FACTOR SCORES RELATED TO PROFITABILITY
ON CAPITAL 1963

Factor	High profit rank	Low profit rank	p
I' organizational cohesiveness	27.36	30.62	0.025
II' formality in decision making	38.84	44.47	0.01
IV' decentralization	26.58	25.22	0.01
V' personalized management	26.49	24.27	0.001

[2] The factor scores used in this analysis are approximations. The heavily loaded items (shown in earlier tables) were scored for a given factor, but were not differentially weighted. The increase in precision which would have resulted would have been minimal, and the absence of a cross-validation sample argued against any need for added precision.

Decidedly surprising is the fact that all four factors are significant in Table 13 and two in Table 12. The two nonsignificant factors in Table 12 show differences in the same direction as those in 13. It will be recalled that profitability had very small loadings on all four factors after rotation. In both Tables 12 and 13, profitability is associated with greater cohesiveness, more formality (bureaucratic routines), centralization, and tendency away from personalized management. It thus seems fair to conclude that outcomes are affected by style in dm even when some effort has been made to exclude the effects of profitability statistically.

CHANGES IN PROFITABILITY.   The last, and most severe, test of any measure of real-life variables is its ability to predict outcomes at a later date. In the present instance, data were collected in the winter and spring of 1964. Since *Fortune Magazine* obligingly publishes its list of the 500 largest corporations annually, and provides rankings on profitability on sales and capital each year, we were tempted to see if our dm indexes predicted change in profitability.

Profit ranks were taken for 1958, 1963, and 1965. Change scores were computed for 1958–1963, 1958–1965, and 1963–1965. If dm indexes recorded relative managerial efficiency, perhaps they would correlate with these change scores. We therefore correlated the four factor scores with these six change scores, a total of 24 correlations. Not a single one reached the 0.05 level of significance. We must conclude that the hypothesis that dm predicts increase or decrease in profitability has been disconfirmed.

DISCUSSION

Data confirm the author's expectations—and hence, perhaps, are suspect—in that they contradict the assumptions of classical theory. Individual executives and variant forms of corporate organization do have significant effects on the dm process. Profit is a major goal but by no means the only one, and most executives agree that in some instances they reject profit in favor of some other value.

The data lend considerable support to the view of the firm as a coalition (24). Strong divisions within the company may get their way without regard to the welfare of the whole (item 24), VPs exaggerate importance of their divisions (item 7), some chief executives actually prefer this (item 18), and factionalism at the top is by no means rare (item 25). Factor IV' points to a common pattern or type of corporation which is relatively decentralized, a set of almost autonomous units under a central umbrella which may be little more than a financial holding company.

On the other hand, support is available here for the positions taken by Likert (23) and McGregor (29) in favor of participative management. Involvement of all executives (item 4) and concern by the chief that all be satisfied (item 10) are associated with high executive morale, satisfaction with the dm process, and profitability. The small decision-making echelon at the top of a large corporation has some attributes in common with the small groups studied by experimental social psychologists, and with the committees studied by Collins and Guetzkow (8). Communication patterns are important; and the efficiency of centralized structure, with concomitant loss of satisfaction for those on the periphery, seems to be involved in these results.

Leadership is also important. The distinction between "mediator" and "arbitrator" styles (45) and the contrast in the present data between bilateral talks and wider executive participation may be related to the now traditional distinction between "consideration" and "structuring." A chief executive who wants all affected executives to participate and be satisfied is certainly closer to the "consideration" pole than are those who disregard such matters.

These data do not support the hypothesis that a vigorous personality may win a decision against opposition with a stronger power base. The social role, or control of organizational power, seems generally more significant. This conclusion, of course, requires qualification. Most of the men contacted in the earlier study (45) were judged to have vigorous, aggressive personalities. It can reasonable be assumed that respondents in this survey were similar. One does not become a VP in a large American corporation by passive–dependent behavior. Personality differences on this dimension therefore may have been relatively small, thus obscuring any significant trends.

It is important to say a word about the problem of corporate goals. We must replace the concept of a single utility, profit maximization, with the concept of multiple utilities. Industrial psychologists should recognize this as an extension of the problems encountered with personnel test validation. Reliance on a single criterion measure, such as quantity of production, or incentive earnings, proved hopelessly oversimplified. According to research findings, personnel decisions should be based on multiple criteria with minimum cutting scores on a number of predictor variables rather than a single regression equation. The personnel manager wants to hire workers who will have good absentee and tardiness records, will aceept supervision, and will produce at a high level in quality and quantity. There is a point on each of these beyond which the employee is unacceptable regardless of how good he is on other aspects of performance. Thus the manager accepts a "satisficing" solution with respect to several variables.

The problem of corporate goals must be handled in the same manner. Executive decisions must balance costs against customer goodwill, efficient production against union resistance, pricing policy against political repercussions. The executive in such cases seeks a satisficing level for the other outcome measures and then attempts to maximize profit. Various executives may be more interested in maximizing for their own division than for the firm. Inevitably, optimization becomes a delusion if taken literally. Corporate dm is guided by numerous values, only one of which is profit maximization.

32

Unprogrammed Decision Making

Peer O. Soelberg
Massachusetts Institute of Technology

The paper presents a framework for describing human-problem solving and decision-making processes. The analysis departs from traditional utility and probability theory. It suggests that decision values are better described as partially ordered sets of constraining goal attributes, and that decision uncertainty may be adequately represented as ranges of "likely" values on each alternative's uncertain goal attributes. The resulting decision process model is fitted to the protocols of several points-in-time interviews of M.I.T. graduate students making job decisions. A set of key hypotheses in this fitted model are then tested on another sample of graduate students the following year. The model suggests how managers' unprogrammed decision making may be improved.

The paper summarizes findings and conclusions from the author's recent book, *A Study of Decision Making: Job Choice.* Cambridge, Mass.: Massachusetts Institute of Technology Press. Reprinted by permission from *Industrial Management Review,* VIII, No. 2 (1967), 19–29.

The research reported below has implications for management practice if one accepts the following three propositions: (1) information processing and decision making are central functions of modern organizations; (2) in order to improve management decision making it is useful to know how organizations presently make decisions;[1] (3) as long as people remain the chief instrument of corporate policy, a key feature of management decision making will be the choice processes of individual human beings.

This paper is a report on how individuals make important, difficult and highly judgmental decisions. It has become customary to contrast so-called unprogrammed with more highly programmed types of decisions (26, pp. 169–82). The latter are choices or actions that follow routinely from the decision maker's application of explicit decision rules to whatever stimulus or input data face him in his task environment.

The management of most companies' daily operations abounds with highly programmed decisions. Consider merely the routinized rules that normally guide the everyday management of inventories, production schedules, machine and manpower allocations, cost estimation, mark-up princing, etc. A famous description of highly programmed decision making is G. P. E. Clarkson's portfolio selection study, in which he demonstrated that the investment decisions made by a bank trust officer were so well programmed that his decisions could be predicted by a computer six months after his investment rules had been elicited by an interviewer and described as a computer program (7).

In contrast, this study focuses on highly unprogrammed decision making, a subject that usually gets relegated to the mystical realm of managerial "judgment."[2] Every day critical decisions are produced for which the decision maker can explicate no identifiable rules or preprogrammed decision procedure. This is not to say that a person may not be following some sort of generalized guidelines when rendering his so-called judgment. But if you asked him directly, he would insist that the unprogrammed problem confronting him had to be solved in its own unique context. Moreover, observing him solve the problem, you would find:

> The decision maker applied few special-purpose rules when arriving at his choice.
> The decision maker might not even be able to specify, a priori, the nature of an ideal solution to his problem.
> A number of the decision criteria that he wished to apply were not operational before he tackled the problem.
> Many of his choice alternatives were unknown when he started out.

---

[1] The second proposition parallels the now familiar argument regarding why engineers ought to know the science underlying their engineering rules of thumb. The less validated the engineering principles are, the more an engineer needs to understand the science on which his practice rests.

[2] It is of interest to note that, prior to Clarkson's study, the trust officer also felt that his investment decisions were highly unprogrammed and "judgmental."

Information about the alternatives' consequences and relative worth was not immediately available from the task environment.

Yet it is precisely this type of unstructured or unprogrammed decision making that forms the basis for allocating billions of dollars worth of resources in our economy every year. Ironically, until we understand the nature of such human decision processes better, our sophisticated computer technology will be of slight aid in making these types of decision. In other words, the potential pay-off to management of a scientific understanding of the economic, psychological, and sociopolitical "laws" of nonprogrammed human judgment is enormous.

AVAILABLE THEORIES

Traditional economists have long tried to get along with little more than the concepts of "utility" and "probability" for explaining unprogrammed choice among uncertain alternatives (3). A utility function is an assumed linear preference ordering of all possible combinations of the goods and services that a person values, and as such is felt by economists to be an adequate basis for describing any decision maker's value structure. Likewise, objective (or personal) distributive probability measures are felt to capture the essence of how decision makers think about the "factual" connections which they are believed to perceive between each of the available solution alternatives and the possible, but uncertain, consequences of their choosing a specific alternative (34, pp. 200–78). It does not take much observation of decision makers in action to convince oneself that the mathematical elegance of the probability–utility concepts may be a deceptive property that easily can mislead anyone interested in arriving at empirically testable descriptions of decision behavior.

The best known exception to traditional probability–utility theory appears in the work of Herbert Simon. The latter's notion of limited rationality, his "means–ends satisficing" model of information processing and his insistence on attaining a close correspondence between the intermediate outputs of his process simulation models of problem solving, and observable verbal behavior, have significantly reoriented and vitalized social science research on decision making (35, 36, 37, 40, 41).

Simon characterizes unprogrammed decision making in terms of the following three-phase process model (39).

Intelligence. Finding occasions for making a decision;
Design. Finding, inventing, developing, and analyzing alternative courses of action;
Choice. Selecting a particular course of action from those available.

In our research we used the following, slightly expanded phase structure as a framework for analyzing unprogrammed decision processes (42):

PARTICIPATION

The decision maker is somehow induced to work in a given task environment, in which he is then motivated to attain one or more nontrivial objectives.

RECOGNITION AND DEFINITION

The decision maker surveys his task environment, discovers, selects, or is somehow provided with problems, and then defines operationally the particular problem he intends to solve.[3]

UNDERSTANDING

The decision maker investigates his task environment, trying to develop an appropriate set of event classifications (ie., concepts) in order to formulate and test hypotheses about the apparent cause–effect relationships in the environment. The latter in turn suggest design operators for, or help generate, viable solution alternatives.

DESIGN AND EVALUATION

The decision maker develops or searches for alternative courses of action. Rather than estimating probabilities to attach to a set of mutually exclusive consequences associated with each alternative, the decision maker searches "within" each alternative until he feels he has enough information about each important goal attribute of that alternative, or until he exhausts his search resources. If the alternative is not rejected, the decision maker assigns some value measure, or range of possible values, to each goal attribute, but does not yet compare these values across goal attributes and alternatives.

CHOICE REDUCTION

The decision maker reduces his set of investigated viable decision alternatives to a single one, i.e., he makes a choice.

IMPLEMENTATION

The decision maker introduces and manages his solution in the task environment.[4]

---

[3] Problem recognition for the decision maker may arise from: (1) the discovery of a barrier to progress toward an objective, (2) a request from others within the organization, (3) a performance indicator dropping below a target level, (4) perception of a previously "coded problem" pattern. Problem definition for the decision maker may take these forms: (1) a description of differences between status and goal along one or more attributes, (2) a description of strategy associated with a previously encountered problem with a similar stimulus configuration, (3) a prescription of an ideal solution to the encountered problem.

[4] This phase of decision making, usually critical for practical purposes, is customarily left out of formal decision models (the consequences of which operations research consultants have had to discover the hard way).

FEEDBACK AND CONTROL

The decision maker receives and evaluates information from the task environment regarding the effects of his implemented decision, and if required, either changes his problem definition, modifies his goals or strategies, or takes appropriate follow-up action. Thus nonlinear dynamics is introduced into the decision making process (17).

This framework was our point of departure for re-examining the literature of decision making and problem solving in search of testable hypotheses that would either make operational or be incompatible with our process outline.

RESEARCH STRATEGY

In order to explore empirically the detail structure of the above generalized decision process, we should obviously have to investigate, at great length, the information processes of a large number of decision makers solving many different types of problems. The specific unprogrammed decision situation we chose to study sought to focus on decision makers who were:

1. Well trained for problem solving, as well as able and motivated to talk at some length about their information processing while they were actually engaged in producing their decisions;

2. Highly involved with the problem confronting them, it being personally important for each to reach the "right" decision;

3. Quite unfamiliar with the type of problem with which they were faced; they had encountered few such problems before and did not expect to do so again in the near furture;

4. Engaged in making the decision over a long period of time (several weeks) in order to minimize possible observer measurement effects, yet allow a number of observations to be made at different phases of the decision process;

5. Easily and inexpensively accessible to the investigator in reasonable number (in order to minimize our idiosyncratic interpretation of data from individuals, by enabling immediate cross comparison of the thinking-aloud protocols of a fairly large sample of decision makers).

The above criteria for choice of subjects were designed to help us focus on as pure and "uncontaminated" a set of decision process observations as we thought could be found in industrial practice. M.I.T. Sloan School of Management Master's and doctoral candidates, making postgraduate job decisions, fitted this bill reasonably well. In addition to satisfying our research criteria, these subjects would allow us readily to test whatever rejectable hypotheses might be generated by our initial phase of investigation, on succeeding years' samples of graduating management aspirants.

Initially our goal was to design a longitudinal (i.e., periodic "over time") questionnaire that could chart efficiently and adequately the course of our subjects' job decision processes. For that purpose we put together an elaborate set of questions, which took three or four hours every week to complete. This was clearly too long, trying as it did to cover every possible theoretical contingency. For example, one part of the questionnaire was derived from probabilistic utility theory. In this part the decision maker was asked to identify, weight, and then rate whatever goal dimensions he felt entered into his decision. It turned out that the goal weights which the subjects provided during decision making could not be trusted; the reported weights varied quite unreliably both with respect to the specific alternatives that the decision maker referred to when answering the goal weight questions, and with the temporal phasing of the decision process.

We therefore had to give up the questionnaire as a poor job. It had become obvious that unless our questionnaire was made up largely of items that were closely compatible with the manner in which the decision maker actually stored and manipulated his decision information "internally," during his own thinking about the problem, the answers he provided to our questions would, for explanatory as well as predictive purposes, be spurious at best and entirely misleading at worst.

We therefore resolved to rely, almost exclusively at first, on periodic, open-ended, and highly detailed interviews with the decision makers. These interviews provided our first insight into some rather surprising aspects of unprogrammed decision making. Preliminary analysis of nearly 100 open-ended interviews, each ranging from one-half hour to two and one-half hours in length, with 20 different decision makers over three- to five-month choice periods, provided the basis for our first Generalizable Decision Processing model (for short, GDP-I) (42). The latter was first presented at Carnegie Institute of Technology in June, 1964.

Each interview protocol was thereafter reduced to comparable format by the following three-step method: First, each protocol was transcribed verbatim and its decision phase structure, according to GDP-I, was annotated in the margin. Thereafter the relevant protocol contents were summarized in a synoptic coding language derived directly from the variables and process hypotheses of GDP-I. This provided us with decision process data that were comparable across subjects. Finally the current state of each person's decision making and his active solution alternatives at that point in time, were entered on a multidimensional, Gantt-type process chart. The standardized data produced by the last two steps of the analysis served as our basis for quantifying each protocol. Fitting these data to the hypotheses of our generalizable decision process model provided (post hoc) support for a number of GDP-I hypotheses, relating principally to the phases in our above process outline, labeled design and evaluation and choice reduction. The more interesting hypotheses that were supported by the data are summarized below:

The decision maker defines his career problem by deriving an ideal solution to it, which in turn guides his planning of a set of operational criteria for evaluating specific job alternatives.

The decision maker believes a priori that he will make his decision by weighting all relevant factors with respect to each alternative, and then "add up numbers" in order to identify the best one. In fact, he does not generally do this; and if he does, it is done *after* he has made an "implicit" selection among alternatives.

The decision maker will search in parallel for alternatives, by activating one or more "alternatives generators"—procedures which, once activated, allow him to search passively, by deciding whether or not to follow up investigating particular ones of a stream alternatives presented by his generators.

The decision maker will usually be evaluating more than one alternative at any one point in time, each evaluation consisting of a *series* of investigation and evaluation cycles.

Evaluation during the search phase takes the form of screening each alternative along a number of noncompared goal dimensions; no evidence of factor weighting is apparent at this stage.

Search will not necessarily halt as soon as the decision maker has identified an acceptable alternative (one that is not rejected by his various screening criteria); conversely, when he ends his search for new alternatives, he will usually have more than a single acceptable alternative in his "active roster."

When the subject terminates his search for new alternatives before his search resources run out, he will already have identified a favorite alternative in his roster of acceptable alternatives; this alternative (his choice candidate) can be identified by considering his primary goal attributes (usually one or two) alone.

At the point of search termination a person generally will *not* have compared his alternatives with one another, will not possess a transitive rank ordering of alternatives, and will refuse to admit that his implicit choice has been made.

Before a decision maker will recognize his choice explicitly, he will engage in a sometimes quite lengthy (two or three months) confirmation processing of his roster of acceptable alternatives; alternatives *will* get compared to each other, factor by factor.

During confirmation processing the roster of acceptable alternatives, if greater than two, quickly will be reduced to two alternatives—the choice candidate and a "confirmation candidate." If only one alternative, the choice candidate, is viable at this time, the decision maker will try to obtain another acceptable alternative (confirmation candidate) as soon as possible "in order to have something to compare it with."

Confirmation processing aims to resolve the residual uncertainties and problems connected with the choice candidate, and to arrive at a decision rule which shows unequivocally that the choice candidate dominates the confirmation candidate—Pareto dominance being the ideal goal strived for.

During confirmation processing a great deal of perceptual and interpretational distortion takes place in favor of the choice candidate, to the detriment of the confirmation candidate; goal attribute "weights" are arrived at, or changed, to fit the perceived data and the desired decision outcome.

The decision is "made" when a satisfactorily Pareto-dominant decision rule has been constructed, or when the decision maker runs up against an inescapable time deadline during confirmation processing.

LIMITED GENERALITY OF THE PROBLEM STUDIED

Though our process hypotheses of job decision making have been stated in readily generalizable form, it should be obvious that the GDP-I model, as it stands, is by no means applicable to *any* unprogrammed problem situation. Some of the characteristics limiting the problem situations to which our hypotheses should apply are the following:

The alternatives are well defined and separately identifiable. Instances of unprogrammed decision alternatives that are not well defined are common in research and development work, for example. In such a case, the problem solver must laboriously seek out at least one feasible alternative before he can begin to choose among alternatives. His prime obejctive is not to select a "best" alternative among several acceptable ones, but merely to invent a single solution that works. For GDP-I to be applicable without modification, the task environment must be susceptible to the use of "search generators," procedures that present the decision maker with streams of reasonable alternatives, thus allowing him to search passively for alternatives by screening out undersirable possibilities.

Another limitation of our job choice study as a basis for generalizing about human decision processes may derive from the interactive relationship of the job seeker versus his alternatives. The latter are by no means passive pebbles to be picked at leisure. Whether or not a job possibility is to be a viable alternative for the decision maker depends on the employer's making an offer. Nevertheless, we *could* (to preserve generality) relegate the question of whether or not an alternative is "viable" to being just another goal attribute to be evaluated by the decision maker.

A third limiting characteristic of the class of decisions described above derives from the fact that the choices we studied were individual processes, largely controlled by single persons. The social or interpersonal aspects of organizational decision making are therefore not captured by the GDP-I model. Indeed, studying and providing for the effects of interpersonal group variables represents, in the author's opinion, the single most promising direction in which the GDP-I model should be developed.

A fourth obvious limit of generalizing from any model derived from observations of job decisions derives from the definiteness, or discreteness, with which solutions to the defined problem are arrived at. In contrast, we easily can think of decision problems to which solutions are found only gradually, or for which decisions have to be made repeatedly (in which case we might expect homeostatic decision rules to develop that would help the decision maker *adapt* to a preferred alternative).

A FOLLOW-UP STUDY

Our initial study provided insight into the information processes of unprogrammed human job decisions and laid the groundwork for the design of a predictively valid questionnaire instrument for testing some of the key hypotheses in the GDP-I model. In contrast to the protocol "curve fitting" exercise reported above, our follow-up investigation was thus truly a "prediction study." All hypotheses, with process-valid measures of their variables, were specified a priori. Moreover, disregarding our personal belief in the GDP-I model, most other decision models yielded small prior likelihoods that the hypotheses we set out to test were in fact true. To most orthodox theorists our predictions would appear to be "shots in the dark."

To keep the study manageable we focused on the design, evaluation, and choice reduction phases of the decision framework outlined above. We were particularly intrigued with the confirmation process that had been identified in the interview protocols. We wanted to test our ability to identify the onset of confirmation processing, which, if it took the form we were postulating, should enable us to predict the job decisions that people would make far in advance of their admission that they had made up their minds. The following six hypotheses, therefore, are merely consecutive building blocks of one long process hypothesis, derived to establish the existence of the confirmation process. A longitudinal job choice questionnaire was designed with quadruple redundancy checks for each item, to operationalize the variables in the hypotheses. The hypotheses, derived from GDP-I, took the following form:

1. Search for new alternatives ends a significant period of time before the decision maker (referred to as Dm) is willing to admit having made his decision.

2. In observation periods prior to the end of his search for new alternatives, Dm will, more often than not, already have available one or more acceptable choice alternatives.

3. When Dm ends his search for new alternatives, he will report significant uncertainty about which alternative he will select as his choice.

4. Should Dm not have obtained a firm job offer from more than one acceptable alternative at the time of search termination, he will have tried hard, and will usually have obtained, at least one other acceptable offer (according to GDP-I, in order to have something with which to compare his choice candidate) by the time he is ready to announce his decision.

5. When Dm ends his search for new alternatives, his favorite alternative can be identified by asking him a set of simple questions. When Dm's subsequent confirmation processing of alternatives ends, i.e., at the time of choice announcement, his decision will be to select that alternative.

6. Effective or perceptive dissonance reduction, in the form of a "spreading apart" of Dm's liking for his accepted versus rejected alternatives, will *not* generally be observed after choice has been announced.

Those familiar with aspiration-level, sequential search choice models may recall that according to this theory the first four hypotheses should not be reasonable. Similarly, according to cognitive dissonance reduction theory, the sixth proposition would be disturbing.

RESULTS OF THE FOLLOW-UP STUDY

Below we can no more than summarize the findings pertaining to the above six hypotheses, based on data from 256 questionnaire response sets provided by 32 members of the 1965 graduating class of M.I.T. Sloan School of Management Master's and doctoral candidates. Each decision maker in the sample provided answers to eight biweekly questionnaires over the period in which he made his job decision. (For a small number of persons—a different subset with respect to each hypothesis—the path of their decision processes, as recorded by the questionnaires, provided inadequate data with which to test a given hypothesis. Thus each total reported below may add to less than 32.)

HYPOTHESIS 1

Twenty-seven of 31 Dms (87 percent) terminated the search for new alternatives 10 days or more before the date on which they reported having made their decision. Fifteen of 31 Dms terminated search three weeks or more before choice was made.

HYPOTHESIS 2

Using a highly conservative measure of an alternative's acceptability, 17 of 24 Dms (74 percent) reported having available one or more acceptable alternatives two weeks or more before they terminated search for new alternatives.

HYPOTHESIS 3

The average personal probability distribution of 28 Dms reporting, at time of search termination, regarding the likelihood that they would choose either the alternatives that we independently had identified as being their "choice candidate," their second most preferred alternative, and "all other alternatives," was respectively: (0.29, 0.24, 0.47). In other words, great uncertainty was expressed by Dms at the time of search termination regarding which alternative they were to choose.

HYPOTHESIS 4

Thirteen of 16 Dms (81 percent) who did not have, or had not been promised, an offer from more than one alternative at time of search termination, did report having at least one such other offer in hand before they made their decision.

HYPOTHESIS 5

Twenty-five and one-half of 29 Dms (87 percent) (one-half since one Dm could reasonably be classified either way) eventually selected as their final decision that alternative which at the time of search termination, one to 12 weeks earlier (median of three weeks), had independently been identified as their favorite alternative, i.e., choice candidate.

HYPOTHESIS 6

No Dm reported a consistent dissonance reduction "spreading apart" of his liking for accepted versus rejected alternatives over the periods of observation immediately following decision commitment. However, two Dms exhibited what we might call latent dissonance reduction, i.e., one with took effect two or more weeks *after* Dm had committed himself to the decision. Nine of 26 Dms (35 percent) showed an *initial* "spreading apart" effect of their relative liking for alternatives, a gap which, however, was reduced again in subsequent periods of observation. Ten of 26 Dms (38 percent) exhibited no change whatever in their reported liking differentials in the observation periods following choice. The remaining five exhibited postchoice dissonance *expansion*, i.e., they narrowed down their liking differential between alternatives after they had made their decision.

In summary, the six decision process hypotheses described above were supported rather convincingly by the data in our longitudinal prediction study.

CHIEF IMPLICATIONS FOR A THEORY

Below are some of our study's more central implications for decision theory, which may not be obvious from the above, severely summarized report of our findings.

First, scalar utility theory is a poor way of representing the structure of human values. Decision value attributes are usually multidimensional; they are not compared or substituted for each other during choice. No stable utility weighting function can be elicited from a decision maker prior to his selection of a preferred alternative, nor do such weights appear to enter into each person's decision processing. His noncomparison of goal attributes during the alternatives' screening and selection phase also obviates the decision maker's need for, and the reasonableness of our postulating the existence of, a multidimensional utility indifference map.

Second, probability theory, either in its objective frequency or personal estimate Bayesian form, does not provide adequate representation of how our decision makers perceived and dealt with uncertainty during their unprogrammed decision making. The "probability" indices with which our highly trained decision makers provided us were neither additive nor cardinally scaled. It seems that a decision maker does not normally think of his choice alternatives in terms of multiple consequences, each of which is then seen to depend conditionally on a specific reaction to his decision by the task environment. Instead he thinks of each choice alternative in terms of a set of noncomparable goal attributes. Uncertainty in this context is more appropriately represented in terms of equally likely *ranges* of a specific alternative's rating along its various uncertain goal attributes. In other words, decision uncertainty rarely takes the form of a "pure" or probability-risk *consequence* uncertainty. More commonly, uncertainty—a nonadditive quantity—is associated with the decision maker's personal evaluation of an alternative's uncertain attributes.

The mathematics of how most decision makers compare such multiple-attribute uncertainty-ranged alternatives is quite simple, but unfortunately would take too much space to illustrate here (42). By the same token of limited rationality, one might argue that it is the simplicity of Dm's information processing computations that effectively prevents him from operating with the m conditional probability distributions for each alternative which, according to distributive probability theory, the decision maker *should* be associating with each multiconsequence, multivalued alternative.

Third, search for alternatives is a parallel process, i.e., several potentially acceptable alternatives are considered by the decision maker at one time. This contrasts with the hypothesis of sequential search aspiration level models. In addition, a subject's evaluation of an alternative is a multistage affair; at each step new information is collected and evaluated about a subset of attributes of the given alternative. In other words, search *within* alternatives is as important a process for us to understand formally as the traditionally described search *across* alternatives.

During the search phase the decision maker does not view his evaluation of alternatives as final. Alternatives that fall short on important goal attributes are rejected immediately. But acceptable alternatives are merely put into the decision maker's "active roster," with little or no systematic comparison performed across the different acceptable alternatives, until the person is ready to make his final decision. In other words, the decision maker may well continue to search for new alternatives, even though he has already discovered a perfectly satisfactory one (one that was not rejected by any of his important goal attributes).

Fourth, making the final decision, what we have called decision confirmation, takes place *after* the decision maker has terminated search for new alternatives. This appears to be a highly involved and affectively a most painful process for a person to engage in. This is the period during which the decision maker has to reject alternatives that seem perfectly satisfactory to him, in some ways perhaps better than the one he finally ends up choosing. It is at this point that the decision maker is forced systematically to compare patently noncomparable alternatives.

It is a major thesis of this study that persons generally solve this problem in the simplest manner conceivable, by not entering into this difficult period of decision making until one of the alternatives can be identified as an implicit "favorite." In other words, decision making during its confirmation phase is an *exercise in prejudice*, of making sure that one's implicit favorite will indeed be the "right" choice. This proposition gives the key to a surprising degree of predictability in decision making, demonstrated with the data of hypothesis 5 above, in which we predicted 87 percent of the career jobs taken two to eight weeks before the decision makers would admit that they had reached a decision.

It is not feasible here to go into detail regarding the nature of confirmation processing (42) yet the following are some of its more outstanding characteristics.

The criteria that the decision maker uses for identifying his favorite alternative are very few; not more than one or two of what we have called *prime* goal attributes account for most of the observed variance.

The decision maker's comparison among alternatives quickly reduces to a pro–con argument between two, and only two alternatives (see hypothesis 4), the object of the decision maker being to bring his perception of the facts, and his evaluation of goal attributes, into line with his predisposition that the preferred choice candidate dominates his second-best alternative (which we call the confirmation candidate) on all important goal attributes, secondary and primary.

The decision maker finally makes his decision when he has constructed a satisfactory decision rule—a goal weighting function, if you please—that enables him to *explain* the Pareto dominance of his choice candidate (unless, of course, the decision maker is forced by some deadline to make his decision before that time. If so, he will still choose his choice candidate, but with much more expressed uncertainty about the "rightness" of his decision).

Fifth, dissonance reduction, in the sense that it has been described by Leon Festinger (14), must be viewed as a conditional phenomenon. In a loose sense, confirmation processing might be viewed as part of the decision maker's "dissonance reduction" process. But according to Festinger, the onset of dissonance reduction awaits the decision maker's *commitment* to this choice, which in our data is synonymous with the point of the person's choice announcement. In this study dissonance reduction after that point in time was observed in only 35 percent of the cases; in all of them the effect dissipated during subsequent periods of observations.

We propose as a testable explanation of our observations: Postchoice dissonance reduction will be observed only when the person, at the time of choice commitment, is not satisfied with his confirmation decision rule—i.e., with the intellectual rationale for why he chose the way he did. Thus dissonance reduction constitutes an *affective* compensation on the part of the decision maker for his lack of a socially acceptable, cognitive justification for his behavior.

This hypothesis also explains the observed second-order dissonance reduction effect: With time we expect all men to be able to invent better and better rationales for why they behaved as they did. Correspondingly, we should observe that any initial affective (dissonance reduction) compensation, with which a person first may be protecting his decision, will be dissolved over time as his intellectual argument gets better.

IMPLICATIONS FOR MANAGEMENT PRACTICE

Let us conclude by considering briefly some lessons of these findings for management. The reader can surely think of some other implications; nevertheless, here are a few obvious ones:

1. Our generalizable decision process model (GDP-I) should help a manager to recognize when others have reached an implicit decision, i.e., when they are merely confirming their favorite alternative. Such knowledge should enable managers not to waste time or resources or lose face by remaining party to a choice process that for most purposes has already been closed. This lesson should be particularly useful in situations where a manager or his company has been cast in the role of "confirmation candidate" by the decision maker.[5]

2. The existence of a confirmation process that goes into effect prior to public choice commitment emphasizes the desirability of getting one's alternatives into the decision process early. On bids for government research and development contracts, for example, Edward Roberts has uncovered evidence that a bidding company needs to get in there well before the official invitation to bid on a contract has left the government agency—that at this time one can predict with disturbing success which firm will get the contract, simply by looking at the order of names on the list of those invited to bid (33).

3. The confirmation process also suggests a way of manipulating decision deadlines in a manager's favor. If he has evidence that his company happens to be his adversary's favorite alternative, the manager can safely clinch the deal by imposing a stringent deadline on decision making, trust to dissonance reduction to carry the day, and save himself time, needless anxiety, and the risk of that rare alternative arriving on the decision maker's horizon in time to upset the apple cart.

4. The existence of the confirmation process also explains the often observed asymmetry of administrative decision making. Once made, decisions are usually very hard to unmake, or to get remade. A most obvious explanation of this is that a manager balks at having to go through all the pain of changing his tailor-made decision rule to fit a new pair of alternatives. (That *might* sound too much like "rationalizing," and thus go against the grain of men who like to think of

---

[5] As the IMR was going to press the author received the following letter from the chairman of the department of management of a large eastern university.

It may interest you to know that we used the results of your study in our faculty recruiting this year. If a prospective faculty member selects you as number one, there is little you have to do. If he selects you as number two, however, there is little you can do to change this. I found that people who had us as number one on their lists were quite willing to provide a number of clues to the effect that they would be willing to join us. On the other hand, those who saw fit to join our faculty, were, in general, quite noncommittal about their intentions. It is on this basis that I made my predictions as to whether we were number one or at some lower ranking in the applicant's mind. This model worked perfectly.

themselves as orderly, rational decision makers.) Besides, the decision rule offers ready arguments, in m dimensions, why few alternatives can be expected to be as good as the chosen one. And these arguments get themselves strengthened and elaborated as time passes—partly through the self-fulfilling prophecy which will bias all future interactions between a manager and his rejected versus accepted alternatives.

The implication for action is that a manager must "watch" his own subsequent interactions with a rejected alternative, such as a subordinate he has not promoted, in order to avoid setting up self-fulfilling chains of interactions between himself and the rejectee. Similarly, the latter should take the manager's postchoice prejudices somewhat "philosophically," and not see the latter's behaviors as necessarily reflecting a personalized form of beastliness.

5. Our description of the nature of the confirmation process also offers a complementary explanation of the observed difficulty of changing people's cognitive attitudes. As soon as the manager is successful in winning a battle on one secondary point in the decision maker's rule, the latter will quickly mend his breach, either by pooh-poohing that particular goal attribute, or by countering with a compensating argument along some other goal dimension. Only if the manager can zero in on the decision maker's *primary* goal attributes (often carried around in a person's head quite inaccessibly, in the form of some uncommunicable existentialist "feel" for the problem situation), can the manager hope to change a person's decision behavior. Even then, the manager faces the difficult task of demonstrating convincingly to his opponent that this person's old favorite is indeed dominated by the manager's own favorite alternative. (This proposition might, incidentally, help explain why public debates are so ineffective as a means of changing anyone's political allegiance or voting behavior.)

IMPROVEMENT OF MANAGEMENT DECISION

This study has implications for how management decision making might be improved. Three of these implications are given below:

1. A manager should work on integrating his formal models of rational decision making with his intuitive, judgmental, common-sense manner of solving choice problems and seek to adapt the former to fit the latter, rather than submit to a bastardization of his intuition in the name of some modern mathematical technique. Mechanical aids to management decision, like computer-based management information systems, will (and should) be resisted to the extent that their structure is incompatible either with the manner in which a manager codes relevant information for his own use, or the manner in which the manager intuitively feels that information should be reduced for arriving at a decision.

To be more specific, a formal goal attribute weighting scheme, an imposed set of operating decision rules, or an explicit framework for estimating and operating with personal probabilities, will be circumvented by reasonable managers, we hypothesize, to the extent that the area in which the technique is to be applied has not been carefully chosen to match the structure of the decision maker's intuitive (culturally learned) process of working through multivalued and uncertain decision alternatives. This is *not* to say, however, that a manager should not try to educate his personal decision-making judgment, although the question of which are the more effective techniques for accomplishing this remains a hotly debated issue in our schools of management. We would recommend that a major part of the manager's initial effort in this regard be directed toward a more explicit understanding of his personal processes of exercising managerial judgment in a variety of decision situations.

2. One way that a manager might start training himself to make better decisions would be to become more aware of his personal predispositions and prejudices (i.e., of his prime goals) when operating in different task contexts. Rapid feedback regarding his apparent decision behavior from people whom the manager trusts and respects should be of much aid in that regard. The attempt to avoid forming opinions early about complex sets of alternatives seems from anecdotal evidence to create an uncomfortable state of tension in most people. Perhaps the manager might try devising private "holding" heuristics to allow "sufficient" unbiased information about his available alternatives to be collected, and to prevent him from modifying his decision criteria until he has reached an explicit decision to start doing so. (A counterargument, which we do not advocate, is that decision making and action taking under time pressure are so difficult to get accomplished under any circumstances, that a manager needs to use all the short-cuts and tension-reducing rules of thumb that he can devise, just to make a decision, even if in some cases such heuristics will lead him to very biased solutions.)

3. Our theory leads us to expect that different managers will exhibit different degrees of the tendency to commit themselves to alternatives early in the decision process. Perhaps such a predisposition could be effectively counteracted simply by pointing out to a manager that this is the way he tends to operate. But perhaps the characteristic is sufficiently difficult or expensive to change that we should consider developing standard laboratory testing problems to help screen out of critical managerial positions those persons who too early, on too meager evidence, jump to conclusions about solutions to complex problems.

33

Who Are the
Risk-Takers in Decision Making?

Yeshayahu Rim
Technion-Israel Institute of Technology

Reprinted by permission from the March–April 1966 issue of *Personnel Administration*, copyright 1966, Society for Personnel Administration, 485–87, National Press Building, 14th and F Streets, N. W., Washington, D. C. 2004.

Lord Adrian, in his Jephcott Lecture on "Priorities in Medical Responsibility," says.

> The mind of a committee is often swayed by circumstances and motives which have no business to move it, our likes and dislikes of our colleagues, our anxiety to be finished, or our fear of showing our ignorance. . . . Yet the group can often discover some rules which satisfy our conscience, often because there are less anxious members who can lead us, and the decision we reach in the end will help society to form its own judgments of what ought to be done to preserve its future (1).

Professor Jones wrote that

> Many decisions are taken by open committees; and when time and security considerations allow, this is a reasonable method, even though it sometimes produces a result less sensible than would have been arrived at by any single member of the committee. The railway gauge of Ireland, for example, seems to have been settled in this manner—the average of all other national gauges was taken, and the result was 5 feet 3 inches; the Irish thus had a new gauge and their rolling stock was not interchangeable with that of any other railway. The common agreement necessary for members of a committee to come to a conclusion often does not go far enough, especially in those important decisions where an element of uncertainty and risk has to be accepted (21).

Over the last few years some research has been undertaken to find out more about the constitutions under which decisions involving risk are taken by individuals and groups.

Stoner's discovery (46) that group decisions are more risky than individual decisions is, as Marquis (27) comments,

> contrary to the common belief that committees are typically cautious, compromising and conservative, and that authority or decisions in a business enterprise should, therefore, be given to a responsible individual rather than to a group.

Marquis (27) confirmed the basic finding that individuals tend to shift their decision preferences after group discussion in the direction of greater risk taking. The results of his experiment also indicate that the shift in the risky direction is characteristic not only of unanimous group decisions, but also of personal decisions made by designated leaders and of individual decisions made by members who had no assigned responsibility.

Marquis concludes that the group decision itself is not the essential feature that results in the personal shifts toward greater risk taking, since this also occurred when discussion alone resulted in such shifts.

> The best lead at the moment is that the members whose initial decisions were the more risky are disproportionately more influential. But why? Are they more respected? Do they have more information? Do they talk more? Are they more persistent, or more argumentative? Or are the more cautious members more susceptible to influence from others?

This paper reports on some relations between personality characteristics of group members and their risk-taking behavior. Specifically, we examine whether certain variables of personality and interpersonal behavior are related to risk taking before and after group discussion, and to shifts in risk taking due to group discussion. In addition, we attempt to find whether certain personality traits distinguish those who influence others to take greater risks and those who are influenced to take such risks.

PROCEDURE:
MEASURES OF RISK-TAKING BEHAVIOR

Six out of the 12 problems developed by Wallach and Kogan (47), some or all of them also used by Stoner and Marquis, were used to obtain measures of risk taking.

A typical problem reads like this:

Mr. A., an electrical engineer who is married and has one child, has been working for a large electronics corporation since graduating from college five years ago. He is assured of a lifetime job with a modest, though adequate salary, and liberal pension benefits upon retirement. On the other hand, it is very unlikely that his salary will increase much before he retires. While attending a convention, Mr. A. is offered a job with a small, newly founded company with a highly uncertain future. The new job would pay more to start and would offer the possibility of a share in the ownership if the company survived the competition of the larger firms.

Imagine that you are advising Mr. A. Listed below are several probabilities or odds of the new company's proving financially sound.

Please check the *lowest* probability that you would consider acceptable to make it worthwhile for Mr. A. to take the new job.

    1 in 10
    2 in 10
    3 in 10
    4 in 10
    5 in 10
    6 in 10
    7 in 10
    8 in 10
    9 in 10

Mr. A. should not take the new job, no matter what the probabilities.

A subject's score of risk taking consisted of the sum of the lowest probability designated by him on all six problems.

The subjects recorded their individual decisions in the six decision problems (initial socre). Then the group was asked to discuss each problem in turn, arrive at a unanimous decision, and record it on different copies of the same set of problems (group-decision score). The groups had no leader or chairman, and the experimenter did not interfere in the lively discussions. After the recording of the unanimous decision, each subject recorded again, on a third copy of the set of problems, his private personal decision ("after"-score).

Having found out what kind of subjects change more, it was of interest to find what kind of subjects bring about the change in the risky direction; in other words, whose initial scores are nearest to the final group-decision scores? It may be assumed that it is these subjects who bring about the shift, i.e., who persuade the other group members to adopt risk-taking behavior.

Difference scores were therefore calculated, reflecting the extent to which any subject's initial score differed from the group-decision score (D_1). The lower this score, the nearer is the subject's initial score to the final group-decision score.

It was also thought of interest to compare the group-decision score with every subject's after-score, in order to find out to what extent different subjects are influenced by the group decision or stick to their initial score. It will be recalled that this after-score was recorded by S as his personal attitude after he knew the group decision. Accordingly, difference scores (D_2) were calculated, reflecting the extent to which any subject's after-score differed from the group-decision score.

PROCEDURE: SUBJECTS

Over 750 subjects, in 150 groups of five, four, or three subjects each, took part in the investigations reported. They were students, teachers, school principals, nurses, foremen, army officers, members of a kibbutz, etc.

The first investigation was concerned with finding out the relationship between neuroticism and extroversion, two important dimensions of personality, and risk taking. The results showed that highly extroverted subjects tended to be riskier than others in their initial decisions, and also to be influential in the group situation. They persuaded the other group members to shift their decisions in the risky direction. In addition, it was found that subjects scoring high on neuroticism were the least influential.

The second study's aim was to investigate the relationship between risk taking and the need for achievement. The latter was measured by the subjects' ranking of eight job incentives, in terms of how important each incentive would be for him in selecting a job and feeling well on the job. The four incentives defining the need for achievement were:

1. Opportunity to learn new skills.
2. Freedom to assume responsibility.
3. Good prospects for advancement.
4. Recognition from supervisors for initiative.

The results showed that those subjects for whom the above four incentives were most important tended to be both riskier in their initial decisions as individuals and influential in the group situation.

The next investigation was concerned with the relationship between social attitudes and decisions involving risk.

As Eysenck (12) showed, social attitudes can be regarded as being determined by two factors. One of these factors is the well-known Radicalism–Conservatism continuum (*R*-factor). The other, which is quite independent of the first, was called Tough-mindedness versus Tender-mindedness (*T*-factor). Detailed experimental analysis disclosed that while the *R*-factor could truly be called a major dimension of social attitudes, the *T*-factor appeared essentially as a projection onto the field of social attitudes of certain fundamental personality traits. Eysenck showed that there is a close relationship between tough-mindedness and extroversion on the one hand, and between tender-mindedness and introversion on the other. It was also found that there was a distinct tendency for though-mindedness to be associated with both aggression and dominance.

We found that those high on tough-mindedness and average on radicalism–conservatism were riskier than others in their initial decisions; those influential in the group situation, however, were above average on both radicalism and tender-mindedness.

In the fourth study, the relationship between dominant interests and risk-taking was investigated. Allport–Vernon–Lindzey's Study of Values (2) was administered; this questionnaire estimates the relative prominence of six basic interests or motives in personality: the theoretical, economic, aesthetic, social, political, and religious.

The results indicate that individuals whose theoretical, economic, and political interests are high tend to be riskier than others in their initial decisions, and that those influential in the group situation, i.e., bringing about the shift in the risky direction of those more cautious, have high theoretical interests, above-average economic, and low social interests.

Another investigation focused on the relationship between risk taking and tolerance vs. intolerance of ambiguity. Budner (5) defined intolerance of ambiguity as the tendency to perceive, i.e., to interpret ambiguous situations as a source of threat. Ambiguous situations are identified as situations characterized by novelty, complexity, or insolubility.

Our results indicate that those individuals who are tolerant of ambiguity tend to be riskier in their initial decisions, and also to be influential in the group situation.

Next, we were concerned with interpersonal values. We used Gordon's Survey of Interpersonal Values (19), which was designed to measure certain critical values involving the individual's relationships to other people or their relationship to him. The six values measured were support, conformity, recognition, independence, benevolence, and leadership.

It was found that those whose highest values were recognition and leadership tend to be riskier than others in their initial decisions and are the influencers in the group discussion, leading the other group members' shift in the risky direction.

The scales of recognition and leadership are defined by Gordon as follows:

Recognition: Being looked up to and admired, being considered important, attracting favorable notice, achieving recognition.

Leadership: Being in charge of other people, having authority over others, being in a position of leadership or power.

The following investigation studied the relation between risk taking and Machiavellianism, a disposition to manipulate interpersonal relationships.

The Machiavellianism scale consists of statements and paraphrases taken from Machiavelli's books, *The Prince* and *The Discourses*, and was constructed recently by Christie (6).

The results showed that high intial risk is taken by subjects scoring at both extremes of the scale, i.e., very high or very low. However, only the high-scoring subjects, i.e., those holding the Machiavellian attitude, are influential in the group situation.

Another series of experiments was devoted to the relation between inner–other-directedness and risk taking. Riesman's theory of social character (32) asserts that, in general, human beings can be grouped into three major types of social character. Tradition-directed people are oriented in the traditional ways of their forefathers; inner-directed people turn to their own inner values and standards for guidance in their behavior, while other-directed persons depend upon the people around them to give direction to their actions.

Two measures of inner–other-directedness were used: a questionnaire developed by Kassarjian (22) and the ranking of adjectives "according to their importance for you," some of which are characteristic of inner-directedness, others of other-directedness.

The adjectives decisive, forceful, imaginative, independent, and self-confident were assumed to be characteristic of inner-directedness.

The results showed that the inner-directed subjects tended to take high initial risks and to influence others to follow them in this direction.

The last investigation was concerned with leadership attitudes. The two leadership dimensions consideration and structure, as measured by Fleishman's Leadership Opinion Questionnaire (16) are defined as follows:

Structure (S): Reflects the extent to which an individual is likely to define and structure his own role and those of his subordinates toward goal attainment. A high score on this dimension characterizes individuals who play a more active role in directing group activities through planning, communicating information, scheduling, trying out new ideas, etc.

Consideration (C): Reflects the extent to which an individual is likely to have relationships characterized by mutual trust, respect for subordinates' ideas, and consideration of their feelings. A high score is indicative of a climate of good rapport and two-way communication. A low score indicates the supervisor is likely to be more impersonal in his relations with group members.

The subjects taking part in this experiment were head nurses (women) and foremen and supervisors in industry (men).

The results showed that those subjects scoring high on both structure and consideration tended to take high initial risks and to influence their colleagues in the group situation.

SUMMARY

In summary, then, it seems that the risk-taking individual who is disproportionately influential in a group situation is an extrovert, has a high need for achievement, is tolerant of ambiguity, and is above average in radicalism and tendermindedness; his theoretical, economic, and political interests are high, as are his interpersonal values of leadership and recognition; he is good at manipulating interpersonal relations; he is inner-directed, and high in consideration and structure.

Questioning
the Managerial Implications of
Making Decisions

1. Would you expect different results from those reported by Stagner if his questionnaire had been administered, not to executives, but to a comparable set of middle managers? How so?

2. How does Soelberg's model of unprogrammed decision making modify the classical problem-solving approach of defining the problem, searching for alternative solutions, selecting a solution, and evaluating the solution, etc.?

3. Accepting Rim's summary statement, in what areas can the risk-taking manager be expected to make his greatest contribution to the organization? To what extent might the manifestation of his personal characteristics create difficulties for the organization?

4. Evaluate this statement: The forces that eventually mold the most effective decisions are initially unpredictable and nonrational.

References

1. Lord Adrian, "Priorities in Medical Responsibility," *Proceedings of the Royal Society,* LVI, No. 7 (1963).

2. Allport, G. W., *Study of Values, Manual of Directions*, rev. ed. Boston: Houghton Mifflin Company, 1951.

3. Arrow, K. J., "Utility, Attitudes, Choices: A Review Note," *Econometrica,* (1958), 1–23.

4. Bowman, E. H., "Management Decision Making: Some Research," *Industrial Management Review*, III, No. 1 (1961), 56–63.

5. Budner, S., "Intolerance of Ambiguity as a Personality Variable," *Journal of Personality*, XXX, No. 1 (1962).

6. Christie, R., and R. K. Merton, "Procedures for the Sociology Study of the Value Climate of Medical Schools, Part II," *Journal of Medical Education*, XVIII (1958), 124–53.

7. Clarkson, G. P. E., *Portfolio Selection: A Simulation of Trust Investment.* Englewood Cliffs, N. J.: Prentice-Hall, Inc., 1962.

8. Collins, B. E., and H. Guetzkow, *A Social Psychology of Group Processes for Decision Making.* New York: John Wiley & Sons, Inc., 1964.

9. Cyert, R. M., W. R. Dill, and J. G. March, "The Role of Expectations in Business Decision Making," *Administrative Science Quarterly*, III (1958), 307–40.

10. ——, H. A. Simon, and D. B. Trow, "Observation of a Business Decision," *Journal of Business*, XXIX (1956), 237–48.

11. Dalton, M., *Men Who Manage.* New York: John Wiley & Sons, Inc., 1959.

12. Eysenck, H. J., *The Psychology of Politics.* London: Routledge & Kegan Paul, Ltd., 1954.

13. Feldman, J., and H. E. Kantner, "Organizational Decision Making," in *Handbook of Organizations*, ed. J. G. March. Skokie, Ill.: Rand McNally & Co., 1965.

14. Festinger, L., *Conflict, Choice, and Dissonance Reduction.* Stanford University Press, 1964.

15. Fisk, G., ed., *The Psychology of Management Decision*. Lund, Sweden: CWK Gleerup Publishers, 1967.

16. Fleishman, E. A., *Manual for Administering the Leadership Opinion Questionnaire*. Chicago: Science Research Associates, 1960.

17. Forrester, J. A., *Industrial Dynamics*. New York: John Wiley & Sons, Inc., 1961.

18. "The *Fortune* Directory: The 500 Largest U. S. Industrial Corporations," *Fortune*, LXIII, No. 1 (1963), 177–96.

19. Gordon, L. V., *Manual for Survey of Interpersonal Values*. Chicago: Science Research Associated, Inc., 1960.

20. Harsanyi, J. C., "Measurement of Social Power, Opportunity Costs, and the Theory of Two-Person Bargaining Games," *Behavioral Science*, VII (1962), 67–80.

21. Jones, R. V., "Science and the State," *Nature*, CC (1963), 13.

22. Kassarjian, W. M., "A Study of Riesman's Theory of Social Character," *Sociometry*, XXV (1962), 213–30.

23. Likert, R., *The Human Organization: Its Management and Value*. New York: McGraw-Hill Book Company, 1967.

24. March, J. G., "The Business Firm as a Political Coalition," *Journal of Politics*, XXIV (1962), 662–78.

25. ———, *Handbook of Organizations*. Skokie, Ill.: Rand McNally & Co., 1965.

26. ———, and H. A. Simon, *Organizations*. New York: John Wiley & Sons, Inc., 1958.

27. Marquis, D. G., "Individual Responsibility and Group Decisions Involving Risk," *Industrial Management Review*, (1962), 8–23.

28. Marschak, J., and R. Radner, "The Firm as a Team," *Econometrica*, XXII (1954), 523 (Abstract).

29. McGregor, D. M., *The Human Side of Enterprise*. New York: McGraw-Hill Book Company, 1960.

30. Mueller, E., A. Wilken, and M. Wood, *Location Decisions and Industrial Mobility in Michigan*. Ann Arbor: University of Michigan, Institute for Social Research, 1961.

31. *Poor's Register of Corporations, Directors, and Executives*. New York: Standard & Poor Corporation, 1963.

32. Riesman, D., *The Lonely Crowd*. New Haven, Conn.: Yale University Press, 1950.

33. Roberts, E. B., "Questioning the Cost Effectiveness of the R & D Procurement Process," in *Reseach Program Effectiveness*, eds. M. Yovits *et al*. New York: Gordon & Breach, Science Publishers, Inc., 1966.

34. Rothenberg, J. F., *The Measurement of Social Welfare*. Englewood Cliffs, N. J.: Prentice-Hall, Inc., 1961.

35. Simon, H. A., *Administrative Behavior*. New York: The Macmillan Co., 1947.

36. ——, *Models of Man.* New York: John Wiley & Sons, Inc., 1957.

37. ——, "Theories of Decision Making in Economics and Behavioral Science," *American Economic Review*, IL (1959), 253–83.

38. ——, *The New Science of Management Decision.* New York: Harper & Row, Publishers, 1960.

39. ——, *The New Science of Management Decision*, rev. ed. New York: Harper & Row, Publishers, 1966.

40. ——, *The Shape of Automation for Men and Management.* New York: Harper & Row, Publishers, 1965.

41. ——, A. Newell, and J. C. Shaw, "Elements of a Theory of Human Problem Solving," *Psychological Review*, LXV (1958), 151–66.

42. Soelberg, P., *A Study of Decision Making: Job Choice.* Cambridge, Mass.: MIT Press, 1966.

43. ——, "Structure of Individual Goals: Implications for Organizations Theory," in *The Psychology of Management Decision*, ed. G. Fisk. Lund, Sweden: CWK Gleerup Publishers, 1967.

44. Stagner, R., *The Psychology of Industrial Conflict.* New York: John Wiley & Sons, Inc., 1956.

45. ——, "Resolving Top-Level Managerial Disagreements," *Business Topics*, XIII (1965), 15–22.

46. Stoner, J. A. F., "Comparison of Individual and Group Decisions Involving Risk" (Master's thesis, Massachusetts Institute of Technology, Sloan School of Industrial Management, 1961).

47. Wallach, M. S., and N. Kogan, "Sex Differences and Judgment Processes," *Journal of Personality*, XXVII (1959), 555–64.

48. White, H. C., "Management Conflict and Sociometric Structure," *American Journal of Sociology*, XLVII (1961), 185–99.

49. Zalkind, S. S., and T. W. Costello, "Perception: Some Recent Research and Implications for Administration," *Administrative Science Quarterly*, VII (1962), 218–35.

Resolving Conflict

Conflict in formal organizations can be depicted as a non-zero sum game permitting competition and cooperation for which there are acceptable and nonacceptable solutions. In this case, the presence of mutual trust is critical. But often the conflict that arises between organizational departments, between union and management, or in the line–staff relationship is, unfortunately, a zero-sum game. That is, if one side wins, the other loses. A common pattern of highly predictable outcomes dominates such controversy.

When union and management play a zero-sum game, each has certain well-known competitive strategies. But when negotiations can produce some satisfaction to both sides, a variety of collaborative arrangements is possible.

The experimental study by Porat points out that cultural differences can explain differences in approaches to labor negotiations in an organization. His analysis identifies the variant approaches utilized by British and American managers to resolve conflict arising out of the bargaining situation.

Seiler takes advantage of the case study method to examine the nature of interdepartmental conflict. He concludes that one way to deal with ambiguity and conflicting points of view arising between groups of people within an organization is to involve the members in a critical examination and clarification of organizational goals.

The handling of differences between individuals is the focus of the paper by Mann. He offers six specific steps in dealing with the essence of conflict—the breakdown of communications. His approach stresses continual restatement of the feelings and ideas of each party in elimination of interpersonal misunderstandings.

34

Planning and Role Assignment in the Study of Conflict Resolution

Avner M. Porat
University of Rochester

A negotiation exercise in which two samples of managers, one from the United States (N = 54) and one from the United Kingdom (N = 118) was used to present cross-cultural behavioral differences in a conflict resolution situation. The three areas examined were the effect of the issues involved in the union management of exercises, the role assignment of the bargainer, and the impact of the preplanned strategy on the negotiation. Results show that differences in the approach of both samples to resolving the conflict were related to economic, cultural, and social differences. Further differences were related to the familiarity of the participant with his assigned role.

This work was supported by Contract NONR 624(14), Group Psychology Branch, Office of Naval Research, and the Ford Foundation. Many contributed to the various phases of data collection and analysis. The data were drawn from the data bank of the International Research Groups on Management (IRGOM) at the Management Research Center, University of Rochester, and were collected by members of IRGOM in the United States and United Kingdom. Susan McMeekin, William Whittaker, and Brian Giles helped in various stages of the analysis. Reprinted by permission from Technical Report 28, Contract Number N00014–67–A–0398–002, NR 171–029, University of Rochester, 1969.

447

Members of today's organizations are frequently called upon to participate in activities aimed at resolving conflict. Whether he is in a business, government, social, or other type of organization, various situations call for the organization's member to negotiate with other persons within or outside his organization in order to reduce or eliminate an existing or potential conflict. Further, in many cases, the conflict can be classified as an intergroup conflict where the individual acts as a representative of a given group, negotiating with representatives of other groups. Examples are labor versus management, staff versus line, sales versus production departments, legislative versus executive branches, etc.

In a paper summarizing the results of an earlier version of the same simulation used in this paper, Bass (2) reviewed the contributions made by social scientists representing various disciplines to the study and understanding of conflict resolution under bargaining situations. According to Bass, economists, interested in the exchange of value, have pursued rational and deductive formulations of the problems with heavy emphasis on the mathematics of game theory (6, 16, 18). Political scientists, such as Mack and Snyder (14), have constructed generalizations from surveys of historical material. Psychologists have focused on such factors as the socio-emotional aspect of in-group/out-group identification (4, 22) and the implications of reinforcement theory on resolving the conflict (15). In the present study, several of the above disciplines were utilized to explore cultural differences in approaching conflict-bargaining situations. The author used a management–union bargaining simulation to examine cross-cultural differences between participants in a conflict resolution simulation and their experiences in adjusting to imposed organizational and goal constraints.

ELEMENTS OF CONFLICT AND NEGOTIATIONS

In cases where conflict has to be resolved through reaching a negotiated agreement, the situation contains a number of common rational and emotional elements. Often the conflicting parties share a common fate. They must resolve their conflict to avoid mutual social and economic losses or in other cases to survive and prosper (2). This is especially true if the parties are engaged in a non-zero sum situation, in which both lose if each seeks only to maximize its own gain at the expense of the other side. Yet, both can gain when they compromise at a less than maximum return for each.

Not every non-zero sum situation will produce the cooperative behavior needed for mutual rewards. Often competitive strategies develop to the detriment of all concerned (19). Only if the parties can develop mutual trust through appropriate communication, and if they are oriented toward each other's welfare, can a cooperative solution be developed (10). The conditions which affect the emergence of this needed trust are influenced by the goals of the person(s) participating in the effort to resolve the conflict. His goals, in turn, are influenced by the constraints which are dictated by organizational considerations. These can be divided into three fundamental types.

The issues involved. The bargainer will be influenced by the specific issues under negotiation. The content of the conflict and the impact of its continuation or elimination on the goals and objectives of his organization will considerably affect the degree of cooperation he will exhibit in resolving the conflict and the final form of resolution. The influence of the issues' content increases when they are of qualitative types. When this is the case, preferences, ideologies, and perceptions increase the difficulty of resolving conflict. For example, an issue of adding union representatives to the board of directors of a company in union–labor negotiations can be much more difficult to agree on than the question of raising wages by "x" cents per hour.

The bargainer's function. By representing an existing unit, the bargainer necessarily fulfills a given role. His behavior in this role is influenced by his knowledge or perspective of what the role is supposed to represent. The same person will usually act differently if he is representing his department in an interdepartmental conflict compared to the way he would behave in representing his organization toward the outside world. In other words, the role he assumes and his goals will vary according to the function he is representing in a given conflict situation.

The preplanned strategy. A person representing a group is bound by the goals, plans, and guidelines laid down by the group or parts of it. The strategy the bargainer has planned or had planned for him will influence his behavior during the negotiation period with the other party. Prenegotiation planning of strategy will affect at least his initial behavior during the meeting with the other party. Once the session is under way, the outcomes will be heavily influenced by his flexibility to adjust to developing situations, or in other words, his commitment or lack of it to the initial strategy (2).

All the above can be further influenced by the personal traits of the persons involved in the negotiations and their cultural affiliation. The latter will often influence their perceptions of the situation and their attitudes toward the priorities and needs in planning their strategy and resolving the conflict (12).

METHOD

Employing two samples of managers, from the U.S. and England, a non-zero sum union-company bargaining game originated by Campbell (8) and modified by Bass (3) was employed to examine the three differential effects of: the issues involved, role behavior and the planning of the strategy, and the interaction of these variables with the cultural affiliation of the participants.

THE PROBLEM

Exercise Negotiations (3) requires participants to engage in a management–labor negotiation session. Half of the group takes the role of the union and the other half the role of company negotiators. The following initial statement is given to all participants:

> The purpose of the exercise is to give you an opportunity to practice and see how well you do in negotiating with another party about a set of contractual issues.

All participants receive written background information about a small textile firm, and its union, concluding with the paragraph:

> The three-year contract has now expired. Negotiations broke down in the final week with both sides adamant in their positions. The only agreement reached was that each side would select a new bargaining agent to represent it, scheduled to meet today (the first day of strike) in an attempt to reach a quick solution and avoid a long strike.

CONTRACT ISSUES

There are five issues for bargaining:

1. a hospital and medical plan
2. wages
3. a sliding scale for increases in cost of living
4. night shift differential
5. vacation pay.

Each participant receives a graphic statement of the current union and company positions and the financial cost to the company in thousands of dollars for a two-year period. A summary of the entire union and company positions and the possible in-between settlement points are shown in Chart 1. On each issue final settlement was allowed only on one of the prespecified points on the chart.

ASSIGNMENT AND DATA COLLECTION

Participants then read an independent community survey concerning the five issues which had to be negotiated. The survey shows at what level other companies in the particular community and industry have settled the same issues. In addition, union representatives receive a more detailed, one-page memorandum explaining the assignment as a union representative, ending with the statement:

> You are to do the best possible job you can to get a good settlement of the contract for labor. Union members were dissatisfied with the last contract three years ago and there is serious danger of division in the ranks of the union if a more satisfactory contract is not achieved in these negotiations. It is essential to labor, however, that the contract be settled in this bargaining period. We realize that this involves compromises on both sides, and you are appointed to carry out binding negotiations for us. Remember, your job is to reach a settlement, one that is good for labor, in this negotiating period.

Company representatives receive a similar one-page company memorandum explaining the company position.

After reading the instructions, the company and union representatives meet

CHART 1
ISSUES FOR BARGAINING

1. Hospital and Medical Plan:

   Past Contract: Company paid 1/4 cost, employee paid remaining 3/4

   UNION: demanded company pay full cost

   COMPANY: refused to pay more than 1/4

	proportion of company payment				
COMPANY	1/4	2/4	3/4	4/4	UNION
Total Money Value per 2 years	0	6,000	12,000	18,000	

---

2. Wages:

   Past Contract: $1.94 per hour

   UNION: demanded an increase of 16 cents per hour

   COMPANY: refused outright

	cents increase per hour										
COMPANY	00	02	04	06	08	10	12	14	16	18	UNION
	0	8000	16000	24000	32000	40000	48000	56000	64000	72000	

   Value per 2 years

---

3. Sliding Pay Scale to Conform to Cost of Living:

   Past Contract: pay scale is fixed through the term of the contract

   UNION: demanded pay increases in proportion to increases in the cost of living

   COMPANY: rejected outright

COMPANY	NO	YES	UNION
Total Money Value per 2 years	0	20,000	

---

4. Night Shift Differential:

   Past Contract: an extra 5 cents per hour is paid for night work

   UNION: demands a 5 cent increase to 10 cents per hour

   COMPANY: rejected

	cents increase per hour						
COMPANY	0	1	2	3	4	5	UNION
	0	1,000	2,000	3,000	4,000	5,000	

   Value per 2 years

---

5. Vacation Pay:

   Past Contract: 2 weeks paid vacation for all workers with one year service

   UNION: wants 3 weeks paid vacation for workers with 10 years service

   COMPANY: rejected

	2 wks. for 1 yrs. service	3 wks. for 20 yrs. service	3 wks. for 15 yrs. service	3 wks for 10 yrs. service	
COMPANY					UNION
Total money Value per 2 years	0	500	2,000	5,000	

451

separately in teams of five or six and map out their respective bargaining strategies for 30 minutes. Each team member of a company, or union team, records his own team strategy, which he helped develop. Then the union and management teams pair off so that each union man meets with one company man to negotiate individually the five issues. According to the rules, each ten minutes of bargaining costs the company $10,000 in profits and the workers $10,000 in lost financial benefits. The cost attached to time for both parties makes this a non-zero sum game. If all five issues are not settled within the 50-minute negotiating limit, the strike goes on, a deadlock is declared, and a $100,000 penalty is imposed on each side. Once an S leaves the team strategy planning session and starts the individual negotiating, he is given no opportunity to consult with other team members, but he is free to refer to the team-written plan.

From the data supplied from each negotiating team, the total costs of settlement to the company (total gain for workers), total costs of negotiations to company and union, total cost to company (cost of settlement plus cost of negotiations), and net gain or loss for workers (amount of settlement minus cost of negotiating) are computed. Each member of the negotiating team then answers six questions concerning his planned and actual strategy.

SUBJECTS

Data on 54 managers from the United States and 118 managers from the United Kingdom were drawn from the files of the International Data Bank on Management Behavior at the Management Research Center, University of Rochester. The data in the data bank were collected by members of the International Research Groups on Management (IRGOM) as part of an extended effort to accumulate cross-cultural data on management behavior around the world. Ss of the present report were all middle-level managers participating in a manager's workshop in their respective countries. The activity was part of the scheduled training program and occurred prior to the assignment of readings or discussions of conflict resolution and/or negotiation problems. The U.S. managers were, on the average, five years older than the British subjects (41.8 years of average age versus 36.2). Also, the U.S. Ss had slightly more full-time working experience than their British counterparts (19.9 years versus 17.9) and a longer time period spent with the same company (12.7 years versus 10.5 years). However, none of these differences was statistically significant.

RESULTS

RESOLVING THE CONFLICT

Under the conditions of the simulation, each side had to make decisions on its competitive versus cooperative approach to the negotiation. The competitive aspect was emphasized by the company's need to hold concessions to a minimum to retain a competitive position in the textile industry while the union, on the other hand, had to obtain a wage and benefit settlement equal to or better than the community average to satisfy and consolidate its membership. The need to cooperate with each other was emphasized by the interests of both parties to reach an agreement quickly, thereby reducing the penalty associated with lengthy negotiations. A cost of $1000 per minute of negotiating time was equally taxing to both the union and the company, until the agreement was reached on all five issues and the contract signed by both parties.

The results presented in Table 1 show that the average British negotiating pair was more successful in balancing the competitive and cooperative motives. The mean cost of contracts signed by the negotiators in both samples is somewhat higher than would be a midway ($60,000) settlement between initial union and management positions, or the average contract attained by the unions in the competing plants, as was indicated in the background information given to the Ss. At the same time, while the mean U.S. contract was $3500 higher than the mean settlement in a British contract, the difference was not statistically significant.

TABLE 1

RESULTS OF THE NEGOTIATION

Issue	Mean of Possible Settlement	Mean of Actual Settlement			Percent of Total Package		
		U.S.	U.K.	Test of Significance	U.S.	U.K.	Test of Significance
No. of Pairs		27	59		27	59	
1. Health plan	$9,000	$10,222	$8,276	*	15.2	13.0	‡
2. Wages	36,000	37,630	32,690	*	56.0	51.2	‡
3. Sliding pay scale	10,000	14,074	17,586	*	20.9	27.6	‡
4. Night shift differential	2,500	3,481	3,810		5.2	6.0	
5. Vacation pay	2,500	1,852	1,405		2.8	2.2	
a. Total settlement (1–5)	60,000	67,259	63,767		100.0	100.0	
b. Total cost of negotiation	25,000	35,593	23,103	†			
c. Cost to company (a + b)	85,000	102,852	83,466	†			
d. Gain to union (a − b)	35,000	31,667	37,259				

*Statistically significant difference of means at $\alpha = 0.05$ level.
†Statistically significant difference of means at $\alpha = 0.01$ level.
‡Statistically significant difference of proportions at $\alpha = 0.01$ level.

The average British pair reached an agreement in significantly less time than the average American pair. It took the average British pair only 23 minutes to reach a settlement, compared to an average of close to 36 minutes for an American pair. This resulted in a combined settlement and strike cost which represented a reduced layout for the British company representative compared to his American counterpart ($83,466 versus $102,852) and a higher net gain for the union ($37,259 and $31,667, respectively).

Significant differences existed with regard to the settling of individual contract items in both samples. In the American sample, a higher dollar settlement was reached with regard to the hourly pay, giving the workers an average wage increase of close to $5000 more than their British counterparts. The U.S. contracts also represented a higher allocation to company contribution to "hospital and medical plan" costs. At the same time, the British agreements showed a higher settlement on the items of "sliding pay scale to conform to cost of living" and on payment for "night shift differential."

THE BARGAINER'S FUNCTION

A frequent drawback preventing quick conflict resolution in a face-to-face bargaining situation is the different goals and objectives of the negotiators. Their individual goals can be influenced by their group affiliation, their previous experience with similar situations, and their perceptions of the task at hand. In the present study all Ss were managers, with half of them assigned a familiar organizational affiliation; i.e., the role of a manager representing his company, and the second half assigned a "stranger" organizational affiliation; i.e., that of a union representative. The results indicate that the role assignment has considerable effect on the formation of different goals, which in turn affected the outcomes of the negotiation.

Each S was asked to indicate what was his primary goal when he set up his strategy. The results for the three major goals, covering 85 percent of the goals indicated, are presented in Table 2, with significant perceived differences occurring within samples, due to the difference in roles, and between the two samples. Settling close to the community average was a goal sought by British union

TABLE 2
Ss' RESPONSES INDICATING THEIR PRIMARY GOAL
IN SETTING UP BARGAINING STRATEGY
(in Percentage)

	N	Settle Close to Community Average		Avoid Continuing Strike		Minimize Company's Cost or Maximize Union's Gains	
		Union	Management	Union	Management	Union	Management
U.K.	116	44.8	11.9	5.2	27.2	34.5	52.5
U.S.	54	40.7	37.0	3.7	29.5	25.9	25.9
Total	170	43.5	19.8	4.7	26.7	31.8	44.2

** Z-test shows statistically significant difference at $\alpha = 0.01$.
* Z-test shows statistically significant difference at $\alpha = 0.05$.

representatives and American union and management but not by the British managers.

The biggest differences between union and company representatives existed in the British sample, with the majority of management people choosing as the primary goal minimization of company cost, while the largest group of union representatives chose to settle close to the community average. In the British sample a statistically significant difference existed between the union and management representatives for the three major goals. In the American sample a significant difference existed only with regard to the goal of strike avoidance, where 26 percent of the company representatives chose it as a major goal compared to 4 percent of the union representatives. Approximately the same percentage of union and management representatives chose each of the two other goals.

THE PREPLANNED STRATEGY

In conducting the negotiations, the average negotiating team in both samples felt that their actual strategy, compared to their prebargaining planned strategy, was more similar than different (Table 3). This was a result of a fairly high level

TABLE 3
DIFFERENCES IN STRATEGY PLAN

	$N = \dfrac{\text{U.K.}}{118}$	$N = \dfrac{\text{U.S.}}{54}$	Significant Difference Level, α
Approach Best Describing Strategy (percentage distribution)			
Package deal	65.3	55.6	
Trading off items	16.9	33.3	0.05
One issue at a time	0.8	5.6	
Setting maximum and minimum Limits for negotiating each issue	14.4	3.7	0.05
Other	2.6	1.8	
Initial Bargaining Approach (percentage distribution)			
Start with most important issue	33.9	20.4	
Start with an unimportant issue	15.3	14.8	
Start by trying to find out opponents' goals	42.4	61.1	0.05
Other	8.4	3.7	
Difference of Actual Strategy from Planned one (Mean) (1 = exactly the same; 9 = completely different)	3.46	3.21	
Degree of Commitment to Prebargaining Strategy Plan (Mean) (1 = not at all committed; 9 = completely committed)	6.79	6.72	

of commitment to their planned strategy as expressed by the participants after the sessions were completed (6.79 on a scale of 1 to 9 in the British sample and 6.72 in the American sample). Yet in both samples, the union representatives felt more committed to their group strategy than did the company representatives.

Differences existed between the two samples with respect to their strategy approach as developed in the planning groups prior to the beginning of the bargaining. The groups were free to develop any strategy they chose, and, in both samples, the majority preferred to develop a strategy for achieving a package deal. The package deal approach was more popular in the British sample, where 65 percent used the term to describe their strategy compared to 55 percent in the U.S. sample. Proportionally, twice as many Americans (33 percent of sample compared to 17 percent in the British sample) described their strategy in terms of trading off items. When this is combined with the strategy of settling one issue at a time, we notice that close to 40 percent in the American sample were involved in negotiating one or two individual items at a time. A relatively large group in the British sample (14 percent) chose to approach the problem by setting maximum and minimum limits to each issue; thereby further increasing the difference between the British and American approaches.

Our final area of inquiry concerned the initial bargaining approach, as we assumed that this was the period when the bargainers were under the heaviest influence of the group planning session. Over 60 percent of the American Ss began by trying to find out their opponents' goals, compared to 42 percent in the British sample. At the same time close to half of the British negotiators started immediately with the issues to be negotiated, with over two-thirds of this group starting with the most important issues (Table 3). In other words, a higher percentage of British managers preferred to get down immediately to the task at hand and took the straightforward approach which, again, might explain some of the differences in the length of the negotiating time.

DISCUSSION

Differences in the negotiation results between the two samples cannot be solely attributed to the differences in perceived commitment to the strategies. However, behaviorally, one could infer that the American were more committed to their own strategy groups than were the British. To this end, Bass (2) indicated that American managers, planning in groups, were more committed to their plan and ended up with a higher proportion of deadlocks than did those who planned their strategy individually. Further, the results raise the hypothesis that, in the U.S., bargaining has become more ritualistic and an end in itself than would be the case in Britain.

Several of the variations can be at least partially explained by differences of social emphasis, resulting from economic and historical reasons. Compared to the U.S., the U.K. is more advanced in social welfare, with the majority of health benefits covered by the state. In the U.S., in the last decade, the trend has been for employers to cover an increasing proportion of the health benefits, such as Blue Cross and Blue Shield. This can explain the difference in the amounts assigned to the health plan.

With regard to salary, the negotiators, in both samples, might have been influenced by the general salary level in each country. According to a United Nations survey (24), the hourly average earnings of a manufacturing worker in the U.S. are almost 50 percent higher than those of his British counterpart. At the same time, the consumer price index has been rising almost twice as fast in Britain in the last five years as compared to the U.S. (24), making the British negotiator more sensitive to protecting the worker from inflation and increasing the allocation to a sliding pay scale.

With regard to perceived functions and goals of the bargainer as a company or union representative, the differences between the two samples can be attributed to the different stages of union development in both cultures. The leadership of the unions in the U.S. has become almost as professional since World War II as are the managers of large corporations. Many managers in American business view labor negotiations as similar in nature to any other negotiations between two companies and set their goals accordingly. There is also less difference perceived in social values between union and management executives in the U.S. and, therefore, there is little need for a manager to change his major goal when he assumes the role of a union representative. In Britain, on the other hand, despite nationalization of several large industries, there seems still to exist a social difference between union and management which results in different perceptions of roles. The British managers perceived that, as union representatives, their main role was to achieve a settlement close to the community average while the company representatives were primarily interested in minimizing their companies' expenses.

In both samples, management representatives were more concerned with avoidance of strikes than were union representatives, pointing to the feeling that strikes, in general, are more costly to the company as a whole than to a union member who can seek another job or who is supported by strike funds. In other words, the problem of resource allocation is heavily influenced by well-rooted social belief in both parties' being in a constant conflict and having different goals.

Overall, in both samples, Ss representing the union perceived themselves as more committed to their group strategy than their counterparts in the company's role. One explanation for this result might be the unfamiliarity with the role environment for a practicing manager who is assigned the role of a union representative. The Ss in the management role might have felt more at ease in their role and, therefore, less bound by the group decision. In other words, group dependence might be negatively correlated with previous experience with a given situation or role.

Finally, the results raise the question to what degree the popularity of given management concepts influence the strategy and behavior of persons in a conflict resolution situation. Today's American managers are influenced by the teaching of new decision theories that emphasize the sequential approach (9, 13, 23), while their British counterparts are leaning toward the "classical" approaches to decision making which emphasize a complete review of the total problem before a specific decision is made. If this assumption is valid, it can explain the much larger proportion of the American sample, relative to the U.K. sample, choosing to solve one issue at a time. It might also be one of the reasons for the prolonged negotiation time in the U.S. sample, since a large group in this sample was involved in a sequential approach to bargaining rather than an overall solving of the conflict. No attempt was made to resolve this question in the present paper; rather, the question is posed as an interesting take-off hypothesis for further research.

CONCLUSIONS

The results presented here point out that the cultural differences between the two samples can explain, at least in part, different approaches to conflict resolution within an organizational system. The participants in the simulation were influenced by their cultural, social, and economic beackground in settling the various issues within the package. Further differences existed in the selection and formulation of the bargaining strategies which, in turn, influenced the outcomes of the conflict. Work is presently under way to analyze similar data obtained from other countries to see if more refined variables can be isolated and their effects on conflict resolution be established.

A final word should be directed toward the method used for data collection. Evidence was presented to the effect that the assignment of an unfamiliar role, i.e., the role of a union negotiator, to a group of Ss can result in some significant differences between them and those playing a role that they associate with in everyday life, i.e., the role of management for our Ss. At the same time, reports from persons who observed the simulation in action, as well as from participants, indicated that there existed a high level of involvement on the part of the Ss in both roles. This is at least partially achieved by the similarity of the problem to real-life experiences faced by managers who need to resolve conflict in many areas of work. Therefore, the simulation also provides important training experience, in addition to collection of research data, and makes it possible to reach some point on the line between a laboratory experiment and real-life situations, with all the pros and cons that such an approach involves.

35

Diagnosing
Interdepartmental Conflict

John A. Seiler
Harvard Business School

The cases cited in this article have been taken from the case and project research files of the Harvard Business School and are reproduced by permission of the President and Fellows of Harvard College. Reprinted by permission from *Harvard Business Review*, September–October 1963, 121–32. © 1963 by the President and Fellows of Harvard College; all rights reserved.

"Purchasing and production are always at each other's throats. I don't know why they can't get along better."

"If the way research and engineering work together were typical for all departments in our company, our executive vice president would be out of a job. Somehow those guys are able to work out their disagreements."

"Sales and production just refuse to deal with each other. Every time a decision is needed, someone higher up has to do a lot of hand-holding or head-knocking. Why won't they bargain?"

If you live in an "interdepartmental world" and particularly if you have some responsibility for what goes on between departments, chances are the phrases, "I don't know why they . . . ," "Somehow those guys . . . ," and "Why won't they . . . ?" in the statements just quoted are not strangers to you. Businessmen are frequently perplexed by the way groups deal with one another. There is certainly cause for wonderment. Interdepartmental problems not only are complicated, but they have received relatively little attention from those not directly engaged in coping with them. Perhaps if we take a look from the firing line at some typical interdepartmental conflicts, we may be able to isolate those aspects which are harmful to productivity and those which represent stimulating and productive competition.

TRADITIONAL EXPLANATIONS

Why are some interdepartmental relationships successful and others not? Managers typically find themselves advancing one or the other of these explanations:

One popular opinion is the "personality clash" theory, which holds that stubborn prejudices and differences in ingrained personal styles (none of which are actuated by organizational influences) are behind nonproductive relations. As compelling as this explanation often seems to be, it fails to account for the fact that we seldom, if ever, encounter a group composed of people with identical or even closely similar personalities. Lacking evidence of such group identity, it is difficult to imagine an intergroup conflict between two "group personalities." This reasoning also fails to account for interdepartmental relations which are characterized by high productivity *and* some degree of personal antagonism. While personality differences undoubtedly play a part, they alone comprise an inadequate explanation of productive and nonproductive relations.

Another view holds that failure in interdepartmental relations is the result of "conflicting ideas." This theory asserts that nonproductive relations occur between groups whose respective memberships are so different in terms of skills, training, job activities, personal aspirations, and so on that they cannot possibly find a common area in which to communicate. While this explanation seems to apply to some nonproductive relations, it is not unheard of to find an advanced research group which works quite effectively with a nontechnical, highly consumer-oriented sales group. Seemingly, at least, groups can differ on many counts without a breakdown occurring in their relations. Furthermore, it is not unusual to find groups with remarkably similar points of view which seem to go out of their way to make trouble for each other. Something in addition to different points of view must be playing a part in forming the character of these relationships.

A third popular explanation for nonproductivity puts the blame on competition between groups for authority, power, and influence. Breakdowns occur because each department operates from an entrenched position which, if compromised, will bring the group nothing but defeat and loss of influence. Many nonproductive relationships seem to display characteristics of this kind. But if this theory is to be sufficient unto itself, the only productive relationship would be one in which either or both of the groups had no desire or opportunity for influence over the other. Under these conditions, passivity would seem to be a requirement for productivity. Yet the most highly productive relations appear to take place between aggressive, confident, and high-achievement departments. Apparently other determinants, in addition to competition for prestige and power, must be operating to make interdepartmental relations successful or unsuccessful.

While no one of these theories is a sufficient explanation of why group relationships turn out the way they do, each has enough sense behind it to make it attractive. Consequently, what is needed is some way of pulling them together into a new and more useful way of thinking about interdepartmental conflicts. This is what I propose to do in this article.

BALANCE OF ENERGY

Fundamental to understanding why some relationships are productive and others less so is a recognition that people have limited energies. When a multitude of demands are made on us, we naturally assign priorities to them. If the demands for organizationally productive work take second place to other demands, then the organization loses out. Demands on departments can also be viewed in this way. If a department's energies are consumed by plottings of defense and attack, little time will be left for devotion to more fruitful business. Consequently, departments, too, must assign priorities to demands on their energy.

Some demands, of course, are more crucial than others. For example, when a car is heading directly at us, our total mental, physical, and emotional energy is absorbed by the endeavor to escape collision. There is little or no energy left for other pursuits. Similarly, when in business we find ourselves truly challenged by a difficult task, most of our capacity for attention tends to be absorbed in that one endeavor. In most cases, however, we are not so singly motivated but, instead, are caught between complex and conflicting demands on our energies to which we must assign some sort of priority.

GROUP CONTROL

The setting of priorities by groups is not much different. Groups are, after all, only interdependent individuals who keep their group membership because it is valuable to them. The uniqueness of a group, that which makes it more than the simple addition of its members' wishes and actions, lies in its ability to motivate member behavior toward goals which are attractive to the entire group but which are not attainable by any member alone. Primary among these goals, of course, and basic to group life in general, is the satisfaction of a person's need to belong to something. But groups provide more than simple social satisfaction to their members. They also provide protection from other groups and individuals. They contain power which can be used to gain liberties, self-respect, and prestige for their members. In return for these benefits, the member submits to group discipline.

When a group's existence is threatened by such changes as a formal reorganization which will disperse its members, by rumors of layoff or firing, or by technical change disrupting the relationships among members, the full energy of the group is mobilized. There is a tightening of member discipline, particularly centering on the activities most likely to thwart any alarming changes. On such occasions, the only "work" done is that which protects the group from jeopardy. On the other hand, when groups do not fear for their survival, but see before them a challenging opportunity to work together toward an end of positive value to the group, all their energies become absorbed by the project they are working on.

Energies freed from defense will seek outlets in activities which strengthen the group's ability to survive in the long run and which add zest to the life of its members. If the work formally available to the group is dull and lacking in challenge (or if other obstacles such as restrictive supervisory actions or lack of member skills get in the way), activity is likely to be predominantly social in character. If the work is challenging, and obstacles are not present to hinder its meeting the challenge, the group is likely to find its formal assignment a satisfying outlet for the application of its energy.

With these ideas about available group energy in mind, let us look at four case situations to see how these ideas can be used fruitfully. Each of these real-life examples represents a particular way in which group energies become absorbed as they try to work with another group.

I.
PRODUCTIVE FOCUS ON TASK

Company A developed and manufactured ethical pharmaceuticals. The activities required to transform a product idea into a marketable item were performed in sequence by subunits of the research, engineering, and production departments. An idea would first take form in a research department test tube.

It would then be evaluated by research chemists and chemical engineers in the pilot plant. Next, new process equipment would be designed by mechanical engineers and job designs laid out around the equipment by industrial engineers. Actual plant construction and placement of equipment were accomplished by construction engineers, and, finally, production responsibility was assumed by production chemists. The members of these formal units agreed that research had the highest prestige of all the work groups and that the relative prestige of the other units declined in the order in which each became actively involved in the new product sequence.

The engineering and research departments were housed in their own buildings some distance from each other and from the plant. The chemical engineers worked most closely with the research chemists—sharing many ideas with them because of the similarity in their training, their work, and their aspirations. The chemical engineers also worked closely with the mechanical engineers in the pilot plant and in process equipment design. The chemical and mechanical groups shared a number of ideas, though the mechanical engineers and research chemists thought quite differently about most things. The mechanical engineers worked closely with the industrial and construction engineers, who in turn were in close contact with factory personnel. These four latter groups shared similarities in background and in ideas.

Company A had an outstanding reputation for important production innovations and rapid development of ideas into mass-production items. Nevertheless, there was frequent argument among research, engineering, and production as to who should take responsibility for the product at what point in the development sequence. Engineering wanted control at the pilot plant. Production wanted control from the time the product entered its physical domain. Research wanted control, as one of its members put it, "until the actual factory yield reaches the theoretical yield."

The boundaries of control were actually somewhat difficult to pinpoint. Research was in command until factory problems seriously affecting quality were solved, except that research decisions were subject to engineering veto (in turn subject to top-management arbitration) anywhere beyond the pilot plant. In spite of continual argument about control jurisdiction, there were few engineering vetoes that ever reached arbitration.

The physical, mental, and emotional energies of these departments appeared to be devoted to the work at hand to a very high degree. While not absent from their relationships, conflicts took the form of tension between the inherently opposing values of quality and economy. The result was a competitive balance between the extremes of both. Why was conflict not destructive in this situation? There are basically three reasons:

1. Each of the three departments represented a social unit in which members could find not only satisfaction for their needs to belong, but also job interest, promotion opportunity, and so on. No one of these departments suffered from internal fragmentation.

2. At each point of significant interdepartmental contact, the members of

the interacting groups agreed on certain important ideas as to how work should be accomplished. Wherever technical interdependence required intergroup contact, the groups tended to view each other and their common work with a markedly similar appreciation.

3. The hierarchy of authority among the departments was identical to the informally agreed-upon prestige hierarchy among these departments. This hierarchy was determined by the technical work limits set by one department for another, and by the initiation of activity by one department for another. The work done by research, for example, limited what the chemical engineers could work on but, at the same time, was the impetus which set the chemical engineers to work on each new product. The same was true of relationships down through the development sequence.

Very simply, then, when a man (or a group) told another what to do and when to do it, he did so as a member of a group of superior prestige, as agreed on by both groups. We might say that the orders which passed from one group to another were "legitimate," since most workers feel that it is legitimate in our society for a person of higher prestige to direct the activities of someone with less prestige, while it is illegitimate for the opposite to occur.

Thus, in the Company A situation, departmental energies were not consumed by internal activities designed to make the department a socially satisfactory place to live nor by struggles to communicate across abysses of viewpoint differences. Because authority was being exerted by socially legitimate persons and groups, little if any energy was wasted in jockeying for prestige positions. There was an abundance of group energy left for work and for contest over the organizationally desirable balance of quality and economy. Furthermore, since the work itself was intrinsically rewarding and since supervisory practices encouraged work satisfactions, Company A's interdepartmental relations were highly productive, despite continual battles over quality versus economy.

The three elements—internal social stability, external value sharing, and legitimate authority hierarchy—comprise a triumvirate of measures which indicate the extent to which departmental energy will tend to be freed for productive work. These factors can be thought of as minimum requirements for interdepartmental effectiveness. For, in their absence, it is highly unlikely that either intrinsically interesting work or encouragement from supervision will achieve much in the way of productivity increases.

II.
WASTEFUL CONFLICTS OF IDEAS

Company B designed, manufactured, and sold precision electronic instruments to scientific laboratories and industrial firms. The sales department was composed primarily of long-service, socially prestigious men (including the president) who had been instrumental in establishing what was referred to as a "family atmosphere" in the company. The sales department was the center of the dominant ideas in the company about how employees should behave.

During the manpower disruptions of World War II, the production department attracted a group of men who had started as workmen and had worked their way up the management ladder, often by transferring from one company to another. These men were perceived by the rest of the company (and even by themselves) as "rough diamonds." Their ideas about personal comportment were very different from those held dear in the sales department.

At the close of the war, certain irregularities in the behavior of top-level, old-line production management were laid bare by the rough diamonds. When the culprits were discharged, they left the rough diamonds in control of production.

At the same time, however, certain checks and balances—in reaction to the ease with which the wartime irregularities were committed—were built into the organization at the expense of production's jurisdiction over such functions as purchasing and stock control. These restrictions were highly resented by the new production regime which felt it was being punished by the "family" school, some of whose members (the discharged old-line production men) were the real culprits. This "injustice" widened an already considerable gap between sales's and production's views of "how things ought to be."

Sales and production came in contact primarily when the quarterly production schedule was being set and whenever sales initiated changes in the schedule within quarters. On these occasions tempers flared, walkouts occurred, and the services of the vice president–controller were required for mediation. Sales's concern for meeting customers' special desires was pitted against production's concern for uninterrupted runs of each instrument in the company's catalog.

Unlike the Company A situation where a balance was struck between quality and economy, in Company B the contest between customer satisfaction and economical production resulted in a breakdown of relations. Furthermore, the production department became an armed camp in which each junior member of the group was strictly warned against dealing with the sales department lest the latter influence production activities at less than the top hierarchical level of the department.

To make sure that sales could not infiltrate production, top production executives allowed the bulk of production's members little influence over internal production affairs. For its part, sales spent a great deal of time devising power plays to force production to deviate from set schedules. Top sales officials wasted hours personally exerting their authority in production offices to obtain schedule deviations. Retributions in the form of ultimatums and unprofitable scheduling "trades" of one instrument for another resulted. Sales's two subsections, scientific and industrial, vied with each other to see who could get the best production deal in the schedule, often at each other's and the company's expense.

In Company B, while the work itself was challenging and although supervision circumscribed that interest only to a modest degree (by removing purchasing and stock control from production's jurisdiction), relationships were relatively nonproductive between sales and production. Minimal standards of performance were met only by the intervention of a vice president in routine sales–production affairs. Energies were not absorbed in an effort to right an illegitimate authority sequence, for sales's commands were legitimated by sales's superior prestige, but in dealing with the breach of communication between two groups whose backgrounds and ideas were diametrically opposed in many important ways.

In turn, each department's internal relations, used as a means of combating the outgroup, absorbed a great deal of effort. Production kept a tight hold on its members, which caused subordinate frustrations, while sales was constantly patching the relations between its own two subgroups. Any work accomplished between the two groups was based on the question, "Will this effort strengthen our position in the battle with the other department?" Almost never could the two groups be said to agree that their combined efforts were satisfying to both, or even to one, of the parties.

The nonproductive conflict between these two departments can be viewed as the result of energies consumed by attempts to right an irreconcilably imbalanced trade (11). By sales's values, sales's ideas should have dominated, tempered only by "practical" economic considerations. (In other words, production should have provided information on which sales could base its decisions.)

By production's values, however, production ideas received too little weight, if, indeed, they were accorded any weight at all. Production believed that sales information should be added to production information and the decision should then be a cooperative one. For sales to achieve its idea of balance, production had to forfeit its idea of balance, and vice versa. So the conflict was irreconcilable. As the mathematicians put it, the two departments were playing a zero-sum game. One's gain was the other's loss, because their different ideas of what was "right" made it so.

III.
ILLEGITIMATE AUTHORITY CONFLICTS

Company B's production department was engaged in another, but quite different, cross-departmental relationship of nonproductive character. The production engineering department (formally considered a peer of the production department) took research designs and translated them into parts lists, production drawings, and fabrication and assembly specifications, and in addition processed engineering change orders (ECOs). Much of production's work—both its content and its timing—depended on production engineering's efforts, since Company B's product designs were constantly changing.

Thus, production engineering was seen by production as telling production what to do and when to do it. On the other hand, production engineering was composed of men with skills no greater than, in fact, quite similar to, those possessed by production members. Production felt itself capable of performing not only production engineering's tasks but the more important tasks of job design and methods work which were within production's jurisdiction but outside production engineering's.

The two departments had almost no face-to-face contact. Communication between them was conducted through memos carried by lowly messengers. Production managers spent an inordinate amount of time checking for consistency among the various items produced by production engineering. When errors were discovered (as they seldom were), a cry of victory would ring out across the production office. A messenger would quickly be dispatched to carry the offending material back to production engineering, amply armed with a message elaborately outlining the stupidity which had produced such an error. The lack of direct contact between the two departments (other than this aggressive kind) made it impossible for technically desirable accommodations between the two departments to be made. The most common topic of production conversation centered about "those goddam ECOs," in spite of the fact that production originated as many ECOs (making changes for its own convenience) as did any other department.

In this case, energies were heavily focused on the impropriety of a low-prestige department like production engineering calling the tune for an equally prestigious or even superior department like production. Production devoted its energies to rebalancing trade between the two departments. In other words, production's prestige could be maintained only by calling more tunes than it danced. This rebalancing process had little to do with accomplishing any work. Yet it consumed vast amounts of production management time (particularly that of the factory superintendent who, of all people, checked every drawing); and, in the last analysis it failed its purpose, since the tide was too great to be stemmed, no matter how much energy was devoted to the effort.

IV.
VALUE AND AUTHORITY CLASHES

Company C designed, manufactured, and distributed a large variety of electronic tubes of advanced design. One of its most rapidly selling tubes had a poor cost record—primarily, it was finally agreed, because of design inadequacies. In the process of trying to reduce costs through fabrication and assembly changes, the industrial engineering department had generated an idea for basic tube redesign. Several industrial engineers experimented informally with the new idea and achieved favorable results. When the matter was brought to the attention of the research department, it found its full schedule would not permit it to take over and develop the new idea. The industrial engineering inventors were given authority to continue development of the new tube. A development schedule was set and a development budget assigned to the industrial engineers.

For a time, progress was satisfactory. Then, when some metallurgical problems developed, the research department stepped in to make tests in an attempt to solve the problem. Conflict immediately developed. The industrial engineers maintained that the research department was unfair to the new tube because of the unrealistic way it conducted its tests. Research found it could get no cooperation in its desire to use industrial engineering equipment to conduct part of its investigation. Contact between the two groups dropped to zero and investigations were conducted in parallel, though each group technically required the other's resources. Development schedules became a farce as one data after another passed without expected accomplishment.

The industrial engineers had become engaged in the project in the first place because, as one of its members put it, "I was particularly displeased with our department's general position in the company and felt we didn't really have a chance to show what we could do." One of the members of research mentioned that he thought of the industrial engineers as "just dumb, stupid, and no good." There was no meeting ground on the value which the two groups could bring to a common project. Nevertheless, there was general agreement that the research people possessed considerably greater prestige than did the industrial engineers.

In Company C, interdepartmental conflict became so energy consuming that relationships were broken off entirely, to the detriment of the project at hand. Normally, research would have held the authority position—and legitimately so, according to its superior prestige. Pressured by scheduling circumstances and by the different points of view concerning what industrial engineering's role should be, the normal authority sequence was turned topsy-turvy. Industrial engineering did the prestige work of invention, directing research to carry out routine tests.

Suddenly, each group attempted to behave in such a way that its own view of a proper relationship would predominate. Research criticized industrial engineering's work and tried to force the industrial engineers back into the subordinate role of helping with tests. Industrial engineering, which always had been eager for a chance to get its "teeth into something," was enjoying the fruits of its initial invention (which, incidentally, later proved to be basically sound). Feeling that its desires were being violated, it tried to keep control of the prestige activities and went out of its way to "prove" that research was barking up the wrong tree.

None of these activities had any necessary relationship to developing a new tube. All energies were devoted to forcing one group's values on the other and maintaining what were believed to be legitimate prestige positions. The two departments were playing another zero-sum game in which what seemed positive trading for one was inevitibly interpreted as negative trading by the other.

VARYING VIEWPOINTS

In each of these four cases, the forces siphoning energy away from productive work have been of a particular kind. In each instance, relationships within groups were at least socially satisfactory. (In Company B, the production group did enforce limits on member influence, but this discipline, because it was viewed as group defense, did not lessen cohesion within the department.) The work of the various groups was intrinsically interesting to group members. Supervision was relatively permissive in allowing group members to "complicate" their lives about the work itself. Obviously, these elements are not always present in organized situations. Equally obvious from our cases is the fact that these elements, by themselves, do not result in effective interdepartmental relations, though they may be considered to contribute to such relations if other conditions are also met.

FOCAL POINTS

What the above cases focus on are the troubles caused by differences in point of view and legitimacy of authority. What these cases teach about group conflicts arising from these two trouble sources is just as true for our understanding of the interrelationships of individuals, for intergroup problems are only special cases of interpersonal issues. The only difference between them is the complexity of dealing with the problem, since the individual persons in our cases are representatives of social groups. Thus, their behavior cannot be modified by actions which are based on the assumption that groups respond exactly as do individuals. In short, the causes of conflict are similar, but the remedies are different.

What happens when groups suffer from authority and viewpoint conflicts is summarized in Figure 1. Like any diagram dealing with a limited number of factors, Figure 1 runs the danger of implying that these cause-and-effect tendencies represent all that need be known about interdepartmental relations. Such an implication, were it intended, would, of course, be fatuous. Research in the area of interdepartmental problems has scarcely begun. Furthermore, we have already noted that other factors can be expected to intervene and render the exhibit's hypotheses, as they should be called, inoperative. Three of these factors have been emphasized—group cohesion, job interest, and supervisory practices.

Once we allow for these mitigating factors, however, we will find it useful to conceive of interdepartmental relations as though they were subject to the dominant influences cited in the diagram. The manager can make this concept more relevant personally if he reviews his own observations of interdepartmental conflict to see how they compare with the kind of analysis described here.

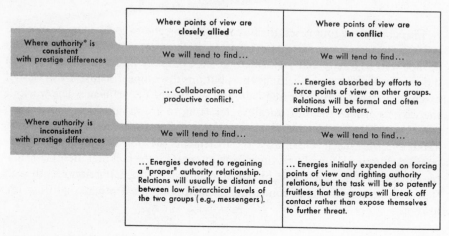

FIGURE 1
DOMINANT INFLUENCES
IN INTERDEPARTMENTAL RELATIONS

	Where points of view are closely allied	Where points of view are in conflict
Where authority* is consistent with prestige differences	We will tend to find...	We will tend to find...
	... Collaboration and productive conflict.	... Energies absorbed by efforts to force points of view on other groups. Relations will be formal and often arbitrated by others.
Where authority is inconsistent with prestige differences	We will tend to find...	We will tend to find...
	... Energies devoted to regaining a "proper" authority relationship. Relations will usually be distant and between low hierarchical levels of the two groups (e.g., messengers).	... Energies initially expended on forcing points of view and righting authority relations, but the task will be so patently fruitless that the groups will break off contact rather than expose themselves to further threat.

* As indicated by work flow.

PLAN FOR ACTION

While the primary purpose of this article has been to explain certain types of interdepartmental problems, the question inevitably arises, "Suppose some sense can be made of interdepartmental difficulties by this kind of thinking; what then do we do with this understanding, even if it does prove to be accurate? How would we go about applying it to lessen interdepartmental conflicts in our company?" Let's look at some action ideas which stem from what has already been said.

STOP, LOOK, AND LISTEN

As frustrating as it might seem, the first suggestion is to stop to see if action is required and, if it is, whether it is feasible. It often may be wise to heed the admonishment (in reverse of the usual form), "Don't just do something, stand there!" The basis for this wisdom lies in the fact that formal organizations often display some of the characteristics of a biological organism, particularly insofar as the latter has some capacity to heal itself. The administrator, if this contention be true, may find the role of the modern physician attractive. He attempts to control the environment so that natural healing processes can take place unhindered within the human body. Here are some examples of where such inaction might be appropriate:

Take the case of Company A. Should something be done to alter jurisdictions among Company A's departments? Or are the natural tensions between these departments, the energies to expand jurisdiction, operating in precisely the most beneficial way for the organization? The best advice in this case seems to be to keep an eye on that tension. Watch that it does not degenerate subtly into another Company C situation. If it moves too far in that direction, then action is required.

This example helps clarify an issue which we have been flirting with throughout this article: the problem of distinguishing productive from nonproductive conflicts. It may not suffice to say that conflict is productive if the parties to it end up satisfied and get there under their own steam. In any particular case, in the heat of a tight scheduling situation, many an administrator has interpreted *any* disagreement as nonproductive and has succumbed to the temptation to interfere. If schedules then have to be junked, the blame is thrown on the groups in disagreement. Had the administrator satisfied himself about the basic conditions within which the fighting groups were working, and listened carefully to see if the fights were *working* or *warring* arguments, he might have saved himself and his organization much trouble.

A case more dramatic than that cited above, and one where action seemed inappropriate, takes us back to the Company B organization. The production department, as might be suspected from what we already know about it, was striving to enlarge its domain to conform to its own ideas about production's importance. This striving provoked a potential clash with the research department when the frequency of special orders began to increase rapidly. Special orders required research design but not production engineering attention, the work of the latter group being devoted to mass-production items. Thus, research would naturally be required to deal directly with production in the case of special orders. Inevitably, production—as isolated historical instances had convinced research—would attempt to dominate these relationships whenever it could.

To avoid this eventuality, research developed a small production unit of its own, though production was fully capable of doing special work. This "organizational invention" of the research department, stepping into work for which it was neither intended nor formally responsible, eliminated the need for contact with production and sidestepped the inevitably nonproductive conflict which would have resulted. The invention was costly in many ways, particularly in terms of valuable research time and space. But on balance it appeared to be the most adequate short-term resolution to a basic interdepartmental problem.

There are a host of other examples of this kind of self-regulation. Many of these measures are rather simple and expedient, if not conducive to removal of the basic causes of nonproductive conflict. Chief among these is the use of what may be called "expendable linkers" as go-betweens in conflicted interdepartmental relations. For example, a production department was observed to assign to its least important member the task of liaison between itself and other departments, where such expediting connoted the use of illegitimate authority. The expediter himself threatened no one, and adopted a most passive demeanor.

Communication then took place not between main contenders who could only lose by such contact but through a neutral intermediary. The cursing went unheard by those for whom a damaging response would have been required.

Other examples involve the use of formal procedures or instruments such as the production schedule, fought over maybe once a quarter, but exerting independent authority betweentimes and keeping sales and production away from each other's throats. None of these is an ideal solution to interdepartmental problems, but each is likely to emerge as a practical expedient in a difficult situation. The administrator may find his short-run problems solved if he is aware of the importance of these often unnoticed "inventions." Furthermore, if he wants to do away with these sometimes awkward mechanisms, he had better make sure he has something with which to replace them.

TYPES OF RESOLUTION

Our cases (and there are unlimited examples like them) have shown that some interdepartmental difficulties go beyond the capacity of the groups to resolve them at anything but a survival level, if that. That level may well be, and often is, intolerable for the organization as a whole. Let us look at the two alternative types of resolution.

First are the resolutions which arise in response to conflicts of authority. In such cases the work flow designed into the organization (e.g., the passage of blueprints from production engineering to production) violates the notions of the organization's members as to who legitimately should, by right of superior prestige, tell whom what to do. Although such problems are not restricted to particular hierarchical levels of the organization, they do tend to become more intense wherever prestige relations are ambiguous or under threat. The higher one goes in many organizations, the more these conditions tend to apply. There are several ways of resolving such problems:

1. An obvious solution is to take whatever steps are available to reduce prestige ambiguity and threat. For example, if Company B's management had realized how pertinent production's resentment at being rated "second class" was to the interdepartmental problems in which it was involved, investigation might have produced ways of clarifying production's status and of enriching its participation in important decisions. Instead, the factory superintendent was the last to be admitted to the executive council and was not accorded vice presidential rank, as were most other department managers. Management failed to take these steps because it feared domination by the superintendent. Yet more careful diagnosis might have revealed that the superintendent's striving for dominance was a result of his impression that management thought him unworthy of participation in decisions for which his expertise was, in fact, badly needed. The circle was vicious.

2. Another step in reducing the amount of nonproductivity in illegitimate authority relations is to reorganize subunits of the organization in such a way that authority and prestige become consistent. In Company B's production engineering and production relationship, such reorganization could have taken the

form of incorporating production engineering into production's domain, much as was done in Company A, where the chemical engineers had been removed from research and placed in the engineering department. With production engineering subject to production's control, yet sharing many ideas with both research and production, a mingling of points of view could have been achieved and authority questions dealt with from within.

The very same kind of potential authority difficulty was avoided in Company B because scheduling was incorporated within production's jurisdiction. Another way of justifying such a resolution of conflict is to note that production's technical functions, as well as those of production engineering, were so closely allied and overlapping that to separate them was to form a barrier across which required contact was extremely difficult and at times impossible. Unfortunately, once again Company B's management so feared production dominance that its inclination was much more to reduce production's domain than to enlarge it.

3. Another extremely clear example of how structural reorganization can resolve not only the authority legitimacy problem, but also have side effects in bringing clashing points of view into sufficient harmony for communication to recommence, is contained in the actual resolution of the Company C difficulty reported above. The obvious solution was to take the research initiative away from the industrial engineers and put it back where prestige relations said it belonged, with research. The solution appeared obvious only because the breakdown between the two departments was so catastrophic.

Equally obvious before that breakdown was the apparently logical belief that the people who invent something should continue to develop it, both because the inventors would logically appear to be most expert in understanding the invention and because it is only fair that productive effort should be rewarded by continuing responsibility and credit. In fact, change was not instituted until the industrial engineers became so thoroughly frustrated by their continuing design failures that they could entertain the idea that their "baby" might be reorganized into more "proper" channels. Although costly in some ways and probably unconscious, management's decision to do nothing at first to set the interdepartmental relations back into the normal work pattern allowed industrial engineering to become receptive to such a change when it finally was made.

This crucial aspect of conflict resolution—receptivity to change—brings us to the second major strategy for helping departmental energies engage in constructive action instead of working against members of another department. This strategy involves what might be called intergroup counseling, therapy, or training. Conflicts in points of view are susceptible only to this strategy, short of complete personnel turnover in one or the other of the warring departments. And, because authority illegitimacy must inevitably engender conflict of viewpoint, it too can be mitigated, if only partially, by intergroup training. Several aspects of this strategy are worthy of attention, though the subject is a difficult and complex one.

Some studies show that intergroup conflict resolution hinges on a particular type of training which seeks an integration of viewpoints by making warring groups realize they are dependent on one another (21). Such a strategy tends to work more readily when both groups fear some external threat to both of them. This idea is not greatly different from the idea contained in the observation that members of families may fight viciously with one another but when an outsider attacks one of the family, the family abandons its differences to fight together against the intruder. It seems obvious from the analysis presented in this article, however, that this strategy is operable only when prestige–authority issues are not present.

A number of researchers, teachers, and managers have begun to explore more direct methods for reducing point-of-view conflict. Some have pointed out that bringing group representatives together to explore their differences is usually doomed to failure since representatives, if they are to remain such, must be loyal to their respective groups (5). Simple measures to increase contact also appear fruitless, because negative stereotypes end up simply becoming reinforced by the contact.

Other measures have proved more effective. Although they vary in form, almost all of these contain the following basic element: The groups in conflict must be brought together as totalities under special conditions (20). The goal of all these conditions is to reduce individual and group anxieties sufficiently so that a point of view can not only be made explicit but can be heard by those who do not share it. This procedure requires not only considerable candor between groups, but also candor within each group and within the individual himself. Naturally, sessions in which such training is supposed to take place can be extremely threatening and should be mediated by an external agent to keep threat within manageable bounds and help guide the groups into explorative rather than recriminative behavior (1).

CONCLUSION

Seldom, if ever, do problems of nonproductive conflict exist in isolation. It is extremely likely that wherever such conflict is found it has been engendered by organizational and emotional maladjustments, each of which has fed upon the other. It would make sense, then, to attack interdepartmental problems while fully realizing that they may be spun into the warp and woof of the organization's fabric. Such an attack has far-reaching consequences for the organization. It means, for example, that the goals of the organization must be critically examined, since these tend to influence the way in which the work of the organization has been divided up and division of labor is at the core of interdepartmental problems.

Because goals, in turn, are heavily influenced by the organization's environment and by the way in which that environment is interpreted by executives and directors, the environment and the process by which it is interpreted also must come under scrutiny. Do those in control have a clear idea of their company's relation to its market? If not, why not? Have they made clear to the other members of the company the job to be done and what that job requires of each subelement in the organization (7)?

These questions are fundamental to the building of an organization. Without answers to these questions, any attempt to resolve an illegitimate authority problem usually is a patch-up job, likely to create as many problems as it cures. Furthermore, without these answers, the members of the organization cannot avoid feeling that their relationships to each other are ambiguous—and aimless ambiguity is a breeding ground for insecurity, defensive behavior, and sapped energy.

Involving the members of an organization in the pursuit of clarifying the organization's goals—in establishing a meaningful identity for the firm—is, perhaps, the soundest process for tapping into the wells of productive energy (17). Such a pursuit, carried on openly and sincerely, cannot help but raise issues of interdepartmental ambiguity, illegitimacy, and conflicting points of view to a level where they can be re-examined and dealt with. An easy process? No. But as "old wives' tales" have told us, no remedy is without pain.

36

Handling Misunderstandings and Conflict

Floyd Mann
University of Michigan

The approach proposed here for dealing with misunderstandings was first stated by Carl Rogers in 1951. See Carl Rogers, *On Becoming a Person*. Boston: Houghton Mifflin Company, 1961, Chapter 17. Reprinted by permission, University of Michigan, Center for Research on Utilization of Scientific Knowledge.

DEALING WITH
BREAKDOWNS IN COMMUNICATION

Real communication is very hard to achieve. We tend to judge, to evaluate, to approve or disapprove before we really understand what the other person is saying—before we understand the frame of reference from which he is talking. This tendency of most humans to react first by forming an evaluation of what has just been said, to evaluate it from our own point of view, is a major barrier to mutual interpersonal communication.

Progress toward understanding can be made when this evaluative tendency is avoided—when we listen with understanding—when we are actively listening to what is being said. What does this mean? It means to see the expressed idea and attitudes from the other person's point of view, to sense how it feels to him, to achieve his frame of reference in regard to the thing he is talking about.

This sounds simple, but it is not.

To test the quality of your understanding, try the following. If you see two people talking past each other, if you find yourself in an argument with your friend, with your wife, or within a small group, just stop the discussion for a moment, and for an experiment, institute this rule of Carl Rogers: "Each person can speak up for himself only *after* he has first restated the ideas and feelings of the previous speaker accurately—and to that speaker's satisfaction."

This would mean that before presenting your own point of view, it would be necessary for you to really achieve the other speaker's frame of reference— to understand his thoughts and feelings so well that you could summarize them for him. This is a very effective process for improving communications and relationships with others. It is much more difficult to do behaviorally than you would suspect.

What will happen if you try to do this during an argument?

You will find that your own next comments will have to be drastically revised. You will find the emotion going out of the discussion, the differences being reduced. There is a decrease in defensiveness, in exaggerated statements, in evaluative and critical behavior. Attitudes become more positive and problem solving. The differences which remain are of a rational and understandable sort—or are real differences in basic values.

What are the risks? The obstacles? What are the difficulties that keep this bit of knowledge from being utilized?

Try this and you risk being influenced by the other person. You might see it his way—have to change your position. There is the risk of change. In this sense, listening can be dangerous—and courage is required.

There is a second obstacle. It is just when emotions are strongest that it is most difficult to achieve the frame of reference of the other person or group.

A third party, who is able to lay aside his own feelings and evaluations, can assist greatly by listening with understanding to each person or group and clarifying the views and attitudes each holds. A third-party catalyst may, incidentally, have great difficulty in intervening and proposing the use of this approach. Any intervention into a heated discussion can be interpreted by one party or the other to the dispute as someone taking the other person's side. This is especially true if the third party asks you to try and state the other person's ideas and feelings when you have not really been listening, but thinking what you should say next when he pauses to take a breath.

Another difficulty stems from our notions as to what it is proper to ask a person to do in a discussion. It seems quite within good taste to ask a person to restate how he sees the situation. But to ask him to restate the other man's position is not consistent with our common-sense ways of handling differences. The one who would change the pattern—try to break out of the vicious circle of increasingly greater misunderstanding—must have enough confidence in himself to be able to propose something different. He will have to have an appreciation of how to go from dealing with misunderstandings to handling conflict and using differences—of how differences can be used to find more elegant solutions to problems. Equally useful will be an awareness that thesis, antithesis, synthesis is a potential outcome from a developmental discussion of differences. Discussions in which one person loses and the other wins seldom solve anything permanently. When a person senses a win–lose situation developing, it should be interpreted as a clue to the need for a new approach, a search for alternate solutions, to be sure that there is not another answer to the problem.

The greatest difficulty of all of course is to learn to use the rule when you yourself are in an increasingly heated verbal exchange. Not to be dependent on a third person to intervene when you create or are a party to a growing misunderstanding is real evidence of understanding the approach proposed here. The full value of this rule is available to us only when each of us can note that we are getting increasingly irritated, angry, and unable to communicate effectively—when we can use these signals to identify the situation in which we are personally involved and even trapped in which the rule might be employed—*if* we could retrieve the rule from our memory, and *if* we could behaviorally use it in an effective manner.

ON HANDLING CONFLICT

What should a person do if after carefully checking his understanding of the other person's ideas and feelings, he finds the differences are real—they stem from different value assumptions and premises? There is no longer any misunderstanding, each person understands the other's position and believes the other's value premises are inappropriate.

A first step might be to check to see if this is a difference that has to be worked through. Is the difference important enough to be sharpend further and a search for a solution undertaken jointly? Is there real interdependence between the persons who no longer are misunderstanding each other but have found there is truly a conflict? If the two parties do have to work together—if the differences in positions taken appear to jeopardize the attainment of an important common purpose—and if there is time to begin to recognize the meaning of these differences—then one or both of the parties need to move ahead toward the positive confrontation and resolution of these differences.

A useful step at this point is often to be sure once again that you understand the other man's position and that the other person understands the difference between the values you hold and those he holds with regard to the issue at hand. This may be done by asking the other person if you really understand his position in a very directive manner—even using leading questions that imply that you do not believe that he would want to hold that position if he fully understood the value implications of it, and accepted the common goals toward which you are both working. If this step indicates goals are not common and shared, this needs to be clarified. There may have simply been a misunderstanding about what the common purpose was in this instance. If after this has been done the differences still remain, it is then essential to check out the values that are held in common. Often it is helpful to move up the hierarchy of values which might be shared to find overarching values which are subscribed to jointly. Once these have been identified and common goals have been restated, the present differences need to be reviewed in terms of these newly stated facts. Differences with regard to the immediate problem are often resolved by this process.

If they are not, then both parties might agree to a problem-solving approach—using another value which they might hold in common—and to adopt one or the other's recommended course of action for the time being. This should be done with the explicit understanding that they will later review carefully the outcome and decide what actual experience has indicated about their different approaches and value premises. They could even use the orderly, systematic collection of data and analysis to test what is the best position or the better way of proceeding.

PRACTICE AND REPRACTICE

It is essential not only to be aware of these ideas about how one might deal with breakdowns in communication and move on to the positive confrontation of differences, but to be able to recognize when these ideas are relevant and might be used, and more importantly to be able to put these ideas into action behaviorally. Cognitive awareness alone is not enough; the behavioral skills necessary to adopt, adapt, and utilize this approach is also essential. Skills as complex as these, requiring dropping old habit patterns of handling conflict which were supported perhaps with deep inclinations to move away from rather than face up to confrontations, can only be changed through practice and repractice. Often a tangential requirement is being able to handle another's expressions of hostility and distrust.

This approach is not easy to incorporate into a person's intellectual and behavioral everyday ways of living with others. But it can be learned—and shared with others. It is not a panacea, but it is an approach that leads steadily and rapidly toward better interpersonal relations. It is relevant to a good deal of what is necessary for self-government. The other man's point of view is valued. His ideas and feelings—and probably yours in return—are treated with human dignity.

THE ACTION STEPS

Now what do you really have to remember to do?

1. Watch for breakdowns in communications between others or between yourself and others.
2. Intervene to suggest the use of the rule to ensure understanding of the other person's ideas and feelings.
3. Stress the restatement of both ideas and feelings to the satisfaction of the participants to the conflict.
4. If misunderstandings have been resolved, but differences still remain, have participants check to see what other values or goals they hold in common.
5. Relate the present differences in value assumptions to these larger, broader goals, values, and reasons for interdependence.
6. If differences are still unresolved, suggest selection of one alternative course of action, but build in commitment to subsequent review and evaluation.

Questioning the Managerial Implications of Resolving Conflict

1. What implications for earlier resolution of union–management negotiations do you see arising out of the data analyzed by Porat?

2. How would you, as a top-level executive, attempt to solve the interdepartmental problems outlined in the four case studies presented by Seiler? How do your methods differ from those proposed by Seiler? Why?

3. Put yourself into the role of a personnel manager who has just read the paper by Mann. You are convinced that his technique will minimize organization-wide conflict, and your boss agrees with you. You have been given the go-ahead to implement a program to reduce interpersonal differences. How do you proceed?

4. The debilitating effects of intra-organizational conflict are fairly obvious. What are the less obvious circumstances under which such conflict can be productive?

References

1. Argyris, C., *Interpersonal Competence and Organizational Effectiveness*. Homewood, Ill.: Irwin-Dorsey, 1962.

2. Bass, B. M., "Effects on the Subsequent Performance of Negotiators of Studying Issues or Planning Strategies Alone or in Groups," *Psychological Monographs*, LXXX, No. 614 (1966).

3. ——, *Exercise Negotiations. A Program of Exercises for Management and Organizational Psychology*, 3rd ed. Pittsburgh: INSTAD, 1967.

4. Blake, R. R., and J. S. Mouton, "Competition, Communication, and Conformity," in *Conformity and Deviation*, eds. I. A. Berg, and B. M. Bass. New York: Harper & Row, Publishers, 1961.

5. ——, *Group Dynamics—Key to Decision Making*. Houston, Texas: Gulf Publishing Co., 1961.

6. Boulding, K. E., *Conflict and Defense: A General Theory*. New York: Harper & Row, Publishers, 1962.

7. Brown, W., *Exploration in Management*. London: William Heinemann Ltd., 1960.

8. Campbell, R. J., "Originality in Group Productivity, III: Partisan Commitment and Productive Independence in a Collective Bargaining Situation. Columbus: The Ohio State University Research Foundation, 1960.

9. Cyert, R. M., and J. G. March, *Behavioral Theory of the Firm*. Englewood Cliffs, N. J.: Prentice-Hall, Inc., 1963.

10. Deutsch, M., "Conditions Affecting Cooperation, I: Factors Related to the Initiation of Cooperation; II: Trust and Cooperation," Final Technical Report, NONR-285(10), New York University Research Center for Human Relations, 1957.

11. Gouldner, A., "The Norm of Reciprocity: A Preliminary Statement," *American Sociological Review* (1960), 161–78.

12. Haire, M., E. E. Ghiselli, and L. W. Porter, *Managerial Thinking*. New York: John Wiley & Sons, Inc., 1966.

13. Lindblom, C. E., "The Science of 'Muddling through,' " in *Readings in Managerial Psychology*, eds. H. J. Leavitt and L. R. Pondy. Chicago: The University of Chicago Press, 1964.

14. Mack, R. W., and R. C. Snyder, "The Analysis of Social Conflict—Toward an Overview and Synthesis," *Journal of Conflict Resolution*, I (1957), 212–48.

15. Osgood, C., "Psychological Concepts in Arms Control and/or Graduated Unilateral Disarmament," *American Psychologist*, XVII (1962), 358(a).

16. Rapoport, A., and A. M. Chammah, *Prisoner's Dilemma: A Study in Conflict and Cooperation*. Ann Arbor: The University of Michigan Press, 1965.

17. Rice, A. K., *The Enterprise and Its Environment*. London: Tavistock Publications, 1963.

18. Schelling, T. M., "Bargaining, Communication, and Limited War," *Journal of Conflict Resolution*, I (1957), 19–36.

19. Scodal, A., J. S. Minas, P. Ratoosh, and M. Lipetz, "Some Descriptive Aspects of Two-Person Non-Zero Sum Games," *Journal of Conflict Resolution*, III (1959), 114–19.

20. Shepard, H. R., and R. R. Blake, "Changing Behavior Through Cognitive Change," *Human Organization*, XXI (1962), 88.

21. Sherif, M., ed., *Intergroup Relations and Leadership*. New York: John Wiley & Sons, Inc., 1962.

22. ——, O. J. Harvey, *et al.*, *Intergroup Conflict and Cooperation: The Robber's Cave Experiment*. Norman: University of Oklahoma Press, 1961.

23. Simon, H. A., *The Shape of Automation for Men and Management*. New York: Harper & Row, Publishers, 1965.

24. United Nations Statistical Office, *United Nations Statistical Yearbook, 1967*. New York: United Nations Organization, 1968.

PERSPECTIVES
ON
THE FUTURE

Among the many trends of consequence to the operating manager today are those involving the impact of the computer on management. Some reasonable understanding of automated information processing is becoming mandatory for managers in many industries and companies. However, other managerial decisions calling for greater analytic consideration, and for awareness of the changes occurring in the environment outside the organization, are equally significant to the manager who would avoid obsolescence. He needs an awareness of the impact on his own organization, his job, and himself of such issues as the generation gap, the population explosion, the rapidity of technological change, rising expectations, and the internationalization of business activity. Part III is an effort to explore these issues to see some of their likely effects on the managers in the decades ahead.

Managing

in the Future

The manager is, perhaps above all, a decision maker. Then it comes as no surprise that the most rapid technological advances in recent times have been in response to his eternal desire to improve his ability to solve problems and make choices. He has seen fit to cause machines to be built to free him of routine matters, to provide him with precise data for making precise decisions, and even to make decisions for him.

The use of computers in organizations has and will continue to generate wide discussion and controversy over the implications of their adoption for human organizations. Such speculations focus not only on decision processes, but on the behavior of managers in the midst of rapid technological change. Michael assesses the effect of computer technology on organizational behavior. He foresees a significant impact on management principles to the extent that increased knowledge and control over decision-making processes will place an increasing burden on managers to be "wise men" and to carefully weigh the moral and ethical implications of their policies.

The future decision-making processes of managers is given extensive treatment by Myers. He predicts that in addition to advances in computer technology, far-reaching changes in the labor force, in urban affairs, and in multinational business ventures will force corporate management to become more concerned about proper utilization of human resources within the organization.

Some of the most pressing labor force issues that managers will have to contend with are related to the surge of today's youth into business organizations. The article by Rukeyser challenges any notions that the "generation gap" has caused university students to become disenchanted with careers in business. He describes a situation in which progressive corporations are most successful in attracting young people who quickly establish their worth. The implications of this influx for future managerial behavior will bear close watching in years to come.

Bennis builds on many of the issues brought out in this and in previous chapters to develop some perspectives on the organizations of tomorrow. He forecasts the decline of bureaucracy and the evolution of a new organizational concept conditioned by the industrial demands of the future.

37

Some Long-Range Implications of Computer Technology for Human Behavior in Organizations

Donald N. Michael
University of Michigan

Reprinted from *The American Behavioral Scientist*, IX, No. 8 (April 1966), 29–35, by permission of the publisher, Sage Publications, Inc.

In 1962, I wrote:

> Computers are especially useful for dealing with social situations that pertain to people in the mass, such as traffic control, financial transactions, mass-demand consumer goods, allocation of resources, etc. They are so useful in these areas that they undoubtedly will help to seduce planners into inventing a society with goals that can be dealt with in the mass rather than in terms of the individual. In fact, the whole trend toward cybernation can be seen as an effort to remove the variabilities in man's on-the-job behavior and off-the-job needs which, because of their non-statistical nature, complicate production and consumption. Thus, somewhere along the line, the idea of the individual may be completely swallowed up in statistics. The planner and those he plans for may become divorced from one another, and the alienation of the individual from his government and individual from individual within government may grow ever greater (21).

That was four years ago. Today I should like to speculate further on the possible implications for human behavior in organizations in the light of the computer's capabilities and in the perspective of the needs of tomorrow's society and its individual members.

I will argue here that a combination of circumstances—for example, the size of our population, the complexity of the social welfare programs needed to operate a technologically based society effectively and felicitously, the increasing availability of powerful and esoteric techniques for planning and implementing these programs, and an insufficiency of highly skilled professionals to do all that needs to be done—will push and pull us toward an increasingly rationalized society in which the computer plays a powerful role.

I will also argue that a variety of behavioral pressures—chiefly the inability of institutions to change as fast as their role in society requires, plus the need to give meaning to the roles of many professionals whose average ability is displaceable by computers—will encourage the persistence and proliferation of nonrationalized patterns of behavior.

I don't think these counterpressures will result in a stalemate. Rather, there will be an increasing separation between operating missions, life styles, and social roles for those institutions and individuals involved in rationalized activities compared to those involved in nonrationalized ones. Just how wide this bifurcation will become remains to be seen.

By "rationalization" I refer to those activities and attitudes which are applied to the systematic implementation of efficiency and effectiveness. The computer, by virtue of its ability to manipulate enormous amounts of data and to simulate the behavior of complex human and material systems, becomes the core component conceptually and organizationally, as well as materially, in modern rationalization methods. Here I shall speak more of rationalization than of computers because its techniques and associated attitudes extend, in principle, beyond the computer. In fact, the true application of rationalization would include the deliberate introduction of opportunities for the operation and display of the extrarational, the whimsical, the ineffable. In some cases today, those conducting highly rationalized activities using the understanding provided by the behavioral sciences, recognize these factors as significant for efficiency, and doubtless others will do so in the future. But the emphasis will often be on "cold" logic, partly because the decision makers will be ignorant of or indifferent to the role of the extralogical, partly because the actual significance of the extra-logical may be unknown in the particular program, and partly because a particular situation may, in fact, require that cold logic be given the highest priority.

However, one way or another, in enough important situations to make the trend significant for our expectations and understanding of coming developments, the computer will necessarily be the core and dominant guide to rationalized processes. Increasingly, the attempted solutions to social problems will be statistical solutions, partly because the aggregate needs of large societies lend themselves to statistical solutions and partly because the techniques for defining as well as solving those problems depend so much on the statistical methods and "world views" of the social technicians and their computers. This is very important—the people who will be turned to for advice in *defining* what the problem is as well as how it can be *solved*, will be those who because of their techniques will define the problem as a statistical problem. Already planners and administrators are tending to place undue emphasis on—that is, coming to value most—those aspects of reality which the computer can deal with just because the computer can do so. The individual—the point off the curve—becomes an annoyance.

In what follows, then, it is the implications of rationalization for human behavior which we will explore, recognizing that for the vast most part the computer will be the basis of and the opportunity for this increased rationalization.

In order to appreciate the context in which problems and opportunities for individual growth and organizational process will present themselves, it is necessary to keep in mind some circumstances which will both push and pull this society toward increasing rationalization.

Of the many factors which will influence the use of computers, certain demographic characteristics of this country over the next two decades will be overriding. We expect around 235 million people in the United States by 1975, about 250 million by 1980, and a world population of 4 billion by 1977. Over the next decade the number of women between the ages twenty and twenty-nine—prime child-bearing age—will increase from 12.1 million to 18 million. There will be 7 million more families in 1970 than in 1964. About half the population will be twenty or under by 1975, and during the same period the number of those over sixty-five will increase almost 20 percent. This is based on the unlikely assumption that no major medical developments will increase the length of life for more people. According to President Johnson in his message on housing and urban development, by 1980 approximately 30 million more people will be living in metropolitan areas than in 1960. Our cities will be merging into a mega-lopolis stretching from Norfolk to Bangor, from Minneapolis to St. Louis, from San Francisco to Santa Barbara. Even our present concept of a "city" will alter significantly as physical mobility becomes ever greater, communications ever more accessible, and new developments and towns sprawl feverishly over the countryside in answer to the implacable demand for new dwellings for the growing population.

These numbers, transformed into potential demands on the society, point to a second factor pushing us in the direction of greater rationalization: greater complexity among the conditions with which the society will have to deal. Eliminating poverty is one such condition; appropriate education for high rates of occupational change and increasing amounts of leisure time is another, the multiple problems of environmental pollution, traffic, water resources, crime control, and tax bases, which will increasingly plague those cities now fusing into megalopoles, represent still others. All these problems will overlap and interact on a scale of mutual influence which has never before confronted those trying to sense the areas of problems and opportunities for the public welfare or for the private sectors of the economy. Extraordinarily powerful conceptual methods will be necessary to cope with such complexity.

A third factor has to do with the sheer scale of the efforts involved in coping with tomorrow's problems and in taking advantage of tomorrow's opportunities. Small efforts and hesitant programs simply won't do. Supporting the evolution of emerging nations will require enormously expanded programs operating over many years. Smaller wars, such as in Korea or Viet Nam, will be a continuing drain on resources. Space and oceanography will consume huge material and skilled human resources, as will the city building and rebuilding necessary for coping with our growing population. While estimates vary, it is probable that we will have to introduce 30 million *new* dwelling units over the next thirty-five years. Almost any socially worthwhile program will take unprecedentedly large investments in humans and hardware, to say nothing of dollars.

A fourth factor, and a relatively radical consideration for Americans, will be a growing requirement for long-time planning. We don't expect to get to the moon by 1970 by ad-libbing that program from day to day. Nor did we build the Polaris submarine system on a hit-or-miss basis. Similarly, it will become increasingly apparent that planning an education system adequate for the future will mean research on learning, teacher selection, preparation, and so on, which will have to be initiated years before it is applied in the classroom. City building will require that plans be worked out so the city can evolve systematically over one to two decades. So too with large-scale oceanographic programs aimed at developing an undersea farming or colonizing capability. So too with packaging long-range developmental progams for emerging nations. But such programs cannot be turned on and off easily. Too much material and psychological and political commitment is involved. Research, development, and capital investment programs are built into everything from congressional "porkbarrels" to university empires, and the subsequent interlocking of vested interests produces a supporting inertia of commitment of formidable proportions. Hence, in some parts of public and private institutions, there will be greater need for and application of powerful rationalized methods for initially assigning program priorities, for evaluating program progress, and for terminating or modifying programs when they no longer merit high priority.

A fifth factor encouraging rationalization will be the persisting shortage of qualified professionals and managers. We don't turn out many of these—mainly because we don't know how. We will, of course, make increasing attempts to mass-produce excellence and wisdom but if we do succeed it won't be in the next decade or so, and it won't be on a scale commensurate with the increasing demand for first-rate minds to guide our ever more complex society. Even now we are short of top-flight professionals and managers to the point of jeopardizing, or at least inhibiting, the full growth of socially desirable programs. Therefore, we can expect organizations to develop more careful selection of the problems to which the experts apply their skills and more careful organization of activities to insure that these skills are efficiently used.

The conservation of the highly skilled will encourage rationalization in another way, one which will have novel effects on organizational arrangements: There will be increasingly extensive use of technicians and subprofessionals to do the nonessential work of the professional. We have the precursors of this type of occupation with the teacher's aide and the laboratory technician. The aide will be used along with the computer to lighten the enormous burdens of many professionals, especially at the higher levels. To develop such aide roles will require a careful breakdown of the essentials and nonessentials of skills and procedures within the professional task. As a result, what the professional does and how he or she does it will become a more precise and more rationalized activity with an increasingly rationalized state of mind associated with it.

In addition to these pushes toward rationalization, there will be strong pulls in that direction. In the first place, we can expect very substantial increases in the knowledge needed to understand and manipulate society and to alter its institutions. Without the enormous abilities of the computer there would probably be only modest improvements over the next couple of decades in the ability of the social sciences to predict and control behavior, but I believe the computer will change this. On the one hand, the computer provides the social scientist with the means for combining in complex models as many variables as he wants in order to simulate the behavior of men and institutions. In the past it has always been argued that, aside from conceptual limitations, the behavioral scientist simply couldn't deal with as many variables as were important in understanding and predicting human behavior. Now he can. Of course, he will be limited to those variables which can be logically manipulated, which leaves out a lot of human behavior. But it includes a great deal too. Then he can test these models against conditions representing "real life." For, on the other hand, the computer provides a unique capacity for collecting and processing enormous amounts of data about the state of individuals and society today—not ten years ago, not five years ago, but today. Thus the behavioral scientist not only can know the state of society *now* to the extent it is represented by these data, but he can use them to test and refine his theoretical models.

Already the computer has impressively improved our ability to describe the way men analyze and solve certain types of problems. It has substantially increased our ability to predict how various populations with specific background characteristics will deal with conflicting information on political issues. And it has complicated election day ethics by predicting the outcome on the basis of East Coast votes before West Coast voting is finished. It also provides the technology for teaching four- and five-year-olds to read.

With such expanded knowledge we can expect institutions to arrange their missions and approaches to take advantage of the potent methods available. In fact, we are already familiar with the use of computerized data for student and personnel screening and assignment, and in defense department strategic planning and weapons systems research and development.

In the second place, our society emphasizes technology and science as the most efficacious means for solving problems. This belief, combined with the proliferation of scientists and technologists newly turned out by our universities, presages an increasingly influential role for these people. Since society and its leadership are eager for their contributions to hardware development and to information useful for policy planning and implementation, we can expect more of them in decision-making and policy-planning positions in government and industry. And in those positions we can expect that their temperamental tendencies and trained capacities, as well as trained incapacities, will result in greater emphasis on and attraction to rationalized procedures for dealing with the issues society poses.

In the third place, there are now many frustrated decision makers and policy planners deflected from using their potentially rationalized approaches to these issues. Others in the system refuse to give them the information they need, using the privileged information they possess to block planners and decision makers higher up. And still others in the system are able to redirect programs and to obscure the results because those in planning and policy have inadequate means for discovering or verifying what has happened "out there" or "down the line." Naturally, planning and policy people will be attracted to institutional arrangements which would remove these impediments to systematic planning and its systematic implementation. Rationalization and particularly the vast capacities of the computers used as data banks to store, compare, and process information will be more and more attractive to those whose farsighted plans are now blocked by shortsighted, indifferent, or contrary human beings with other less inclusive plans to implement. This will give further impetus to the trend toward centralized decision making, planning, and operations management—for the resources needed to bypass present barriers are the same ones which can be more effectively used by centralized planning personnel to reach out, through their computers and related techniques, into the working environment and obtain from them much better data than ever before available for planning, for managing, and for evaluation.

What, then, are some implications of increased rationalization for the management role from the top of the hierarchy, where the major decisions and plans are made, to the bottom, where they are carried out (recognizing, of course, that plans and policies have, to some extent, been generated by middle-management actions as well)? The implications will vary in degree and impact in different types of institutions at different levels. I will not differentiate carefully here: Our present understanding of these trends probably doesn't merit precise analysis.

Those who have analyzed management in relation to computer-using systems concur that the quality of management in government or industry will change and that those doing the tasks of management will need more flexibility, imagination, and fundamental intelligence than is now usually required. This will be so because organizations will be far less dependent on men to do routine decision-making tasks which require little originality, imagination, or high levels of intelligence. There is every reason to believe that over the next twenty years computers will come to have a fairly substantial capability for doing routine kinds of "thinking" of the sort which now preoccupies middle management. Some of you are familiar with the comments on these matters of Leavitt and Whisler from the *Harvard Business Review*. Let me quote Paul Ginsberg of General Electric:

> Future development of electronic computers gives promise of providing to humans a capability to effectively cope with vastly more complex problems than currently can be solved. When this capability has been achieved, a single manager or decision maker will be responsible for tasks that today require delegation among many individuals. Fewer decisions will be required since more complex problems imply formulations that encompass many more actions. The tendency will be to centralize the control within the political and economic organizations. This will be accomplished by a reduction in the number of echelons existing within an organization, and also at any given level fewer components of equal rank will be required to effectively carry on the activities assigned to that echelon. As a result of these changes, fewer managers will be making decisions that control the actions of more individuals than we see today. The checks and balances on the decision maker will be reduced, since he is then a member of a group with fewer total members to criticize and restrain his actions. Subordinate individuals in an organization who are directly affected by the decisions rendered will be in a weaker position than they are today. Their ability to detect and counter undesirable actions will be reduced, since they will *not* have an increased ability afforded by the computers to understand the more complex problems comprehended by centralized management.

One thing seems clear, whatever the manager's tasks, organizations which are cybernated will not require as many managers per organization as they do now. It need hardly be added that many of those who are presently specialized clerks and repositiories of information (and this includes those executives who have been useful chiefly as "live" data banks) will be eliminated as duplication of information storage is eliminated and as individual offices lose their own specialized and restricted data processing and information storage systems. Also, outlying branches of institutions will need fewer clerks, data processors, and information retrievers; their small computers will tie into the central one, making it possible for data to be processed automatically and returned speedily by teletype from the central computer.

Whereas government and industry presently deal with lessened employment needs in the white- and blue-collar echelons (chiefly by waiting for the natural attrition of turnover), this is not so likely to be a plausible solution to reduction in management and other middle-level professional personnel, such as the middle-level engineer whose tasks are being performed increasingly by computers. Such jobs do not "turn over" as quickly or as regularly as nonprofessional ones; presently, much of the psychological and financial security of these positions is tied closely to the particular company involved. Thus, persons employed at these levels will have to be deliberately and explicitly fired. Furthermore, firings will not always be "across the board"—although in some cases a "percentage reduction" in a division of, say, a given type of engineer, will be the procedure. This means that managers may have to single out for firing persons with whom they have worked closely. Clearly, this will produce much emotional stress on those who do the firing. Moreover, if this is a frequent enough pattern, it's likely to engender anticipatory hostility and certainly a cynical sense of "replaceability" in those who work for the higher echelons and who sense themselves as potential victims of rationalization.

Some organizations may begin to recruit management for their hard-nosed ability to fire their fellow workers when firing is needed. Others may choose to make themselves attractive to the public and to case their own consciences by deliberately eschewing such practices, inventing instead featherbedding methods for holding on to their middle-level professionals or at least cushioning the transition. Indeed, it may well be that over the next two decades a major task for those who do make the grade in management will be to figure out acceptable forms of featherbedding for their less successful associates. After all, this is not a new experience in our society; we are not surprised at men being "kicked upstairs" or having positions "invented" for them. Another approach that will undoubtedly receive much attention will be the attempt to reorganize the tasks of management so that those partial tasks which can't be done by computers can be transformed into full-time roles for live middle-level managers and engineers. Top management will also have to invent new ways of giving middle management some kind of involvement in the organization as those functions which they used to perform and which used to provide this sense of involvement become depersonalized through rationalization.

Certainly a hard-nosed approach to terminating the jobs of middle-level professionals is not going to encourage loyalty to the organization. Lacking loyalty and security, many of those who now work overtime in an effort to further enmesh themselves in the higher echelons of the organization may find the ends not worth the effort. Moreover, as the average school provides a better quality of education for thier children, and as living conditions across the nation homogenize, the incentives to stay with a given organization will also decrease. It is likely, then, that at least in industry we can expect increasing mobility among middle-level personnel who, additionally motivated by the knowledge that at any time they may become the victims of rationalization, coolly and cynically seek out the best possibilities for themselves.

It may well be that later in the next two decades this country will find it is gaining a new supply of aggressive middle-level professionals who are not so security oriented as those of the last few decades, and who harbor the aggression—perhaps the hostility—and certainly the drive to take risks and push hard in this kind of environment. Here I am speaking of the products of the antipoverty programs, those who will come out of the slums still harboring many of the dog-eat-dog values of childhood, and moreover, guilt-ridden at their separation from and rejection of their uneducated parents. This will be a latter-day version of the syndrome of the American-born second generation, who dealt with guilt and hostility toward their immigrant parents through hard-driving, ulcer-producing ambitions.

Developing basic techniques in and keeping up with the technology of rationalization will require that decision makers and policy planners continue their education throughout their managerial careers. This pressure for learning and relearning is already beginning, and it is quite likely that men in midcareer will find themselves increasingly useless to their organizations unless they can keep up. At present, re-education in midcareer is a new experience for most professionals, including managers. And evidently for many it is an emotionally difficult experience. To all the other insecurities of upper-middleclass life is now added the threat of being dispossessed from it becaue of failure to pass the new tests for professional advancement, tests which reflect on one's own intellectual abilities. The tension will be shared by the families of those confronted with the new requirement. In this tension and its resolution lie new challenges for the family, especially for the status-conscious, heavily indebted families of suburbia.

Since management people with training in quantitative techniques will be in ever greater demand, top management will look covetously at research and engineering groups as a source of talent. Such creative people may not make better policy planners and decision makers than others with similar quantitative technique experience, but top management may think they will, and indeed, some of those in R & D may aspire to the higher status of top management roles. In the past, a major reward for innovation and competence has been to move the person into a managerial postion. Thus, competing skill needs as between management and R & D will be exacerbated.

Because management will be a highly competitive, intellectual, and political activity, with a high proportion of washouts, young people will be less inclined to move into this field unless they feel quite sure they have the special talents needed, and top management will be less inclined to send its junior people for further training unless it is fairly certain that they will measure up to the next requirements. Since these requirements will be changing rapidly during this time and demanding more and more facility and expertise in management, there will be a premium on aptitude-testing techniques.

We should expect, then, an efflorescence of and improvement in selection techniques and, as these things usually go, they will be applicable to the rest of the laboring force as well. This means that with the growing sophistication of testing techniques for predicting aptitudes and success and their growing application, there will be a lessening sense in the individual of the feeling that one can make of the world what one wishes. In other words, we are in for a modern form of Calvinism in which the evidences of foreordainment will not be found in the Bible but in the psychological test. Such a reduction in the individual's sense of potency and ability to make his own way in the world will inevitably produce profound changes in values about the individual and freedom.

I've said enough already to suggest that there will be strong counterpressures to those pushing for greater rationalization. An explication of these counterpressures will help us foresee other trends in organizational processes which are intimately related to the existence of the computer because these pressures will tend to counteract the enlarged utilization of the computer.

Describing a major source of opposition, the Prentice-Hall *Report on Business* says: "there is . . . little doubt that computer installations are severely resisted at the management level by groups who fear a shift in the balance of power at a management level. This in fact has taken place in many installations" (27). Conventional administrative and political styles will persist in many places—or at least fight very strong rear-guard actions—because some of those threatened by the new demands of greater rationalization are strong members of existing institutional power hierarchies. It is one thing to fire workers with whom one neither identifies as a person nor shares power. It's another thing to fire—or be able to fire—a colleague who but for the grace of God might be you or who has the power leverage to resist.

Three consequences follow: Management, anticipating internal strife at its own level, will often delay this painful reorganization by going slowly in the use of computers; or management may push ahead but, as suggested earlier, go to great efforts to make featherbeds for its peers; or various parts of management may act to sabotage those computer-based activities which threaten it. Thus, in many organizations we can expect a variety of efforts intended to contain the pressures to rationalize. How long they can hold out will depend on how successful their more computerized competition is at doing what the footdraggers are supposed to be accomplishing—whether it's making profits or monitoring a government-sponsored re-education program. Of course, higher levels of rationalization won't always lead to more effective actions; the results might be quite the contrary when logic-based techniques are imposed in Procrustean fashion on activities better realized through the operation of the extrarational. But doubtless there are many activities which will be done better through imaginative application of the computer, and in these cases the long-run consequence will be to demolish the obfuscators and foot-draggers. The process will be uneven, however, and during the next couple of decades we can expect to see many embattled and successful holdout organizations, or parts of organizations, whose special appeal for those working in them will be their "old-fashioned" and "more human" approach. Speaking of his own organization, one executive put it this way: "We examined the possibilities of putting in computers, and even though we knew they could help us do a better job, we decided not to go ahead because they would cause drastic human dislocations" (10).

A second counterpressure results from the complexity of the issues to be dealt with combined with the effectiveness and ubiquitousness of "public information" or public relations definers of "reality." These sources of selected and slanted information will make it possible to present an image of rationalization even when the "facts" may come closer to business-as-usual disorganization, if not chaos. The "war on poverty" is a precursor of this sort of pseudo-or semi-rationalized activity. It appears much more rationalized than it is in fact. This is not to say there is no effort to rationalize the program; at some levels, especially near the top, the effort is very real. But as the program diffuses into the operational areas, it becomes much more subject to political patronage, empire building, emotional and operational vested interests, and so on. The "systems approach" at the Federal level often gives way to local pushing and shoving, which is publically cloaked as "refining programs and procedures," or "encouraging local participation." Sometimes it is but often it most definitely is not. It may be that eventually the program will become rationalized down as well as up the line, but for reasons we shall discuss later it and future social welfare programs like it may not become rationalized very far.

This leads to a third pressure militating against rationalization. Increasingly, this society will have to find a meaningful role for all the average professionals mass-produced by an essentially uninspired, although improved, educational system. For the fulsome use of the computer is, as we have seen, already displacing the mediocre manager and engineer; programmed learning could displace the mediocre teacher, and so on. We could stop their displacement by thwarting the trends toward rationalization but, as pointed earlier, this is unlikely except on a voluntary basis and often there will be very real and pressing needs for rationalization which would make its inhibition very dangerous to the national welfare as well as to the viability of competing organizations. An alternative to deliberately proscribing rationalization in order to preserve professionals' jobs would be to invent and pay for new roles for the displaced and the unhired, which, at the same time, would facilitate the conduct of social welfare programs. If the programs were properly designed, even the use of average talents would make them more effective than past efforts in the social welfare field. Temporarily, at least, their contribution would be a meaningful one.

Paying well for mediocre service, of course, has its analog in that this affluent society pays very well for mediocre material goods. But a true precedent exists on a grand scale already: The government pays for enormous amounts of mediocre research and development, either directly through grants and contracts or indirectly through the tax privileges it offers foundations and other nonprofit organizations. It is generally conceded that much of what now passes for scientific and technological research is trivial and second rate. In the words of the late Norbert Wiener: "I am rather skeptical about crash projects, and a great deal of the apparent science explosion comes from the use of many people who are labeled and popularly understood as scientists in this mass work that comes in crash projects. . . . So I say that one of the needs of science at the present is to keep the monkeys away from the typewriters" (34).

But research does keep many average physical scientists and engineers pleasantly and affluently busy, and it supports a huge infrastructure of managers, project and program review committees, proposal writers, and public information manufacturers. What is more, a review of the parallel and overlapping social welfare research and demonstration programs of the various government agencies clearly demonstrates that there can't possibly be enough first-class people to do the work, and that the activated and proposed studies and actions are at best only vaguely related to any systematic set of concepts or goals. There are exceptions, of course, and there will be more over time. But using the vast and growing army of average-ability professionals in government, industry, universities, and private agencies in such ways that they can retain their self-respect and remain affluent consumers of our increasing productivity will require the establishment and persistence of operationally sloppy social welfare programs. In this sense, the poverty prgram, for example, becomes an end in itself rather than a means to another end. It is a splendid device not only to alleviate unemployment-based poverty from the bottom, but to prevent it from creeping up the skilled scale. Of course, it will take highly rationalized activities at some levels to insure that such poorly rationalized activities fulfill their purpose at a supportable social and economic cost.

Both the resistances and the counteractions to rationalization will encourage behavior different not so much in kind as in degree from the past. In some quarters, there will be more emphasis on and more appeal in face-to-face relationships and intimate self-enlarging experiences. These are the means par excellence of avoiding or compensating for the depersonalized existence of highly rationalized operations. They are also the means for finding a dignified role not potentially replaceable by a machine. That is, not replaceable as long as the success of the face-to-face relationship is not measured primarily in terms of profit making or efficiency. Finally, it is a means for throwing a monkey wrench into rationalized machinery, for face-to-face relationships always have the potential for placing on the system demands which cannot be met statistically or even "logically."

The most evident expression of this last counterresponse to rationalized systems is the social protest-type activity, such as the Berkeley demonstrations, sit-ins, and other nonviolent devices for disrupting the system. Bending punchcards and overloading the mayor's switchboard so he can't get calls in or out are other actual examples. We can expect more inventions of protest behavior as a way to give personal meaning in a world too big and too complex to find other ways of identifying with its larger trends and circumstances.

However, protest and other face-to-face activities, such as teaching and Peace

Corps involvements, will themselves have a tendency to become rationalized. Using these resources efficiently and effectively will impose its own demands for organization and structure. But again, the interstices of these programs and projects will be able to harbor many unrationalized souls and activities. Those who find their roles being transformed into highly rationized ones will either capitulate or spin off new activities rich in human turmoil and confusion. And so on.

This process is not new, of course, but it will show itself with new intensity, I think, as efforts increase to rationalize many areas which now run sloppily untroubled by up-to-date knowledge about their impact—or lack of it—and unconcerned with planning a decade or more ahead.

A second form of reaction to greater rationalization, for those affluent enough, will be more self-indulgence—or self-social welfare, if you will. People will "owe it to themselves" to get back to themselves and closer to others, to get out of the computerized world of work and into the immediate world of direct experience. Look at all the indulgent attention we are giving the poor to help them lead the good life. Novelty and sensation seeking will be pursued on an expanding scale as will be more deliberate and systematic efforts to enlarge one's "sense of self."

In addition to the proliferation of already familiar ways of getting more "kicks" and culture out of living, a less familiar method seems to be an excellent bet for widespread popularity. I refer to psychedelic, or hallucinogenic, or experience-widening chemicals. Now prohibited by the government except for licensed research, these agents are nevertheless being used quietly by all sorts of people, many of them sober and sensible, enthralled with the intensity of immediate aesthetic and emotional experience available in this way. The toxicity level of these agents seems to be remarkably small for most people. They are nonhabit forming and could be produced very cheaply. They may provide a splendid counterbalance to the constraints of highly computerized, systematized work environments, thereby allowing some the best of both worlds, much as the drudgery and privation of the medieval peasant was made more bearable by the vision of heaven and the splendor of the Church. Legally or illegally, I expect these chemical agents to be in wider use in the years ahead.

Finally, let me draw your attention to another existential factor of exceeding importance, one which vastly complicates the whole issue of when the computer will be used and when it will not. There is no reason to suppose that during the next couple of decades our understanding of the human condition will be so broad and deep or the versatility of the computer so great that we will be able to make wise and sufficient decisions solely by using computers and related techniques. On the other hand, there is every reason to believe that we will have a far deeper and broader understanding of the human condition as a result of the capabilities of the computer.

New knowledge and technologies will be available to decision makers and policy planners as a basis for the increasingly potent manipulation of man and his environment. At the same time, the complexity of the issues dealt with, plus greater clarity about what is known reagrading the issue, will confront these social "movers" with the humanistic necessity of making decisions and plans which transcend in their content and consequences those included in a purely rationalized approach to the situation.

The challenge we face is that of somehow developing wise men who understand the limits of human knowledge and have the integrity and courage to withstand the great pressures to value most about the society those aspects of it which can be comprehended and dealt with within the compass of the computer and rationalized activities.

Furthermore, the public (whatever that means) will be an inadequate arbiter, for the problems will be too complex and the techniques for defining and coping with them too esoteric for even the college graduate to know which policy most meets his own long-run interests. The general situation is illustrated by a statement by Harry Schwartz of *The New York Times:*

> ... the public seems happily content with little or no knowledge in situations where adequate explanation must rest directly upon the concepts and techniques of mathematics. It is as if there were a tacit agreement between those who direct this country's mass media and the rest of us; they will not offer, and we will not demand, anything to do with serious mathematics. There are exceptions, of course, but these are rare (29).

In all, top leadership in many organizations will find that while the computer relieves them of minor burdens, it will enormously increase the demands on them to wrestle with the moral and ethical consequences of the policies they choose and implement. In the past, the executive has been able to avoid facing many of these consequences by claiming he had too little knowledge about the real world or too little control over it to feel very much responsibility for the consequences of his feeble attempts to deal with that essentially unknown and powerful environment. With the new tools at his command, he will be able to use this "out" less and less. The implication is clear to me: The top-level manager and decision-making professional will have to seek intensively for wisdom all his life. Of course, he will have to be a perpetual student of the techniques of rationalized decision making, but even more, a student of the humanities. If he is not wise—if he is unthinking or singleminded in his application of the computer—he will fail eventually and our society too will fail under such leadership. But providing wise men in the numbers and at the rate needed is a challenge whose outlines we can see only dimly. Our desperate task is to transform this vague appreciation into wise men. We should have begun yesterday. It is by no means clear that we can provide them in time. Nor is it clear that we cannot. But we must do much more than just hope.

38

Management Decisions
for the Next Decade

Charles A. Myers
Massachusetts Institute of Technology

Among the most crucial developments confronting corporate management in the decade ahead will be rapidly changing labor force patterns, accelerating utilization of computer systems, recurring urban crises, and continuing expansion of international business activity. These four areas that vitally affect the firm itself and the environment in which it functions may initially appear to be unrelated. This paper integrates them, however, by showing that the resolution of the problems in each area will require better utilization of human resources.

This paper was adapted from an address delivered at the 1968 Sloan Convocation for Alfred P. Sloan Fellows and the Program for Senior Executives. The author wishes to thank Professor Douglass V. Brown for his comments on an earlier draft. Reprinted by permission from *Industrial Management Review*, X, No. 1 (1968), 31–40.

INTRODUCTION

Recently, considerable attention has been focused on the year 2000 and beyond. Herman Kahn, who wrote first about thermonuclear war, has now turned the attention of his Hudson Institute to a series of statements about the turn of the century. Kahn is bolder than most prophets. He lists as one of the characteristics of our society: "Business firms are no longer the major source of innovation" (16). Another prophet is Daniel Bell, a sociologist at Columbia University, who heads an American Academy of Arts and Sciences group that is also attempting to assess our society at the year 2000. He has coined the phrase "post-industrial society" to describe the United States at that time. Bell defines the post-industrial society "as one in which the organization of theoretical knowledge becomes paramount for innovation in the society, and in which intellectual institutions become central in the social structure" (4).

The American Management Association, through its American Foundation for Management Research, held a conference early this year, publishing papers and discussion under the title, *Management 2000* (17). The speakers at the conference, on the whole, did not predict as sharp a break with the present as Kahn and Bell visualize. These forecasts about the turn of the millennium (only 32 years away) have initiated considerable thought within the business community.

The intent here is to stimulate further thought about the future by suggesting developments likely to occur in the next decade which will be of paramount significance to management. The effort is more limited, both in scope and in time horizon, than the current predictions about the year 2000 and beyond. The areas considered are further limited to developments with implications for management decisions. No projections are made concerning international crises or political elections, for example, not because they are without significance for managment, but because the uncertainty associated with these events discounts their importance for current management decisions. By selecting a time horizon of the next decade instead of the next century, projections can be made with greater certainty. Furthermore, the validity of forecasts about the year 2000 by Kahn and Bell is in part dependent on the response of corporate executives to the developments of the next decade discussed here.

Four areas of sufficient importance to warrant in depth consideration are:

1. Changes in the composition of our labor force which accentuate some of the problems managers have already had in dealing with better educated and differently motivated employees, and the shortage of competent managers accentuated by these labor force changes;
2. Rapidly increasing use of computer systems and management science techniques;
3. Further crises in our cities, particularly in the urban ghettos where the persistent problems of black disaffection and hard-core unemployment will not go away during the next decade, or even the decade after that;

4. Expanding involvement of the multinational corporation, not only in Western Europe but also in developing countries.

The implications for management decisions of these all-important areas are discussed in the sections which follow.

CHANGES IN THE LABOR FORCE AFFECTING MANAGEMENT

Recent labor force projections by the Bureau of Labor Statistics of the United States Department of Labor, extending to 1975, provide a basis for analyzing emerging population and manpower patterns.[1] According to those projections, the population picture in 1975 will possess the following characteristics:

1. There will be an absolute *decrease* in the age group, 35–54. The number of males 35–44 years of age, the prime age group from which most top managers will be recruited, will be 7.3 percent lower than the 1965 figure. Unless increased efforts are made to develop more managers, a smaller group of men will be dealing with the tougher problems of the next decade. The significance for management development efforts and for those managerial philosophies and organizational climates which best develop managers on the job is obvious.

2. There will be a 30 percent increase in the number of people in the age group, 15–24. Although many will be students, a substantial portion will be in the labor force. Their expectations in an affluent society will diverge from their elders' much as the values of today's youth do. To recruit and motivate young people who have a myriad of options (further graduate study, overseas and domestic service, etc.), management must adjust to these expectations. The increase in this age group provides challenges from other vantages. The market which has emerged to satisfy young people's desires—for sports cars, clothing, rock music—is likely to grow at a rate exceeding the one-third numerical expansion of this young group.

3. An expansion of nearly 40 percent will take place in the age group, 25–34. This group will be comprised of today's teenagers and young adults, whose behavior and values have led to much head-shaking by their elders. Although the 25s to 34s may sober up a bit with the usual family responsibilities, managers will certainly have to accommodate themselves to the behavior of this new generation. Tomorrow's young people may not be called hippies, but they are likely to continue questioning society's values and rebelling against society's constraints. Managers will have to tolerate considerable diversity in those they hire in the next decade. The challenge of providing opportunities which will

---

[1] The usual assumptions about the continuation of past economic, employment, and productivity trends were made in preparing these projections. It was also assumed that the Vietnam war would end by January 1, 1970, and that defense expenditures would drop to the prewar level. *Manpower Report of the President* (18) contains some of this information.

interest these future managers must be met if they are to contribute enthusiastically to organizational objectives. Job enlargement, less detailed control of job responsibilities, and business involvement in social problems will be necessary, if indeed anything will attract capable people in this age group to industry from other alternatives now available.

4. The age group 55 and over will increase 17 percent by 1975. In part this reflects increasing longevity, and will necessitate re-examination of rigid compulsory retirement policies and/or more efforts to prepare employees (including executives) for retirement. Perhaps people in this age group should look forward to two occupations, one before compulsory retirement and one after, one full-time and one part-time. Adequate provision must be made for the reduced income of retirement years. Someone has pointed out that while many organizations retire their chief executives at 65, this is about the age when United States Senators and Representatives become chairmen of important Congressional committees.

5. Nearly four-fifths of the young adults (23–34) in the 1975 labor force will be high school graduates; one-fifth will be college graduates or beyond. This heavy influx of educated people is both an asset and a challenge to management. Employees will be better educated but will also have greater expectations for their careers. This is the upper end of the educational ladder. At the lower end will be a minority "underclass," the 7 percent with less than eight grades of schooling, whose educational handicap in the working world will be especially severe.

6. The upper and lower ends of the occupational ladder in 1975 will reflect earlier educational backgrounds. The number of professional and technical employees at the top will grow twice as fast (by 45 percent) from 1965 to 1975. As a further indication of the impact of advancing higher education on our occupational structure, there were only 3.8 million professional and technical employees in 1947 and 8.9 million in 1965. By 1975, if current projections are accurate, there will be 12.9 million. (It is worth noting that earlier projections have frequently fallen short of their marks.) At the bottom of the occupational ladder, excluding farm workers, are the people classified as "laborers." Their share in the labor force will shrink from 5 percent in 1965 to 4 percent in 1975. There will be proportionally fewer jobs for those with brawn but not much education.

To sum up this brief review of the 1975 labor force projections, proportionately fewer managers will have to recruit and develop increasing numbers of better-educated younger people (as compared to 1965), including more professional and technical employees. A review of employment and retirement policies for the increasing number of older workers will be required. Finally, help in developing methods for removing educational deficiencies at the lower end of the occupational scale, particularly for nonwhites, will present a critical challenge to managers.

USE OF COMPUTERS
IN MANAGEMENT DECISION MAKING

Perhaps by the year 2000, computer programs will have so high a degree of artificial intelligence that there will be no need for managers. In the next decade and beyond, however, the intelligent use of computers is more likely to extend rather than replace the manager's capacities, relieving him of much routine and structured work. By enhancing the productivity of individual managers, computer systems of the '70s will help overcome the shortage of competent managers. The increasing complexity of the managerial job, within the enterprise and especially in the realm of the enterprise's interactions with its external environment, will require all the support managers can extract from computers and related management science techniques. Accounting, inventory control, production scheduling and control, marketing, purchasing, customer ordering, and shipping, among others, have all benefited from computer applications. There will be further extensions in these areas.

The development of data banks which permit the building of realistic models of relationships among the areas mentioned above will help managers to simulate decision alternatives, narrowing the range from which informed managerial judgment must choose. As one goes higher in the managerial ranks, however, the problems for decision become less structured. This consideration led many of the participants at a 1966 Sloan School conference on the impact of computers on management to conclude that "in the year 2000, managers in man–machine systems will still be dealing with ill-strutcured problems" (23).

Computerized management information systems have already helped to integrate various functions and branches of the enterprise, but the "total management information system," mentioned so often in recent literature but not yet realized, may emerge within the next decade. Apart from the technical problems of designing a system to cover a large enterprise, there is the critical question of how the system will be designed to provide information at different points in the organization. Simply stated, who will have access to what information, and when? This question is related to the contrasting managerial philosophies which Douglas McGregor called Theory X and Theory Y in his book, *The Human Side of Enterprise* (19). A top management which accepts Theory X assumptions (management by centralized direction and control) will probably be able to exercise tight control through a computerized total management information system. But a Theory Y management, concerned about developing subordinate managers through integration and self-control, will suggest that a computerized total management information system be designed to provide data for subordinate managers so that they can monitor their own progress toward organizational objectives and take corrective action before their superiors order them to do so. As Professor Jay W. Forrester put it in summing up his impressions of the conference on computer impacts mentioned earlier: "It appears that we can use computers and information technology to create more confinement or more freedom" (23). Top managers should have little difficulty deciding which approach will attract and motivate the better educated, professionally trained people who will appear in greater numbers in the 1975 labor force.

If computers free managers of a considerable amount of the routine, structured parts of their work, managers will, I believe, have more time for the ill-structured problems. Areas of managerial activity of an ill-structured nature include the establishment of organizational objectives, the selection, development, and motivation of subordinates,[2] and the imporvement of constructive relations with nonmanagerial employees and their unions. More attention to the interaction of the enterprise with federal, state, and local governments and with the community from which it draws both employees and public support will be necessary. These aspects of the managerial job, because they are difficult to define in advance, will require broadly trained people who are sensitive to social as well as technical changes.

THE URBAN CRISIS: ITS SIGNIFICANCE FOR MANAGEMENT

When Senator Edward Kennedy finally spoke publicly after the assassination of his second brother, he said in a speech to the Worcester (Mass.) Chamber of Commerce: "Guns and gas are being stockpiled against crime and riots—bad schools and housing, no jobs and an inadequate passion for justice—these are being neglected." Some managers feel that these problems are best left to politicians and to governments. This feeling is shared by critics of business from the left, who contend that govenment action is the only answer. In contrast, an increasing number of businessmen are becoming more and more involved in trying to deal with some of these "basic causes." The view that "corporations do the most good for society when they just stick to business and maximize their profits" is no longer so adamantly defended by corporate leaders (1). In the decade ahead, managers will become more involved in urban problems, including supporting that kind of business-government partnership that has evolved in some of our recent federal and local manpower training programs. There is no way to avoid this commitment, or to escape the consequences of the urban crisis.

---

[2] A recent Sloan School thesis reports that five chief executives of five different organizations had 64 percent of all their interpersonal contacts with their own subordinates. See Mintzberg (22).

Last May, the challenge was presented to management in these words:

Today, there is another great social change now aflame in which business has an unperformed social responsibility—one as inescapable, I believe, as the responsibility for operating at a profit. I refer to that concerning the natural aspirations of those who call themselves the black minority, and I include within the problem the natural aspirations of those in other minority groups—not excluding the minority of the white race who also need training, better education, more adequate housing, and more real opportunities to exercise their inherent capacities to make their own way in our busy, highly competitive American environment (8).

Perhaps surprisingly, this is not a statement by a social critic of management, unless you would so characterize Roger M. Blough, Chariman of the Board of the United States Steel Corporation.

The manpower decisions which managers will face in the next decade will not be greatly different than they are today. The problems mentioned by Senator Kennedy and Mr. Blough will not be solved tomorrow. Migration from the South to northern cities is likely to continue. More children will be born under the handicaps of the ghetto. And, unless more is done to expand job opportunities for Negroes, high rates of teenage and young adult unemployment will persist.

Within the past year or two, managers have become actively involved through their companies in the hiring and training of the hard-core unemployed, the so-called "disadvantaged." Currently, industry is addressing the problem under government supported and business-run programs, such as the National Alliance of Businessmen's "Job Opportunities in the Business Sector," headed by Henry Ford II. There will be further efforts, possibly with either direct government subsidy or tax credits to compensate for the added training and associated costs incurred in hiring people lacking minimum qualifications.

But the task of supervisors and managers does not end with just hiring and minimal training. A variety of decisions will have to be made beyond this initial phase. How much remedial education should be provided? Will standards of performance and discipline be relaxed until the disadvantaged are fully productive? What will this require in the training of supervisors and middle managers, and in communication with regular employees who may resent what appears to them to be pampering and perhaps reverse discrimination? And what about upgrading to better jobs? In facing up to these questions, managers may have to revise their preconceptions. No business leader has made this point more lucidly than Virgil E. Boyd, President of the Chrysler Corporation, in a speech in Detroit last June.[3]

I thought I knew what "hard core" meant, until we became involved in this area. I was wrong. Hard core refers not to those without steady jobs, but to those who are

---

[3] The full, unpublished text was made available to me by the Public Relations Department of the Chrysler Corporation. Shorter excerpts appeared in *The New York Times* (24).

not equipped for any job. Not the unemployed, but the unemployable—those who are unable to fill out even a simple job application. . . . These people who have been pushed into the backwaters of our society can't read simple words such as "in" and "out" signs on a door. It comes right down to blackboard drills, teaching letters that spell common colors, so they can read the instruction card that tells them to put a blue or a green seat belt or a steering wheel on a car as it comes down the assembly line. It entails teaching simple addition, so that they can count boxes of parts they take off a supplier's truck.

And it goes much deeper than that. For example, some of these people signed on for job training—with an "X" of course—but failed to show up. And many of those who did report were very late. . . . Naturally, a lot of people in my company—just as in many other companies—quietly nodded their heads and reaffirmed everything that they had always known to be true. They were more than ever convinced that all the people who aren't working just don't want to work. . . . But those of us who reacted to the demands for help from industry had made a commitment, an agreement with the government, and we intended to meet it. So we set out to find what really was wrong.

We started by sending people out to find out why all those X's never showed up for work. The answer, in many cases, was childishly simple. If you can't read, how do you know what it says on the destination signs of the many buses that go by on a given busy street? . . . It didn't take long to establish another fact—only one in five owned an alarm clock. Why? Because they'd never had to be any particular place at any particular time before. So we took them into the plants and showed them men, just like themselves, who owned cars, and clothes, and houses, and that they owned them because these men lived within the rules of an industrial society and showed up for work, on time, every day.

And this is the point at which some of our established, competent people began to revise those things which they knew to be true. They changed their thinking because once these hard-core people knew how, and why, to come to work, their attendance and tardiness record was *500 percent better* than the average of all our employees. . . . Further, we found that while the majority of the hard-core people had only a third to fourth grade reading ability, they also fell within a very acceptable range of I.Q. And given sufficient motivation and direction, they performed at the average level within a relatively few weeks.

Mr. Boyd concluded:

Perhaps the possibility of these results with the unemployables should have been obvious to us all along. But it wasn't, and we have made an important discovery, and a change in attitude that is critically important to the resolution of the urban crisis. We have recognized that it is not only possible but definitely to our advantage to help the chronically unemployed, and that with a lot of help, and some patience, they will help themselves.[4]

The next decade will bring such discoveries to many managers. The involvement which initiates these discoveries will be a terribly important component of the solution of our urban crisis.

---

[4] For a comprehensive review of other business efforts, see (12).

Speaking to a group of Detroit businessmen, a black militant leader, Frank Ditto, is reported to have said: "If you cats can't do it, it's never going to get done" (9). Whether private firms can do it will depend not only on their increased commitment, but also on the capacity of the economy to generate enough (increasing) demand to provide the job opportunities which are needed. A general unemployment rate around 3.5 to 4.0 percent means very tight labor markets for most adult male members of the labor force (2.1 percent for white males 20 years of age and over in 1967). But it also means unemployment rates of double this for nonwhites (4.3 percent for the same age group), and very high rates for teenagers. Among the young men under 20 years of age in the labor force, the unemployment rate of nonwhites was double that of whites in 1967; 26.5 percent of the nonwhite teenage labor force was unemployed (18). This situation persisted while the number of employed Americans increased by over 1.5 million from 1966 through 1967 to a total of nearly 77.4 million employees in civilian jobs.

With the further expansion and younger composition of our labor force in the next decade, we will need public policies that support continued economic growth and keep unemployment rates below the 4-percent level. We cannot tolerate the 6-percent unemployment rates which prevailed on the average in 1958 and again in 1961. If public policy decisions are not committed to this objective, then we shall see higher rates of unemployment in the next decade, and the number of impoverished families in the United States (those earning less than $3000 a year) will continue to be as high as 5 million. With unemployment falling more heavily on nonwhites than on whites, the consequences for continued urban unrest and protest are worth pondering. The costs of the urban crisis will be met one way or another, and decisions by management leaders will be computed in the costs and the benefits.

EXPANDING ROLE OF THE MULTI-NATIONAL CORPORATION

The fourth and final area of management decisions in the next decade involves the expanding role of the multinational corporation. Just as management faces social and technical changes which will affect its decisions within the American society into the late 1970s, so it also looks abroad and sees new opportunities as well as new problems in other societies. These opportunities and problems, much as on the domestic front, will involve to a large extent the utilization of people.

Even though many multinational corporations have headquarters in the United States, some of their international operations have nationals of other countries in top management positions. The president of IBM World Trade in New York, for example, is a Frenchman. These multinational firms have also developed managerial talent for their operations abroad. This has led another

Frenchman, Jean-Jacques Servan-Schreiber, author of the French best-seller translated and published here this year as *The American Challenge*, to analyze the secret of American business success in Western Europe as due not to the "technological gap," but to "human factors—the ability to adapt easily, flexibility of organizations, the creative power of teamwork . . . Beyond any single explanation, each of which has an element of truth, the secret lies in the confidence of the society in its citizens. . . *What counts is the determination to liberate and show confidence in man at every level.*"[5]

Perhaps this is not true of every American enterprise, but a growing number of managers in the United States are turning to those managerial philosophies and organizational structures which emphasize the development of people and their initiative in the achievement of organizational objectives. If this view is correct, and it enjoys substantial support from behavioral science research, then American leadership of multinational corporations in the next decade will have a comparative advantage. It is possible to borrow technology, but it is more difficult to emulate the intangibles of managerial competence and leadership.[6]

At the same time, American managers working with nationals of other countries in international operation abroad have an opportunity to raise the level of competence of the nationals they employ, a competence which will help the American multinational company survive some of the understandable nationalistic urges of the host country by helping build the country's own human resources. The American firm operating abroad cannot ignore the foreign educational systems, which are a prime source of future managers. The firm will increasingly be called upon to assist in the upgrading and expansion of those systems, particularly in the new schools of management that are springing up not only in Western Europe but also in many developing countries. New management schools have occasionally had the help of American management schools also, as in the case of the Sloan School's assistance to the Indian Institute of Management in Calcutta.

The red tape and frustrations involved in direct investment in less-developed countries are well known. American managers in the next decade will be required to decide which national partners to approach on joint ventures, what degree of control to exercise, and how managerial responsibilities are to be shared (32). Beyond this, the multinational corporation in the next decade will find itself "a world enterprise," generating tensions in very nationalistic nations, and, in the words of the President of the Pfizer Company, becoming "agents of change, socially, economically, and culturally" (25).

To the extent that American managers are involved in multinational operations, their commitment to the *development* of people rather than exclusively to

---

[5] Servan-Schreiber also notes that "a century ago, (de) Toqueville saw this essential, indeed fundamental, characteristic of the New World." See (30, pp. 252, 266).

[6] Robert S. McNamara says in his new book: "In my view, the technological gap was misnamed. It is not so much a technological gap as it is a managerial gap." See (20).

the *direction* of people will ease the problem of their acceptance as "agents of change." They will listen and understand first, then act. They will learn the language, work to understand the culture, and develop relations with people in society at large as well as in the world of business. They cannot remain in American "islands" abroad.

CONCLUDING OBSERVATIONS

The four areas of management decisions in the next decade discussed above are not all-inclusive. They are, however, among the most important. Furthermore, there is a theme common to all of them: The major challenge for management is better utilization of people, utilization of the young and better-educated members of the labor force, more effective use of management talent by aiding rather than replacing managers with computers, utilization of the untapped resources of the "disadvantaged," and the development of nationals of other countries through the multinational corporation.

In an address to the 1968 National Conference of the British Institute of Management last March, under the title, "Education for Management and Technology in the 70s—An American Forecast," President Howard W. Johnson of M.I.T. articulated the central theme in these words:

> Societies will be strong economically in proportion to their management systems, their ability to harness technology in the service of the market, including the individual but also societal needs—for education, transportation, housing, health, adequate food, clean air and water. The leadership of this management system demands rare and imaginative men, and I am persuaded that the corporate task of the 70s will be to provide the climate in which such men are nurtured and their abilities brought to full flower within the corporate frame. The world is changing with such speed that only the adaptive and innovative can keep the pace.

Servan-Schreiber has phrased it this way: "All clichés to the contrary, American society wagers much more on human intelligence than it wastes on gadgets ... this wager on man is the origin of America's new dynamism" (30). The managerial decisions discussed above will be important in determining whether this statement can still be made at the end of the next decade.

39

How Youth is Reforming
the Business World

William S. Rukeyser
Associate Editor
Fortune magazine

Reprinted from the January 1969 issue of *Fortune* magazine by special permission;
© 1968 Time Inc.

As this decade began, General Mills of Minneapolis was a corporation in the doldrums. Its cozy world of flour mills, Wheaties, and Betty Crocker, so satisfyingly stable when the economy was weak, was proving to be a bit too stable in years of national plenty. Sales were in a slump, and stiff competition was pinching margins in bulk flour, which accounted for over a quarter of General Mills's sales. The company's attempts to enter such fields as electronics and animal feed were unprofitable. Internally, General Mills was sedate and stratified. Promotions came hard. Management was dominated by the family of James Ford Bell, who founded General Mills in 1928.

But though the managers were steeped in tradition they were not intoxicated by it. Since the early 1960s, there has been a metamorphosis at General Mills, a fundamental upheaval in product lines, organization, and attitudes. And to a surprising extent, the changes have been wrought by young people—specifically, by a remarkable group of men in their twenties and early thirties.

A harbinger of the transformation was the hiring in 1960 of Louis F. Polk, Jr., then thirty years old, as special assistant to the controller's department staff. Educated at Andover, Yale, and the Harvard Business School and fresh from a vice-presidency at a Bendix Corp. subsidiary, Bo Polk quickly became both an instigator and an emblem of rapid change in the company. Polk was named vice president and chief financial officer in 1961, and was a member of the board of directors from 1964 until a month ago, when he left General Mills and entered a highly publicized contest to become president and chief executive officer of Metro-Goldwyn-Mayer.

Shortly after Polk's arrival, General Mills became a youth-conscious corporation. It stepped up its college recruiting program, and began actively seeking men with master's degrees in business administration. Because it was seriously determined to accommodate their skills and because its problems embodied a classic managerial challenge, the company succeeded in drawing some unusually talented young men to Minneapolis. One of them was Henry H. Porter, Jr., twenty-seven and just out of the business school at Harvard when Polk hired him as his assistant in 1962. Recalls Porter: "I did feel I was being used productively from the beginning. I had zero legal experience, but one of the first jobs I had was to sell a cat-food plant in Boston. And I was deeply involved in getting us out of our electronics business."

Ending some of the ill-starred forays into diversification was a necessary prelude to the renaissance at General Mills. Also, the company, with strong support from its growing group of young managers, closed nine of its seventeen flour mills around the country. All together, operations that had been producing over $200 million in annual sales—about one-third of the total—were discontinued. In 1962 these operations had a combined loss of about $8 million. In the process, General Mills freed some $100 million of cash for other ventures.

A chance to put some of the money to work came along in 1964, when company researchers turned up a novel discovery: a product made with a food base, which could be sold as a toy. A market study run by Craig A. Nalen, another young executive working for Polk, indicated little chance of success for that particular product. But Nalen and Polk became intrigued with the general field of crafts, toys, and games, and spurred the company into a series of acquisitions, beginning with Rainbow Crafts, a small outfit producing a modeling compound known as Play-Doh. (The toy company's thirty-five-year-old sole owner was so buoyed by freedom from entrepreneurial burdens that he immediately enrolled in the Harvard Divinity School.) Among the division's three subsequent acquisitions was Parker Brothers, maker of Ouija boards and Monopoly. In the fiscal year ended last May, the new division's operating profit was $5,267,000, or 6.6 percent of the company's total.

The boost to earnings has been so resounding that General Mills has set up a New Ventures Department—a kind of free-form assemblage of salaried entrepreneurs in their twenties and thirties. The hope is that its members will descry profitable new businesses, develop a strategy for entry through acquisition or internal development, and then operate the new enterprises as divisions or subsidiaries. By such corporate devices, General Mills is catching and keeping young people, and establishing a new managerial environment.

THE NOW GENERATION
LOOKS AT MANAGEMENT

The degree to which U.S. corporations are being shaped by the new college graduates they seek and hire marks one of the important new paths taken by business in this decade. Educated young people are bringing impressive skills to business, and making equally impressive demands. Companies wise enough to accommodate to both are reaping benefits. But along the way they have had to upend everything from training programs and organization charts to salary scales and the way top executives allocate their time.

One reason young people are having such an impact on business is simply that there are so many of them taking corporate jobs. This point serves as a corrective to those worrisome reports that the Now Generation is shunning business careers. Recent surveys, including a major one by the College Placement Council in Bethlehem, Pennsylvania, indicate that around half of all college seniors are at least considering careers with business firms. This evidence is bolstered by the popularity of almost all institutions offering training in management skills: Enrollment in graduate schools of business and commerce has more than doubled since 1960. This school year, according to the American Council on Education, more college freshmen expect to major in business than in any other area.

Judged by sheer numbers, then, business continues to look attractive on campus. But certain important groups of students must be excepted. Some dissidents who are intelligent and serious are highly critical of business, and they may eventually wield considerable influence over the environment in which business operates. Even among nonactivists, many students—including a disproportionate number of the most academically gifted—will choose teaching and government posts, which pay much higher salaries and enjoy greater prestige than they did even a few years ago. Edward E. Booher, chairman of McGraw-Hill Book Co., notes with some amazement, "Recently one of my worthy young associates seriously remarked that working for a book publisher devoted to the improvement of learning and the spread of knowledge and information was almost as exciting and important as working for the federal government. And this was intended as a compliment!"

For all their growing appeal, nonbusiness fields still only gnaw at the peripheries of the annual crop of potential executives. Corporate recruiters generally dismiss the notion that they are losing many good applicants because of student sentiment against business. The most strident antibusiness rhetoric comes from students who were never very likely to become businessmen anyway. And top scholars have always been strongly attracted to teaching, the professions, and other nonbusiness pursuits.

IN SEARCH OF THE WHOOPING CRANE

Companies continue to seek potential managers largely among engineers, scientists, M.B.A.s, and graduates of smaller, nonurban liberal-arts colleges—groups not wholly untouched by the new movements in campus thinking, but still conspicuous for lack of radicalism. While business certainly needs bright people, the skills of successful management are not necessarily associated with unusual academic distinction. Says Lee A. Iacocca, an executive vice president of Ford Motor Co., "I don't always look for the valedictorian—he doesn't always fit. It takes a certain breed of youth to get into our business, which is the epitome of the rat race. You get 15,000 parts to flow together properly, then another year out it's another model. A lot of people are not cut out for it."

The draft, the Peace Corps, and the graduate schools absorb so many graduating seniors these days that the twenty-two-year-old with a bachelor's degree—once the most common prey for recruiters—is rapidly becoming what one New York personnel executive calls "the whooping crane of the labor market." To take an extreme example, only 6 percent of Harvard's class of 1968 went directly into business. But many of these young people will, of course, eventually be seeking corporate jobs.

It may be good for business to have a certain number of talented potential executives choose government or academic work. The fortunes of a lot of companies depend increasingly on the decisions of government agencies; any success the agencies have in attracting capable people should be good news for these companies. Men and women who enter academic life do not necessarily slide irretrievably beyond the horizon of the business world, either. The research they carry out in many disciplines can be helpful to business, and a fair number of them will end up on company payrolls as consultants. Furthermore, some of those who begin careers in other fields intend one day to enter business full time. Some young lawyers who go to work for federal regulatory agencies are motivated partly by the knowledge that two or three years of such experience will greatly increase their value to industry—and with it their starting salaries.

"I INTERVIEWED I.B.M."

The sense that many businessmen have of a shortage of trained young man-power reflects not an actual lessening of the supply of people, but a quite staggering upsurge in industry's demand for college graduates. Because of the low birth rates of the depression years, the number of men aged thirty-five to forty-five has been declining nationally since 1963. Since this is the age group most commonly found in middle- and upper-middle management positions, an unusual number of those positions have to be filled by younger men. This quirk of demography coincides with a rapid and prolonged economic expansion, an explosion of technological change, and the historic shift from blue-collar to white-collar employment, all of which have increased the need for highly educated managers. The convergence of these trends has resulted in an unprecedented and sometimes undignified scramble by corporations to court the young.

Because the demand for their services so greatly exceeds the supply, young graduates are in a strong position to dictate terms to their prospective employers. This power—rather than any new political orientation or social awareness—accounts for most of the singular impact this generation is already having on corporations. On the whole, the impact has been healthy. In the classic manner of business-oriented people, young employees are demanding that they be given productive tasks to do from the first day of work, and that the people they work for notice and react to their performance. The demand is provoking an unusual amount of attention and sympathetic action by business. Corporations are recognizing that even inexperienced manpower is a scarce resource. They are reviewing their procedures to see how they can use costly young employees more efficiently. This is disturbing bureaucratic peace in some companies, but the results could be beneficial all around.

To anyone who has been absent from the postgraduate job market for a few years, the current relationship between young job seekers and their prospective big-business bosses is almost unbelievable. Revealingly, and without a trace of irony, students almost invariably refer to their talks with corporate recruiters by saying, "I interviewed I.B.M. [or whomever]"—not, "I was interviewed." Despite some slackening of the rush to recruit graduates after the minirecession of 1967, the good student at a well-regarded school can still expect multiple job offers. If he has a technical degree, an M.B.A., or—better yet—both, he can run his total into the dozens if he is so inclined.

The amount of time, money, and energy that corporations put into their annual recruiting drives is stupendous, particularly when it is realized that the whole idea of large-scale college recruiting is fairly new to most companies. Organizations with heavy requirements for technically trained people have been familiar presences on the campus for decades, of course; A.T. & T., General Electric, and the oil companies are prime examples. But most companies have arrived in force much more recently. Ford did some scattered recruiting as far back as the 1940s, but the company did not formally establish a college recruiting department until 1959, when it hired 285 college graduates. In 1969 the company plans to send recruiters to 200 colleges and universities in an effort to hire 1750 people at a direct recruiting cost of some $1,300,000. This figure does not include the time of 400 line executives at Ford, each of whom spends several days a year actively recruiting on campuses.

In organizations with a pressing need for M.B.A.s, notably banks and management-consulting firms, even top management now recruits. The First National City Bank of New York augments its year-round recruiting efforts at Harvard and a few other graduate schools of business by sending annually what a personnel executive calls "a traveling road show" consisting of the chairman, the president, and other top officials to entertain groups of students at dinner. The personnel man recalls wryly, "When I first went to work here eighteen years ago, I saw a vice president—and didn't see another one for a long time."

THE END OF DESTITUTION

Corporations are wooing technical and business students at the more prestigious colleges with an intensity once reserved for the recruitment of unusually well-coordinated high-school quarterbacks. There circulate dark legends, some of which are probably rooted in fact, of joyrides in company planes, trips to Hawaii, and Lucullan feasts. Such extreme inducements are not at all usual, partly because they are thought likely to repel more good prospects than they attract. But expense-paid cross-country trips to inspect plants and meet executives are now common. And most big companies have started reimbursing new employees for the costs of moving from college to the first job. An eastern bank has found that even this generosity may be insufficient; one of its freshly graduated M.B.A.s expressed chagrin when the bank declined to pay the cost of shipping more than one of his two cars.

The most easily measurable effect of this competition for graduates has been its dramatic impact on starting salaries. These have been rising at a rate of 5 to 10 percent annually for several years. Today scarcely any college man need consider offers to start at less than $6000 a year, or around $120 a week. Many students with bachelor's degrees are offered as much as $9000 or so, depending on such variables as their major field of study and the type of company involved.

For those with graduate degrees, according to the College Placement Council, *average* industrial starting wages scale upward from over $10,000 for an M.S. in chemistry to approximately $16,000 for a new Ph. D. in electrical engineering. For M.B.A.s from the dozen or so top business schools, offers normally start above $10,000, average around $12,000, and are not at all unusual at as much as $14,000. Even lawyers can now avoid the period of postgraduate destitution that used to be deemed good for their professional souls; last winter the large Wall Street law firms, in an apparent bid to offset the growing appeal to young lawyers of work for government and antipoverty agencies, raised their basic salary from $10,500 to $15,000.

Young applicants insist that they are less concerned with pay than with other job values. But this insistence reflects their ability to choose among various high-paying positions, rather than any asceticism. "Some of my liberal friends," relates an M.B.A. candidate at the University of Pennsylvania's Wharton School, "want me to work for the National Labor Relations Board at $7000 a year. I can't quite do that. I'm not that much of a martyr." As Ford's Lee Iacocca notes, "Kids say that aren't interested in money alone. But it's sure good for openers."

The escalation of starting pay has spread shock waves through the entire salary structure. Companies often find themselves in the anomalous position of having to promise more to a new graduate than they are paying people already in their employ for a year or two. Since the word about starting pay gets around quickly, companies have to raise other salaries too. After the law firm of Cravath, Swaine & Moore pioneered the $15,000 starting salary last February, one of its partners received two boxes of candy and a valentine from a group of junior lawyers down the street at Nixon Mudge Rose Guthrie Alexander & Mitchell.

The effects of this big push from the bottom are not concentrated solely among younger employees. The push has been compressing the range of salaries at upper levels as well. The management-consulting firm of McKinsey & Co. has completed a study of the compensation of nearly 48,000 executives (defined as the highest-paid 1 percent of all employees) in eighty-six large companies. The study found that, between 1956 and 1967, lower-level executives got bigger percentage increases in compensation than their superiors; this pattern was unvarying, from the lowest-paid 30 percent of executives, whose compensation rose 54 percent in the eleven years, to the highest-paid 1 percent of the group, who had only a 23 percent rise. Using statistics adjusted to avoid distortions caused by exceptional individuals at either end of the pay scale, the study indicated that in 1967 the average sixty-five-year-old executive was paid $33,000, or only a bit more than half again as much as the $20,000 averaged by executives at age thrity. Arch Patton, a McKinsey director, comments: "In too many instances, companies are paying their newest executive trainees almost as much as men with considerably more experience and demonstrably greater value."

DRAINING THE MESSENGER POOL

Many companies that have hired large numbers of M.B.A.s—whose pay has risen even faster than that of most—are actively examining their job definitions to see if some of the work now done by M.B.A.s can be handled instead by people with only bachelor's degrees or even by graduates of two-year colleges. In addition, Ford, Lockheed, and some other large employers have expanded their "cooperative education" arrangements with a number of colleges. In the co-op program, undergraduates alternate trimesters of college with trimesters of work for the participating company. Most of the students in the programs have joined their co-op companies full time after graduation, and personnel men are enthusiastic about them. Says Lockheed's manpower administrator, Kaye R. Kiddoo: "They fit in better than *anyone*."

Still, the demand for M.B.A.s is likely to remain strong, partly because the business schools attract a disproportionate share of the most promising people who intend to go into business (see "The M.B.A.—the Man, the Myth, and the Method," *Fortune*, May, 1968). Retailers, utilities, railroads, and other companies that so far have made only light use of professionally trained managers are likely to compete more vigorously for them in the future. In manufacturing, college graduates have so far been concentrated overwhelmingly in staff positions at corporate headquarters rather than line jobs at the plant level; companies are gingerly moving toward correcting this imbalance, and at least one—Fairchild Camera & Instrument Corp.—has even started using M.B.A.s as foremen.

When wages were low, companies could afford to use new employees as mail sorters or messengers. Long training programs, frequently boring and purposeless, were common. But with the rise in costs, such practices have become uneconomic. Companies that emphasize training rather than quick responsibility generally find it harder to recruit bright students. "If there's one change, it's away from formal training and tours," says an automotive executive. "Good people want a task where they can say, 'I made money, I did something, I invented something.' They want to work for a living and have the satisfaction of having someone say, 'It's okay.' " J.C. Penney frequently makes young graduates department managers in stores after only a year or so of training; the average used to be closer to five years. Similarly, General Electric—which long has had intricately structured training programs, some of which amount almost to internal graduate schools—has lately introduced more flexible and shorter programs for its best new M.B.A.s. Explains Robert J. Canning, G.E.'s manager of college recruiting and relations, "They don't want to audit expense accounts, and we don't want a $12,000 clerk."

BEYOND THE PARKING LOT

The trend toward providing "meaningful work" for inexperienced employees has spread even to summer jobs. To get the people they want—and to keep them interested in permanent employment after graduation—quite a few firms now put students to work on projects that can be completed over a summer. Projects have ranged from computer-programming work and comparisons of companies' fringe benefits to full-fledged studies of potential acquisitions. So far, this kind of summer job has been offered almost exclusively to candidates for whom the competition is greatest—those studying for technical and business degrees. For other students, summer work still often means parking cars, stacking boxes, or filling in for vacationing clerks. But companies that have experimented with projects for summer employees are enthusiastic about the quality and usefulness of the work performed, and many of them no longer look upon the practice simply as a recruiting tool.

Some companies have met the new needs without abandoning their formal training programs. I.B.M. expects most of its people to attend courses inside and outside the company continually in order to keep up with its fast-changing and complex technologies. Officials affirm that employees welcome, rather than resist, this kind of purposeful training. I.B.M. is perennially one of the nation's most attractive corporations to college graduates. Last year it hired thirty new graduates of Cornell University, while 310 of the 427 companies that interviewed on the Cornell campus failed to hire a single student. Such appeal to students is hard to maintain, even for I.B.M. There are indications that some students may be reassessing the desirability of working for companies that have had great success in hiring bright graduates; the students worry that the executive pipeline may already be clogged with talented young people. Henry Porter of General Mills, a vice president at thirty-four, explains, "A person my age can be a model and encouragement, but also a cork in the way."

MILD ADVERSITY AT MERRILL LYNCH

Some companies can overcome resistance to long training, and even to low starting pay, simply by the magnitude of the eventual rewards they hold out. The college graduates in the junior executive program at Merrill Lynch, Pierce, Fenner & Smith are in training for a period of fifteen to twenty-one months. Even those with M.B.A. degrees start at a noncompetitive $575 a month, and can look forward to only token raises while in training. But at the end of it all, they can join Merrill Lynch's 4000-strong corps of brokers, whose 1967 median income was $26,400. Last year over a thousand young men and women applied for the twenty-five places in the junior-executive program.

The majority of companies can count on no such willingness to endure even mild and temporary adversity. The recent much-heralded increase in executive turnover is mostly explained by the restlessness of *young* executives (see "Why It's Harder to Keep Good Executives," *Fortune*, November, 1968), and there is no reason to believe that this restlessness will diminish. With surprising unanimity, business students say that they expect to stay with their first employer for only about three years. Thus companies have another powerful incentive to put young people quickly into tasks commensurate with their skills and salaries. The firm that does not get its money's worth out of a new man in the first couple of years may never get it.

Some companies are avoiding brand-new graduates because of their penchant for moving on. Litton Industries likes to hire managers who have worked elsewhere for a few years and have already taken their "first bounce." "We look for that experience that allows a person to evaluate his job in terms of what else he might be doing," says Ralph H. O'Brien, a Litton vice president. "The fellow right out of school always thinks the grass must be greener on the other side." Because its corporate staff is compact and because it is thought to be an unusually exciting company to work for, Litton can fill its needs without prowling the universities. Most companies cannot.

DEPRECIATION OF EXPERIENCE

The competition to sign up young people has been accompanied by a widespread change in corporate attitudes toward the value of experience. The freshness of outlook that young people can provide is more prized today. Bo Polk, who was deeply involved in General Mills's withdrawal from its unremunerative feed business, recalls, "The sacred cows said that we just couldn't get out of the business—it was too integrated and too interrelated in the rest of our business, we couldn't take the loss, et cetera. Fundamentally the withdrawal was a creative solution brought about by people who didn't know the feed business, who were not emotionally involved, and were determined to solve the problem."

Of all the attributes of this generation of college students, none is more characteristic than its vocal involvement with the great social and political questions of the day. Students who choose business careers tend to be a well-barbered, Republican-leaning lot, often condemned by their more fiery classmates as Philistines and materialists. But however unsatisfactory they may be by the yardsticks of the new left, these students do share many of the concerns of their peers, and particularly their determination to do something about racial injustice and the crisis of the cities. One of the most enthusiastically supported activities among M.B.A. candidates at the Wharton School is Business Practice Services (headed by one of the school's fourteen Negro graduate students), which sends teams of students into Philadelphia ghettos to advise black shop owners and entrepreneurs on such basic matters as how to keep a ledger. Companies are finding their social programs among the easiest of their activities to staff.

Of course, social concern within corporations extends far beyond the ranks of young employees. It often originates in the boardroom, not among junior executives. Moreover, support for social initiatives cuts across the barriers of age. Ford discovered that some of the warmest endorsements of the ghetto-hiring program instituted after the 1967 Detroit riots came from line supervisors who wanted a chance to help in alleviating problems of race and unemployment.

"WILL I BE ABLE TO DO SOMETHING?"

Companies sometimes appeal to the social consciousness of young people in their recruiting literature. General Electric stresses its involvement in the fight against polluted rivers and rare diseases. I.B.M. invites graduates to "help us make the world a better place to live in." But as in the past, the inducements that attract the most capable and sought-after people going into business are usually less abstract. "Students are more concerned with their own roles in their careers than with vague generalities about the social conscience of business," Franklin E. Smith, a 1968 graduate of Harvard, writes in the *MBA* magazine. "No matter how socially responsible business may be, students will not enter it if they are convinced that they will have little part in that responsibility . . . The biggest question these people seem to have is not one about social responsibility or pay, but 'will I be able to do something which is a challenge, an intellectual exercise, something creative and useful?' "

Comparisons between generations are almost always tendentious. One experienced personnel man sums up his new duties by saying, "We're dealing with a lot of tender little egos. They have to be told they're loved quite frequently." But young people today, for whom affluence and electronic communications are the routine stuff of existence, are certainly more cosmopolitan and better educated than their predecessors. Business does well to adjust its policies and procedures to these new conditions. Although many of the changes now coming about have been forced upon suspicious managements by the vagaries of the labor market, they are mostly for the better. There never was any special virtue in dissipating the initiative of young people by giving them menial positions, underpaying them, and in general causing them to feel insignificant. With remarkable consistency, the companies that have gone furthest in meeting the needs and wants of their young employees are the most enthusiastic about the performance of the new generation of businessmen.

40

Organizations of the Future

Warren Bennis
Massachusetts Institute of Technology

This article is adapted from a talk presented at the 22nd National Conference, American Society for Training and Development, May 2–6, 1966, Pittsburgh, Pa. Subsequently, several colleagues helped me edit the manuscript to avoid some possible traps and misstatements, and I am grateful to them: Charles Myers, Donald Marquis, Bill Humes, Ted Alfred, Dave Sirota, Charles Savage, Robert Kahn, Bill McKelvery, and Dave Kolb. They do not necessarily endorse the ideas expressed, of course. Reprinted by permission from the September–October 1967 issue of *Personnel Administration*, copyright 1967, Society for Personnel Administration, 485–87, National Press Building, 14th and F Streets, N. W., Washington, D. C. 20004.

Recently, I predicted that in the next 25 to 50 years we will participate in the end of bureaucracy as we know it and the rise of new social systems better suited to twentieth century demands of industrialization (5). This forcecast was based on the evolutionary principle that every age develops an organizational form appropriate to its genius and that the prevailing form of pyramidal-hierarchical organization, known by sociologists as "bureaucracy" and most businessmen as "that damn bureaucracy," was out of joint with contemporary realities.

I realize now that my prediction is already a distinct reality so that prediction is foreshadowed by practice.

I should like to make clear that by "bureaucracy" I mean the typical organizational structure that coordinates the business of most every human organization we know of: industry, government, university, R & D labs, military, religious, voluntary, and so forth.

Bureaucracy, as I refer to it here, is a useful social invention, perfected during the Industrial Revolution to organize and direct the activities of the business firm. Max Weber, the German sociologist who developed the theory of bureaucracy around the turn of the century, once described bureaucracy as a social machine.

The bureaucratic "machine model" was developed as a reaction against the personal subjugation, nepotism, cruelty, and capricious and subjective judgments that often passed for managerial practices during the early days of the Industrial Revolution. Bureaucracy emerged out of the need for more predictability, order, and precision. It was an organization ideally suited to the values and the demands of Victorian Empire. And just as bureaucracy emerged as a creative response to a radically new age, so today new organizational shapes and forms are surfacing before our eyes.

I shall try first to show why the conditions of our modern industrialized world will bring about the decline of bureaucracy and force a reconsideration of new organizational structures. Then, I will suggest a rough model of the organization of the future. Finally, I shall set forth the new tasks and challenges for the training and development manager.

WHY IS BUREAUCRACY VULNERABLE?

There are at least four relevant threats to bureaucracy. The first is a human, basically psychological one, which I shall return to later on, while the other three spring from extraordinary changes in our environment. The latter three are: (1) rapid and unexpected change, (2) growth in size where volume of organization's traditional activities is not enough to sustain growth, and (3) complexity of modern technology where integration of activities and persons of very diverse, highly specialized competence is required (28).

It might be useful to examine the extent to which these conditions exist right now.

RAPID AND UNEXPECTED CHANGE. It may be enough simply to cite the knowledge and population explosion. More revealing, however, are the statistics that demonstrate these events:

Our productivity per man hour now doubles almost every 20 years rather than every 40 years, which was true before World War II.

The federal government alone spent 16 billion in R & D activities in 1965 and will spend 35 billion by 1980.

The time lag between a technical discovery and recognition of its commercial uses was 30 years before World War I, 16 years between the wars, and only 9 years since World War II.

In 1946 only 30 cities in the world had populations of more than one million. Today there are 80. In 1930 there were 40 people for each square mile of the earth's land surface. Today, there are 63. By the year 2000, there are expected to be 142.

GROWTH IN SIZE.   Not only have more organizations grown larger, but they have become more complex and more international. Firms like Standard Oil of New Jersey (with 57 foreign affiliates), Socony Mobil, National Cash Register, Singer, Burroughs, and Colgate-Palmolive derive more than half their income or earnings from foreign sales. A long list of other, such as Eastman Kodak, Pfizer, Caterpillar Tractor, International Harvester, Corn Products, and Minnesota Mining and Manufacturing make from 30 to 50 percent of their sales abroad (3). General Motors's sales are not only nine times those of Volkswagen, they are also bigger than the gross national product of The Netherlands and well over those of a hundred other countries. If we have seen the sun set on the British Empire, it will be a long time before it sets on the empires of General Motors, ITT, Royal Dutch/Shell and Unilever.

TODAY'S ACTIVITIES REQUIRE PERSONS OF VERY DIVERSE, HIGHLY SPECIALIZED COMPETENCE.   Numerous dramatic examples can be drawn from studies of labor markets and job mobility. At some point during the past decade, the U.S. became the first nation in the world ever to employ more people in service occupations than in the production of tangible goods. Examples of this trend are:

In the field of education, the *increase* in employment between 1950 and 1960 was greater than the total number employed in the steel, copper, and aluminum industries.

In the field of health, the *increase* in employment between 1950 and 1960 was greater than the total number employed in automobile manufacturing in either year.

In financial firms, the *increase* in employment between 1950 and 1960 was greater than total employment in mining in 1960 (15).

Rapid change, hurried growth, and increase in specialists: With these three logistical conditions we should expect bureaucracy to decline.

CHANGE IN MANAGERIAL BEHAVIOR

Earlier I mentioned a fourth factor which seemed to follow along with the others though its exact magnitude, nature, and antecedents appear more obscure and shadowy due to the relative difficulty of assigning numbers to it. This factor stems from the personal observation that over the past decade there has been a fundamental change in the basic philosophy that underlies managerial behavior. The change in philosophy is reflected most of all in:

A new concept of *Man*, based on increased knowledge of his complex and shifting needs, which replaces an oversimplified, innocent push-button idea of man.

A new concept of *power*, based on collaboration and reason, which replaces a model of power based on coercion and threat.

A new concept of *organization values*, based on humanistic–democratic ideals, which replaces the depersonalized mechanistic value system of bureaucracy.

These transformations of Man, power, and values have gained wide intellectual acceptance in management quarters. They have caused a terrific amount of rethinking on the part of many organizations. They have been used as a basis for policy formulation by many large-scale organizations. This philosophy is clearly not compatible with bureaucratic practices.

The primary cause of this shift in management philosophy stems not from the bookshelf but from the manager himself. Many of the behavioral scientists, like McGregor or Likert, have clarified and articulated—even legitimized—what managers have only half registered to themselves. I am convinced that the success of McGregor's *The Human Side of Enterprise* (19) was based on a rare empathy for a vast audience of managers who were wistful for an alternative to a mechanistic conception of authrotity. It foresaw a vivid utopia of more authentic human relationships than most organizational practices allow. Furthermore, I suspect that the desire for relationships has little to do with a profit motive per se, though it is often rationalized as doing so (2). The real push for these changes stems from some powerful needs, not only to humanize the organization, but to use the organization as a crucible of personal growth and development, for self-realization (33).

CORE ORGANIZATION PROBLEMS

As a result of these changes affecting organizations of the future, new problems and tasks are emerging. They fall, I believe, into five major categories, which I visualize as the core tasks confronting organizations of the future.

1. *Integration* encompasses the entire range of issues having to do with the incentives, rewards, and motivation of the individual and how the organization succeeds or fails in adjusting to these needs. In other words, it is the ratio between individual needs and organizational demands that creates the transaction most satisfactory to both. The problem of *integration* grows out of our "consensual society," where personal attachments play a great part, where the individual is appreciated, in which there is concern for his well-being, not just in veterinary-hygiene sense, but as a moral, integrated personality.

2. The problem of *social influence* is essentially the problem of power and how power is distributed. It is a complex issue and alive with controversy, partly because of an ethical component and partly because studies of leadership and power distribution can be interpreted in many ways, and almost always in ways which coincide with one's biases (including a cultural leaning toward democracy).

The problem of power has to be seriously reconsidered because of dramatic situational changes that make the possibility of one-man rule or the "Great Man" not necessarily "bad" but impractical. I am referring to changes in the role of top management. Peter Drucker, over 12 years ago, listed 41 major responsibilities of the chief executive and declared that "90 percent of the trouble we are having with the chief executive's job is rooted in our superstition of the one-man chief" (11). The broadening product base of industry, impact of new technology, the scope of international operations, make one-man control quaint, if not obsolete.

MANAGING CONFLICT

3. The problem of *collaboration* grows out of the very same social processes of conflict and stereotyping, and centrifugal forces that divide nations and communities. They also employ furtive, often fruitless, always crippling mechanisms of conflict resolution: avoidance or suppression, annihilation of the weaker party by the stronger, sterile compromises, and unstable collusions and coalitions. Particularly as organizations become more complex they fragment and divide, building tribal patterns and symbolic codes which often work to exclude others (secrets and noxious jargon, for example), and on occasion to exploit differences for inward (and always fragile) harmony. Some large organizations, in fact, can be understood only through an analysis of their cabals, cliques, and satellites, where a venture into adjacent spheres of interest is taken under cover of darkness and fear of ambush. Dysfunctional intergroup conflict is so easily stimulated, that one wonders if it is rooted in our archaic heritage when man struggled, with an imperfect symbolic code and early consciousness, for his territory. Robert R. Blake in his experiments has shown how simple it is to induce conflict, how difficult to arrest it (7). Take two groups of people who have never been together before, and give them a task that will be judged by an impartial jury. In less than one hour, each group devolves into a tightly-knit band with all the symptoms of an "in-group." They regard their product as a "masterwork" and the other group's as "commonplace," at best. "Other" becomes "enemy"; "We are good; they are bad. We are right; they are wrong" (27).

Jaap Rabbie, conducting experiments on the antecedents of intergroup conflict at the University of Utrecht, has been amazed by the ease with which conflict and stereotype develop.[1] He brings into the experimental room two groups and distributes green name tags and green pens to one group and refers to it as the "green group." He distributes red pens and red name tags to the other group and refers to it as the "red group." The groups do not compete; they do not even interact. They are in sight of each other for only minutes while they silently complete a questionnaire. Only 10 minutes is needed to activate defensiveness and fear.

In a recent essay on animal behavior, Erikson develops the idea of "pseudo-

---

[1] Personal communication, January 1966.

species" (13). Pseudo-species act as if they were separate species created at the beginning of time by supernatural intent. He argues:

> Man has evolved (by whatever kind of evolution and for whatever adaptive reasons) in pseudo-species, i.e., tribes, clans, classes, etc. Thus, each develops not only a *distinct sense of identity* but also a conviction of harboring *the* human identity, fortified against other pseudo-species by prejudices which mark them as extraspecific and inimical to "genuine" human endeavor. Paradoxically, however, newly born man is (to use Ernst Mayr's term) a generalist creature who could be made to fit into any number of pseudo-species and must, therefore, become "specialized" during a prolonged childhood. . . .

Modern organizations abound with pseudo-species, bands of specialists held together by the illusion of a unique identity and with a tendency to view other pseudo-species with suspicion and mistrust. Ways must be discovered to produce generalists and diplomats, and we must find more effective means of managing inevitable conflict and minimizing the pseudo-conflict. This is not to say that conflict is always avoidable and dysfunctional. Some types of conflict may lead to productive and creative ends.

4. The problem of adaptation is caused by our turbulent environment. The pyramidal structure of bureaucracy, where power was concentrated at the top, seemed perfect to "run a railroad." And undoubtedly for the routinized tasks of the nineteenth and early twentieth centuries, bureaucracy was and still is an eminently suitable social arrangement. However, rather than a placid and predictable environment, what predominates today is a dynamic and uncertain one in which there is a deepending interdependence among the economic and other facets of society.

5. Finally, the problem of revitalization. As Alfred North Whitehead says:

> The art of free society consists first in the maintenance of the symbolic code, and secondly, in the fearlessness of revision. . . . Those societies which cannot combine reverence to their symbols with freedom of revision must ultimately decay. . . .

Growth and decay emerge as the penultimate conditions of contemporary society. Organizations, as well as societies, must be concerned with those social structures that engender buoyancy, resilience, and a "fearlessness of revision."

I introduce the term "revitalization" to embrace all the social mechanisms that stagnate and regenerate with the process of this cycle. The elements of revitalization are:

> An ability to learn from experience and to codify, store, and retrieve the relevant knowledge.
> An ability to "learn how to learn," that is, to develop methodologies for improving the learning process.
> An ability to acquire and use feedback mechanisms on performance, to develop a "process orientation," in short, to be self-analytical.
> An ability to direct one's own destiny.

These qualities have a good deal in common with what John Gardner calls "self-renewal." For the organization, it means conscious attention to its own evolution. Without a planned methodology and explicit direction, the enterprise will not realize its potential.

Integration, distribution of power, collaboration, adaptation, and revitalization are the major human problems of the next 25 years. How organizations cope with and manage these tasks will undoubtedly determine the viability and growth of the enterprise.

ORGANIZATIONS OF THE FUTURE[2]

Against this background I should like to set forth some of the conditions that will determine organizational life in the next two or three decades:

1. THE ENVIRONMENT. Rapid technological change and diversification will lead to interpenetration of the government with business.

Partnerships between government and business will be typical. It will be a truly mixed economy. Because of the immensity and expense of the projects, there will be fewer identical units competing for the same buyers and sellers. Organizations will become more interdependent.

The four main features of the environment are:

Interdependence rather than competition.
Turbulence and uncertainty rather than readiness and certainty.
Large-scale rather than small-scale enterprises.
Complex and multinational rather than simple national enterprises.

2. POPULATION CHARACTERISTICS. The most distinctive characteristic of our society is, and will become even more so, education. Within 15 years, two-thirds of our population living in metropolitan areas will have attended college. Adult education is growing even faster, probably because of the rate of professional obsolescence. The Killian report showed that the average engineer required further education only 10 years after gaining his degree. It will become almost routine for the experienced physician, engineer, and executive to go back to school for advanced training every two or three years. Some 50 universities, in addition to a dozen large corporations, offer advanced management courses to successful men in the middle and upper ranks of business. Before World War II, only two such programs existed, both new, both struggling to get students.

All of this education is not just "nice," it is necessary. As Secretary of Labor Wirtz recently pointed out, computers can do the work of most high school graduates—cheaper and more effectively. Fifty years ago education was regarded as "nonwork" and intellectuals on the payroll were considered "overhead."

---

[2] Adapted from an earlier paper by the author, "Beyond Bureaucracy," *Trans-Action*, July–August 1965.

Today the survival of the firm *depends* on the effective exploitation of brain power.

One other characteristic of the population which will aid our understanding of organizations of the future is increasing job mobility. The ease of transportation, coupled with the needs of a dynamic environment, change drastically the idea of "owning" a job—or "having roots." Already 20 percent of our population change their mailing address at least once a year.

3. WORK VALUES. The increased level of education and mobility will change the values we hold about work. People will be more intellectually committed to their professional careers and will probably require more involvement, participation, and autonomy.

Also, people will be more "other-directed," taking cues for their norms and values from their immediate environment rather than tradition. We will tend to rely more heavily on temporary social arrangements (31). We will tend to have relationships rather than relatives.

4. TASKS AND GOALS. The tasks of the organization will be more technical, complicated, and unprogrammed. They will rely on intellect instead of muscle. And they will be too complicated for one person to comprehened, to say nothing of control. Essentially they will call for the collaboration of specialists in a project or a team form of organization.

There will be a complication of goals. Business will increasingly concern itself with its adaptive or innovative-creative capacity. In addition, meta-goals will have to be articulated; that is, supra-goals which shape and provide the foundation for the goal structure. For example, one meta-goal might be a system for detecting new and changing goals; another could be a system for deciding priorities among goals.

Finally, more conflict and contradiction can be expected from diverse standards of organizational effectiveness. One reason for this is that professionals tend to identify more with the goals of their profession than with those of their immediate employer. University professors can be used as a case in point. Within the university, there may be a conflict between teaching and research. Often, more of a professor's income derives from outside sources, such as foundations and consultant work. They tend not to be good "company men" because they divide their loyalty between their professional values and organizational goals.

ORGANIC–ADAPTIVE STRUCTURE

5. ORGANIZATION. The social structure of organizations of the future will have some unique characteristics. The key word will be "temporary"; there will be adaptive, rapidly changing temporary systems. These will be "task forces" organized around problems-to-be-solved by groups of relative strangers who represent a diverse set of professional skills. The groups will be arranged on an organic rather than mechanical model; they will evolve in response to a problem rather than to programmed role expectations. The "executive" thus becomes a coordinator or "linking pin" between various task forces. He must be a man who can speak the diverse languages of research, with skills to relay information and to mediate between groups. People will be evaluated not vertically according to rank and status, but flexibly and functionally according to skill and professional training. Organizational charts will consist of project groups rather than functional groups. This trend is already visible today in the aerospace and construction industries, as well as many professional and consulting firms.

Adaptive, problem-solving, temporary systems of diverse specialists, linked together by coordinating and task evaluating specialists in an organic flux—this is the organizational form that will gradually replace bureaucracy as we know it. As no catchy phrase comes to mind, I call this an organic-adaptive structure.

6. MOTIVATION. The organic–adaptive structure should increase motivation, and thereby effectiveness, because it enhances satisfactions intrinsic to the task. There is a harmony between the educated individual's need for meaningful, satisfactory, and creative tasks and a flexible organizational structure.

There will, however, also be reduced commitment to work groups, for these groups, as I have already mentioned, will be transient structures. I would predict that in the organic–adaptive system, people will learn to develop quick and intense relationships on the job, and learn to bear the loss of more enduring work relationships. Because of the added ambiguity of roles, time will have to be spent on continual rediscovery of the appropriate organizational mix.

AMERICANS PREPARED

The American experience of frontier neighbors, after all, prepares us for this, so I don't view "temporary systems" as such a grand departure. These "brief encounters" need not be more superficial than long and chronic ones. I have seen too many people, some occupying adjacent offices for many years, who have never really experienced or encountered each other. They look at each other with the same vacant stares as people do on buses and subways, and perhaps they are passengers waiting for their exit.

Europeans typically find this aspect of American life frustrating. One German expatriate told me of his disenchantment with "friendly Americans." At his first party in this country, he met a particularly sympathetic fellow and the two of them fell into a warm conversation which went on for several hours. Finally, they had to leave to return to their homes, but like soul-mates, they couldn't part. They went down into the city street and walked round and round on this cold winter night, teeth chattering and arms bound. Finally, both stiff with cold, the American hailed a cab and went off with a wave. The European was stunned. He didn't know his new "friend's" name. He never saw or heard from him again. "That's your American friendship," he told me.

That *is* American friendship: intense, spontaneous, total involvement, unpredictable in length, impossible to control. They are happenings, simultaneously "on" and transitory and then "off" and then new lights and new happenings.

A Swiss woman in Max Frisch's *I'm Not Stiller* sums it up this way: "Apparently all these frank and easy-going people did not expect anything else from a human relationship. There was no need for this friendly relationship to go on growing" (14).

TRAINING REQUIREMENTS FOR ORGANIZATIONS OF THE FUTURE

How can we best plan for the organizational developments I forecast? And how can training and development directors influence and direct this destiny? One thing is clear: There will be a dramatically new role for the manager of training and development. Let us look at some of the new requirements.

1. TRAINING FOR CHANGE. The remarkable aspect of our generation is its commitment to change, in thought and action. Can training and development managers develop an educational process which:

Helps us to identify with the adaptive process without fear of losing our identity?
Increases our tolerance for ambiguity without fear of losing intellectual mastery?
Increases our ability to collaborate without fear of losing individuality?
Develops a willingness to participate in our own social evolution while recognizing implacable forces?

Putting it differently, it seems to me that we should be trained in an attitude toward inquiry and novelty rather than the particular content of a job; training for change means developing "learning men."

2. SYSTEMS COUNSELING. It seems to me that management (and personnel departments) have failed to come to grips with the reality of social systems. It is embarrassing to state this after decades of research have been making the same point. We have proved that productivity can be modified by group norms, that training effects fade out and deteriorate if training goals are not compatible with the goals of the social system, that group cohesiveness is a powerful motivator, that intergroup conflict is a major problem facing modern organization, that individuals take many of their cues from their primary work group, that identification with the work group turns out to be the only stable predictor of productivity, and so on. Yet this evidence is so frequently ignored that I can only infer that there is something naturally preferable (almost an involuntary reflex) in locating the sources of all problems in the individual and diagnosing situations as functions of faulty individuals rather than as symptoms of malfunctioning social systems.

If this reflex is not arrested, it can have serious repercussions. In these new organizations, where roles will be constantly changing and certainly ambiguous, where changes in one subsystem will clearly affect other subsystems, where diverse and multinational activities have to be coordinated and integrated, where individuals engage simultaneously in multiple roles and group memberships (and role conflict is endemic), a systems viewpoint must be developed. Just as it is no longer possible to make any enduring change in a "problem child" without treating the entire family, it will not be possible to influence individual behavior without working with his particular subsystem. This means that our training and development managers of the future must perform the functions of systems counselors.

3. CHANGING MOTIVATION.   The rate at which professional–technical–managerial types join organizations is higher than any other employment category. While it isn't fully clear what motivates them, two important factors emerge.

The first is a strong urge to "make it" professionally, to be respected by professional colleagues. Loyalty to an organization may increase if it encourages professional growth. Thus, the "good place to work" will resemble a super-graduate school, abounding with mature, senior colleagues, where the employee will work not only to satisfy organizational demands but, perhaps primarily, those of his profession.

The other factor involves the quest for self-realization, for personal growth which may not be task related. That remark, I am well aware, questions four centuries of encrusted Protestant ethic. And I feel uncertain as to how (or even *if*) these needs can be met by an organization. However, we must hope for social inventions to satisfy these new desires. Training needs to take more responsibility for attitudes about continuing education so that it is not considered a "retread" or a "repair factory" but a natural and inescapable aspect of work. The idea that education has a terminal point and that adults have somehow "finished" is old-fashioned. A "drop-out" should be redefined to mean anyone who hasn't returned to school.

However the problem of professional and personal growth is resolved, it is clear that many of our older forms of incentive, based on lower echelons of the need hierarchy, will have to be reconstituted.

4. SOCIALIZATION FOR ADULTS.   In addition to continuing education, we have to face the problem of continuing socialization, or the institutional influences which society provides to create good citizens. Put simply, it means training in values, attitudes, ethics, and morals. We allot these responsibilities typically to the family, to church, to schools. We incorrectly assume that socialization stops when the individual comes of age. Most certainly, we are afraid of socialization for adults, as if it implies the dangers of a delayed childhood disease, like whooping cough.

Or to be more precise, we frown not on socialization, but on conscious and responsible control of it. In fact, our organizations are magnificent, if undeliberate, vehicles of socialization. They teach values, inculcate ethics, create norms, dictate right and wrong, influence attitudes necessary for success, and all the rest. The men who succeed tend to be well socialized and the men who don't, are not: "Yeah, Jones was a marvelous worker, but he never fit in around here." And most universities grant tenure where their norms and values are most accepted, although this is rarely stated.

Taking conscious responsibility for the socialization process will become imperative in tomorrow's organization. And finding men with the right technical capability will not be nearly as difficult as finding men with the right set of values and attitudes. Of course, consciously guiding this process is a trying business, alive with problems, not the least being the ethical one: Do we have the right to shape attitudes and values? We really do not have a choice. Can we avoid it? How bosses lead and train subordinates, how individuals are treated, what and who gets rewarded, the subtle cues transmitted and learned without seeming recognition, occur spontaneously. What we can choose are the mechanisms of socialization—how coercive we are, how much individual freedom we give, how we transmit values. What will be impermissible is a denial to recognize that we find some values more desirable, and to accept responsibility for consciously and openly communicating them.

5. DEVELOPING PROBLEM-SOLVING TEAMS. One of the most difficult and important challenges for the training and development manager will be the task of promoting conditions for effective collaboration or building synergetic teams. In synergy, individuals actually contribute more and perform better as a result of a collaborative and supportive environment. They play "over their heads," so to speak. The challenge I am referring to is the building of synergetic teams.

Of course, the job isn't an easy one. An easy way out is to adopt the "zero synergy" strategy. This means that the organization attempts to hire the best individuals it can and then permits them to "cultivate their own gardens." This is a strategy of isolation that can be observed in almost every university organization.

[Until universities take a serious look at their strategy of zero synergy, there is little hope that they will solve their vexing problems. The Berkeley protests were symptomatic of at least four self-contained, uncommunicating social systems (students, faculty, administration, trustees) without the trust, empathy, interaction (to say nothing of a tradition) to develop meaningful collaboration. To make matters even more difficult, if possible, academic types may, by nature (and endorsed by tradition) see themselves as "loners" and divergent to the majority. They all want to be independent together, so to speak. Academic narcissism goes a long way on the lecture platform but may be positively disruptive for developing a community.]

Another approach has the same effect but appears different. It is the pseudo-democratic sytle, in which a phony harmony and conflict avoidance persists.

In addition to our lack of background and experience in building synergy (and our strong cultural biases against group efforts), teams take time to develop.

They are like other highly complicated organisms and, just as we wouldn't expect a new-born to talk, we shouldn't expect a new team to work effectively from the start. Teams require trust and commitment and these ingredients require a period of gestation.

Expensive and time consuming as it is, building synergetic and collaborative frameworks will become essential. The problems that confront us are too complex and diversified for one man or one discipline. They require a blending of skills, slants, and disciplines for their solution and only effective problem-solving teams will be able to get on with the job.

6. DEVELOPING SUPRA-ORGANIZATIONAL GOALS AND COMMITMENTS.   The President of ABC (the fictitious name of a manufacturing company) was often quoted as saying:

> The trouble with ABC is that nobody aside from me ever gives one damn about the over-all goals of this place. They're all seeing the world through the lenses of their departmental biases. What we need around here are people who wear the ABC hat, not the engineering hat or the sales hat or the production hat.

After he was heard muttering this rather typical president's dirge, a small group of individuals, who thought they could wear the ABC hat, formed a group they called the ABC HATS. They came from various departments and hierarchical levels and represented a microcosm of the entire organization. The ABC HATS group has continued to meet over the past few years and has played a central role in influencing top policy.

It seems to me that training and development managers could affect the development of their organizations if they would encourage the formation of HATS groups. What worries me about the organization of the future, of specialized professionals and an international executive staff, is that their professional and regional outlook brings along with it only a relative truth and a distortion of reality. This type of organization is extremely vulnerable to the hardening of pseudo-species and a compartmentalized approach to problems.

Training and development can be helpful in a number of ways:

> They can identify and support those individuals who are "linking pins," individuals who have a facility for psychological and intellectual affinity with a number of diverse languages and cultures. These individuals will become the developers of problem-solving teams.
>
> They can perform the HATS function, which is another way of saying that training and development managers should be managers who keep over-all goals in mind and modulate the professional biases which are intrinsic to the specialists' work.
>
> They can work at the interfaces of the pseudo-species in order to create more intergroup understanding and interface articulation.

Today, we see each of the intellectual disciplines burrowing deeper into its own narrow sphere of interest. (Specialism, by definition, implies a peculiar slant, a segmented vision. A cloak and suit manufacturer went to Rome and managed to get an audience with His Holiness. Upon his return a friend asked him, "What did the Pope look like?" The tailor answered, "A 41 Regular.") Yet, the most interesting problems turn up at the intersection between disciplines and it may take an outsider to identify these. Even more often, the separate disciplines go their crazy-quilt way and rely more and more on internal standards of evidence and competence. They dismiss the outsider as an amateur with a contemptuous shrug. The problem with intellectual effort today (and I include my own field of organizational psychology) is that no one is developing the grand synthesis.

Organizations, too, require "philosophers," individuals who provide articulation between seemingly inimical interests, who break down the pseudo-species, and who transcend vested interests, regional ties, and professional biases in arriving at the solution to problems.

To summarize, I have suggested that the training and development director of the future has in store at least six new and different functions: (1) training for change, (2) systems counseling, (3) developing new incentives, (4) socializing adults, (5) building collaborative, problem-solving (5) building collaborative, problem-solving teams, and (6) developing supra-organizational goals and commitments. Undoubtedly there are others and some that cannot be anticipated. It is clear that they signify a fundamentally different role for personnel management from "putting out fires" and narrow maintenance functions. If training and development is to realize its true promise, its role and its image must change from maintenance to innovation.

I have seen this new role develop in a number of organizations, not easily or overnight, but pretty much in the way I have described it here. It might be useful to review briefly the conditions present in the cases I know about:

The personnel manager or some subsystem within personnel (it might be called "employee relations" or "industrial relations" or "career development") took an active, innovative role with respect to organizational goals and forcibly took responsibility for organizational growth and development.

Second, this group shifted its emphasis away from personnel functions per se (like compensation and selection) and toward organizational problems, like developing effective patterns of collaboration, or fostering an innovative atmosphere or reducing intergroup conflict, or organizational goal-setting and long-run planning.

Third, this group developed a close working relationship to various subsystems in the organization, an organic, task-oriented relationship, not the frequently observed mechanical "line–staff" relationship.

Fourth, they were viewed as full-fledged members of the management team, instead of the "head-shrinkers" or the "headquarters group." This was the hardest to establish in all cases, but turned out to be the most important. In fact, in one case, the man responsible for spearheading the organizational development effort has recently taken an important line job. The reverse happens too. Line management participates in so-called personnel activities, almost as if they are an adjunct to staff. Distinctions between line and staff blur in this context and an organic linkage develops, often serving as a prototype of a collabora-tive, problem-solving team.

One single factor stands out in retrospect over all others. There was always the conviction and the ability to make the training and development department the leading edge, the catalyst for organizational change and adaptability. Rather than performing the more traditional role, these groups became centers for innovation and organizational revitalization, and their leaders emerged as change-agents, the new managers of tomorrow's organizations.

I should now add another point in conclusion. It emerges from the previous points. They describe a far more autonomous, organizationally influential, self-directed role than trainers have been given or have asked for in the past.

If the training group is to be concerned with adult socialization, for example, it would be myopically irresponsible if not worse for them to define socializa-tion in terms of momentary needs of the organization. Rather, they must take at least some of the responsibility for enunciating the goals and conditions of the enterprise. In a way, their systems counseling function is "organizational soci-alization." If they take responsibility for socializing both the members as people and the organization as a human system, then they must have values and stand-ards which are somehow prior and outside both.

In fact, the emerging role I outline (Table 1) implies that the roles of the top management and training director become more interchangeable than ever before.

TABLE 1
HUMAN PROBLEMS CONFRONTING CONTEMPORARY ORGANIZATIONS

Problem	Bureaucratic Solutions	New Twentieth Century Conditions
Integration The problem of how to integrate individual needs and organizational goals.	No solution because of no problem; individual vastly oversimplified, regarded as passive instrument; tension between "personality" and role disregarded.	Emergence of human sciences and understanding of man's complexity; rising aspirations; humanistic–democratic ethos.
Social Influence The problem of the distribution of power and sources of power and authority.	An explicit reliance on legal–rational power, but an implicit usage of coercive power; in any case, a confused, ambiguous shifting complex of competence, coercion, and legal code.	Separation of management from ownership; rise of trade unions and general education; negative and unintended effects of authoritarian rule.
Collaboration The problem of producing mechanisms for the control of conflict.	The "rule of hierarchy" to resolve conflicts between ranks and the "rule of coordination" to resolve conflict between horizontal groups; "loyalty."	Specialization and professionalization and increased need for interdependence; leadership too complex for one-man rule or omniscience.
Adaptation The problem of responding appropriately to changes induced by the environment.	Environment stable, simple, and predictable; tasks routine; adapting to change occurs in haphazard and adventitious ways; unanticipated consequences abound.	External environment of firm more "turbulent," less predictable; unprecedented rate of technological change.
"Revitalization" The problem of growth and decay.	Underlying assumption that the future will be certain and basically similar to the past.	Rapid changes in technologies, tasks, manpower, raw materials, norms and values of society, goals of enterprise and society all make constant attention to the process of revision imperative.

Questioning
the Managerial Implications of
Managing in the Future

1. How can an organization best alleviate the anxiety likely to develop throughout its structure when sweeping programs of automation are undertaken? What responsibilities, if any, does it assume when jobs are replaced by machines?

2. Predict two sources of change in the manager's environment, in addition to those posed by Myers. Evaluate the applicability of his conclusions to the areas you choose.

3. What do you suppose will be some eventual effects on traditional management principles of the youth influx described by Rukeyser?

4. To what extent do you agree with the predictions made by Bennis? What additional evidence can you offer to support your view?

5. Why do we look to the future when there are so many problems to be solved today? What do we hope to gain?

References

1. Albrook, R. C., "Business Wrestles With Its Social Conscience," *Fortune,* LXXVIII, No. 2 (1968), 89–91ff.

2. Argyris, C., *Interpersonal Competence and Organizational Effectiveness.* Homewood, Ill.: Irwin-Dorsey, 1962.

3. Barber, R. J., "American Business Goes Global," *The New Republic,* CLIV (April 30, 1966), 154. 14–18.

4. Bell, D., "The Year 2000—The Trajectory of an Idea," *Daedalus,* XCVI, No. 3 (1967), 639–55.

5. Bennis, W., "The Decline of Bureaucracy and Organizations of the Future." (Invited address presented to the Division of Industrial and Business Psychology at the American Psychological Association meeting, Los Angeles, Calif., September 5, 1964).

6. ——, "Beyond Bureaucracy," *Trans-action,* III (1965).

7. Blake, R. R., H. A. Shepard, and J. S. Mouton, *Managing Intergroup Conflict in Industry.* Houston, Texas: Gulf Publishing Co., 1964.

8. Blough, R. M., "The Public Life of Private Business," address at Annual Meeting, American Iron and Steel Institute, New York, May 23, 1968.

9. *Business Week,* February 3, 1968, p. 59.

10. "Computers: How They're Remaking Companies," *Business Week,* Special Report, February 29, 1964.

11. Daniel, D. R., "Team at the Top," *Harvard Business Review* (1965), 74–82.

12. "Dealing the Negro in," *Business Week,* Special Report, May 1968, pp. 64–68ff.

13. Erikson, E., "Ontogeny of Ritualization." (Paper presented to the Royal Society, June 1965.

14. Frisch, M., *I'm Not Stiller.* Harmondsworth, Middlesex: Penguin Books, 1961, p. 244.

15. Fuchs, V. R., "The First Service Economy." *The Public Interest* (1966), 7–17.

16. Kahn, H., and A. J. Wiener, *The Year 2000*. New York: The Macmillan Co., 1967.

17. *Management 2000*. Hamilton, N. Y.: American Foundation for Management Research, 1968.

18. *Manpower Report of the President* (Washington, D. C.: Government Printing Office, April, 1968).

19. McGregor, D. M., *The Human Side of Enterprise*. New York: McGraw-Hill Book Company, 1960.

20. McNamara, R. S., *The Essence of Security*: *Reflections in Office*. New York: Harper & Row, Publishers, 1968.

21. Michael, D. N., *Cybernation*: *The Silent Conquest*. Santa Barbara, Calif.: Center for the Study of Democratic Institutions, 1962.

22. Mintzberg, H., "The Manager at Work—Determination of his Activities, Functions, and Programs by Structural Observation" (Doctoral dissertation, Massachusetts Institute of Technology Sloan School of Management, 1968.

23. Myers, C. A., ed., *The Impact of Computers on Management*. Cambridge, Mass.: Massachusetts Institute of Technology Press, 1967.

24. *The New York Times*, Book Review Section, February 21, 1965.

25. *The New York Times*, June 11, 1968, p. 54.

26. Powers, J. J., "The Multinational Company" an (Address given at the Semi-Annual Meeting of the Manufacturing Chemists' Association, New York, November 21, 1967).

27. *Report on Business*, Englewood Cliffs, N. J.: Prentice-Hall, Inc., December 16, 1961, p. 17.

28. Rogers, C., "Dealing with Psychological Tensions," *Journal of Applied Behavioral Science*, I, No. 1 (1965), 6–24.

29. Rubenstein, A. H., and C. Haberstroh, *Some Theories of Organization*, rev. ed. Homewood, Ill.: Irwin-Dorsey, 1966.

30. Servan-Schreiber, J.-J., *The American Challenge*. New York: Atheneum Publishers, 1968.

31. "On Temporary Systems," in *Innovation in Education*, ed. M. B. Miles. New York: Columbia University, Teachers College, Bureau of Publications, 1964, pp. 437–90.

32. Tomlinson, J. W., "A Model of the Joint-Venture Decision Process in International Business (Doctoral dissertation Massachusetts Institute of Technology Sloan School of Management, 1968.

33. *The Varieties of Religious Experience*. New York: Modern Library, Inc., 1902, pp. 475–76.

34. Wiener, N., "Intellectual Honesty and the Contemporary Scientist," *The American Behavioral Scientist*, VIII, No. 3 (1964), 16.

Managing
Multinationally

The world of work is rapidly shrinking, and its facets are becoming more interdependent as modern technology brings the humans inhabiting the earth closer together. One result of this convergence is that we need to know the details of management philosophy and employee attitudes in cultures other than our own. If we are committed to nurturing the growth of certain less-developed nations or if we seek simply to profitably interact with other cultural industrializations, we must understand them in terms of the traditional values and practices that may dictate organizational behavior different from our own.

Webber agrees with the position that the common foundations of business act to bring managers of the world closer together, but he also identifies culture as an element taking us in the opposite direction. He argues that world-wide uniformity in management philosophy will be slow in coming because of the difficulty in reconciling differences in cultural values, beliefs, and traditions.

The age of the multinational corporation is upon us. Lee proposes a method for overcoming some of the disruptive effects of cultural differences in such an organization. His systematic framework advises the overseas American manager to discard his "American-calibrated culturometer" that evaluates behavior in other cultures in terms of American norms.

Perhaps a more visible way to overcome divergent tendencies in cross-cultural contact is to extensively prepare those who will take part in multinational operations. To this end, Peter proposes certain conditions that must be understood and met before cross-cultural management training can meet the desired goal of maximum transnational transfer and application of managerial skills.

41

Convergence or Divergence?

Ross A. Webber
University of Pennsylvania

Technology, education, and pragmatic response, all foundations of business, suggest an emerging commonality; but culture may be a disruptive element.

For the information concerning students playing a game of interpersonal conflict, the author is indebted to Professor David W. Conrath of the Wharton School of Finance and Commerce. Reprinted by permission from *Columbia Journal of World Business*, IV, No. 3 (1969), 75–83.

"A specter is haunting Europe." In such chilling terms over one hundred years ago Karl Marx and Friedrich Engels announced the doomed future of capitalism and the glories to come of communism. Today, equally frightening specters haunt Europe as well as Asia, Africa and the New World. They are the dual terrors of instant annihilation in a nuclear Armageddon or gradual starvation on an overcrowded planet. In recent years these two concerns have produced more international cooperation than any other. Both the Soviet Union and the United States have attempted to limit the spread of nuclear weapons. Every nation and international institution encourages economic development. If anything, more has been done on the latter than the former. As never before, mankind sees salvation in economic development.

The peoples of the world share a great common force—their human nature. Whatever myriad and bizarre forms the pursuit of wants takes, we all share certain needs. As soon as one need is relatively satisfied, a new one emerges. The hierarchical model of these human needs implies motivational dynamism. To be sure, some of the more somnolent societies have not yet started to climb this ladder, but eventually they too will set out on what is a never-ending quest. The underlying dynamism of man's needs is apparent. Increasingly mankind is becoming united in the belief that economic growth is vital for satisfaction of the full range of human needs. Religious and secular alike now see economic development as a worthy task for the best brains and toughest muscles.

Whether the ultimate objective of this growth is sensual enjoyment or spiritual fulfillment is irrelevant—at least in the short run. "Greed is the tie that binds," according to the cynic. Whatever the moral implications, economic interests are exerting powerful unifying pressures. In 1968 the World Council of Churches (Protestant and Orthodox) and the Roman Catholic Church announced "the most advanced and ambitious Christian unity experiment yet undertaken." What was it? A conference on world cooperation for economic development held in Beirut, Lebanon. The director of the program was a Catholic priest who was paid by both sponsors—the first time this had been done. The Reverend Dr. Eugene Carson Blake, Secretary General of the World Council, was quoted as having remarked when the idea of the joint appointment was first raised that "you really discover mutuality when you start *paying* together."

The forces for convergence in managerial philosophy and practice stem from this common economic orientation. In recent years, a number of articles and books have suggested that such convergence is taking place (4, 8, 11, 17, 18). Nonetheless, it is a subject which should be stated in the form of a question, the answer to which depends upon cultural factors and the organizational level under consideration. This distinction is frequently ignored. At the top of the firm and in the relationship of man to machine, there does seem to be convergence. Governments are playing larger economic roles in capitalist countries; markets more in socialist countries. In both, managers of many large firms have gained substantial power and autonomy. Similarly, the basic technology of the industrial age is very much alike in Oshkosh, Minsk and Brazzaville.

In the middle, however, where managers communicate, motivate and make decisions, convergence may be less dramatic, for it is here that cultural differences have their sharpest impact. Here, there are forces both of uniformity and diversity. A common economic motivation is manifest in technology, education and philosophy; diversity is found in time, natural resources, demography and, most important, culture. The factors fostering uniformity appear to dominate at the macro-economic and the micro-technical levels—the place of business in the nation and the use of modern technology in the plant. The forces of divergence, however, assert stronger influences on the philosophy and practice of managers within the firm.

TECHNOLOGY

Whether macro or micro, the most common argument for convergence is the imperative of industrialization itself. Technology—like the language of mathematics—is universal. By obeying laws of reason and science, men of varying cultural and ideological positions presumably can agree on the best machine design or most desirable production system. For the most part, this technology is Western. The hardware of Europe and the United States is spreading over the globe so that the machine tended by the U.S. worker may be more modern, but it is not fundamentally different from that of the Indian or Brazilian workers where industrialization is just taking place. Demands for attention, response and care exerted by the machines on their human operators are essentially identical.

If there is only one best technology, and if a country desires to industrialize, the resulting engineering of work tends to affect occupations similarly. Traditional manual systems of power and manufacture are eliminated or reduced to marginal importance. Elaborated division of labor and graduated skill levels emerge. The unskilled "hired man," "handyman" or "millhand" all tend to become irrelevant; witness how difficult it is for unskilled minority groups in cities to find jobs—jobs they could usually obtain in rural areas years ago. The dumb, phlegmatic, oxlike Schmidt that Frederick W. Taylor made famous 50 years ago has become the literate and fairly articulate Smith with skills that management needs and for which substitutes are much harder to find.

As skill rises, power rises also. Employees are given responsibility for more expensive equipment and more critical decisions. Since a manager in this situation finds it difficult to supervise everyone, his subordinates' commitment to work conscientiously becomes more important. The need for subordinate consent gives them influence. Power may become less unilateral and management less autocratic.

The imperatives of the machine cannot be confined to the shop. Off the job, a man's position in society tends to change and the social structure becomes more open. Choosing one's parents is still important, but it should become less so. What a man does takes on increasing importance instead of what a man is. This leads to convergence.

The same technology calls for much the same occupational structure around the world—in steel, in textiles, in air transport. The occupational role of a man gives him a place in society that affects his behavior in many ways. Also, there comes to be a growing diversity of occupations and of levels of management, and no really clear-cut dividing lines are visible to all. The occupation takes the place of the class (8).

In corroboration, it has been demonstrated that industrialization tends to be associated with greater opportunity for the relatively modest-born (10). The performance of the high achiever becomes the determinant of success, rather than nepotism.

More sophisticated techonology and greater educational requirements give workers more mobility. With skill there is additional freedom to move—as has occurred in the U.S.S.R. in the postwar era. When Ivan has a skill which the state needs, and for which a number of plant managers are willing to pay, it is not easy to limit his mobility without recourse to expensive and inefficient policing.

Technology, therefore, exerts a major force toward making work and society more similar wherever industrialization occurs: fewer unskilled jobs, greater division of labor, less paternalistic or autocratic management, social level defined by occupation and greater opportunty for the son to move higher up the occupational and social ladder.

EDUCATION

Industrialization must be served, and education becomes a servant. Complex technology and sophisticated organization require training in a variety of specialties. Vast expansion of the educational system is required to support this industrialization, but subsequently, people demand education as a right over and above any contribution it makes to economic growth. The way of life facilitated by industrialization calls for other specialists to attend to needs off the job.

In short, an industrial society must educate its people. Workers must be literate so that they can understand instructions, follow directions and keep records; and so that managers, engineers and civil servants can be trained to operate the new mixed public and private production system. Beyond that are the needs for doctors, lawyers, scientists, professors and other professional personnel.

The correlation of educational development and per capita income suggests that higher income is associated with expanded education—although cause and effect are not entirely clear (7). The demand for education and educated people supplements and coincides with management's demand for capable people regardless of their origins. One result: a leveling of economic and social disparities. The scarcity of skilled persons is gradually reduced, lessening their economic advantage; a greater number of intelligent people are needed; the advantages of the highly born are undermined.

With industrialization the gap between managers and workers does not disappear. Managers will remain substantially more educated than workers, but the workers' education will improve. The relative gap between a high school and college education in an industrialized country is less than that between the "no education" of workers and the "some education" of managers in less-developed nations.

PHILOSOPHY

Jet-set is the term applied—partly enviously, partly critically—to the modern elite flying among the capitals of the world. They may be a force for uniformity. If the elite of the economic world become a true elite—the most effective and productive people regardless of birth or advantage—they may become more alike in their pragmatism. Ideology should fade because of its irrelevancy for the problems faced. Man has a great ability to maintain belief in false ideology in the face of contradictory evidence, but realism may replace it.

It is probable that the aims of economic development (elimination of poverty, greater choice in business occupation, a better life) are more universally accepted today than ever before. This commitment to economic development tends to undermine adherence to ideological principles—to the dismay of dogmatists of both left and right who with equal indignation cry out that we are sacrificing our integrity (be it capitalist or socialist), compromising our principles (be they Marxian or Smithian), and flirting with the devil (be he solid red, or red, white and blue striped)—all in the name of economic expediency (9, 13, 16).

IDEOLOGIES CHANGE

"No one can touch the United States in industrial management," a Communist official of the Czechoslovakian Institute of Management has stated, echoing what many Eastern European economists elsewhere have believed but dared not say. The Institute presents an unabashedly U.S.-influenced program of case studies, industrial games, marketing, sociology, psychology, research and development and other Western techniques that until relatively recently were either unknown or unmentionable in the Communist world. Jaroslaw Jirasek, the director of the program, says, "We are in a very bad position after those years when entrepreneurial decisions were made by centralized management. It is not easy to change men's minds," he maintains, "but if we cannot change men's minds, we must change the men because one clever man cannot be replaced by a thousand idiots."

The reason for these changes? Economics. Faced with serious economic problems, Czechoslovakia "has no choice but to change and in a very short time. Otherwise, we will not be able to keep in the front of the European Movement."

Most managers, owners, politicians and customers want efficiency. Hindering ideologies, beliefs and dogmas surrender to economic pragmatism. In obtaining this efficiency, knowledgeable men—rather than family members or political appointees—are needed to make the important decisions. This implies managerial autonomy. The large-scale production characterizing industrialization requires enormous capital accumulation and complex technology involving elaborate organization. Risk must be minimized in order to facilitate and safeguard the expenditure of time and money to initiate the operation. Communist enterprise managers and corporate executives all desire to minimize uncertainty; they want to control everything that can adversely affect their organization. As John Kenneth Galbraith has said, this means autonomy and control: autonomy from uncontrollable pressures be they market or bureaucratic in origin; as much control as possible over prices, supply and demand.

To manage this organization effectively, executives must be free of interference from incompetent owners or ignorant politicians. In the Galbraithian thesis it is assumed that only professional managers and specialists have the knowledge necessary to run modern complex enterprises. The result: Organizational decisions are increasingly centralized in professional management. For a socialist country this implies decentralization from state decision making; for the capitalist nation, it means increased central control by human decision makers (usually corporate planners and executives) versus impersonal control of the market. In either system, the central government has responsibility to decrease uncertainty stemming from economic cycles—especially by insuring a high level of total economic demand.

NATIONAL IMPLICATIONS

Observing these economic developments, a prophet might maintain that national societies will become more alike because nations are irrelevant and will disappear. In politics, we have heard these arguments for a long time from Communists, Nazis, United World Federalists and super United Nations supporters; from men as different as Karl Marx, Adolf Hitler, Wendell Willkie and Pope John XXIII. All have argued that national governments and boundaries divide men, promote war and compound the human tragedy. Always, however, economic interests, as well as military and political factors, presumably contradicted their unrealistic and, in some cases, frightening arguments.

Exploitation of markets, protection of industry, enrichment of the mother country, insulation from foreign depressions or inflations, and, frequently, defense of liberty itself have all called for strong national boundaries. Currently, however, the economic pressures may be changing—or are starting to change. Adam Smith's old fear of corporations growing and spreading beyond the control of market and government apparently is coming true. It is suggested that we are moving toward a world of very large multinational firms and very small entrepreneurial firms of the one-man-show variety. For many reasons the middle-sized concern will wither or be gobbled up by the monster multinationals—so much so that by 1985 some three hundred multinational companies may dominate the world economy (12).

In short, modern business firms, capitalist or socialist, are transcending national boundaries. Governments only get in the way. A veteran observer of international developments recently wrote:

> An industrialized world is held together by the larger number of corporate bodies and by their widening role. The corporation groups the nationals into a new loyalty —a functional identity across all borders. The day may well come when the majority of people in all nations will have their functional loyalties to one or more supranational corporate bodies. They may well become conscious of basic commitments, values, and interests unrelated to the state or the nation (15).

It was the dream of Marx and the early Socialists that workers everywhere would perceive their common interests, throw out the anachronistic nation-states and institute a Communist society in which national boundaries would disappear. These dreams were consumed in the fires of World War I when the working men of the Western world marched to battle in the names of their respective fatherlands. They went willingly and even happily if the accounts of the era can be believed. It is ironic that now the more potent forces for internationalization are the business interests so hated by early Socialist reformers.

The forces of uniformity in economic activities and management are potent. Does this mean inevitable similarity around the globe?

Inevitable is a vague term. "Inevitably" there will probably be convergence in managerial, economic—and even political—philosophy and practice. Nonetheless, it is a long way off for there are forces of diversity as well. Time, basic resources and demography may be touched on briefly. Culture requires more consideration.

TIME

Modern technology is grafted on to societies at different times, when the societies are at different states of economic development. When this technology is introduced into a culture, it is not automatically accepted. Stresses are produced. These may be suppressed, but the tensions spring up elsewhere. Society may adapt to suit the technology, but unintended changes also occur in other institutions. This cycle of stress, accommodation and new stress may dampen out, but the process is undoubtedly gradual. Thus, the introduction of modern technology and industrialization into Japan produced factories and machines very like Great Britain. Nonetheless, life within the plants has not been identical. The countries were different at the onset of development so the stresses produced in the two countries were different: family-centered in Japan, class-centered in Great Britain. The unanticipated and uncontrolled propagation of this stress affects different aspects of each culture producing new diversity at the same time that the forces of uniformity are being felt.

BASIC RESOURCES

The natural resources of countries differ, and this limits the pace and direction of development. Technology may eventually diminish the importance of natural resource differences: Atomic power can substitute for water power, plastics for wood, man-made materials for natural. However, these differences are real, and they cause management to differ because each industry lends a characteristic style to its managerial philosophy and practice. Thus a textile-dominated nation will tend to develop different management from that of a petroleum-rich country.

DEMOGRAPHY

The density of population obviously varies and exercises a divergent influence. A relatively empty country is likely to have a different course of development than a heavily populated one. The United States has always had higher wages, and labor recruitment was more difficult than in Europe. Labor efficiency was more critical, and a significant increase in the standard of living was made easier. High valuation of the individual worker and the attention that he deserves were more common. Barriers to immigration and man's uncertain ability or unwillingness to control births suggest that these differences will not soon disappear.

CULTURE

We are immersed in a sea. It is warm, comfortable, supportive and protecting. Most of us float below the surface; some bob about catching glimpses of land from time to time; a few emerge from the water entirely. That sea is our culture. Most of us act, think and dream in terms of the norms and standards we have absorbed from the culture in which we are reared. That which our culture values, we value; that which our culture abhors, we abhor. By education or experience, some of us become aware that there are other values and beliefs that make sense too—as much or more than our own. But we see them hazily and, all too often, with age the awareness slips away. A few, very few, are able to escape, overcome parochialism and see the world more objectively. But escape is by no means entirely desirable. We can feel alone and unsure when the comfortable values of our old culture fall away, become irrelevant and are replaced by nothing.

WHAT IS "RIGHT"?

Culture is a great source of security that tells us frequently what is "right" and "good." The problem, as numerous anthropologists have pointed out, is that what is right and good may appear irrational and unpredictable. Kissing is an example. In Micronesia, the idea of putting mouth on mouth is unthinkable. For the anti-oral Micronesians, the "female breast has no sexual significance; it is an organ for providing food for the nursing infant." The U.S. mammary culture "must seem very queer to non-breast-loving cultures" (1).

Culture influences what behavior is approved or disapproved. This in turn affects management. Consider two students who are playing a game of interpersonal conflict. Each contestant has two strategies from which he may choose with the following results: If both choose Strategy A, each receives $3.00; if both choose Strategy B, each receives $2.00; if they split on Strategies AB or BA, each receives $1.00 (see Figure 1).

FIGURE 1

		Player #1	
		A	B
Player #2	A	$3.00	$1.00
	B	$1.00	$2.00

Given this matrix, upon repeated plays Master of Business Administration candidates from the United States tend to stabilize on Strategy A and earn $3.00. Such is not the case for students from Korea. Korean students at the same school tend to select strategy B and earn $2.00. Why?

Perhaps cultural factors cause the difference. It would appear that the Koreans will not cooperate. Either they distrust each other, or they want to minimize the earnings of their competitiors even more than to maximize their own. Depriving another would seem to be more important than individual gain—in contrast to the U.S. attitude.

Of course, this experiment does not prove that personal noncooperativeness is characteristic of Korean society. If it were, however, it would have implications for management. Organization size might have to be limited to facilitate central control since unsupervised cooperation is not likely. Top management might be afraid to delegate authority because they are not sure that subordinate managers will work in the organization's interest. Whatever the actual situation, cultural factors can influence organizational behavior and management.

In all cultures, existing institutions, ideologies and practices have lives of their own. They are persistent in the face of change. Bare bottoms are an issue in Tanzania, where President Julius Nyerere has ordered the Massai tribe to alter their mode of dress. The haughty Massai, who have long considered themselves superior to their more advanced countrymen, are strongly resisting the government directive to cover up the one buttock that they produly bare. The Massai's vanity will probably give way to the demands of a more sophisticated state, but it will not be an easy battle. Attitudes toward life and acceptable behavioral patterns are slow to change even under the pressures of economic necessity. They will probably change only as little as necessary to adapt to the new technology of modern industrialization. Residual cultural differences will remain for a long time.

Uniqueness is really the basis of diversity. At any moment, every country is unique in its cultural factors, economic development, natural resources and demographic characteristics. Some of these may be similar to other countries, but the net mix is unique. The values, beliefs and habitual behavior patterns strongly resist change because they impart security.

The impact of these forces on management as a whole cannot be analyzed. Because the factors of uniformity and diversity affect the various aspects of management differently, we need to distinguish among three relationships in management. These are the three levels or interfaces: (1) man and his work, (2) man and man (superior–subordinate, lateral and diagonal relations) and (3) organization and its environment. Table 1 summarizes the elements.

Arithmetic does not help. At present, there is no way of totaling the forces for uniformity and those for diversity in a single country to obtain a net number suggesting the rate or direction of movement. The arguments for convergence and divergence vary on the three interfaces.

TABLE 1
THE ELEMENTS AND THEIR RELATIONSHIPS

Forces of Uniformity	Managerial Interfaces	Forces of Diversity
Technology	Man–Work	Cultural inertia
Education	Man–Man	Time and stage of development
Pragmatic philosophy	Firm–Environment	Natural resources
		Demography

MAN AND WORK

The case of convergence in the relationship between man and his work—especially man and the machine—is compelling. Technological and economic pressures are so clear and strong that work for the average man will tend to become more alike. His equipment, his portion of the task, his training for the job, the expectation that he appear and be on the job not at his own volition but that of the employer—all will tend to be similar in the not very distant future.

FIRM–ENVIRONMENT

Similarly, the forces of convergence are strong on the relationship between the firm and its environment—customers, competitiors and government. The growth of professional managers administering fairly autonomous firms is widespread in both capitalist and socialist countries. They must be relatively free from interference by ignorant owners, politicians and bureaucrats. Managers must also be responsible to customers and know what goods are needed. As the Russians found out, managers can produce unwanted goods which pile up in warehouses. Recently, Premier Aleksei N. Kosygin called on Soviet industry to overcome the gap in consumer goods between the Soviet Union and the

United States. Invoking the example of "capitalist monopolies," he urged Soviet management to reduce delays in producing and marketing new consumer products. "In the capitalist countries," he said, "the monopolies are obliged to react quickly to the needs of the customers and produce modern types of products and search for new rational forms of organization of production and its control." Just how monopolistic firms are "obliged" is not entirely clear. If the market forces them to respond, then they must not be completely monopolistic. Still, the point is valid: Some avenue of influence from customers to managers is essential and is apparently developing in the Communist states.

MAN AND MAN

Less clear is convergence in the man to man, superior–subordinate, and peer relationships within the organization. There is a possible trend toward strengthening of the subordinate's importance and bargaining power through his increased knowledge and the more intricate technology he operates. This implies greater responsiveness by superiors to subordinates. More democracy may be inevitable in economic organizations because of the two-way flow of influence arising out of technical sophistication and employees' skills; fear and power become less effective (14).

Equality in decision making and harmony of interests are not implicit in this evolution of influence processes. If the prediction has validity, conflict and bargaining between interest groups will undoubtedly characterize the more democratic business firm just as they do every democratic state. The hierarchical structure may change, but the general shape will remain. Differentiated positions in a hierarchy are probably essential because they reflect fundamental functions in the managerial process.

Superiors and subordinates will remain, but the basis of motivation may have to be shifted. With industrialization, government-generated security and improved living standards, management can no longer concentrate its appeal on low-level physical and security needs. Higher drives for competence, achievement and autonomy become relevant. If the manager wants to tap the ability of skilled subordinates, he must gain their commitment. This means he must provide opportunities on the job to satisfy higher needs. At least among managers, there seems to be a universality of higher level drives for self-actualization in several nations and various cultures (5). As man gains freedom from slavery to basic needs, he will attempt to satisfy drives higher in the hierarchy of needs.

These higher needs are not necessarily more noble; striving for ego satisfaction or power can be brutal. But management must respond to them. Satisfied needs are irrelevant for motivation. To obtain commitment and effort, management must motivate by appealing to the next appropriate level of unsatisfied needs. If the hierarchy of needs is truly universal, management the world over will have to provide opportunities for participation, competence and autonomy. From civil rights to education, from poor ghetto dwellers to affluent students, in Washington and Warsaw, the most profound social revolution in the world today is the struggle for democratic processes in decision making.

In addition, in the drive for efficiency there are pressures to impersonalize the managerial process. Family membership, social class, religion, perhaps even color may tend to lose their centrality as criteria for hiring and promotion decisions in favor of judgment about ability and potential.

SLOW PROCESS

Despite these forces for uniformity in managerial philosophy and practice, however, the process will be slow. Managerial leadership is affected by demographic conditions causing labor shortage or excess. If excess, management is unlikely to be overly concerned about employees. Even more important, the diversity of cultural values, beliefs, habits and traditions exerts profound influence on managerial relations. Patterns of respect, awe, contempt and deference are deep-seated. What is thought desirable or worthy in life will influence interpersonal relations, especially leadership style.

A comparative study of similar U.S. and Norwegian factories demonstrates that a worker's positive response to more participative management in the United States is not matched in a different cultural setting (3). In Norway the workers are suspicious and antagonistic. Other studies indicate the different values attributed to direction versus persuasion as managerial tactics in different cultures (5). German managers place high value on the former, low on the latter; Japanese managers vice versa; and Americans in between (although closer to the Japanese). Cultural factors also influence the methods and directions of communications in South American and North American organizations. Complaints, suggestions and criticisms just do not flow upward in a Venezuelan company (19).

Cultural factors such as attitudes toward authority, achievement and personal risk exercise more influence on the interpersonal aspects of management than on the man–technology or firm–environment interfaces. The forces of uniformity are less clear and imperative on the methods management uses to communicate, coordinate and motivate. The sharp differences existing in these processes between U.S. and foreign companies, and indeed between domestic firms, testify to the divergence in managerial philosophy and practice that exists, and may always have, within organizations. For a long time at the least, cultural factors will exert a strong and differentiating influence upon managerial philosophy and practice: less on technological and production decisions, less on the relations of man and job, less on the firm's relationship to its customers and society; but more on the methods of motivation, patterns of communication and styles of leadership.

42

Cultural Analysis
in Overseas Operations

James E. Lee
Wisconsin State University

Reprinted by permission from *Harvard Business Review*, March–April 1966, 106–114.
© 1966 by the President and Fellows of Harvard College; all rights reserved.

The purpose of this article is to expose the natural *self-reference criterion*—the unconscious reference to one's own cultural values—as the root cause of most international business problems overseas and to offer an analytical approach designed to reduce its influence when it comes to solving such matters.

The resident general manager of an American company in Italy recently characterized the three major difficulties which he, as a U.S. businessman overseas, faces:

1. Communicating with U.S. headquarters.
2. Adapting to local cultural differences.
3. Keeping up with rapid changes in the international political and economic situations which affect his company's operations.

The first two problems (the third is beyond the scope of this article) are of course different aspects of the same problem—that of business adaptation. This general manager, like many another, cannot operate the same way he could back home. Not only must his products be altered to fit local overseas market needs, but the organization and the policies by which it is run are different. Furthermore, he must behave differently as a resident manager, and act as a buffer for the differences between his operation and corporate headquarters in the United States. And even though his profits are up to expectations, his New York superiors are afraid that he has "gone native" from the way he defends his position on controversial matters.

In this case while the manager, his organization, and his products seem to have succeeded in adapting to the foreign environment, his company headquarters has not. In other cases, the situation is even less healthy. Products have failed to find predicted markets; factory operations have bogged down; and resident managers have returned to the United States without finishing their normal tours of duty.

Business literature is not without advice for the U.S. manager overseas who needs to know something of the customs of other peoples. Edward T. Hall, in his article, "The Silent Language in Overseas Business," provided a number of examples of how the behavior of certain foreign businessmen must be considered by the American who would do business with them (6).

Although the mapping of the customs of various cultures is a necessary beginning to the cultural adaptation process, there is a limit to the value of increasing the customs inventory without a schematism in which they become more than isolated bits of information.

In this presentation I will suggest a framework of three general classes of business adaptation and discuss some of the pitfalls of the self-reference criterion (SRC) as it relates to each. I will also propose a system of cultural analysis for business adaptation in these key areas.

BUSINESS ADAPTATION

The term adaptation, as it is used throughout this article, refers to the achievement of business goals with a minimum of problems and setbacks due to the various manifestations of cultural conflict. These goals can be of many magnitudes or types—from the reduction of tea-break time to the opening of a factory or the launching of a product. Their achievement will depend, however, on the conflict-free operation of the business plan—on successful overseas adaptation.

The three general classes of business adaptation—product, institutional, and individual—vary in degree of adjustment necessary from none, or token, to comprehensive (very rare).

PRODUCT MODIFICATION

A product can be sold "as is" abroad; it can be slightly modified to fit technical specifications such as voltages or laws; or it can be redesigned to fit better a special local need. For example, products such as Camel cigarettes, Maidenform bras, and raw chemicals are rarely modified.

A second, almost token, degree of adaptation characterizes most products. Automobiles (carburetion and timing for different octanes) and appliances (for local power supply differences), are examples. There are many failures in this category, however. Consider:

> An American firm making offset duplicating machines introduced its equipment, with altered electric power specifications, to a developing country which was very proud of its own paper manufacturing facilities. Unfortunately, the widely varying dimensions of the local paper required greater adjustment than the machines could make. It would have been a blow to the country's national pride to use precious foreign exchange to import paper because its own was inferior. Consequently, many of these machines already purchased with foreign exchange are still idle.

How did the SRC play its role here? The American businessman himself tends to take such national pride lightly because he has no parallel in his own personal cultural experience. Moreover, his SRC for direct foreign exchange pressure on his own individual small purchases abroad is almost nil. He is therefore unable, using the unconscious SRC as a guide, to predict the abrupt halt in sales in what appears to be a growing market. Consider this second example:

> The managers of a joint-venture tobacco company in an Asian country were warned that their proposed new locally named (a token adaptation) and manufactured filtered cigarettes would fail. Filters had not yet been introduced there. Nevertheless, the resident Western managers, along with their local executives whose SRC was dominantly Western because of their social class and education, puffed smugly on their own U.S. filtered cigarettes while the product flopped, leaving the company with idle equipment and unrecovered setup and launch costs.
>
> The basic reason for the prediction of failure was a difference in fear of death—especially from cancer of the lungs. A life expectancy of 29 years in that Asian country does not place many people in the lung cancer age bracket. Moreover, for those in this age bracket, there is not the general cultural value of sanitation, the literacy rate, or a *Reader's Digest* type of magazine to motivate them to give up unfiltered cigarettes.

How did the Western-oriented tobacco company's management miss these two critical factors? I suggest that it was, again, the operation of that perfectly normal human mechanism—the SRC.

A third degree of product adaptation (comprehensive) is rarely observed. This is not because of a dearth of potential products peculiar to the needs of other cultures. Rather, the cultures capable of designing and manufacturing new products select and design almost all of them on a self-referenced basis.

For example, there is no small, low-priced, durable, Western-designed car for the tremendous potential market in non-Western cultures. Why? Because the Western automotive builder is not naturally inclined to design cars whose specifications are really foreign to his own culture. Imagine a Detroit designer's attitude toward a one-wheel chain drive, single-cylinder car. (More on this later.)

Or imagine an American architerct's reaction to an angle-iron framed, $10' \times 10' \times 12'$, fiberboard dwelling which is bolted together and costs about $400. Such a house is *needed* in many of the developing countries of Asia, Africa, and South America. In these countries the vast majority of the popuation live somewhat unofficially on someone else's land in their own shacks or huts. They often have to pay bribe money to government officials or employees of the land-owner to remain. The threat of eviction operates to keep their houses inexpensive and of a temporary design which is not very mobile. Yet research has shown that the dwellers of many of these huts would like a better house and that some of them have enough cash savings to afford a better structure. The only possible alternative for them now, however, is to buy a house *with* land, which because of its extremely high cost is out of the question for all but a very small percentage of them.

Inexpensive fiberboard (made from indigenous materials) bolted to an angle-iron frame would be a great improvement over their current houses and could be dismantled easily if they were faced with eviction. In one Asian city of 2.5 million people, about two thirds of the population live in shacks or huts which cost less than $100. The monsoons destroy them about every three years, and they must be replaced. A survey conducted by graduate business students in Karachi has indicated that 2 percent of the hut owners would like to buy—and could immediately afford, without credit—a $400 house. At $50 per-unit profit, this would appear to be an attractive business proposition which is adapted to another culture.

But this is not the kind of business proposition that would be likely to interest an American businessman. Why? I suggest that his SRC makes this so farfetched that such a product would be unlikely to occur to him, and if it did, it would hardly appeal to him.

INSTITUTIONAL BEHAVIOR

The second general class of adaptation can be seen as a group of complex subprocesses:

1. Identification and negotiation with particular partnership capital.
2. Negotiation of entry with government and other business institutions.
3. Adaptation of the organization structure to fit conditions abroad.
4. Selection and development of the foreign national manpower.
5. Adaptation of the policies to which the organization is to be committed.

Failures of an entire branch, division, or factory do not lend themselves to clear-cut analyses, but usually stem nonetheless from an adaptive failure, due to the SRC influence, in one or more of the above processes.

In Pakistan, for example, many of the executive secretaries to the managing directors of American subsidiaries are Christians. If we start with the assumption that secretaries must be women (American value), this is the only course open. But Pakistan is a Muslim, not a Christian, culture, and we have placed a minority squarely in one of the seats of power and influence in the company. This affects the American company's ability to *adapt*, since it impedes normal communications flow and offers a visual symbol of what might be construed as criticism of Islam.

Lest the reader get the notion that these adaptive errors are peculiar to businessmen, it should be pointed out that U.S. embassies, agencies such as AID, and American military personnel abroad also operate on the SRC. In 1961, for example, 20 percent of the local employees on the American Embassy roster in Pakistan were Christians, a group which even now constitutes less than 1 percent of the population. At that time the embassy's local news-release liaison man was a non-Muslim whose job it was to "sell" Muslim editors on using USIA news releases. The reasons for having him in this job were that he was intelligent, cooperative, and energetic. I was never able to convince the man's superior that he might be all these things but perhaps also be the *wrong* man for the job.

In a sense, institutional adaptation is a kind of summation of the individual adaptations of those running the institution. But there is more to it than this. There are the headquarters personnel and corporate policies. Suppose, for instance, that a U.S. firm transplants its American open-door grievance policy. The American management abroad may be surprised to find that this policy does nothing for productivity. Instead it may reduce it.

This is not to suggest that hearing grievances is a bad practice. But it must be remembered that the American industrial grievance system has *evolved* as a function of cultural change; that is, the individual American worker, his foreman, his union, the government, and U.S. business managers have evolved their definition and grievance resolution patterns together over a long period of time. And so have the peoples and institutions of other cultures. The culture conflict arises, then, when the specific American version of grievance—meaning a complaint arising out of and in the course of employment—is assumed for the foreign version, and the American-evolved policy is superimposed on a group of people in the foreign culture.

Throughout the developing countries of the world, grievance often means any complaint whatsoever. For many of these workers, almost all complaints have historically been taken to one of the following: the family head, the *patron*, the landlord, or the colonial or local government administrator. In these cultures the systematization of complaints—civil, criminal, labor—with understood indications for the particular authorities who resolve them has not evolved to the American stage. For example:

> A worker in India under an American open-door policy might complain that "Lalji is unfair" to him. He would ask his foreman to do something about it. The foreman might discover that Lalji is the owner of a water buffalo that has twice knocked down the aggrieved's *juggi* (straw house). He might also discover that this particular man, Lalji, is not—nor has he ever been—an employee or supplier of the company.

Thus the American company which operates abroad with policies which assume that the term grievance is interpreted the same all over the world will necessarily suffer internal conflict. The assumption of understanding of other concepts which are integral with the American managerial system can also bring problems. For example, if the local understanding of such concepts as authority and responsibility differs from the American understanding, adaptation of both policy and behavior is necessary.

In order to get a sample of how different some foreign views of these concepts might be from American views, I once asked a group of 96 bilingual graduate business students in Pakistan to write down synonyms in their non-English tongue for each of a number of English words. Among these words were "authority," "responsibility," and "grievance." The students gave 17 different synonyms for authority, but only 6 for responsibility; 47 gave the same word for authority, while 88 gave the same word for responsibility. For grievance there were 16 different synonyms given, including pain, sorrow, uneasiness, bad blood, grief, unhappiness, hardship, difficulty, brawl, malice, and worry.

Such imprecise understandings of these concepts—coupled with an organization structure and policies which because of their SRC base require the assumption of American understanding all around—are bound to produce confusion and conflict between the American resident manager and his local officers and employees. This conflict often inhibits adaptation and the achievement of the full business potential for such an institution or organization.

INDIVIDUAL ADJUSTMENT

As I mentioned earlier, the process of adjustment of the American to the foreign culture has been given attention in the literature, primarily through the descriptions of certain foreign customs and how American businessmen should respond to them. Also, the formal indoctrination programs of Americans and their families are beginning to exhibit curricula which include studies of the American culture as well as the foreign culture. (American University's Business Council for International Understanding is an example.)

Unfortunately, the individual's adaptive behavior cannot be made subject to the same kind of detailed analysis that a single product or institutional policy can. The individual is constantly responding to the overseas environment from an American value system base. Walter Ong, a long-time observer of overseas Americans, describes it this way:

> Our own great American achievement has somehow become a positive psychological handicap. The United States has been a vast and successful working machine for converting into ourselves persons from every nation of the world. . . . We cannot make ourselves over, even imaginatively, into other people. . . . Our thoughtlessness is caught in our assumptions that what we do is never chauvinistic or nationalistic, though what others do may well be. Thus for British missionaries to teach cricket or Canadian missionaries to teach lacrosse would be chauvinistic, but for American missionaries to teach baseball is not spreading American culture but merely enabling the benighted natives to be human beings (2).

Foreign observers often see our SRC more as an American-axis-of-the-universe phenomenon. A Mexican businessman, when confronted with an American businessman's remark that "time is money," asked simply, "Whose time—yours or ours?" Appropriate adaptive behavior for an American would not be to assume the Mexican attitude toward time. Rather, his goal would be to inhibit his SRC while gaining an understanding of the values of the foreign environment in which he finds himself. This will increase his tolerance level for the "strange" behavior he observes. He will then be better able to discover, on a rational basis, ways to manage which are less disruptive to those whose efforts he manages. This new understanding and acceptance, along with the reduction of conflict, further permits him to gain fulfillment of his own personal needs by eliminating unnecessary frustration.

CURBING SRC

In my opinion the SRC habit is one of the most difficult to break. It is a habit which in some circumstances helps us to survive and succeed. Experience gives us the SR3 as a tool which helps us face new situations, occasionally even in other cultures. Therefore, its curbing must be specific, not general; there are numerous situations in other cultures where it helps business to succeed.

The success of the Singer sewing machine the world over may have been accidental as it happened, but if Singer had approached the question of its possible success by the SRC—American women like to sew their own clothes; therefore other women must also like to make clothes—the success would have been the same.

This same SRC approach would not work so well today, however, because America is fast turning into a ready-made-clothes culture. Thus the sewing machine market is being taken over by other cultures—particularly Japan and Italy—whose SRC still roughly matches the world market for home sewing needs and whose technical level is up to the design, manufacture, and distribution of the machine. Even now it can be predicted that this market will eventually be taken over by still other cultures as the current holders of this market grow into a ready-made SRC situation.

ANALYTICAL FRAMEWORK

It is true that other cultures whose economies are moving them into line with the American SRC are numerous enough to keep the U.S. export or manufacturing market expanding. The neglected markets and overseas operational opportunities, however, will go relatively untapped by U.S. business until a more rational and systematic approach—based on cultural analysis—is taken for product development and institutional–individual adaptation. I believe that American business should begin to move in this direction.

The cultural analysis system described in the following pages—as an effective way to check the SRC influence in business adaptation—is a modification of the habitual thinking pattern of the anthropologist, who has the inveterate habit of looking at any item of behavior as functional within the total cultural system of which it is a part. When this new thinking pattern is applied to business, it can be seen as a four-step procedure:

Step 1—Define the business problem or goal in terms of the American cultural traits, habits, or norms.

Step 2—Define the business problem or goal in terms of the foreign cultural traits, habits, or norms. Make no value judgments.

Step 3—Isolate the SRC influence in the problem and examine it carefully to see how it complicates the problem.

Step 4—Redefine the problem without the SRC influence and solve for the optimum business goal situation.

Since the analysis is to serve adaptation in several areas of international business activities, its use must necessarily be flexible.

PRODUCT PROCEDURE

A decision in this area, for example, will most often start with an existing product or a suspected market for a known product category. Cultural analysis applied here would be patterned somewhat along these lines:

Step 1—List the American (or Western) traits, economics, values, needs, or habits that are fundamental to the success of the product here in the United States.

Step 2—List the related traits, economics, values, needs, or habits in the proposed market culture and compare them with those in step 1.

Step 3—The SRC can then be seen to account for the differences between steps 1 and 2.

Step 4—These differences, if they are significant, serve as the warning signal that the product idea should be modified or discarded, or that the product should be designed to fit the market needs listed in step 2.

Let us take an actual product adaptation example now, and follow the above four-step analysis procedure. In 1963 the European division of an American auto manufacturer withdrew its assembly operation from Karachi under government pressure to manufacture automobiles or sell out. Considering this as the product problem it was in the beginning, how might the cultural analysis approach have proceeded at the time of the company's entry there in the late 1950s?

Step 1. Western culture in the 1950s was characterized by transportation needs geared to traits of speed, promptness, relative eonomy, comfort, and style. The U.S. and European superhighways demanded a cruise speed of 60 to 70 miles per hour, and 80 to 100 octane gasolines were available. References to horsepower per pound and per cubic inch were creeping into automotive advertising, and a two-car family market was opening up in the United States. Manufacturing techniques were very sophisticated, and foreign exchange was not a businessman's problem. Raw material and power supplies were abundant. These comprised the rationale for the existence of the European model as a product design.

Step 2. Pakistan was a culture characterized by a strong desire to be mobile, but with an extremely low skill and technological level. It was accustomed to a camel-cart pace, prideful of its Islamic heritage, and competitive with India, which was already manufacturing automobiles. Only 60 octane gasoline was available, and there was extreme pressure on foreign exchange. The bicycle owner was equivalent to a late-model used car buyer in America; the Vespa owner equivalent to the owner of a new Pontiac; and the Opel owner equivalent to the owner of several Cadillacs. Consumer credit was a future hope; the national speed limit was (and still is) 35 miles per hour; and the total number of automobiles registered was less than 50,000. Population at that time was about 80 million, of which less than 15 percent were literate. Less than 1 percent of the family heads were estimated to earn more than $100 per month.

Step 3. The significant differences between steps 1 and 2 appear to suggest strongly that the needs on which the European model were originally based did *not* exist in Pakistan, and that the product problem was too great to consider modification.

Step 4. If we were to choose to find or design a product to fit Pakistan's cultural and economic specifications, we would probably discover that such a car—the King Midget, manufactured by Midget Motors of Athens, Ohio— actually exists in America with a 15-year shakedown life behind it. The King Midget sells for $680, is made of angle, channel, and strap iron. In addition, it has few castings and no compound body curves. Capital investment for a 1200-per-year volume in Pakistan would be about $100,000 in hard currency and an equivalent amount in the local currency. Manufacturing skill level needs are low, and the foreign exchange requirement per unit would be less than $100. The car, which would sell for approximately $1000, would have a cruising speed of 40 miles per hour, and would go 80 miles on a gallon of low octane gasoline.

The main reason that this vehicle and the portion of the world market in which some 2 billion people live have not gotten together is that the car is

manufactured by two former aircraft mechanics—not automotive designers—
on an SRC basis for highly specialized U.S. markets which do not exist in other
cultures: the senior middle-class couple in retirement housing developments
in Florida, the "Detroit rebel" two-car family, and others. It is not likely that
even the automotive industry's leaders would undertake a similarly adapted
design for the Pakistani market because of their "big car luxury" production
approach—unless the SRC is removed from the Detroit designers' frame of
reference.

INSTITUTIONAL PATTERN

Organizations must adapt in a very complex environment overseas. They
have to begin by adapting to the various institutions in the foreign culture, but
they must also adapt to certain U.S. institutions—such as the U.S. government
and corporate headquarters back home. The same major institutions constitute
the business environment both in the foreign culture and in the United States.
However, the character of the interrelationships and their importance to success
of the enterprise are not the same. These overseas institutions—financial,
government, labor, and marketing—are not fitted together in the same way
they are in the United States, and the American SRC is often of little help in
understanding the total institutional system or the ideal behavior patterns for
adaptive entry into the system.

One of the most common early steps in many countries is the selection of
partnership capital. This initial "marriage" can itself have far-reaching effects
on the over-all adaptation of the new enterprise. To illustrate:

> In one South American country an American company found that its SRC ("money
> is money") led it astray. It is true that Americans *do* take a brief look to see if it is
> "clean" money and if it has government sanction, but these are often only super-
> ficial examinations. This particular U.S. company joined with a small group of local
> capitalists who were destined to be removed from the position of having moderate
> power in their government to that of having none. Five years after the partnership
> was formed, the American firm began to suffer raw materials import license delays
> and other forms of harassment at the hands of the foreign government. The Ameri-
> cans are currently in a holding operation, wondering what to do about their joint
> venture which is slowly going downhill.

What would be the cultural analysis steps in approaching the selection of
partnership capital?

Step 1. American capital is generally selected on the basis of adequacy and
demonstrated integrity.

Step 2. The foreign capital may be selected on the basis of business and
government connections, social class, and political comers in the family group.

Step 3. The American SRC influence will be to underestimate the role of
government in business and industrial operations, and to overestimate the
adequacy of warning signs available to Americans to show up the wrong capital.

Step 4. To eliminate the American SRC influence would require that the
methods of selecting partners—as they are practiced in the foreign country—

be carefully studied first, after which the partners or stockholders can be chosen as nearly as possible on this basis without jeopardizing the relationship with those institutions which are important to the company's success.

Closely related to the above SRC influence are the maladapted hiring practices of American companies abroad. Even a superficial examination of any foreign country will reveal how much more provincialism there is, on the average, than the U.S. businessman is accustomed to here in America.

Thus, if the American firm overseas always hires the "best" man who applies for each job vacancy, it is asking for trouble. Although people from different factions from the same foreign city or community may apply for work at the company's gate, it does not necessarily follow that they will work well together. It would never occur to U.S. businessmen to question seriously the hiring of an Iowa-born machinist to work beside an Ohioan or Arizonan. This faith in the defactionalization of America may not be fully justified, but the American–foreign difference is sufficient that the SRC should not be carried over to the rest of the world. It has to be curbed until the American management overseas is aware of the extent of the communitization or factionalization of the peoples who will appear at the hiring gate.

For example, a Western-oriented paper mill (not American in this case) in East Pakistan which hired Bihari refugees from India to work with the native Pakistani Bengalis suffered a minor antimanagement labor disturbance which grew into an interethnic riot and cost over 500 workers' lives. The essential error here was the confidence that the workers' common Islamic religion would override status, language, economic, and personal value differences.

(An American result of the same kind of SRC was the mixing of Catholics—Irish and Italian—in early New England industry on the assumption that they would necessarily work well together because of a common religion.)

INDIVIDUAL ADAPTATION

Of all the cultural characteristics which appear to present individual adaptation problems for Americans overseas, the so-called time-value differences are probably the most common. Much of what appears in the literature about the various attitudes of other peoples toward time is misleading, in my opinion. Consider the following examples:

1. A foreigner makes an appointment to see an American businessman in the American's office, but shows up 45 minutes late.

2. A foreigner will not get down to discussing the heart of the matter for which he made an appointment.

3. A foreign subordinate promises to have a certain job finished by Wednesday, let's say; but later evidence would indicate that this deadline could not have been met and, furthermore, that there probably had been no serious intent on his part to try to meet it.

These would appear to represent important differences in temporal values. Careful analysis will show, however, that the time designation for some of these traits is artificial due to the SRC of the super time-conscious American culture. This superficial trait description tends to obscure the real considerations necessary for cultural adaptation. While the first of the above examples may possibly be labeled a time-value difference, the second and third examples actually point up behavioral differences in directness and in superior–subordinate relationships. Proceeding with the four-step cultural analysis here will prevent us from making such mistakes—much as a "Stop, Look, and Listen" sign serves as a systematic interruption in our natural behavior when we approach a railroad crossing. This can be illustrated by a brief analysis of the first of the above examples, and then an even more condensed analysis of the second and third.

EXAMPLE 1—LATENESS FOR APPOINTMENTS. What is the origin of American promptness? Are all Americans prompt? Is this promptness related to economic superiority? Americans have had the means to be on time for several generations. Good public transportation, many clocks and watches, and much practice should be considered partly responsible. And Americans have the good fortune of being descended from time-conscious ancestors going back several centuries (step 1).

In the foreign culture one can often readily see poorer transportation and communications facilities. In most poor cultures there will be some kind of religious fatalism and get-through-the-day carryover from centuries of survival struggles which inhibit the development of the trait of planning very far in the future. Moreover, it will be evident that the capabilities (education and skills) of those on whom a planned event depends are inferior (step 2).

Our SRC can be seen to have prevented our noting carefully the basis on which on-time behavior depends. It has therefore produced expectancies on our part which are inconsistent with actual situational demands (step 3).

Our analysis thus far would indicate that under the circumstances a certain looseness in the other culture's time system is both desirable and functional. How can the American adapt to this system? One solution, of course, would be for him to begin to plan on lateness in others as a rule. He can often arrange to be busy with other work until the foreigner arrives. He should also try to take comfort in the knowledge that his foreign visitor, when he does finally arrive, will be patient until the American's substituted activity can be broken off. This is because the foreigner has developed a patience to fit the necessary looseness of his own culture's time system. Conversely, if the appointment is at the foreigner's office, the American should take his briefcase so he can be busy with other work until the foreigner can see him (step 4).

On a broader scale, the American can adapt to delays in general by keeping more irons in the fire. The American must also keep in mind that the foreigner operates on his own SRC and will probably assume that the American, like his own people, will be patient and understand the delay.

EXAMPLE 2—POSTPONEMENT IN GETTING DOWN TO BUSINESS. In America the nature of business relationships has evolved to a more formal level, while they are still on a more interpersonal level for the foreigner.

His culture's system for "guaranteeing" integrity has not necessarily evolved to match the American's. The American businessman must set aside his SRC assumptions of well-policed business ethics and must seek to develop the kinds of interpersonal relationships which, coupled with the foreign ethical system, will support the business relationship. The U.S. businessman who does not fight the interpersonal system will usually find that the rapport-establishment period is both shorter and more pleasant than will the American who insists on an SRC approach.

The previously mentioned adaptive behavior of increasing the number of projects underway is also helpful in adapting to the stretched-out time cycles due to the slower pace in establishing relationships.

EXAMPLE 3—FAILURE TO KEEP PROMISES. The foreigner's broken promise made to a superior, as seen by the American, is famous as an Oriental trait. Actually, this trait is to be found in most of the cultures of low literacy and low economic development level. The SRC of the American holds that it is better to tell the boss an agreed-on deadline cannot be met than to have him find out later. Moreover, this trait can only be developed in a country where (1) confession is considered good for the soul, (2) the employee has other courses of action open to him if the boss is displeased, (3) the confessor cannot be immediately or easily replaced, and (4) only the eight-hour loyalty is the rule instead of lifetime service with obligations to be on call at all times.

The foreigner operates on a more interpersonal system (the institutions in his culture are not well developed), and a part of this system is to avoid disagreements or embarrassment. In his system confession can be very dysfunctional. Moreover, he feels that he can be more easily replaced, and that he has little recourse if he is fired (his own SRC).

One simple, but often resisted, solution to the problem is to take greater care in seeing to it that assignments are attainable and *well* understood, especially the time schedule aspects, even if it means voluntarily repeating most assignments. This is far more efficient than suffering the continued surprises of important schedules unmet.

Individual cultural adaptation requires constant observation of local behavior in terms of the cultural values which govern it. At the same time, the American behavior patterns must be continuously examined for origins, and some appreciation developed for each of the two behavioral systems as functional. The American managerial behavior must be altered if it is dysfunctional enough to seriously disturb the value orientations of those on whom the success of the overseas company depends.

CONCLUSION

Cultural adaptation of an individual, an institution, or a product demands a certain level of knowledge of the traits of the American culture and a similar level of understanding of the foreign culture. In my opinion there is no substitute for this knowledge in building the understanding that produces the tolerance level necessary to the objectivity required for adaptation.

The first step in this process is the isolation of the American self-reference criterion habit as a biasing influence. From this point, the knowledge acquired may be used in the solution of business problems in adaptation. Instead of measuring foreign cultures with an American-calibrated "culturometer," the American value system is set aside and a more internationally objective measurement system used in both cultures. The SRC-free approach, which begins with two sets of cultural measures, permits a better bicultural "fit" to be discovered for the improvement of American business abroad. This SRC-free approach—cultural analysis—is further seen to apply to product, institutional, and individual manager adaptation abroad.

43

Management Training
for Cross-Cultural Application

Hollis W. Peter
University of Michigan

Reprinted by permission from *The Quarterly Journal of AIESEC International*, IV,
No. 3 (1968), 15–22.

575

When I was invited to participate in this AIESEC Seminar, I readily accepted the proposed title for my speech, which was "The International Training Program." However, in thinking about what might contribute to our general purpose of learning more about the international transfer of management skills, it seemed to me that we should focus on management training for cross-cultural application.

The word cross-cultural is better than international, which may carry with it some particular meaning of relationships between governments or formal activities between countries. We should be concerned primarily with ensuring that managers can manage more effectively in a variety of cultures, whether the transfer and application cross national boundaries or not.

Let me illustrate the difference. A young manager from a European country who goes for training and experience to a large corporation in the United States would expect to make some adaptations in transferring what he had learned to the situation in a similar business in his own country. An American colleague would have somewhat greater adaptations to make to the European country. If, however, both the European and American colleagues in the corporation were asked to manage part of a different enterprise in certain parts of the United States, they might find that even greater efforts were required to transfer and adapt their skills than either would have to make in Europe. Let us say that they were asked to manage a local enterprise of Navajo Indians on their reservation, or to manage students in a large university on the West Coast, or function in a business involving quite a separate set of unions than they had met before. It is not the national boundaries that make the greatest problems of transfer and adaptation for management, but the extent of differences in the cultural characteristics of the groups that are to be managed. There are cultural boundaries to be bridged between different age groups and social classes.

Sociologists have defined culture as the sum total of ways of living built up by a group of human beings, which is transmitted from one generation to another.

Without trying to provide a fuller description of culture, we should keep in mind that cross-cultural transfer of management skills does not mean simply adaptation to another culture. It also means that managers are deliberately seeking to influence other people and inevitably their cultures, in constructive ways which are necessary to achieve fully the objectives of their organization. Managers are both agents and carriers of culture change. Those of you who are not sociologists or anthropologists may want to explore more fully what is really meant by this word "culture." I recommend as a most readable little paperback book Professor Hall's *The Silent Language in Overseas Business* (6), which does a good job of explaining the many dimensions of culture, as well as showing how spoken language is only one means of communication and influence.

INDUSTRIAL ORGANIZATIONS AS SUBCULTURES

One interesting aspect of cross-cultural training is the effect of the business or industry itself as a subculture within the larger national or other cultural boundaries. We hear phrases like "he's a Shell man," or "he's an IBM type." Whether particular ways of thinking are part of the selection process, the type of industry or the individual company is not specified. I learned from my study of 500 Shell managers in ten countries that there is something to this. The Royal Dutch Shell Group of Companies, for example, operating in over 100 countries and employing as many nationalities, does have some aspects of a separate subculture. This is only partly because everyone is in the same group of companies. The oil industry, and certainly Royal Dutch Shell, includes quite a number of distinct businesses, each having its own technological requirements, traditions, and processes. Finding, producing, refining, transporting, and marketing oil, gas, and their myriad byproducts and transformations have in common only the basic raw material. Moreover, there are differences between Shell and other major oil companies, all in the same business and with similar technologies. Yet, because of history, national origins, and patterns of tradition, Shell men both see themselves and are in fact different from other oil men in some of their shared values, norms of behavior, and accepted ways of doing things—aspects of culture.

One effect of the Shell culture, supported in part by the high mobility of assignment of Shell managers and technical men around the world, is that it becomes a homogenizing force, helping to even out the great variety of national cultural traits which employees bring into their early work with this group of companies. This is not attributable entirely to the organization nor to a deliberate set of values, as the complex task requirements of the oil industry are remarkably similar in all parts of the world, and call for similar behavior. The result of these forces, however, is that Shell men, regardless of nationality, do have considerable homogeneity of beliefs, attitudes, and styles which have developed as appropriate to their activities and staff composition. This means that while there are some dissimilarities between the Shell subculture and those of other oil companies, there are greater differences between all oil men and traditional members of the national groups from which they are drawn.

One practical effect of industrial organizations as subcultures is that they can greatly facilitate the transition which an individual member must make between his own and another national culture. All of us have experienced the benefits of meeting other members of our own organization in strange surroundings, and finding how helpful their advice has been in bridging two cultures. In this sense a business organization operating across national or cultural boundaries is a "half-way station," or as one anthropologist put it, a "greased tube" which facilitates the smooth entry of individuals into a new cultural situation.

A SYSTEMS VIEW OF MANAGEMENT

It is often helpful to look at a business enterprise in terms of the various systems which comprise it. Management is concerned with men, material, money, machines, and in any business there are component subsystems that must be coordinated to achieve the desired over-all objectives.

I do not intend to explore or even to review with you the aspects of management and training which are needed to prepare a manager, for example in financial and accounting methods, in budgeting, or in the appreciation and use of computers. These, and other aspects of management which are oriented to the engineering and physical side of the business are important. However, as I will discuss more fully later, these aspects of managing present relatively fewer problems of cross-cultural transfer and application than do others.

It is with the components of managing which are concerned with the effective operation of the social system within a business that we are primarily interested for cross-cultural adaptation.

THE BUSINESS FIRM AS A COMPLEX SYSTEM

One of the central tasks of a manager is to view his organization as a social arrangement, because it is composed of people rather than physical objects. Managers are needed to provide coordination among the different people and groups who are performing specialized tasks which contribute to the organization's mission. The total enterprise is essentially made up of two systems, the technical and the social. The problems with which managers must deal result from adapting the technical and social systems to each other at their many interfaces, and also from problems within the social system itself. The engineers and technical specialists handle the problems strictly within the technical system. From this systems view of organizations comes the concept of joint optimization first developed by the Tavistock Institute of Human Relations. As stated by the management of Shell U.K. Ltd., which prepared a management philosophy document with Tavistock help:

> The company must manage both a social system, of people and their organization, and a technical system of physical equipment and resources. Optimization of its over-all operations can be achieved only by jointly optimizing the operations of these two systems; attempts to optimize the two independently of each other, or undue emphasis upon one at the expense of another, must fail to achieve optimization for the company as a whole.

In speaking of the social system of an enterprise Dr. A. T. M. Wilson of Unilever, formerly Director of the Tavistock Institute, has said that an organization can be thought of as having five components:

1. An organization has a group of objectives, linked both to internal activities and to external situations.
2. Individuals and groups of people with different orientations, knowledge, experience, and skills.
3. A social structure of functions and specialized roles.
4. Some kind of value system which reflects the slowly changing customs or work culture of the organization.

5. Related to this value systems is a fluctuating level of morale, a general attitude of the constituent groups and individuals toward the problems of cooperating in their functions and tasks.

If managers are to make the most of the people in their organizations, they must ensure that all five components are compatible with each other.

MANAGEMENT TRAINING AS ONE MEANS OF DEVELOPMENT

I have suggested that managing is a social process, and is concerned with problems of the organization that include not only the people and their relationships, but also company objectives, value systems, morale, and related attitudes, since all are interrelated. Does this require any special management development and training?

We do not question the need for formal preparation, both prior to and in addition to later work experience for engineers and others who operate the technical systems. It might seem equally obvious that those who manage people in a complex sociotechnical system must also be developed and trained to be effective. However, there is still the widespread belief held by many traditional managers that one learns managing only by managing, by trial and error, without reference to what has been learned by others who may have been more successful. However, the necessity of planned programs of management development and training is recognizaed in more progressive organizations as being necessary for three main reasons:

1. There is a need for more managers and for better managers than can be provided through normal work experience, i.e., without special programs for accelerated development.
2. There is too much failure in normal managerial experience and too little opportunity to understand the reasons for failure to rely exclusively on this method of acquiring appropriate knowledge and skills.
3. There is ample evidence that most managers can be improved, and potentially good managers developed, through planned programs including management training.

Let us look first at the range of management development methods, and then at management training with special attention to cross-cultural transfer and application.

In addition to training, there are many other methods for developing managers for improved effectiveness. These include:

1. Indoctrination programs
2. Job rotation
3. Performance appraisals
4. Apprenticeships
5. Junior management boards
6. Special projects and assignments

7. Professional conferences
8. Coaching and sponsorship
9. Communication media.

Management training is assuming an increasing importance in business and industry for several reasons. Unparalleled developments in industrial technology have taken place within the last two decades, and the rate of technological change is increasing. Along with technological change have come more complex organizations that induce a wide diversity of products and operate in a worldwide market. Recent developments in information technology, especially the use of computers, are helping to solve the increased problems of coordination and integration of activities, but provide additional training needs for managers. Operations research and other newly emerged disciplines employing sophisticated techniques also require a greater understanding of mathematics, statistics, and calculus than ever before. Managers today, and especially tomorrow, must be numerate as well as literate. In short, the rapid pace of change requires that more training be provided.

Much has also been learned about man's motivation to work and the satisfactions he receives from work. Managers are expected not only to develop themselves but their subordinates, and need not only better understanding of human behavior in the work situation, but skill training to be more effective leaders and trainers. Fortunately, a good deal has also been discovered in the last several decades about the learning process, and how learning is related to training. Training is better than it ever was, but not yet good enough. If you are interested in the relationship between industrial training and learning processes, one very good new paperback book on the subject is *Training in Industry: The Management of Learning*, by B. M. Bass and J. A. Vaughan, published in 1966 by Wadsworth Publishing Company in California and by Tavistock Publications in London. The Royal Dutch/Shell Group of Companies is fairly typical of large multinational firms in its concern for developing managers in many countries. As H. W. Atcherley, Group Personnel Coordinator, said last year, "Business and industry are in the process of a managerial revolution and future developments will certainly call for managers of a very different kind."

In Shell, management training has recently been given new priorities which emphasize the responsibility of the operating companies to ensure that managers at all levels are equipped with the knowledge, skills, and attitudes required for their jobs in each country, and which stress that managers should be familiar with environmental problems and the part that can be played by the application of social science knowledge in achieving company objectives.

ASSUMPTIONS WHICH UNDERLIE MANAGEMENT TRAINING AND DEVELOPMENT

It is all too easy to accept that management training and development is a good thing, especially for facilitating cross-culture application, without examining the assumptions which underlie such training programs. If we are to make progress, we must, however, be explicit about these assumptions and our state of knowledge regarding them. Before commenting on some of these basic assumptions, I call your attention to the excellent article "Foreign Management Trainees in the Industrial Culture" by Saxberg and Gaedeke in the *AIESEC Quarterly Journal* of February–April 1968, which touches on some of these same assumptions.

The first assumption is that the characteristics of the "ideal" manager are known, and that those who plan training programs also know what this ideal is. There is some but considerably less than full agreement on these characteristics, in spite of a wealth of research primarily on managers in the United States. The problem is a difficult one to solve partly because successful managerial behavior changes, depending on the particular needs and environments in different businesses in different periods of time; the ideal is not one but various combinations of qualities. Nevertheless, a few companies have reached the point where they know enough about their successful managers to make practical use of this knowledge in selection for management development. One recent report on this research in the States is *Predicting Managerial Success*, John Myers (ed.), Ann Arobr, Michigan, Foundation for Research on Human Behavior, 1968. It is heartening to learn that replication in Norway, Denmark, and the Netherlands of some work done in the United State on the early identification of managerial potential shows that the particular research methods used are almost culture-free. We need, however, a great deal more rigorous research in other culture settings to learn how culture-bound such research findings on managers are, and what is needed in each culture setting.

A second assumption to which I have already referred, is that something approaching the ideal manager can be developed. Here again the evidence is accumulating that, given certain moderate levels of intelligence, temperament, personality, and achievement, all of which can be measured or tested for, planned development activities do make a difference and are worth the cost.

The third assumption, that men and women of managerial potential can be correctly selected, is linked to the second. The organization requirement is to do this early enough to provide time for planned developmental activities. Common errors in most companies are: (1) underestimating the potential for growth of its average employees, and (2) focusing too much attention too early on a small select group, to the exclusion of others who may have equal or greater managerial potential but who are less visible at the time such choices are made, or who are later starters.

The fourth assumption is that the management trainers, and those who plan training programs, know how to develop, influence, and change the management trainees in desirable ways. The low status and inadequate preparation of many professional trainers in industry reminds me of a visit made by several livestock experts to the horse corral of an underdeveloped Indian tribe. The experts were shocked to learn that the sorriest horse in the herd was being used as the stud for breeding—the explanation given was that this horse just wasn't good for anything else! Industrial trainers must themselves be highly skilled in a variety of techniques not only for imparting information, but in influencing the attitudes and behavior of managers. Line managers must themselves feel and be responsible for specifying the training of other younger managers, even where some training activities are carried out by specialists.

A fifth assumption is that the recipient of management training understands the purpose of the training and will cooperate in allowing himself to be changed. This is where the attitudes and motivation of trainees are vitally important, and where involvement and some degree of guidance and control must usually be in the hands of the trainee.

A related assumption is that the recipient is able to change in the expected direction. If the changes involve conflict with strongly held beliefs or values, or if the trainee has a rigid authoritarian personality, he may simply be unable to change his attitudes or acquire certain managerial skills important in managing others, particularly those with quite different beliefs (i.e., from other cultures).

A last general assumption is that the training program creates the right conditions for learning, influences, and self-development. We recognize that the climate of the work situation can sometimes be detrimental to on-the-job learning of various kinds, but hardly ever think of training situations failing for this reason. Are the things being learned those that the trainer intends, or something quite different?

I recall an episode from my childhood in China, when my father, a medical missionary, was using exhibits in a traveling tour of villages to train the villagers in better health practices. One such exhibit was a gigantic model of a common housefly constructed in perfect detail by a Chinese craftsman. The lecturer was explaining how the fly carried filth and disease to people's food on its hairy legs. My father, in a proper scientific manner, was randomly interviewing members of the street audience as the troop of exhibits and lecturers passed by. His question to one man was, "Do you now understand why you must keep flies off your food?" to which the man replied, "No, but I can understand how you Americans are worried, with flies that size in your country!"

SOME KEY ASPECTS OF MANAGEMENT TRAINING FOR CROSS-CULTURAL APPLICATION

Management can no longer be considered simply an art or an instinctive process; most good managers are made, not born that way. Consequently, as management is gradually becoming more scientific and professional, there is more emphasis on developing managers through training rather than discovering them.

At the present time it is not feasible to describe a complete curriculum for developing good managers; however, our current task is to focus on those aspects of management training which are particularly important for cross-cultural transfer and application of managerial skills. I will propose several, and suggest also how they are provided by certain kinds of training:

1. Managers must themselves recognize that their own, and their subordinates' beliefs, attitudes, motives, and values are as relevant to improving organizational performance as the wide range of technical abilities, knowledge, and skills which they fully appreciate must be acquired and used. The relations among several of these elements can be shown in the simplified paradigm of Figure 1. Management training should, then, include an appropriate component dealing with beliefs, attitudes, values, and motives.

FIGURE 1

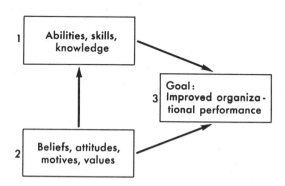

2. The beliefs, attitudes, and values of managers, as well as of their subordinates, are largely determined by the cultural influences to which they have been exposed. Some of these beliefs may be dysfunctional in one's own culture or elsewhere and may restrict improved managerial performance. For example, the belief that good managers are born, not made, limits interest in training and development, since such stimuli are seen as unnecessary or wasted effort. Similarly the managerial belief that workers are naturally stupid and lazy does not encourage people being helped to grow and develop within their capabilities which are usually greater than appreciated; this results in underutilization of human resources. The culturally determined beliefs, some of which interfere with the requirements for good management should be examined and dealt with in management training and education.

3. Good managers need to know enough about motivation to successfully tap the variety of motivational forces in subordinates and the additional group forces which contribute to achieving organizational goals; poorer managers tend to have an oversimplified or incomplete model of human motivation in their minds and rely more heavily on financial rewards and threats of punishment. Management training should give trainees the additional power that present knowledge of motivational forces can provide, whether such training is based on the Herzberg concepts of dissatisfiers versus motivators, or the Maslow concept of a hierarchy of needs. Even more, the management training

process itself should incorporate motivational principles which permit intrinsic rewards for trainee accomplishment and thereby greatly strengthen the learning process itself.

4. Since managers deal not only with individuals but with work groups, their own of which they are the leader, and others, they can usually improve their performance by increasing their knowledge of group dynamics, and by tapping group forces more effectively.

This area of managerial knowledge and skills is particularly relevant when the manager realizes that leadership is not a simple quality, but a relationship with subordinates. The appropriate style of leadership in fact depends on at least three factors: (1) the personality and preference of the manager, (2) the capabilities and expectations of his subordinates, and (3) the nature of the problem and of the situational requirements. If one considers the range of possibilities of even the last two of these factors in different cultural settings, it makes even more imperative training which allows the manager to learn the necessary diagnostic and adaptive skills to be an appropriate leader wherever he may be.

In describing some of the key aspects of management, especially for cross-cultural application, I have also been describing the ideal cross-cultural manager. To summarize: Among other things, he is aware of cultural influences governing his own beliefs and attitudes as well as others'; he sees cultural relativity in proper perspective. He understands how values and attitudes, as well as knowledge and skills, determine behavior. He appreciates the wide range of human needs and motivations on the job and tries to create a work environment and personal leadership which allow these motivations to be tapped for achieving organizational and personal goals. He is sensitive in his interpersonal relations and knows how to work effectively with different groups and individuals.

What kinds of training can and do provide the opportunity for managers to acquire these attitudes and to learn these skills and to make the appropriate changes in their own managerial behavior?

TRADITIONAL METHODS FOR CROSS-CULTURAL MANAGEMENT PREPARATION

The traditional approaches of orientation before departure for work in another cultural setting tend to focus exclusively on providing a fund of information on such topics as:

The organization sponsoring the work—its mission, structure, policies, and procedures.

Matters of personal concern—housing, health information, and educational facilities for the children.

The host country—its history, economics, geography, social institutions, and customs.

Questioning
the Managerial Implications of Managing Multinationally

1. In contrast to Webber's stand, some have claimed that management principles are universal throughout the world. If you were told to design a study to determine whether or not culture was a source of variance in the way organizations are managed, how would you operationally define each of the management principles you select as dependent variables in your study? Would you expect any of them, more so than others, to differ across cultures?

2. In absence of better information, reference to one's own SRC is a natural reaction to new and strange situations. Propose a training technique for enabling and persuading managers to discard their SRC when making cross-cultural contact.

3. Which assumptions and necessary conditions of the international training program described by Peter are different from those relevant to any domestic management development program? What are the essential differences between two such training programs?

4. What personal characteristics would you expect of a man who has proven himself to be successful in managing multinationally?

References

1. Bates, M., *Gluttons and Libertines*: *Human Problems of Being Natural*. New York: Random House, Inc., 1968.

2. Cleveland, H., *et al.*, *The Overseas American*. New York: McGraw-Hill Book Company, 1960, p. 131.

3. French, J. R. P., J. Israel, and D. As, "An Experiment on Participation in a Norwegian Factory," *Human Relations*, XIII (1960).

4. Haberstroh, C. J., "Organizational Structure: Social and Technical Elements," *Industrial Management Review*, III, No. 1 (1961), 64–77.

5. Haire, M., E. E. Ghiselli, and L. W. Porter, *Managerial Thinking*. New York: John Wiley & Sons, Inc., 1966.

6. Hall, E. T., "The Silent Language in Overseas Business," *Harvard Business Review*, XXXVIII, No. 3 (1960), 87.

7. Harbison, F., and C. A. Myers, *Education, Manpower, and Economic Growth*. New York: McGraw-Hill Book Company, 1964.

8. Kerr, C., J. T. Dunlop, F. Harbison, and C. A. Myers, "Industrialism and World Society," *Harvard Business Review*, XXXIX, No. 1 (1961), 113–26.

9. Marko, K., "Soviet Ideology and Sovietology," *Soviet Studies*, University of Glasgow, 1968.

10. McClelland, D. *The Achieving Society*. Princeton, N. J.: D. Van Nostrand Co., Inc., 1961.

11. Moore, W. E., "Global Sociology: The World as a Singular System," *The American Journal of Sociology*, LXXI, No. 5 (1965), 475–82.

12. Perlmutter, H., "The 300: Some Reflections on the Future of the International Business Firm." (Lecture given at Chief Executive Conference, *Business International Roundtable*, Bermuda, January 1968).

13. Pethybridge, R., "The Assessment of Ideological Influence on East Europeans," *The Public Opinion Quarterly*, XXXI, No. 1. (1967), 38–50.

14. Slater, P. E., and W. G. Bennis, "Democracy is Inevitable," *Harvard Business Review*, XLII (1964).

15. Tannenbaum, F., "The Survival of the Fittest," *Columbia Journal of World Business*, III (1968).

16. Terestchenko, V., "Advertisingwise, Here's Looking at You," *Industrial Marketing,* LII, No. 8. (1967), 65–67.

17. Thompson, E. H. D., "Is a World-Wide Philosophy Emerging? *Management International,* 1965.

18. Tinbergen, J., H. Linnemann, and J. P. Pronk, "The Meeting of the Twain," *Columbia Journal of World Business,* I (1966).

19. Whyte, W. F., *Men at Work.* Homewood, Ill.: Richard D. Irwin, Inc., 1961.

NAME INDEX
(Italicized numbers indicate articles)

A

Lord Adrian, 434
Alderfer, C. P., 247, 248
Allen, L. A., 153
Allport, G. W., 220, 221
Anderson, J., *295-300, 374-381*
Argyle, M., 342
Argyris, C., 177, *353-373*
Atcherley, H. W., 580
Atkinson, J. W., 225, 247
Avery, R., 258

B

Bakunin, M., 173
Bamforth, K., 177, 179
Barrett, R. S., 35
Bass, B. M., 29, 35, 62, *60-71, 113-120, 170-181,* 171, 448, 449, 456, 580
Bavelas, A., 178
Becker, H. S., 558
Bell, D., 506
Bell, J. F., 517
Bennis, W. G., 28, 37, 172, 177, *527-542*
Berelson, B., 19
Berg, N., 153
Berlew, S. E., 258
Blake, R. R., 180, 531
Blumberg, A., *158-169*
Booher, E. E., 519
Bough, R. M., 511
Bowman, E. H., 401
Boyd, J. B., 174
Boyd, E., 511
Bray, D. W., 258
Budner, S., 437
Bunker, S. R., 174
Burns, T., 135, 137, 153, 302

C

Cain, L. D., Jr., 257
Campbell, R. J., 449
Caplow, T., 258
Centers, R., 247
Christie, R., 438
Churchman, C. W., 153
Cioffi, F., 342
Clarkson, G. P. E., 418

Coates, C., 247
Collins, B. E., 416
Costello, T. W., 401
Cyert, R. M., 153, 401

D

Dalton, M., 400
Davis, R. D., 29
Davis, W. A., 246
Day, R. C., 340
Deep, S. D., 171
Delbecq, André L., *72-78*
Dent, J. K., 10, 16
Dickson, W. J., 151
Dill, W. R., 302, 401
Ditto, F., 513
Drucker, P., 3, 531
Dunnette, M. D., *85-93*

E

Eber, H. W., 340
Emery, F. E., 28
England, G. W., *7-16*
Erikson, E., 257, 531
Eysenck, H. J., 436

F

Feld, S., 247
Feldman, J., 400
Festinger, L., 429
Fisch, G. G., 146, 153
Fleishman, E. A., 133
Flowerman, S., 220
Forrester, J. W., 510
French, J. R. P., 221
Friedlander, F., *27-38,* 180
Frisch, M., 536

G

Galbraith, J. K., 554
Gardner, G., 342
Ghiselli, E. E., 97, *235-244*
Ginsberg, P., 497
Glaser, B. G., 258
Glasser, W., 277
Golembiewski, R. T., *158-169*

Management development (*cont.*)
    and organizational processes, 140-157
    personality needs and expected benefits from, 201-209
    training for change, 536
    zig-zag mobility in, 156
Management games; *see* Carnegie Tech Management Game *and* Organizational simulations
Management-labor dichotomy, 265
Management Research Center, 452
Management theory
    classical theorists, 47, 153
    deductive school of, 153
Management training; *see* Management development
Managerial Grid, 180, 375, 376
M. I. T. Sloan School of Management, 421, 426
Matrix organization; *see* Organizational design
Merrill, Lynch, Pierce, Fenner & Smith, 524
Motivation; *see also* Need hierarchy *and* Supervision
    changing motivation in future organizations, 537
    expectancy theories of, 225
    factors in the success of managers, 235 ff.
    growth and deficiency motivation, 135
    motivational climate of the organization, 229
    n Achievement, 247
    participative management theory of, 111
    paternalistic system of, 106
    and path-goal attitudes, 226 ff.
    scientific management approach to, 107
    theory X, 509
    theory Y, 262, 509
Multi-national companies, 507, 513-515, 554-555

N

National Industrial Conference Board, 149
National Training Laboratories, 372
Need hierarchy, 94, 246, 266; *see also* Motivation
    examination of in an organizational setting, 245-260
Needs; *see* Motivation *and* Need hierarchy
New York Times, 504
Non-zero sum game; *see* Conflict

O

Organizational change; *see also* Organizational development
    effective managerial performance in, 129-139
    future organizations, 527-542
    laboratory approach to, 158-169
Organizational climate, 135, 142, 150, 236; *see also* Motivation
Organizational communication; *see* Communication
Organizational decision making; *see* Decision making
Organizational design, 45-59, 77, 78
    cross-functional teams, 59
    differentiation in, 48 ff.
    integration in, 49 ff.
    linking groups, 78
    matrix organization, 59
    overlapping group memberships, 77, 78
    project group or task force, 78
Organizational development, 170-181; *see also* Organizational change *and* T-groups
Organizational goals, 7-16, 17-26, 27-38; *see also* Decision making
    correlates of perceived importance of, 17-26
    and expected managerial behavior, 8-10
    profit maximization, 8 ff., 30, 400 ff.
    satisficing, 29, 30
    societal components of, 30 ff.
    supra-organizational goals, 539-541
    variability of, 11-15
Organizational objectives; *see* Organizational goals
Organizational simulations; *see also* Carnegie Tech Management Game
    Exercise Compensation, 114
    Exercise Life Goals, 115
    Exercise Negotiations, 449
    Exercise Objectives, 115
    Exercise Organization, 62
Organizations
    closed system, 29
    informal; *see* Informal organization
    open-energy system, 28
    organic-adaptive structure, 534, 535

P

Participative management; *see* Supervision; Motivation; Scanlon Plan
Pay; *see* Compensation
Performance appraisal, 376; *see also* Management development
Profit maximization; *see* Organizational goals
Protestant ethic, 537

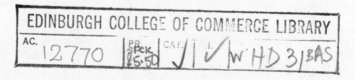